Transactions
of the
Royal
Historical
Society

SIXTH SERIES

XI

CAMBRIDGE
UNIVERSITY PRESS

Published by the Press Syndicate of the University of Cambridge
The Edinburgh Building, Cambridge CB2 2RU, United Kingdom
40 West 20th Street, New York, NY 10011–4211, USA
10 Stamford Road, Oakleigh, Melbourne 3166, Australia
Ruiz de Alarcón 13, 28014 Madrid, Spain

First published 2001

ISBN 0 521 815606

SUBSCRIPTIONS. The serial publications of the Royal Historical Society,
Royal Historical Society Transactions (ISSN 0080–4401) and Camden Fifth Series
(ISSN 0960–1163) volumes may be purchased together on annual subscription.
The 2001 subscription price (which includes postage but not VAT) is £60
(US$99 in the USA, Canada and Mexico) and includes Camden Fifth Series,
volumes 17 and 18 (published in July and December) and Transactions Sixth
Series, volume 11 (published in December). Japanese prices are available from
Kinokuniya Company Ltd, P.O. Box 55, Chitose, Tokyo 156, Japan. EU
subscribers (outside the UK) who are not registered for VAT should add VAT
at their country's rate. VAT registered subscribers should provide their VAT
registration number.

Subscription orders, which must be accompanied by payment, may be
sent to a bookseller, subscription agent or direct to the publisher: Cambridge
Univeristy Press. The Edinburgh Building, Shaftesbury Road, Cambridge CB2
2RU, UK; or in the USA, Canada and Mexico: Cambridge University Press,
Journals Fulfillment Department, 110 Midland Avenue, Port Chester, NY
10573–4930, USA. Prices include delivery by air.

SINGLE VOLUMES AND BACK VOLUMES. A list of Royal Historical
Society volumes available from Cambridge University Press may be obtained
from the Humanities Marketing Department at the address above.

Printed and bound in the United Kingdom by Butler & Tanner, Frome and London

CONTENTS

Contents

TRANSACTIONS OF THE
ROYAL HISTORICAL SOCIETY

PRESIDENTIAL ADDRESS

By P. J. Marshall

BRITAIN AND THE WORLD IN THE EIGHTEENTH CENTURY: IV, THE TURNING OUTWARDS OF BRITAIN

READ 24 NOVEMBER 2000

I

THESE addresses have tried to chart Britain's rise by the end of the eighteenth century to a position as a worldwide power that eclipsed all her European rivals. In particular they have traced the vicissitudes of an empire of rule over territory and peoples that grew greatly in the aftermath of the Seven Years War, suffered huge amputations in 1783, but was set on further expansion in the 1790s. In this final address I want to turn to Britain itself and the engagement of the British people with their empire.

The turning outwards of Britain towards its empire can be measured in many ways: in terms of trade, of the movements of people seeking land, commercial opportunities or civil and military office, of the scale of the deployment of the forces of the British crown overseas in war and peace, and of the attention given to empire by governments, by parliament and in public debate through pamphlets, the press or the petitions, such as those stimulated by the prospect of war with the American colonies or by the campaign against the slave trade. Nearly all theses indicators show a sharp upward trend in the later eighteenth century. The dispatch of increasingly purposeful voyages of exploration, the gathering in of every sort of 'curiosity' from overseas and their display in museums and private collections, the huge outpouring of travel writing and human and natural histories, the depiction of scenes and people by artists professional and amateur are all indications of an increasing intellectual involvement with empire. Seeking a strand that

I

might put all these different types of engagement into some sort of common focus is a daunting task. I want, however, to try to formulate some generalised propositions as to how British people saw themselves in relation to their empire in the later eighteenth century.

I would like to begin with a specific example, the formidable figure, in more senses than one, of General James Grant, the laird of Ballindalloch in Banff in the north-east of Scotland. Now seriously corpulent, Grant had been governor of East Florida and had seen much hard fighting in America in both the Seven Years and the American Revolutionary Wars. In retirement he entered parliament and lived mostly in London, returning to Ballindalloch every summer with 'his retinue of attendants and his black cook, in his state coach'.[1] As a man who had gained fame and fortune from empire, he was by no means unusual in the north east of Scotland. Other Grants were launched on commercial ventures throughout the empire[2] and were to make distinguished careers in the East India Company's service. James Fraser set a pattern which many Scottish 'nabobs' were soon to follow when he returned in 1749 from Surat in western India to Reelig near Inverness with a large fortune and a fine collection of manuscripts and miniatures.[3] Recruiting men for the new Highland regiments to fight overseas was a highly commercialised activity on many estates.[4] Migrants from Elgin and Banff were particularly involved in the development of the Ceded Islands in the West Indies after 1763, as Inverness was later to be in Demerara after 1796.[5] General Grant reflected on this West Indian connection with northern Scotland in a letter of April 1792 which he wrote to his old friend Lord Cornwallis, telling him about the progress of the campaign against the slave trade, of which Grant thoroughly disapproved; he thought abolition would be 'contrary to the rights of men'. 'Petitions', he wrote,

have been pouring in from every part of the Island, and a great number indeed from Scotland, some of them from Highland Parishes, where the Fools who sign the Petitions at the Black Smiths shop, which is the Country Coffee House, never saw the Face of a Black, and there is not one of the parishes from whence there are not some

[1] See biography of him by Edith, Lady Haden-Guest in *The House of Commons: 1754–1790*, ed. Sir Lewis Namier and John Brooke (3 vols., 1964), I, 531.
[2] David Hancock, *Citizens of the World: London Merchants and the Integration of the British Atlantic Community 1735–1785* (Cambridge, 1995), 48–59.
[3] See forthcoming article in *The New Dictionary of National Biography*.
[4] Andrew McKillop, 'Military Recruiting in the Scottish Highlands, 1739–1815: The Political, Social and Economic Context' (Ph. D. thesis, University of Glasgow, 1995).
[5] Douglas Hamilton, 'Patronage and Profit: Scottish Networks in the British West Indies, c. 1763–1807' (Ph. D. thesis, University of Aberdeen, 1999), 97, 106.

of the better Farmers Sons sent to the West Indies and employed in the different plantations as overseers.[6]

This brief extract suggests two obvious conclusions. In the first place, that the eighteenth-century turning towards empire, at least in certain regions like the Highlands of Scotland, was intense, but that it was also an ambiguous one, taking forms which may be no easier for us to reconcile than they were for General Grant. How could the same kind of people seek employment in the West Indies and petition for the abolition of the slave trade?

Throughout the history of the British empire people have been able to take apparently contradictory positions about the empire because it meant different things to them and reflected different aspirations. Ambiguity of meaning and aspiration was inherent in the lack of precision in defining the British empire at any time in its existence. The essentials of the late eighteenth-century empire of rule, setting aside the East India Company's provinces about which much remained unresolved, were that it consisted of dominions of the king, acquired by conquest or cession or by right of discovery and first settlement. Those who lived in the king's dominions were his subjects; they owed allegiance to him and by the eighteenth century were deemed to be 'subordinate unto and dependent upon' the British parliament.[7] By common usage, the king's subjects were British subjects.

That apparently bald statement of the law, in essence derived from Calvin's case of 1608,[8] masked questions of a depth and complexity that were to be debated throughout the whole span of Britain's imperial experience. Could the concept of a British subject be stretched to include peoples whom the seventeenth-century lawyers, if they had been aware of their existence, never envisaged in their wildest imaginations as passing under British rule? Was British subject in any respects a uniform category? For instance, did this enormously extended body of British subjects have any obligations and rights in common beyond the obligation to obedience and the right to protection implied by allegiance to the British crown? Under what circumstances, if any, were British subjects who did not live in Britain to be regarded as 'Britons'? In particular, how far did the powerfully emotive concept of the 'rights of Englishmen' apply outside England?

Seen from a British point of view, was the extension of empire to be a process by which Britain exported its values and institutions throughout the world, assimilating more and more people to a common

---

[6] Letter of 22 April 1792, Public Record Office, PRO, 30/11/270, fo. 95.
[7] The Declaratory Act, 1766, 6 Geo. III, c. 12.
[8] *'The Empire of the Bretagnes', 1175 to 1688. The Foundations of a Colonial System of Government*, ed. F. Madden and D. Fieldhouse (Westport, Ct., 1985), 29–40.

Britishness, so that the British became a worldwide people? Would empire fulfil the vision of its future enunciated by the Bostonian radical James Otis in 1766, when he hoped that the British empire 'may be prospered and extended till all men shall become truly free and rejoice as brethren in that Liberty which God has made them free and their right to which is indefeasible'?[9] Otis was expressing, if in an extreme form, an ideal of an 'empire of liberty' that was held by many colonial Americans and other radically minded people.[10] An alternative version was that of an extended empire based on a recognition of diversity and, perhaps inevitably, of hierarchy. In that case, would those who lived under British rule remain separately demarcated peoples, in spite of their status as British subjects, being treated in different ways thought appropriate to them by their rulers, according to gradations of civility or savagery or even to concepts of racial difference? If that version prevailed, would the Britishness of those who lived in the British Isles, instead of extending itself throughout the world, remain an exclusive category, perhaps becoming more sharply defined by empire?

Crudely simplified, great questions of uniformity or diversity, of equality or hierarchy, were raised in an acute form in the late eighteenth century and remained unresolved when the British empire disintegrated in the later twentieth century. While all historians of empire would surely accept that both of these simplistically identified trends were to influence British views of empire over the next two hundred years of imperial history, the established verdict is undoubtedly that hierarchy rather than equality generally prevailed. The majority of British people are assumed to have come to see their empire as marked by diversity and hierarchy and to have been extremely reluctant to extend, or no doubt in their view, to dilute concepts of an exclusive Britishness, which empire helped to emphasise. Moreover, such attitudes are seen to have been firmly in place by the beginning of the nineteenth century.[11] While there is undoubtedly strong evidence in support of such a conclusion, as General Grant discovered on his summer jaunts to Ballindalloch, British responses to empire in the late eighteenth century were by no means uniform or predictable. A debate was under way that was to last for at least another one hundred and fifty years. In the eighteenth century this debate was mainly conducted in terms of two great contemporary preoccupations, law and religion.

[9] Letter to D. De Berdt, 8 September 1766, University of Virginia, microfilm 1714, Lee family papers, reel I.

[10] Fred Anderson, *Crucible of War: The Seven Years' War and the Fate of Empire in British North America, 1754–1766* (New York, 2000), 746.

[11] Notably in C. A. Bayly, *Imperial Meridian: The British Empire and the World 1780–1830* (1989).

II

In the mid eighteenth century the most enthusiastic exponents of the equality of British subjects throughout the empire were likely to be colonial Americans, white West Indians or British radicals. For them the legal basis of that equality must be the universal application of English law. All the peoples of the empire were entitled to benefit from 'the common law and such general statutes of England as are securative of the rights and liberties of the subject'.[12] Whites in the American and West Indian colonies had long insisted on this and British minorities living among newly conquered alien populations made the same claims. British merchants living in Quebec argued that to subject them to French law would be to make them 'slaves, when the inhabitants of all the other colonies are Freemen'.[13] The British in Calcutta claimed 'certain rights inherent in *Englishmen* ... which no Power on Earth can legally deprive them of'.[14]

The main trends in British legal thinking in the late eighteenth century were, however, against the indiscriminate extension of English law throughout the empire. As new peoples with diverse legal systems were brought into the empire, there was a marked tendency to accept this legal diversity and to allow new British subjects the continuing use of their own laws. This was particularly the view of Lord Mansfield. He insisted on the principle that conquered Christian peoples kept their own laws until the king specifically gave them new ones and believed that changes in the laws of conquered peoples ought to be avoided as far as possible. English courts must be willing to judge cases according to foreign law, which could be known 'as well as our own', if the judges had 'the law stated to them'. Englishmen living in colonies where the law of conquered peoples remained in force must conform to it.[15]

The clause in the Quebec Act of 1774 that guaranteed that 'the Laws of Canada' should still be applied in cases concerning 'Property and civil Rights' was a clear endorsement of Mansfield's view.[16] On the same principle, Spanish law was preserved in Minorca and Roman-

---

[12] Cited in Jack P. Greene, *Peripheries and Center: Constitutional Development in the Extended Polities of the British Empire and the United States 1607–1788* (Athens, Ga., 1986), 28.

[13] Speech of counsel on Quebec Bill, 31 May 1774, *Proceedings and Debates of the British Parliaments Respecting North America*, ed. R. C. Simmons and P. D. G. Thomas (6 vols., Milwood, NY, 1982–9), 4, 498.

[14] *Journals of the House of Commons*, 38, 97.

[15] See his judgements on Fabrigas *v.* Mostyn and Campbell *v.* Hall, both in 1774, *A Complete Collection of State Trials*, ed. T. B. and T. J. Howell (33 vols., 1816–26), 20, 231, 290, 323, and his letter to G. Grenville, 24 December 1764, *The Grenville Papers*, ed. W. J. Smith (4 vols., 1852), 2, 476–7.

[16] 14 Geo. III, c. 83, sec. 8.

Dutch law would remain in force at the Cape and other colonies later taken from the Netherlands. The most acute problem of legal diversity within the empire was, however, presented by the acquisitions of the East India Company. It could be argued that these were not the dominions of the king either by conquest or by settlement, but had been entrusted to a private body, the East India Company, by the Mughal emperor, and that therefore their populations were not British subjects. An act of 1773 indeed made a distinction between the great mass of 'the inhabitants' and a tiny minority of 'British subjects', presumably those born in Britain.[17] The formal assertion of British sovereignty over India was to be delayed until 1813. Yet whatever its right to do so, there could be no doubt that from 1765 the East India Company possessed *de facto* power over the administration of justice in its provinces. In Calvin's case it had been laid down that 'infidel' laws automatically lapsed in any territory acquired by the king. There was, however, almost total unanimity in British opinion that there could be no question of the Company's setting aside the Hindu and Islamic law that the British had inherited in favour of any extension of English law. Existing law must be preserved even if the courts that administered it were reformed. Underlying such views were deeply engrained stereotypes about Indian society. Indians, especially Hindus, were taken to be the most conservative people on earth and their laws were presumed to be inextricably intermixed with their religion. Habituated to despotic rule, they would regard the principles of equality before the law and personal freedom embodied in English law as a violation of what was sacred to them. Even if this were not so, the publication in 1776 of the first English version of the so-called 'Codes' of Hindu law[18] suggested that Hindu law by the criterion of satisfying human needs had much to commend it.

Radicals might condemn any deviation from the full application of English law throughout the empire as evidence of compromises with despotism, but British opinion generally took pride in the way in which diverse legal traditions appeared to have been accommodated within the empire, even if the accommodations now appear to historians to have been rather limited ones. In the Indian case in particular, what was taken to be Hindu or Islamic law was applied with British assumptions about the sovereign power invested in the state, equality before the law, the nature of property rights or the appropriateness of punishments.[19] There were, moreover, clear assumptions of superiority

[17] 13 Geo. III, c. 63, secs. 14, 16.
[18] *A Code of Hindu Laws, or Ordinations of the Pundits*, trans. N. B. Halhed (1776).
[19] J. D. M. Derrett, *Religion. Law and the State in India* (1968); Jörg Fisch, *Cheap Lives and Dear Limbs: The British Transformation of the Bengal Criminal Law, 1769–1817* (Wiesbaden,

and inferiority underlying the accommodation of other legal systems within the empire. English law was seen as the law of an advanced, sophisticated, commercial society. Other societies incorporated within the empire had not evolved to the same degree and therefore laws appropriate to what was assumed to be their less advanced condition should remain in force.

For a large class of people within the eighteenth-century empire whether English law or another system prevailed was hardly material, since they remained virtually outside the protection of any form of law and few accorded them the status of British subjects. These were the slaves, whose numbers under British rule grew so rapidly in the later eighteenth century. Although slavery was found to have no basis in English law, there had been no effective use of the crown's prerogative powers against colonial slave laws and the position of slaves in Britain itself remained formally unresolved throughout the century. The most sympathetic recent scholarly treatment of Mansfield's approach to the Somersett case of 1772 and to other cases involving slaves suggests that he would grant redress for acts of injustice inflicted on individual slaves brought before him, but that he would not challenge the validity of slavery in Britain and thus precipitate a crisis for the commercial interests that would be at stake in such a challenge.[20] Those interests were later to be challenged by political rather than by legal action. Religious activists were to be the driving force behind that political challenge.

III

The late-eighteenth-century empire prided itself not only on its toleration of legal diversity but on its increasing toleration of religious diversity as well. Lord North, Pitt or Dundas may seem unlikely candidates to be regarded as magistrates, worthy of being compared with the Antonines, who, in Gibbon's words, could not be 'actuated by a blind, though honest bigotry, since the magistrates were themselves philosophers',[21] but they presided over an empire in which all shades of Protestantism enjoyed freedom, in which the penalties against Catholics had been much relaxed, and which in India enforced Hindu and Islamic law, endowed *madrasas* and Hindu colleges and supervised

1983); Radhika Singha, *A Despotism of Law: Crime and Justice in Early Colonial India* (Delhi, 1998).

[20] James Oldham, 'New Light on Mansfield and Slavery', *Journal of British Studies*, 27 (1988), 45–68.

[21] *The History of the Decline and Fall of the Roman Empire*, ed. J. B. Bury (7 vols., 1896–1900), I, 34–5.

the administration of Hindu shrines, soon to include, much to the
scandal of many British Christians, the great temple complex at
Jagannath.

In spite of mounting tension between Anglicans and other Protestant
denominations in much of North America, there was a wide consensus
that Britain's Atlantic empire in the mid eighteenth century was
sustained by a union of Protestants against its Papist enemies. For the
Virginia Presbyterian, Samuel Davies, George II had been the patron
of 'the Dissenter as well as the Conformist'.[22] The British Anglican
John Brown agreed that, faced by a Papist threat even after victory in
the Seven Years War, all Protestant denominations in the colonies
should unite on 'principles of religious freedom', since 'the contending
religious interests are nearly equal'.[23] Right up to the Revolution British
ministers resisted all applications from colonial Anglicans to authorise
the appointment of a bishop in America. It was reported that they
were unwilling to alienate opinion in the colonies and thus that 'political
considerations' were overriding 'religious ones'.[24]

To the mounting dismay of zealous Protestants on both sides of the
Atlantic, political considerations were also inclining British governments
to seek accommodations with the old enemy, Popery. Penal laws against
Catholics were in force in Britain and in most colonies. After the Seven
Years War, however, a sizeable Catholic population was incorporated
into the empire in Quebec and Grenada. In the Act of 1774 the
Catholics of Quebec got something more than a bare toleration: in
Mansfield's words their clergy were given the right to 'a decent and
moderate maintenance'.[25] The papers of ministers show that for them
the religious settlement in Quebec was as much a matter of political
calculation as resisting Anglican pressure for a colonial bishop had
been.[26] Any link in the mind of the British government between the
conciliation of French Canada in 1774 and the impending crisis in the
thirteen colonies is yet to be substantiated, but within a year ministers
were discussing the advantages to be gained from using Canadian
troops against Americans.[27] By then the need to draw on Catholic
manpower for the forces of the crown had become a major incentive

[22] *Sermon ... on the Death of his Late Majesty King George II* (Boston, [1761]), 22.

[23] *On Religious Liberty* (1763), iii.

[24] N. Rogers to T. Hutchinson, 2 July 1768, Massachusetts Historical Society, Hutchinson
Transcripts, 25, 267.

[25] Cited in Philip Lawson, *The Imperial Challenge: Quebec and Britain in the Age of the American
Revolution* (Montreal, 1989), 132.

[26] E.g. Alexander Wedderburn's Report, 6 December 1772, *Documents Relating to the
Constitutional History of Canada, 1759–1791*, ed. A. Shortt and A. G. Doughty (2 vols.,
Ottawa, 1907), I, 427–8.

[27] See letters between Suffolk and Germain, 15, [16] June 1775, William L. Clements
Library, Germain Sackville MSS, 3.

for relaxing the penal laws in Britain and Ireland. Military needs have been clearly shown to have been behind the North government's prompting of the 1778 Irish Relief Act and a proposed bill to relieve Scottish Catholics.[28] In the 1790s even more urgent reasons were leading to fresh instalments of conciliation in Ireland. The Catholics of Ireland must be preserved from the contagion of French republicanism. Henry Dundas's letters about the extension of the Irish franchise in 1793 show how far British ministers had departed from any idea of a Protestant empire. It was an inescapable fact, he wrote, that Catholics were 'the majority of the Irish nation'. In the past that inescapable fact had been the rationale for the penal laws; now it was the rationale for relief from them.[29]

Hindus were assumed to constitute the vast majority of the population of the Company's Indian provinces with Muslims as an important minority. As men like Warren Hastings were well aware, an ecumenical distribution of religious patronage had been one of the ways in which the Indian rulers of the successor states to the Mughal empire as well as the emperors themselves had consolidated their authority. It behoved the British successors to them to do the same. A considerable body of writing was also making the case that Hinduism at least merited sympathetic toleration, since it was based on sophisticated philosophical beliefs and instilled admirable moral precepts.[30]

Underlying policies that sought to accommodate a diversity of laws and religions within the empire was a clear sense of imperial insecurity. Toleration was needed to consolidate precarious new dominions, especially in India and Canada, and to mobilise resources to the full for desperate struggles against Bourbon and Revolutionary France. The limited changes in religious matters that had official sanction were also aimed at shoring up a precarious empire: that is by instilling principles of order in British people overseas by Anglican church establishments in Nova Scotia and Quebec and later in the West Indies and British India. There were, however, increasingly powerful unofficial pressures for the most part from British dissenters and evangelical Anglicans, that sought not just to preserve the empire through toleration but to change it fundamentally by transforming it into an instrument of God's purposes on earth through the propagation of Protestant Christianity in all parts of it.

This vision of a truly Protestant British empire went much further than the mid-eighteenth-century ideal of a transatlantic empire of free

[28] Thomas Bartlett, *The Fall and Rise of the Irish Nation: The Catholic Question 1690–1830* (Dublin, 1992), 84–6; Robert Kent Donovan, 'The Military Origins of the Roman Catholic Relief Programme of 1778', *Historical Journal*, 28 (1985), 79–102.

[29] Cited in Bartlett, *Irish Nation*, 171.

[30] *The British Discovery of Hinduism in the Eighteenth Century*, ed. P. J. Marshall (Cambridge, 1970).

Protestant communities. It embraced the non-European peoples of the empire: native Americans and Africans and later Indians and the peoples of the Pacific.

To many British people, victory in the Seven Years War seemed to be a clear sign that the British empire was especially favoured by God and that much was to be expected in return. Expectations were at first focused principally on the conversion of the native Americans, who seemed for so long to have fallen under the machinations of Catholic missions from New France. These aspirations mostly perished with the war against revolutionary America. Yet even before the outbreak of that war attention was shifting to Africans. They too must be gathered to Christ, both in America and in Africa itself. To a new generation of committed Christians, slavery and the slave trade were the great obstacles to this. They were increasingly seen as crimes by which Britain and its empire were negating God's providential purposes for them and for which they would be judged and suffer divine retribution. The British empire must be purged of those great sins.

Although the attack on the slave trade attracted support from large sections of the political elite and was ultimately to succeed in 1807 as a government measure, it was driven by the commitment to it of individual activists and of a great popular following. The country-wide network of committees set up after 1787 has been seen as a crucial stage in the establishing of a claim by the middling orders of British society to a role in public life.[31] These committees used the press or public meetings to incite the mass signing of petitions to parliament. The evidence of their success is overwhelming. Nearly 400,000 people are estimated to have put their names to 519 petitions in 1792, the year in which General Grant saw petitions being signed at Highland blacksmiths' shops and in which they were also being signed by a wide band of urban working people throughout Britain.[32] Historians have interpreted opposition to the slave trade as symbolic of wider aspirations and discontents. It has been linked to a whole series of largely middle-class reform movements and to working men's sense of the violence being done to their way of life by the rise of new industries.[33] Such arguments are cogent, yet, whatever its underlying impulses, abolitionism still constituted a massive popular attempt to transform an empire which enslaved Africans.

[31] J. R. Oldfield, *Popular Politics and British Anti-Slavery: The Mobilisation of Public Opinion Against the Slave Trade, 1787–1807* (1998 edn), 118–19.

[32] Seymour Drescher, *Capitalism and Antislavery: British Mobilization in Comparative Perspective* (Basingstoke, 1986), 80–6.

[33] E. g. Oldfield, *Popular Politics*; Drescher, *Capitalism and Antislavery*; David Brion Davis, 'Reflections on Abolitionism and Ideological Hegemony', *American Historical Review*, 92 (1987), 797–812.

It also inescapably involved popular engagement with questions of who Africans were and what was due to them. That Africans were fellow men and that the state of slavery was in no way a natural one for them were generally uncontroversial beliefs, long sanctioned by Christian doctrines of monogenesis. Proponents of slavery rarely tried to contradict them.[34] Yet to concede common humanity was not necessarily to concede very much. For most eighteenth-century opinion Africans were a people sadly degraded by their historical experience and the environment in which they lived. This meant that even for abolitionists some form of subordination, even, if for tactical reasons, a reformed slavery, was the inevitable future envisaged for nearly all Africans in the British empire. Africans might have the potential for a full life, but that would take a long time to be realised. At the most there seems to have been a growing acceptance, although this was rarely spelt out, that Africans were British subjects and that they were entitled to the protection of the law. Even the West Indian legislatures began to concede some niggardly measure of protection and slavery became legally unenforceable in Britain.

Yet the radical edge to eighteenth-century abolitionist rhetoric is unmistakable. It is clear even in Wesley: 'Liberty is the right of every human creature, as soon as he breathes the vital air; no human law can deprive him of that right which he derives from the law of nature.'[35] For Peter Peckard, who asked the famous question, 'Am I not a man and a brother?', Africans like all men had 'an absolute *Right* to Life, to Limb, to Property and to Liberty'. To deprive them of 'these blessings' was, he believed, 'an action absolutely indefensible and highly criminal'.[36] In the early 1790s the language of rights became more strident in abolitionism. To the alarm of Wilberforce and others working for broad political support in the House of Commons, radical societies such as the London Corresponding Society or the Manchester Constitutional Society, emerged as 'the most vociferous champions of abolition in the country generally'.[37] The Sierra Leone project in its early form seems to represent an attempt to endow Africans in practice with the rights claimed for them. For Granville Sharp it was 'an Establishment for FREEDOM in Africa', where the black settlers were to run their own affairs under his frank pledge system.[38]

[34] Anthony J. Barker, *The African Link: British Attitudes to the Negro in the Era of the Atlantic Slave Trade, 1550–1807* (1978).
[35] 'Thoughts upon Slavery', in *Works of John Wesley* (1872 edn, 14 vols.), 11, 79.
[36] *Am I not a Man and a Brother?* (Cambridge, 1788), 94.
[37] Roger Anstey, *The Atlantic Slave Trade and British Abolition, 1760–1810* (1975), 277–8; David Turley, *The Culture of English Anti-Slavery, 1780–1860* (1991), 156–77.
[38] Stephen J. Braidwood, *Black Poor and White Philanthropists: London Blacks and the Sierra Leone Settlement* (Liverpool, 1994), 130–2. On Sierra Leone, see also Christopher Fyfe, *A History of Sierra Leone* (Oxford, 1962), 16–37; Michael J. Turner, 'The Limits of Abolition:

Abolitionism was intended to purge the British empire of the sins which threatened it with divine displeasure. For most Christian enthusiasts missionary endeavour throughout the empire was the necessary corollary of the abolition of the slave trade. This could not be entrusted to the Anglican church in the West Indies or to the Societies for the Propagation of the Gospel or the Promotion of Christian Knowledge, who appeared to have achieved so little. It would be done by groups of Methodists or by voluntary societies, acting independently of government and of most of the established church, and identified with dissent in the Baptist and London Missionary Societies or with Anglican evangelicals in the Church Missionary Society after 1799. Like sections of the anti-slave trade movement in the 1790s, such societies were associated with political and social radicalism at home. Sydney Smith's jibes about pious 'tinkers' or 'little detachments of maniacs', 'who would deliberately, piously and conscientiously expose our whole Eastern empire to destruction' are well known.[39] Although usually cautious in practice in deferring to authority, the new societies posed an implied challenge to official policies overseas, be it the gradual reform of slavery in the West Indies, respect for Cape Dutch susceptibilities in South Africa or the long established policies of avoiding conflict with Hinduism and Islam in India. In place of official caution and accommodation, dictated by concern for the fragility of empire, the new missionary societies offered a vision of equality for converted Protestants throughout the empire. Bold as this vision might be, even the most radical missionaries could rarely transcend the conventional stereotypes about debased African nature that required a long period of white tutelage, and with their vituperative attacks on the depravity of Hinduism and Islam they did much to propagate new stereotypes about debased Indian nature as well.[40]

In the early nineteenth century both the abolitionist and the missionary movement came under a degree of official patronage, which enabled them to win their great victories with the ending of the slave trade in 1807 and the increased access to India of 1813. By then they had lost many of their radical associations and were becoming partners in imperial purposes, if never entirely comfortable ones.[41] In the later

---

Government, Saints and the "African Question", c. 1780–1820', *English Historical Review*, 122 (1997), 319–57.

[39] *Edinburgh Review*, 12 (1808), 173, 179.

[40] For India, see P. S. E. Carson, 'Soldiers of Christ: Evangelicals and India, 1784–1833' (Ph. D. Thesis, London University, 1988); for the West Indies, see Mary Turner, *Slaves and Missionaries: The Disintegration of Jamaican Slave Society, 1787–1834* (Urbana, 1982).

[41] For the 'taming' of the missionaries, see Elizabeth Elbourne, 'The Foundation of the Church Missionary Society: The Anglican Missionary Impulse', in *The Church of England*

1820s abolitionists were again to rebel against official procrastination and missionaries always felt a sense of 'self-sufficiency' under 'divine superintendence', not that of government, as Professor Porter has so felicitously put it.[42] Yet in the last decade of the eighteenth century the abolitionists and the new missionary societies had offered and apparently won wide popular endorsement for a prospect of empire very different from the official one.

IV

I have suggested that two by no means mutually exclusive ways of ordering the empire were in contention in the later eighteenth century. Empire could be seen as an extension of Britain, as more and more people throughout the world were absorbed into a universal Britishness, based on a common system of law and rights and a common Protestantism for all its denominational divisions. This had been the vision of much colonial American opinion and of those who sympathised with their cause in Britain. Perhaps paradoxically, some of the most articulate of those who were regarded by Americans as their enemies also envisaged them as part of a greater Britain; this was the ultimate argument why Americans should pay British parliamentary taxes.[43] A Britishness that united communities of British origin across the Atlantic had always been a selective one and it could only embrace a limited part of the new empire that was emerging after 1763; in any case it was shattered by war and American independence. New aspirations for the propagation of British values throughout the world were, however, to emerge in the 1780s and to flourish into the next decade. Freedom from slavery and evangelical Protestantism were to be spread throughout the empire and beyond. What was envisaged was something like *la grande nation* being propagated by revolutionary France. It too was a hegemonic programme: the terms for liberation were set in Britain and the equality to true believers that it appeared to offer was in practice strictly circumscribed by what amounted to racist assumptions. Yet it was in its way a revolutionary programme, involving popular mobilisation in Britain on a large scale and threatening the accommodations with local elites on which the British empire was built overseas.

---

c. 1689–c. 1833: From Tradition to Tractarianism, ed. John Walsh, Colin Haydon and Stephen Taylor (Cambridge, 1993), 263–4.

[42] Andrew Porter, 'Religion and Empire: British Expansion in the Long Nineteenth Century, 1780–1914', *Journal of Imperial and Commonwealth History*, 20 (1992), 379.

[43] Eliga H. Gould, *The Persistence of Empire: British Political Culture in the Age of the American Revolution* (Chapel Hill, 2000), chapter 4.

Such a programme was hardly likely to commend itself to the rulers of an empire engaged in a bitter struggle with revolutionary France. They countered it, however, as much by incorporating versions of its objectives into official policy as by outright suppression. Hostility to slavery and free access to the empire for all Christian denominations became maxims of an imperial regime that in other respects accepted a plurality of legal systems and of religious practices and which generally abstained from intervention in the very wide definition that it gave to what constituted the private lives of its subjects. Toleration of diversity, albeit a diversity that must accept certain non-negotiable British fundamentals, such as the maintenance of a British interpretation of law and order, respect for property rights and British notions of probity in government, was to remain the dominant note of British imperial rule throughout the history of the empire.

So diverse was the empire assumed to be that the peoples of the British Isles seem rarely to have envisaged themselves as citizens of a greater Britain that incorporated the peoples of the empire in a common Britishness with them. In legal terms the empire always remained a *mélange* of separate colonies, protectorates or dominions. The concept of common citizenship of the Commonwealth or of 'the United Kingdom and Colonies' was legally unknown until 1948, and then the only common right conferred on these citizens was that of access to Britain,[44] a right that was quickly to be abrogated. In the absence of any concept of common citizenship, the peoples of the empire tended to be ordered in public debate in Britain according to whatever hierarchical system was then in vogue, be it progress towards civility or innate racial characteristics. Britain's supremacy in this ranking was rarely questioned.

A mental ordering of the empire that placed its peoples into separate compartments, arranged hierarchically on principles that demonstrated British superiority no doubt constituted only a limited turning-outwards for most British people. Nevertheless, as in the later eighteenth century there were always groups with aspirations to apply universal principles to the empire and thus to bring about change in it, changes that might even effect transformations in Britain itself. The missionary impulse may have lost some of its subversive edge but it grew greatly in numerical strength in the later nineteenth century. Radically minded reformers in the early nineteenth century sought fundamental change in the empire by such means as the codification of law, the rigorous application of free market principles or the scientific redistribution of land. If revolutionaries from the right, imperial federationists and exponents of imperial preference could still be revolutionaries, seeking

---

[44] 11 and 12 Geo. VI, secs. 1 and 4.

a new Britain as well as a new empire. Some of them, such as Leo Amery, embraced a wider imperial patriotism, 'blended with and yet transcending our several national patriotisms'.[45] So it was too for some liberal-minded people who envisaged Britain's future in a multi-ethnic Commonwealth of equal nations.

So by a long and winding road we return to General Grant, his black cook, his state coach and the Highland blacksmiths' shops where vexatious petitions were being signed against the slave trade in 1792. Such petitions were not, as Grant seems to have thought, a gesture of renunciation of empire in a part of Britain that was reaping the benefits of empire to the full. They were a sign that people's aspirations for empire embraced the propagation of moral principles throughout the world as well as the garnering of wealth and power for individuals and for the nation. Such aspirations ostensibly sought to unite the peoples of the empire with the people of Britain rather than to emphasise their differences. The programmes for unity were, however, British ones, were dependent to a considerable degree on British power for their propagation and they too had barely concealed hierarchical assumptions. Thus, like the efforts made to categorise the apparent differences of humanity, they too constituted a hegemonic ordering of the world. In the present historiographical climate, in which the ideological underpinnings of empire receive as much attention as the economic or political ones, it would be excessively naive to expect anything else. Even so, we should not try to simplify the aspirations behind the so-called imperial project. We will have a very restricted understanding of the influence of empire on Britain's history if we do. In the later eighteenth century people of a radical disposition as well as those of a conservative one were staking their claims to order the empire. They were to continue to do so for the next one hundred and fifty years.

[45] Wm Roger Louis, *In the Name of God, Go! Leo Amery and the British Empire in the Age of Churchill* (New York, 1992), 32.

THE BLUES, THE FOLK, AND AFRICAN-AMERICAN HISTORY

By Marybeth Hamilton

READ 21 JANUARY 2000 AT THE UNIVERSITY OF WARWICK

ON a stifling Saturday in Texas in June 1937 a twenty-six-year-old African-American musician, Robert Johnson, stepped to the microphone in a makeshift recording studio in a disused warehouse atop a Buick showroom. Johnson had grabbed a ride west from his native Mississippi to make it to the recording session in Dallas, one more journey in a life that had been spent by and large on the road. In contemporary parlance, he was a songster: an itinerant guitarist and maker of songs who scraped together a living wherever he found it, performing on street corners and in juke joints in the Deep South, sometimes drifting north, even reaching New York City, but always heading south again. That he recorded at all came down largely to luck; luck, and the exigencies of the Great Depression, which cut deeply into record company profits and forced the so-called 'race record' companies, which sold to an almost entirely black market, to look for cheap talent, Southern performers with local reputations who might appeal to regional markets. Johnson was one of many who caught a talent scout's ear in the Mississippi Delta in the late 1930s. On that Saturday in Dallas he recorded fifteen songs, among them a haunted blues called 'Hellhound on my Trail'.

> I got to keep movin', I've got to keep movin'
> Blues fallin' down like hail, blues fallin' down like hail
> Blues fallin' down like hail, blues fallin' down like hail
> And the days keeps on worryin' me
> There's a hellhound on my trail, hellhound on my trail
> Hellhound on my trail[1]

Today, Robert Johnson has become a major pop music phenomenon. The first stirrings of this were felt in the 1960s, when Johnson's recordings were reissued on a two-volume LP, but it crested in 1990 with the release of *Robert Johnson: the Complete Recordings*, a CD anthology that brought together all of Johnson's songs and two recently discovered

---

[1] Robert Johnson, 'Hellhound on my Trail', *Robert Johnson: the Complete Recordings* (Columbia C2K 46222/467246–2[UK]).

photographs of the man himself, the only photos of Johnson known to exist. Alongside the CD came extensive publicity chronicling Johnson's brief, violent, mysterious life: his death by poisoning at age twenty-seven, and the legend that he had sold his soul to the Devil at a Delta crossroads in return for prowess on the guitar. The anthology sold one million units, with the first 400,000 bought up in only six months. Johnson's face can now be found on postcards, t-shirts, posters, and guitar polishing cloths; it also stares out from the covers of recent works of popular musical history: Greil Marcus's *The Dustbin of History* and Francis Davis's *The History of the Blues*. As for 'Hellhound on my Trail', it is broadly acclaimed as the apex of the blues tradition: 'Johnson's crowning achievement', writes critic Peter Guralnick, a stark, terrifying cry of despair. The dark intensity of his music has made Johnson the most celebrated of all blues singers. 'To my generation', writes Guralnick, 'Johnson became the embodiment of the existential wandering blues-man, burdened by a despair that spoke of not just black suffering but the anguish at the heart of the human condition.'[2]

Johnson's importance lies not on the popular level alone. He has res-onated just as strongly for scholars of African-American history – most recently, for the historian Leon Litwack in his sweeping study of the turn of the century American South, *Trouble in Mind: Black Southerners in the Age of Jim Crow*. Johnson's dark vision looms over the text: two of the book's eight chapters take their titles from Johnson's songs, and the lyrics of Johnson's 'Hellhound on my Trail' provide the closing words of the book. For Litwack, 'Hellhound on my Trail' is both prototypical blues and an archetypal tale of the Jim Crow experience, and Johnson himself a black Everyman adrift in the Mississippi Delta, a haunted soul who articulated black Southerners' profound alienation, their experience as 'a new gen-eration of interior exiles . . . exiles in their own land'.[3]

Litwack's book is by no means singular. For the last two decades, the blues of the Mississippi Delta have provided a luminous focus for a revitalised African-American history, one engaged with the experience of the forgotten and faceless black masses. Beginning with Lawrence Lev-ine's monumental *Black Culture, Black Consciousness: Afro-American Folk Thought from Slavery to Freedom*, published in 1977, historians have turned to blues as a key form of folk culture, echoing with the voices of the inarticu-late, with experiences that historians had for too long ignored. As his-torical evidence, its value lies in its sheer directness. As Litwack puts it, to listen to Robert Johnson 'is to feel – more vividly and more intensely than any mere poet, novelist, or historian could convey – the despair, the

[2] Peter Guralnick, *Searching for Robert Johnson* (London, 1990), 2.
[3] Leon Litwack, *Trouble in Mind: Black Southerners in the Age of Jim Crow* (New York, 1998), 478.

thoughts, the passions, the aspirations, the anxieties, the deferred dreams, the frightening honesty of a new generation of black Southerners and their efforts to grapple with day-to-day life, to make it somehow more bearable, perhaps even to transcend it'.[4] What Johnson's blues provides, in other words, is a kind of audio snapshot of the innermost truths of the past. As Litwack writes, quoting the Delta blues chronicler Robert Palmer: 'How much history can be transmitted by pressure on a guitar string? The thoughts of generations, the history of every human being who's ever felt the blues come down like showers of rain.'[5]

In what follows I want to reflect upon this idea of the blues as history transmitted by a guitar string. More precisely, I want to interrogate historians' use of the blues and raise questions about what I can only describe as their romance with this particular form of historical evidence. It is, I think, curious to hear an historian as sophisticated as Litwack frame the blues in this straightforwardly populist way: as the voice of the folk, the pure and unmediated cry of the masses. That reverence for the music's evidentiary powers recalls nothing so much as the claims made, decades ago, for oral history: that it allows us to bypass the dangers of historical interpretation by removing the need for an historian, that it enables us to communicate with the past directly by presenting pure images of past experience.[6]

At the root of the problem lies historians' conceptualisation of the blues as folk culture. In using that label, both Litwack and, in particular, Levine take care to distinguish their approach to folk music from what might be called a traditionalist view: the folk as isolated preindustrial peasantry; folk culture their spontaneous, unschooled creation, a creation endangered as the cheap, tawdry products of commercial mass culture eat away at the foundations of traditional life. Instead, and drawing on revisionist folklorists of the 1960s, they emphasise folk music as process: the interaction between marginal peoples and the songs they sing, whatever their origin, whether absorbed at the cradle, sung in the fields, or learned from the Victrola or juke box. Folk music is any song through which a people expresses its own needs and values. And the folk itself is 'any group of people whatsoever who share at least one common factor ... a group [that] for whatever reason has some traditions that it calls its own'.[7]

Yet despite this disclaimer, there is an unspoken process of selection at work in these histories. If in theory any song can be a folk song, in practice some always seem to be more folkish than others. In using the blues as a

---

[4] Ibid., 457.

[5] Ibid., xvii.

[6] Michael Frisch, 'Oral History and Hard Times: A Review Essay', in The Oral History Reader, ed. Robert Perks and Alistair Thomson (London and New York, 1998), 29–37.

[7] Alan Dundes, 'The American Concept of Folklore', Journal of the Folklore Institute, 3 (1966), quoted in The Dictionary of Anthropology, ed. Thomas Barfield (Oxford, 1997), 195.

window on folk consciousness, historians draw their evidence from the same clutch of singers, with the voices of Charley Patton, Son House, above all Robert Johnson heard over and over and over again. Embedded in historians' use of the blues as folk culture are unexplored assumptions about authenticity in African-American art and experience, about what is peripheral and what stands at the core. At the core is the blues of the Mississippi Delta, a music whose 'folkness' lies in its raw emotion, in Robert Johnson's unvarnished terror and pain.

That the Delta was the original home to the blues has been an article of faith for recent historians – and here I refer not just to music journalists, but to scholars of African-American history. Nowhere else in the South, writes Samuel Charters, could have bred a music so raw, so primal: nowhere else was so cut off from the currents of modern life.[8] And nowhere else did racial oppression rule with such ferocity. In the Delta time had effectively stopped – it remained a quasi-feudal region still stuck in the dynamics of slavery. Those circumstances shaped the blues in its natural state, a music of peculiar power and purity, an intensely emotive, deeply personal music permeated by alienation and anguish.

This paper maps the historical roots of this vision of folk authenticity. Historians have been so eager to hear the Delta blues as the direct voice of black folk experience that they have neglected the process of cultural recycling that has given listeners in our era readier access to some visions of blues than to others. More specifically, they have neglected the blues revival of the late 1950s and 1960s, when white Americans and Europeans rediscovered a music that African-Americans were leaving behind. Those years saw a flood of aficionados, record collectors and folk music enthusiasts, head south from Memphis and north from Vicksburg armed with tape recorder, camera, and notepad, determined to cut through the dross churned out by the commercial record companies and capture the sound of the real thing. The real thing was the Delta blues, the name they devised for the rough, impassioned voices they had encountered on scratchy 78s and heard reissued on new LP compilations: singers like Skip James, Charley Patton, and Robert Johnson. In those recordings these new listeners heard what historian Miles Orvell has called the 'incandescence' of the authentic: impassioned voices echoing with pain and privation, emanating from a flat, water-logged, primitive landscape seemingly untouched by the modern world.[9]

Yet the aficionados of the blues revival were not the first song hunters to scour the Delta. That path was forged two decades earlier, when an interracial team, the black sociologists Lewis Jones and Charles Johnson

---

[8] Samuel Charters, *The Bluesmen* (New York, 1967), 27–32.
[9] Miles Orvell, *The Real Thing: Imitation and Authenticity in American Culture, 1880–1940* (Chapel Hill, 1989), xvi.

of Fisk University and the white folklorist Alan Lomax of the Library of Congress, surveyed black music in Coahoma County, Mississippi, the first attempt by the Library of Congress's Archive of Folk Song to join forces with an historically black university and document forms of African-American music inaccessible to whites working alone. In 1941 Lomax, Jones and Johnson assembled a team of black fieldworkers based in Coahoma County's capital, Clarksdale, who interviewed residents about musical taste, musical activity, and their use of sheet music, radio, juke-boxes, and records. Those sessions smoothed the way for Lomax, who arrived in the summer of 1942 and made over 200 hours of field recordings: from children's game songs, spirituals, field hollers and work songs to party songs, brothel tunes, and blues.[10]

Owing in large part to Lomax's reminiscence of the project, his award-winning 1993 memoir *The Land Where the Blues Began*, the Coahoma County study has been celebrated largely for the local musicians it captured on record: a tractor driver on a cotton plantation, Son House; and a shy, sleepy-eyed sharecropper named McKinley Morganfield, who would soon move to Chicago and, under the stage name of Muddy Waters, help change the face of popular music.[11] My focus, however, is not on the findings but on the tale that its architects shaped to make sense of them. In their reports and memos written during and after the project, Lomax and Jones identified the blues as the Delta's key form of black music. Yet this was not the Delta blues as we now perceive it, bred by isolation and anguish. This was a music of sex and modernity, rooted in national currents of industrialising black life.

Modernity and urbanisation are the keynotes of the tale Jones and Lomax set out. The Delta it depicts was fast-paced and worldly, par-ticularly in contrast to 'the Hills', the counties east of the Delta, where families had deep roots in the soil and traditional mores seemed fully in force. In the Delta no one stayed in one place for long, and its young people were scorning the church, experimenting with sex, immersing themselves in a mass-marketed world of jukeboxes, automobiles and motion pictures.[12] More jarringly, the Delta blues we would recognise was nowhere in evidence. Surveying the black bars of Clarksdale, Lewis Jones

---

[10] Alan Lomax, 'The folk-song survey in collaboration with Fisk University', undated memo c. September 1941 in Alan Lomax Archive, Hunter College, New York City (hereafter ALA-HC); Alan Lomax, 'A memorandum about the July trip to Coahoma County: Functional approach to the study of folklore', undated memo in ALA-HC; Alan Lomax, 'Folk Culture Study: suggested field procedures', undated memo c. September 1941 in ALA-HC. Some of this material can also be found in Fisk University Mississippi Delta Collection, Archive of Folk Culture, Library of Congress, Washington, DC (hereafter AFC-LC).

[11] Alan Lomax, *The Land Where the Blues Began* (New York, 1993).

[12] Lewis Jones, 'The Mississippi Delta', undated ms. (probably late 1940s), 61–2, in ALA-HC.

found not a single local musician on the jukeboxes: not Charley Patton, not Skip James, not Robert Johnson. Top sellers in 1942 were the same as they were in black districts across the US: Louis Jordan, Lil Green, Count Basie, Fats Waller.[13] This was not the case in Clarksdale alone. Late one night Alan Lomax stumbled on a juke joint on the edge of a cotton field and opened the door to find a blaring jukebox and a roomful of people jitterbugging to Duke Ellington.[14]

The Coahoma County study presents an interpretive problem: a legendary moment when the Delta blues was discovered – but not in the form that has passed into legend, not in the form that we expect to find. In what follows I want to explore this tale, focusing on its guiding assumptions and the sense of mission that drove its creators. The Coahoma County investigators, like the Delta blues fans who followed, shaped their vision of the blues of the Delta in part out of political and cultural commitments, their sense of what was real in black secular music in an urban, industrial, mass-market world where African-Americans looked less like a 'folk' than ever before. Eventually, one tale of the Delta blues triumphed. But as historians of popular memory have argued, dominant accounts of the past take shape in part through their struggles with others, a process by which certain tales 'achieve centrality and luxuriate grandly; others are marginalised or excluded.'[15] The Coahoma County study presents one such excluded story. Through it we can begin to explore what was pushed to the margins when the Mississippi Delta was reimagined as the locus of African-American folk authenticity, or, as Alan Lomax would eventually phrase it, the land where the blues began.

What is perhaps most unsettling about the Coahoma County study to anyone who has ever picked up a blues book or CD is that it was not premised on a conviction that the blues had its roots in the Mississippi Delta. As I have already noted, for today's blues chroniclers that origin seems incontrovertible, though a few will admit that in point of fact they have precious little direct evidence to go by. As a music of a denigrated, impoverished class, the early blues left few traces behind it – no reliable accounts of performances, no thorough transcriptions of lyrics. While historians agree that the AAB verse form first appeared in the early twentieth century, even that is less fact than inference: nothing resembling that form appears in nineteenth-century ballad hunters' reports. Otherwise, all comes down to guesswork. No one knows who sang the first blues, or where they sang it, or when.

---

[13] 'List of records on machines in Clarksdale amusement places', Folder 7 (Lists), Fisk University Mississippi Delta collection, AFC-LC.

[14] Alan Lomax field notes, July 1942, ALA-HC.

[15] Popular Memory Group, 'Popular Memory: Theory, Politics, Method' in *Oral History Reader*, ed. Perks and Thomson, 75–86.

With all certainties absent, scholars rely on tales told retrospectively by well-placed observers about encountering the blues for the first time. Far and away the most frequently told of those tales is one that first appeared in 1941, the year that saw the launch of the Coahoma County study, in *Father of the Blues*, the autobiography of the African-American composer W. C. Handy. Handy describes how he first heard the blues around 1903, late one night in the Mississippi Delta, as he dozed on a railway platform waiting for a train that had been delayed nine hours. A dream-like figure appeared before him: a 'lean, loose-jointed Negro', his clothes in rags, his shoes in tatters, his face etched with the sadness of ages. On his guitar he strummed a haunting refrain, 'the weirdest music I ever heard. The tune stayed on my mind.'[16]

In the past forty years Handy's story has been told over and over again, in liner notes, journal articles, and books written by chroniclers eager to assert the primacy of the Delta in blues history with little hard evidence to back that claim up. One might label it, now, a foundation myth, a tale used to convey something true and essential about the origins of the blues tradition. To its enthusiasts, the blues expresses fundamental emotions, timeless echoes of black – indeed, human – suffering. It makes sense that it would enter history not through its invention but through its discovery, encountered as Handy encountered it, in the form of a sorrowful wanderer adrift in the Delta, appearing before him as if from a dream.

Yet powerful and ubiquitous as that tale is now, in the early 1940s it had nothing like that sort of resonance. Certainly not for Alan Lomax or Lewis Jones, though both had read *Father of the Blues*. Underpinning and guiding their study was a very different blues origins tale: one that rooted the blues in the city, in the urban sexual underground. The 'Delta blues', by these lights, was an urban import, originally part of the red-light district that had sprung up in Clarksdale in the early twentieth century, when railroad construction tied the Delta into the national economy and opened it up to the currents of black city life.

The first thing to say about this genealogy is how common it was in the interwar period. Discussions of blues in the national press routinely rooted the blues in the 'southern underworld' of cities like New Orleans, where it expressed and stimulated 'outlaw emotions'.[17] Such a tale, heavily laden with stereotypes, clearly played on white notions of black immorality; yet, even to racial progressives, it did seem to make a kind of empirical sense. Since the earliest years of its recorded history, the blues *had* celebrated 'outlaw emotions': overtly sexual hits like 'Black Snake Moan', 'Meat Cutter Blues', 'Tight Like That', and 'I Got the Best Jelly Roll in Town',

---

[16] W. C. Handy, *Father of the Blues* (New York, 1941), 78.
[17] 'Enigmatic Folk-Songs of the Southern Underworld', *Current Opinion* (September 1919), 165–6.

laden with culinary and animal double entendres that brought the feeling, sensing, tasting body vividly to mind.[18]

For intellectuals in the interwar era, coming to terms with the blues meant engaging with this sexual music. More than a few regarded it with a mix of dismay and distaste. The sociologist Forrester Washington, writing in 1928, spoke for many when he lamented the salaciousness of the recordings issued by race record companies, recordings he claimed were spreading urban disorder into the farthest flung corners of the black rural landscape.[19] Buried within such comments were early stirrings of a social science critique decrying the 'pathology' of black urban life, a critique that would reach its peak of intensity after World War Two. But what is striking about the Delta study of 1942 is the absence of such moralistic laments. Alan Lomax, Lewis Jones and Charles S. Johnson found a vibrant authenticity in black sexual song, a sense of the music's 'incandescence' that had its roots in the politics of the Popular Front.

Born in Texas in 1916, Alan Lomax was raised on the study of folk music: his father, John Lomax, collected cowboy ballads and African-American song in the early twentieth-century American south. The elder Lomax was a conservative southerner for whom collecting folklore was a nostalgic attempt to salvage pristine rural traditions.[20] That preoccupation was not, however, shared by his son. By the late 1930s, when he joined the Library of Congress, Alan Lomax was active in left-wing cultural circles and committed to revitalising folkloric practice along progressive lines.

Integral to that revitalisation was the documentation of sexual song. In the folk song hunts in the late 1930s and 1940s, Lomax sought out and recorded obscene material, depositing the disks in the Library of Congress. He had inaugurated this practice in 1938 in an extraordinary three-day interview with the jazz pioneer Jelly Roll Morton, who sat at his piano and recreated the sound of the blues of the Storyville brothel, songs so explicit in their sexual content that they remained buried in the archives for a full fifty years. (See the appendix at the end of this article, for lyrics.) Three years later, on the Coahoma County study, Lomax's directives to the Fisk fieldworkers targeted sexual and scatological material: party songs, dirty jokes, and 'toasts', the ritualised abusive humour that he saw as a vital form of African-American culture.[21] He even restaged his Jelly

[18] On sexuality in blues recordings, see Paul Oliver, 'The Blue Blues', in Oliver, *Screening the Blues: Aspects of the Blues Tradition* (Cambridge, 1968), pp. 164–261.

[19] Forrester Washington, 'Recreational Facilities for the Negro', *The Annals of the American Academy of Political and Social Science* 130 (November 1928), 279.

[20] Jerrold Hirsch, 'Modernity, Nostalgia, and Southern Folklore Studies: the Case of John Lomax', *Journal of American Folklore* 150 (Spring 1992), 183–207.

[21] See Alan Lomax, 'Folk Culture Study: Suggested Field Procedures', 2, in ALA-HC, where Lomax specifies 'sexual or skatological [sic] songs' as one of the song types to be collected and researched on the study. For examples of obscene material collected on

Roll Morton session by interviewing ex-brothel pianist Jaybird Jones, sitting him at his piano, pumping him for anecdotes of Clarksdale's red-light district.[22] The result was disks full of obscene songs, rhymes and tales that the Library of Congress catalogued with the Greek symbol 'delta' to denote its erotic content and render it off limits to all but specialist scholars.

In recording sexually explicit material, Lomax broke with a generation of American song collectors whose works lamented the obscenity of black secular song while refusing to provide any evidence of it. Accounts of Negro folk music published in the early twentieth century by Howard Odum, Guy Johnson, Gates Thomas and Newman White were suffused with distaste for the salaciousness of what they encountered. 'The real problem of the Negro work-songs is not to find them, but to get them selected, classified and expurgated for publication so that the point and quality of the songs are not impaired', wrote Gates Thomas in 1926. 'Pornography is such an organic part of their structure that it cannot be excised without destroying the point of the songs.'[23] Yet in the song collections they published, obscene material was excoriated and excised, for, as Odum explained, 'these songs come ill-harmonised to the soft, stirring melodies of a folklife'.[24]

As Odum suggests, more than simply obscenity laws led folklorists to expurgate sexual song. Early twentieth-century song collectors had a sense of the authentic folk voice rooted in Victorian ideas of uplift. The beauty of 'soft, stirring melodies of a folklife' lay in their purity of spirit, their echoes of a divine presence, which enabled listeners to transcend gross physicality and experience something of the sublime.[25] Rooted in pristine peasant communities, folk song moved the listener to spiritual catharsis. While African-American spirituals seemed to serve this func-tion, sexual song did not. Its relentless double entendres mired listeners in the physical, in a world of black snakes, boiled cabbage, and jelly rolls.

That Alan Lomax recorded this material owed to a political vision that attempted to disentangle the concept of folk music from its Victorian moorings. He shared that vision with other left folklorists involved in WPA lore-gathering programs: Benjamin Botkin, Herbert Halpert and

the study, see Lomax's interview with David Edwards, on AFS 6615a, Fisk University Mississippi Delta Collection, AFC-LC, and *Land Where the Blues Began*, 375–9.

[22] Alan Lomax interview with Jaybird Jones, AFS 6662A and 6663A, Fisk University Mississippi Delta Collection, AFC-LC.

[23] Gates Thomas, 'South Texas Negro Work Songs', *Publications of the Texas Folklore Society* 5 (1926), 155, quoted in Paul Oliver, *Screening the Blues*, 164.

[24] Howard Odum, 'Social and Mental Traits of the Negro: Research into the Conditions of the Negro Race in Southern Towns', *Studies in History, Economics, and Public Law*, 37 (1910), 165–7; see also Howard W. Odum and Guy Johnson, *The Negro and His Songs* (Chapel Hill, 1925), 166.

[25] Ronald Radano, 'Denoting Difference: the Writing of Slave Spirituals', *Critical Inquiry* 22 (Spring, 1996), 506–54.

Mary Elizabeth Barnicle. Sexual song – even commercial 'race records', which Lomax studied appreciatively in the late 1930s – formed part of what Botkin termed 'living lore'.[26] Unlike its Victorian predecessor, 'living lore' was not confined to rural communities. As 'folklore in the making', it proliferated in the metropolis: in the songs and tales of city labourers and the 'symphony' of urban night-life.[27] Rooted in a Popular Front ethic of interethnic solidarity and industrial unionism, the concept of 'living lore' affirmed a radically inclusive American culture, celebrating the vitality and creativity of the diverse communities industrialisation had spawned. Its authenticity lay in its audible social dynamics. As Botkin explained, living lore – like 'the blues and reels and the work songs and "hollers" of the Black South' – was an 'expression of social change and culture conflict'.[28]

That search for expressions 'of social change and culture conflict' drove Lomax throughout the Delta study. He particularly noted conflicts around sex. Percolating through the obscene songs and toasts he recorded were sexual hostilities that he, along with the Fisk team, attributed to the region's high rates of mobility, involving black women at least as much as black men. In the old days, said one informant, 'a woman couldn't just get up and go once she done left home and been married to a man ... But nowadays they is practically all free. They can do most they wants to do. Leave when-so-never they get ready, run round with white men, and most everything.'[29] Adding to the tension was a sexual system that allowed sex between white men and black women but forbade it between white women and black men. 'To tell you the truth', said share-cropper Joe Cal, it's only 'the white man and the nigger woman' 'that ain't slaves in this here man's land'.[30]

From the perspective of folklore studies, Lomax's project marked a sharp break with the past. Previous hunts for black song in Mississippi

[26] B. A. Botkin, 'Folklore as a Neglected Source of Social History', in *The Cultural Approach to History* ed. Caroline F. Ware (New York, 1940), 311–12.

[27] B. A. Botkin, 'WPA and Folklore Research: "Bread and Song"', in *The Conservation of Culture: Folklorists and the Public Sector* ed. Burt Feintuch (Lexington, 1988), 259.

[28] Botkin, 'Folklore as a Neglected Source of Social History', 312. Insightful discussions of Botkin can be found in Hirsch, 'Modernity, Nostalgia, and Southern Folklore Studies', 199–203; and in Jerrold Hirsch, 'Folklore in the Making: B. A. Botkin', *Journal of American Folklore* 100 (1987), 3–38. For a sweeping analysis of Popular Front cultural politics, see Michael Denning, *The Cultural Front: the Laboring of American Culture in the Twentieth Century* (London and New York, 1997).

[29] Quoted on p. 104 of Samuel Adams, 'Social Change in the Delta', undated ms. in ALA-HC. Though the Lomax Archive's copy of this manuscript is attributed to John Work (a Fisk University musicologist who helped set up the study of Coahoma County), it is clearly authored by Adams, a fieldworker on the study: much of the text can also be found in Samuel Adams, 'The Acculturation of the Delta Negro', *Social Forces* 26 (1947), 202–5.

[30] Adams, 'Social Change in the Delta', 104.

had focused on spirituals, and virtually none had explored the Delta, a region deemed too new, too unstable, to merit serious folkloric investigation. As the head of the state's folklore programme cautioned Lomax, 'there are no folk songs and folklore typical of the Miss. Delta, since the region has been opened up and settled comparatively recently, and then largely by people from other parts of the state, including the hills where most of the folk material is to be found'.[31] Yet it was precisely the Delta's modernity that appealed to Lomax. 'It is a folklorists' illusion that folklore communities are pure, that the pure old tradition is the one most worth studying', he observed.[32] To hunt for songs in the Delta was to strike a blow against folkloric nostalgia, to show how a modernising region was creating new forms in the face of relentless conflict and change.

The Fisk sociologists, for their part, sought evidence of conflict too. Yet the agenda of Lewis Jones and Charles Johnson looked not to folkloristics but to social science, its prescriptions for African-American life. Indeed, their concerns, not those of Lomax, had targeted the Mississippi Delta to begin with.[33] Jones and Johnson were out to challenge the 'caste and class' model of race relations forged by anthropologists who in the mid-1930s had transformed the region into a pilgrimage site for students of American racial dynamics.

Paramount among such studies was John Dollard's 1937 *Caste and Class in a Southern Town*, researched fifty miles south of Clarksdale in Indianola in neighbouring Sunflower county.[34] Dollard's book probed the psychological mechanisms underpinning the South's racial order, arguing that its social relations were structured by the interaction of caste and class. Class, within the black community, was a new development – new since the late nineteenth century, when economic and educational changes had seen the emergence of a small black elite. Yet the privileges that ordinarily accompanied middle- and upper-class status were continually thwarted by an iron-clad caste system that held all African-Americans to be contaminating, a brutal, degrading system that felt little different from slavery.

By the 1940s the caste model dominated the social science understanding of race, exerting a hold so tenacious as to leave a few social scientists – particularly black ones – uneasy. What had begun as a useful

[31] Memo from Eri Douglass to Jerome Sage ('Subject: Data for Mr. Alan Lomax'), 29 October 1942, Folder 10 (Correspondence October 1942–January 1947), Fisk University Mississippi Delta Collection, AFC-LC.
[32] Lomax field notes, July 1942, ALA-HC.
[33] As late as July 1941, Lomax was suggesting southwestern Tennessee as the focus for the study, as it 'is slightly more stable than the Delta area'. Lomax to Charles S. Johnson, 30 July 1941, Folder 8 (Correspondence 1939–41), Fisk University Mississippi Delta Collection, AFC-LC.
[34] John Dollard, *Caste and Class in a Southern Town* (New York, 1937).

framework for untangling the South's complex social dynamics had turned into a model for race relations across the US that framed African-Americans as helpless victims and ruled out any prospect of change.[35] The caste model dictated that the fundamental change was impossible: black Americans acquiesced in their own subjugation, channelling their hostilities into aggression towards their own group.

Among the dissenters from the caste paradigm, none were better placed to challenge it than Charles Johnson and Lewis Jones. Since the 1930s, Fisk's Institute of Social Science had carried out regional studies showing the dynamism of social and economic patterns across the black South. The moving force behind those studies was Charles Johnson. He had come to Fisk in 1928 after seven years in New York, where as editor of the journal *Opportunity* he championed the writers of the New Negro movement. At Fisk he returned to the scholarly agenda he had absorbed at the University of Chicago, where he trained in sociology as the protégé of Robert Park. The regional studies he launched at Fisk echoed Park's 'human document' tradition, using ethnographic fieldwork methods, intensive interviews and participant observation, to probe subjects' interior worlds. The South they depicted was rife with changes in farming, welfare provision, and education. Above all it was teeming with migrants, black men and women seeking new opportunities who, as Park argued in the late 1930s, 'had gradually ceased to exhibit the characteristics of a caste'.[36]

With their emphasis on migration and the reshaping of the plantation economy, those regional studies had always challenged the caste model, but in turning to the Delta's musical culture the Fisk team confronted them head on. In *Caste and Class in a Southern Town*, John Dollard had pointed to the region's sexually expressive leisure as a lynchpin in the caste system, a gain that whites allowed to lower-class blacks that reconciled them to subjugation. Race records and juke joints, music and dancing encouraged uninhibited physical indulgence, a sensual experience denied to whites. As Dollard put it,

> [The poor Negro] has accessible pleasure possibilities which are abandoned in large degree by ... middle-class white people. His impulse expression is less burdened by guilt and less threatened by his immediate social group; the essence of the gain lies in the fact that he is more free to enjoy, not merely free to act in an external physical sense, but

[35] See James B. McKee, *Sociology and the Race Problem: the Failure of a Perspective* (Urbana and Chicago, 1993).
[36] Robert Park, introduction to Bertram Wilbur Doyle, *The Etiquette of Race Relations in the South* (1937), xxii. On Johnson and Fisk, see Richard Robbins, *Sidelines Activist: Charles S. Johnson and the struggle for Civil Rights* (Jackson, Mississippi, 1996).

actually freer to embrace important gratifying experiences.[37]

That illusion of freedom stabilised the caste system, allowing even the most denigrated to benefit from the status quo.

The Fisk team disagreed. As they saw it, the rise of the blues within the Delta had in fact *unsettled* the caste system by tying African-Americans into a mass-market black culture that celebrated mobility, pleasure and individual licence. The enthusiasm it inspired had weakened the church (the one force, they believed, that had the power to reconcile blacks to their own subjugation).[38] Above all, it had fed racial pride. 'Negroes making music are of the same nature as my own and to me they are the best in the world', one informant told fieldworker Samuel Adams. 'When a nigger sings, he sing with more emotion. Ain't nothing no white man do sincere.'[39]

Echoing through this Delta blues the Fisk team heard a new voice of black self-assertion. Fuelling that voice was economic and social change. As New Deal agricultural subsidies spurred planters to mechanise and rationalise cotton production, the quasi-feudal tenancy system declined, and planters who once voiced a sense of paternalist responsibility for tenants now hired them in the picking season and paid them off at the end of the day. Farm labourers, for their part, picked up stakes if better wages were offered elsewhere. 'Substitution of the wage relationship for the traditional sentimentalities has been accompanied by much mutual suspicion and fear', Jones and Johnson noted. The result, as they saw it, was intense animosity and a new sense of identity among black workers. Blacks in the Delta, wrote fieldworker Adams, 'are ceasing to be a folk people'.[40] Jones and Johnson concluded: 'Over the past ten years the changes may be summed up in the suggestion that a rural proletariat has developed.'[41]

In the blues of the Delta, the Fisk team heard the voice not of the folk, but of the black proletariat – secular, urban, flouting tradition. Their stress on the music's modernity echoed Sterling Brown, Langston Hughes and other African-American intellectuals who like Charles Johnson had come of age in the New Negro movement. And in describing it as a proletarian music they evoked a rallying point for some of the American left: a vision of African-Americans as a revolutionary vanguard. Like Richard Wright, like Langston Hughes, they sought the radical potential of African-American culture. It was not surprising that they heard the

[37] Dollard, *Caste and Class*, 391.
[38] See Lewis Jones, 'The Mississippi Delta', undated ms. in ALA-HC.
[39] Adams, 'Social Change in the Delta', 63.
[40] Adams, 'Acculturation of the Delta Negro', 202.
[41] Charles S. Johnson and associates, *To Stem This Tide: a Survey of Racial Tension Areas in the US* (Boston, 1943), 27–30.

Delta blues as, in essence, politicised, rife with the tensions bred by wage labour and by the sexual volatility that migration brought in its wake.

In the years that followed World War Two, the Lomax/Fisk tale of the Delta blues vanished from the historical annals. It disappeared partly because it never received a proper airing. The book that Jones and Lomax intended to write became an impossibility by late 1942, as their collaboration degenerated into a morass of professional jealousy. In truth, it had been tense from the beginning. Privately, Lomax had railed against the laziness and incompetence of the Fisk field workers. Lewis Jones, in turn, resented Lomax: a white boy from Washington radiating authority, given to peremptory memos upbraiding the Fisk team for their insufficiently musicological focus. Within weeks of completing the fieldwork, the investigators began jockeying for position as the study's primary spokesman, creating such a level of acrimony that the Library of Congress temporarily removed Lomax from the project. In 1947, when Lomax began preparing a book on the Delta, Fisk refused to loan him the field recordings. Lomax responded with a furious letter, and all contact between the two parties ceased.[42]

But in the end their narrative did not collapse so much as it was obliterated by a new generation of folk-song enthusiasts who rejected the vision of blues that had shaped it. The 1950s saw a growing enchantment with the power and purity of rural American cultures. In coffee houses, on university campuses, and at music festivals across the US, that enchantment gave birth to a folk revival. Yet this folk-song movement had a different tone from its predecessor in the interwar era, when songs of marginal peoples were taken up for their illumination of social struggle. 'For those of us whose revival began around 1958', writes Robert Cantwell, such political associations 'would have been, in our naive and compliant youth, a barrier to any enthusiasm for folksongs.'[43] Instead, revivalists embraced folk music for its 'real and human values', its heartfelt poetry.

In a Cold War culture that marginalised radicalism, song hunters recoiled from the politicised vision that had guided the folk-song hunts of the Popular Front. The folklorist Frederic Ramsey, who travelled South making recordings in the mid-1950s, wrote, 'I ... looked vainly [in previous studies] for accurate and convincing accounts of the persons who

[42] On tensions among the investigators during the fieldwork, see Alan Lomax field notes, July 1942, ALA-HC. On the disintegration of the collaboration, see B. A. Botkin to Harold Spivacke, 27 October 1942; Alan Lomax to Charles Johnson, 2 January, 1947; Alan Lomax to John Work, 2 January 1947; all in Folder 10 (Correspondence October 1942–January 1947), Fisk University Mississippi Delta Collection, AFC-LC.
[43] Robert Cantwell, *When We Were Good: the Folk Revival* (Cambridge, MA, 1996), 22.

were making [black] music.'[44] Revivalists sought a new kind of accuracy that distanced itself from what Samuel Charters called the 'sociological' thrust of interwar writing on black song.[45] Imprisoning artistry in an ideological straitjacket, those accounts could not illuminate the blues. 'If the blues simply mirrored the protest of the moment they would finally have little more than an historical interest, like the songs of the suffragettes or the Grange movement', wrote Charters. Instead, the African-American poured into the blues 'his personal and immediate experience', creating 'a poetic language' that spoke of 'a larger human reality', timeless truths of alienation and loss.[46]

In that sense, the blues revival formed part of a depolitisation of cultural inquiry in the Cold War US, a movement of intellectuals away from radicalism and towards a new role as 'guardians of the self', champions of the personal against the forces of political conformity.[47] Yet while the revival's architects sought to erase all political distortions, their own vision was informed by politics – in particular, by intensifying postwar attacks on the 'tangle of pathology' overtaking black life.[48] Mounting fear of black urban disorganisation lent added force to revivalists' conception of blues as a fundamentally rural music, suffused with the anguish of slavery, born in an isolated, primitive landscape cut off from the modern world.

It took a few years for that vision of blues to root itself in the Mississippi Delta. In his pioneering 1959 book *The Country Blues*, Samuel Charters barely mentioned Mississippi; his raw, archaic black music grew out of the rural South as a whole. And while his friend Frederic Ramsey included the Delta on his Southern song hunt, he did not seem to think that the blues had its roots there. 'Don't know what the Delta along the way will hold', he wrote to Moses Asch of Folkways Records as he embarked on his journey in 1954. 'Probably at least one good blues singer.'[49]

The idea of something called the 'Delta blues', the deepest, purest form of the music, began circulating in the early 1960s, boosted by three seminal LPs: the first Robert Johnson anthology, entitled *King of the Delta Blues*

---

[44] Frederic Ramsey, Jr., *Been Here and Gone* (New Brunswick, 1961), xi.

[45] Samuel Charters, *The Country Blues* (New York, 1959), xii.

[46] Samuel Charters, *The Poetry of the Blues* (New York, 1963), 17, 173.

[47] The phrase 'guardians of the self' is from Wilfred McClay, *The Masterless: Self and Society in Modern America* (Chapel Hill, 1994), 226, quoted in Daryl Michael Scott, *Contempt and Pity: Social Policy and the Image of the Damaged Black Psyche, 1880–1996* (Chapel Hill, 1997), 73. For a discussion of postwar intellectuals and cultural inquiry, see Andrew Ross, *No Respect: Intellectuals and Popular Culture* (New York and London, 1989), 42–64.

[48] See Scott, *Contempt and Pity*, pp. 71–91. The phrase 'tangle of pathology' was coined by Daniel Patrick Moynihan in US Department of Labor, *The Negro Family: the Case for National Action*, Washington, DC, 1965, 29.

[49] Frederic Ramsey to Moses Asch, 28 June 1954, Frederic Ramsey personal correspondence folder, Folkways Collection, Center for Folklife Programs and Cultural Studies, Smithsonian Institution, Washington, DC.

Singers, and two albums put together by record collector Pete Whelan for his Origins Jazz Library label: *The Mississippi Blues* and *Really! The Country Blues*, a compilation of tracks by Delta-born artists. The title of the latter – *really* the country blues – was a slap at Samuel Charters, whose book *The Country Blues* had neglected the Delta and thus failed to capture what Whelan saw as the music's most authentic form. 'Wasn't Charters' country blues real?', an interviewer asked Whelan thirty years later. 'It was real', he replied, 'but not real enough.'[50]

The 'realness' of the Delta blues lay in its rough-hewn sound, its heated, primal emotion, and the primitive character of the song form. As one of its early champions explained: 'The voice is dark and heavy, often thick and congested, with a peculiar crying quality . . . and suffused throughout with an emotional intensity that is all but overpowering (the words seem almost torn from the singer's throat).'[51] These were barely songs at all – more a rhythmic wail of anguish, in which 'monosyllabic cries' expressing 'strong, uncontrollable feelings' often 'carr[ied] far greater meaning than do the song's words'.[52] They were raw, unvarnished, in the most profound sense, an intense distillation of the music of slavery, 'only a step from the wordless field cries and hollers of an older generation'.[53] Such a music could only have been born in the Delta: nowhere else had perpetuated the dynamics of slavery in such a pure form, and nowhere else had been so completely cut off from commercial culture. Yet raw as they were, they voiced sentiments that were startlingly contemporary. As Pete Welding wrote of the greatest of the Delta bluesmen, Robert Johnson, 'His songs are the lonely, impassioned, unanswered cries of disaffected, disoriented, rootless modern man, purposeless, without direction or power, adrift at the mercies of the fates.'[54]

That the Delta seemed a natural landscape for this music of existential loneliness had much to do with social changes that transformed the look and feel of the region itself. Pilgrims who went there in the early 1960s absorbed in the romance that they had woven around the music found a very different landscape than had greeted the Fisk investigators twenty years earlier. With railroad lines overgrown or pulled up and two-thirds of its black population having fled to the north, the Delta of the mid-1960s did look more isolated, more remote than ever before. Add to that all that had happened in the previous decade to push the region to the forefront of white liberal consciousness: the horrific lynching of 14-year-old Emmett

[50] Joel   Slotnikoff,   'Pete   Whelan   Interview',   http://www.bluesworld.com/PeteWhelanInterview.html.

[51] Pete Welding, 'Stringin' the Blues', *Down Beat* (1 July 1965), 22.

[52] *Ibid.*

[53] *Ibid.*

[54] Pete Welding, 'Robert Johnson: Hellhound on His Trail', *Blues Unlimited* 82 (June 1971), 16.

Till for the crime of whistling at a white woman: the reissue of John Dollard's *Caste and Class in a Southern Town*, given a new life on university reading lists: and, above all, the Mississippi Freedom Summer campaigns for civil and political rights – all painted a grim portrait of the Delta as a region still stuck in the mid-nineteenth century, the most benighted place on earth.

For blues revivalists, only that setting could have bred a music so permeated by alienation and anguish. It proved to be a powerful vision – powerful enough, indeed, to sway Alan Lomax. In the years following the Second World War, Lomax moved away from the focus on social conflict that had guided him in the era of the Popular Front. By the time he wrote his account of the Coahoma County study, his magnum opus *The Land Where the Blues Began*, in 1993, he had largely discarded the vision that had once led him to Jelly Roll Morton. If in 1938 Morton's sexual blues provided 'a rich evocation of underground America', in 1993 they were commercial, superficial, and inauthentic: 'the blues of the professional jazzman are never quite the real thing'.[55] The real thing was the blues of the Delta, a music of 'anomie and alienation' that had its roots in a region where slavery had never ended, that was cut off from the forces of the modern world.

It had taken Lomax fifty years to publish an account of the Mississippi Delta. 'He agonised over that book', says his daughter. 'He lived with that material for a long time.'[56] That he so substantially rewrote his field notes speaks volumes for the shift in his once radical vision. But perhaps it also tells us something about the limits of that vision itself. As the Fisk sociologists may well have sensed, Lomax was not documenting black music as part of a fight against racism. Fundamentally, he was fighting what he called 'cultural grey-out', the dominance of world music by the faceless, sentimental tunes churned out by the corporate song hacks of Tin Pan Alley. Capturing the blues at the grass roots formed part of the battle for a full-blooded music – a battle that for Lomax was charged with democratic romance. He wrote of making field recordings, 'Every time I took one of those big, black, glass-based platters out of its box, I felt that a magical moment was opening up in time. Never before had the black people, kept almost incommunicado in the Deep South, had the chance to tell their story in their own way.'[57]

It's hard to tell what Lomax's informants made of this process, but evidence suggests that some of them had a take on the sessions that was rather more straightforward. 'Dear sir', wrote Muddy Waters two months after Lomax recorded him in his cabin on the outskirts of Clarksdale.

[55] Lomax, *Land Where the Blues Began*, 440.
[56] Anna Lomax Chairetakis, telephone conversation with the author, February 1999.
[57] Lomax, *Land Where the Blues Began*, xi.

'This is the boy that put out Bur Clover Blues and First Highway Blues and several more blues. Want to know did they take. Please sir if they did please send some to Clarksdale Miss please sir answer soon to M G Morganfield.'[58]

That the twenty-six-year-old Morganfield felt obliged to call himself a boy in writing to the twenty-five-year-old Lomax suggests that, despite all hopes of inspiring trust, the South's racial etiquette still impinged on the study. Moreover the letter suggests something more, something that Lomax never seems to have recognised: Morganfield assumed that he was a talent scout for a commercial record company. Clearly, there were some elements of the Delta's modernity that even Alan Lomax did not want to hear.

Appendix
'Wining Boy Blues' (Jelly Roll Morton), recorded by Alan Lomax at the Library of Congress, June 1938. Found on Jelly Roll Morton, *Winin' Boy Blues* (Rounder CD 1094)

[58] McKinley Morganfield to Alan Lomax, 21 September 1941, Folder 11 (Correspondence: individual informants), Fisk University Mississippi Delta Collection, AFC-LC.

(speaks): This happen to be one of my first tunes in the blues line down in New Orleans in the very early days when people first thought of playing piano in that section. Of course, when a man played piano, the stamp was on him for life, the femininity stamp, and I didn't want that on so of course when I did start to playing the songs were kinda smutty a bit, not so smutty but something like this.

(sings): I'm the winin' boy, don't deny my name (× 3)
I can pick it up and shake it like Stavin' Chain,
I'm the winin' boy, don't deny my name

I had a gal, I had her in the grass
I had that bitch, had her in the grass (× 2)
One days she got scared and a snake ran up her big ass,
I'm the winin' boy, don't deny my name

I had that bitch, had her on the stump (× 3)
I fucked her till her pussy stunk
I'm the winin' boy, don't deny my name

Nickel's worth of beefsteak and a dime's worth of lard (× 3)
I'm gonna salivate your pussy till my penis gets hard,
I'm the winin' boy, don't deny my name.

Every time the changin' of the moon (× 3)
The blood comes rushin' from the bitch's womb,
I'm the winin' boy, don't deny my fuckin' name

I want about ten sweet bitches to myself (× 3)
The one I like I'm gonna keep her to myself
I'm the winin' boy, don't deny my fuckin' name

A PROFANE HISTORY OF EARLY MODERN
OATHS

By John Spurr

READ 10 MARCH 2000

IT was a dark November night in 1680 when a gang of masked men burst into Robert Robinson's isolated house, waking the household with the clatter of their riding boots, swords and muffled curses, and snarling at Robinson, 'Old rogue, where is thy money?' After ransacking the room and breaking open a chest, another of the gang 'did hold a Bible to Robert Robinson to swear whether he had any more gold or silver than what they had taken from him'. Robinson swore that he had no more and 'Mr Lodge did laugh when he heard Robert Robinson sworn.' Now the burglary of Robert Robinson's house near the village of Old Hutton, Westmorland, at about 1.00 am on 4 November 1680 had some very odd features, but none so curious as Mr Lodge's laughter when the old man was forced to swear. Edmund Lodge was the local schoolmaster and curate. In 1678 he had leased Robinson's house for three years and the old man was now a 'tabler' or lodger in his own home. In time Lodge would move on to be the vicar of Clapham in Lancashire, where he died in 1696. But before then he would be tried and acquitted as one of this band of coiners and robbers. Some of these same desperadoes said that the raid on Robinson's house had been Lodge's idea. Circumstantial evidence suggests that Lodge had told the thieves that Robinson had more than £40 in a chest 'ready to be taken away'; and when the gang broke in, Lodge indulged in a lot of phoney-sounding play-acting with them – one thief shouting at him, 'damn you for a dog, hold your peace or I will cut your flesh from your bones'. So the testimony of one of the burglars 'that Mr Lodge did laugh when he heard Robert Robinson sworn' is plausible.[1] It is also intriguing. What was it that made Mr Lodge laugh?

The answer may be staring us in the face. In the burglary at Hutton the purpose, language and ritual of an oath were being grotesquely perverted, and Edmund Lodge may simply have been so malicious or so nihilistic that he took a delight in that perversion. As a Christian, never mind a clergyman, Lodge would have been well aware that oaths

---

[1] The case is recounted in A. Macfarlane, *The Justice and the Mare's Ale – Law and Disorder in Seventeenth-Century England* (Oxford, 1981), 47–60, esp. 51.

were 'the safest tie of conscience', the 'highest obligations possible'.[2] The year after the burglary Dean John Tillotson preached a sermon to the assizes at York on the familiar topic of oaths and their obligation.

> An oath is a sacred thing, as being an act of religion and an invocation of the name of God: and this whether the name of God be expressly mentioned in it or not. If a man only say, I swear, or I take my oath, that a thing is or is not ... or if a man answer upon his oath ... or if a man swear by heaven or by earth, or by any other thing that hath relation to God; in all these cases a man doth virtually call God to witness; and in so doing he doth by consequence invoke him as a judge and an avenger, in case what he swears be not true ... a curse upon ourselves is always implied in case of perjury.[3]

In short, an oath is a provisional self-curse. A profane oath is one sworn in inappropriate circumstances, to support a lie or a frivolous statement. It is a breach of the third commandment's ban on the misuse of God's name. So much was common knowledge.

As a seventeenth-century English Protestant clergyman, Edmund Lodge would have been taught a rigorous line on oaths. Although, for most theologians and divines 'the Lord teaches us how to swear' in Jeremiah iv. 2, 'thou shalt swear in truth, in judgment and in right-eousness', the application of these cardinal principles was a complex business requiring much discussion in print, pulpit and university. The main rules were that oaths are either 'assertory' – stating a matter of fact – or 'promissory' – committing the swearer to a future action. Oaths are to be sworn in the plain sense of their words and in the sense of those who imposed them. An oath cannot be lawful if it obliges the swearer to an unlawful act. Even a rash or coerced oath binds: a promissory oath binds even if it is to your disadvantage, discomfort and inconvenience (but not if it would lead to self-destruction). In their theoretical treatment of oaths and the difficulties to which they gave rise, English Protestants frequently considered the hypothetical case of 'a Traveller falling amongst Theeves, who with their swords at his breast, should threaten him with death, unless he sware unto them to ransome his life'. Not only was it lawful to promise the ransom and 'ratifie the promise with an oath', but the oath had to be kept; 'for however the person be unworthy, yet our faith, whereby we bound our selves to God, ought to be kept'. After all, in the last resort the victim

[2] Isaac Barrow, *Theological Works*, ed. A. Napier (9 vols., Cambridge, 1859), II, 44–6.
[3] John Tillotson, *Sermons* (12 vols., 1757), ii, 65–6.

did have a choice, his life or his oath.[4] This casuistical point was not lost on the wider public who lapped up polemical pamphlets and rogue literature which explored identical dilemmas.[5] It would not be too fanciful, therefore, to suppose that Lodge was recalling this casuistry as he heard the terrified Mr Robinson swear on the Bible.[6] And that may be all that we can say about this unsavoury episode. It was simply an instance of criminals profaning a solemn oath with the possible complicity of a far from resolute clergyman. Or, perhaps, we can go a little further and seek a more general framework, a proper history of early modern oaths, against which we might more fully comprehend Mr Lodge's momentary mirth.[7]

I

'An oath is a sacred thing ... an act of religion', said Tillotson in 1681. And it is still claimed today that 'oaths are encountered among all peoples and in all cultures. They are a primal symbol of religion.'[8] Universal and timeless oaths may be, but they are not, of course, universally effective. Complaints of perjury and profane swearing were as familiar in the distant past as they are today. It is surely only realistic, then, to conclude that oaths are a necessary but imperfect device in a fallen world, a constant requirement and yet constantly broken: as Professor Nelson has remarked 'oaths operated no more, and no less, as a kind of judgment of God in the ninth than in the twentieth century: they solemnized proceedings and reduced the risk of perjury'.[9] Perhaps Edmund Lodge's hilarity is no more than the cynical laughter of a man who believed with Polonius that oaths are 'springs to catch woodcocks', traps for the simple-minded and opportunities for the unscrupulous.[10]

There is, however, an alternative view. Oaths, it could be argued,

---

[4] Robert Sanderson, *De Juramenti: Seven Lectures Concerning the Obligation of Promissory Oaths* (1655), 137–8; John Tombes, *Sephersheba: Or, The Oath-Book* (1662), 105–7. These authors pride themselves on the strictness of their teaching compared to Catholic casuists such as Becanus and Azorius and even to Cicero.

[5] See Misorcus, *The Anti-Quaker* (1676), 13–14; [Richard Head], *Jackson's Recantation, or, the Life and Death of the Notorious High-Way-Man* (1674), sigs. C3v–C4v.

[6] Robinson's was, of course, an assertory rather than a promissory oath.

[7] I have been engaged on such a history of oaths and swearing for some time. I am grateful to the British Academy for the award of a post-doctoral fellowship between 1987 and 1990 that enabled me to begin work on the subject.

[8] *The Encyclopedia of Religion*, ed. M. Eliade (16 vols., New York, 1987), xv, 301; also see H. Silving, 'The Oath', *Yale Law Journal*, LXVIII (1958–9).

[9] J. L. Nelson, 'Dispute Settlement in Carolingian West Francia', in *The Settlement of Disputes in Early Medieval Europe*, ed. W. Davies and P. Fouracre (Cambridge, 1986), 60.

[10] *Hamlet*, I, iii, line 115, in *William Shakespeare – The Complete Works*, ed. P. Alexander (1951), 1034.

are part of the world we have lost. Once near universal, they have waned in popularity and effect. This is a view which often supposes a movement towards 'reason': oaths are seen as a property of 'primitive' or even 'superstitious' societies which really did believe that God could strike you down for blasphemy, but as societies 'advanced' they acquired better, more rational, means of guaranteeing performance and truth than an oath and developed more sophisticated (or vestigial) notions of God and his *modus operandi*. This evolutionary account of oaths makes certain assumptions. First, it assumes that at some stage oaths exercised a widespread power over individual consciences. It is common to find assertions in the literature that everyone trusted oaths, that 'in the sixteenth century and before, oaths ... were one of the strongest ties binding society together'.[11] Secondly, the equation of oaths with a less rational mentality implies that oaths *as such* had absolute power, that, for example, an oath creates an obligation where none previously existed or that an oath compels belief even when that belief contradicts other evidence and reason. Thus Maitland asserted that the oath was 'the primary mode of proof' for the Anglo-Saxons and that 'the oath, if duly made, was conclusive'.[12] A. J. Gurevich states that medieval culture placed credence in oaths 'on the grounds that truth inheres in the oath, and a solemn act of this nature cannot be carried out against the will of God'.[13] A third related assumption is that oath belief is an index of religious belief, that waning fear of oaths is a consequence of a declining belief in the deity, or at least in divine surveillance of and intervention in the human world.[14] And this is where the early modern period comes into the story.

Historians have noticed two distinct tendencies in the history of sixteenth and seventeenth-century oaths. One is that oaths were becoming a favoured tool of the secular authorities: Paolo Prodi is only the latest scholar to have argued that the early modern state's monopolisation of oaths represents a sacralisation of power and the first steps towards the 'secular oath'.[15] The other tendency, however, runs counter to this. Oaths and oaths-taking are often alleged to be in crisis during these centuries: 'oaths, in general, were not taken as seriously

---

[11] R. L. Greaves, *Society and Religion in Elizabethan England* (Minneapolis, 1981), 680.

[12] Quoted by P. Wormald, 'Charters, Law and the Settlement of Disputes in Anglo-Saxon England', in *Settlement of Disputes*, ed. Davies and Fouracre, 151.

[13] A. J. Gurevich, *Categories of Medieval Culture* (1985), 175; cf. P. P. Howell, *A Manual of Nuer Law* (1954), 219–20.

[14] L. Kolmer, *Promissorische Eide im Mittelalter* (Regensburger Historische Forschungen, 12; Kallmünz, 1989), 362; also see the editor's remarks in the 'Postface' to *Le Serment*, ed. R. Verdier (2 vols., Paris, 1991), II, 429–36.

[15] Paolo Prodi, *Das Sakrament der Herrschaft – Der politische Eid in der Verfassungsgeschichte des Okzidents*, trans. J. Else (Berlin, 1997); originally published as *Il Sacramento del Potere* (Bologna, 1992).

as they had been in earlier centuries', says one historian, there was a 'declining belief in the awesomeness of the oath'; by the 1690s, according to another, 'only Quakers and perhaps some baptists feared oaths as a matter of religion'; in the seventeenth century 'oaths had lost their point', says Christopher Hill, as England was moving 'from oaths to self-interest'.[16] Viewed in this light Mr Lodge's laughter becomes a tiny, but revealing, moment in a crisis of the early modern conscience.

It seems then that we must choose between two views of the history of oaths and oath-taking: one a steady-state in which oaths are pragmatically justifiable because they bind some of the people some of the time; and the other a story of declining belief in their 'awesomeness'. Both interpretations exhibit a certain reverence towards oaths; they take the oath at the estimation of the 'oath-specialists', the clergy and the lawyers who formulate the rules governing oaths and compose the litanies of complaint when those rules are broken or disregarded. In this paper, however, I want to suggest another approach to the history of oaths. I want to essay a profane rather than a reverential history. This is a distinction borrowed from Richard Trexler. In his polemic for a profane rather than reverential history of popular religion, Professor Trexler exhorts us to overhaul our definitions of religion, to conceive of religions as sets of social behaviour rather than as communities bound by doctrines.[17] My ambitions are more modest. I simply want to see if we can step outside some of the assumptions and preoccupations of the two approaches just sketched: I seek not to dethrone but to supplement them. But how am I to go about constructing a profane history of oaths?

It would seem logical as a first step to take Christianity and the Christian God out of the picture. This, however, turns out to be decidedly old hat. After all the existence of pagan oaths was for early modern preachers and lawyers conclusive proof of a natural law of respect for oaths: 'the reverence of an oath is natural to us, and implanted in us'.[18] In 1647 John Digby, earl of Bristol, pronounced oaths

---

[16] B.J. Shapiro, *Probability and Certainty in Seventeenth-Century England* (Princeton, 1983), 186; C.J. Sommerville, *The Secularization of Early Modern England* (Oxford, 1992), 143; C. Hill, *Society and Puritanism in Pre-Revolutionary England* (paperback edn, 1969), 371.

[17] See Richard Trexler, 'Reverence and Profanity in the Study of Early Modern Religion', in *Religion and Society in Early Modern Europe 1500–1800*, ed. K. von Greyerz (1984). The distinction was an early modern commonplace. 'Honour and Reverence consist onely in a separation from vulgar usage, in setting a greater value upon, in retaining more veneration for one then we commonly do for others', while 'to profane' is to break down that separation: John North, *A Sermon Preached before the King at Newmarket October 8 1671* (Cambridge, 1671), 20–1.

[18] John Allen, *Of Perjury* (1682), 10.

the highest and strongest obligations that can pass from man to God, from nation to nation, from subjects to their prince, or prince to their subjects, or from man to man, and this is not only so declared in scripture, but was undoubtedly part of that natural and moral law which was by God planted in the hearts of man even from the creation.[19]

In a judgement of 1744 Chancellor Hardwicke ticked off Sir Edward Coke for his early seventeenth-century definition of an oath as the act of a Christian. Oaths, said Hardwicke, 'are as old as creation and their essence is an appeal to the supreme being as thinking him the rewarder of truth and the avenger of falsehood'.[20] Just a few decades later French revolutionaries were crowning their festivals with elaborate oaths. In Mona Ozouf's opinion

> the sacrality of the oath, for the men of the Revolution, derived from the fact that it made visible the act of contracting, which was conceived as the fundamental feature of sociability ... [but it was also combined] ... with those invocations that linked it to a necessary transcendence and those curses intended to show the extent to which the contractual commitments presupposed individual abdication.

This comment illuminates the two sides of the oath: its role in human transactions; and its invocation of a superior, usually transcendent, authority.[21]

The latter, the invocation of a 'necessary transcendence', is often seen as fundamental to the oath. It arises naturally in discussions of the validity of oaths made between individuals who do not believe in the same god. What mattered here was that an individual swore by his or her own god. Hobbes acknowledged the commonly held sentiment that 'there is no swearing by anything which the swearer thinks not God'.[22] Protestant divines were unanimous that a Christian's promissory oath to an infidel was valid. And Jews and Muslims were sworn on their own holy books in Christian courts. There is a nice question here about whether an oath by a false god is really as convincing to Christians as

[19] [John Digby], *An Apologie of the Earl of Bristol* (1647: reprinted Caen, 1656), 31.

[20] Quoted in *Boland and Sayer on Oaths and Affirmations: Second Edition*, ed. W.J. Fell and A.G. Keats (1961), 1.

[21] M. Ozouf, *Festivals and the French Revolution*, trans. A. Sheridan (Cambridge, Mass., 1988), 280; also see C. Langlois, 'Le Serment Révolutionnaire 1789–1791: Fondation et Exclusion', in *Serment*, ed. Verdier, II, 394; J.C. Colfavru, 'Le Serment', *Revolution Françaises*, 2 (1888); T. Tackett, *Religion, Revolution and Regional Culture in Eighteenth-century France: The Ecclesiastical Oath of 1791* (Princeton, 1986). In so far as I have been able to ascertain, French revolutionary oaths are of the 'je jure' or 'nous jurons' formula and what seems to be at stake for the conscience is less what people swear by than what they swear to.

[22] Thomas Hobbes, *Leviathan* (Everyman edn., 1914), 73.

an oath by the true God. Some Christians engaged in curious double think: Grotius, for instance, maintained that if an individual swears by false gods, he shall be bound 'because, though under false notes, yet in a generall notion, he looks upon the Deity; wherefore the true God, if he swears falsly, interprets it to be done to his dishonour'.[23] On occasion Lollards, who generally refused to swear oaths, apparently extracted oaths of secrecy from those orthodox individuals whom they were seeking to enlighten.[24] In *Titus Andronicus* Aaron the Moor requires an oath from the Roman Lucius, and observes that 'an idiot holds his bauble for a god, / And keeps the oath which by that god he swears'.[25] In other words Aaron recognizes that an oath binds those who are credulous enough to believe themselves bound; are there perhaps shades of Edmund Lodge to be discerned in the figure of wicked Aaron?

It is Aaron's own atheism, of course, which represents the serious challenge to the sanctity of oaths. When he first demands the oath, Lucius asks him, 'who should I swear by? thou believest no god; / That granted, how canst thou believe an oath?' 'What if I do not? as, indeed, I do not,' replies Aaron, 'yet for I know thou art religious, / And hast a thing within thee called conscience.'[26] Although he was happy to rely on the oaths of believers, Aaron himself acknowledged no 'transcendence', no God, and so he could never offer or be bound by an oath. This is precisely why Locke and even Hobbes believed that atheists were beyond the pale of civil society.[27] It is why in 1880 the atheist Charles Bradlaugh declared that the oath had 'a meaningless character' for him and why in return he was not allowed to swear the oath of allegiance and take his seat as an MP.[28] Yet whether the oath was spurned or sworn, it is in these cases still treated with respect, with reverence. A truly profane treatment, on the other hand, would contemplate with equanimity the prospect of oaths being sworn and received by godless individuals like Aaron and Bradlaugh; and it would do so because it is concerned with oaths as forms of behaviour.

[23] *The Illustrious Hugo Grotius Of the Law of Warre and Peace*, trans. C[lement] B[arksdale] (1655), 234.
[24] I infer this from the cases reported in S. McSheffrey, *Gender and Heresy: Women and Men in Lollard Communities 1420–1530* (Philadelphia, 1995), 12, 101.
[25] *Titus Andronicus*, v, i, lines 70–80, in *Shakespeare*, 895.
[26] *Ibid.*
[27] *John Locke: Epistola de Tolerantia: A Letter on Toleration*, ed. R. Klibansky and J.W. Gough (Oxford, 1968), 135; Hobbes quoted in R. Tuck, *Philosophy and Government 1572–1651* (Cambridge, 1993), 344.
[28] W. L. Arnstein, *The Bradlaugh Case: A Study in Late Victorian Opinion and Politics* (Oxford, 1965), 40–44. A contrast is provided by a Christian like Eamon De Valera who in 1927 subscribed an oath of fidelity to the British monarch while declaring that 'I am not taking an oath'; see T. R. Dwyer, *Eamon de Valera* (Dublin, 1980), 75–6.

II

Oaths are speech acts. They are utterances that also do things. Oaths can be said to determine or control other utterances and future events. In a judicial setting, for instance, an effective oath can determine another utterance such as a verdict and hence an event such as an acquittal or conviction. What makes any utterance 'effective' is that it meets certain conditions, the 'conditions of felicity' as Austin called them, namely that it follows conventional procedure, is uttered in appropriate circumstances and by and to appropriate people, and is performed in a proper frame of mind.[29] It is not difficult to imagine how various oaths might meet such conditions:

> He first gave me the oath to look over, and then took a little Greek testament from a bag, gave it open into my hand, and himself read the oath aloud to me, while I kept two fingers of the right hand on the open book. After this I was for restoring the book to him, but he guided my hand with the book to my mouth, to be kissed, which is a form usual in all oaths in England.[30]

This is a German tourist's account of taking the oath of admission to the Bodleian Library, Oxford, in 1710. The solemnity of this oath was more than matched by oaths of office or by oaths in the courts of law. Oaths, however, are exchanged in many less formal circumstances: in Essex around 1511 John Grey addressed a young woman, 'Elizabeth, and if ye may fynde in your hert to love me above all other, her[e] and afor God, I plight you my trouth.'[31] Oaths and swearing were at home in the good company of the alehouse or the bowling green. John Bunyan complained that it would provoke a sober man to anger if one should swear to a notorious lie 'and yet thus do men deal with the holy God: They tell their Jestings, Tales and Lies, and then swear by God that they are true'.[32] These are all oaths in a strict sense, and most contemporaries, unlike Bunyan, were able to distinguish between those that should be treated seriously and those that are mere badinage. Confirmation, if needed, of this truism is afforded by the anthropological and the medieval literatures. An analysis of oaths in one Kenyan

[29] See J. L. Austin, *How to do Things with Words*, ed. J.O. Urmson (Oxford, 1962).

[30] The diary of Z. C. von Uffenbach quoted in J. B. Major, *Cambridge under Queen Anne* (1911), 377.

[31] W. H. Hale, *A Series of Precedents and Proceedings in Criminal Causes, Extending from the year 1475 to 1640: Extracted from the Act Books of the Ecclesiastical Courts in the Diocese of London* (1847), 88–9. Troth-plighting is not strictly swearing an oath, it is the 'afor God' which differentiates this example; on troth-plighting see D. Cressy, *Birth, Marriage and Death – Ritual, Religion and the Life-Cycle in Tudor and Stuart England* (Oxford, 1997), 267–76.

[32] John Bunyan, *The Life and Death of Mr Badman*, ed. J.F. Forrest and R. Sharrock (Oxford, 1988), 28.

community has shown that they are used jokingly, as part of verbal play, and this informal use is signalled by smiles and laughter, by forms of address and verbal construction. When a similar oath is used in dispute resolution or as a group oath, then it is elaborated with ritual. Medieval Europeans, too, could rank oaths on a scale from the jokily conversational to the formal or, as some would have preferred, from the profane to the sacred.[33]

Oaths, then, are speech acts elaborated by ritual and context to perform a variety of functions. These rituals and contexts have not been much explored. The very gestures with which oaths are sworn are no doubt significant. In many languages verbs for swearing are derived from roots meaning 'to grasp' or 'to hold'.[34] Taking an oath often involves holding or touching inanimate objects. In the Christian West swearing oaths has been associated with altars, relics, crucifixes and holy books for many centuries: it was considered remarkable in 794 when Bishop Peter of Verdun took an oath 'without relics and without the holy evangels, only on the heart of God', while an oath sworn in twelfth-century England on a 'troper' or service book, rather than the gospels, was open to question. Oaths were still being sworn on holy relics in the seventeenth century in Wales and Ireland.[35] Particularly significant oaths were sworn on the consecrated host. In Ireland in 1488 Sir Richard Edgecumbe 'devised as sure an oath as he could' to bind the earl of Kildare to the new Tudor king: the earl attended mass and then 'holding his right hand over the holy host' (which had been consecrated and divided into three) he 'made his solemn oath of ligeance unto our sovereign lord King Henry VII'.[36] Medieval oaths were usually taken with either the right hand or the first two fingers raised or the hand laid on the holy object: oaths of fealty of course involved another set of gestures entirely.[37] Not that the

[33] C.A. Kratz, 'Genres of Power: A Comparative Analysis of Okiek Blessings, Curses and Vows', *Man*, 24 (1989); J. Ziolkowski, 'Saints in Invocations and Oaths in Medieval Literature', *Journal of English and Germanic Philology*, 87 (1988).
[34] See R. Ó Huiginn, 'Tongu da dia toinges mo thuath [I swear by the God by whom my people swear] and related expressions', in *Sages, Saints and Storytellers*, ed. D. Ó Corrian, L. Breatnach and K. McCone (Maynooth, 1989), 337. I am grateful to Professor Ralph Griffiths for alerting me to this essay.
[35] For a survey see N. Hermann Mascard, *Les reliques des saints – La formation coutumière d'un droit* (Paris, 1975), 235–70; and for the examples cited P. J. Geary, *Furta Sacra – The Theft of Relics in the Central Middle Ages* (Princeton, 1978), 43–4; R. Bartlett, *England Under the Norman and Angevin Kings 1075–1225* (Oxford, 2000), 180; G.H. Jones, 'Celtic Britain and the Pilgrim Movement', *Y Cymmrodor* 23 (1912), 352–3; R. Gillespie, *Devoted People – Belief and Religion in Early Modern Ireland* (Manchester, 1997), 33–4.
[36] 'The Voyage of Sir Richard Edgecumbe, 1488', in *Hibernica: or, Some Antient Pieces relating to Ireland* (1757), 32–5.
[37] J-C. Schmitt, *La Raison des Gestes dans l'Occident Medieval* (Paris, 1990), 99, 291, 321; B. Guenée, *Un Roi et son Historien* (Paris, 1999), 413–14; F. Koller, *Der Eid im Münchener Stadtrecht des Mittelalters* (Munich, 1957), 44.

two categories of swearing could always be kept separate in practice: the oath of an entrant to one of fifteenth-century Stamford's gilds was sworn on the Bible, but began 'I shall trewe man be to god almighty, to our lady seynt Mary and to that Holy Virgin and Martyr St Katherine'; the ritual concluded with kissing the book and drinking a round with the brethren.[38]

From the later middle ages, however, an attenuation of the ritual around solemn oaths becomes apparent and it seems to be due to several, quite distinct, factors, including changing legal practice, pressure from secular rulers, and in due course the impact of Protestant scruples in some areas.[39] By 1640 John Ley could describe various English procedures, including the raising of three fingers in acknowledgement of the Trinity: but the 'commonly known manner' is to lay one's hand on the Bible or gospels while swearing and finish 'with so help me God in Jesus Christ, sealing all up with kissing the book'. 'The first and purest use of oaths', exemplified by Abraham in Genesis xiv. 22, claimed one preacher, was 'to mention the name of the Lord with lifting up the hand to heaven'. In 1686 the Massachusetts colonist Samuel Sewell swore the oath of allegiance: 'I read the oath myself holding the book in my left hand and holding up my right hand to heaven' – a procedure which led to some tension with English officials who preferred to lay their hands on the book and kiss it.[40] Obviously these exiguous and bloodless early modern swearing rituals were still able to arouse passions. Yet Sewell's account also reminds us of a crucial reality: some oaths were read. The implications of literacy for the act of swearing are vast. Reading an oath for oneself, reading it aloud, and underwriting it, 'sub-scribing' it, with your mark or your signature, surely represent very different experiences from reciting an oath or giving verbal assent to a form read out by someone else? This may prove to be one of the

[38] English Gilds, ed. T. Smith (Early English Text Society, original series, 40, 1870), 188–9.

[39] See E. Cohen, The Crossroads of Justice: Law and Culture in Late Medieval France (Leiden, 1992), 57–61, 69–70; J. de Vigurie, 'Contribution à l'histoire de la fidélité. Note sur le serment en France à l'époque des guerres de religion', Annales de Bretagne et des Pays de l'Ouest, 82 (Rennes, 1975), 291; J.E. Tyler, Oaths, their Origin, Nature and History (1834), 58; Tombes, Sephersheba, 40, 49. It was not a necessary consequence of a Bible-centred piety that the book itself should be despised; Lollards, for example, revered the holy book as an object: see M. Aston, Lollards and Reformers: Images and Literacy in Late Medieval Religion (1984), 109–10.

[40] John Ley, A Comparison of the Parliamentary Protestation with the Late Canonical Oath (1640), 30–3; Edward Bowles, The Dutie and Danger of Swearing (York, 1655), 8; C. Evans, Oaths of Allegiance in Colonial New England (Worcester, Mass., 1922), 41. Also see H. Consett, The Practice of the Spiritual or Ecclesiastical Courts (1685), 99–100, and, for examples of kissing the book at King's Lynn and London, see The Journal of William Schellinks' Travels in England 1661–1663, trans. and ed. M. Exwood and H.L.Lehmann (Camden Society, fifth series, I, 1993), 155, 167.

most significant distinctions between the different phases of the history of oaths and swearing.

Once sworn what oaths do at a human level is to create or modify relationships between two or more people. As the earl of Bristol observed, they are not only 'the highest and strongest obligations that can pass from man to God' but also 'from nation to nation, from subjects to their prince, or prince to their subjects, or from man to man'.[41] Oaths bind lovers, just as they adjudicate between litigants. They are constitutive of communes, gilds, fraternities, professions and institutions. They are at the heart of covenanting communities and bonds of association. They forge solidarity between those caught up in the same situation: 'we whose names are hereunto subscribed do in the presence of almighty God solemnly swear that we will stick to and be true to one another ... so help me God', was the oath of the frightened royalist garrison in Hereford in 1646.[42] Oaths bound individuals who found themselves caught up in a single process. It might, for instance, be law enforcement: as so many speeches from the bench told them, constables, jurors and magistrates were sworn to present without favour and affection and to do justice; 'we are not only sworn, but we have likewise made a covenant with God to be just according to our oaths'.[43] But oaths might just as easily bind law-breakers: rebels like the pilgrims of 1536 who swore the oath of the honourable men to restore the church and suppress the heretics; conspirators like the initial five Gunpowder plotters; or criminal gangs, or perjurers or the profane.

Paradoxically it is when oaths are disputed, when they divide people from each other, that their communicative function is revealed most starkly. Oaths would not be in dispute, after all, if they did not mean something significant to both parties. Confronted by oaths some dissident individuals or groups took refuge in obfuscation. When a wealthy Suffolk mercer named Nicholas Smyth was sued for his tithes in 1552, he claimed to have 'discharged his conscience' so far as payment was concerned, but would only answer 'by his honestie and fidelitie, and not by vertue of his othe'.[44] In 1629 a suspected Catholic priest excused himself from taking the oath of allegiance by claiming that he did not know the meaning of the words 'equivocation' or 'allegiance'.[45] Others challenged the appropriateness of an oath. John

[41] Digby, *Apologie*, 31.

[42] *The Diary of Henry Townshend*, ed. H. Willis Bund (4 parts in 2 vols., Worcestershire Historical Society, 1915–20), III, 266.

[43] William Smith, *The Charge given by Sir William Smith Bt at the Quarter Sessions ... at Westminster ... 24 April 1682* (1682), 8.

[44] R.A. Houlbrooke, *Church Courts and the People during the English Reformation 1520–1570* (Oxford, 1979), 127.

[45] *Reports of Cases in the Courts of Star Chamber and High Commission*, ed. S.R. Gardiner (Camden Society, new series, 39, 1886), 195–6.

Lilburne refused the *ex officio* oath before Star Chamber in 1637 because
he could find no warrant for such an oath of inquiry in the Bible.
'When I named the Word of God, the court began to laugh, as though
they had had nothing to do with it.' The conventicler Robert Bye
was also laughed at when he described himself in High Commission as
'Christ's freeman': 'I am indeed and good earnest', he expostulated
and cited Hebrews vi. 16; 'I dare not take this oath. An oath is for the
ending of controversie, but this is made to be but the beginning of
controversie.'[46] The word of God contained no warrant for open-ended
oaths: indeed, the danger of swearing when the scope of the oath is
unknown was well attested by Herod's rash oath to Salome. Perhaps
the most common tactic was simply to take an oath in one's own sense.
According to Samuel Butler, the perjured churchwarden, that stock
figure of the seventeenth century, 'interprets his Oath, as *Catholics* do
the Scripture, not according to the Sense and Meaning of the Words,
but the Tradition and Practice of his Predecessors; who have always
been observed to swear what others please, and do what they please
themselves'.[47] Yet nothing could prevent such individuals taking the
oaths in their own sense and assuming office.[48] The exasperation
aroused by this subversion of oaths paled in comparison with that
provoked by the long line of 'deviants' or 'heretics' who refused to
swear at all. Their dread of oaths was built upon a reverence for the
divine prohibition in the Sermon on the Mount (Matthew v. 34–7;
James v. 12). Some groups like the Quakers were willing to subscribe
to the content of all oaths of loyalty and veracity, they would perform
other speech acts such as 'affirming' or 'declaring', but they could not
do this thing called 'swearing' and that, of course, is precisely what the
state required of them.[49]

In all of these examples swearing an oath is regarded by both sides
to the dispute as a serious and solemn matter; each thinks it is the
other side that is guilty of profanity or sacrilege by imposing oaths
needlessly or twisting their significance. I would contend that the
argument holds true even for cursing and profane swearing, the casual
swearing by God, Christ, his life, blood and wounds, or the common

[46] *Ibid.*, 309.
[47] Samuel Butler, *Characters*, ed. C.W. Daves (Cleveland, 1970), 169.
[48] J. Spurr, 'Perjury, Profanity and Politics', *The Seventeenth Century*, VIII (1993), 38.
[49] On the heretical tradition of refusing oaths see Prodi, *Sakrament*, 291–328; A. Vauchez, 'Le Refus du Serment chez les Hérétiques Médiévaux', in *Serment*, ed. Verdier, II, 257–63; Nicolau Eymerich, *Le manuel des inquisiteurs*, glossed by Francisco de Pena, trans. L. Sala-Molins (Paris, 1973), 127–8, 137, 197; Aston, *Lollards and Reformers*, 111; A. Hudson, *Lollards and their Books* (1985), 134; R. Bauman, *Let Your Words be Few: Symbolism of Silence and Speaking among Seventeenth-Century Quakers* (Cambridge, 1983), 95–119. There were many other Christians, including clergy, whose orthodox piety led them to shun oaths wherever possible.

cursing of 'damn me' and 'pox on it'. Although the content of this swearing, its blasphemy and Catholic overtones, antagonised Protestant reformers, the godly also had a much more instinctive reaction to swearing. Profane swearing was one of the worldly activities against which the godly defined themselves: their conversions included a renunciation of swearing, and thereafter many were deeply troubled by proximity to swearers and their speech. The profane swearers, on the other hand, rarely explained themselves. But many of the godly suspected that they used their swearing as a mark of difference; that the English royalist 'dammees' – so-called in the 1640s 'because "God damm me" was become a common curse, and as a byword among them' – swore to proclaim their utter difference from puritans who would swear 'by nothing but indeed'.[50]

So if we attend to oaths and swearing as forms of behaviour, as counters in human transactions, we see not only what a range of oaths was used, from the solemn and formal to the bragging and obscene, but also how dependent their meaning was upon context and conventions. The conditions that make an oath in support of an alehouse boast effective are clearly very different from those that make a witness oath in court credible. But these are both oaths and both susceptible to historical analysis. At this point in the discussion the context of oaths moves centre-stage. Indeed it could fairly be objected that in several of my examples the context is more important than the oath itself; that oaths are repeatedly subordinated to other considerations, such as political allegiance or biblical literalism. So I turn to contexts and to three in particular, casuistry, politics, and, if we can resurrect them, the conventions of mundane speech.

III

Oaths – like vows, promises and lies – were meat and drink to early modern casuists. Casuistry, the moral science of applying general rules to particular dilemmas, to 'cases of conscience' as they were called in England, offered an explicit and religious frame of reference for oaths. Since the principles were clear and severe, the casuistry inevitably tended to concentrate on exceptions and evasions. Medieval and early modern Catholic casuistry developed in directions which seemed to exploit ambiguity and encourage laxity. In 1515 Sylvester's *Summa summarum* argued that if a man was compelled by thieves to swear an

<hr/>

[50] See P. Seaver, *Wallington's World – A Puritan Artisan in Seventeenth-Century London* (1985), 64; D. Underdown, *Riot, Revel and Rebellion: Popular Politics and Culture in England 1603–1660* (Oxford, 1985), 89, 178; *The Autobiography of Richard Baxter*, abridged by J.M. Lloyd-Thomas and ed. N.H. Keeble (1974), 36; *The Non-Dramatic Works of Thomas Dekker*, ed. A.B. Grosart (5 vols., 1884–6), II, 21.

oath that he would pay them a sum of money, he was not obliged by his oath if he had added 'subaudiendo in animo suo' – inaudibly in his mind – a clause such as 'provided I already owed you that money'.[51] This was the famous 'mental reservation' which was to become so vexed an issue when Jesuits used it to evade answering the Elizabethan and Jacobean authorities. It convinced Protestants that the Catholic clergy and, above all, the Jesuits had discharged the laity from the obligation of all oaths and bonds given to heretics: 'an oath on a papist's conscience is like a collar on the neck of an ass, which he will slip on for his master's pleasure, and slip off again for his own.'[52] Although the casuistry taught at Douai to these missionaries did not belittle the significance of oaths or telling the truth – after all a martyr's crown lay that way – it did suggest that when imposed by a judge without due authority an oath does not oblige the swearer, 'or only obliges him as far as he intended it should oblige him when he took it'. It is 'more prudent' for a missionary not to take an oath when dragged before the heretics, but 'he can swear sophistically, or can reply sophistically to their individual questions'.[53] In general Protestant casuistry developed in reaction to the perceived laxity of Catholic teaching, and therefore Protestant casuists took a predictably stern line on oaths and their obligations. They advised the refusal of any oath that seemed at all ambiguous and – as we heard in Tillotson's sermon – they portrayed almost every solemn verbal construction as an oath.

In the political arena oaths operated under murkier rules. There is something perplexing about the ease with which princes and nobles could offer a solemn oath at one moment and repudiate it at the next. The duke of Norfolk was blunt about where his loyalties lay during his negotiations with the rebellious pilgrims of 1536: as he told the king, 'none oth nor promes made [to the rebels] for polecy to serve you myn only master and sovereign' could outweigh his loyalty to Henry.[54] But where did that leave the duke's reputation and integrity? In 1484 Sir

---

[51] Silvestro Mazzolini da Priero quoted in J.P. Sommerville, 'The "New Art Of Lying"': Equivocation, Mental Reservation and Casuistry', in *Conscience and Casuistry in Early Modern Europe*, ed. E. Leites (Cambridge, 1988), 172; cf. the thirteenth-century view of Thomas of Chobham quoted in R. Bartlett, *Trial by Fire and Water: The Medieval Judicial Ordeal* (Oxford, 1986), 80–1.

[52] *The Diary of John Ward AM, Rector of Stratford upon Avon*, ed. C.M. Severn (1927), 306.

[53] E. Rose, *Cases of Conscience: Alternatives Open to Recusants and Puritans under Elizabeth I and James I* (Cambridge, 1975), 90; *Elizabethan Casuistry*, ed. P. J. Holmes (Catholic Record Society Publications, 67, 1981), 52. Elsewhere Catholics believed that they were the victims of other religions that taught that 'it is lawful to swear a false oath with the mouth, yet break it in the heart'; B. Pullan, *The Jews of Europe and the Inquisition of Venice* (1983; reprinted 1997), 19.

[54] M.H. and R. Dodds, *The Pilgrimage of Grace and the Exeter Conspiracy* (2 vols., Cambridge, 1915), I, 259–60; Henry later reminded him of this assertion, II, 15.

Rhys ap Thomas, political boss of South Wales, promised Richard III that he would stop all invaders and took the oath of allegiance required of him 'though with some heart's grief I confess, and reluctancy of spirit'. 'Whatever, sir, other men might reckon of me, this is my religion, that no vow can lay a stronger obligation upon me in any matter of performance, than my conscience.' He advised Richard that 'the pressing of vows and oaths upon subjects, no way held in suspect, hath often times wrought even in those of soundest affections, a sensibility of some injury done to their faith'. Did this affront sway Sir Rhys when the bishop of St David's came to persuade him that the vow to Richard was a rash inconsiderate oath that could be repudiated in favour of a new oath of allegiance to Henry Tudor?[55] Sir Rhys clearly believed that faith and conscience are better safeguards than imposed oaths. Although to grasp fully the decisions and rationalisations of such men we would need to explore their aristocratic ethos in depth, surely we are justified in suspecting that 'honour' has a part to play? Throughout this period the English nobility asserted (not always successfully) their right to give evidence on honour rather than oath.[56] And if we look to the honour codes of Mediterranean societies, we see that oaths were subservient to other values and needs. Sixteenth and seventeenth-century Venetian nobles freely confirmed their illegal and theoretically dishonourable private deals, especially their election-fixing, with oaths to each other. The state's response was to impose oaths by which the nobles swore that they had not made such arrangements or that they would disregard them when voting. As one observer noted, most nobles 'threw the fear of God to the winds ... although they went to the oath as a matter of course, everyone swore falsely'.[57] The standard accounts of honour argue that the intention of the swearer is paramount. Within the code of honour a man can only commit his honour by his own free will. Offering an oath, like telling a lie or making a promise, only binds someone if he intends it to: if he respects the person to whom he swears and invokes that which is sacred to him, then the oath-taker is bound and breaking his oath will dishonour him. But if the swearer never intended to perform his obligations or if the oath is coerced then his honour remains unsullied.[58] I do not know whether such thinking

[55] R.A. Griffiths, *Sir Rhys ap Thomas and his Family – A Study in the Wars of the Roses and Early Tudor Politics* (Cardiff, 1993), 201, 203.

[56] For exceptions to the rule that nobles testified on their honour, see J. Hawarde, *Les Reportes del Cases in Camera Stellata*, ed. W.P. Baildon (1894), 275, 426.

[57] J. Walker, 'Honour and the Culture of Male Venetian Nobles, c. 1500–1650' (PhD thesis, Cambridge University, 1998), 130–1. I am grateful to Dr Walker for discussing this issue with me. Also see D.E. Queller, *The Venetian Patriciate* (Urbana, 1986), 60, 70, 110–11.

[58] J. Pitt-Rivers, 'Honour and Social Status', in *Honour and Shame – The Values of Mediterranean Society*, ed. J.G. Peristiany (1965).

ever permeated South Wales, but it makes good sense of Sir Rhys ap Thomas's stance.

My third frame of reference for oaths is far more diffuse than a code of honour or a system of casuistry. Perhaps I can characterise it as the sceptical, often inconsistent, attitude displayed towards mundane oaths as people encountered them in their daily lives. We know that people used oaths; that quarrels and violence were accompanied by 'great oaths and curses'; that when unmarried women in labour were interrogated by midwives about the paternity of their bastards, they responded with oaths – one mother averred that 'as she and her child should part asunder' her statement was true, another that 'as ever she should look God in the face' she could not name the father of her baby.[59] What we do not know is how they regarded their own oaths. A helpful point of comparison is offered by Maureen Flynn's work on sixteenth-century Castilian blasphemy. Ordinary Spanish Christians refuted the inquisitors' attempts to interpret their impetuous curses as if they were intentional and literal blasphemies. The inquisitors regarded speech as a direct expression of pre-linguistic thoughts and intentions; the laity saw their own outbursts as 'slipping from the tongue' when they had 'lost themselves' or become possessed by the force of anger; and Flynn proposes that their blasphemies represent momentary and imaginary assertions of personal independence in the face of over-whelming adversity.[60] There are, however, no inquisitorial archives in which the common English man and woman can explain their oaths. We are forced instead to exploit such oblique sources as fictions, entertainments and proverbs.

We have to follow Henry Parrot the epigrammist into the world of Nanus, a dwarfish witty man who will tell you with oaths how he lives by 'trickes, tobacco, strumpets and good clothes'. Or let Parrot introduce you to Lalus:

> Lewd Lalus, came to me six crowns to bórrow,
> And swore (God damn him) he would pay't tomorrow,
> I knew his word as currant as his bond,
> And therefore gave him but three crowns in hand,
> This I to part with, he to take was willing,
> And thus he gain'd, and I sav'd fifteen shilling.[61]

[59] Quoted in S. Hindle, 'The Shaming of Margaret Knowsley: Gossip, Gender and the Experience of Authority in Early Modern England', *Continuity and Change*, 9 (1994), 402, 417.

[60] M. Flynn, 'Blasphemy and the Play of Anger in Sixteenth-century Spain', *Past and Present*, 149 (1995), 43–7; also see W. Monter, *Frontiers of Heresy: The Spanish Inquisition from the Basque Lands to Sicily* (1990), 166.

[61] Henry Parrot, *Lacquei ridiculosi* (1613), Book I, epigrams 142 and 201; also see Henry Fitzgeffrey, *Satyres and Satyricall Epigrams* (1617), Book II, sig. D3v, 'Aenigma'.

In the demi-monde oaths are always negotiable; they are part of the game, a means of deceit, and it is only the naive lover or the gull who will trust in them. Most English people did not inhabit such a world, but they did experience it vicariously. They laughed at the satirists' town gallant, especially at his seductive new invented oath, 'let me be Damn'd, and my Body made a Gridiron to Broil my Soul on, to Eternity, if I do not Madam love you confoundedly'.[62] They roared at the braggart Captain Bobadill as he swore 'Body o'Caesar' and 'by Pharoah's foot' and other 'such dainty oaths'. And they shook their heads over Otway's atheist, Daredevil, who is chastised for a casual profanity, 'damn me, Sir'. And who replies, 'Words mere words.' 'We use a hundred of 'em in conversation, which are indeed but in the nature of expletives, and signifie nothing; as Dam'me, Sir, Rot me, Sir, Confound me, Sir, which purport no more than So, Sir; And, Sir; or Then, Sir, at the worst.'[63]

In these fictions, oaths can and do deceive. Lovers' oaths, for instance, are conventionally not worth the sigh with which they are uttered; 'men's vows are women's traitors', ran the proverb.[64] Other deceptive oaths were altogether more sinister. Allot's *Wits Theater of the Little World* (1599) recounts the ruse of Cleomenes who swore to his friend Archonides that he would attempt nothing unless his friend 'should be at one end' of it, and then decapitated his unfortunate pal and kept his head in a basin of honey so that he could always consult him before any adventure.[65] Equally charmless is Parrot's epigram on Caius, accused of rape 'for stealing secretly to his maid's bed' but who escaped conviction since he 'took his oath (nor did he swear amiss), / He went not unto her bed, (for t'was his.)'[66] This is the tip of a whole literature that delights in the trickery of oaths. In this playful world oaths can mislead both the gods and humans. There was a pronounced medieval interest in the ability 'to swear a literal truth which the divine powers must verify, but to cast the oath in such a way as to deceive one's fellow mortals'.[67] In medieval literature – Tristan and Isolde, Amis and Amiloun, for instance – these deliberately equivocal oaths were characteristically vindicated by an ordeal. The *locus classicus* is Isolde's

---

[62] *The Character of a Town Gallant* (1680), 3.
[63] *Ben Jonson*, ed. C.H. Herford and P. Simpson (10 vols., Oxford, 1925–50), III, 317, 320, 321; *The Works of Thomas Otway*, ed. J.C. Ghosh (2 vols., Oxford, 1932), II, 328.
[64] W.C. Hazlitt, *English Proverbs and Proverbial Phrases* (1869), 280.
[65] Robert Allot, *Wits Theater of the Little World* (1599), 123–4.
[66] Parrot, *Lacquei*, Book II, epigram 17.
[67] R.J. Hexter, *Equivocal Oaths and Ordeals in Medieval Literature* (Cambridge, Mass., 1978), 3.

oath.[68] Although this oath and the whole episode should always be construed within the particular version of the Tristan romance in which it appears, the nub was that illicit lovers overcame tyranny by disguising the lover as someone disreputable or disgusting – a madman or beggar – who manages to touch his beloved before the ordeal, so that she can swear 'if I've touched any man but this creature let the fire consume me'. 'The key here', says one scholar of these oaths, 'is the absolute power of truth, a power which can force supernatural beings, contrary to their own knowledge and, at times, will, to hand down a decision vindicating the guilty and condemning the innocent.'[69] Although this motif has a claim to universality, several scholars have speculated that 'this literary depiction of a God who could be thus easily fooled may be a later reflection of genuine problems of conscience'.[70]

The cheating of and through oaths lived on into the early modern period. It is prominent in treatment of lovers' vows or in jest books. And it can be either quite light-hearted or rather dark. Consider for instance a troubling play like *Arden of Faversham* – a tragedy (or perhaps a tragi-comedy) significant for its supposed psychological realism and its mundane setting – but a play whose language resounds with oaths and curses.[71] Alice Arden's love for Thomas Mosby overcomes her marriage vows ('love is a God and marriage but words'), and yet after having sworn her husband's death and having achieved it, she falls to recriminations against lovers and their vows, 'what cannot oaths and protestations do, / When men have opportunity to woo?' An audience may easily have read the character of Alice as another instance of female trickery and of the equivocal and deceptive nature of women's

[68] Useful in this are H. Hattenhauer, 'Der gefälschte Eid', in *Fälschungen im Mittelalter* (Hannover, 1998), II, 667–72; *The Saga of Tristram and Isönd*, ed. P. Schach (Lincoln, Nebraska, 1972), 91–3; L. Seiffert, 'Finding, Guarding and Betraying the Truth: Isolde's Art and Skill, and the Sweet Discretion of her Lying in Gottfried's Tristan', in *Gottfried von Strassburg*, ed. A. Stevens and R. Wisbey (1990); J. Gilbert, 'Gender, Oaths and Ambiguity in *Sir Tristrem* and Béroul's *Roman de Tristran*', in *The Spirit of Medieval English Popular Romance*, ed. A Putter and J. Gilbert (2000).
[69] Hexter, *Equivocal Oaths*, 3.
[70] P. Hyams, 'Trial by Ordeal: the Key to Proof in the Early Common Law', in *On the Laws and Customs of England*, ed. M.S. Arnold (1987), 98. Some evidence of this is available in H. Fichtenau, *Living in the Tenth Century – Mentalities and Social Orders*, trans. P.J. Geary (Chicago, 1991), 404–15; L. Jefferson, *Oaths, Vows and Promises in the First Part of the French Prose Lancelot Romance* (Bern, 1993).
[71] *The Lamentable and True Tragedie of M. Arden of Feversham* (1592) – I quote from the 1971 Scolar Press facsimile. There is a modern edition, *The Tragedy of Master Arden of Faversham*, ed. M. Wines (1973); and oaths in the play are the subject of some interesting comments in F. Whigham, *Seizures of the Will in Early Modern English Drama* (Cambridge, 1996), chapter 2.

sexuality and language.[72] Oaths fly about the drama, impelling and
impeding the action: oaths to love and oaths to murder Arden, oaths
sworn by Black Will and by the servant Michael, but they are oaths
backed by lust, greed and physical fear – when Will is reminded of his
oath to kill Arden, he scoffs, 'Tush, I have broken five hundred oaths;
/ But woulds't thou charm me to effect this deed, / Tell me of gold,
my resolution's fee'.[73] There is no constant line on oaths: Black Will is
utterly cynical; Dick Reede, the wronged sailor who curses Arden, is
transparently honest, but is nevertheless sanctimoniously warned that
curses like arrows shot into the sky have a nasty habit of landing on
the archer's head. Mosby swears an archetypal trick oath: as the
conspirators crowd around the hapless Arden on the evening of his
murder, Mosby swears, 'Yet, Arden, I protest to thee by Heaven, /
Thou ne'er shalt see me more after this night' – which is, of course,
literally true since a few moments later Mosby brains Arden with his
tailor's iron.[74] Earlier Alice puts her finger on a vital issue when she
asks her lover, who has promised not to pursue her:

> What, shall an oath make thee forsake my love?
> As if I had not sworn as much myself,
> And given my hand unto him in the church!
> Tush, Mosby, oaths are words, and words is wind,
> And wind is mutable. Then I conclude,
> 'Tis childishness to stand upon an oath.[75]

'Oaths are but words, and words but wind' is one of those early
modern proverbs we cannot escape. It is here in Arden; 'oathes are
but wordes' claims a piece by George Ruggles, and another by Nathaniel
Field; the proverb is quoted by Samuel Butler in *Hudibras* and it is
alluded to by Hobbes.[76] It was even heard in real people's mouths: in
1604 a Cheshire gentleman William Reynolds was alleged to have
urged one Peter Norris 'not to care what to sweare for oathes are but
words[,] words are but wind and winde is but mutable and therefore
[it is] but [a] childish trick to make account of an oath': words which

[72] *Arden*, sigs. A3r, J1r; cf. Gilbert, 'Gender, Oaths and Ambiguity'.
[73] *Arden*, sig. D2r.
[74] *Arden*, sig. I1r.
[75] *Arden*, sig. B4r.
[76] George Ruggle, *Club Law*, ed. G.C. Moore Smith (Cambridge, 1907), 95; Nathaniel
Field, *Amends for Ladies* (1618), B4r; Samuel Butler, *Hudibras*, ed. J. Wilders (Oxford, 1967),
II, 2, 197–8; Thomas Hobbes, *De Cive: The English Version*, ed. H.M. Warrender (Oxford,
1983), 60–1.

some may think to be suspiciously close to those of Alice Arden.[77] But Reynolds could certainly have read the phrase in tracts or heard it from the pulpit: Edward Bicknoll, writing on hypocrisy in 1579, remarked that 'for our safety the lawyer teacheth us this lesson, to trust few or none upon their words, words are but wind, bind every man's bargain sure by writing'. A century later a moralist pleaded 'let us not say, our words are wind, for why? / ... Rash oaths are such a wind, that hurry men / Into the devil's black and noisome den'. While preaching on the subject of idle words, Philip Henry ran two old saws together, noting in his diary that 'tis a proverb, words are but wind, and tis truth, that's an ill wind that brings nobody good.'[78] Whatever their sources, these quarrelsome Cheshire neighbours knew all about oaths. Norris was 'reported and knowne to be a swearer and blasphemer of Gods holy name' who 'maketh little accomnpte what he sweareth', said one deponent. But this same witness had been chided for his own oath by Norris, who observed 'I wuld not have sworn such an oath howsoever it had happened with me; for I have read in a booke how dangerous a thing it is for a mans soule to forsweare himselfe.'[79]

Casuistry, political life, and mundane speech as reflected by literature are only three of the many contexts for swearing oaths. Yet I am especially struck by the prominence in all three of the swearer's intentions and the swearer's room for manoeuvre. Whether one calls it 'sophistry', 'honour', 'playfulness' or 'profanity', swearers exercised a substantial degree of freedom over the significance of their oaths. Once that truth has been noted, however, this remains a rather static account of oaths and swearing. Perhaps a more dynamic history will emerge if we now consider the tension between what oaths were and what reformers and others wished them to be.

IV

Even the most reverential account of oaths has to acknowledge that they have taken many forms over the last millennium. Christianity has done much over the centuries to promote oath-taking, but originally the medieval church embraced existing oaths, oaths inherited from Roman Law, rituals of fidelity and fealty, and elsewhere. At first the

[77] Public Record Office, STAC 8/288/16, fo. 35. I am grateful to S. Hindle, 'The Keeping of the Public Peace', in *The Experience of Authority in Early Modern England*, ed. P. Griffiths, A. Fox and S. Hindle (1996), which brought this source to my attention. A similar instance from Sussex is reported in C. Herrup, *The Common Peace: Participation and the Criminal Law in Seventeenth-Century England* (Cambridge, 1987), 112.

[78] Edward Bicknoll, *A Sword agaynst Swering* (1579), sig. iiv; T.I., *A Cure for the Tongue-Evill* (1662), 13; *The Diaries and Letters of Philip Henry*, ed. M. H. Lee (1882), 50–1.

[79] PRO, STAC 8/288/16, fos. 17, 11.

effort was to relocate oath-taking to the church's sphere: hence in 803 Charlemagne – who had his own reasons for fostering oaths – decreed that all oaths should be sworn either in a church or on holy relics. As the laity were persuaded to resolve their disputes or guarantee their promises by coming to church to swear, they were simultaneously taught that God and his saints would exact a terrible vengeance from perjurers.[80] In Brittany by the ninth century oaths at church were supplanting the traditional uses of sureties, individuals whose duty it was to see that an obligation was performed.[81] Churches were keen to establish their right to administer oaths, principally through their control of altars and relics, and to promote the oath as a tool of settlement either in itself or as an ancillary to the ordeal or the duel. For the clergy the oath was a preferable decisory mechanism to the ordeal because they thought it worked in a different way. In their eyes, an oath did not test God as did an (autonomic) ordeal. God was not bound to respond in a predictable way: a false oath would not *necessarily* produce instant death for the false swearer.[82] When the fourth Lateran Council repudiated the ordeal, the oath's dominance was assured and it became, in Professor Bartlett's words, 'the cornerstone of medieval judicial procedure'.[83]

It is, of course, misleading to speak of *the* medieval oath: oaths have never been monolithic. Medieval canon law distinguished between *iuramentum* – a legal oath of the kind one might swear when entering a gild and the breach of which was a venial sin – and *sacramentum*, a more solemn oath the violation of which was perjury and a mortal sin. More to the point the middle ages excelled at making and taking oaths: a point amply sustained by simply listing the oaths of homage and liegance, the oaths of chivalry, the oaths of fraternity, the oath-helping or compurgations, the vows of pilgrimage, chastity or celibacy, the oaths of jurors and office-holders, the frequent exemptions and indulgences from existing oaths, the cheating of oaths, and of course the quotidian swearing by the saints, the Virgin, and 'the members', the

---

[80] E. James, 'Beati pacifici: Bishops and the Law in Sixth-Century Gaul', in *Disputes and Settlements*, ed. J. Bossy (Cambridge, 1983), 33. On Charlemagne's motives see S. Airlie, 'Narratives of Triumph and Rituals of Submission: Charlemagne's Mastering of Bavaria', *Transactions of the Royal Historical Society* (sixth series, IX, 1999), 95, 107–8.

[81] W. Davies, *Small Worlds: The Village Community in Early Medieval Brittany* (1988), 81–3.

[82] There is a large but scattered literature on these themes. I have particularly benefited from Kolmer, *Promissorische Eide*; Y. Bongert, *Recherches sur les cours laïques de Xe au XIIIe siècle* (Paris, 1949), 205–10; James, 'Beati pacifici'; K. Uhalde, 'Proof and Reproof: the Judicial Component of Episcopal Confrontation', *Early Medieval Europe*, 8 (1999); H. Pryce, *Native Law and the Church in Medieval Wales* (Oxford, 1993); R. Stacey, *The Road to Judgement: From Custom to Court in Medieval Ireland and Wales* (Philadelphia, 1994); Bartlett, *Trial by Fire and Water*.

[83] Barlettt, *Trial by Fire and Water*, 30.

physical parts, of Christ. In the midst of such profusion, confusion was almost inevitable. Different types of oath and swearing seemed to merge into each other, as we saw in the case of the entry oath to the Stamford gild, and as other scholars have observed in the way that Occitan troubadours alluded, even quoted, their castellans' oaths of fidelity in their songs about the bonds of love, or in the gestural similarities between oaths of homage to a lord and the attitude of prayer to Christ.[84]

In the face of all this cheerful confusion and irreverence it was perhaps not surprising that the late-medieval clergy were ever more insistent that a solemn oath was a binding obligation, perjury was a sin, and profane cursing and swearing were unacceptable. As one scholar has remarked of the fourteenth-century campaign to curb sins of the tongue, this 'pastoral discourse on deviant speech had an uncommon power because of its composition by a militant literate elite, its claims to govern all speech, its authorities (biblical, patristic, philosophical), its use in confession (the gateway to the Eucharist), and its advocacy by supposedly every priest as a religious teacher'.[85] This statement strikes an early modernist forcibly. Here, *mutatis mutandis*, is the agenda of the sixteenth and seventeenth-century reformers in a nutshell. The clerical concern to control and curb the oath clearly has a long history. If one goes back no earlier than the fourteenth century, the catechisms and preachers are recognisably pursuing the same goals as those of the seventeenth century; from Thoresby and Manning to Baxter and Allestree their materials are the same: Jeremiah iv. 2 is quoted by Chaucer's Parson and Pardoner in the 1380s, as it is by Bishop Gibson in the 1725 edition of his *Admonition against Swearing*, and by every English anti-swearing tract between. Although I am less familiar with the continental literature, this theme seems to be just as prominent in Catholic Europe.[86] The mounting concern with blasphemy, the movements for the reformation of manners, and the campaigns to clean up popular pastimes and the stage, are all well attested. Even the romance literature was susceptible to these pressures. Unlawful oaths to marry by already married heroes were punished with leprosy in some French versions of the story of Amis and Amiloun, while R.J. Hexter argued that the Middle English version of c.1330 was the first in which a connection was drawn – by a heavenly voice sent

[84] F.L. Cheyette, 'Women, Poets, and Politics in Occitania', in *Aristocratic Women in Medieval France*, ed. T. Evergates (1999), 160–1; V. Reinburg, 'Hearing Lay People's Prayer', in *Culture and Identity in Early Modern Europe: Essays in Honour of Natalie Zemon Davis*, ed. B. Diefendorf and C. Hesse (Ann Arbor, 1993), 23–6.
[85] E.D. Craun, *Lies, Slander and Obscenity in Medieval English Literature – Pastoral Rhetoric and the Deviant Speaker* (Cambridge, 1997), 9.
[86] See, for one example, Jean Benedicti, *La Somme dez Pechez* (Rouen, 1608), 50–1, 57.

from Jesus no less – between Amiloun's trick oath and his subsequent contraction of leprosy.[87]

While clerical authority seemed to be bearing down on swearing from at least the fourteenth century, political authority was struggling to harness the power of oaths. Both in France and England the fifteenth century saw widespread breach of sworn obligations and oaths of loyalty, but as the early modern sovereign state slowly emerged it sought to rehabilitate and reinvigorate the bond of the solemn oath between subjects and their rulers.[88] Scholarly attention has focused on the constitutional role of oaths sworn by rulers at their coronations and on oaths of allegiance offered by their subjects. D.M. Jones, for instance, has argued for the emergence of an oath-based approach to allegiance in England by the early seventeenth century. The Tudor state had succeeded to the church's role as arbiter of the individual conscience and then set about investing loyalty oaths with obligations arising from conscience.[89] The first attempt to shackle subjects by their oaths was the ad hoc oath contained in Henry VIII's 1534 Act of Succession. This set a pattern followed by the Elizabethan Act of Supremacy of 1559 and the Jacobean Oath of Allegiance of 1606, by a string of loyalty tests in the 1640s and 1650s, and by the oaths of allegiance and orthodoxy imposed under the restored monarchy. Far more than a constitutional device, oaths testing political trustworthiness and ideological commitment were part of the apparatus of the state in France, in the German lands, and in England. Officials, teachers and clergymen were required to take confessional oaths, and in some territories the entire population or all male householders were required to attest their allegiance on oath.[90] Meanwhile royal and civic authorities

---

[87] Hexter, *Equivocal* Oaths, 33–6, but it should be noted that this connection is more in the nature of a choice – a test of Amiloun's bond to Amis – rather than a punishment. This interpretation should be read in the light of *Amis and Amiloun*, ed. M. Leach (Early English Text Society, original series 203, 1937), lines 1093–1104, 1250–96; Leach's comments at lxiii–lxv; O. Kratins, 'The Middle English *Amis and Amiloun*: Chivalric Romance or Secular Hagiography?', *Publications of the Modern Language Association*, 81 (1966), 350–1.

[88] See Guenée, *Un Roi*, 422–3, 461–2; J. Sherborne, 'Perjury and the Lancastrian Revolution of 1399', *Welsh History Review*, 14 (1988–9); J. de Vigurie, 'Les serments de sacre des rois de France (xvie, xviie et xviiie siècles)', in *Hommage à Roland Mousnier – Clientèles et Fidélités en Europe à l'Epoque Moderne*, ed. Y. Durand (Paris, 1981), 57–69; K. Colberg, 'Der Eid des Königs: Kaiser Sigismund und das "Schwurverbot"' in *Staat und Gesellschaft im Mittelalter und der frühen Neuzeit – Festschrift für J. Leuschner*, no editor (Hanover, 1983); Prodi, *Sakrament*, 197–244.

[89] D.M. Jones, *Conscience and Allegiance in Seventeenth-Century England – The Political Significance of Oaths and Engagements* (Rochester, New Jersey, 1998).

[90] K. Schreiner, 'Iuramentum Religionis: Entstehung, Geschichte und Funktion des Konfessionseides der Staats-und Kirchendiener im Territorialstaat der frühen Neuzeit',

were also eager to throw their weight behind or even annexe clerically initiated campaigns against blasphemy, profane swearing and perjury.[91] Oaths were simply too useful to neglect. Early modern England, for example, saw the increasing use of oaths in tax assessments, the swearing of witnesses in pre-trial examinations by the justices, the creation of a criminal offence of perjury, the use of oaths of inquiry like the *ex officio* oath, and procedural changes which had minor local officials swearing to the truth of their presentments about the state of the highways or the value of cargoes.[92]

It is tempting to discern a 'project' behind all these late medieval and early modern trends. Oaths are to be reduced to a single universal bond between the individual and God. The oath retreats into the private area of the individual's personal relationship with God. The sanctions of the oath shrink to the great fear of eternal punishment, other considerations, such as honour or shame or reputation, are discounted. Simultaneously the oath becomes an irresistibly attractive tool of the authorities. For it is a powerful, infrangible, obligation which can bind the individual to the big political entities, the nation and the national church. Hence the state, aided and abetted by the church, imposes a multiplicity of oaths on the population. Paradoxically oaths multiply, just as the social construction of an oath and of the act of swearing is becoming narrower. That at least *may* be the ideological enterprise. But if so, then this project was doomed to create and reveal its own failures.

In England it was claimed that the succession of contradictory loyalty oaths had undermined the credibility of all oaths. Henry VIII's bishops and clergy had all broken their oaths of loyalty to the papacy; when Boleyn fell, Henry replaced the 1534 oath of allegiance, now described as 'vain and annihilate', with another, and in due course that too became 'vain and annihilate'. 'The frequent forfeited oaths and repeated

---

Der Staat, 24 (1985); G. Strauss, *Law, Resistance, and the State: The Opposition to Roman Law in Reformation Germany* (Princeton, 1986), 111, 153–4; Vigurie, 'Contribution à l'histoire de la fidélité', 292–3.

[91] See E. Blemas, 'La montée des blasphèmes à l'age moderne du Moyen age au XVIIe siècle', in *Injures et blasphèmes*, ed. J. Delumeau (Paris, 1989).

[92] See Michael Dalton, *The Countrey Justice* (1618), 125–6, 264–5; Hindle, 'Keeping the Public Peace', 220–1; M.D. Gordon, 'The Invention of a Common Law Crime: Perjury and the Elizabethan Courts', *American Journal of Legal History*, XXIV (1980); J.G. Bellamy, *Criminal Law and Society in late Medieval and Tudor England* (Gloucester, 1984), 23, 45–7, 110; J.G. Bellamy, *The Criminal Trial in Later Medieval England* (Gloucester, 1998), 34, 102, 105–6, 108, 109; J.H. Langbein, *Prosecuting Crime in the Renaissance: England, Germany, France* (Cambridge, Mass., 1974); J.R. Kent, 'The Centre and the Localities: State Formation and Parish Government in England, c.1640–1740', *Historical Journal*, 38 (1995), 387–90; P. Langford, *Public Life and the Propertied Englishman 1689–1798* (Oxford, 1991), 98–118.

perjuries' of the Civil War and Interregnum were even more damaging.[93] The bad faith of the church and state was undeniable. Oaths were imposed and then buttressed by coercion or by financial bonds and penalties. It was no coincidence that the Nun of Kent and her followers were executed on the very day that 'all the crafts in London were called to their halls and ... sworn on a book' to bear true allegiance to Queen Anne Boleyn. Nor that Walpole tried to ensure a good turn out for a loyalty oath in 1723 by spreading rumours of a punitive tax on those who refused to swear.[94] The state imposed oaths while claiming that they added nothing to existing obligations. The oath of allegiance, for instance, merely confirmed an existing natural allegiance from subjects to their sovereign that 'was due by the law of nature thousands of years before any law of man was made'.[95] An oath therefore can bind even those who have not taken it. This is an admission that while the state claimed such oaths were universal, they were applied selectively. The very phrasing of oaths betrays the authorities' lack of conviction: oaths were heaped with provisos and caveats, that the oath was being taken 'willingly and ex animo', 'without reservation', 'heartily, freely and willingly', or in the words of the oath of allegiance: 'all these things I do plainly and sincerely acknowledge and swear, according to these express words by me spoken, and according to the plain and common sense and understanding of the same words, without any equivocation or mental evasion or secret reservation whatsoever'. These very oaths were quite consciously imposed on those who were not expected to keep them. Many of the seventeenth-century oaths imposed on Catholics were designed to identify 'recusants' or Catholic dissenters without all the tiresome business of proof and trials. An oath – or strictly an abjuration (a renunciation on oath of certain propositions) – was tendered, and refusal was the offence.

It is, in my opinion, quite likely that such misuse damaged the credit of oaths and oath-taking. My concern today, however, has been less with the attempts of church and state to channel oath-taking into one narrow stream than with the broader tradition of irreverent or profane oath-taking. In other words, I have suggested that we read the teachings of the clergy and the exhortations of the state alongside Parrot's epigrams or *Arden of Faversham*. And if we do, the argument that 'oaths had lost their point' in early modern England will be revealed for the optical illusion which it is – an illusion manufactured in large part by those who sought to restrain the free play of oaths. There is always a

---

[93] John Gauden, *A Discourse Concerning Publick Oaths* (1662), 9.
[94] R. Rex, 'The Execution of the Holy Maid of Kent', *Historical Research*, 64 (1991), 219; Langford, *Public Life*, 104.
[95] Sir Edward Coke quoted in Jones, *Conscience and Allegiance*, 73.

risk in protesting too much. By repeating so often that oaths are words 'clothed about with death' or that 'oaths are edged tools, and not to be played with', the preachers, statesmen and moralists perhaps only revealed how little reverence their contemporaries displayed for oaths.

V

In 1534 when Henry VIII imposed his first loyalty oath, the Imperial Ambassador Chapuys joined with those who 'laugh at the king, and not without reason, for his presuming that oaths violently obtained from his people can make his quarrel good and ensure obedience; whereas on the contrary, it only proves that laws and ordinances that require being sworn to are no good at all. This is the way in which people talk privately among themselves.'[96] Laughter again – Mr Lodge has not been forgotten, but neither have I quite got the joke yet (you may perhaps think that I have killed it). I have tried to show that Lodge lived in a world that both revered and profaned oaths. We should not limit ourselves to the reverential view of an oath as a single action invoking a transcendent God with potentially serious consequences. For that, after all, is to read the oath as it was presented by the preacher and the magistrate. And their construction of the oath never did impose itself to the exclusion of all others. No, we also need the profane reading of oaths as a form of behaviour and a protean behaviour at that. Oaths as they were acted were of all kinds – playful, witty, profane, perjured, solemn and binding – and they were part of human interaction, for all that they invoked God. This plurality is evident in the continuing pleasure given by tales, in chapbooks, ballads, and on stage, of oaths thwarted or broken. Or in the ineradicable tendency of some in the alehouse to tell their jests and lies and then swear that they are true. Or in the plain fact that much recorded early modern speech was peppered with profane oaths. I am not arguing that everyone refused to take oaths seriously or that those who swore profanely did not swear solemnly; I am suggesting that they retained the choice. People used oaths in many different, and even mutually inconsistent, contexts. Thus a man might swear profanely in the alehouse, yet still expect his solemn oath to be taken seriously; he might make a sacred vow and then consult the casuists to escape its consequences. People swore as they wished. The ambivalence is there in the evidence of proverbs: it was common wisdom that 'swearing and lying be very near kindred' and yet it was also said, perhaps for all we

---

[96] *Calendar of State Papers Spanish, Henry VIII, 1534–5* (1886), v. i. 131; also see Chapuys' own arguments to the English Council, *Letters and Papers, Foreign and Domestic, of the Reign of Henry VIII* (1883) vii, 263–8.

know by the very same people, that 'oaths are but words, and words but wind'. Was it simply these self-evident, contradictory and profane truths that set Mr Lodge laughing on that bleak winter's night in Westmorland?

RETHINKING POLITENESS IN EIGHTEENTH-CENTURY ENGLAND: MOLL KING'S COFFEE HOUSE AND THE SIGNIFICANCE OF 'FLASH TALK'

The Alexander Prize Lecture

By Helen Berry

READ 7 APRIL 2000

HISTORIANS are rightly suspicious of axioms, those capsules of historical 'truth' that pass into the received wisdom about a particular time period. Part of our job is to explode historical myth, to scrutinise and re-evaluate existing versions of the past. Yet how hard it is to think outside of the paradigms that are the legacy of an impressive bibliography and a legion of footnotes. I myself became aware of one particular paradigm regarding the cultural history of early modern England in the course of postgraduate research. I found myself straying across one of those temporal boundaries that arises from the chronological fragmentation imposed by textbooks and course syllabuses. In short, I moved from the pre-Civil-War period, with which I was then more familiar, into the early years of the long eighteenth century. It appeared to me that the literary sources from the late 1600s, which were the subject of my doctoral research, had much in common with the popular literature of earlier periods – the almanacs and chapbooks so well described by Bernard Capp, Margaret Spufford and others.[1] The popular press of the last quarter of the seventeenth century seemed familiar territory: monstrous births, providential occurrences, and various forms of advice to young people were as much the staple diet for readers of cheap print in late seventeenth-century London as they had been in the era of Gouge and Whateley. The observation of such continuities had little relevance, however, since the preoccupation of

[1] Margaret Spufford, *Small Books and Pleasant Histories: Popular Fiction and its Readership in Seventeenth Century England* (2nd edn, Cambridge, 1989); Bernard Capp, *English Almanacs, 1500–1800: Astrology and the Popular Press* (Ithaca, NY, 1979). A version of this paper was read at the University of Leicester conference organised by Rosemary Sweet and Penny Lane, 'On the Town: Women and Urban Life in Eighteenth-Century England' (May 1999). Peter Burke, Anthony Fletcher, Elizabeth Foyster, Jeremy Gregory, Vivien Jones, Alison Rowlands and Heather Shore provided additional remarks and references, for which I am most grateful.

historians studying this later period had changed. Instead of mapping the material and textual continuities between popular seventeenth-and eighteenth-century literature, which seemed to me to exhibit certain powerful similarities across time, the imperative was now to use such sources to map the changes which forged the eighteenth-century *zeitgeist*, the new 'culture of sensibility'.[2]

Accusations of neglect regarding the different contextual circumstances in which the printed word was produced will no doubt follow. Who can deny that profound changes were taking place in English society at the end of the seventeenth century? Urbanisation, the continuing expansion of colonial trade, the rise of the middling sorts – the story is well known, and repeated in any history book that covers the period 1660–1800.[3] An ever-increasing number of people of 'middling' rank, we are told, profited from trade and were able to purchase a luxurious lifestyle, which in turn fuelled the growth and diversification of a capitalist economy.[4] Somewhere between Habermas's theory of the bourgeois public sphere, and Paul Langford's excellent account of the expansion of commercial culture in eighteenth-century England, a paradigm was born: that during the 1700s, English people became obsessed with manners and the cultivation of new and ritualised forms of behaviour, necessitated by their co-existence in an increasingly complex urban environment.[5] The theme of these novel social codes, which encompassed all forms of human action in the public sphere, from conversation to body language (and here Norbert Elias[6] has been highly influential) may be summarised in one word – politeness.

My dissatisfaction with the paradigm of politeness grew during my research into the early coffee-house periodicals by the entrepreneurial London publisher, John Dunton. Allegedly, Dunton's function in the literary realm was to bear witness to the coming of Addison and

---

[2] The phrase is taken from G. J. Barker Benfield, *The Culture of Sensibility: Sex and Society in Eighteenth Century Britain* (Chicago, 1992).

[3] See for example Peter Earle, 'The Middling Sort in London', *The Middling Sort of People*, ed. Christopher Brooks and Jonathan Barry (1994), 141–58; Penelope Corfield, *Class by Name and Number in Eighteenth-Century Britain* (Oxford, 1991); Margaret Hunt, *The Middling Sort. Commerce, Gender, and the Family in England, 1680–1780* (Berkeley, Ca., 1996); John Brewer, *The Pleasures of the Imagination: English Culture in the Eighteenth Century* (1997); Stephen Copley, 'Commerce, Conversation and Politeness in the Early Eighteenth Century Periodical', *British Journal for Eighteenth Century Studies*, 18 (1995), 63–75; Anna Bryson, *From Conduct to Civility: Changing Codes of Conduct in Early Modern England* (Oxford, 1998).

[4] Lorna Weatherill, *Consumer Behaviour and Material Culture* (1988), 13–14, 167–9 and *passim*.

[5] Jürgen Habermas, *The Structural Transformation of the Public Sphere; an Inquiry into a Category of Bourgeois Society*, trans. Thomas Burger (Oxford, 1992); Paul Langford, *A Polite and Commercial People. England 1727–1783* (Oxford, 1989).

[6] Norbert Elias, *Power and Civility. The Civilizing Process*, II (Oxford, 1982).

Steele.[7] His periodicals, such as the extraordinary *Athenian Mercury*, were (according to the existing historiography) all about politeness. My reading of seven years' issues of the periodical from the 1690s yielded a somewhat different conclusion: that men and women, under the licence of anonymity, were anything but polite in the frank questions which they put to Dunton's secret society of 'learned men', those self-appointed 'agony uncles', the 'Athenian Society'.[8] Nor were their questions confined to tea-pouring and polite forms of address, although these were also present in the text. Instead, they took the opportunity, in an era of considerable political censorship, to ask the broadest range of questions about the world around them, how it worked, and what was its meaning. They wanted to know everything, from the mechanics of their own bodies, to the orbit of the earth. Their inquisitiveness extended beyond the minutiae of etiquette, and although they realised the necessity of good relations within their community, in particular the importance of reputation in an economy founded upon credit, this was not the *sine qua non* of their being. Coffee-house conversations, stimulated by reading Dunton's periodicals, must have been more truly eclectic than even Habermas had imagined.

What, then, were the parameters of politeness? How much did it really preoccupy eighteenth-century English people, even those in the burgeoning metropolis and provincial urban centres? If indeed an obsession with manners became one of the defining features of the middling sort, and a characteristic theme of Augustan literature written by highly influential social commentators from Addison to Johnson, what consequences were there in the daily encounters between those who appropriated polite behaviour in varying degrees, or not at all? For the historian, this raises the problematic question of sources – just what was going on in the streets and coffee houses of London over two hundred years ago? Moving, as I am, towards a critique of politeness, there is also the uncomfortable realisation that, in order to test its limits, one must accept the paradigm of its influence as a cultural phenomenon. For the purpose of this survey, however, I shall choose to engage with, rather than reject, the hypothesis that politeness, or rather an awareness of the importance of correct deportment and speech prescribed according to gender and status, was something which was increasingly discussed in the public sphere of print culture. What interests me here is the way in which discussion of this subject generated, rather than precluded, a fascination with *impolite* behaviour. The

---

[7] See for example J. Paul Hunter, *Before Novels: the Cultural Construction of Eighteenth-Century English Fiction* (New York, 1990), 12–18.

[8] For details about the Athenian Society, see Gilbert D. McEwen, *The Oracle of the Coffee House: John Dunton's Athenian Mercury* (Huntington, Ca., 1972).

psychological mechanism behind this phenomenon, I suggest, is comparable with that observed by Lyndal Roper in her survey of witchcraft in sixteenth-century Germany. Professor Roper argues that religious repression, rather than successfully marshalling the populace into piety, had the reverse effect: of nurturing those 'vices' that the church was attempting to suppress.[9] Could not a similarly repressive civil code of outwardly conformist behaviour in eighteenth-century England nourish an underbelly of impolite resistance? A challenge to the hegemonic status of politeness is the logical corollary to the cautious observation that the middle classes were not inevitably 'rising'. In the eighteenth century, not everyone was going up in the world – neither was it necessarily a more polite place. This may seem to be a truism, yet within the existing historiography, it is almost impossible to find a dissenting voice. Where are the hidden transcripts of impolite thought, speech and action in eighteenth-century England?

The *Life and Character of Moll King, Late Mistress of King's Coffee-House in Covent-Garden*, published in 1747, is a little-known pamphlet describing the career and life history of one of the more colourful women to have emerged from obscurity in early Georgian London.[10] Born of humble origins, Moll was later known to Fielding and his contemporaries as the proprietor of one of the capital's most infamous coffee houses. This brief account of Moll's extraordinary life promises a revelatory story about a scandalous woman who was notorious by name to Londoners in the early to mid-1700s. As such, it is part of a genre of popular texts from the early eighteenth century in which the central figure was a woman of dubious reputation. The most famous of these was Defoe's *Moll Flanders*, but there are many others. The *Life and Intrigues of the late Celebrated Mrs Mary Parrimore* (1729) is an account of the 'Tall Milliner of 'Change-Alley', a prostitute who received the attentions of Jews, Quakers and Irishmen.[11] Another example is the *Life of the Late Celebrated Mrs Elizabeth Wisebourn*, bawd to the infamous prostitute Sally Salisbury.[12] The practice of celebrating legendary women of low birth in ballads and cheap print dates from a much earlier period, to at least the late

[9] The 'contradictory effects on human beings of disciplinary legislation', and argued as a result that repression is 'part of a double process which also creates, rather than represses, its opposite', in Lyndal Roper, *Oedipus and the Devil. Witchcraft, Sexuality and Religion in Early Modern Europe* (1994), 146, 160.

[10] Anon., *The Life and Character of Moll King, Late Mistress of King's Coffee-House in Covent-Garden ... containing a true narrative of this well-known lady, from her birth to her death* (1747).

[11] Anon., *The Life and Intrigues of the Late Celebrated Mrs Mary Parrimore* (1729).

[12] Anodyne Tanner, *The Life of the Late Celebrated Mrs Elizabeth Wiseboun, Vulgarly Call'd Mother Wybourn* (n.d., 1721?). For an account of Sally Salisbury, see Vivien Jones, 'Sex Work, Satire, and Subjectivity: Prostitute Narratives', paper delivered at the 'Luxury and Aesthetics: Sense and Excess' conference, University of Warwick, July 1999.

sixteenth century, from that doyenne of Elizabethan lowlife, Long Meg of Westminster, to Moll Cutpurse (in real life, Mary Frith).[13] Such women lived by their wits, and were associated with sexual licence and criminal activities, yet were often celebrated as unruly popular heroines. What distinguishes the *Life and Character of Moll King* from these and other texts from the mid-eighteenth century is the account it contains of the peculiar 'cant' or slang known as 'flash', a linguistic phenomenon which presents the opportunity we have been seeking to challenge the axiom of polite culture.

Like many of the prostitute narratives mentioned above, the *Life and Character of Moll King* is based upon the life history of an actual person. A summary of Moll's story, and an examination of the broadest possible range of contemporary sources about the landlady and her coffee house, form a necessary backdrop to our enquiry, before we can proceed to consider the significance of 'flash'. According to the *Life and Character*, Mary, or Moll King (her maiden name is unknown), was born in Middlesex in 1696. Her ne'er do well father was a shoemaker, and, when still very young, our heroine was 'obliged to get her Bread in the Streets with her Mother'.[14] As a consequence, Moll was later unable to hold down a job as a servant, since 'being much us'd to the Streets, she could not brook Confinement within Doors'.[15] Her familiarity with urban street life is suggestive of independence and a wild, untamable nature, as well as denoting the more obvious implication of sexual disrepute. Moll's education was 'not more polite, than that of the Nymphs of either *Billingsgate* or *Covent-Garden Market*'.[16] As a young woman, Moll was 'tolerably handsome and very sprightly'. She flirted with many suitors, having many 'Sweethearts' before settling upon her first husband, Tom King. Tom was described in the *Life and Character* as 'a young Fellow of [Moll's] own calling': other contemporary sources confirm that Tom had in fact been educated at Eton.[17] A whiff of scandal accompanied their marriage since Tom and Moll were 'tack'd together' hurriedly at a Fleet wedding.[18] The circumstances are unknown, and their possible reasons for resorting to clandestine marriage are manifold. The social disparity between the pair would

---

[13] Bernard Capp, 'Long Meg of Westminster: A Mystery Solved', *Notes and Queries*, new series, 45 (1998), 302–4. My thanks to Professor Capp for this reference.

[14] *Life and Character*, 1–4.

[15] *Ibid.*

[16] *Ibid.*

[17] Thomas Harwood, *Alumni Etonenses; or, a catalogue of the provosts and fellows of Eton College and King's College, Cambridge* (Birmingham, 1797), 293: 'A.D. 1713. THOMAS KING, was born at West Ashton in Wiltshire, went away Scholar, in apprehension that his Fellowship would be denied him, and afterwards kept that Coffee-House in Covent-Garden, which was called by his own name.'

[18] *Life and Character*, 5.

have certainly presented a powerful obstacle to the match in ordinary circumstances.[19]

The Kings made sufficient fortune from their coffee house business to enable them to purchase an estate near Hampstead.[20] After Tom's death in 1737, according to the *Life and Character*, Moll remarried, a Mr Hoff or Huff, who tried unsuccessfully to lay hands on her money, but Moll kept her property, and her first husband's name, until her death on 17 September 1747. The registers of St Paul's Church, Covent Garden, confirm that 'Thomas King from Hampstead' was buried on 11 October 1737, and that a 'Mary Hoff Widow, from Hampstead in Middx.' was buried on 27 September 1747.[21] Parish records thus not only verify the existence of Tom and Mary, and their final place of residence, but provide the additional detail that Moll outlived both of her husbands. The register of St Paul's also contains a reference to the Kings' only (surviving?) child, 'Thomas son of Thomas King by Mary his Wife', who was christened on 13 November 1733.[22]

The history of Moll's career suggests that she was the epitome of an early eighteenth-century urban woman with little to lose and much to gain, resolutely entrepreneurial and materially successful throughout her different life stages, first as a young married woman, then later as a widow. From a young age, she showed every sign of being an entrepreneurial woman with an eye for the main chance. One of her early trading ventures was to buy a great quantity of small nuts wholesale and then retail them 'after the Price rose surprizingly', making a handsome profit of 'upwards of £60'.[23] Moll's success in selling snacks inspired her next venture. She and her husband rented a 'little house or rather Hovel' in Covent Garden market and set up a coffee house to provide refreshment to the market sellers, charging the going rate of 1d. for admission and a dish of coffee.[24] We do not know the precise date on which the coffee house opened. 'Mary King' is one of nine people named among the recognizances (bonds) for victualling licences in the London borough of Westminster for 1728.[25] The licensing register for 1730 provides a more positive identification, since it lists

[19] P. Rushton, 'Property, Power, and Family Networks: the Problem of Disputed Marriage in Early Modern England', *Journal of Family History*, 2, no. 3 (1986), 205–19. See also R. B. Outhwaite, *Clandestine Marriage in England, 1500–1850* (Cambridge, 1995), 54–73.

[20] *Life and Character*, 13.

[21] William H. Hunt (ed.), *The Registers of St. Paul's Church, Covent Garden, London: Burials*, Harleian Society, 36 (1908), 359, 429. The date of Tom's death has previously been recorded as 'unknown': see Bryant Lillywhite, *London Coffee Houses. A Reference Book of Coffee Houses of the Seventeenth, Eighteenth and Nineteenth Centuries* (1963), 596.

[22] *Life and Character*, 22; Lillywhite, *Coffee Houses*, 597.

[23] *Life and Character*, 7.

[24] Aytoun Ellis, *The Penny Universities: A History of the Coffee Houses* (1956), 45.

[25] G[reater] L[ondon] R[ecord] O[ffice]/WRLV/37/fol. 29.

'Thomas King the Market' among the victuallers in St Paul's Covent Garden.[26] Their initial custom was mainly among market traders, but late opening hours made King's coffee house attractive to those who were out at night for pleasure rather than business – people of fashion, hell-raisers, rakes and beaux, who brought with them an entourage of hangers-on and prostitutes. By 1732, King's coffee house had become a fashionable port of call for the drunken sparks of the town. In this year, Fielding's *Covent-Garden Tragedy* posed the question, '*What Rake is ignorant of* King's *Coffee-House?*'[27] Moll and her husband soon found that there was not enough space to accommodate the number of people who flocked to their all-night venue. They responded first by buying the house next door, and then a third adjoining property, but even so their coffee house was still full to capacity most nights.[28]

King's coffee house profited from its proximity to Drury Lane, and was conveniently located next door to the new Covent Garden Theatre, which opened in 1733. It was only a few paces from watering holes such as the Fleece, the Rose, and the Shakespeare Tavern in Russell Street.[29] At the time, there were several other notable coffee houses in the Covent Garden area, such as Bedford coffee house, Button's (the leading literary coffee house), and Tom's (popular with the nobility),[30] but King's had a distinctive character of its own. An engraving by Hogarth in 1738, the year after Tom King's death, verifies its existence, and bears out the reports that it was a notoriously riotous place. 'Morning', set in Covent Garden, is the first of a series of paintings which Hogarth executed on the theme of 'The Four Times of the Day'.[31] Moll's coffee house is in the foreground of the painting, and is indeed little more than a shack, dwarfed by St Paul's Church to the rear. In Hogarth's scene, it is early morning, and Covent Garden is covered in snow, but, bleary-eyed and dishevelled, a couple of rakes have just emerged from the coffee house and are busy fondling prostitutes, oblivious to the market sellers and churchgoers who pass by. Meanwhile, inside the coffee house, a woman (most likely Moll herself) attempts to restrain a rowdy crew who have drawn their swords. Someone's wig is knocked off in the fight, and Hogarth captures the moment just as it flies through the air and out of the doorway.

Another glimpse of Moll in action is contained within a mock-heroic poem, also published in 1738, under the title of *Tom K—'s: or, the PAPHIAN GROVE. With the various HUMOURS of COVENT GARDEN.*

---

[26] GLRO/WRLV/1/20.

[27] Henry Fielding, Prologue to *The Covent-Garden Tragedy* (1732).

[28] *Life and Character*, 7–8.

[29] R. Webber, *Covent-Garden: Mud-Salad Market* (Letchworth, 1969), 56, 62.

[30] *Ibid.*

[31] Jenny Uglow, *Hogarth. A Life and a World* (1997), 304–5.

This bawdy, mock-heroic poem, in which whores are elevated to the status and charm of goddesses from classical mythology, depicts Moll coming out from behind the serving counter to greet her customers with a rhyming couplet:

> Shall I prepare a Negus, or d'ye choose
> To sip of *Turkish* Berry the boyl'd Juice.[32]

A plate illustration that accompanies this verse shows yet another fight taking place: this time, the bald heads of the gentlemen whose wigs have been knocked off are shown in full view. Moll's only assistant in this general confusion is 'tawney *Betty*', described in an explanatory note as 'the Black Girl that attends with the Coffee'.[33] Thus stark contemporary commentaries were produced, in visual and textual form, which confirm the exotic and unruly character of Moll King's coffee house.

How did King's fit into the broader context of coffee-house society at this time? Coffee houses differed greatly in the social composition of their clientele and the nature of transactions which took place on the premises.[34] Lectures in natural philosophy could be heard at Man's near Charing Cross or Garraway's in Exchange Alley, while the Grecian coffee house in the Strand was closely associated with the Royal Society.[35] Child's in St Paul's churchyard was frequented by the clergy, and the Marine coffee house by merchants. Moll's was clearly one of the seedier coffee houses, yet it was popular and attracted fashionable men-about-town.[36] Hogarth's painting of King's coffee house shows gentlemen in fine clothing (perhaps even courtiers) as customers. Finely clad gentlemen are also shown in the only surviving illustration of the interior of King's coffee house – the plate illustration to the mock-heroic poem, the *Humours of Covent Garden*. King's coffee house seems to have had an unusually wide social mix of male customers, from courtiers to Covent Garden market traders and pimps. Moll kept her business at one remove from actual brothel-keeping, but her coffee house was closely associated with (and profited from) prostitution, a link which was certainly made by contemporary commentators. Hogarth's

---

[32] Anon., *Tom K—'s: OR, THE PAPHIAN GROVE. With the various HUMOURS OF COVENT GARDEN, The THEATRE, L— M— ton's , &c.* (1738), 29–30. A caricature of the landlady from *Covent Garden in Mourning, a Mock Heroick Poem* (1747) is reproduced in E. J. Burford, *Wits, Wenches and Wantons. London's Low Life: Covent Garden in the Eighteenth Century* (1986), 52.

[33] *The Paphian Grove*, 53.

[34] Stephen Pincus, 'Coffee Politicians Does Create: Coffee Houses and Restoration Political Culture', *Journal of Modern History*, 67 (1995), 807–34.

[35] Larry Stewart, *The Rise of Public Science: Rhetoric, Technology, and Natural Philosophy in Newtonian Britain, 1660–1750* (Cambridge, 1992), 143.

[36] *Ibid.*, 144–5.

painting of 1738 firmly associated King's coffee house with whores, while the reputation of Moll King's as a place where drunken sparks consorted with prostitutes at all hours of the day and night continued even after the landlady's death. The hero of Smollett's *Roderick Random* (1748) retired there at two o'clock in the morning after a drunken binge ('Banter and I accompanied Bragwell to Moll King's coffee-house, where, after he had kicked half a dozen hungry whores, we left him asleep on a bench').[37]

King's coffee house became one of the favourite targets of the Middlesex J.P. Sir John Gonson, a fanatical whore-hunter and zealous supporter of the Reformation of Manners campaign. Hogarth depicted him arresting a prostitute in her room in Drury Lane in the *Harlot's Progress* (1732).[38] According to the *Life and Character*, Gonson brought twenty indictments against Moll for running a disorderly house, but the landlady usually escaped prosecution because of a lack of incriminating evidence.[39] Moll and her husband removed the rope ladder to their upstairs bedroom during business hours, and prostitutes at Moll's had to retire to a suitable 'bagnio' (one of the nearby Turkish baths) with their clients. As a result, Gonson failed to find anything suspicious on the premises during his regular spot-check visits.[40] Moll perhaps had too much commercial sense to allow her business to be closed down under suspicion that she was running a bawdy house. The words of Moll's namesake, Moll Flanders, seem particularly apposite in this instance: 'THUS my Pride, not my Principle, my Money, not my Vertue, kept me honest.'[41]

Surviving court records confirm that Moll was a continual headache to the guardians of the king's peace. Middlesex quarter sessions records indicate that 'Mary, wife of Thomas King, yeoman' was charged jointly with Maria Johnson on 29 August 1732, for an assault which took place upon 'Jane Walthoe, spinster' in the parish of St Paul's, Covent Garden.[42] The case was eventually settled on 10 January 1733, when the accused paid a fine of twelve shillings. 'Mary King late of the parish of St Paul Covent Garden in the County of Middlesex Widow' was

---

[37] Tobias Smollett, *Roderick Random* (1748), ed. David Blewett (Harmondsworth, 1995), 278.

[38] Sir John Gonson, 'Knighted May 14, 1722, of the Inner Temple (at Whitehall)', in *The Knights of England*, II (1906), 282. Gonson's name appears as one of the presiding Justices of the Peace for Middlesex during the 1730s; see for example P[ublic] R[ecord] O[ffice]/KB10/fol. 23. See also Robert Shoemaker, *Prosecution and Punishment. Petty Crime and the Law in London and Rural Middlesex, c.1660–1725* (Cambridge, 1991), 86, 249.

[39] *Life and Character*, 16–17.

[40] *Ibid.*, 8–9.

[41] Daniel Defoe, *The Fortunes and Misfortunes of the Famous Moll Flanders* (1722), ed. G. A. Starr (Oxford, 1981), 61.

[42] GLRO/MJ/SR/2579/fol. 55.

also indicted for assault, this time upon one William Lewis, on 30 January 1738, although there is no record of this indictment proceeding further through the courts.[43] If this is indeed Moll King, the same woman named in the indictment of 1733, her description in the 1738 case as a widow would be consistent with the timing of her first husband Tom's death in October 1737. The name of 'King, Mary Wife of Thomas' also appears in the index of indictments brought before the King's Bench during the 1730s.[44] One indictment dates from the period of Moll King's second marriage to Mr Hoff. This time it was for running a disorderly house, and it was issued to 'John Hoffe of the parish of Saint Paul Covent Garden within the Liberty of Westminster in the County of Middlesex Yeoman and Mary his Wife' on 23 January 1739.[45] The plausibility that this was indeed Moll, charged jointly with her second husband for profiting from running an immoral and disorderly coffee house, is heightened by the precise detail of their abode in Covent Garden, the timing of the indictment (issued the year after Hogarth executed his painting of King's coffee house, and two years after the death of Mary's first husband, Tom) and the nature of the charge, which tallies with contemporary observations about the character and infamy of King's coffee house.

Exploration of the widest range of relevant contemporary sources has thus enabled us to confirm both the landlady's existence and the nature of her business. From this, we may conclude that Moll's coffee house served as a space in which the rules of polite conduct were temporarily suspended. One illustration of this, as we have seen, was its strong association with violence and prostitution. Another important aspect of the 'impoliteness' of King's coffee house, however, derived from the landlady's own special contribution to the cultural landscape of eighteenth-century London – her promotion of a form of urban slang known as 'flash'. It is to a closer examination of flash talk that we now turn our attention.

It is well known that the earliest coffee houses were dubbed 'penny universities', in reference to the minimum entrance charge, and the fact that many subscribed to weekly news-sheets and periodicals, which

[43] GLRO/MJ/SR/2691/fol. 65.

[44] See for example PRO/IND 1/6672 Trinity Term, eighth year of George II's reign (9 June–30 Nov., 1734). The name of Mary King is also listed for the Hilary Term in the eleventh year of George II's reign (13 Jan.–15 April, 1738).

[45] The accused were charged according to the formulaic language of the courts with running a 'certain renoun ill governed disorderly House' where 'at unlawful times as well as in the night as in the day ... [they] remain Tipling Drinking playing Whoring and misbehaving themselves To the Great Damage and Disturbance of all their Neighbours' PRO/KB10/24/1/fol. 43.

were made freely available to customers. In reference to the idea that coffee houses were places of learning, the author of the *Life and Character of Moll King* records that Moll King's coffee house became known as 'King's College', which would have cemented a common identity between Moll's customers, and satirised the notion that people who went to Moll's did so for scholarly reasons. Initiation into membership of 'King's College' depended, it seems, not just upon the payment of a penny, but upon the adoption of a particular set of attitudes and habits, and an encoded form of language. According to the author of the *Life and Character of Moll King*, 'Players' and 'witty Beaux' would accost each other in a London street by saying '*Are you for* King's *College to Night, to have a Dish of* Flash *with* Moll?'[46] The purpose of talking in the slang known as 'flash' was to delineate the members of 'King's College' from those outside of their circle. 'Flash' was thus a shibboleth which marked out the fashionable and streetwise *cognoscenti* from other citizens.

The following excerpt is a dialogue in flash talk represented in *The Life and Character of Moll King*. The dialogue is supposed to have taken place between Mrs King and 'one of her best Customers, before her House was frequented by people of Fashion'. The speaker here is Harry Moythen, possibly from the nearby parish of St Martin-in-the-Fields,[47] identified in the text as the man who was 'stabb'd some Time ago by *Dick Hodges*, the Distiller':

Harry. To pay, *Moll*, for I must hike.

Moll. Did you call me, Master?

Harry. Ay, to pay, in a Whiff.

Moll. Let me see. There's a Grunter's Gig, is a Si-Buxom; two Cat's Heads, a Win; a Double Gage of Rum Slobber, is Thrums; and a Quartern of Max, is three Megs: – That makes a Traveller all but a Meg.

Harry. Here, take your Traveller, and tip the Meg to the Kinchin. – But *Moll*, does *Jack* doss in your Pad now?

Moll. What *Jack* do you mean?

Harry. Why, *Jack* that gave you the little brindle Bull Puppy.

Moll. He doss in a Pad of mine! No, Boy, if I was to grapple him, he must shiver his Trotters at *Bilby*'s Ball.

Harry. But who had you in your Ken last Darkee?

Moll. We had your Dudders and your Duffers, Files, Buffers and Slangers; we had ne'er a Queer Cull, a Buttock, or Porpus, amongst

---

[46] *Life and Character*, 10.

[47] Harry Moythen, of the Parish of St.Martin-in-the-Fields, was indicted by John Murphey for assault at the King's Bench in Middlesex on 11 July 1738. PRO/KB10/24/2/fol. 48.

them, but all as Rum and as Quiddish as ever *Jonathan* sent to be great Merchants in *Virginia*.

Harry. But Moll, don't puff:-You must tip me your Clout before I derrick, for my Bloss has nailed me of mine; but I shall catch her at *Maddox*'s Gin-Ken, sluicing her Gob by the Tinney; and if she has morric'd it, Knocks and Socks, Thumps and Plumps, shall attend the Froe-File Buttocking B[itc]h.[48]

'Flash', our commentator observed, 'can scarcely be understood but by those that are acquainted with it'.[49] Doubtless the dialogue is the fictitious invention of the author of the *Life and Character of Moll King*, written in order to entertain the reader. The dialogue aimed, however, to convey to the reader the experience of overhearing 'flash' being spoken in a coffee house. The obscure meaning and burlesque manipulation of language was intended to provoke curiosity (a glossary is provided for 'translation' at the end of the pamphlet) and amusement. The author of the dialogue also implied that part of the pleasure gained from actually speaking flash (or perhaps, from reading it aloud?) was that it was both secretive and exclusive, the delicious irony being that it denoted entry into a counter-culture of libertines and wits rather than one of the ancient universities.

A common term for colloquial speech in the seventeenth and early eighteenth centuries, particularly when associated with criminals, was 'cant', which Samuel Johnson defined as 'A corrupt dialect used by beggars and vagabonds'.[50] Some of the earliest recorded forms of 'cant' date from Elizabethan times, in Thomas Harman's *Caveat for Common Cursetours* (1556) and Robert Greene's *Art of Coney-Catching* (1591). There are similarities between flash and earlier recorded cant vocabularies, which suggests the continuous use of commonly known slang words across time. A *whyn*, for example, had been the cant term for a penny since the 1530s.[51] Thomas Harman's text from the mid-sixteenth century records that the cant term for an orphan girl was *kinchen mort*, while the glossary in the *Life and Character of Moll King* two hundred years later

---

[48] *Life and Character*, 11–12.

[49] *Ibid.*, 10.

[50] Eric Partridge, *Slang Today and Yesterday. With a Short Historical Sketch and Vocabularies of English, American and Australian Slang* (1933), 3. See also Peter Burke, 'Introduction', in Peter Burke and Roy Porter (eds.), *Languages and Jargons. Contributions to a Social History of Language* (Cambridge, 1995), 3. Samuel Johnson, *Dictionary of the English Language*, 1 (1755). Dr Johnson's *Dictionary* also defines 'flash' in the sense of 'Empty; not solid; showy without substance', a meaning which it has preserved in modern usage.

[51] A. L. Beier, 'Anti-Language or Jargon? Canting in the English Underworld in the Sixteenth and Seventeenth Centuries' in Burke and Porter (eds.), *Languages and Jargons*, 88.

lists the meaning of the word *kinchen* as 'a little child'.[52] The lexicon of flash was therefore not entirely new – it drew upon much earlier oral culture – but it appears to have thrived particularly in certain urban spaces, such as Covent Garden market, and among the customers of Moll King's coffee house. The appearance of the term flash to describe this linguistic phenomenon is verified through its mention in a variety of different sources from the late seventeenth century onwards. The use of 'flash' in this sense may be traced to at least 1699, where it is mentioned by the anonymous 'B. E.' in *A New Dictionary of the Terms Ancient and Modern of the Canting Crew, in its several Tribes of the Gypsies, Beggars, Thieves, Cheats, &c.* This was the first dictionary to record ordinary slang, and was designed to be 'Useful for all sorts of People (especially Foreigners) to secure their Money and preserve their Lives, besides very much Diverting and Entertaining, being wholly New'. The meaning of *Flash-ken* in the *Canting Crew* is given as 'a House where Thieves use, and are connived at'. The *New Oxford Dictionary of English* records that the archaic use of the word flash was in the context 'of or relating to thieves, prostitutes, or the underworld, especially their language'.[53] This was certainly the sense in which the term was still being used in the early nineteenth-century when a Middlesex magistrate reported 'I have seen children not more than seven or eight years of age into the trade of picking of pockets, under the eyes of adults ... and when in the next stage of their education they are introduced to Flash-houses'.[54]

Clues to the original meaning of flash terms in the early eighteenth century are given in the 'KEY to the Flash Dialogue', a glossary at the end of the pamphlet about Moll King.[55] Certain words and phrases suggest their association with the nocturnal bonhomie of coffee houses north of the Thames (Southwark is referred to as *T'other side*). A *Gage of Rum Slobber* was a 'Pot of Porter'; *Rum* or *Quiddish* meant 'Good-natur'd', a *Porpus* was 'an ignorant swaggering Fellow'. Other flash words seem very familiar. To *hike* was to go home, to *Doss* was to sleep, a *Pad* was a bed, an *Old Codger* was an old man. Flash was associated with small commercial transactions – there are several terms for money in the glossary: *Si-buxom* was sixpence, *Thrums* was threepence, a *Cat's Head* was a half-penny. Part of the original purpose of speaking flash, it seems, was in order to make veiled references to criminal activity. Some phrases refer to dodgy deals and swindles performed by London

---

[52] Partridge, *Slang*, 45; *Life and Character*, 24.

[53] *OED* (Oxford, 1998), 698.

[54] Quoted in Heather Shore, 'Cross Coves, Buzzers and General Sorts of Prigs. Juvenile Crime and the Criminal "Underworld" in the Early Nineteenth Century', *British Journal of Criminology*, 39 (1999), 10.

[55] *Life and Character*, 23–4.

traders; *Dudders* were 'Fellows that sell Spital-fields Handkerchiefs for India ones'; *Duffers* were 'Those who sell British Spiritous Liquors for Foreign'. There are also references to other illicit or immoral activities. *Files* were pickpockets, *Buffers* were 'Affidavit-Men' and *Slanders* were dealers, or 'Thieves who hand Goods from one to the other, after they are stole [*sic*]'.

How do we interpret the production of a 'flash' glossary for readers in the early eighteenth century, who presumably were not of the same social or economic milieu as those, like Harry Moythen, who formulated and deployed street slang to veil their illegal or immoral activities? One possible explanation arises from Foucault's observation that the greater the rigidity of prevailing social norms, the greater the danger, and therefore pleasure, in transgressing them.[56] The author of the *Life and Character of Moll King* anticipated that the reporting of coarse speech would elicit a scandalised yet fascinated response from 'polite' readers (whom he calls 'Persons of Modesty and Understanding') – the very people who were prohibited from talking flash. In this case, the author's profit depended upon readers' interest in subjects which were beyond the realm of 'polite' discussion in the public sphere.[57] John J. Richetti has observed that eighteenth-century popular fiction could have produced 'gratifying fantasies of freedom – moral, economic and erotic' for the reader who was otherwise constrained by social mores.[58] Vivien Jones has argued in a similar vein that the relationship between eighteenth-century conduct literature and pleasure was problematic and 'potentially more productive' than a 'straightforwardly repressive' model would suggest.[59]

Where was the source of pleasure for eighteenth-century readers in reading about Moll and her 'flash talk'? We may infer from contextual evidence relating to broader social and economic circumstances that the publication of the *Life and Character of Moll King* posed a direct challenge to the restraining impact of a 'culture of sensibility', since flash talk transgressed the polite codes of social deference and genteel discourse that preoccupied so many contemporary authors. For example, one of the principal rules of eighteenth-century polite society

<hr/>

[56] Michel Foucault, *History of Sexuality*, II: *The Use of Pleasure*, trans. Robert Harley (Harmondsworth 1987), *passim*.

[57] Brean Hammond, for example, comments that 'protocols were established governing behaviour in newly emergent public spaces, including the textualized public spaces of established literary genres', in his *Professional Imaginative Writing in England, 1640–1740: 'Hackney for Bread'* (Oxford, 1997), 9.

[58] See John J. Richetti, *Popular Fiction Before Richardson. Narrative Patterns: 1700–1739* (Oxford, 1969), 29–30, 35.

[59] Vivien Jones, 'The Seductions of Conduct: Pleasure and Conduct Literature', in *Pleasure in the Eighteenth Century*, ed. Roy Porter and Marie Mulvey Roberts (1996), 108–32.

was the avoidance of references to bodily functions, but this taboo was gloriously disregarded in flash talk.[60] Thus, the flash term for a woman drinking or wetting her mouth was *sluicing her Gob*. Sex, that ultimate indelicate subject, was referred to openly, and in the bluntly explicit language of the marketplace: in a fine example of synecdoche, a *Buttock* was the flash term for a whore. This overt reference to female sexuality may be contrasted with the synchronic cultural process by which higher status women were being elevated as the harbingers of civility through elaborate and courteous address.[61] Flash had no words for respectable women; it was preoccupied only with lower status women of ill repute and their criminal activities; thus, a *Froe-File-Buttock* was a female pickpocket. Flash words were certainly gendered. Unlike Latin or Greek, flash was a form of obscure speech which was accessible to female 'wits' and women of the town, and it could thus not be used safely by men as a means of excluding women from understanding their conversation. Indeed, it appears as though the credit for encouraging flash talk rests with a woman – Moll King herself. The pamphleteer commented that flash was 'very much us'd among Rakes and Town Ladies',[62] and the additional *frisson* of a woman indulging in vaguely erotic and burlesque 'plain talk' may well be imagined. The implications of talking flash thus also had gendered dimensions. A gentleman who spoke flash was revelling in its impoliteness; a woman could also use it to this effect, but in doing so she was indicating her questionable virtue.

Another pleasurably subversive aspect of flash was its potential to disrupt status hierarchies. Flash talk was represented as being popular at first, not among genteel fops, but among the lower sorts such as Harry Moythen who frequented Moll King's coffee house in the early days. Flash was infused with the blunt-speaking of street vendors and criminals, but was apparently later adopted by coffee-house customers from among the higher ranks of society. Engaging in 'flash talk' was characterised by the author of the *Life and Character of Moll King* as a subversive act on the part of the elite speaker. We know from the study of modern linguistics that language is stratified according to particular social and occupational groupings, and that the relationship between the language which is peculiar to marginal groups (such as 'thieves, junkies ... convicts, political terrorists, street vandals') and the 'norm

---

[60] One of the preconditions of developing civil society is that 'the most animalic human activities are progressively thrust behind the scenes of men's communal social life and invested with feelings of shame', in Elias, *Power and Civility*, 230.

[61] Lawrence E. Klein, 'Gender, Conversation and the Public Sphere in Early Eighteenth-Century England', in *Textuality and Sexuality: Reading Theories and Practices*, ed. Judith Still and Michael Worton (Manchester, 1993), 105–7.

[62] *Life and Character*, 10.

language' of the dominant culture, is essentially antagonistic.[63] Eighteenth-century rakes who by definition did not abide by prevailing codes of normative behaviour were at liberty to engage in flash talk at the coffee houses, since they were sufficiently secure in their status to flaunt linguistic conventions as a mark of their general disregard for prevailing social mores. As Anna Bryson has remarked, 'self-conscious defiance of modesty and decency in speech' was the mark of a libertine, who gained gratification from 'transgressing the rules which, according to the discourse of civility, constrain[ed] the expression of impulse'.[64] Thus, the decision as to whether to talk flash, and its signification, depended very much upon the context: whether the conversation was located in the street or in a coffee house; the social status and gender of the speaker and audience.[65] As the author of the *Life and Character of Moll King* stated, if flash were spoken in the wrong context, or if deployed by one of a lower social standing than these fashionable men-about-town, then the speaker risked being 'looked upon not to be very well bred'.[66]

The account of flash in the *Life and Character of Moll King* of course cannot be regarded as a faithful representation of eighteenth-century oral culture. We do not know precisely who, if anyone, was using this slang and in what context. Conceivably, the author could have made up the flash dialogue and glossary entirely by cobbling together extracts from earlier works such as the *Canting Crew*. Words such as *File*, *Froe* and *Buttock* (meaning whore) appear in the 1699 edition of the text by 'B. E.' as well as in the *Life and Character*, although there are a considerable number of new words and phrases in the latter work, such as *Bilby's Ball* and *Darkee*.[67] The analysis in this paper has concentrated upon the significance of the pamphlet about Moll King as a means of communicating to the eighteenth-century reader the potential for subversive forms of speech, since very little can be inferred about the place of 'flash' in the so-called eighteenth-century 'criminal underworld' (in itself a problematic concept) or its degree of originality or authenticity.[68] The significance of the publication of the *Life and Character of Moll King* is thus that it gave some degree of legitimation to, and

[63] Allon White, 'Bakhtin, Sociolinguistics and Deconstruction', in *The Theory of Reading*, ed. Frank Gloversmith (Worthing, 1984), 125–7.

[64] Bryson, *Courtesy to Civility*, 251, 253.

[65] These crucial factors affecting human behaviour are elaborated in Bourdieu's construction of the *habitus* as the variable 'systems of dispositions' characteristic of different groups of individuals in social space. Pierre Bourdieu, *Distinction. A Social Critique of the Judgment of Taste*, trans. Richard Nice (1984), 6.

[66] *Life and Character*, 13.

[67] B. E., *Canting Crew*; *Life and Character*, 12, 23–4.

[68] Heather Shore proposes that the criminal 'underworld' is properly conceived as a network of 'criminal exchange and communication'. See 'Juvenile Crime', 11, 15.

recognition of, the possibility of 'impolite' alternatives to the prevailing normative culture. Representing flash as a fixed text with a printed glossary may, at one extreme, be interpreted as the production of a fictitious guide, intended for those who wished to keep up with the imagined habits of the fashionable beau monde. In this sense, the glossary of flash generated its own inverted code of politeness: the *Life and Character of Moll King* functioned as a low-life version of the periodical publications of Addison and Steele, those mediators of taste and fashion in the public sphere. It was with considerable irony that the author of the *Life and Character of Moll King* described the sample of flash dialogue between Moll's customers, as 'a Specimen of the great Politeness of these sort of Gentry'.[69]

To conclude, there is a great deal of difference between isolating a key word such as 'politeness' as means of gaining insight into long-distant *mentalités*, and transforming the quest for references to such words into a historical fetish. Such an approach elides contemporary resistance to (or even blissful unawareness of) the top-down attempts of 'polite' didactic authors to influence cultural change. The *Life and Character of Moll King*, as I have argued, poses a challenge to the current trend of regarding the growth of a culture of sensibility in the 1700s as axiomatic. Interest in 'flash talk' as a cultural phenomenon among mid-eighteenth century readers raises the possibility that fashionable slang was used in certain urban spaces as a means of cutting across social boundaries. The account of flash talk in the *Life and Character of Moll King* illustrates how codes of polite conduct could generate rather than preclude alternative forms of interaction, of which language was a key part. I have suggested that the text may be interpreted as a 'discourse of impoliteness', one that requires us to rethink politeness itself, not as a uniformly observed set of rules, nor as an attribute which all were striving to attain, but as a potentially repressive social force that eighteenth-century men and women, given the opportunity, took peculiar pleasure in transgressing.

[69] *Life and Character*, 11.

FIFTEENTH-CENTURY DURHAM AND THE PROBLEM OF PROVINCIAL LIBERTIES IN ENGLAND AND THE WIDER TERRITORIES OF THE ENGLISH CROWN

Proxime Accessit, Alexander Prize 1999

By Tim Thornton

IT is remarkable when an historical interpretation has stood almost unchallenged for one hundred years. Yet this is the case with the approach to the history of the county palatine of Durham outlined by G. T. Lapsley in 1900; it is a story of the steady decline of this once highly autonomous jurisdiction which has been retold by virtually all those who have written on the subject since.[1] It is even more remarkable when that interpretation has acted as a vital support for two much more far-reaching paradigms. In the case of Lapsley's interpretation of Durham, these extend not just elsewhere in the British Isles but also to North America. On the one hand is the approach to the territories of the English crown as a precociously centralised polity, characterised by the effective authority of the crown's institutions and the rapid decline of what little provincial particularism had once been present.[2] With Lapsley's Durham a pale shadow of its former self by the fifteenth century, historians have been able to propose that even the strongest of the ancient palatinates was effectively defunct and the power of the centre unopposed.[3] On the other hand, there is the paradigm which

---

[1] Gaillard Thomas Lapsley, *The County Palatine of Durham: A Study in Constitutional History* (1900); Constance M. Fraser, 'Prerogative and the Bishops of Durham, 1267–1376', *English Historical Review* [hereafter *EHR*], 74 (1959), 467–76; Jean Scammell, 'The Origin and Limitations of the Liberty of Durham', *EHR*, 81 (1966), 449–73. I would like to thank Cliff Davies, Ralph Griffiths, Mark Ormrod and Tony Pollard for their patient and helpful comments on this paper.

[2] Marxist work, e.g. A. L. Morton, *A People's History of England* (1938); Whig historiography, e.g. George Macaulay Trevelyan, *England in the Age of Wycliffe* (1899, 4th edn 1909); his *History of England* (1926, 3rd edn with corrections 1952); and more recent influential interpretations such as Mervyn James, *Family, Lineage and Civil Society: A Study of Society, Politics and Mentality in the Durham Region, 1500–1640* (Oxford, 1974); Philip Corrigan and Derek Sayer, *The Great Arch: English State Formation as Cultural Revolution* (Oxford, 1985).

[3] E.g. recently D. M. Loades, *Power in Tudor England* (Basingstoke and London, 1997), 33.

sees English North America as the scene of a conflict between the direct authority of an ambitious crown and a burgeoning desire for local self-government which was eventually successful.[4] If Durham's palatinate was an archaism by the fifteenth century, then its use in the early seventeenth century as a model for the proprietary charters, beginning in Maryland and which rapidly succeeded chartered companies as the main form of government for the new colonies, was no obstacle to the growth of local political confidence and assertiveness as against Westminster.[5] Fundamentally, both paradigms are accounts of state-formation with the state totalising and individualising, in England to produce a relatively homogeneous national state, in North America to provoke rebellion and independence.

In theory, at least, at their height the bishop's regalities in Durham were even more extensive than those of the other palatine lords in England, the earl of Chester and the duke of Lancaster.[6] They included a Chancery and an Exchequer, and a court system; and unlike the earl of Chester, the bishop had his own mint. Like the earl of Chester, the bishop of Durham issued his own writs and excluded those of the king. And like the people of Cheshire, the community of Durham did not send representatives to the English parliament. There were differences between the palatinates of Chester and Durham, of course: the bishop was not a member of the royal family, and Durham's administrative system resembled that of a neighbouring English shire while Chester's was similar to that of a Welsh marcher lordship. Hence in Durham, the bishop appointed his own justices of assize and of the peace, his own sheriff, coroners and other officers. Yet there were in both

[4] Jack P. Greene argued for the acceptance of considerable autonomy in early seventeenth-century America thanks to the distance from the centre and lack of an effective force that could be deployed by the central authority: *Peripheries and Center: Constitutional Development in the Extended Polities of the British Empire and the United States, 1607–1788* (Athens, Ga., and London, 1986), esp. chapter I. Greene developed the approach of Charles H. McIlwain, *The American Revolution: A Constitutional Approach* (New York, 1923). Cf. Stephen Saunders Webb, who emphasised strong central rule through military governorships: 'Army and Empire: English Garrison Government in Britain and America, 1569 to 1763', *William and Mary Quarterly*, third series, 34 (1977): 1–31; *idem, The Governors-General: The English Army and the Definition of Empire, 1569–1681* (Chapel Hill, NC, 1979).
[5] William Hand Browne, *Maryland: The History of a Palatinate* (Boston and New York, 1912) 20, saw the lord's powers as potentially 'oppressive'; Bernard C. Steiner, 'Maryland's First Courts', *Annual Report of the American Historical Association*, 1 (1901): 213–29, esp. 221, 228, as 'quaint' and 'archaic'. Even A. F. McC. Madden, a believer in the relevance to America of medieval 'empire', relied for his account of Durham on Lapsley: '1066, 1776 and All That: The Relevance of English Medieval Experience of "Empire" to Later Imperial Constitutional Issues', in *Perspectives of Empire*, ed. John E. Flint and Glyndwr Williams (1973), 9–26.
[6] Lapsley, *Durham*, chapter 2; R. L. Storey, *Thomas Langley and the Bishopric of Durham, 1406–1437* (1961), chapter 2; A. J. Pollard, *North-Eastern England during the Wars of the Roses: Lay Society, War, and Politics 1450–1500* (Oxford, 1990), 160–3.

palatinates the institutional trappings of power, authority and government: around Palace Green in Durham were the head offices of the administration of the palatinate. This physical apparatus of power was allied to a no-less-impressive set of cultural traditions supportive of the palatine community and its privileges. These traditions had at their heart St Cuthbert, but they encompassed the leading members of the palatine community, the barons, and, for example, the myths surrounding the Conyers of Sockburn family.[7]

Lapsley believed that the impact of Edward I's policies on Durham, and especially of his relations with Bishop Antony Bek, produced both an expression of advanced claims for palatine liberties and clear signs that their days were numbered. Others who have examined the development of political relationships in the British Isles more recently have placed great significance on the same period. Rees Davies, for example, based his presidential lectures on the observation that '[i]n 1400 the British Isles and Ireland were still a collection of peoples, albeit now much more clearly of four peoples than had been the case in 1100'.[8] Robin Frame has concluded that in place of a relatively loose assemblage of political power across these islands, the realms of England and Scotland reinforced their grip on their core territories while losing the borders and peripheries, especially Gaelic Ireland, to unstable and disorganised local rule.[9] So powerful and striking was King Edward's intervention in Durham, as in other territories as diverse as Wales and the Isle of Wight, that it seems almost futile to continue the story of local autonomy.[10] Whilst the shell of privilege remained, the substance had been hollowed out by the unstoppable centralising forces of the English crown, the Westminster administration and national politics. For Lapsley, the fourteenth century saw a 'perplexed toleration' of the Durham palatinate. Thereafter, 'the logical consequences of clearer vision were delayed by the disorders of the fifteenth century; and when, under the vigorous policy of the Tudors, the blow fell, the Bishops no longer had any care to avert it'.[11] That assumption has never been thoroughly tested. Given its immense importance in the historiography of England and North America, it is time that it was.

[7] St Cuthbert's day gathering: *Registrum Palatinum Dunelmense*, ed. T. D. Hardy, Rolls Series (1873–8) [hereafter *RPD*], IV, 435; Lapsley, *Durham*, 108. Barons: *ibid.*, 63–7; Robert Surtees, *The History and Antiquities of the County Palatine of Durham* (1816–40), III, 243–5.

[8] *Domination and Conquest: The Experience of Ireland, Scotland and Wales, 1100–1300* (Cambridge, 1990); 'The Peoples of Britain and Ireland, 1100–1400, I: Identities', *Transactions of the Royal Historical Society*, sixth series, IV (1994), 1–20; 'II: Names, Boundaries and Regnal Solidarities', V (1995), 1–20; 'III: Laws and Customs', VI (1996), 1–23; 'IV: Language and Historical Mythology', VII (1997), 1–24 (quotation at sixth series, IV, 20).

[9] *The Political Development of the British Isles 1100–1400* (Oxford, 1990).

[10] N. Denholm-Young, *Seigneurial Administration in England* (Oxford, 1937), 99–108.

[11] Lapsley, *Durham*, 76.

The tests we may apply are based on the three predominant strands in the current debate on state-building in early modern Europe. The first assesses such issues as dispute resolution and control over economic resources, especially through fiscal means, seeking to find the source of the authority expressed thereby.[12] The second strand is a longer-standing one: it examines the decisions of major 'national' representative institutions in legislating local jurisdictions out of existence and expressing through themselves the collective identity of the whole.[13] The third looks to personal relationships, especially in fora such as the court, whereby powerful individuals in the localities were recruited to central political alignments, whatever the apparent continuities of local political structures.[14] There is no doubt that challenges possibly related to these issues took place. But what is more important is their limitations and specific nature: none seriously challenged the fundamental position of the palatinate.

First, jurisdiction and dispute settlement. Sovereignty was closely allied to the role of supreme arbiter in conflicts and this was a major reason for the growth of equity jurisdictions at Westminster in the fifteenth and sixteenth centuries. Chancery and Star Chamber dealt, among other things, with challenges to lesser jurisdictions, denial of justice in franchisal courts being a common theme of bills in both central courts.[15] Yet litigation involving Durham seems to have been virtually absent from either court until well into the sixteenth century.

Before 1485, just seven Chancery cases are attributed to Durham.[16] Even so, many of these attributions are dubious. Some cases do not really affect Durham's jurisdiction, for example those suits which

---

[12] Esp. Michael Braddick, 'State Formation and Social Change in Early Modern England: A Problem Stated and Approaches Suggested', *Social History*, 16 (1991), 1–17.

[13] E.g. G. R. Elton's *The Tudor Revolution in Government: Administrative Changes in the Reign of Henry VIII* (Cambridge, 1953).

[14] A varied historiography stemming partly from Norbert Elias's work on the court in early modern Europe: *Die höfische Gesellschaft. Untersuchungen zur Soziologie des Königtums und der höfischen Aristokratie mit einer Einleitung: Soziologie und Geschichtswissenschaft* (Neuwied and Berlin, 1969); and partly from K. B. McFarlane's work on the English nobility, e.g. *The Nobility of Later Medieval England* (Oxford, 1973); *England in the Fifteenth Century*, intro. G. L. Harriss (1981).

[15] Nicholas Pronay, 'The Chancellor, the Chancery and the Council at the End of the Fifteenth Century', in *British Government and Administration: Studies Presented to S. B. Chrimes*, ed. H. Hearder and H. R. Loyn (Cardiff, 1974); Franz Metzger, 'The Last Phase of the Medieval Chancery', in *Law-Making and Law-Makers in British History: Papers Presented to the Edinburgh Legal History Conference*, ed. Alan Harding (1980); J. A. Guy, *The Cardinal's Court: The Impact of Thomas Wolsey in Star Chamber* (Hassocks, Sussex, 1977).

[16] Figures based on the county allocations in the List and Index Society calendars. Cf. thirteen attributed to France outside Calais; Wales thirty; Channel Islands four.

challenged the activities of officials of Newcastle-upon-Tyne.[17] Others
dealt with issues of church property which were pleaded in Chancery
without regard to jurisdictional boundaries affecting non-clerical cases.[18]
Before 1485, in fact, we have evidence of only two cases which seem
to affect Durham's jurisdiction.[19] Even when, after 1485, cases relating
to Durham came before Chancery, there was a likelihood that the
court would refuse to deal with them. Where Chancery action is
recorded in one case, concerning lands in Yorkshire, Leicestershire,
Nottinghamshire and Durham, the injunction related to land in the
first three counties but was silent on the subject of land lying in
Durham.[20]

Bundles	Dates	Durham
3–29	10 Ric. II–5 Ed IV	1 (0.0142%)
30–67	1463–85	5 (0.0543%)
68–75	Uncertain	1 (0.0700%)
76–377	1485–1515	19 (0.124%)
378–457	1515–18	3 (0.122%)
458–600	1518–29	2 (0.0419%)
601–694	1529–32	9 (0.381%)
695–712	1532–33	1 (0.187%)
713–934	1533–38	9 (0.126%)
935–1094	1538–44	9 (0.153%)
1095–1172	1544–47	5 (0.159%)
1174–1186	1547	1 (0.235%)
1188–1267, 1269, 1316–17, 1271–85	1547–51	19 (0.560%)
1286–1315, 1268, 1270, 1318–24	1551–53	4 (0.308%)
1325–1397	1553–55	6 (0.230%)
1398–1488	1556–58	11 (0.339%)

In the sixteenth century, however, there was undoubtedly a growth in
the number of cases from Durham dealt with in Chancery. This growth
has, however, been exaggerated in recent work: Christopher Kitching's
essay on this period masks details of this growth by using a broad
statistic for the entire sixteenth century of 'up to' two hundred cases;
his assertion of the popularity of Chancery needs to be qualified. The
situation in which the county contributed very few cases to Chancery

[17] The one relatively securely dated case before 5 Edward IV, Public Record Office,
London [hereafter PRO], C 1/12/144 (seizure of a ship freighted from Aberdeen to
London, and carrying it to Shields) cannot be called a Durham case. C 1/64/291, /67/44
(Newcastle).
[18] PRO, C 1/48/477; /66/382.
[19] PRO, C 1/56/259; /69/416.
[20] PRO, C 1/402/44.

indeed continued into the 1540s.[21] Even in that decade the growth that occurred was very limited: it was only really in the reign of Edward VI that the county palatine was referred to in more than one-third of one per cent of Chancery cases.[22] This was, however, a fourfold increase in proportionate terms on the period 1538–47. The difficulties of Bishop Tunstall at this point were responsible. The crisis in Tunstall's authority, worsening through 1550 and ending in his deposition in December of that year, left a vacuum. There is no doubt that John Dudley, duke of Northumberland, intended to retain the palatinate, if in the crown's hands and not those of the bishop, but there are signs that this produced a slight increase in the numbers seeking justice in the Westminster Chancery.[23] Thereafter, even though Mary restored Tunstall and his diocese, the trail for litigants to Westminster had been opened.[24] Their number did not, however, dramatically increase: even under Elizabeth there were only seventy-three cases from Durham treated in Chancery.[25]

A similar situation existed in Star Chamber. Among the cases in the Public Record Office class known as 'Star Chamber Proceedings: Henry VII' Durham is unrepresented.[26] Among the cases allocated to Henry VIII's reign, Durham attributions appear very infrequently, in six cases to be precise. Again, some of these can be excluded since they either raise clerical issues or do not in fact relate to Durham itself.[27] And unlike Chancery, in Star Chamber there is little sign of even the slightest increase in Durham litigation in the reign of Edward VI.[28]

[21] Cf. demands during the Pilgrimage of Grace that injunctions, *subpoenas*, and privy seals be sent less frequently into the more distant counties of the realm; Durham may have been part of this concern: *Letters and Papers, Foreign and Domestic, of the Reign of Henry VIII, 1509–47*, ed. J. S. Brewer, J. Gairdner and R. H. Brodie (1862–1910) [hereafter *LP*], xi. 1182, 2(7).

[22] Cf. Christopher Kitching, 'The Durham Palatinate and the Courts of Westminster under the Tudors', in *The Last Principality: Politics, Religion and Society in the Bishopric of Durham, 1494–1660*, ed. David Marcombe (Nottingham, 1987), 49–70, at 54–9. He conceals slow growth behind a statistic for the whole sixteenth century of 'up to' 200 cases (my calculation is 171).

[23] D. M. Loades, 'The Dissolution of the Diocese of Durham, 1553–4', in *Last Principality*, 101–16, at 102, 104; *Calendar of Patent Rolls* (1901–) [hereafter *CPR*], *Edward VI*, v. 175, vi. 177.

[24] D. M. Loades, 'The Last Years of Cuthbert Tunstall, 1547–1559', *Durham University Journal*, 66 (1973), 10–22.

[25] *Calendars of the Proceedings in Chancery in the Reign of Queen Elizabeth* (1827–32); Kenneth Emsley and C. M. Fraser, *The Courts of the County Palatine of Durham from the Earliest Times to 1971* (Durham, 1984), 76.

[26] There is only one non-English case: PRO, STAC 1/65 (Flintshire).

[27] Kitching, 'Durham Palatinate and the Courts of Westminster', 58, with no precise figures, again provides too enthusiastic an account of Durham involvement. Clerical case: PRO, STAC 2/1/40. Murder in Scotland: /1/181. That leaves /5/22; /15/186–7; /20/52; /31/33.

[28] Edward VI, two cases: PRO, STAC 3/5/69, /7/82; and /6/83. Philip and Mary, two related cases: STAC 4/1/14; /6/63.

A major reason for this failure to take the route to Westminster was the success of the Durham Chancery's equity jurisdiction. This directly contradicts the tendency of writers such as G. V. Scammell to emphasise the institutional infertility of the palatinate.[29] In the fifteenth century the chancellor of Durham took over from the bishop's council the role of giving judgement, and by 1478 there are signs of recognisable actions in equity there, and even of a decree under Bishop Fox (episcopate 1493–1502). Decrees were systematically entered from 1519.[30]

Thomas Wolsey's position as bishop of Durham (1523–9) and lord chancellor played some part in the number of Durham cases coming to Chancery and Star Chamber during the years to 1529; what is perhaps surprising is that this influence acted to *reduce* the number of cases, not to increase them. In Chancery, Durham cases represented a lower proportion of the court's business under Wolsey than at any time since the beginning of Edward IV's reign. A problem-solver like Wolsey, if he held both local and central office, did not inevitably seek central solutions,[31] and Wolsey may have been responsible for a major reorganisation of the Durham Chancery.[32]

A study of equity jurisdiction therefore suggests the degree to which Durham jurisdiction was unchallenged in one field until at least Elizabeth's reign.[33] Contrary to received opinion, a study of taxation, another crucial expression of political power and identity, shows that challenges could occur, often driven by elites in England who wished to spread their common burdens wider, but that they were defeated, often through the direct intervention of the king and those around him. In Durham, the fourteenth century saw the emergence of a discrete taxation system that excluded the rapidly developing mechanisms of Westminster parliamentary taxation.[34] A charter of 1302 suggests procedures for allocating common obligations already existed there,

[29] Scammell, 'Origins and Limitations of the Liberty of Durham', 463–4.

[30] Emsley and Fraser, *Courts of Durham*, 75–8; Lapsley, *Durham*, 188–9. PRO, DURH 4/1 is the first surviving decree book, 1633; earlier material can be recovered from Durham University Library, Mickleton MS 38 (index volume).

[31] Noted Kitching, 'Durham Palatinate and the Courts of Westminster', 49. Cf. Wolsey's assertion of his rights: W. Hylton Dyer Longstaffe, 'Cardinal Wolsey's Instructions to his Officers at Durham', *Archæologia Æliana*, second series, II (1858), 39–40. When Wolsey ordered a murderer seized from the Tynemouth sanctuary, it was to the Durham sheriff that he was to be delivered: *LP*, III (2). 3095 (12 June 1523).

[32] John Spearman, *An Enquiry into the Ancient and Present State of the County Palatine of Durham* (Edinburgh, 1729), 55–6; Lapsley, *Durham*, 189.

[33] The council in the North's share of Durham business highlights further the absence of a shift to dispute resolution through royal authority at the centre. On the council, Lapsley, *Durham*, 259–63.

[34] Durham was exempt as church land until William II's grant that no geld be levied in *Nordteisa*, 1096x8: *Regesta Regum Anglo-Normannorum, 1066–1154* (Oxford, 1913–69), I, no. 412.

and in 1314 a tax was voted to the bishop.[35] In 1344, the community voted the bishop contributions towards his expenses in buying off the Scots, and in 1348 for defending the county's privileges.[36] It is hard to find signs of regular local taxation thereafter, as for example developed in Cheshire; Durham had not only established its independence from English taxation but also from a parallel system that might ultimately be driven from Westminster.[37]

Faced by fiscal experimentation late in Edward III's reign and in that of Richard II, the Durham community persisted in its attempts to exclude English taxes. Initially the county was subject to common English levies, such as the tax of half the country's wool in 1338.[38] Yet the government was willing to recognise the county's privileges, and when the fifteenth and tenth emerged as the standard form of par-liamentary subsidy, Durham was excluded.[39] Many authorities, most recently Mark Ormrod writing of the English parish subsidy of 1371, have assumed that areas like Durham were effectively part of the English grants of this period. Yet although the occasions for taxation might be the same, and in this case Durham's contribution was included in the overall target of £50,000, Durham insisted on agreeing its own taxes and, for example, assessing, collecting and spending them.[40]

More importantly, whatever was done in 1371, the regime guaranteed that it would not be a precedent,[41] a guarantee effective against the poll taxes of 1377–81.[42] Another parish-based subsidy in 1427–8 attempted to tax all householders 'withyene ... this saide Royaume', but its general

---

[35] 1302: *RPD*, III, 43, 64; Lapsley, *Durham*, 118–19, 272. 1314: *RPD*, II, 686; Lapsley, *Durham*, 119, 272; *Scriptores Tres, Historiæ Dunelmensis*, ed. J. Raine, Surtees Society, IX (1839), cxiii.

[36] 1344: *RPD*, IV, 273–7; Lapsley, *Durham*, 119, 272. 1348: DURH 3/31, m. 4d, curs. 30; Lapsley, *Durham*, 119–20, 273.

[37] Lapsley suggested taxation was unnecessary with defence handled through general border mechanisms: *Durham*, 120.

[38] *RPD*, IV, 225–8; Lapsley, *Durham*, 298.

[39] *Northern Petitions*, ed. C. M. Fraser, Surtees Society, CXCIV (1982 [1981]), 161, 271–2; cf. *Calendar of Close Rolls* (1902–) [hereafter *CCR*], *1346–9*, 3. G. L. Harriss, *King, Parliament and Public Finance to 1369* (Oxford, 1975).

[40] W. M. Ormrod, 'An Experiment in Taxation: The English Parish Subsidy of 1371', *Speculum*, 68 (1988), 58–82, esp. 77–9. Ormrod claims the 1371 precedent was used in fifteenth-century taxation demands, citing Storey, *Langley*, 55; Lapsley, *Durham*, 298–9, which do not show this but simply discuss what they wrongly see as the successful *Westminster* taxation of 1436 and 1450.

[41] PRO, DURH 3/31, m. 5; *Scriptores Tres*, pp. cxlii–cxliii (20 Nov. 1374); cf. *Rotuli Parliamentorum*, ed. J. Strachey and others (1767–77) [hereafter *RP*], II, 461; Lapsley, *Durham*, 117, 298.

[42] Cf. W. H. B. Bird,'Taxation and Representation in the County Palatine of Chester', *EHR* 30 (1915), 303 (Cheshire, Durham and the 1379 tax). The 1380 parliament demanded the inclusion of the Cinque Ports, Cheshire and Durham; the king accepted the inclusion of the former, but not Durham or Cheshire: *RP*, III, 94. *CPR*, *1377–81*, 628.

failure included a lack of response from Durham.[43] The income tax of October 1435 covered 'every Shire of Ingelond', but in 1436 the people of Durham eventually made their own grant. In return, in 1437, they again received letters of indemnity.[44] In 1450, a subsidy again intended the inclusion of Durham, for all 'withyn youre said Royalme' were liable.[45] This tax is crucial to Lapsley's account, for he believes it was met only by 'ineffectual protest'.[46] Yet although the government tried to impose the tax in Durham, it failed.[47] Unpopular generally, in November 1450 the subsidy had still not been apportioned.[48] While many shire officials were distrained in March 1451, those of Durham were not: the attempt had been abandoned.[49] Durham was included in the grant of archers made to Henry VI in 1453, but only on its own terms.[50] The next income tax was attempted in 1472, and this time the intention to involve Durham was absolutely specific and insistent. Commissioners were to be appointed 'as Commissions have been custumably used to be sent for the levye of xv^{mes} and x^{mes} afore tyme graunted, and into the Bisshopriche of Durham and all other places necessary'.[51] But on 8 January 1474 there were still no returns from a group of northern counties, including Durham. The grant was therefore transmuted to 590 archers, of which Durham was to provide 300.[52]

---

[43] RP, IV, 318; *Inquisitions and Assessments Relating to Feudal Aids* (1899–) (nothing for Durham); cf. Roger Virgoe, 'The Parliamentary Subsidy of 1450', *BIHR*, 56 (1982), 124–38, at p. 127. The broadly similar 1431 subsidy was completely withdrawn: RP, IV, 369–70, 409–10.

[44] RP, IV, 486–7; PRO, DURH 3/44, m. 12, curs. 78; cf. *Calendar of Fine Rolls* (1911–) [hereafter CFR], *1430–7*, 257–62, 267–9; *Proceedings and Ordinances of the Privy Council of England*, ed. N. H. Nicolas (1834–7), IV, 343. 1437: *CPR, 1436–41*, 4; Storey, *Langley*, 55. This came shortly after the successful defence of palatine privileges, including those relating to taxation, in 1433: *Scriptores Tres*, ccxxviii–ccxxxv; Lapsley, *Durham*, 241–2; Storey, *Langley*, 116–34.

[45] RP, V, 172–4; Virgoe, '1450', 133.

[46] '[E]loquent of the change which had occurred within the government of the palatinate.' Lapsley dates the tax to 1449, when the parliament began: *Durham*, 118, 298–9. This became the point of reference for later writers, e.g. *Northern Petitions*, 161.

[47] The 1437 indemnity was enrolled immediately after the demand for collection: PRO, DURH 3/44, m. 12, curs. 77–8.

[48] Ralph A. Griffiths, *The Reign of Henry VI: The Exercise of Royal Authority, 1422–1461* (1981), 381, 396; Virgoe, '1450', 133; RP, V, 172–4. Cf. Cheshire's outraged response: Henry Davies Harrod, 'A Defence of the Liberties of Chester, 1450', *Archaeologia*, second series, VII (1900), 71–80, at 75–7; George Ormerod, *History of The County Palatine and City of Chester*, 2nd edn rev. and enlarged by Thomas Helsby (1882), I, 45–6; Dorothy J. Clayton, *The Administration of the County Palatine of Chester 1442–85*, Chetham Society, third series, XXXV (1990), 126–7.

[49] CFR, *1445–52*, 207; Virgoe, '1450', 133.

[50] RP, V, 232; Griffiths, *Henry VI*, 432.

[51] RP, VI, 4–5.

[52] RP, VI, 113–15; C. D. Ross, *Edward IV* (1974), 214–18. The 1481 benevolence again saw the northern counties asked for men not money: Roger Virgoe, 'The Benevolence

There are signs that subsequent regimes had begun to learn this lesson. The income tax of 1489 was based on that of 1472: the act was to apply to all 'issues and profyttes in England, Wales and the Marches of the same'. Commissions were to be sent 'into every shire, and to every Cyte ... as Commyssions have been custumably used to be sent, for the Levye of xv^{es} and x^{es} afore tyme graunted, and to all other places necessarie', although, significantly, this time none was specified.[53] The Lords made a separate grant of their own taxation, but this specifically excluded Northumberland, Cumberland and Westmorland, while it explicitly included Wales and the marches.[54] Resistance included the murder of the earl of Northumberland, and Polydore Vergil says that the Durham palatinate was involved. The tax was translated into a fifteenth and tenth in 1490, thereby excluding Durham.[55]

By the end of Henry VII's reign, the king and his ministers had stopped trying to include Durham in national taxes. A crucial factor was probably the arrival of Richard Fox as bishop of Durham in 1493. The levy of 1497 from its conception had no application in Durham: it was based on 'every shire chargeable with the seid xv^{mes} and x^{mes}', and no commission was appointed for Durham.[56] The pattern of acts explicitly excluding Durham was continued with the grant in 1504 of a sum of £30,000 in lieu of feudal aids. No commission was appointed for Durham, although the act stated that 'every Shire w^{t}in this Realme' should contribute.[57] This is suggestive, since the purpose of the tax was not exclusively financial. Henry intended to survey tenures, a foundation of his policy of exploiting feudal rights. If a latter-day Domesday Book was intended, it was to include the northern counties, but not Durham. In fact, the antiquarianism of the Westminster grant of 1504 followed experimentation in the mapping of feudal rights by Bishop Richard

of 1481', *EHR*, 104 (1989), 28–30, at 37. Bishop Booth, chancellor (1473–4) during this negotiation, retired 'weary and tired by the endless task' of managing parliamentary business, of which it must have been an important part: *The Crowland Chronicle Continuations: 1459–1486*, ed. Nicholas Pronay and John Cox (1986), 133.

[53] *RP*, VI, 420–1.

[54] *RP*, VI, 423–4.

[55] *RP*, VI, 438–9; *The Anglica Historia of Polydore Vergil AD 1485–1537*, ed. and trans. Denys Hay, Camden Society, third series, LXXIV (1950), 38–9; Raphael Holinshed, *Chronicles of England, Scotland and Ireland* (1807), III, 769; Lapsley, *Durham*, 299 (he dates this 1488); M. A. Hicks, 'The Yorkshire Rebellion of 1489 Reconsidered', *Northern History*, 22 (1986), 39–62. Hicks conflates the grant of £75,000 with the Lords' grant, for he suggests that the former, like the latter, exempted the border counties: pages 40, 42, 47, 50. Only £27,000 of the £75,000 intended had been received.

[56] *The Statutes of the Realm* (1810–28) [hereafter *SR*], II, 644–7.

[57] *SR*, II, 675–82 (esp. p. 675) (Northumberland, Cumberland and Westmorland were included).

Fox in the palatinate of Durham through a *quo warranto* enquiry.[58]

In 1512 a grant of subsidy was explicitly intended to cover all counties, including 'liberties frauncheses sayntuaries auncient demeane and places exampte', yet no commissions were appointed for Durham, the other northern counties or Cheshire.[59] A similarly inclusive clause was a feature of the 1513–14 act, but this again failed to produce commissions for Durham.[60] By the time the 1514–15 parliament came to pass its subsidy act, an exclusion clause for Durham and the rest pronounced them 'utterly acquyted and discharged'.[61] There was perhaps an attempt to include Durham during the drafting of the 1512 and 1513–14 acts, but one that was successfully resisted early enough to prevent commissions being appointed to assess the taxes. Durham's position was accepted in time for it to be written into the 1514–15 act; the 1523 subsidy also included an exemption.[62]

Most notably, Durham sustained its exemption from English subsidies through the 1530s and 1540s, when Wales and Cheshire were for the first time included.[63] The 1534 statute, atypical in its drafting,[64] included Cheshire, if only by implication, but Durham had explicit exemption. The 1540 subsidy confirmed that Westminster taxation was here to stay in Wales and Cheshire, but Durham's privileges were confirmed.[65]

Legislative interference was even less threatening. Durham remained

---

[58] PRO, DURH 3/61, m. 11, curs. 48–9; Lapsley, *Durham*, 34–5. Cf. Harold Garrett-Goodyear, 'The Tudor Revival of Quo Warranto and Local Contributions to State Building', in *On the Laws and Customs of England: Essays in Honor of Samuel E. Thorne*, ed. Morris S. Arnold, Thomas A. Green, Sally A. Scully and Stephen D. White (Chapel Hill, NC, 1981), 231–95, at 236; R. Stewart Brown, 'The Cheshire Writs of Quo Warranto in 1499', *EHR*, 49 (1934), 676–84; J. Beverley Smith, 'Crown and Community in the Principality of North Wales in the Reign of Henry Tudor', *Welsh History Review* [hereafter *WHR*], 3 (1966–7), 145–71.

[59] Henry VIII, c.19; *SR*, III, 75; R. S. Schofield, 'Parliamentary Lay Taxation, 1485–1547' (PhD thesis, Cambridge University, 1963), 198–203.

[60] Henry VIII, c.17; *SR*, III, 105–19 (a note of places 'wherof there be no Comissioners retorned and affiled to this acte', listed Cheshire, Cumberland, Northumberland, Westmorland and Wight, but with no mention of Durham); Schofield, 'Parliamentary Lay Taxation', 204–9.

[61] Henry VIII, c.26; *SR*, III, 156–67. A proviso now dealt with those avoiding tax by 'removing into the excepted Counties'.

[62] 14 & 15 Henry VIII, c. 16 (*SR*, III, 230–41); Schofield, 'Parliamentary Lay Taxation', 213–18.

[63] Henry VIII, c. 19; *SR*, III, 516–24. Cheshire: *LP*, VII, 1496; PRO, E 179/85/2–3. G. R. Elton argued this statute was revolutionary, but for different reasons: 'Taxation for War and Peace in Early Tudor England', in *War and Economic Development: Essays in Memory of David Joslin*, ed. J. M. Winter (Cambridge, 1975), 33–48. Wales (1543): Glanmor Williams, *Recovery, Reorientation and Reformation: Wales, c. 1415–1642* (Oxford, 1987), 267.

[64] Schofield, 'Parliamentary Lay Taxation', 215.

[65] 32 Henry VIII, c. 50; *SR*, III, 824. Only under James I did it fall: Schofield, 'Parliamentary Lay Taxation', 145. 3 Jac. I, c. 26 exempted Durham (*SR*, IV(2), 1108–26, esp. 1124–5); 7 Jac. I, c. 23 made no mention of it (*SR*, IV(2), 1187–1201).

unrepresented in the Westminster parliament until after the Civil War.[66] In general, English statutes were observed,[67] but there might be special provision in general legislation to take account of Durham's privileges. For example, in Edward IV's last parliament, an act making Berwick the staple, along with Carlisle, for the Scottish trade, included a saving clause for Bishop William Dudley.[68] And many legal innovations respected palatine liberties with the result that Durham did not feel their force. Even on such a controversial issue as liveries, in 1468 a statute stated that no action was to lie within the counties palatine of Lancashire, Cheshire or Durham.[69]

If Antony Bek had suffered under the scrutiny of Edward I's officers, then in many areas the bishops of Durham had successfully reasserted their rights. Bek had lost the right to an independent customs system in Hartlepool; but the right was recovered in the 1330s.[70] While the lands of rebels such as Bruce and Balliol had been taken by the crown, the bishops continued to assert their rights of forfeiture through the next centuries, and the oft-repeated claim that Elizabeth's seizure of the earl of Westmorland's lands in 1570 was the end of the privilege is exaggerated at least.[71]

It is therefore hard to see the fifteenth and early sixteenth centuries as a period of institutional centralisation weakening the Durham palatinate. If anything, the trend was towards a confirmation of its powers in jurisdiction, taxation and statute. This might still allow for the working out of perhaps the greatest threat to the autonomy of the palatinates, that which might be effected through the political authority which the king possessed there. Whatever the jurisdiction of the courts

---

[66] Andrew W. Foster, 'The Struggle for Parliamentary Representation for Durham, c. 1600–41', in *Last Principality*, 176–201.

[67] Lapsley, *Durham*, 125–7; Storey, *Langley*, 54–5.

[68] Edward IV, c. 8; *SR*, II, 475–6.

[69] 8 Edward IV, c. 2; *SR*, II, 426–9. This confirmed existing laws against liveries (1 Henry IV, c. 7; 7 Henry IV, c. 14; *SR*, II, 113–14, 155–6), extended to Lancashire and Cheshire in 1429 (8 Henry VI, c. 4; *SR*, II, 240–1); but it stated no exigend should be awarded 'by any of the Justices for the Time being, within the said Counties Palatine' of Lancashire and Cheshire 'against any Person or Persons, upon any Information, Suit, or Process to be made by Force of this Ordinance' (428). The statute instead provided that actions might be brought in the courts of Durham, Lancashire, Cheshire and Hexham (426–7). Cf. M. A. Hicks, 'The 1468 Statute of Livery', *Historical Research*, 64 (1991), 15–28, esp. 21, whose emphasis on Durham, Lancashire and Cheshire seeking exemption because of a lack of confidence in their own judicial systems should be corrected.

[70] C. M. Fraser, *A History of Antony Bek* (Oxford, 1957), 86–7, 191, 199; *Northern Petitions*, 270–1 (no. 202); *RPD*, IV, 221–2, 264–5; *CCR, 1337–9*, 39; Lapsley, *Durham*, 276–7.

[71] Lapsley, *Durham*, 42–50; *Northern Petitions*, 160, 240; *CPR, 1266–72*, 63; *RPD*, III, 28–32; PRO, DURH 3/77, m. 32 (1544), 1570 and after: 13 Elizabeth, c. 16, no. 6 (*SR*, IV(I), 551); M. J. Tillbroke, 'Aspects of Government and Society of County Durham 1558–1642' (PhD thesis, Liverpool University, 1982), 72. Lapsley, *Durham*, 47.

and parliament at Westminster, the king appointed the bishop and royal patronage and political authority might brush aside the apparent boundaries of jurisdiction. One of the major strands in the historiography of the palatinates has been the insistence that factional politics at court meant that the personnel and powers of the administration became an arm of court politics.[72] Equally, the prime focus for local identification might be the connection of a nobleman, and as his fortunes revolved increasingly round the court, so 'bastard feudal' connections might undermine palatine autonomy. In other words, the prime focus for politics in the shire might become the same alignments of curial and noble politics that mattered, we are told, everywhere else. We should be careful before assuming this. First, we must deal with the argument that says that the palatinate decayed because it became too close to the crown. It has been suggested that the course of English politics interrupted the proper influence of the crown in the Durham palatinate in the appointments of Bishops Dudley (1476) and Shirwood (1484). Professor Pollard has pointed out how in both cases the king passed over the keeper of the privy seal, the post-holder who had frequently received the bishopric previously, and chose instead someone close to him personally. Dudley had no experience of public administration, but in him Edward IV was selecting a man who was among his closest servants, as dean of the chapel royal. In Shirwood, Richard III chose the archdeacon of Richmond and a member of his close clerical connection.[73] To suggest that Dudley weakened the palatinate because he co-operated closely with Gloucester begs the wider question of the reasons for Edward's allocation of immense power in the north to his brother: the bishop worked with the king's power in the north, as Edward chose to constitute it. Of course, when Edward made Richard his commander in the north for the Scottish wars of the 1480s, Dudley followed suit in making him his lieutenant – not to do so would have been more destructive of royal authority in the region.[74] If there is something odd in these appointments, it is in Richard III's acceptance that Shirwood would remain in Rome, and his assumption of control

[72] N.B. the 'over-mighty courtier' of the work of Eric Ives (e.g. 'Court and County Palatine in the Reign of Henry VIII: The Career of William Brereton of Malpas', *Transactions of the Historic Society of Lancashire and Cheshire*, 123 (1971), 1–38) and Steven Gunn (e.g. 'The Regime of Charles, Duke of Suffolk, in North Wales and the Reform of Welsh Government, 1509–25', *WHR*, 12 (1985), 461–94).

[73] A. J. Pollard, 'The Crown and the County Palatine of Durham, 1437–94', in *The North of England in the Age of Richard III*, ed. A. J. Pollard (Stroud, 1996), 67–87, at 83–4; A. J. Pollard, 'St Cuthbert and the Hog: Richard III and the County Palatine of Durham, 1471–85', in *Kings and Nobles in the Later Middle Ages*, ed. Ralph A. Griffiths and James Sherborne (Gloucester, 1986), 109–29, at 115–23; Pollard, *North-Eastern England*, 374, 388–9.

[74] PRO, DURH 3/54, m. 11; Lapsley, *Durham*, 307.

in Durham other than through the person of the bishop. Yet although the king kept the temporalities in his own hands until August 1485, he did not, as he might have, merge the administration with that of the council in the North, but ruled the area through the structures of the palatinate, with Sir Richard Ratcliffe probably appointed steward of Durham. It has been argued that close royal servants brought the palatinate into the crown's orbit. As in Ives's Cheshire, courtiers prospered in the locality due to their contact with the king, and in the court their influence was supported in part by the knowledge of their powerful local roots: Ratcliffe is a classic example.[75] Given this it is significant that Henry VII chose not to appoint another absentee diplomat to Durham, but an activist bishop. Replacing Shirwood with Fox was hardly an example of Tudor centralisation. Dudley and Shirwood may not have represented the succession of keepers of the privy seal – this is to place too much emphasis on the office and not what the office represented. They were what keepers had been: close, trusted clerical servants of the crown and this was not destruction by the crown but support for palatine autonomy, since these bishops, and arguably even a man like Ratcliffe, did not subject the palatinate to the centre but brought a commitment to palatine privileges to the heart of court and government.

The other side of this argument is that involvement in the normal patterns of English politics meant that the palatinate was undermined when it became enmeshed in the noble feuding of the fifteenth century. Ralph Griffiths has recently attempted to provide a territorial context for the Wars of the Roses:

> Some historians lay responsibility squarely on the nobility and greater gentry, their fluctuating fortunes and in some cases, echoing the opinions of contemporaries, their overweening power and ambition and their mutual jealousies. But if that explanation is to hold water, it must be given a territorial and governmental context, and the most satisfying one lies in the more distant provinces of the realm and the dominions.[76]

This causes us to turn to the case of Robert Neville, significant in that his elevation to Durham is often seen as the low point of the independence of the bishopric – *vis-à-vis* the nobility – in the fifteenth century. Yet we must be cautious: the most obvious cause for this caution occurred during the period of Henry VI's minority. The death

---

[75] Pollard, 'Cuthbert and the Hog', 123: 'overmighty household men'.
[76] 'The Provinces and the Dominions in the Age of the Wars of the Roses', in *Estrangement, Enterprise and Education in Fifteenth Century England*, ed. Sharon D. Michalove and A. Compton Reeves (Stroud, 1998), 1–25, at 24.

of Bishop Langley in 1437 coincided with a difficult period in Henry's transition to full powers, and the result of the activity of Cardinal Beaufort in the council was the appointment of Robert Neville to the bishopric. This was, on the most immediate level, a piece of family aggrandisement on behalf of the sons of Joan Beaufort and the Nevilles of Middleham. But did that make the bishop the 'lackey' of an 'over-mighty subject' and the Neville connection?[77] In spring 1439, after the appointment of his brother George, Lord Latimer as Durham chamberlain and the grant of an annuity there to another brother, Edward, Lord Abergavenny, Robert Neville attacked Barnard Castle with a great multitude of men, banners flying.[78] What is most notable is that Bishop Robert did this after the death of Richard Beauchamp, earl of Warwick, when the successors to his interests in Barnard Castle and elsewhere were the Nevilles of Middleham: Richard's heir was married to Salisbury's daughter. In this case, only a few months after his appointment to the bishopric on the basis of his Beaufort/Neville connections, Robert Neville was acting for the bishopric's interests against those of his own family. Of course, in the subsequent history of his episcopacy, Neville never again acted so directly against his own kin, but the interests of the palatinate remained central to his actions. After 1448 the Scots had the advantage in border conflicts. In 1449–50 it was in Durham itself that a truce was signed, but James II broke it with impunity in 1455. In the 1450s, when the Scottish border was so often under threat, the bishop's actions, albeit in support of Salisbury and his allies, were driven in large part by a concern for the security of his own palatinate.[79] In local tradition, Neville was remembered as a bishop who built a new home for the palatine administration's Chancery and Exchequer; his was also the successful defence of the palatinate's exemption from Westminster taxation in 1450.[80]

It is significant that political challenges from the crown and nobility tended to centre not on the palatinate's status and internal operation but on its boundaries. Even there, palatine authority retained strength. The overlordships of Barnard Castle and Hart were particularly con-troversial. Although Edward I had declared them forfeit to the crown as a consequence of the resistance of Balliol and Bruce, the bishops of Durham never accepted that they were rightfully the crown's. The story of Barnard Castle is relatively well known. The crown resisted challenges to its position there, and the lordship became part of the

[77] Pollard, 'Durham', 77.

[78] *CPR, 1436–41*, 371–2, 408.

[79] Pollard, *North-Eastern England*, 221–4, surveys these border struggles; cf. Griffiths, *Henry VI*, 734, on Richard of York's concerns; Antonia Gransden, *Historical Writing in England* (1974–82), II, *c. 1307 to the Early Sixteenth Century*, 274–87, on Hardyng.

[80] *Scriptores Tres*, 147; Lapsley, *Durham*, 190, 271.

royal demesne in 1483. That said, when the Beauchamp succession was thrown into doubt in 1459 by the rebellion of the earl of Warwick, it was Bishop Neville who enacted the confiscation.[81] In 1470 Bishop Booth recovered his rights there, and when Gloucester took control of the lordship in 1474 he did so without a clear grant on the king's patent roll.[82] A deliberate refusal to confront the issue finally in the king's favour is also apparent in the phraseology of the licence to Gloucester to found his college there in 1478, when Barnard Castle was said to lie in 'the Bishopricke of Duresme', although it was the king who made the grant.[83] And in reality it was the bishop's administrative and judicial system which operated there, not the king's.[84] Less well known, but equally important, is the story of Hart and Hartlepool. In 1461, Edward IV recognized Bishop Booth's right in Hart, and in 1485 Lord Clifford was restored to the lordship by Bishop Shirwood.[85]

We are therefore left with the conclusion that the real constraint on the palatinate was its relationship with the crown, as had always been the case,[86] and yet also with a recognition that this relationship in practice meant a high degree of independent action on the part of the palatinate and its communities. This can only be understood if we reinterpret the nature of kingship and the kingdom in fifteenth-century England away from a rigid polarity of interest between centre and locality and between crown and nobility. To propose that some of the palatine officers and bishops 'went native' is to assume an opposition between the free and forceful operation of the prerogatives of the bishopric, on the one hand, and the interests of the Westminster administration and the crown, or of the nobility, on the other. This is plainly not the case. Hence the record of Bishop Booth, who was close to Queen Margaret of Anjou, and has been described recently as Edward IV's 'loyal and trusted agent in the North'.[87] He took on the prior of Durham and asserted his feudal rights over the convent's lands; he revived the Durham mint and added the prerogative of coining halfpennies to that of minting pennies. In 1466 he appointed a lawyer, Thomas Morslaw, as his steward, thereby ending a period in which important noblemen, such as Morslaw's predecessor, John Neville, at that time earl of Northumberland, had held the post. Yet of course

[81] Michael Hicks, 'The Forfeiture of Barnard Castle to the Bishop of Durham in 1459', *Northern History*, 33 (1997), 223–31.
[82] Pollard, 'Cuthbert and the Hog', 110–11.
[83] *CPR, 1476–85*, 67; William Dugdale, *Monasticon Anglicanum* (1673), III(2), 203; Pollard, 'Cuthbert and the Hog', 116.
[84] Pollard, *North-Eastern England*, 149, n. 14.
[85] Pollard, 'Durham', 69.
[86] Esp. Scammell, 'Origin and Limitations of the Liberty of Durham'.
[87] Pollard, 'Durham', 82.

Booth pressed particularly firmly for his rights over Barnard Castle. This was a campaign to remove the lordship from royal control, and hence might be seen as 'going native'. In the 1470s Booth duly received a grant from the king of Barnard Castle 'according to your rights and title'.

Booth's case is a reminder that we should be aware of other ways of reading the experiences and interests of those in power in Durham. Four of the fifteenth-century bishops suggest another context in which these men operated: the culture of palatinate administration and society. Bishop Langley's background was in Lancashire and the service of the Duchy and palatinate there.[88] Bishop Neville's ancestry and connections were obviously primarily aristocratic, but as a scion of the earls of Westmorland he had forebears who had been at the centre of Durham society for many generations. Bishop Booth was closely related to some of the most important administrators in the fifteenth-century Cheshire palatinate, the Booths of Dunham Massey, a family steeped, in both lay and clerical life, in the culture of palatine privilege, especially given their origins in Lancashire.[89] So too was Bishop William Dudley, as the third son of John, Lord Dudley, who possessed estates in Cheshire. After Oxford, William's first benefice was at Malpas in south-west Cheshire in 1457. Lord Dudley himself had been prominent in the resistance to the 1450 subsidy in Cheshire.[90] For all four, palatine liberties were an essential part of their outlook on political life.

This is, of course, not true of Richard Fox, but like the others he was provided to Durham as one of the most trusted servants of the king. Yet he pursued the interests of the bishopric in ways that some might see as being against those of the Westminster administration. Fox's period in control of the bishopric saw him attempting to use the power of the bishopric to put down the nuisance of the men of Tynedale and Redesdale, perhaps a classic central government objective;[91] but at no point did he ever allow the priorities of Westminster to outweigh those of the bishopric. One of the most striking phrases from his letters of the period is his warning to Thomas Castell, prior of Durham: 'Doubte you not, broder, I shall no thyng desyre you to doo that shall be hurt or preiudice to the mitre of that my church'. As Marjorie Howden, the editor of his episcopal register commented, 'the dignity of the mitre was never forgotten or made subservient to secular

---

[88] Storey, *Langley*, 4–8.

[89] Clayton, *Administration of Chester*, 173–5.

[90] A. B. Emden, *A Biographical Register of the University of Oxford to A.D. 1500* (Oxford, 1957–9), I, 600; Clayton, *Administration of Chester*, 77–80, 84, 86, 89; Harrod, 'Defence of the Liberties of Cheshire', 71–80.

[91] *The Register of Richard Fox, Lord Bishop of Durham, 1494–1501*, ed. Marjorie Peers Howden, Surtees Society, CXLVII (1932), 80–4.

business'.[92] As we have seen, Fox's episcopacy saw the end of efforts to tax Durham from Westminster. Fox was responsible for a *quo warranto* campaign in the bishopric which clarified and strengthened the bishop's position. Fox was particularly insistent on his rights in Hart, which offended the Cliffords. At least one writer in Durham, the chronicler associated with the name of William de Chambre, believed that his translation to Winchester was due to the devotion of this key minister of the crown to the rights of his bishopric: *ratione controversiæ ortæ inter eum et comitem Cumberlandiæ pro jure de Hartilpoole*.[93]

Fox was an exceptional man, but his interest in Hart is not so inappropriate a point at which to conclude. Durham's palatinate status, if understood in the way suggested here, was not seriously undermined in the fifteenth century and emerged from Henry VII's reign strengthened. Michael Hicks has recently posed the question of why, in Barnard Castle and Hart, the nobility preferred powerful crown authority to that of a more easily overawed bishop.[94] The answer, it seems on reflection, is that they did not. All parties preferred what seems to us to be ambiguity, sometimes tense, more often not. In the contemporary mind this was a respect for palatine privilege which was not unchallengeable, especially at the margin, but which was thoroughly supported by the contemporary legal and political culture of custom and particularism. In that environment, the palatinate could only thrive. In particular, the palatinate was the obvious model to turn to when territorial expansion demanded the establishment of forms of authority and government. It was natural that Durham should be explicitly used as a model when statute was used in 1483 to extend new palatine powers for Richard of Gloucester in areas of southern Scotland to be conquered by him; it was just as natural in the grants in the new world in the early seventeenth century as English America took shape.[95] In both these contexts, strong provincial juridictions were neither archaic nor simply necessary but an obvious solution to the challenges of the fifteenth and the seventeenth centuries.

[92] *Register of Fox*, xxxii.
[93] *Scriptores Tres*, 150, ccccxlix–ccccliv.
[94] Hicks, 'Forfeiture of Barnard Castle'.
[95] *RP*, vi, 204–5; A. Grant, 'Richard III and Scotland', in *North of England*, 125–6.

EUROPE REMADE: PURITY AND DANGER IN LATE MEDIEVAL EUROPE*

By Miri Rubin

READ 19 MAY 2000

SOME of the most cherished arrangements, the most comforting statements, the most confident claims about the nature of a society living under a divinely sanctioned sacramental–sacerdotal order, were given very different meanings in late medieval Prague, Paris and Pontefract. Such divergence and difference had always been a pattern of European life, as variety applied not only to climate, economic systems, language and political institutions, but also to devotional styles. The consolidation of sameness which was attempted – and to a significant extent achieved – by the church between 1100 and 1300, was offered through a single system of law, of preferment, of ritual. This was embedded within a set of understandings about the relationship of ecclesiastical hierarchy to salvation as well as to social order. Yet by around 1400 doubt and discomfort had attached to several of the touchstones of this world view – eucharist, pope, clergy – and thus hindered the flow of communication and cooperation which both underpinned and represented it. The authority to discern truth was in the hands of rulers and prelates who, in turn, were empowered or catalysed by professional thinkers and communicators – scholars, preachers, teachers, lawyers and poets. Words mattered greatly because they could conjure a vision of possible peace and remedy. They were spoken in tens of universities, hundreds of city councils, in a growing number of representative assemblies. Polities – be they territorial lordships, cities or even at times the Emperor – were pressing these thinkers and communicators to help in the work towards revival, purification and healing, away and against schism, pollution and war. How is the confidence to judge and discern spiritual and ethical truth ever regained by institutions or by individuals? More than ever before we witness preoccupation with the re-ordering of a Christian world through the re-establishment of social, economic and ethical order.

These preoccupations with authority and truth manifest some of the

*I wish to thank Ros Allen, Marilyn Desmond, Kantik Ghosh, Steven Gunn, Gareth Stedman Jones, and John Watts for their illuminating comments in discussion of parts of this paper. I have also benefited greatly from discussions with Renate Blumenfeld-Kosinski about her recent work on prophets and visionaries during the Great Schism.

abiding concerns of all people with the drawing of boundaries around the holy, the gaining of access to the pure, and the distancing of self and loved ones from the polluted and the dangerous. When the institutions meant to promote and endorse sacramental promise and truth in teaching were beset by very public cracks – as they clearly were c.1400 – some unusual voices of challenge penetrated through the fissures more clearly than before. Such voices of prophetic comment were both the product and the symptom of the state of indeterminacy in several spheres: the voices of Bridget of Sweden (1303–73), of Catherine of Siena (1347–80), and of the less well known Constance of Rabastens (d.1386), Marie Robine (d.1399) and Jeanne-Marie de Maillé (d.1414).[1]

Schism in the church did not only cloud ecclesiastical theory and disrupt church bureaucracy, it had real consequences for households, polities, marriages, all of which depended on an intricate system of approval and endorsement related to the smooth handling of sacramental practice and ecclesiastical law and custom. For as the poet Guillaume of Salvarville wrote c. 1400, false popes made false prelates, who in turn made false priests, whose sacramental efficacy in a whole area of essential activities was put into question.[2] This sense of disruption and danger became suddenly apparent to a wide range of layfolk. Constance of Rabastens's visions of 1384–6 (which were recorded in Occitan by her confessor Raymond of Sabanac and survive in a Catalan version) reflected an abhorrence of the French position in the crisis of the church.[3] Her vision of August 1385, on the day of the Assumption of the Virgin had Christ appealing to her in agony:

I was once crucified, and another time I have been crucified, and this is a greater offence than that committed by Pilate who delivered me to death, because they would not accept the real pope which I had made, and they created another.[4]

In another section of her comments Constance encouraged Gaston

[1] André Vauchez, 'Female prophets, visionaries, and mystics in medieval Europe', in The Laity in the Middle Ages: Religious Beliefs and Devotional Practices, ed. and intro. Daniel E. Bornstein, trans. Margery J. Schneider (Notre Dame, Ind., 1993), 219–29.
[2] Zenon Kaluza, 'Note sur Guillaume de Salvarville auteur de deux poèmes sur le grand schisme', Mediaevalia philosophica polonorum 19 (1974), 162; Daniel E. Bornstein, The Bianchi of 1399. Popular Devotion in Late Medieval Italy (Ithaca, NY, 1993), 199–200.
[3] Renate Blumenfeld-Kosinski, 'Constance de Rabastens: Politics and Visionary Experience in the Time of the Great Schism', Mystics Quarterly, 25 (1999), 147–68.
[4] 'E una veu fou crocifiat, e altre veu ells me ban crucifiat, e es maior la offensa que no fo di Pilat, quant me liura a mort, car lo Papa vertader que yo havia fet no han vulgut tenir, ans ne han fet un altre, e aço som los cardenals qui eren, e la vertadera eleccio del altre, ço es del primer', N. Valois and Amédée Peguès, 'Les révélations de Constance de Rabastens et le Schisme d'Occident (1384–86)', Annales du Midi, 8 (1896) 241–78; at c.62, 272.

Fébus, the Count of Foix, to try and convince the king of France, Charles VII, to join the single true Roman pope, and to prefer crusade to schism.[5] Constance named the culprits; opportunists like the bishop of Autun who preferred a cardinal's hat from Clement VII to that offered first by Urban VI. Here is an impatient lay voice, speaking with the authority of simple devotion, and from that position criticising the arrangements of kingdoms and prelates. Her bishop, that of Toulouse, had Constance arrested, and forbade the copying and recounting of her visions. Constance's voice was of a type which was to occupy thinkers and leaders greatly in this period: was its charisma God-sent or a feminine dissimulation, and who was empowered to decide?

The major moral and political conundrum was the question of authority and truth. Prophets such as Constance forced this question urgently since their voices were heard now perhaps more willingly as traditional sources of pronouncement began to falter or were hopelessly contradictory in message.[6] A specific genre developed in these decades, one which nonetheless attempted to provide criteria for judgement: texts on discernment and proof, *probatio* or *discretio spirituum*.[7] Such works recommended investigations ranging from medical tests to the decoding of textual signs and examination of the effect of visions, to priests and prelates who were faced with the pastoral and judicial task of discernment. In late medieval Europe this ancient genre was rediscovered; almost every leading intellectual produced a contribution to it, and in parallel medics and lawyers too were seeking new forensic procedures for the distillation of judgement and diagnosis.

Sometimes such writing was prompted by a specific case presented for discernment. The Chancellor of the university of Paris, Jean Gerson (d.1429), was sent for assessment by Jean Morel, canon of St Denis of Reims, an account of the visions of the devil experienced by Ermine of Reims (d.1396). Ermine had migrated from the Vermandois to Reims with her aged husband in 1384 and was widowed in 1393. In her widowhood she became a local religious notable, following a series of visions of the devil with which she was visited. She came to receive pastoral care from the canons of Val des Ecoliers, and its sub-prior, Jean Le Graveur, recorded her visions. Gerson consulted members of

---

[5] Vauchez, 'Female prophets', 224–5.

[6] On prophecy and apocalyptic expectation around these decades see Roberto Rusconi, *L'attesa della fine: crisi della società, profezia ed apocalisse in Italia al tempo del Grande Scisma d'Occidente (1378–1417)*, Istituto storici Italiano per il medio evo – studi storici 115–18 (Rome, 1979), 17–35.

[7] Rosalynn Voaden, *God's Words, Women's Voices. The Discernment of Spirits in the Writing of Late-Medieval Women Visionaries*, York Studies in Medieval Theology, 3 (Woodbridge, 1999), 34–50.

the theology, canon law and medical faculties of the University of Paris, and the resulting tract of late 1401 (some claim 1408), *Iudicium de vita sanctae Erminae*, was as much an assessment of a Christian spirit as that of the conduct of a Christian body.[8] Although Ermine never pronounced on anything but her visions of the devil, never made explicit political comments as others had done, her words convey the sense of imminent danger from devils closing in. The power of the master of darkness may have seemed particularly active in 1396, since in that year a long-standing papal supporter, once a papal secretary, now a canon of Reims, Jean of Varennes, turned against the pope of Avignon, and preached his views publicly in the city. On Palm Sunday Jean de Varennes launched a series of sermons calling for the pope to convene a council and for both popes to resign. He expressed a frustration which others shared, including some theologians of Paris. When called to pronounce on the dossier gathered around Ermine's visions, Jean Gerson opined that she was a good person, but that her visions should remain of local, limited circulation.[9]

Gerson was prompted again to writing on discernment when Bridget of Sweden's (1303–73) canonisation of 1391 was questioned at the Council of Constance in 1415. Gerson supported her canonisation (which was confirmed by John XXIII), in his *De probatione spirituum*, even as he doubted some of her visions, as he did those of women more generally.[10] Gerson strove to provide useful mnemonics and formulae respecting discernment, as he had done in *De distinctione verarum revelationum a falsis* of 1400–1: a vision was after all a little like a coin, to be tested by the senses:

> humility gives weight
> discretion malleability
> patience durability
> truth shape
> and charity gives colour.[11]

Echoing the rhythm of confessional interrogation he suggested that visionary experience should be tested:

---

[8] *Entre Dieu et Satan. Les Visions d'Ermine de Reims (d.1396)*, ed. Claude Arnaud-Gillet, Millenio medievale 3 – 'la tradizione profetica' (Florence, 1997), 21–2.

[9] *Entre Dieu et Satan*, 18–20 on John of Varennes, 21–7 on Gerson's judgement.

[10] *Oeuvres complètes*, IX, ed. Palémon Glorieux (Paris, 1973), no. 448, 177–85; on women as religious arbiters see 'De examinatione doctrinarum', *Oeuvres complètes*, IX, 458–75 of 1423. In the year of his death, 1429, he penned a defence of the claims to prophecy made for Joan of Arc, *De puella aurelianensi* IX, 661–5.

[11] 'Humiltas dat pondus; discretio flexibilitatem; patientia durabilitatem; veritas configurationem; caritas dat colorem', Jean Gerson, *Oeuvres complètes*, III, ed. Palémon Glorieux (Paris, 1962), no. 90, 39.

Ask who, what, by what means, to whom, how and whence?[12]

Jean Gerson's *oeuvre* was thus constantly and committedly engaged in facilitating discernment of truth. His own hesitations and changes of direction attest the difficulty of discernment, particularly over the visions received by layfolk, lay women.[13] As we have seen, although he accepted Ermine to have been a genuinely pious person, he was circumspect about the value of her example, and all but abandoned her cause by the time of *De probatione spirituum* of 1415. Furthermore, he advised those, like him, engaged in discernment and advice, to avoid pandering to visionaries, and refrain from encouraging them in their sense of holiness. The approach must be sceptical:

> and in particular and above all he should consider whereby this person has been moved to reveal her secret ... and be especially cautious lest you applaud such a person, so that by praising her you may not suggest that she is someone saintly and worthy by reason of her revelations and miracles.[14]

The sacerdotal–sacramental structure which had encompassed the life and aspirations of Christians since the twelfth century demanded a great deal from the clergy and fostered high expectations of them. These had turned into a nemesis – for they had given rise to a related, reciprocal discourse on clerical insufficiency, which might be called anti-clerical.[15] The liturgical, pedagogic and pastoral roles which came to be linked with the celibate clergy were enormous – could anyone hope to fulfil them adequately? Could most priests meet the personal qualities which would validate their operation as sacramental performers? On such an ambitious cultural system it is worth citing the

[12] 'Tu quis, quid, quare, cui, qualiter, unde, require', Jean Gerson, *Oeuvres complètes*, IX, no. 448, 180.

[13] For an illuminating discussion of this area see Dyan Elliott, 'Authorizing a Life: the Collaboration of Dorothy of Montau and John Marienwerder', in *Gendered Voices: Medieval Saints and their Interpreters*, ed. Catherine M. Mooney (Philadelphia, Pa., 1999), 168–91.

[14] 'praesertim in principio consideret acriter quare movetur haec persona secretum suum pandere, super quo fiet ista consideratio? Cave praeterea ... ut non applaudas tali personae, non obinde laudes eam, non mireris quasi sanctam dignamque revelationibus atque miraculis', Jean Gerson, *Oeuvres complètes*, IX, no. 448, 181. On the constant preoccupation with authorisation of women's visions and voices by reformers of female houses see Hans-Jochen Schiewer, 'Auditionen und Visionen einer Begine. Die "Selige Schererin", Johannes Mulberg und der Basler Beginenstreit; mit einem Textabdruck', in *Die Vermittlung geistlicher Inhalte im deutscher Mittelalater*, ed. Timothy R. Jackson, Nigel F. Palmer and Almut Suerbaum (Tübingen, 1996), 289–317.

[15] For aspects of anti-clerical sentiment see Kaspar Elm, 'Antikelrikalismus im deutscher Mittelalter', *Anti-Clericalism in Late Medieval and Early Modern Europe*, ed. Peter A. Dykema and Heiko A. Oberman, Studies in Medieval and Reformation Thought, 51 (Leiden, 1993), esp. 4–5.

opinion expressed in 1961 by Mary Douglas, that 'it is possible for the structure to be self-defeating'.[16] Indeed, most influential teachers of the period were not to be found among secular clergy, not even among bishops, but among the cohorts of elite and professional preachers: trained, specialised and possessing a developed sense of their importance and mission. What of the parish priest? He baptised, he offered communion and consoled the dying.

The position adopted by engaged layfolk, such as the Brethren and the Sisters of the Common Life, betokened not so much a distaste for the clergy, but a dis-engagement from lay dependence solely on parochial life. A very great respect for the sacraments, led such folk to infrequent reception of communion, and to the understanding that among the Brethren only very few should be ordained. According to the founder Geert Groote (1340–84) and later Gerard Zerbolt (1367–98) the search for ordination seemed perilous to the soul, as it reflected the aspirant's ambition and pride. Another type of cure of souls could be provided outside priestly office: that of love, and guidance and encouragement – in short, an educational mission, such as was indeed developed by the Brethren.[17] The *vitae* of Brethren and Sisters, assiduously composed and circulated in these milieux, included examples of perfect lives lived in the modest estate of the un-ordained: a brother of Deventer resisted ordination despite the urging of his uncle, a Dean of St Severinus, and yet he was said to have been glorified for 'he had to die in such a humble clerical, or rather semi-lay state'.[18] Thus the Brethren and Sisters read and worked, copied manuscripts and above all taught, circulating the divine word outside the parochial sacramental framework. Their leaders tried to avoid institutional arrangements which might give rise to the only too visible infelicities of the ecclesiastical order: the houses of Sisters were fully under the management of urban authorities, somewhat like hospitals. In several houses of the Brethren administrative affairs were entrusted to urban magistrates; indeed, in some cases this was the provision made by lay patrons, to allow Brethren, according to Gerard Zerbolt, to be free of wrath and to lead a virtuous life.[19]

[16] Mary Douglas, *Purity and Danger: an Analysis of the Concepts of Pollution and Taboo* (London and New York, 1966), 141.

[17] G. H. Gerrits, *Inter Timorem et Spem: a Study of the Theological thought of Gerard Zerbolt of Zutphen (1367–1398)*, Studies in Medieval and Reformation Thought 37 (Leiden, 1986), 189.

[18] 'quod in tam humili statu clericali, quin pocius, semi-laicali debeat mori' in John Van Engen, 'Late Medieval Anticlericalism: the Case of the New Devout', in *Anti-Clericalism in Late Medieval and Early Modern Europe*, ed. Dykema and Oberman, 34.

[19] On other forms of anticlerical expression see Albrecht Klassen, 'Anticlericalism in Late Medieval German Use', in *Anti-Clericalism in Late Medieval and Early Modern Europe*, ed. Dykema and Oberman, 91–114.

The dangers of such a mixed life were manifest. A full attack on the Brethren and Sisters was mounted by the Dominican Matthew of Grabow (d. after 1421) towards the end of the Council of Constance. Matthew argued that religious striving should occur only within religious orders, and under the discipline of vows.[20] Jean Gerson leapt to the defence of these northern communities, and successfully rebutted the criticisms in 1418, and in a revised tract of 1422 *De perfectione cordis*: at the heart of his answer was the reminder, that neither Christ, nor Mary, nor the apostles, nor any members of the primitive church had taken vows.[21] Gerson abhorred the notion that only the religious could strive; simple people, like Ermine, could possess what he called 'an erudition of the heart', suffused by scripture.[22] Why even Mary, unlearned and simple, was able to burst into a chant of praise of perfect harmony when the miracle of Elizabeth's conception was revealed to her.[23] In the heat of debate against a Dominican friar Gerson defended the striving of the responsible and educated layfolk of the North; yet he was truly torn over the issue of lay participation and initiative, and was to remain so.[24]

In a variety of regions in innumerable ways the boundaries between sacerdotal provision and lay action were being tested and redrawn. The sacramental edifice so painstakingly built in the twelfth and spread in the thirteenth century, was challenged not only by those groups which questioned its operations – such as English Lollards with their alternative view of the sacraments and their unique style of preaching, or the Bohemian Hussites with their challenge to priestly authority.[25] Awareness and action were alive among lay communities and are

[20] Heiko A. Oberman, *Masters of the Reformation: the Emergence of a New Climate in Europe*, trans. Dennis Martin (Cambridge, 1981), 53.

[21] 'extra religiones factitias, potest aliquid cum voto simplici vel sine voto, christianam religionem in suis praeceptis et consiliis perfecte observare', 'Contra conclusiones Mathaei Graben O.P.', *Oeuvres Complètes*, x, ed. Palémon Glorieux (Paris, 1973), no. 499, 71–2; D. Catherine Brown, *Pastor and Laity in the Theology of Jean Gerson* (Cambridge, 1987), 46–8; Christoph Burger, *Aedificatio, Fructus, Utilitas: Johannes Gerson als Professor der Theologie und Kanzler der Universität Paris*, Beiträge zur historischen Theologie, 70 (Tübingen, 1986), 159, 182–3.

[22] Mark Stephen Burrows, *Jean Gerson and De Consolatione Theologiae (1418). The Consolation of a Biblical and Reforming Theology for a Disordered Age*, Beiträge zur historischen Theologie, 78 (Tübingen, 1991), 135–6.

[23] 'Collectorium super Magnificat', *Oeuvres complètes*, viii, ed. Palémon Glorieux (Paris, 1971), no. 418, 165.

[24] On his attitude to the devotional life developed in the Low Countries see Geert Warnar, 'Mystik in der Stadt. Jan van Ruusbroec (1293–1381) unde die niederländische Literatur des 14. Jahrhunderts', in *Deutsche Mystik in Abendlandische Zusammenhang. Neue erschlossene Texte, neue methodische Ansätze, neue theoretische Konzepte*, ed. Walter Haug and Wolfram Schneider-Lastin (Tübingen, 2000), 685–6.

[25] František Šmahel, 'The Hussite Critique of the Clergy's Civil dominion', in *Anti-Clericalism in Late Medieval and Early Modern Europe*, ed. Dykema and Oberman, 83–90.

evident from a variety of sources. Not least from the accounts of the
visitations such as those of the archdeacon of Josas in the Ile-de-
France between 1458 and 1470.[26] Here archdeacon and churchwardens
habitually confronted lack and loss – of vessels, of persons, of fabric, of
Latin, of midwives for quick baptism *in extremis*. These documents,
crafted by cleric and laypeople, although formulaic, express a tone of
determined engagement with the task of making the pale local parish
resemble somewhat more that colourful sacramental–sacerdotal order
which was preached, taught and desired.

More scathing, more eloquent, challenges to the clergy were voiced
in other quarters. A reforming Dominican such as Matthias of Janov
in the 1380s could call for the replacement of lukewarm, or worse,
clergy with the religious, in his advice to Archbishop of Prague, John
of Jenstein (1384–1400):

> And remember meanwhile, just how many devout, chaste, learned
> and humble men, wise and suited to all manner of good work to the
> edification of Christ's body and the people of the church, are shut
> away in houses and cloisters of the Carthusians, what young and old
> men illustrious and well bred are in convents of the order of St
> Benedict, how many remained enmured in houses and cells of the
> Cistercians, how many are hidden in the dwellings of regular friars
> … That is why the holy people of the church, the flock of Christ's
> sheep, remains deserted and impoverished of spiritual men useful to
> them.
>
> Bring forth all these men who are hiding in inner places and
> search them out with the utmost diligence from all parts of the
> world.[27]

In some parts – primarily the great Italian urban communes and the
imperial great cities which possessed a long history of autonomous
action in politics, social planning, and economic direction – initiatives
were perhaps not so dramatic as that just cited, but dramatic they
were. The cities which two hundred years earlier had bred and

---

[26] *Visites archidiaconales de Josas*, ed. J. M. Alliott (Paris, 1902).

[27] 'Et recordare interim, quot et quanti viri devoti, casti, docti et humiles, prudentes
ydoneique ad omne bonum opus in edificacionem corporis Christi plebiumque ecclesie
sunt reclusi in domibus et in claustris fratrum Carthusiensium, quam illustres et bene
indolis iuvenes et senes sunt in conventibus ordinis Sancti Benedicti, quot et quanti
silent inclusi in domibus et cellis fratrum Cisterciensium, quot in penetralibus fratrum
Regularium manent absconditi. Propter quod wulgus sanctum ecclesie et greges ovium
Christi manent desolati a viris spiritualibus utilibus sibi et depauperati.

Produc autem istos omnes viros latitantes sic in penetralibus et conquire ipsos foras
cum summa diligencia ex omnibus partibus mundi', Ruben E. Weltsch, *Archbishop John
of Jenstein (1348–1400): Papalism, Humanism and Reform in Pre-Hussite Prague* (The Hague,
1968), 167, n. 42.

welcomed the new preaching orders were now engaging the super-preacher, whose operations were intimately related to the city's own preoccupation with order. In Siena the Observant Franciscan Bernardino's (1380–1444) moral recommendations were incorporated into the city's law. Such law was to be enforced by an appointed official, the *Captianeo ed Esecutore di Giustizia*, in promotion of good and virtuous living.[28] Bernardino's preaching touched on issues salient to social, gender and political order: strictures against extravagant trousseaus and wedding parties, for example, which linked such display and expense with privation of the poor.[29]

Here issues do not follow a distinction between secular and religious concerns – those of charismatic preachers never do – and so the communes yielded to fiery preachers, whom they appointed. Bernardino's preaching touched on the intimacies of the marriage bed, when addressing the marriage debt, just as it did with relations between artisans and merchants and the restitution of usurious profits. But he was watched vigilantly for his enthusiasm could also be seen as questionable novelty. He was persecuted in Bologna in 1424 for his promotion of the devotion to the Name of Jesus, in an attack led by the Dominican inquisitor which ultimately led to an investigation in Martin V's Rome in 1427. Was Bernardino pure or dangerous? His fortune also demonstrates the unclarity of boundaries, and contention over the appropriateness of forms of worship. Bernardino promoted a cultic emblem which he hoped might offer unity and balm: a disk with the monogramme IHS emblazoned on it, which was to form a focus for city-wide devotional action, beyond faction and party and politics.[30] But opponents saw the emblem as idolatrous, eccentric, and possibly heretical – it too earned him a trial in Rome. Devotional styles were so diverse as to undermine emergence of an authoritative manner in the operation of ritual and cult.[31]

Even if charismatic preachers sometimes worried the city councils that had appointed them, in large parts of Europe they set the tone. In a Lent sermon which considered preaching on feast days Bernardino determined that preaching was no less, but equally important as attendance at mass:

the people, and especially the uneducated, are no less required to

[28] Peter Francis Howard, *Preaching and Theology in the Florence of Archbishop Antoninus, 1427–1459*, Quaderni di 'Rinascimento' 28 (Florence, 1995), 88–9.
[29] Bernadette Paton, *Preaching Friars and the Civic Ethos: Siena, 1380–1480*, Westfield Publications in Medieval Studies, 7 (1992), 224–8.
[30] For the image see Iris Origo, *The World of San Bernardino* (1963), figure xvi (facing p. 17).
[31] Paton, *Preaching Friars*, 275–7.

hear the divine word than to hear the mass; and especially for three reasons: first, is for necessity, second, for utility; and third, for benefit.[32]

Archbishop Antoninus of Florence (1389–1459), an Observant (reformed) Dominican, expressed a more extreme understanding with steely resolve, as he compared sacrament to sermon:

for greater fruit follows from the preached word of God, than from the Body of Christ consumed. Because no one is justified by the sacrament if it is received in an uncontrite and unworthy state, rather this increases sin. Whereas even the most obstinate men, are converted by listening to preaching. Were not the Gentiles converted to the faith by it? And therefore, because of the greater benefit which follows, the work of preaching is privileged above all divine [things].[33]

How very different from the position of the Brethren and Sisters of Common Life in the North; or of St Francis two hundred years earlier.

Here we clearly witness 'institutions' ceding to charisma – in a mirror image of the process which Max Weber had famously observed and analysed at the inception of religions. Yet that was not the solution favoured by all; another model for the enhancement of purity and the avoidance of the danger of moral collapse was on offer in other quarters. Not from the sophisticated council chambers of Italian cities, but from those most mobilised and solemn halls of the university of Paris, from Jean Gerson, as worldly wise as any Florentine silk merchant. While Chancellor of the University, he was also priest to the parish of St Jean-en-Grève on the right bank of the Seine. Gerson's vision of revival and purification was altogether different from the charismatic model. Outside clerical order there could exist no order, no promise of salvation, no dredging of humans out of the pits of sin and the confusion of doubt. Order was the condition of salvation and it required that priests obey theologians, that layfolk obey priests and that women

[32] Bernardino of Siena, *Opera omnia*, III, ed. College of St Bonaventure (Quaracchi, 1956), sermon 10, a.3, c.2, 186–9. On subsequent use of Bernardino's argument see E. Jane Dempsey Douglass, *Justification in Late Medieval Theology: A Study of John Geiler of Keysersberg*, Studies in Medieval and Reformation Thought (Leiden, 1966), 88–90.
[33] 'Quinimmo major fructus sequiter ex verbo Dei praedicato, quam Corpore Christi sumto. Nam per sacramentum nullus justificatur, si accedit indigne et incontritus; sed augetur iniquitas sua. Sed obstinatissimi homines audiendo praedicationem convertuntur. Unde enim Gentiles converti sunt ad fidem, nisi ex praedicatione? Et propterea propter magnum fructus, qui sequitur, est opus praedicationis super omnia divina privilegiatum', in Howard, *Preaching and Theology*, 99. A similar idea is expressed in the earlier, English text *Dives et Pauper* of c.1410, see *Dives et Pauper. A Facsimile Reproduction of the Pynson Edition of 1493*, intro. Francis J. Sheeran (Delmar, NY, 1973), 261.

obey men.[34] Anything but order would result in dissipation:

> This was the old error of the Waldensians and the Poor of Lyon, which Wyclif and his followers had sought to renew, and who were rightly damned for it. Why is that? Lest the hierarchical order of the ecclesiastical power remain unstable, vague and uncertain, so that no one knows for sure whether it is worthy of love or hate.[35]

Gerson was as aware as any parishioner just how frail the system was, and thus how open to ridicule or apathy. Rather than pit against the parish priest the fiery oratory of full-time preachers, rather than encourage lay people to search out ways for themselves, he set out to empower that clergy, to remind it of its tasks and capacities as prime ritual actors, teachers, consolers and preachers too. He took the famous canon 21 of the Fourth Lateran Council (1215), *Omnis utriusque sexus*, to be an authoritative recognition of the centrality and necessity of the parish priest: for confession, penance, and communion.[36]

Concurrently, he believed that if there was to be theology in the University of Paris, this should be a gospel-based mystical theology, 'a clear and savory understanding of those things which are believed in the Gospel', as put in his proposal for the reform of the University of 1402 *Contra curiositatem studentium*.[37] He was thus also strongly opposed to the bull of Alexander V *Regnans in excelsis* published in 1409; in a sermon of 1410 he claimed that the pope had erred in allowing the friars autonomy from ecclesiastical scrutiny in the University of Paris, despite the fact that he recognised the contribution of friar-preachers, and urged Dominicans back to Paris.[38] For Gerson the lowliest curate was superior, in the church's constitution, to any friar. His own Sundays sometimes saw him visiting four churches, preaching in each. He was a leading conciliarist, who believed that the fundamental institution of the church could never change. And in the service of the fundamental

[34] David Luscombe, 'Jean Gerson and Hierarchy', in *Church and Chronicle in the Middle Ages. Essays presented to John Taylor*, ed. Ian Wood and G.A. Loud (London and Rio Grande, 1991), 199–200.

[35] 'hic enim fuit error vetus Waldensium et pauperum Lugduno, qui per Wicleff et sequaces suos renovari quaesitus est, set juste damnatus. Cur ita? Ne hierarchicus ordo potestatis ecclesiasticae maneat instabilis, vagus et incertus cum nemo sciat an amore vel odio dignus sit', Jean Gerson, *Oeuvres complètes*, VI, ed. Palémon Glorieux (Paris, 1965), no. 282, 212.

[36] Louis B. Pascoe, *Jean Gerson: Perceptions of Church Reform*, Studies in Medieval and Reformation Thought, 7 (Leiden, 1973), 153–5.

[37] Jean Gerson, *Oeuvres complètes*, III, no. 9, 249; Monika Asztalos, 'The Faculty of Theology', in *A History of the University in Europe*, I, ed. Hilde De Ridder-Symoens (Cambridge, 1996), 436–7; Steven E. Ozment, 'The University of the Church: Patterns of Reform in Jean Gerson', *Medievalia et humanistica*, new series, I (1970), 112–14; James L. Connolly, *Jean Gerson: Reformer and Mystic* (Leuven, 1927), 82–3.

[38] Connolly, *Jean Gerson*, 108–9.

sacerdotal nature of the church as a saving institution mirroring Christ's own body – even a pope could be removed, so as not to undermine the many sacerdotal bees hard at work in their parishes.

Jean Gerson engaged with the life of the clergy with an intimacy and camaraderie that eleventh and twelfth century masters had never displayed. His attentions bespoke an ethnographic association with the sacerdotal realm. And inasmuch as there is no pastor without his sheep, no priest without parishioners, the laity formed part of any guiding pastoral thrust.[39] Clergy and laity are seen as struggling together – or failing together. In his *De pollutione nocturna et preparatione ad missam* he encouraged priests to believe that God would help them in making the sacrament work, even if they were ill-prepared, and that over-scrupulosity could detract rather than enhance their effect.[40] The treatise (attributed to him) on masturbation[41] and confession, his consideration of chastity, his thoughtful reflections on the nature of dreams and fantasy are practice bound, and treated men and women, lay and priest as engaged in a joint effort towards salvation, equally hampered by weakness and a tendency to sin.

Gerson had answers to every dilemma of clerical work, and insider knowledge too: if hearing confession might inflame passion, then discretion, knowledge of one's body, attempts at self-control were appropriate counter-measures. And when these failed, if unclean thoughts did fill the priest's mind or sexual arousal was felt while listening to the unburdening of another's confession, then this was experienced in the course of delivering a greater good. If the parishioner's desire or thoughts about his or her priest were of great intensity, then even the administrative framework of the church should yield, in allowing the parishioner to confess elsewhere.[42] The parish was the frontier, and every pastoral day a struggle, but upon pastoral care depended the greater good of all.

The priesthood and laity were not alone in their joint and mutual efforts; symbols and ceremonies, like Bernardino's burning emblem, could further heighten experience and reward. Exactly a century before he became its incumbent Gerson's own parish – St Jean en Grève[43] – boasted a miracle following a host desecration accusation against a Jew.

---

[39] Pascoe, *Jean Gerson*, 153.

[40] *Oeuvres complètes*, IX, no. 425, 35–50. On scrupulosity see Sven Grosse, *Heilsungewissheit und Scrupulositas im späten Mittelalter. Studien zu Johannes Gerson und Gattungen der Frömmigkeitstheologie seiner Zeit*, Beiträge zur historischen Theologie, 85 (Tübingen, 1994). See Dyan Elliott, *Fallen Bodies: Pollution, Sexuality and Demonology in the Middle Ages* (Philadelphia, Pa., 1999), 26–9.

[41] I am grateful to Mr Yaron Toren for sharing with me his erudition and as yet unpublished translation of this text.

[42] Elliott, *Fallen Bodies*, 25.

[43] Connolly, *Jean Gerson*, 129–30.

A miracle chapel was built on the site of the Jew's house to keep the miracle host; and Gerson's own parish church was home to the little knife, 'le petit canivet' which the Jew was alleged to have used. A new liturgy was created for the feast, and the parish was woven into the public fabric of late medieval Paris for grand processional events and royal entries.[44]

We do not, alas, know Gerson's attitude to this cult, but we do know that he favoured and valued carefully scrutinised devotion to saints, as is clear from his letter to his sisters, advising them on their weekly devotion.[45] He was after all the great promoter of St Joseph in his influential *Considérations sur saint Joseph* of 1413 and 1414.[45] Joseph was a figure hitherto little revered in the west. Like the decent priest, here was the decent husband and father, provider and protector, of simple but adequate faith. Joseph was an ordinary father alongside an ordinary mother, in a marriage which was real although it was pure, since it was grounded on consent and obedience. Gerson's Joseph, who gained a feast day in 1487, was made out of the legacy of vernacular drama and iconography which rendered Joseph a simple, natural man, who doubted his wife's unexpected conception, and who required a strengthening of faith by way of an angelic intervention.[47] But Gerson turned away from the traditional aspects of Joseph's character which were made to seem ludicrous: his portrayal as small and swarthy, as a Jew, on the margin of important biblical events.[48]

Sixteenth-century reformers delighted in mocking the cult of Joseph's stockings – the garment which Margery Kempe travelled to see in Germany – in which Joseph was said to have swaddled the newborn Christ.[49] Joseph's new cult reformed the person of Joseph to be of noble birth, of gracious conversation, and of a glorifying end, for an understanding of marriage and order came to hinge upon him. Gerson's understanding is here made apparent: Mary and Joseph's marriage

[44] Miri Rubin, *Gentile Tales: the Narrative Assault on Late Medieval Jews* (New Haven and London, 1999), 40–5.

[45] 'Gerson à ses soeurs', Jean Gerson, *Oeuvres complètes* II, ed. Palémon Glorieux (Paris, 1960), 14–17; Patrick B. McGuire, 'Late Medieval Care and Control of Women: Jean Gerson and His Sisters', *Revue d'histoire ecclésiastique*, 92 (1997), 5–37.

[46] 'Considérations sur St Joseph', Jean Gerson, *Oeuvres complètes* VII, ed. Palémon Glorieux (Paris, 1966), no. 300, 63–94, and in 1414, 'Autres considérations sur St Joseph', no. 301, 94–9. His example opened the way for other writers, like Pierre d'Ailly (1350–1420), Bernardino of Siena.

[47] V.A. Kolve, *The Play Called Corpus Christi* (1966), 247–52.

[48] Ruth Mellinkoff, *Outcasts*, I (Berkeley, Ca., 1993), 41, 77–82, 98–9, 222–7 and related images in volume II; on Joseph's doubt see Klaus Schreiner, *Maria: Jungfrau, Mutter, Herrscherin* (Munich, 1994), 50–4.

[49] Gail McMurray Gibson, *The Theater of Devotion: East Anglian Drama and Society in the Late Middle Ages* (Chicago, 1989), 57–9.

demonstrated a clear gendered division of power and function, of a type also expressed in Gerson's and Bernardino's sermons and tracts on marriage and on the marital debt.[50] Gerson thought of their marriage as pure – 'Joseph en son esprit et es vertus de son ame ne bruissoit point par l'ardeur de vil concupiscence' – but also as companionate: how fitting for Mary to have a mate with whom to share her own great secret, and that of her kinswoman Elizabeth's pregnancy.[51] Gerson paints for his readers and hearers a kitchen-sink scene, an:

> occasion de dire a Joseph tout son secret … comme pour reveler le concevement de sainte Elizabeth sterile que Joseph en eust joye.

Joseph was a good father to Jesus: he taught him to walk and marvelled at his progress and growth. Gerson saw Joseph as carefully chosen to enjoy this special relationship:

> Joseph avec ce, estoit esleu de Dieu a converser continuelment en la compagnie du tres bel et tres avenant et delicieux enfant Jhesus, a le porter, a le nourrir, a le baisier par licence et amitié paternelle.[52]

In an ordered Christian universe clearly units of family life respected the natural order of gender, of paternal authority and provision and of maternal nurture; such was the image which Mary and Joseph's recast family nest was to offer.

It was that desire to help and re-establish the image and practice of order – so fundamentally based on gender difference – which led Gerson to participation in the rather precious, and yet extremely revealing and intellectually challenging exchange of letters and opinions known as the *Querelle de la Rose*. This exchange was prompted by Christine de Pisan's *Epître au dieu d'amours* of May 1399, a poem in which a series of Ladies complained against the detractions and abuses heaped upon women by Ovid and Jean de Meung, the thirteenth-

---

[50] On Mary's subordination to Joseph see Brown, *Pastor and Laity*, 216–17.

[51] 'Autres considérations sur St Joseph', 95; Brown, *Pastor and Laity*, 233–5; Pamela Sheingorn, 'Appropriating the Holy Kinship: Gender and Family History', in *Interpreting Cultural Symbols: Saint Anne in Late Medieval Society*, ed. Kathleen Ashley and Pamela Sheingorn (Athens, Ga., 1990), 184–5.

[52] 'Considerations sur St Joseph', 88, 68. An earlier vernacular version of Mary's visit to Elizabeth, which mentions Joseph's support to Mary appears in Gerson's contribution to *La Vie de Nostre Benoit Sauveur Ihesucrist et la Saincte Vie de Nostre Dame*, ed. Millard Meiss and Elizabeth H. Bateson (New York, 1977), 11 ('pour la consoler et secourir, avecques elle se partit de son hostel son mary, Joseph'). Nurture of the young was particularly important to Gerson, see Brian Patrick McGuire, 'Education, Confession and Pious Fraud: Jean Gerson and a Late Medieval Change', *American Benedictine Review*, 47 (1996), 310–38. I am grateful to Yaron Toren for bringing this article to my attention.

century continuator of the early thirteenth-century poem.[53] The *Querelle* was launched in the following year with a treatise by Jean de Montreuil, Provost of Lille, and erstwhile secretary to the Dukes of Berry, Burgundy and Orleans. His treatise is now lost but Christine responded to it in mid-1401. She described Jean de Montreuil's position to be the defence of the poet, and of his 'excessive imputations and most untruthful criticisms and degradations of women as exceedingly wicked creatures'.[54] Gerson's contribution was the *Traité* also known as the *Vision* of 18 May 1402[55] – his sole contribution to the *querelle*, although he mentioned the *Roman de la Rose* and its moral implications in the notes for his sermon cycle, *Poenitemini* of 1402/3.[56] What was at stake here? How did the theologian come to participate in a debate about a poem about love and seduction, the epitome of vernacular verse which by this time was known in most parts of Europe?

Gerson's interest was kindled by the moral implications of the *Querelle*. The gendered double standard which the *Roman de la Rose* seemed to promote was insidious, a danger to the very purity of Christian household morality:

> Its extreme error is occasion for sin, in blasphemies, in poisonous doctrines, in the destruction and desolation of poor Christian souls ... in harm to charity ... in the dissipation of faithfulness of both married and single.[57]

The lively descriptions, the poem's playful mingling of the divine and lofty with the lewd and earthy, was an attarction likened by Gerson to vice.[58] The poem's licence was a counterblast to the careful physical structures of control and guidance which Gerson had been structuring in pastoral writings for priests and laity alike.[59]

The pastoral project of moral order in households based on gendered hierarchy was undermined by the poem's profligate privileging of the

---

[53] *Poems of Cupid, God of Love*, ed. Thelma M. Fenster and Mary Carpenter Erler (Leiden, 1990), on the debate 7–9, on the poem 10–15; Jillian M.L. Hill, *The Medieval Debate on Jean de Meung's Roman de la Rose*, Studies in Medieval Literature, 4 (Lewisten, NY, 1991).

[54] *La Querelle de la Rose: Letters and Documents*, ed. Joseph L. Baird and John R. Kane, New Studies in the Romance Languages and Literatures, 199 (Chapel Hill, NC, 1978), 46–56.

[55] *La Querelle*, 70–91; Hill, *The Medieval Debate*, 105–41.

[56] *La Querelle*, 162–4. For the sermon, Jean Gerson, *Oeuvres complètes*, VII*, ed. Palémon Glorieux (Paris, 1968), no. 371, 833–41.

[57] *La Querelle*, 90.

[58] Sylvia Huot, *The Romance of the Rose and its Medieval Readers: Interpretation, Reception, Manuscript Transmission* (Cambridge, 1993), 22–3.

[59] Brian Patrick McGuire, 'Sexual Control and Spiritual Growth in the Late Middle Ages', in *Tradition and Ecstasy: the Agony of the Fourteenth Century*, ed. Nancy Van Deusen, Claremont Institute of Mediaeval Music – Musicological Studies, 62/3 (Ottawa, 1997), 126–8.

desires of one member of the pair over the other's, following the manner of sexually and amatory comportment which the poem taught men – or did it teach – to develop and perfect. Genius's defence of sexual expression as obedience to nature, was rebuffed by Jean Gerson as mere slavery to the body, an idea which he was to develop further in his writings on the maintenance of the celibate life. Gerson's intervention was a cry for order, a plea for correction, and his disgust made him an ally of Christine. Inasmuch as Christine appreciated that words could harm and representation mattered in constructing people's lives – so did Gerson. It is interesting to note that Gerson's attack was as much on the text as on the illuminations which sometimes accompanied it.

Christine de Pisan's view of a reformed world was one in which intellectuals, writers – secular like herself and clerical like Gerson – operated with responsibility, towards moral *utilitas*, in a Christian universe.[60] Christine strove in her own *oeuvre* towards such rethinking of kingship and war, family and conjugal life. Like her, other thinkers and actors preoccupied with renewal and purification took a holistic view of the social body; any moral transformation had to touch on all areas of life. Mirroring the preoccupation with the family was the discussion of work, and a reform of business ethics was imagined by figures such as Pierre d'Ailly in Paris, and Henry of Langenstein (1325–97) in Vienna, in their writings on usury. Discussions of usury were occasions for theorising on work, profit, investment, trust, and the resulting ideas were spread through campaigns of preaching by Observant Franciscan preachers such as Bernardino of Siena, Giovanni of Capistrano (1386–1456), or by reform minded prelates such as John of Jenstein (1348–1400), and later the Dominican Observant Archbishop Antoninus of Florence. The discourse on usury touched on the disposition of work and wealth and power. It also became a prominent site for the discussion of Jewish practice, both financial and confessional. In his *Tractatus de contractibus* of 1391 Henry of Langenstein claimed that usury was not work, and usurers were idle, like the Jews who thus enjoyed leisure in which to develop further rebuttals of Christian faith.[61] Within the big imperial cities, debates about usury habitually slipped into discussion of policies towards Jews, a slippage which could be instantiated by groups as diverse as the financiers and guild masters of Nuremberg, and the scholars of the University of Prague. Furthermore,

[60] Renate Blumenfeld-Kosinski, 'Enemies Within/Enemies Without: Threats to the Body Politic in Christine de Pizan', *Medievalia et Humanstica*, new series, 26 (1999), 1–15; Rosalind Brown-Grant, *Christine de Pisan and the Moral Defence of Women* (Cambridge, 2000), 31–2.
[61] Michael H. Shank, *'Unless You Believe, You Shall Not Understand': Logic, University and Society in Late Medieval Vienna* (Princeton, NJ, 1988), 149, 157.

in the fifteenth century and under the influence of a particular type of spin provided by popular (Observant) preachers, the discourse on usury was metamorphosed into a justification for the excision of Jews from the city or region. In Italy this took by the 1460s the form of *monti di pietà* in a wave of foundations of these new charitable banks, which were underwritten by leading merchants and presented as acts of charity, intimately linked to the hope for purification which would follow. Since the *monti di pietà* provided small subsistance loans which were meant to remove the financial need for the presence of Jews, their creation was the precondition for ethical renewal amongst financiers, and expulsion of Jews from tens of cities in Tuscany, Emilia and the Marche.[62]

In the Empire the tone was set by agents such as archbishop John of Jenstein, whose synodal efforts throughout the 1380s condemned the practice of usury, and who had the message preached regularly in Prague's churches. He linked his opposition to king Wenzel to usury and to the prosperity of Jews, suggesting that the well-being of Jews in Prague under Wenzel through the practice of usury, could augur the rule of anti-Christ, as in a Christmas sermon delivered at his Roudnice castle:

> New ills emerge these days, whose advent had been foretold, and is now being fulfilled, and no small sign of it is the prosperity of the Jews, who everywhere multiply and congregate enjoying such immunity, that not surprisingly God's ire is to be feared, lest he permit that anti-Christ come. Because you see well that the clergy and Christians are supplanted in right and liberties and subjected to many injuries, while the synagogue, rather than Christ's church, profits, and among princes above all, a Jew can do more than a nobleman or a prelate.[63]

Here the contest was between Jews and clergy; and by establishing this opposition others could be implied; that the clergy was charitable where the Jews were oppressive, that the clergy were just where the Jews were exploitative usurers. Occasion for such extension was provided by the enactment of exclusionary and inculpating narratives, such as the host

[62] Vittorino Meneghin, *I monti di pietà in Italia dal 1462 ad 1562*, Studi e testi francescani nuova seria, 7 (Venice, 1986).

[63] 'malis cottidie novis emergentibus, que de eius dicta sunt adventu, verificantur, quod inter cetera est non modicum indicium prosperitas Judeorum, qui ubique multiplicantur et congregantur tantaque immunitate foventur, quod nimirum ira domini formidanda sit, ne permittat, ut Antichristus veniat. Nam bene videtis clerum et Christifideles cottidie in suis iuribus et libertatibus supplantari et subici multasque iniurias perpeti et magis synagogam quam Christi proficere ecclesiam et inter principes plus unum posse Judeum quam procerem vel prelatum', Weltsch, *Archbishop John of Jenstein*, 62 n. 89.

desecration accusation or the ritual murder libel. All this became evident in the case of Prague in 1389.

The capital city was just too small for the soaring claims of a reforming archbishop, a king intent on securing credit, a burgeoning scholarly milieu, and a world of burgesses within which resided a prosperous Jewish community. The host desecration accusation which unfolded in 1389 during the King's absence, led to the destruction of the Jewish community, of some 3000 souls. The city council worried about the usurious fats of the Jewish bodies and had them burnt before they contaminated the capital's air. Here the poor played a role too, as the city council hired them – in a self-regarding act of job creation – for the task of burning the Jewish dead. The city was thus purged of the Jews, and cleansed of their usurious odour. The event was remembered in several texts as a popular act of cleansing, of purgation, of redrawing of the boundaries between purity and dangerous usury, posed by Jews and, by association, by the king, their protector.[64]

But that is not all, for the impure habitually brings to mind the purest and most limpid. The cleansing of Prague in 1389 was remembered as an act poignant in its Marian overtones, an act of Marian purification, in those texts which commemorated it, such as the tract on the *Magnificat* by John Lange of Wetzlar.[65] For were not the Jews the inveterate enemies of the Virgin? A particularly dense and fruitful association between the Virgin and the Jews emerged at the heart of Marian devotion, as Jews were habitual protagonists in the miracle tales codified and collected in the twelfth, and then spread into the vernaculars in the thirteenth century. These tales recounted and imaged the saving mercy and inspiring forgiveness of the Virgin; at their end the conversion of the Jew and harmony were achieved.[66]

The Virgin played an emphatic affective role in the spiritualities of monks and of reformed priests – as a feminine presence in a life imagined to be without female intimacy – but she increasingly became something more, protector of orthodoxy, scourge of heretics, tool for the enlightening of those who err, a teacher without words.[67] She played a prominent role in the subjectivity of those seeking purity and renewal in late medieval centuries and was central to their task: the Virgin

[64] Rubin, *Gentile Tales*, 135–6; Frantisek Graus, *Struktur und Geschichte. Drei Volksaufstände im mittelalterlichen Prag* (Singmaringen, 1971), 50–60.

[65] E. S. Bauer, *Frömmigkeit, Gelehrsamkeit und Zeitkritik an der Schwelle der grossen Konzilien. Johannes von Wetzlar und sein Dialogus super Magnificat* (Mainz, 1981); see also Schreiner, *Maria*, 438–40.

[66] Rubin, *Gentile Tales*, 7–28.

[67] On Marian sensibility and attitudes and actions towards Jews see Hedwig Röckelein, 'Marie, l'Egilse et la synagogue. Culte de la Vièrge et lutte contre les Juifs en Allemagne à la fin du moyen-âge', in *Marie. Le Culte de la Vièrge dans la Société médiévale*, ed. D. Iogna-Prat, E. Palazzo, D. Russo (Paris, 1996), 513–31.

provided coherence and inclusion where fragmentation and unmaking were the rule.[68] When Christ's own body and the terms on which it was encountered formed the matter of disagreement in universities and in churches – even being transformed in some regions – Mary's purity was still a possible balm: in its modest demands, in its desire simply to be.[69] For scholars the Virgin came to be associated with the possible harmonisation of disparate and over-qualified knowledge, it offered them a place of safety.

Just as scholarly exegesis threatened to lose its foundation in scripture, as theological novelties lost their grounding in doctrine, visceral devotion and the grounding which it could offer, was a need that writers like Gerson acknowledged. A mystical, affective theology was sought by him, for which several twelfth-century writers provided inspiration.[70] In a letter offered within an *ars dictaminis* of *c*.1400 written by Anselm of Frankenstein, the author begs the Virgin to bless his course of study, and her letter in response followed with ethical guidance and encouragement.[71] In devotional poems the twelve stars of Mary's crown were now likened to the seven liberal arts to which were added theology, medicine, metaphysics, physiology and natural physics. Similarly, in a sermon delivered in Lent 1425 Bernardino saw the Virgin as radiant in knowledge: corporal, rational, spiritual and divine knowledge. She even knew perfectly the movement of the planets:

> Similarly, all the courses of the moon, of Mercury, of Venus, of the sun, of Mars, of Jupiter, of Saturn. In the star-studded sky there is not a single planet whose course she does not know.[72]

But above all Mary was a source of 'compassion to every creature worthy of salvation', and of tranquility 'How can one not believe in Mary, she who has never been surpassed by any creature more benign,

[68] See for example the highly scriptural fifteenth-century Marian Christmas carol from the milieu of *Devotio moderna* in 'A Marian Christmas carol', edited by Andries Welkenhuysen in *Serta devota in memoriam Guillelmi Lourdaux*, i, ed. W. Verbeke (Louvain, 1992), 432–8.

[69] Anne Winston-Allen, *Stories of the Rose. The Making of the Rosary in the Middle Ages* (University Park, Pa., 1997).

[70] Giles Constable, 'Twelfth-century Spirituality and the Late Middle Ages', in *Medieval and Renaissance Studies. Processdings of the Southeastern Institute of Medieval and renaisance Studies summer 1969*, ed. O.B. Hardison Jr (Chapel Hill, NC, 1971), 27–60.

[71] Michael Stolz, 'Maria und die Artes Liberales. Aspekte einer mittelalterlichen Zuordnung', in *Maria in der Welt. Marienverehrung im Kontext der Sozialgeschichte 10. zu 18. Jahrhunderts*, ed. Claudia Opitz, Hedwig Röckelein, Gabriela Signori, Guy P. Marchal and Clio Lucernensis (Zürich, 1993), 95–120.

[72] 'Simile tutti e corsi de la Luna, di Mercurio, di Venus, del Sole, di Marte, di Giove, di Saturno. Del cielo stellato non è niuna stella che Maria non sapesse e non conoscesse l'uffizio suo', Bernardino of Siena, *Prediche volgari*, i, ed. Ciro Cannarozzi (Florence, 1958), no. 11, 163.

mild, peaceful?'[73] It is thus not surprising to find that so many of the formative thinkers and authors already mentioned found devotion to the Virgin, contemplation of the Virgin and the offering of the Virgin in pastoral contexts as a necessary part of their programmes. The mother of knowledge and consoler of the studious also became the patron saint of several new universities of the later fourteenth century, where so much discussion on the purification of Europe took place. The seal of the university of Prague carried the image of the Virgin as in *sedes sapientiae* with the Christ Child on her knee and surrounded by the caption *Alma mater pragensis*.[74]

For those who sought to purify the Christian body Mary was purity itself, a fitting example and catalyst. New feasts and celebrations of her life proliferated: from the debates over immaculate conception, to the histories of her kin, prominently that of her mother Anne and of her siblings. Embracing her comforted priests, offered a symbolic balm to communities in crisis; she recast the moral universe, and could intercept the woes of current politics. John of Jenstein, experienced on 15 October 1378 a vision which he described in a letter to pope Urban VI as showing Christ prodding a black and monstrous Satan, dressed in the episcopal headband (*infula*) and armed with weapons, to pass the papal keys to the anti-pope, surrounded by anti-cardinals, with only the Virgin in the background remote, and unsullied.[75] To end the schism Christ clearly had to be persuaded to stop that prodding of satan, and by whom if not by his mother, the protector of Christian sinners? Only from her could inspiration towards healing and renewal arise. John of Jenstein thus strove for the establishment of a new feast, that of the Visitation, to emphasise the joy felt at the impending incarnation which she was destined to facilitate.[76] He instituted the feast in his own province of Prague, wrote its office, had a stained glass window established in his own castle-chapel, and appealed to the pope for approval. Following the scrutiny of theologians and canonists the feast was accepted, and when John heard the news he exploded with joy:

> Because in the institution of this feast truthfully traps are placed between the serpent and the woman ... she will intercede with the son, so that peace be in her virtue, so that all will recognise the one

---

[73] 'compassione a ogni creatura degna di salute'; 'Come non è da crèdare di Maria, che mai non fu la più benigna, agevole, pacifica creatura di lei?', Bernardino of Siena, *Prediche volgari*, 1, 164, 165. On the use of Mary by the *Bianchi* see Bornstein, *The Bianchi of 1399*, 132–45.

[74] Stolz, 'Maria und die Artes Liberales', 105–6.

[75] Weltsch, *Archbishop John of Jenstein*, 83–4.

[76] On the new feast of the Visitation see Richard W. Pfaff, *New Liturgical Feasts in Late Medieval England* (Oxford, 1970), 40–61, esp. 41–7.

true high pontiff our lord pope Urban VI, so that in God's church we be one as he is one with the father and the holy spirit.[77]

Yet his attempts ultimately failed, since his vision was not shared by his Chapter in Prague. Its canons saw the proliferation of devotional dates as absurd, and demeaning. Again, the clash of devotional styles and political aims, resulted in opposition to the feast in the very province of its birth. This refusal brings to mind some of Luther's later objections to new feasts related to Mary and her kin, created within living memory, like his comments of 1516/17 about the feast of the Conception of the Virgin in a series of sermons on the Ten Commandments:

> posterity will see that we did not live in vain: because we made new feasts and let old ones grow old, if we have done nothing else, this is worthy of eternal praise;

and with a final aside

> Indeed the day of Adam and Eve should be celebrated, for it is predestined.[78]

And this from the man who was to remake piety to the Virgin in a wholly new manner, one which saw her as humble and human, rather than queenly and exalted.[79]

What is striking in the various forms of reform and renewal which we have seen here is that so many were initiated by secular agencies in their role as guardians and stewards of spiritual well-being and social order, moved by preachers, theologians and mystics.[80] Reforms of

---

[77] 'Namque in institucione festi huiusmodi insidie veraciter iam posite sunt inter serpentem et mulierem ... ipsa interpellabit ad filium, ut sit pax in virtute sua, recognoscantque unum verum summum pontificem dominium nostrum Urbanum papam sextum, ut in ecclesia dei nos unum sumus cum [sic] sicut ipse unum est cum patre et spiritu sancto', Weltsch, *Archbishop John of Jenstein*, 90 n. 52.

[78] 'Nec frustra nos quoque vixisse videbit posteritas, quia novis festis fecimus vetera vera veterasse: si nihil aliud fecimus, hoc unum satis est dignum aeterna memoria'; 'Et forte diem Adae et Hevae quoque celebrandum et praedestinatum', in Hans Düfel, *Luthers Stellung zur Marienverehrung*, Kirche und Konfession 157, (Göttingen, 1968), 83. See of 1537 'Sermon on the Gospel of St John, Chapters 1–4', in *Luther's works*, XXII, ed. Jaroslav Pelikan (St Louis, Mo., 1957), 347.

[79] On changes in the cult of St Anne see Kathleen Ashley, 'Image and Ideology: Saint Anne in Late Medieval Drama and Narrative', in *Interpreting Cultural Symbols: Saint Anne in Late Medieval Society*, ed. Kathleen Ashley and Pamela Sheingorn (Athens, Ga., 1990), 111–30.

[80] For the convergence of pious upheaval and civic response see Bornstein, *The Bianchi of 1399*, chapter 6. On the involvement of administrators in prophetic phenomena see Bernard Montagnes, 'Prophétisme et eschatologie dans la prédication méridionale de Saint Vincent Ferrer', *Cahiers de Fanjeaux*, 27 (1992), 331–2.

religious houses were habitually promoted, indeed imposed, by town councils, as in Basel in 1428 when the council required its Dominicans to undergo reform against the desire of the brethren, several sons of leading local families.[81] Cities and princes were founding universities, not as the *studia generalia* of the thirteenth century, but as urban and regional institutions for the making of opinion and advice. Forty such new universities were founded in the fifteenth century, whereas only ten were founded in the fourteenth.[82] They were smaller and poorer institutions, regional in their recruitment and in the careers envisaged by their graduates,[83] but in them the clerics and lawyers, who were to be the administrators of great lordships, cities and provinces, rubbed shoulders. Several were founded by townsmen, as in Louvain, Mainz and Deventer.[84] Initiatives were local; purification went hand in hand with pacification – and often through coercion and violence. A typical reforming ruler, keen to acquire such advice, was Duke Albert V of Austria, who adopted a bureaucratic programme composed by the theologian Nicholas of Dinkelsbühl after the Council of Constance, the *Reformationis methodus*,[85] and soon after expelled the Jews of Austria in 1422. Through his influence reform was also adopted in Bavaria, where the Duke styled himself *princeps in ecclesia*.[86] Cities were the public spheres for moral experimentation and renewal – be this in the penitential processions of Florence, the fiery preaching in Siena, or the austere and sometimes enclosed houses of Brethren and Sisters of the Common Life in Deventer and Leuven.[87] Initiatives could also be launched from the countryside, from noble circles such as that which bred the prophet Jeanne-Marie de Maillé (d. 1414). This was an aristocratic milieu of families in south-west France which fostered Franciscan observance and lay participation, and which promoted the

[81] Bernhard Neidiger, 'The Basle Dominicans between Town and Prince', in *Mendicants, Military Orders and Regionalism in Medieval Eruope*, ed. J. Sarnovsky (Aldershot, 1999), 137.

[82] Jacques Verger, 'Patterns', in *A History of the University in Europe*, 1, ed. De Ridder Symoens, 62–5 and maps on 72–4.

[83] Peter Moraw, 'Careers of Graduates', in *A History of the University in Europe*, 1, ed. De Ridder Symoens, 244–79.

[84] Paolo Nardi, 'Relations with Authority', in *A History of the University in Europe*, 1, ed. De Ridder Symoens, 77–107.

[85] Dieter Mertens, 'Riforma monastica e potere temporale nella Germania sud-occidentale prima della Riforma', in *Strutture ecclesiastiche in Italia e in Germania prima della Riforma*, ed. Paolo Prodi and Peter Johanek, Annali dell'Istituto storico Italo-germanico di Trento, 16 (Bologna, 1984), 174.

[86] H. Rankl, *Die vorreformatorische Landesherrliche Kirchenregiment in Bayern (1378–1526)*, Miscellanea Bavarica Monacensia, 34 (Munich, 1971), 271.

[87] For an analysis of the urban and vernacular context of Netherlandish mystical writing and experience see Warnar, 'Mystik in der Stadt', esp. 695–701.

recognition of their kinswoman Jeanne-Marie's prophecies on the peace of the church and the healing of schism.[88]

Once the expectation that all-embracing answers be pronounced was diminished, local self-help became the rule, and its business ranged from reform of brothels, the settling or incarceration of beggars, sumptuary legislation, in local and regional initiatives. Reforming bishops could exhibit zeal and scepticism even against practices author-ised by popes: thus in pursuit of his pastoral duties in 1405 the Archbishop of Prague sent a commission (one of whose members was Jan Hus) to evaluate the blood-cult of Wilsnack in Saxony. When the commissioners found this well-established and heavily indulgenced cult to be fraudulent, the archbishop did not hesitate to forbid it to his parishioners and have monthly sermons preached against it, despite papal and episcopal support, and the continuing stream of pilgrims. The Wilsnack cult remained contentious until the Reformation. It was a site of struggle not between popular and elite views of devotion, but between the opposing frames of value and worth, the differing devo-tional styles held by prelates and princes and scrutinising polities.[89] This episode also reflects another set of contending aspirations: one which saw in excess and enthusiasm the sign of commitment and a power for the good; and the other, which preferred a quieter, more sustained religious discipline, unspectacular in appearance but transforming in its rigour.

Two stories are often told of the re-formations of the sixteenth century: one has them as the necessary result of the collapse of medieval institutions; and the counter part, which emphasises the preparatory work of fifteenth-century thought, as a 'premature reformation'. The histories I have shared with you fit into neither narrative. Rather, what has been discussed here was an institutional shift in the locus of experiment and discussion – as polities interpreted their political work through programmes of moral reform and renewal.

Inspired by preachers and teachers, adherents of a wide range of traditions, lay and clerical, made attempts which were painful, groping, sometimes blind, to re-establish comforting boundaries between purity and danger, the sacred and the profane. Some craved for the main-tenance of an enhanced, exclusive and celibate body of sacramental actors. Others saw the sacred as embodied in and emerging from communities of members of the Christian body. Still others favoured

[88] André Vauchez, 'A Holy Woman during the Hundred Years War: Jeanne-Marie of Maillé', in *The Laity in the Middle Ages: Religious Beliefs and Devotional Practices*, ed. Daniel E. Bornstein and trans. Margery J. Schneider (Notre Dame, Ind., 1993), 205–15.

[89] Charles Zika, 'Hosts, Processions and Pilgrimages in Fifteenth-Century Germany', *Past and Present*, 118 (1988), 25–64.

the dismantling of cultic action, preferring personal striving, education and community responsibility. It was the indeterminacy and constant disruption of boundaries and the cacophony of dissonant voices appealing to different traditions and gesturing in different directions that produced what strikes the historian as a zigzag of repeated instances both of inspired amities, and of purgative bouts of violence. In these and future decades it was out of these visions and that violence – that Europe, and the regions and peoples whose lives it was newly to discover and transform – was re-formed, re-made.

YEATS AT WAR: POETIC STRATEGIES AND POLITICAL RECONSTRUCTION FROM THE EASTER RISING TO THE FREE STATE

The Prothero Lecture

By R. F. Foster

READ 5 JULY 2000

THIS lecture is named for George Walter Prothero (1848–1922), historian and editor: and one excuse for giving a lecture on W. B. Yeats to an audience of historians is that Yeats actually knew Prothero. They both sat on the Academic Commttee of the Royal Society of Literature and in 1912, after a meeting of this body, Yeats wrote to Lady Gregory:

> I never look at old Prothero for 5 minutes without a desire to cut his throat, he frequently takes the chair and is a very bad chairman ... In the middle of his last [oration] Maurice Hewlett said to Henry James (it was Sir Alfred Lyall's memorial meeting) 'This is dull' to which Henry James sternly replied 'Hewlett, we are not here to enjoy ourselves.'[1]

With that warning, I want to proceed to talk about the theme of the current Anglo-American Conference: which is, of course, war. But I want to talk about the reflections and refractions of war in a certain kind of literary context, and in the context of Irish memory. 'Memory' is a subject which has achieved a historiography all its own, starting – as with so many high historiographical fashions – in the *ateliers* of Paris.[2] But it is not a novel preoccupation in Ireland, where the importance of structured memory has been recognised by the widespread practice of its obverse: therapeutic voluntary amnesia. Until recently, this was conspicuously the case regarding the First World War. For many years the 'Great' War was seen as a topic of some embarrassment: the political correctnesses of the new state established in 1922 demanded that the participation of hundreds of thousands of Irish people in the

---

[1] Allan Wade (ed.), *The Letters of W.B. Yeats* (1954), 565.

[2] See Pierre Nora, *Les Lieux de Mémoire* (Paris, Gallimard, 1984–1992, 7 vols.), translated by Arthur Goldhammer and edited by Lawrence D. Kritzman in three volumes as *Realms of Memory: The Construction of the French Past: Conflicts and Divisions* (New York, 1996), *Traditions* (New York, 1997) and *Symbols* (New York, 1998). Also see Patrick H. Hutton, *History as an Art of Memory* (Hanover, NH, 1993).

war to end all wars, fighting for the British Empire, be forgotten or at best politely ignored. So 'Not talking about the war' was elevated to a fine art in public rhetoric – and this affected historiography too. Over the last twenty years or so, this has been reversed: the war has been seen as centrally important in modern Irish history; the experiences of combatants, the treatment of ex-soldiers, the centrality of the war to the planning of the Easter Rising, have all been topics treated at length in excellent books, and the way that the war interacted with the fortunes of John Redmond's brand of constitutional nationalism has also been closely inspected.[3] Moreover, the war has become an acceptable part of official memory too: symbolised by the restoration of Lutyens's memorial garden at Islandbridge, and by the President of Ireland joining Queen Elizabeth in ceremonies remembering the war dead.

This is all emphatically to the good; it represents a facing up to the many-faceted nature of modern Irish history, and a recognition that there may have been alternative futures to the one that actually happened. At the same time, it should be remembered that during the years 1914–18, the war and what it represented were already, for many nationalists, a subject of some ambiguity and embarrassment. Nor did they have to be revolutionaries. Clearly, some constitutional nationalists were prepared – like the Nationalist MPs Tom Kettle or Willie Redmond – to fight for Britain; equally clearly, others felt more doubt. W. B. Yeats was not a nationalist MP, though he was once suspected of having such ambitions.[4] By 1914, he was also very far from being a revolutionary. But the day after the war broke out, he wrote doubtfully to an Abbey Theatre colleague: 'I wonder how the war will affect the minds of what audience it leaves to us. Neitsze [*sic*] was fond of foretelling wars for the possession of the earth that were to restore the tragic mind, & banish the mass mind which he hated ... In Ireland we want both war & peace, a war to unite us all.'[5]

Redmond, of course, thought that this was exactly what the war effort against Germany would do – specifically, that it would bring a recalcitrant Ulster into line with their comrades to the south. This did not happen; and after the 1916 Rising and its aftermath, the Anglo-

---

[3] See for instance T. Dooley, *Irishmen or English Soldiers? The Times and World of a Southern Catholic Irish Man (1876–1916) Enlisting in the British Army During the First World War* (Liverpool, 1995); Terence Denman, *Ireland's Unknown Soldiers: the 16th (Irish) Division in the Great War* (Dublin, 1992); David Fitzpatrick (ed.), *Ireland and the First World War* (Dublin, 1992); Senia Paseta, *Before the Revolution: Nationalism, Social Change and Ireland's Catholic Elite, 1879–1922* (Cork, 1999); Patrick Maume, *The Long Gestation: Irish Nationalist Life 1891–1918* (Dublin, 1999); Paul Bew, *Ideology and the Irish Question: Ulster Unionism and Irish Nationalism, 1912–1916* (Oxford, 1994) and *John Redmond* (Dundalk, 1996).

[4] See my *W.B. Yeats, A Life: I, The Apprentice Mage, 1865–1914* (Oxford, 1997), 128, for John Butler Yeats's expectations in 1893.

[5] Quoted in *ibid.*, 522.

Irish war, or war of independence, proved to be the 'war that united us all' – if 'we' were to be conceived as the nationalists of twenty-six counties. Other disunities remained painfully evident. Through it all, Yeats remained preoccupied by the effect of the war on the mind. And the way his own intelligence – creative and political – responded to both wars – the Great War and the small Irish war that followed it – is central to the story of his life. In the process he adapted his public persona in order to emerge as a founding father of the new nation in 1922. In this as in so many ways, his biography is the history of his country.

From August 1914, Yeats's attitude towards the war effort epitomises the ambiguities and sensitivities inseparable from the subject in Ireland. He was a convinced Home Ruler, who had given many speeches for the cause (and even made the Abbey Theatre put on a terrible play by Redmond's daughter for nakedly political reasons); even if the arguments he sometimes produced for the need for Home Rule were quint-essentially Yeatsian (including the impartially offensive argument that it would 'educate Catholics mentally and Protestants emotionally').[6] By 1914 he was emphatically an 'establishment' nationalist; he lived part of the year in London, where he was on dining terms with Asquith and Balfour; he would shortly refuse a knighthood; he was far estranged from extreme nationalism. But he also had an early record of Fenian activity, and of criticising the monarchy. From the start of the war, he refused to align himself with public statements on behalf of 'men of letters' condemning Germany, and was careful not to identify the Abbey theatre with official war-effort benefit performances.[7] As news came through from the front, he was critical of the apparent incompetence and 'useless heroism' of the British officer class: 'England is paying the price for having despized [sic] intellect.'[8]

At the same time, to be anti-war in Dublin was effectively to identify yourself as an advanced nationalist, and Yeats elaborately refused to do this – notably when he was to share a platform with the ostentatiously 'advanced' Patrick Pearse at a public meeting, for which Trinity College refused to act as host on the grounds of Pearse's anti-recruiting activities. Yeats trod a very careful line at this meeting, disassociating himself from Pearse's politics while defending free speech: but he noted that when Captain Tom Kettle turned up at the debate in military uniform, fresh from the Western Front where he would subsequently meet his death, he was booed. While Yeats kept apart from the 'bloody frivolity' of the war, it raised issues which could not be evaded, and which

---

[6] See *ibid.*, 448 (a comment he would have dared to make only in America).
[7] *Ibid.*, 523.
[8] A letter to his father, 12 Sept. 1915: misdated in Wade, *The Letters of W.B. Yeats*, 588.

penetrated unexpected areas of life.[9] For instance, attempting to organise a Royal Literary Fund pension for James Joyce (exiled in Trieste) he came up against Edmund Gosse at his most cavilling and blimpish:

> Neither his own letters nor yours expressed any frank sympathy with the cause of the Allies. I would not have let him have one penny if I had believed he was in sympathy with the Austrian enemy. But I felt that you had taken the responsibility in the matter.

Yeats's reply was masterly:

> It never occurred to me that it was necessary to express sympathy 'frank' or otherwise with the 'cause of the allies'. I should have thought myself wasting the time of the committee. I certainly wish them victory, & as I have never known Joyce to agree with his neighbours I feel that his residence in Austria has probably made his sympathy as frank as you could wish.[10]

Thus literary politics were, like every other facet of life, affected by the war. Nor was Yeats as absolutely detached as he liked to pretend. He did give his strategy of detachment poetic form, when Edith Wharton asked him to donate a poem for a war-effort compilation called *The Book of the Homeless*. Close friends and collaborators of his like Edmund Dulac turned out a great deal of work for such enterprises, but Yeats kept himself aloof: he told Henry James (Wharton's inevitable intermediary) that this was the only thing he would write about the war, and the poem conveys a certain impatience at the whole exercise – as well as a contrived staginess. (Great ladies brought out some of the best in Yeats, but also a lot of the worst.)

> I think it better that at times like these
> We poets keep our mouths shut, for in truth
> We have no gift to set a statesman right;
> He's had enough of meddling who can please
> A young girl in the indolence of his youth,
> Or an old man upon a winter's night.[11]

Actually, he did take part in a reading for the Belgian Relief Fund a

---

[9] For the Thomas Davis speech see *Apprentice Mage*, 523–5. 'Bloody frivolity' appears in a letter to Ernest Rhys, 31 May 1916, Kansas.

[10] For this episode, and this exchange, see James Longenbach, *Stone Cottage: Pound, Yeats and Modernism* (Oxford, 1988), 182–3.

[11] This is the first completed version, in the Bienecke Library, Yale University. In *The Book of the Homeless* 'his youth' became 'youth', and was subsequently changed to 'her youth'. There is also a signed transcription in Yeats's hand in the National Library of Ireland (MS 30, 415). The charities in question were the American hostels for refugees and the Children of Flanders Rescue Committee.

year later; and though he kept his head down, wartime conditions impinged on his life in various ways. A boy shouted 'Kitchener wants you!' at him when he was going into his club. The London blackout altered his urban landscape in a way he approved – no more illuminated advertisements for Bovril, he gratefully remarked. While living in the New Forest, his erratic secretary and amanuensis Ezra Pound was taken briefly into police custody for being an 'alien in a prohibited area'.[12] Most bizarrely of all, wartime paranoia interrupted Yeats's experiments in St Leonards-on-Sea with David Wilson, a mildly deranged chemist who had invented a machine which received and amplified messages from the spirit world. Yeats's excitement about this was immense, and he tried to raise money for developing it commercially. But Wilson recklessly published a message received in German, and the police impounded the machine as an illegal wireless: Yeats had to intercede with Gerald Balfour (fortunately interested in psychical research) and highly placed contacts at the Home Office. But he could not stop Wilson being conscripted, and the experiments came to an end. It could have been, Yeats thought, 'the greatest discovery of the modern world'.[13]

This bizarre episode happened in 1917; in that same year, Yeats was in correspondence with the Foreign Office about giving a series of lectures under their auspices in France. But significantly, one of the reasons why this idea was dropped was that he wanted to talk about 'modern Ireland'. And since the events in Dublin of a year before, this was a dangerous subject. Those same events had initiated a process of repositioning in Yeats's own life which would dominate his publication strategies as well as affect the content of his poetry over the next five years – until three-quarters of Ireland emerged into quasi-independence in 1922, and Yeats emerged alongside as the poet of the revolution.

Yeats, like nearly everyone else, was astonished by the Easter Rising of 1916, when Patrick Pearse and his companions defied the majority of their IRB comrades as well as the British empire by launching a hopeless insurrection. Several of his friends noted that his surprise was coloured by his deep dislike of Pearse, whom he had, according to Pound, been denouncing for years as 'half-cracked and wouldn't be happy until he was hanged ... had Emmet mania same as some other lunatics think they are Napoleon or God'. Pound also pointed out, regarding the proclamation of the Republic, '[Yeats] dont like Republics

[12] For the Pound incident see Longenbach, *Stone Cottage*, 260–3. The jeer about Kitchener is reported in a letter from Augusta Gregory to J. B. Yeats, 17 Nov. 1917 (National Library of Ireland, MS 18, 676) and the Bovril reflection is quoted in *Apprentice Mage*, 523.

[13] This episode is explored by Christopher Blake, 'Ghosts in the Machine: W.B. Yeats and the Metallic Humunculus', *Yeats Annual*, forthcoming.

... likes queens, preferably dead ones'.[14] Several of the revolutionaries and their sympathisers had been known to him – some, like Arthur Griffith, founder of Sinn Fein, had become serious enemies. At just this time Griffith attacked Yeats as an 'imperialist' who had gone over to the enemy. 'Mr Yeats is a poseur in patriotism precisely as Chesterton is a poseur in Catholicism.'[15] Others, like Constance Markiewicz, had been friends in his youth and were now – through their extreme politics, socialist as well as republican in her case – estranged. Living in England, Yeats was reliant on letters from friends to find out what had happened: and these provide a fascinating barometer of changing opinions. His sister Lily sent a bracing sketch of some of the principal revolutionaries, which gives a rather different portrait than that which her brother would later build canonically into his poem 'Easter 1916':

> What a pity Madame Markiewicz's madness changed its form when she inherited it. In her father it meant looking for the North Pole in an open boat, very cooling for him and safe for others. Her followers are said to have been either small boys or drunken dock workers. I dont think any others could have followed her. I wouldn't have followed her across a road. I often heard the elder Pearse speak at his school prize days and such things. I thought he was a dreamer and a sentimentalist MacDonagh was clever and hard and full of self-conceit. He was I think a spoilt priest.

As for the alcoholic John MacBride, she added, 'it must have been some humorist who got him the post of water baliff to the corporation'.[16]
Thus we have exactly the 'mocking gibes' that Yeats would later write into his poem of apparent atonement about the rebels, 'Easter 1916'. The letters from his closest friend Augusta Gregory at Coole Park similarly begin with references to 'corner-boys' and 'rabble': but they change, particularly with the executions. Her opinions, in fact, run well ahead of Yeats's. 'It seems as if the leaders were what is wanted in Ireland & will be even more wanted in the future – a fearless & imaginative opposition to the conventional and opportunist parliamentarians.' Particularly significant is an exchange where Yeats sends her articles from the *Westminster Review* stressing the Rising as a German plot; and she retaliates with quotations from Shelley on the execution of people who deliberately risk the death penalty from motives of political idealism: 'persons of energetic character, in whom as in men who suffer for political crimes, there is a large mixture of enterprise & fortitude & disinterestedness, and the elements, though

---

[14] Pound to John Quinn, 1 May 1916, quoted in Longenbach, *Stone Cottage*, 256.
[15] *Nationality*, 29 Jan. 1916.
[16] To John Butler Yeats, 7 May 1916: my thanks to W.M. Murphy for this reference.

misguided and disarranged, by which the strength and happiness of a nation might have been cemented, die in such a manner as to make death not evil but good."[17] These are the very ideas interrogated in the poem Yeats would write about the Rising – 'Easter 1916'. The seedbed of that complex poem contains not only Maud Gonne's remark to Yeats that 'tragic dignity had returned to Ireland', but also Gregory's reflections on Shelley, and the Dublin mockery retailed by Lily – all to be changed utterly.

Yeats wrote 'Easter 1916' over the summer, staying with Maud Gonne in Normandy, with echoes of the European war in the wings; but Ireland had come to the forefront. Equally importantly, he finished the poem at Coole Park, under Gregory's influence again. Appropriately, it is in some ways a classically ambiguous text – as Gonne smartly spotted when she told him it didn't come up to the mark ('My Dear Willie, No I dont like your poem it isn't worthy of you and above all it isnt worthy of the subject.'[18]) The life of the poem is itself a complex subject. Its arrival at Gonne's seaside house, sent from Coole, galvanised arguments between Maud and her daughter over the nature of sacrifice; it was then circulated as a samizdat among trusted friends. In early December Yeats read it at Lindsey House, Cheyne Walk, to a reception so electric that Gregory had to defuse things by declaiming some Hilaire Belloc;[19] it made a ghostly appearance on a draft contents-list for his 1919 collection, *The Wild Swans at Coole*, but subsequently disappeared. Eventually it was published in the *New Statesman* in 1920, and absorbed into the canon of inspirational revolutionary literature, creating phrases recycled into countless chapter and book titles: 'All is changed, changed utterly; A terrrible beauty is born.'

Despite this endorsement, and its future life on posters and tea-towels, 'Easter 1916' is in fact a very ambivalent reaction to the Rising, emphasising the 'bewildered' and delusional state of the rebels as much as their heroism, and moving to a plea for the 'flashing, changing joy of life', as Maud Gonne put it, rather than the hard stone of fanatical opinion, fixed in the fluvial stream of life.

> Hearts with one purpose alone
> Through summer and winter seem
> Enchanted to a stone
> To trouble the living stream.

[17] This series of letters, of mid-May 1916, is in the Berg Collection, New York Public Library.
[18] Nov. 1916: see Anna MacBride White and A. Norman Jeffares (eds.), *Always Your Friend: the Gonne-Yeats Letters 1893–1938* (1992), 384–5.
[19] Daniel J. Murphy (ed.), *Lady Gregory's Journals, vol. I: Books One to Twenty-Nine, 10 October 1916–24 February 1925* (Gerrards Cross, 1978), 20.

The horse that comes from the road,
The rider, the birds that range
From cloud to tumbling cloud,
Minute by minute they change;
A shadow of cloud on the stream
Changes minute by minute;
A horse-hoof slides on the brim,
And a horse plashes within it;
The long-legged moor-hens dive,
And hens to moor-cocks call;
Minute by minute they live:
The stone's in the midst of all.

Too long a sacrifice
Can make a stone of the heart.
O when may it suffice?
That is Heaven's part, our part
To murmur name upon name,
As a mother names her child
When sleep at last has come
On limbs that had run wild.
What is it but nightfall?
No, no, not night but death;
Was it needless death after all?
For England may keep faith
For all that is done and said.
We know their dream; enough
To know they dreamed and are dead;
And what if excess of love
Bewildered them till they died?
I write it out in a verse –
MacDonagh and MacBride
And Connolly and Pearse
Now and in time to be,
Wherever green is worn,
Are changed, changed utterly:
A terrible beauty is born.

A textual analysis of the poem reveals this ambiguity, and also the inheritance in the poem of phrases and reflections which Yeats had been entrusting to notebooks and essays since long before the First World War.[20] But in the mood of 1916, it would be read as republicanism

---

[20] See *Apprentice Mage*, 417–21. The essay is to be found in W. B. Yeats, *Essays and Introductions* (1961), 311–42.

pure and simple. Not only was this still far from being Yeats's position; he was also being accused of pro-Germanism, there were rumours his own Literary Fund pension would be withdrawn, and in fact he visited Asquith to quell these very assertions. And there is another way in which one of the unexpected contingencies of the First World War restrained his actions. He was much involved in the endless campaign to repossess the great collection of paintings which the art conoisseur Sir Hugh Lane (Gregory's nephew) had left to the Dublin National Gallery when he drowned in the *Lusitania* disaster in 1915. The bequest was in an unwitnessed codicil, revoking his previous bequest to the National Gallery in London; the London gallery, and powerful friends in the government, stood on the letter of the law and claimed the paintings belonged to them. (Curzon was seen as a particularly obsessive enemy on this score, though his biographer believes it meant rather less to him than Yeats thought.[21]) Yeats and Gregory spent a phenomenal amount of time, energy and ink fighting this cause. In 1916, they were pursuing it through the corridors of power, by means of Yeats's friendship with Asquith, Birrell and others. But they were also particularly cultivating both Carson and Craig, now influential in government – but also, of course, the leaders of implacable Ulster Unionism. Yeats's chances of keeping them on side, once he had energed as an apologist for the Dublin rebellion, may easily be imagined. His sense of political possibilities was always finely developed; indeed, he told John Quinn that he could include 'Easter 1916' in his next collection only if the war came to an end before then, well aware that in many people's eyes pro-rebel equalled pro-German.[22]

What the years from 1916 to 1920 are remarkable for, therefore, is a good deal of writing that was withheld from publication. There were unambiguously nationalist poems like 'The Rose Tree', Fenian ballads of a kind which Yeats had experimented with in his youth but – apparently – turned resolutely away from in the intervening years. There was a Fenian Noh play, *The Dreaming of the Bones,* dealing with the iniquities of the fatal lovers whose scandal supposedly led to the Normans being invited into Ireland in the twelfth century – whose eternal existence as wandering ghosts is strangely bound in with that of a 1916 rebel, on the run in County Clare. It is a play which departs from Noh conventions in coming down on the side of revolutionary confrontation rather than reconciliation – ending with an invocation of that classical symbol, the red cock of revolution. Yeats was well aware that it packed a strong revolutionary punch – too strong, at the

---

[21] My thanks to David Gilmour.
[22] See Yeats to John Quinn, 16 May 1917, New York Public Library; also Murphy, *Lady Gregory's Journals*, 20.

moment, for it to be performed.[23] And from the summer of 1916, he returned to writing his memoirs.

Like most people's memoirs, these cast more reliable light on the author at the time he was writing them, than the actual events they purport to describe: in fact, he takes sweeping liberties with chronology and personnel, in order to build his pattern. This particular draft was unpublished as such until 1972, but he quarried it for the marvellous volume called *The Trembling of the Veil* that appeared in 1922. In 1916, significantly, Yeats set himself to writing about the 1890s: but with the sharp consciousness that Irish history since Parnell's death in 1891 was going to produce a revolution twenty-five years later. The theme he returns to again and again is the conflict between nationalist propagandist politics and the imperatives of the creative artist: stressing that the artist's influence, while remaining independent, will play its own political part, by radicalising the new Ireland. This was the thesis that he would reiterate again and again, finally and most memorably delivering it as part of his speech of acceptance of the Nobel Prize in 1923, the year after Ireland achieved some kind of independence: an event Yeats would cannily relate to the honour bestowed upon himself.[24]

That is to look ahead. For the moment, he watched as Irish opinion settled in a new direction over 1917–18. This was a period of personal *sturm und drang* for Yeats, from which he emerged with a new wife, a rejuvenated interest in occult and psychical research, and a new home – the Norman tower which he bought in 1916 and had begun to renovate. In Irish politics, helped greatly by a series of government blunders, political support was swinging to Sinn Féin – the party of Yeats's old enemy, Arthur Griffith. Again, the opportunities were provided by wartime conditions: the government's paranoia about the involvement of radical nationalists in a trumped-up 'German plot', for instance, and the great crisis in 1918 over the decision to impose conscription on Ireland if need be. In this year of transition, Yeats's movements repay close attention.

First of all, he finally wrote a war poem: though not in the way that, perhaps, Edith Wharton would have expected. In January 1918, his friend Augusta Gregory's only son Robert was killed flying his plane over Italy: a shattering blow for the Gregory circle. She wanted a memorial of him and Yeats obliged: writing an obituary and several elegies. What is striking is how carefully he avoided the actual circumstances of Gregory's death for king and country. The first attempt, 'Shepherd and Goatherd', is an awkward and archaic piece of pastoral (only achieving interest in a stanza describing Yeats's own evolving

---

[23] See Yeats to Gregory, 11 June 1917, Wade, *Letters*, 629.
[24] W. B. Yeats, *Autobiographies* (1955), 531–72.

theory of the journey of the soul). The most substantial effort, 'In Memory of Major Robert Gregory', is also self-centred – a sombre celebration of the poet's own new state of life (wife, tower, remembrance of dead friends) – written under the firm tutelage of Lady Gregory, to Yeats's irritation. He affected to long for Urbino-style patronage, but disliked being ordered to produce a stanza 'to commend Robert's courage on the hunting field'; he produced it, but confided to his wife 'I have firmly resisted all suggsted eloquence about aero planes and the "blue Italian sky".'[25] Augusta Gregory was allowed to play Isabella d'Este only so far. But this was not only an aesthetic reluctance. To praise the manner of Robert Gregory's death in an Ireland where, in 1918, even moderate nationalist opinion had turned against the war effort, and farmers' sons were determined to stay home and bring in the harvest rather than be conscripted for slaughter in Europe – this would have upset the political balance he was so carefully and discreetly keeping in his public life. So the one poem for Robert in which he faces up to the manner of his death, takes good care to reverse the message of king and country;

An Irish Airman Foresees His Death

I know that I shall meet my fate
Somewhere among the clouds above;
Those that I fight I do not hate,
Those that I guard I do not love;
My country is Kiltartan Cross,
My countrymen Kiltartan's poor,
No likely end could bring them loss
Or leave them happier than before.
Nor law, nor duty bade me fight,
Nor public men, nor cheering crowds,
A lonely impulse of delight
Drove to this tumult in the clouds;
I balanced all, brought all to mind,
The years to come seemed waste of breath,
A waste of breath the years behind
In balance with this life, this death.

This was Yeats's 'war poem' at last, written in June 1918 and published after the war was over, in 1919. But it placed the warrior-airman as an exponent of Nietszchean tragic joy; and attributed to him a lack of sympathy for the imperialist cause which was the exact opposite of what Gregory apparently actually felt. There would be one more

---

[25] W.B. Yeats to George Yeats, 18 May 1918 (private collection). The poem is interestingly analysed in D. Harris, *Yeats, Coole Park and Ballylee* (1974), chapter 5.

Gregory elegy, which was not published in Yeats's lifetime – though that was Lady Gregory's decision, not his. And it would stem from the circumstances of the subsequent war – in Ireland.

For the moment, in 1918, Yeats held back his nationalist writings, and very carefully monitored the plays to be put on at the Abbey, rejecting several as too political for present circumstances; he also refused to be a signatory for the Irish Convention hastily arranged by his old friend George Russell ['AE'], to bring together nationalists and unionists and attempt a compromise Home Rule settlement. 'I dont want to take a political part, however slight, in haste.'[26] Since AE was calling for a pluralist solution to the current impasse, and the greatest possible diversity of thought, this is rather odd: Yeats had spent many years arguing for exactly the same thing. But in late 1918 he was holding back. He cancelled a projected lecture on 'the poetry of the Irish rebellion', privately remarking 'times are too dangerous for me to encourage men to risks I am not prepared to share or approve'.[27] At the same time, there are signs that he had decided the way the cat was going to jump. Interestingly, as early as January 1918 he had suggested to Gregory getting de Valera and Sinn Féin on board the Lane pictures campaign – a full ten months before the general election that proclaimed them the coming power.[28] And when the conscription crisis broke that summer, he took a firm line. The man who had proclaimed that poets had no gift to set a statesman right decided to do just that, approaching Asquith (though warned by Horace Plunkett that 'Squiffy isn't Gladstone') and initiating a correspondence with Lord Haldane which deserves quotation.

> I write to you because you are a man of letters, and we, therefore, may speak the same language. I have no part in politics and no liking for politics, but there are moments when one cannot keep out of them. I have met nobody in close contact with the people who believes that conscription can be imposed without the killing of men, and perhaps of women. Lady Gregory, who knows the country as few know it, and has taken down, for instance, hundreds of thousands of words in collecting folk-lore from cottage to cottage, and has still many ways of learning what is thought about it – is convinced that the women and children will stand in front of the men and receive the bullets. I do not say that this will happen, but I do say that there is in this country an extravagance of emotion which few Englishmen, accustomed to more objective habits of thought, can understand.

[26] To Augusta Gregory, 31 May 1917, Berg Collection, New York Public Library.
[27] W.B. Yeats to Clement Shorter, Wade, *Letters*, 649.
[28] W.B. Yeats to Augusta Gregory, 25 Jan. 1918, Berg Collection, New York Public Library.

There is something oriental in the people, and it is impossible to say how great a tragedy may lie before us. The British government, it seems to me, is rushing into this business in a strangely trivial frame of mind. I hear of all manner of opinions being taken except the opinion of those who have some knowledge of the popular psychology. I hear even of weight being given to the opinions of clergymen of the Church of Ireland, who, as a class, are more isolated from their neighbours than any class known anywhere to me. I find in people here in Dublin a sense of strain and expectancy which makes even strangers speak something of their mind. I was ordering some coal yesterday, and I said: 'I shall be in such and such a house for the next four months.' The man at the counter, a stranger to me, muttered: 'Who, in Ireland, can say where he will be in four months?' Another man. almost a stranger, used nearly those very words speaking to me some two weeks ago. There is a danger of a popular hysteria that may go to any height or any whither. There is a return to that sense of crisis which followed the Rising. Some two months after the Rising I called on a well-known Dublin doctor, and as I entered his room, an old cabinet-maker went out. The doctor said to me: 'That man has just said a very strange thing. He says there will be more trouble yet, for "the young men are mad jealous of their leaders for being shot". That jealousy is still in the country. It is not a question as to whether it is justified or not justified, for these men believe – an incredible thought, perhaps, to Englishmen – that the Childers Committee reported truthfully as to the overtaxation of Ireland, that the population of Ireland has gone down one-half through English misgovernment, that the union of Ireland, in our time, was made impossible because England armed the minority of people with rifles and machine-guns. When they think to themselves: 'Now England expects us to die for her', is it wonderful that they say to themselves afterwards: 'We shall bring our deaths to a different market.' I read in the newspapers yesterday that over three hundred thousand Americans have landed in France in a month, and it seems to me a strangely wanton thing that England, for the sake of fifty thousand Irish soldiers, is prepared to hollow another trench between the countries and fill it with blood. If that is done England will only suffer in reputation, but Ireland will suffer in her character, and all the work of my life-time and that of my fellow-workers, all our effort to clarify and sweeten the popular mind, will be destroyed and Ireland, for another hundred years, will live in the sterility of her bitterness.[29]

---

[29] 10 Oct. 1918, National Library of Scotland.

The preoccupation with hereditary bitterness infecting the accu
mulated efforts to 'sweeten the public mind' anticipates the two grea
poem sequences which the Irish revolution inspired him to produce
'Nineteen Hundred and Nineteen' and 'Meditations in Time of Civi
War'. One war ended in November 1918; another would begin a few
months later, with the shooting of two policemen in County Tipperary
But for the moment, as Ireland descended into guerilla war from
1919, Yeats kept his counsel; to judge from references in his friends
correspondence, he was considered to have lost touch with publi
affairs, immured in his tower with his wife and new baby. It is true
that from time to time he thought of withdrawing altogether, to Ital
or even Japan. He was putting together the beginnings of his bizarre
study of the philosophy of history, *A Vision*, and preoccupied with th
belief that the Christian era was ending, in an apocalyptic downward
spiral of world revolution: his attention to events in Russia was close
than is often realised, and reflected not only in his poem 'The Second
Coming', written at this time (a world-historical poem about world
revolution), but also in the strangely prophetic essay 'If I Was Four and
Twenty', which ends with an odd anticipation of totalitarian rule in
Europe.[30]

In early 1920 Ireland lurched deeper into guerilla war, and Lloyd
George's government responded by sending over the mercenary force
known as 'Black and Tans' and 'Auxiliaries'. For many the actions o
these troops, with their unofficial policy of 'reprisals' against the civilia
population, were what drove once unlikely people to join Sinn Féin
Before they came, Lily Yeats had joked that to be a true Sinn Féiner
you had to believe the RIC were obligingly shooting each other to
make propaganda for the British government; after some experience o
the Tans, she would write in December 1920: 'As you know I was no
Sinn Féiner a year ago, just a mild nationalist, but now–'.[31]

From early 1920 her brother was on a lecture tour in the USA
Here, as so often before his responses to journalists are worth decoding
He was, in a sense, unmuzzled, but also had to keep a wary eye to
Irish-American fenianism: especially as de Valera was touring the States
at the same time. (A meeting was actually arranged, which Yeats
described to Gregory. 'I was rather disappointed – a living man, al
propaganda, no human life, but not bitter or hysterical or unjust.
judged him persistent, being both patient and energetic, but that he
will fail through not having enough human life to judge the human life

---

[30] This is a strangely strident piece of intellectual autobiography, written in the summe
of 1919 for AE's *Irish Statesman*, and deserves closer attention than it usually receives. I
is reprinted in *Explorations* (1962), 263–80.
[31] To John Butler Yeats, 7 June 1920; my thanks to W.M. Murphy for this reference.

of others. He will ask too much of everyone & ask it without charm. He will be pushed aside by others.'[32]) In the event, Yeats's public statements were distinctly un-Republican. He attacked the 'oppression' of the military, criticised censorship, but also stressed the advisability of granting Dominion status and said that Ulster should not be coerced. The British had created Sinn Fein's success by bungling: now they might 'be criminal enough to grant to violence what they refused to reason' (a very conservative reflection indeed).[33] Political fanaticism, he said, was 'a bitter acid that destroyed the soul'; he reprised this in reading his poem about Constance Markiewicz feeding a seagull on her window-ledge in prison, a strange mixture of sympathy and contempt:

> Did she in touching that lone wing
> Recall the years before her mind
> Became a bitter, an abstract thing,
> Her thought some popular enmity
> Blind and leader of the blind
> Drinking the foul ditch where they lie?

And he did not read 'The Rose Tree' or 'Easter 1916'. Sinn Féin sympathies had their limits. Griffith and he, Yeats told a journalist, had not been on speaking terms for some years.[34]

Strangely, at this time, in an instruction from prison, Griffith told his Sinn Féin comrades: 'Mobilise the poets.. Perhaps Yeats will use his muse for his country now.'[35] But he did not. He stayed away from Galway, irritating Gregory with his enquiries about the safety of building materials at his tower; in Oxford, he worked on his philosophical system. But in the autumn and winter of 1920 he also wrote the section of his autobiography called 'Four Years', recalling his London apprenticeship from 1887 to 1891. This looks like an escape from current horrors: but reading between the lines offers a different interpretation. The text is preoccupied by how a 'nation or an individual might achieve, through emotional intensity ... a symbological, a mythological coherence'; and in a passage written at this time, but incorporated into a later volume, he recalled his own early efforts at creating a culturally

[32] W.B. Yeats to Augusta Gregory, 18 May 1920, Berg Collection, New York Public Library: partially quoted in Murphy, *Lady Gregory's Journals*. Yeats not only attended de Valera's public address on 11 May, but may have had a private audience with him at his hotel – requested by the Sinn Féin leader. The republicans hoped to enlist Yeats's public advocacy, but he avoided it.

[33] *Toronto Evening Telegraph*, 3 Feb. 1920, quoted in Karin Strand, 'W.B. Yeats's American Lecture Tours', unpublished Ph.D.thesis (Northwestern University, 1978), 177–8.

[34] *Ibid.*

[35] R. Fanning (ed.), *Documents of Irish Foreign Policy*, 1 (Dublin, 1998), no. 3, 5: a memo from Arthur Griffith to Dail Éireann, issued from Gloucester prison, 23 Jan. 1919.

revolutionary organisation, relating the gestation of his own youthful opinions to what he actually calls 'the future birth of my country'. The artist's integrated life is the platonic parallel for the creation of a national myth. The ringing conclusion of 'Four Years' should be read not only as emotion recollected in an Oxford study, but as a product of observing Ireland in the process of revolution and remaking.

> I used to tell the few friends to whom I could speak these secret thoughts that I would make the attempt in Ireland but fail, for our civilization, its elements multiplying by division like certain low forms of life, was all-powerful; but in reality I had the wildest hopes. Today I add to that first conviction, to that first desire for unity, this other conviction, long a mere opinion vaguely or intermittently apprehended: Nations, races, and individual men are unified by an image, or bundle of related images, symbolical or evocative of the state of mind which is, of all states of mind not impossible, the most difficult to that man, race, or nation; because only the greatest obstacle that can be contemplated without despair rouses the will to full intensity.
>
> A powerful class by terror, rhetoric, and organised sentimentality may drive their people to war, but the day draws near when they cannot keep them there; and how shall they face the pure nations of the East when the day comes to do it with but equal arms? I had seen Ireland in my own time turn from the bragging rhetoric and gregarious humour of O'Connell's generation and school, and offer herself to the solitary and proud Parnell as to her anti-self, buskin followed hard on sock, and I had begun to hope, or to half hope, that we might be the first in Europe to seek unity as deliberately as it had been sought by theologian, poet, sculptor, architect, from the eleventh to the thirteenth century. Doubtless we must seek it differently, no longer considering it convenient to epitomize all human knowledge, but find it we well might could we first find philosophy and a little passion.

And he knew what he was doing. At this time, he wrote to Gregory describing his memoirs: 'they are mainly history of my kind of national ideas & how it formed in my head – the rags I picked off various bushes. I think it will influence young Irishmen in the future, if for no other reason than that it shows how seriously one lived & thought. I know from my own memory of my youth in Dublin how important biography can be in Ireland.'[36]

Moreover, by the late autumn a series of climactic events were pushing him to, at last, coming out on the side of revolution. Near his

[36] 14 Dec. 1920, Berg Collection, New York Public Library.

local Galway town of Gort, the Black and Tans committed two horrific atrocities, when a young mother sitting at her cottage door was shot dead from the back of a lorry, and when two local boys were murdered for 'impudence' and their bodies dragged behind a lorry for miles; meanwhile the Sinn Féin mayor of Cork, Terence MacSwiney, died on hunger strike in prison. Three days before MacSwiney's death (by then inevitable), Yeats published 'Easter 1916' at last – in the *New Statesman*, which had been campaigning for clemency towards him. Simultaneously he accepted a play of MacSwiney's for the Abbey, and redrafted his own play about hunger-strike, *The King's Threshold*. (He carefully published the revised ending in *Seven Poems and a Fragment* in October 1922.) Mac-Swiney's impending death, Yeats remarked hard-headedly to Gregory, 'may make it tragically appropriate'. MacSwiney's own play, while a bad piece of work, 'would greatly move the audience who will see the mayor in the play's hero'.[37] Suddenly the Abbey stage was to be a forum for politics after all. (And the audiences for MacSwiney's play, *The Revolutionist*, reached record levels, reversing a period of declining profits.)

And at this point too, Yeats wrote his last Robert Gregory poem – 'Reprisals', a distinctly agitprop piece about the Black and Tan atrocities at Gort, addressed to Gregory's shade and implicitly contrasting his war-effort and heroic death with the reality of the grubby Empire in whose name mercenary soldiers now were murdering his tenants. But Lady Gregory, who thought it an insincere poem, and disliked the use of her son's name, asked him to withdraw it from the *Nation*, which he did – with some annoyance. 'I had long hesitated before I wrote', he told her, 'as I have hesitated about other things in this tragic situation.'[38] This was certainly true.

But by the spring of 1921 the time for hesitation was past, and he came out on 17 February with a famous denunciation of the government's policy in Ireland, at the Oxford Union, attacking the establishment from, so to speak, inside. An Irish undergraduate, Joseph O'Reilly, has left a description:

> He denounced and defied the English ... In twelve minutes of bitter and blazing attack on the English in Ireland he ended pointing at the busts of the Union's Prime Ministers. 'Gladstone! Salisbury! Asquith! They were Victorians. I am a Victorian. They knew the meaning of the words 'truth' and 'honour' and 'justice'. But you do not know the meaning of them. You do not know the language I speak so I will sit down.

[37] W.B. Yeats to Lennox Robinson, 29 Oct. 1920, Southern Illinois University, Carbondale.
[38] 3 Dec. 1920, Berg Collection, New York Public Library.

There was no acting or posing, added O'Reilly. 'No-one who heard that speech could question his sincerity as an Irish nationalist.'[39]

No one who read his collection *Michael Robartes and the Dancer*, published the same month, could doubt it either: here were, in deliberate sequence, 'Easter 1916', 'Sixteen Dead Men' and 'The Rose Tree'. Griffith's challenge to use his muse for Ireland seemed answered.

Moreover, the re-writing of his political position would continue, in many ways. Notably, it affected the publishing life of the sequence he began just after the publication of '*Michael Robartes and the Dancer*', entitled 'Thoughts on the Present State of the World'. This was, in its way, a war poem: at least, it began as a poem about the apocalyptic world-events of the past few years, posited against the belief held by a deluded bourgeoisie before 1914, that life would go on for ever. 'Many ingenious lovely things are gone / That seemed sheer miracle to the multitude'. Comments in letters, and recurrent phrases and images, establish that he is thinking of the world before the Great War, as well as of ancient Greece and (I believe) the Irish-Georgian Ascendancy. But the poem deliberately shifts to the current Irish war and the Gort atrocities

> Now days are dragon ridden, the nightmare
> Rides upon sleep; a drunken soldiery
> Can leave the mother, murdered at her door,
> To crawl in her own blood and go scot-free;
> The night can sweat with terror as before
> We pieced our thoughts into philosophy
> And planned to bring the world under a rule
> Who are but weasels fighting in a hole.

Thus he introduces 'Reprisals' by another route: but it is linked to preoccupations with historical cycles and world chaos. The interesting thing is that, as time went by, he evidently decided to stress the *Irish* war as the poem's theme, rather than the more cosmic conflict which really lies behind it. Hence his retitling it a few years later by the name we know it: 'Nineteen Hundred and Nineteen'. This has always been something of a conundrum, at least to simple-minded historians, for the poem was written in 1921 and deals with events from 1920. But by choosing that name, some time after the poem was written, he shifts the chronology of the poem away from the Great War and into the Irish war. When he wrote, in 1921,

[39] TS by Joseph O'Reilly, 'W.B. Yeats and Undergraduate Oxford', Harry Ransom Humanities Research Center, University of Texas, Austin.

We who seven years ago
Talked of honour and of truth
Shriek with pleasure if we show
The weasel's twist, the weasel's tooth

he was obviously thinking of 1914: that recurring memory of being assured by a friend watching a military display in the park that this was all part of the past, and modern civilisation had done away with war. But when we read 'seven years ago' in a poem titled 'Nineteen Hundred and Nineteen', we obviously think of 1912, and the passing of the Home Rule Bill, with all its brave hopes. And by the time this title was attached to the poem, readers would know that 1919 was the date when the Anglo-Irish war began. Thus Yeats turned his poem about the dislocations of the world after the Great War into a poem about the Irish war instead. This perfectly parallels the general repositioning of his stance which he pursued since the aftermath of the Easter Rising: which both parallels and expresses a national repositioning of stance, and a certan elision of memory.

From late 1921, the British government entered upon negotiations with Sinn Féin. Yeats continued to write his memoirs, now dealing with the 1890s and returning to the idea that extreme-nationalist abstractions were like the fixed ideas of hysterical people, turning the mind to stone: while Unionist prejudices are their mirror image. At the same time he separates out events, misrepresents the political alignments of the time, draws out the role of himself and his collaborators as the midwives of what was evidently, as he wrote, a revolution drawing to its close. The last words of the volume published as *The Trembling of the Veil*, covering the late eighties and the nineties, announces that 'the coming generation, to whom recent events are often more obscure than those long past, should learn what debts they owe, and to what creditor'. Superficially referring to Gregory, she here stands for Synge and himself too: the makers of drama and language through which revelation had come, with the fabulous moment of the trembling of the veil of the temple.

And as he finished these memoirs, the new dispensation was being born, with the Anglo-Irish Treaty of December 1921. Yeats's private letters show his heavy forebodings, but with remarkable speed he decided to return to Ireland. He had written himself back into Irish history. 'We have to be "that old man eloquent" to the new governing generation', he told Gregory. 'If we write our best, the spiritual part of free Ireland will be in the books & the Free State's struggle with the impossibilists may make even some of our unpopular struggle shine with patriotic fire.'[40] He must have been annoyed when an old sparring-

[40] 12 Jan. 1922, Berg Collection, New York Public Library.

partner reviewed his memoirs and decided that they showed Yeats's
generation had been consigned to history by the Anglo-Irish War. John
Eglinton wrote 'Each new phase of Ireland's political and social history
seems to require new personalities to express it: and just as Griffith and
Collins have blotted out Redmond and Devlin, so the literary influence
of Patrick Pearse and his band has seemed, at all events for the moment,
to cast into the shade the movement in which Mr Yeats was so recently
the protagonist.'[41]

This of course was exactly what Yeats had so strenuously devoted
himself to disproving. And in 1922 he seemed right, and Eglinton
wrong. It was all working out very well – even if the President of the
new Free State was his old enemy Arthur Griffith. The same day as
that letter about making their unpopular deeds shine with patriotic fire,
Yeats sent an equally frank letter to AE:

> I am by constitution a pessimist & never thought they would get so
> much out of Lloyd George & so am pleased nor am I distressed to
> see Madame Markiewicz and other emotional ladies among the non-
> jurors. I expect to see Griffith, now that he is the universal target,
> grow almost mellow and become the fanatic of broad-mindedness
> and accuracy of statement. Hitherto he has fired at the coconuts but
> now that he is a coconut himself he may become milky.[42]

Thus the poet who had no gift to set a statesman right, and who
assured Haldane that he had neither interest in nor aptitude for politics:
and whose dislike of Pearse and enmity to Griffith had been so well
attested in 1914. He even held high hopes that Griffith would make
him Minister for Fine Arts in the new government, and began to plan
how he would apply art to industry, as in Germany: a prospect he
found very tempting. Griffith had more sense than to make Yeats a
minister, but he was appointed a senator, carried out a number of
discreet government missions (notably during the Civil War that
followed), cultivated key ministers like Desmond FitzGerald, Ernest
Blythe and Kevin O'Higgins, and immediately took his place at the
head of prestige cultural events such as the Irish Race Convention and
the Tailteann Games: the cultural comissar of the new order.

Yeats had won his war. His poetry and prose continued to cast an
eye (sometimes cold, sometimes not) back over the events of the Anglo-
Irish War. But in common with so many other Irish people, he practised
a deliberate amnesia about the 1914–18 war which had done so much
to create the conditions for the Irish revolution. In 1928 he famously

---

[41] *Dial*, February 1922.

[42] 12 Jan. 1922, Harry Ransom Humanities Research Center, University of Texas,
Austin.

turned down Sean O'Casey's play about the World War, *The Silver Tassie*, because it seemed to him a subject irrelevant to O'Casey's genius (he told O'Casey that while he had written about the Irish war out of passionate involvement, 'you are not really interested in the Great War', a pronouncement O'Casey ventured, not unreasonably, to contradict[43]). And in the 1930s Yeats excluded most of the First World War poets from his Oxford anthology of modern verse on the grounds that 'passive suffering is not a subject for poetry' . But the path he had followed through those years of European chaos was both a complicated and a self-conscious one, realising throughout the necessity to write himself into the events which were building to revolution all around him and emerging in a position which would have seemed – to say the least -unlikely, considering the political and ideological position he had occupied in 1914.

The same was true of many of his compatriots – not least Arthur Griffith, the newly milky coconut who was suddenly President of Dáil Éireann. But Yeats stands as a powerfully absorbing exemplar of the Irish propensity to therapeutic forgetting: the ability to change footing and gloss over the past. Contemporaries recognised it too. In the heady days of the new state the writer James Stephens recorded a conversation with Griffith. He wanted, reading between the lines, to find out what kind of politician the new President was, and what qualities had enabled him to survive the revolution and emerge at its head. Stephens approached the issue by addressing a hypothetical question.

> 'If by touching a button you could kill a person in China and get all his goods without fear of detection or punishment either here or in hell, would you touch the button?'
> Mr Griffith laughed, but focussed the problem.
> 'I would not touch the button', he averred.
> 'Would Connolly?" I urged. 'Or Montgomery? Or Gogarty?'
> 'Yeats would', said Mr Griffith.[44]

[43] This celebrated exchange was published in *The Observer*, 3 June 1928, and subsequently *The Irish Statesman*. For a discussion of the issues see Garry O'Connor, *Sean O'Casey: A Life* (1988), 246–50.
[44] *Review of Reviews*, 65, no. 317 (March 1922).

THE IMPACT OF NAPOLEON III ON BRITISH
POLITICS, 1851–1880

By J. P. Parry

READ 20 OCTOBER 2000 AT THE UNIVERSITY OF EXETER[1]

NAPOLEON BONAPARTE'S nephew Louis Napoleon was elected President of the French Republic in December 1848. Faced with an obstructive Legislative Assembly, he mounted a *coup d'état* in December 1851 and restored universal suffrage in a new constitution, which was ratified overwhelmingly by plebiscite. The Second Empire was born when another plebiscite in November 1852 granted him the title of Emperor. Napoleon III presided over France until her defeat by Prussia in September 1870 drove him from power and into exile in England, where he died in 1873.

This paper is not about Napoleon III but about the effect of his rule on British politics. It argues that British reaction to him, and to French and European politics more generally, had a profound influence on domestic mid-Victorian political culture. In the 1850s and 1860s, British politicians, the media and public opinion were at their most self-confident about Britain's stability and economic success. They attributed these achievements largely to Britain's constitutional arrangements, which they contrasted pointedly with those in operation on the continent. France was invoked particularly frequently as an example of a badly structured polity. I want to argue that, primarily through this comparison, British national identity became sharply defined in political debate. But another crucial component of national self-confidence was Britain's apparent ability to influence European affairs. Ironically, this depended on maintaining an informal alliance with Napoleon III and France. This created great ambiguity in the response to the Second Empire, which was heightened by the desire of the City and most commercial opinion to cultivate good relations with Napoleon in order to ward off the threat of war and to exploit economic opportunities in France. So it is important to bear in mind that by no means all British reactions to Napoleon III were negative ones. A number of intellectuals,

[1] Professor Derek Beales and Dr James Thompson commented helpfully on an early draft of this paper.

for example, suggested that Britain had much to learn from the French.[2] Nor did Napoleon, thrice an exile in Britain, wish to antagonise her. But my argument is that the negative views of him were the ones that mattered most in politics. In particular, stereotypes of Napoleonic France were very important in explaining why mid-Victorian politics were dominated not just by the Liberal party but by a particular type of Liberalism, emphasising constitutional, moral and patriotic issues. So one sub-theme of the paper is that historians of British politics can benefit from placing their subject in a wider European context – and that the European context was at least as important in shaping British public debate at this time as the imperial and global context.

There are four stages to my argument. I start by exploring the reasons for British suspicion of France before the advent of the Second Empire. Then I consider the specific additional criticisms made of Napoleon's regime after 1851, and the fears expressed about it. Third, and at greatest length, I look at the impact of these criticisms on British politics from 1851 to 1870. Finally, I consider briefly the way in which political debate after Napoleon's fall in 1870 continued to be influenced by the concepts and fears that I have discussed. Each of these stages is divided into two parts. The first part assesses the situation in foreign and defence policy; the second looks at more purely domestic issues. By making this division I aim to bring out more clearly the paradox that a successful British foreign policy usually depended on co-operation with the French but that a leitmotif of British domestic politics was simplistic opposition to 'continental' constitutional habits.

I

At a diplomatic level, the relationship between Britain and France was necessarily dominated by their age-old rivalry and recent prolonged warfare. Palmerston did not doubt that France's greatest goal was 'the humbling of England, the traditional Rival of France, and the main obstacle to French supremacy in Europe and all over the world'.[3] Most of Britain's European influence was exercised in the Mediterranean, where France was her major threat. In Spain in the 1830s and again in the East in the 1850s, a military alliance with France was undertaken as much to prevent her gaining undue advantage in those areas as to

[2] Matthew Arnold is perhaps the best example. It is also important to point out how profoundly some liberals and radicals disliked the increased respect which Napoleon III received from society, business and the press after the 1860 Commercial Treaty – a dislike that was caustically expressed in A.V. Dicey, 'Louis Napoleon: 1851 and 1873', *Fortnightly Review*, 13 (Jan.–June 1873), 197–204.

[3] 1863: R. Millman, *British Foreign Policy and the Coming of the Franco-Prussian War* (Oxford, 1965), 116.

check Russia. Similarly it was the French threat to Northern Italy as much as the Austrian presence there which determined Britain's Italian policy for over twenty years. On top of these strategic anxieties there was a distinct latent psychological fear of French aggression and indeed invasion. This was the legacy of the intense wartime propaganda of the 1800s which warned that Napoleon Bonaparte's invading French mobs would sweep away private property, individual freedom and Protestant religion in an orgy of criminality and uncontrolled animal passion.[4] British public life in the 1850s was dominated by men over whose youths the Bonapartist shadow had fallen.

Despite this instinctive suspicion, however, Britain needed informal understandings with France in order to have the influence in international politics that the public and press expected. Palmerston argued that Britain should choose her allies according to the damage that they could do her in war, and that co-operation with France was the only way to prevent her from 'realising her vast schemes of extension and aggression'.[5] Moreover, French support was a counter-weight to the influence of the 'Northern' or 'Eastern' autocracies, Russia, Austria and Prussia, which would otherwise dominate the continent diplomatically and ideologically. And in the Mediterranean it was important for the British fleet not to be at odds with both France and Russia. All in all, when France was an ally, as in the Spanish Civil War of the 1830s or the Crimean War, Britain might hope to cut a dash in Europe, but otherwise not.[6] Disraeli described Anglo-French concord as 'the key and corner-stone of modern civilization'.[7] Advocates of that concord did not always go unchallenged in British policy-making, but until the 1860s theirs was the dominant official view.

Yet the difficulty of maintaining this pro-French policy can be seen once we turn to consider British public perceptions of French domestic politics. In early and mid-Victorian England, the major continental regimes were very commonly seen as autocratic, heavily centralised and – owing to the presence of large standing armies – militaristic. Representative assemblies and local authorities seemed to have little power. Secret police activities, restrictions on press freedom, and the dominant position of an intolerant (usually Catholic) priesthood ensured

---

[4] S. Cottrell, 'The Devil On Two Sticks: Franco-Phobia In 1803', in *Patriotism: The Making And Unmaking of British National Identity*, ed. R. Samuel (3 vols., 1989), I, 267–8.

[5] M. F. Urban, *British Opinion and Policy on the Unification of Italy 1856–1861* (New York, 1938), 355–6; D. F. Krein, *The Last Palmerston Government: Foreign Policy, Domestic Politics, And The Genesis of Splendid Isolation* (Ames, Ia, 1978), 21–2.

[6] Clarendon, 1864, in J. K. Laughton, *Memoirs of the Life and Correspondence of Henry Reeve* (2 vols., 1898) II, 103.

[7] 9 Feb. 1858, *Hansard['s Parliamentary Debates*, third series], 148, 1060. See also W. E. Gladstone, 'Germany, France, and England', *Edinburgh Review*, 132 (Oct. 1870), 574.

that political and religious liberty was at a discount.[8] In contrast, the general perception, at least among the propertied classes, was that the British Crown was accountable to a parliament which was always on guard against high taxes and military aggrandisement. Crown and parliament both operated within a venerable framework of laws and conventions. Local authority powers were extensive and jealously defended; so were religious toleration and personal and press liberty. At one level or other, political participation – citizenship – was extensive and seemed to give great strength to the regime. Liberties were underpinned by general acquiescence in the rule of law. By the early 1840s, these assumptions were ingrained in British parliamentary argument. There is, of course, a major issue as to how far extra-parliamentary radicals accepted them, and with what qualifications.

However, the point to stress is that the events of the 1840s intensified this sense of British constitutional distinctness and made it the most significant element in political constructions of national identity over the following twenty years – in the process blunting the radical challenge.[9] Britain's self-confidence as an economic power was enhanced by the repeal of the Corn Laws in 1846, the remarkable global dominance attained by British manufacturing products in the 1850s and the spread of responsible government in the white settler colonies at the same time. These developments seemed to demonstrate the benefits of free trade, a libertarian constitution and a Protestant religion encouraging individual responsibility. The European revolutions of 1848 left the British political system largely unscathed but produced a continent split between the forces of repression and republicanism. It became commonplace to praise Britain's political achievement by contrasting it with the reinstatement of autocratic government in most major European states after 1848.[10] *Punch* published two cartoons, 'John Bull showing the foreign powers how to make a constitutional plum pudding' and 'There is no place like home', which graphically illustrate this sentiment.[11]

France occupied a particularly central role in British perceptions of the constitutional failings of the continental regimes. Though the Eastern powers appeared more monolithic in their absolutism, they

[8] B. Porter, '"Bureau and Barrack": Early Victorian Attitudes towards the Continent', *Victorian Studies*, 27 (1983–4), 407–33.

[9] On the radicals, see G. Claeys, 'Mazzini, Kossuth, and British Radicalism, 1848–1854', *Journal of British Studies*, 28 (1989), 225–61.

[10] See e.g. S. Laing, *Observations on the Social and Political State of the European People in 1848 and 1849* (1850); *Manchester Guardian*, 1851, quoted in A. Briggs, *Victorian People: a Reassessment of Persons and Themes, 1851–67* (Harmondsworth, 1965 edn), 57–8; Palmerston, 25 June 1850, *Hansard*, 112, 443; Albemarle, 3 Feb. 1852, *Hansard*, 119, 5–6; H. Reeve, 'Earl Grey on Parliamentary Government', *Edinburgh Review*, 108 (July 1858), 272.

[11] *Punch*, 15, 267, 23 Dec. 1848, and 16, 27–30, 20 Jan. 1849.

John Bull showing the foreign powers how to make a constitutional plum-pudding. Punch,
23 December 1848.

were more distant, less familiar and less immediately threatening.
Nothing contributed more to the British sense of political achievement
than, firstly, the French Revolution of 1789, and secondly, France's
continual oscillation thereafter between monarchy or empire on the
one hand and revolution and 'anarchy' on the other. It was not just
1789 and 1799, but 1830, 1848, 1851, 1870 and 1871 which ensured that
the British public remained so smug about the quiescence of their own
regime. Powerful images, for example from Carlyle's *French Revolution*
(1837) or Madame Tussaud's Chamber of Horrors (permanently housed
in London from 1835), underlined the contrast. The two centrepieces
of the Chamber of Horrors were a real guillotine from Paris, and
Marat – described in the programme as that 'execrable wretch' – after
being stabbed in his bath, while there were also death-heads of the
'sanguinary demagogue' Robespierre and the king and queen.[12] This
was truly an anti-revolutionary exhibition.

There was no shortage of punditry discussing the reasons for French
political instability, and a consensus emerged that the problem was
the over-centralisation of power. The lack of vigorous local political
structures, the destruction of the old aristocracy and the despotism of

[12] *Biographical and descriptive sketches of the distinguished characters which compose the ... exhibition
of Madame Tussaud and sons* (1844), 27–8.

Bonaparte meant that there was a severe shortage of intermediate
institutions between the state and the individual.[13] The Revolution had
greatly reduced the clergy's sphere of influence, weakening the sense of
morality, while changes to property law encouraged a selfish individualism rather than the mutual dependence engendered by the
English trust system.[14] The French people lacked experience and
education in self-government.[15] They could be distracted by material
bribes, sensation or talk of military glory, and failed to see through
utopian dogma. So parties stood for power either on abstract and
unworkable general principles or by appealing to the average avaricious
Frenchman's lust for national grandeur and the seizure of property.
French politics were thus dominated by passion rather than reason
and by the clash of irreconcilable economic principles. Intolerant
of despotism, the French were unsuited to freedom; instability was
inevitable.[16]

II

What impact did Napoleon III's rise to power have on these assumptions
about, on the one hand, France's role in Europe and on the other, her
constitutional instability? The dominant British view was that his regime
would stand or fall depending on whether he could revive his uncle's
glory. His domestic position was necessarily insecure; like all emperors,
he could prosper only by pursuing an assertive and successful policy
abroad.[17] The sensual tastes of the French public would also demand
action, and this would destabilise Europe. Ultimately he was bound to
want, and need, to avenge the great humiliation of Waterloo by turning
to attack England. His sphinx-like silences, and his colourful past,
added to the alarm of the liberal and conservative establishments:
Prince Albert said that he was 'a walking lie' – 'once a conspirator,
always a conspirator'.[18] It was impossible to tell what he was planning,

[13] *Punch*, 15, 266, 23 Dec. 1848; Gladstone, 'Germany, France, and England', 576–80;
J.H. Hippisley, 'The Realities of Paris', *Westminster Review*, 17 (Jan. 1860), 59; H. Reeve,
'France', *Edinburgh Review*, 133 (Jan. 1871), 1–32.

[14] H. Reeve, 'France', *Edinburgh Review*, 133 (Jan. 1871), 16–20.

[15] Sarah Austin, 1848, in J. Ross, *Three Generations of Englishwomen: Memoirs and Correspondence of Mrs John Taylor, Mrs Sarah Austin, and Lady Duff Gordon* (2 vols., 1888), I, 218.

[16] Laing, *Observations*, ch. 7; *The Collected Works of Walter Bagehot*, VIII, ed. N. St. John
Stevas (1974), 183; George Eliot, 1870, in C. Campos, *The View of France from Arnold to
Bloomsbury* (1965), 50; D. Duncan, *The Life and Letters of Herbert Spencer* (1908), 155; J.C.
Morison, 'The Abortiveness of French Revolutions', *Fortnightly Review*, 14 (July 1873), 41–
53.

[17] As the *Times* put it, imperialism needed to demonstrate 'perpetual youth and strength':
13 Jan. 1873, 9. For Bagehot s view in 1867, see *Collected Works*, VIII, 175.

[18] Urban, *British Opinion*, 128, 358.

except that his goals were personal and dynastic advancement rather than the good of the nation. He was willing to use the language of the Rights of Man and the human brotherhood to advance his personal purposes in Italy – to the horror of conservatives – but at the same time most radicals did not believe that someone so despotic, and so dynastic in his ambitions, could be genuine in speaking that language.

Thus suspicion of Napoleon's foreign policy was endemic in Britain. British attitudes to the domestic basis of Napoleon's regime were equally strongly held. Commentators had three major causes for complaint against his system. These produced a powerful stereotype that lasted, in most cases, until the end of his reign.

The first criticism was of the oppression and violence on which Napoleon's power seemed to be founded, especially because of the *coup d'état* of December 1851. At the time of the *coup*, Palmerston, most of the political elite, and many businessmen welcomed it as the best chance for France to recover stability. But the killings passed into legend, often in grossly exaggerated form. For example, A.W. Kinglake's history of 1863, *The Invasion of the Crimea*, recycled the widely believed stories of deliberate mass shootings, torture, transportation and starvation. It rather pedantically identified 'nine kinds of slaughter', suggesting that up to 50,000 may have been killed, as against the soberer estimates of a couple of hundred.[19] (Kinglake, incidentally, had a personal grudge against Napoleon, who, when living in exile in England, had stolen his mistress.) At the time of the *coup*, there was particular shock that fourteen people were shot when hiding behind a carpet that only a few months previously had been admired by the queen herself at the Great Exhibition. Like many who had friends in the Parisian intelligentsia, Dickens never forgave 'the cold-blooded scoundrel at the head of France – or on it',[20] and his *A Tale of Two Cities* (1859) can be seen as a commentary on the dehumanising effects of French state oppression. There was a similarly horrified reaction in England in 1858 to the news that Montalembert had been arrested and tried for publishing a pamphlet which praised English institutions and political culture at the expense of French ones. Napoleon seemed to have no respect for constitutional traditions or press and personal liberties.

A second source of English concern about Napoleon's regime was

---

[19] A.W. Kinglake, *The Invasion of the Crimea; its Origin, and an account of its Progress Down to the Death of Lord Raglan* (8 vols., 1863–87), I, ch. 14, esp. 277, 282. See also e.g. M.S. Hardcastle, *Life of John, Lord Campbell* (2 vols., 1881), II, 299.

[20] 14 Jan. 1852, *The Letters of Charles Dickens*, ed. G. Storey *et al.* (11 vols. to date, Oxford, 1965–99), VI, 575. Dickens and his admirers were greatly offended when in December 1858 a photograph of him on display in a Paris shop was removed by the authorities who, looking at the less than attractive man, thought that it was a wicked caricature of Napoleon III: *ibid.*, VIII, 576 n.3.

that, while oppressive, it was based on universal suffrage; his appeal to the mob allowed him to crush educated criticism. *The Times* commented that 'with all its purple and gold the Imperial Government was heir to the Communistic notions of the Red Republican regime', while Brougham remarked: Napoleon is 'still a socialist in practice'.[21] This combination of autocracy and democracy seemed to symbolise the historical peculiarity and problem of French politics and marked imperialism out as an example to avoid.

This was all the more so because of the third complaint against the Second Empire, the moral corruption of the regime and its destabilising effect on French character, which was already prone, as we saw, to self-indulgence and money-worship. Napoleon's power seemed to rest on unscrupulous flatterers; there were too few men of 'public virtue'.[22] His government gave favours and lavish contracts to businessmen and stockjobbers, something that was particularly distasteful to landed or intellectual English critics of the growth of commercialism. Taxpayers' money was wasted on superficial embellishments to the capital. Such extravagance did not promote solid prosperity; the unrestrained and impatient materialism of the Parisians created a culture of conspicuous consumption, of 'luxury and profligacy', and their city became the 'paradise of the *nouveau riche* and the *demi-monde*'.[23] Because France was so centralised, depraved Paris – described by Freeman as 'a collection of shops and stuck-up people, with the Tyrant's house in the middle'[24] – set the cultural tone for the country. Luxury, mixed with egalitarian ideology, 'brutified' the public sphere and destroyed discipline in the army.[25]

Most commentators took the view that the failings of Bonapartism were ultimately caused by its obsession with the advancement of one man and his dynasty. The system of 'personal rule' was unchecked, arbitrary and self-indulgent; it lacked principle, scruple and public spirit; it spawned materialism and false national pride.[26]

---

[21] *The Times*, 10 Jan. 1873, 7–8; Brougham, 1859, in Laughton, *Reeve*, II, 23.

[22] *The Times*, 11 Jan. 1873, 8; Gladstone, 'Germany, France, and England', 578.

[23] A. Hayward, 'The Personal History of Imperialism in 1870', *Fraser's Magazine*, 2 (Nov. 1870), 638–9; Marquess of Salisbury, 'Political Lessons of the War', *Quarterly Review*, 130 (Jan. 1871), 261; Dicey, 'Louis Napoleon'.

[24] 1861: W.R.W. Stephens, *The Life and Letters of Edward A. Freeman* (2 vols., 1895), I, 295–6.

[25] A.V. Kirwan, *Modern France: its Journalism, Literature and Society* (1863), 356; Hayward, 'Personal History of Imperialism', 640; W.R. Greg, 'Suum cuique: 'The Moral of the Paris Catastrophe', *Fraser's Magazine*, 4 (July 1871), 127.

[26] Kirwan, *Modern France*, vii; F. Greenwood, 'Louis Napoleon', in *The Napoleon Dynasty; or, History of the Bonaparte Family, by the Berkeley Men and Another* (1853); *Spectator* and *Times*, 1870, quoted in D. Raymond, *British Policy and Opinion During the Franco-Prussian War* (1921), 74. Of course, some Englishmen applauded the notion of strong leadership by a Carlylean

The need to secure dynastic survival led to a concentration on foreign adventure and prestige as a distraction from domestic taxes and oppression, but an expensive external policy further disrupted trade and increased expenditure, thus requiring ever more desperate throws of the foreign policy dice: this was the 'relentless logic of a false position'.[27]

'Personal rule' and the 'assertion of absolute force over others', at home and abroad, was what the mid-Victorians usually meant when they used the word 'imperialism'.[28] This was the antithesis of the widespread participation in a political community that secured stability and strengthened man's moral integrity. Much of the British commentary on Napoleon's regime took the form of a comparison with the most famous of Empires, the Roman Empire, the decay of which was generally blamed on materialism, decadence, public extravagance and the pursuit of false glory. Of course Victorian attitudes to ancient Rome were very ambivalent. Rome was credited with practical genius and the spread of law, civilisation and Christianity to distant lands, and many classically educated mid-Victorians saw the British as the modern Romans in those regards.[29] Indeed, Palmerston's most famous oration, on the Don Pacifico debate in 1850, exploited the comparison. But this was not to say that Britain's external policy should emulate Roman imperial practice, and it is a sign of the innate anxiety that such practice might poison British life that Palmerston's critics in that debate immediately twisted his 'civis Romanus sum' allusion so as to suggest an alarming empathy with a 'conquering race' and 'an exceptional system of law'.[30] Criticisms of Napoleon III's domestic and Mexican

---

moral hero. However, Carlyle and his followers despised Napoleon III more than most: e.g. L. Huxley, *Life and Letters of Thomas Henry Huxley* (3 vols., 1903 edn), I, 334, 336.

[27] See Salisbury in 1860 and 1871: P. Smith, *Lord Salisbury on Politics: A Selection from his Articles in the Quarterly Review, 1860–1883* (Cambridge, 1972), 129–30; 'Political Lessons'.

[28] R. Lowe, 'Imperialism', *Fortnightly Review*, 24 (Oct. 1878), 458.

[29] See e.g. Lady Eastlake, 1858, quoted in J. Pemble, *The Mediterranean Passion: Victorians and Edwardians in the South* (Oxford, 1987), 64.

[30] Gladstone, 27 June 1850, *Hansard*, 112, 585–6. Gladstone admitted that he was not opposed to the idea that Britain had a 'duty' on occasion to exercise influence to encourage the development in other countries of 'institutions akin to those of which we know from experience the inestimable blessings'; rather, he objected to doing so in a spirit of arrogance and national pride, and in opposition to the 'principles of public law' (*ibid.*, 582). This, in Gladstone's eyes, was the difference between an English and an imperial policy. Palmerston, however, had argued that intervention of one sort or another was the norm for major powers, so Britain was merely standing up for her interests and principles. Palmerston's use of the Roman comparison was presumably intended to imply no more than that Britain should be ready to act as an arbiter of justice as she defined it. However, he was distinctly sympathetic, by generation and upbringing, to the propagation of classical cultural values in public life – as is shown, among other things,

policy drew heavily on imperial Roman comparisons; during the Montalembert affair the *Daily Telegraph* called him 'the Tiberius of the Tuileries'.[31] And several writers pointed out that the French, like the Romans, had an insatiable desire to dominate and conquer Europe and 'give law' to it.[32] One author, in 1861, argued that England's policy should be 'the working out, on the large field of European history, of that protest against imperialism, political and sacerdotal, on which the constitution of England has been built'.[33] In other words, despite their glorious past services to Europe, the contemporary legacy of the Roman Empire and its child the papacy was a negative one: the continued influence of Caesarist secular practices and Ultramontane ecclesiastical power.[34] In state and in church affairs, a small group of men placed themselves above the law and wielded excessive influence over the lives and thoughts of peoples. As the first country to declare national independence against this system, England's mission was to demonstrate to European public opinion the advantage of political and ecclesiastical self-government.

III

What effects did Napoleon's European policy have on British politics? In the dozen years after 1848, public self-confidence at Britain's ability to shape foreign affairs grew to an all-time high. This was partly because of the beneficial political and economic circumstances outlined earlier, but also because of the disarray of the Eastern powers and the unrivalled opportunities that this threw up for British naval and diplomatic assertiveness – particularly in the Crimea, China and Italy. In addition, the British claimed most of the credit for, and much of the advantage from, the substantial lowering of tariffs in most parts of Western and Central Europe throughout the 1860s. But in all four of these instances, British achievement was crucially dependent on the goodwill of Napoleon III. France supplied the bulk of the soldiers necessary to win the Crimean War, and bore the brunt of the casualties. French diplomatic and military support helped Britain to victory in

---

by his doughty defence of a classical design for the Foreign Office. Incidentally, both he and Gladstone compared the Second Empire to Augustan Rome, neither very censoriously: see F. C. Palm, *England and Napoleon III: A Study in the Rise of a Utopian Dictator* (Durham, NC, 1948), 171, and L.A. Tollemache, *Talks With Mr Gladstone* (1898), 118.

[31] *The Daily Telegraph*, 26 Nov. 1858, 4.

[32] E. A. Freeman, *General Sketch of European History* (1872), 351, 365; Freeman, 'The Panic and its Lessons', *Macmillan's Magazine*, 24 (May 1871), 2; Hayward, 'Personal history of imperialism', 637.

[33] A. H. Louis, *England And Europe: A Discussion of National Policy* (1861), 353.

[34] *Ibid*, 349.

China in 1857–8. It was Napoleon III who ended the stalemate on the Italian question in 1859, setting in motion the train of events that was to create an Italian state respectful of the British constitutional legacy and open to British naval and commercial influence. And it was Napoleon's willingness to sign a commercial treaty with Britain in 1860 which made it necessary for other European countries to make similar agreements among themselves in the following few years.

Despite Napoleon's assistance in all these respects, British public debate in the 1850s was dominated by vehement distrust of his practices and ambitions. This was usually expressed with strident national self-confidence, as in the *Saturday Review*, which made its name and that of its young polemicists like Harcourt in the process. Occasionally, however, panic took over. Napoleon's *coup* of December 1851 sparked off an invasion scare, exacerbated by anxiety at the recent development of steam-powered ships which potentially threatened Britain's naval superiority. The scare led directly or indirectly to the fall of two British governments in 1852, Russell's Whig ministry, when its militia bill was criticised as inadequate, and then the minority Conservative government, in December 1852, after increases in defence expenditure made its budget unattractive. Those – mainly Liberals – who regarded the ending of the Crimean War in 1856 as premature, leaving Russia free to oppress her subject peoples, tended to blame Napoleon for it. Then, in 1858–9, there was a second, longer-lasting crisis. After an attempted assassination of Napoleon planned by Italian patriots living in England, French colonels urged their government to take action against the dens of conspirators across the Channel. This created alarm in the English press, which was fuelled by the completion of the enormous naval base at Cherbourg, and by the building of the first French ironclad battleship. In February 1859 the minority Conservative government announced an increase of naval spending in response to this and the developments in Italy, where Napoleon was fomenting Piedmontese challenges to Austrian rule in Lombardy and Venetia. Austria declared war on Piedmont in late April and Napoleon placed 200,000 men in Italy in eight weeks. This created a crisis in the City of London, led to the formation of volunteer corps up and down the country and contributed to the fall of the Conservative government in June 1859.

Politically there were two major casualties of these panics of 1852 and 1859. The first were the Cobdenite radicals who had seemed poised for great influence after the Repeal of the Corn Laws. They were damaged for two reasons: their association with the cause of peace at a time of anxiety about defence, and the ease with which their opponents could accuse them of an anti-patriotic commercialism. Napoleon's *coup* and the fear of French attack dealt a severe blow to

Cobden's attempt to turn the retrenchment issue into an effective radical cause.[35] Radicalism lost its way, while its opponents were able to cast Cobdenites and Peace Society men as scapegoats for Britain's vulnerability. Alarms were voiced that a preference for taxpayer benefit over national virtue and honour had infected British public life in recent decades and weakened Britain's ability to cope with the autocratic continental threat. The 'commercial classes' were blamed – though in fact politicians of all shades were responsible for the emphasis on tax and tariff cuts since 1815 and the lack of interest in army or navy reform, and in this they undoubtedly reflected public opinion. The Peace Society, revivified in 1848, took years to recover from this negative publicity of 1852–3, as the invasion scare was followed rapidly by the Crimean crisis.[36] Some of the journalists and military men who did most to work up the panic were consciously engaged in an ideological and moral crusade against commercialism. For example, Henry Reeve of *The Times* justified his scaremongering writings by arguing that 'this nation is a good deal enervated by a long peace, by easy habits of intercourse, by peace societies and false economy'.[37] Though no scaremonger, Disraeli emphasised from now until his death the damage done to a patriotic foreign policy by the dominance of 'the commercial principle' in English public life.[38]

But the other casualties were the Conservatives, who were very unlucky that their only brief tenures of office in the twenty years after 1846 occurred during periods of high tension with France. The invasion scares of 1852 and 1859 ruined Disraeli's attempt to formulate budgets that would forge a compromise between town and country interests, draw the sting from the fiscal issue and rid the Conservatives of their sectional and backward-looking protectionist image. Instead, by removing Disraeli from office, the scares gave Gladstone the chance to gain the political prize for a new mid-Victorian fiscal compromise in his budgets of 1853 and 1860, the foundation of his political success.[39]

---

[35] M. Taylor, *The Decline of British Radicalism, 1847–1860* (Oxford, 1995), 216–18.

[36] D. Nicholls, 'Richard Cobden and the International Peace Congress Movement, 1848–1853', *Journal of British Studies*, 30 (1991), 351–76.

[37] Laughton, *Reeve*, 1, 251–3. Though critical of the *Times*'s fervour, Clarendon could only agree on the need to 'rouse our countrymen from the apathetic habits and utilitarian selfishness engendered by a long peace': *ibid.*, 1, 258. Similarly in 1859–60 it was easy to accuse the Cobdenites of 'un-English' attitudes because of their advocacy of a speedy passage for the French commercial treaty at a time when Napoleon III seemed to be using the treaty to try to divert attention from his annexation of Savoy. Hence the storm over Bright's provocative declaration to the Commons, 'Perish Savoy'. For Manners' speech on this, see Urban, *British Opinion*, 404. For Ruskin's criticism of commercial non-interventionists in Italy, see *ibid.*, 208–9.

[38] J.P. Parry, 'Disraeli and England', *Historical Journal*, 43 (2000), 716–23.

[39] *Ibid.*, 711–12.

In both 1852 and 1859, the Conservatives had to increase defence estimates substantially – by £800,000 in 1852 and £1m in 1859. Though Disraeli was a vigorous advocate of cheap defence and good relations with Napoleon III, other Conservatives, especially from an older generation or military backgrounds, overruled him, with the crucial support of Prime Minister Derby. They did so partly because the panics were founded on the perception that parliamentary government was vulnerable in the face of continental autocracy; therefore a weak government found it particularly necessary to over-compensate by a show of defensive vigour.[40] In 1852, the case for increased defence spending was also strengthened by the emotion surrounding the funeral of the duke of Wellington, the great Conservative chief and vanquisher of Bonaparte.

In 1859, the Conservatives had another problem as well, the Italian question. Liberals came together in opposition to Conservative foreign policy because, despite internal differences on how far to *intervene* in favour of Italy, they could agree that the Conservatives' partiality to Austria was endangering Britain's neutrality and position in Europe, and risked a descent into war.[41] The Conservatives had declared too strongly their sympathies for the status quo, for the autocratic Europe of 1815, and thus had encouraged Austria to think that she could attack Piedmont without triggering British anger.[42] But they had also not been forceful enough in warning Napoleon against entering the war.[43] In consequence they looked unpatriotically weak and anti-liberal. In this respect, again, the Conservatives were the victims of bad timing, as the signing of the treaty of Villafranca by Austria and France in July 1859 showed. This treaty appeared to reveal Napoleon in his true colours as an autocrat who shared with Austria the concern to prop up the pope and the forces of reaction in Italy, suppressing liberty.[44] As a result, the new Liberal government had the chance, for the first time in years, to encourage Italian liberalism without playing into the hands of Britain's rivals there. Italy became an ideal issue for Liberals, allowing them to combine national assertiveness with the defence of self-government, and to marry a commitment to constitutional liberalism with a triumphant hostility to France, Austria and the papacy.

[40] See e.g. Sir H. Maxwell, *The Life and Letters of George William Frederick Fourth Earl of Clarendon* (2 vols., 1913), I, 350; Laughton, *Reeve*, II, 13.
[41] See various speakers (e.g. Bury, Palmerston, Bright, Russell) in the debate on the Address, 7, 9, 10 June 1859, *Hansard*, 154, 98, 193, 297.
[42] Urban, *British Opinion*, 190–1.
[43] Lord Stanmore, *Sidney Herbert Lord Herbert of Lea: A Memoir* (2 vols., 1906), II, 166; A.I. Dasent, *John Thadeus Delane Editor of 'The Times': His Life and Correspondence* (2 vols., 1908), I, 310.
[44] See, for example, the cartoon, 'Free Italy (?)', in *Punch*, 37, 37, 23 July 1859.

Bow-wow!! Punch, 19 November 1859.

Thus the events of 1852 and 1859 benefited mainly the Liberals, and in 1859, under Palmerston, they began fifteen years of Liberal dominance of British politics. Palmerston's new government benefited from three policies in particular – the strong show of vigorous support for Italy discussed above, and two others, an active defence programme, and a Commercial Treaty with France designed to demonstrate good relations between the two powers. Though all three policies emerged only after some internal controversy, each proved capable of cementing a broad party and public coalition.

Palmerston's self-consciously patriotic defence policy embraced naval expansion, dockyard fortifications and subsidies to the volunteers. There was broad agreement in favour of naval expansion, specifically technological innovation: four more ironclads were planned in November 1859, to make six in all. This would restore supremacy at sea and make it clear to Napoleon that it would be suicidal for France to attempt to challenge that supremacy. Confidence soon returned that the naval race had been won.[45] Keeping Napoleon in check in this way

[45] M.J. Salevouris, *'Riflemen form': The War Scare of 1859–1860 in England* (New York, 1982), ch. 5. Napoleon's annexation of Nice and Savoy in March 1860, though a slight embarrassment to the government in other ways, was of great political benefit in fomenting popular feeling in favour of extensive defensive preparations.

was a genuine and paramount strategic and diplomatic necessity, but it also brought Palmerston great domestic political benefits. He could consolidate his image as a patriotic leader of a broad-bottom government, someone above domestic faction. And it allowed him to find an issue on which to demonstrate his superior reading of English public opinion to that of Gladstone, his chancellor, and Cobden. This was the issue of dockyard fortifications, which Palmerston felt would convince Napoleon of the foolishness of challenging Britain's naval might. After months of resistance, Gladstone had to agree to a four-year fortification programme and increased military estimates.[46] Palmerston airily told the queen that 'it would be better to lose Mr Gladstone than to run the risk of losing Portsmouth or Plymouth'.[47]

The other attractive Liberal policy stance was to claim that British activity in Europe would now concentrate on the peaceful promotion of liberal principles in politics and economics. Having decisively strengthened its defences, the government could seek good relations with Napoleon – without which British influence in Europe would be difficult to exert. The Commercial Treaty of 1860 was a demonstration to domestic opinion that the Anglo-French alliance was an alliance with a particular purpose: to spread the gospel of free trade and commercial intercourse to more benighted parts of Europe. *Punch* showed the schoolmistress Dame Cobden teaching little Napoleon, in shorts, how to spell the word 'F-R-E-E'.[48] Napoleon's embrace of free trade increased his popularity in the City, and suggested to the more supercilious Englishmen that he was willing to accept English tutelage more generally.[49]

Domestically, the emphasis placed on the Commercial Treaty and its effects had two benefits. First, the financial developments pleased Gladstone, Cobden and their followers and helped to prevent a disruption of the Liberal coalition on the defence issue. Second, the suggestion that British commercial and political ideals were slowly penetrating the continent, as a result of British influence in Italy and the sequence of most-favoured-nation trade treaties after 1860, was very useful because it prevented overt tension within the Liberal party on the issue of intervention abroad. There was still continuing scope for disagreement between non-interventionists and those who hoped for a reconstruction of Europe on the basis of constitutional liberalism. But a confidence emerged among Liberal pundits that the spread of

---

[46] E.D. Steele, *Palmerston and Liberalism, 1855–1865* (Cambridge, 1991), 99.

[47] H.C.F. Bell, *Lord Palmerston* (2 vols., 1966 edn), II, 262.

[48] *Punch*, 38, 37, 28 Jan. 1860.

[49] For example, the *Daily News* remarked of the passages on the Papacy in Napoleon's New Year letter of 1860 that he 'takes a liberal, statesmanlike, and we may add, thoroughly English view of the whole question': Urban, *British Opinion*, 348, 351.

Britain's distinctive political and economic values would be met with less and less resistance from the conservative powers, and that constitutional government and free trade would slowly triumph without the need for expensive wars.[50] It was politically very convenient that international and economic circumstances allowed this optimism to survive until after Palmerston's death in 1865 – despite the ominous failure to work well with Napoleon during the crises of 1863 and 1864.

The Liberals, then, gained enormously from Napoleon's European policy. They were the beneficiaries of the optimism about Britain's global influence which Napoleon's assistance facilitated, they developed a patriotic language in response to his apparent challenge, and then the waning of the challenge added still further to British self-confidence. In the early 1860s, with national defence apparently secure, European tariff barriers crumbling before the British commercial advance, and a liberal Italy breaking the bonds of despotism, that self-confidence seemed highly justified.

IV

Napoleon III also cast a significant shadow in Britain because of the ability of politicians to exploit fears that domestic public life might become contaminated by continental, and particularly Bonapartist, values. The French example was seen as something to avoid because it would both jeopardise British constitutional practices and encourage immorality, specifically materialism. There was already, independently, great anxiety about the spread of materialism in British life, not surprisingly, since Britain had traditionally looked to Protestantism and a public-service aristocracy to supply moral leadership but was now an intensely and increasingly commercial society.[51] In such a context, the threat of a *cultural* invasion from across the Channel – from France in particular but the continent in general – created great alarm about an erosion of British morals, just as concern about a *military* invasion spawned fear of material destruction. These cultural fears had effects on political debate in four areas which I shall examine in turn. They did not just affect the Liberal party, but my argument will be that they crucially shaped the approach and tone of mid-Victorian Liberalism.

[50] J. S. Mill, 'A Few Words on Non-Intervention', *Fraser's Magazine*, 60 (Dec. 1859), 766–76; W. R. Greg, 'Principle and No-Principle in Foreign Policy', *National Review*, 13 (July 1861), 241–73; A. H. Layard, 'England's Place in Europe', *Saint Paul's: A Monthly Magazine*, 1 (1867–8), 275–91; M.E.G. Duff, *A Glance Over Europe: Being an Address Delivered at Peterhead on the 19th December 1867* (Edinburgh, 1867), 57.
[51] See J. P. Parry, *Democracy and Religion: Gladstone and the Liberal Party, 1867–1875* (Cambridge, 1986), 31; *Disraeli, Derby and the Conservative Party: Journals and Memoirs of Edward Henry, Lord Stanley 1849–1869*, ed. J. Vincent (Hassocks, 1978), 175.

Moreover, they helped to unite a coalition that was divided on major issues, by demonstrating that those who differed on those issues nonetheless had common objectives.

The first theme was the importance of defending the British Constitution against continental threats to it. Specifically, Palmerston implied that in Britain parliament, and ministers accountable to parliament, checked the potentially overbearing influence of monarchs. He took care that the press knew of his foreign policy differences with Victoria and especially Albert. Favourable newspapers portrayed Palmerston defending British and liberal interests against domestic opponents at Windsor who favoured the continental autocrats. His dismissal as foreign secretary in December 1851 was widely blamed on the interference of the Court.[52] His resignation from the government in 1853 generated a vigorous press campaign suggesting that his brave policy on Russia was being blocked by Albert, the culmination of a long history of the latter's unconstitutional and destructive interference in domestic politics.[53] In 1859, a number of papers printed letters from correspondents apparently alarmed that the Court, dominating a weak and complaisant minority Conservative government, would take Britain into the Italian war on Austria's behalf.[54]

As the beneficiary of widespread suspicion about Albert's 'Germanic' allegiances, Palmerston could paint himself as a vigorous defender of constitutional liberalism, despite his lukewarmness towards further parliamentary reform, and he sought by this means to reassure Reformers and to marginalise the Reform cry. This was playing exactly the same game as his mentor Canning had played in the 1820s in setting himself up as the liberal opponent of the Holy Alliance and George IV's cottage coterie.[55] Self-satisfaction at Britain's apparent stability and prosperity in contrast to Europe further diminished the urgency of Reform. Though much of the contrast was directed at autocracy in general, the ease with which Napoleon, specifically, exploited universal suffrage to entrench his despotism strengthened the case of those who opposed major franchise changes.[56] Moreover, the invasion scares of 1852 and 1859 effectively killed the Reform campaigns of 1848–51 and 1857–9. One line of Tennyson's famous anti-French poem of 1859,

[52] K. Martin, *The Triumph of Lord Palmerston: A Study of Public Opinion in England before the Crimean War* (1963 edn), 70–1.
[53] R. Williams, *The Contentious Crown: Public Discussion of the British Monarchy in the Reign of Queen Victoria* (1997), 100–2, 161–4.
[54] Urban, *British Opinion*, 207.
[55] J. Parry, *The Rise and Fall of Liberal Government in Victorian Britain* (New Haven, 1993), 39–41.
[56] E.g. Wood's views, 1853, quoted by Disraeli and Russell in *Hansard*, 124, 84–5; R. Lowe, *Speeches and letters on Reform* (2nd edn, 1867), 147, 163; (1853) Hardcastle, *Campbell*, II, 299–300, 312.

'Riflemen form!', ran 'Better a rotten borough or so than a rotten fleet and a city in flames!'[57] Of course, many Liberals remained adamantly committed to Reform; hence its rapid re-emergence after Palmerston's death in 1865. But the chauvinistic constitutional quiescence of Palmerston's era continued to influence Liberalism, first in moderating the scope of the party leadership's Reform proposals of 1866 and 1867, and secondly in weakening radical thinkers' interest in French political ideas and gradually strengthening their view that the 'Anglo-Saxon' constitutional virtues of the United States were those from which Britain could most profitably learn.[58]

The second cause which many mid-Victorian Liberals were anxious to defend also stemmed from the celebration of the unique success of the British Constitution. This was the emphasis on maintaining the vigour and freedom of local, municipal and voluntary activity. The rhetoric of local independence, self-government and laissez-faire was at its most potent in British politics in the 1850s and early 1860s. It contributed to a number of setbacks for state-sponsored social reform; the General Board of Health was abolished in 1858 and Russell's resolutions for an education rate were comprehensively defeated in 1856. Much of the parliamentary discussion on such issues concentrated on the importance of avoiding 'un-English' legislation which would betray patriotic values in favour of continental over-centralisation.[59] Haussmann's reconstruction of the Parisian boulevards was used by metropolitan radicals such as Ayrton as a justification for opposing successfully, many of the proposals for expensive new public buildings and road projects in London.[60]

Perhaps the best example of enthusiasm for English voluntary activity was the volunteer movement, which grew rapidly to about 120,000 men between the summer of 1859 and the autumn of 1860.[61] Admiration for the volunteer corps was based on the fact that it seemed so English –

---

[57] See also Clarendon, 3 May 1859, in '*My Dear Duchess': Social and Political Letters to the Duchess of Manchester, 1858–1869*, ed. A.L. Kennedy (1956), 56. Elcho, a keen volunteer and equally keen Adullamite, argued against the need for Reform in 1865 from his experience as a colonel in a working-class volunteer regiment: C.J. Kauffman, 'Lord Elcho, trade unionism and democracy', in *Essays in anti-Labour History: Responses to the Rise of Labour in Britain*, ed. K.D. Brown (1974), 189.

[58] See Goldwin Smith, 'The Experience of the American Commonwealth', in *Essays on Reform* (1867), and H. Tulloch, 'Changing British Attitudes towards the United States in the 1880s', *Historical Journal*, 20 (1977), 825–40.

[59] J. P. Parry, 'Past and Future in the Later Career of Lord John Russell', in *History and Biography: Essays in Honour of Derek Beales*, ed. T. C. W. Blanning and D. Cannadine (Cambridge, 1996), 159–60.

[60] See Ayrton's parliamentary speeches, and M. H. Port, 'A Contrast in Styles at the Office of Works: Layard and Ayrton: Aesthete and Economist', *Historical Journal*, 27 (1984), 151–76.

[61] H. Cunningham, *The Volunteer Force: A Social and Political History, 1859–1908* (1975), 19

in a variety of ways. To many, its attraction was that it sprang from initiatives within the local community, by gentry, employers, university students or philanthropists; it was the very opposite of a threatening standing army maintained by overbearing taxation imposed by a centralised state. Meanwhile, the heartier spirits could agree with *The Times* that the movement fitted the manliness and athleticism of the national character: the newspaper contrasted plucky English youth with 'the students of a French Lycée, strolling two and two along the Quartier Latin, and playing dominoes over their lemonade; or the pupils of a German professor, who accompany their instructor during the holydays in a botanical ramble'.[62]

The volunteer movement had an attractively inclusive appeal that was capable of uniting political groups who differed on other issues. For example, it won supporters from both camps in the foreign policy debate, interventionists and isolationists. Effective national self-defence would help to protect Britain from the instability created by dynastic rivalries and political turbulence on the continent.[63] It would guard against the threat of invasion but also keep defence expenditure down and frustrate militarist scaremongers, something particularly important to radicals.[64] The movement was inclusive also in the sense that men from all classes and political traditions were able to appreciate its social effects. Some radicals liked the republican symbolism of working-class men being trusted to bear arms to defend their community, and a number of volunteer corps modelled themselves on Garibaldi's Redshirts. The Liberal MP George Melly hoped that the movement would train people to habits of self-government and thus to 'a real Liberalism'.[65] But at the same time it strengthened respect for the military life and in many cases demonstrated the continuing importance of hierarchy in English society. Representatives of the local gentry often put themselves at the head of corps, allowing middle-class volunteers to enjoy the privilege of estate hospitality. Young aristocrats who were to play a large part in Liberal cabinets in future – such as Ripon and Spencer – were particularly prominent in the movement, and wanted it to unite the social classes in a common patriotism. So did the Christian Socialists whom these young Liberal aristocrats often admired. Tom Hughes, for example, hoped that it would 'bind the nation

[62] *Ibid.*, 11.
[63] T. Hughes, 'The Volunteer's Catechism, with a Few Words on Butts', *Macmillan's Magazine*, 2 (July 1860), 192.
[64] *Ibid.*; W.H.G. Armytage, *A.J. Mundella 1825–1897: The Liberal Background to the Labour Movement* (1951), 29.
[65] Though he felt that it would also strengthen Conservatism in parliament: *Journals and Memoirs of Stanley*, 164.

together again' after the money-grubbing of recent years had weakened social ties and higher aspirations.[66]

These arguments demonstrate how far the mid-Victorian Liberal party was from being simply a manufacturing party – how important propertied leadership and concerns about character were to its sense of purpose. One anxiety often expressed in mid-Victorian politics was that the moral fibre of the English citizen must be protected against enervation and decadence, and this concern to defend particular moral values was the third area in which mid-Victorian Liberalism could develop a strongly patriotic tone by making continental comparisons. As we saw, there was a long-standing tradition of associating French culture with sensuality, profligacy and effeminacy, and a tendency to define the character of the ideal Englishman in terms of opposition to it – in terms of character, Protestant virtue and individual responsibility. The satirist Wilkie Collins shrewdly observed at this time that 'the morality of England is firmly based on the immorality of France'.[6] This was reflected in contemporary works of historical fiction, not just *A Tale of Two Cities* but also, for example, Kingsley's *Hereward the Wake* (1866), the story of the last English rebellion against the greedy, lawless but disciplined post-Conquest Norman tyranny.

But two dangers for Englishmen to beware were commonly perceived. One was that the more philistine of the upper classes, the potential leaders of England, would be tempted by the sensuality of Paris, which as Carlyle succinctly put it, was 'nothing but a brothel and a gambling hall'.[68] Looking back in 1870, Queen Victoria regretted the effects of 'horrid Paris' on the morals of her sons – with good reason – and concluded that Napoleon's 'frivolous and immoral court did frightful harm to English society'.[69] The other danger was that the 'intensity of our commercial energy' would make the British middle and working classes especially vulnerable to the adoption of 'demoralizing' habits like the 'French Sunday'. If the law allowed businessmen to open their shops and theatres on Sunday, their urge for profit would make them unable to resist the idea, thus exploiting their workmen, disrupting their own family life and diminishing the place for reflection, religion and culture in society.[70]

In other words, the battle against continental morals was also a battle

[66] 'Volunteer's Catechism', 193.
[67] To Dickens: R. Gibson, *Best of Enemies: Anglo-French Relations since the Norman Conquest* (1995), 225.
[68] R. Christiansen, *Tales of the New Babylon: Paris, 1869–1875* (1994), 17.
[69] *Your Dear Letter: Private Correspondence of Queen Victoria and the Crown Princess of Prussia 1865–1871*, ed. R. Fulford (1971), 300.
[70] W. Arthur, *'The People's Day': An Appeal to the Rt. Hon. Lord Stanley MP Against his Advocacy of a French Sunday* (fifth edn, 1855), 14–15, 37.

against the potential sin in the British themselves. This battle was an attractive cause to many mid-Victorian Liberals, who undertook political crusades in defence of moral values which the crusaders regarded as fundamental to the English character and which were being threatened by continental vice or aristocratic complacency at home. The Administrative Reform Association (1855) and later the Bulgarian agitation were examples of such movements which had a clear patriotic dimension. Protestant Dissenters, though not the only participants in such crusades, were often central to them and increasingly influential in Liberal politics more generally; the intensity with which they manifested their Englishness is a subject worthy of further study. Each campaign of this sort was necessarily divisive, and indeed potentially at odds with the dictates of party loyalty, so it would be wrong to suggest that they strengthened the Liberal party in the short term. What they did, however, was to channel religious and patriotic earnestness into the political arena in a way that contributed markedly to the strength of purpose of many provincial Liberals.

A good example of this kind of patriotic campaign is that against the Contagious Diseases Acts. These Acts (of 1864, 1866 and 1869) made possible the compulsory hospitalisation, inspection and detention of prostitutes in garrison towns who were suspected of carrying venereal disease. The regulation of prostitution was well-established in France and Prussia, and the Acts owed a great deal to the admiration in army, medical and social science circles of the effects of regulation on public hygiene and military efficiency in those countries. The extension of the system to eighteen towns, in 1869, was the catalyst for the intensely fought crusade against the Contagious Diseases Acts led by Josephine Butler, which was finally successful in the 1880s. This campaign is much discussed in modern historiography as an assertion of women's equality before the law, and rightly so. But it was an attempt to secure that equality in face of a threat, a 'Continental system of legislating on behalf of vice and against women',[71] which had 'found a footing in our land'. The campaigners against the legislation insisted that it violated the basic principles of the English Constitution, by denying an equal moral and legal standard for men and women. The repealers argued that 'the Napoleonic system' removed guarantees of personal security for women, put their freedom and reputation in the hands of the police, and threatened to brutalise them. At the same time, state regulation of prostitution made 'the path of evil...more easy to our sons'. And it deprived individual citizens of the duty to patrol moral standards themselves, thus weakening the sense of individual responsibility and

[71] J. L. Paton, *John Brown Paton: A Biography* (1914), 133. Paton was Principal of the Congregational Institute.

humanity without which a virtuous polity could not exist. An 'evil thing' was 'threatening our land', and 'a practical repentance' was necessary from parliament and government.[72] In other words, their leaders saw such campaigns as patriotic struggles for the soul of England.

Confidence in the superiority of British political and moral values led naturally into the fourth and final element of the mid-Victorian Liberal worldview that I want to mention – the vision of the white settler colonies, and to some degree, the United States, as agencies which could assist 'English' ideas to play a dominant part in the progress of the world. It was in the 1840s and early 1850s that the British political elite began to display unmistakable signs of confidence about the stability and prospects of the settler colonies, a confidence manifested particularly in the policies of constitutionally minded Whigs like Russell and Grey after 1846 and in the views of the younger Colonial Reformers like Buller and Gladstone.[73] It was increasingly argued that the energy and enterprise of the English character could develop the natural resources of the vast colonial and American territories, but that some form of self-government was essential if these settlers were to become 'true citizens' of 'British communities'.[74] Between 1846 and 1853, the principle of representative government was established in most of the settler colonies in Canada, Australia, New Zealand and the Cape. This was stimulated by a number of local factors, of course, but the process was greatly facilitated at Westminster by the pronounced contrast between the success of constitutional, religious and economic liberalism in Britain, and the autocracy, protectionism and civil strife of the continent. The colonies were to be exemplars of English rather than continental practices. This conception of them continued to be very commonplace.[75] Indeed, when a panic about overpopulation and unemployment in Britain re-emerged at the end of the 1860s, there was much interest in these schemes to encourage emigration to the empire, since these would bring the double benefit of assisting the spread of the English race throughout the world and avoiding the alternative, an 'inhuman' and 'immoral' restriction on the propagation of English stock by the 'French vices' of birth control.[76]

[72] *Josephine E. Butler: An Autobiographical Memoir*, ed. G.W. and L.A. Johnson (Bristol, 1909), 88–90, 94–6, 113–24.

[73] J. M. Ward, *Colonial Self-Government: The British Experience, 1759–1856* (1976), 232.

[74] Lord John Russell, in *ibid.*, 241; R. Koebner and H.D. Schmidt, *Imperialism: The Story and Significance of a Political Word, 1840–1960* (Cambridge, 1964), 69–71; D. Steele, *Lord Salisbury: A Political Biography* (1999), 17–18.

[75] Reeve, 1852, in Laughton, *Reeve*, I, 261; Thring, 1865, in Koebner and Schmidt, *Imperialism*, 81; Taylor, *Decline of British Radicalism*, 218–19; Forster, 1875, in *The Concept of Empire: Burke to Attlee 1774–1947*, ed. G. Bennett (1953), 260.

[76] E. Jenkins, 'Two Solutions', *Fraser's Magazine*, 3 (Apr. 1871), 451–6.

But this confidence about the role of the colonies was very far removed from 'imperialism', indeed was often perceived as its opposite. England's mission was for the cause of freedom, celebrating libertarian ideas and individual enterprise, in contrast to a self-aggrandising, overbearing state- or dynastic-driven imperialism like Napoleon III's.[77] In the 1850s and 1860s there was general confidence at home in England's world role *because* it was defined in terms of the dissemination of her constitutional and moral values. This meant that domestic discussion of the future of the empire could remain crucially vague on major issues: how much territorial expansion the empire required, how British power over natives should be exercised, whether 'representative government' would naturally lead to independence, whether the United States was a threat to the empire or an informal part of it.[78] This vagueness allowed Liberals whose instincts were hostile to the formal extension of empire to co-operate with those whose views were to become very different.

In all these four ways, then, comparison between Britain and the continent helped mid-Victorian Liberalism to develop a strongly patriotic appeal, focused on 'English' constitutional and moral values – and to blunt internal differences on substantive policy issues. In arguing this, I am *not* saying that these appeals were consciously shaped by any individual leaders, and in particular I am not saying that Palmerston himself should be credited with much of the direction of the party over which he presided. Indeed, Palmerston was not always popular with his coalition or indeed with the public at large. Some Liberals and radicals regarded his foreign policy as mere bluster.[79] At times, his pursuit of good relations with Napoleon lost him support, most obviously during the Orsini affair of 1858, when he was accused of surrendering the liberties of Englishmen to please a foreign despot – even of planning to 'annex' Britain 'for police purposes to France'.[80] In 1858, as during Napoleon's wartime state visit to England in 1855, a number of radicals claimed that Palmerston's eagerness to do Napoleon's bidding symbolised autocratic sympathies in the British as well as the French government.[81] Palmerston's lukewarmness towards parliamentary reform obviously played an important part in these tensions.

Palmerston's contribution to the success of mid-Victorian Liberalism

---

[77] See e.g. Russell, in Koebner and Schmidt, *Imperialism*, 93.

[78] On the problem of the USA, see the difference of opinion between Dilke and Froude: Koebner and Schmidt, *Imperialism*, 87, 99.

[79] For Harcourt, see e.g. M.M. Bevington, *The Saturday Review 1855–1868: Representative Educated Opinion in Victorian England* (New York, 1941), 64–5.

[80] Urban, *British Opinion*, 103; *Letters of Dickens*, VIII, 522.

[81] Taylor, *Decline of British Radicalism*, 291–300; M. Finn, *After Chartism: Class and Nation in English radical politics, 1848–1874* (Cambridge, 1993), 177–86.

was less significant but still important. The fact that political debate, explicitly or implicitly, centred on a comparison between 'Englishness' and continental practices played to his strengths. In an era in which patriotism, in all its manifestations, was the major bond between Liberals, Palmerston, 'the English mastiff', was without doubt the best representative of that patriotism. He was the most suitable leader because he appeared to be the most above faction, the symbol of England and the best interpreter of her constitutional and international mission. His coalition was divided on many issues, but the constant comparisons with Napoleon and France assisted very greatly in keeping it together, by subordinating these divisions to a frequently unquestioning emphasis on the points of patriotic agreement.

V

The final part of this paper considers the very different situation caused by the French defeat in war and the fall of Napoleon III in September 1870. The changed state of affairs in Europe meant that 1870 was a watershed in British politics as well.

First, the enfeeblement of France by Prussia dealt a great blow to Britain's influence in European affairs. Isolated in Europe, she could not prevent Prussia from taking Alsace and Lorraine, or Russia from deneutralising the Black Sea. So Gladstone could not project the same patriotic aura as Palmerston. Indeed his government acquired a reputation for inglorious parsimony in defence expenditure. Gladstone and several other ministers drew the rational conclusion from the collapse of the Second Empire that British naval spending could, if anything, fall.[82] But the service ministries and much of the press campaigned against economy, exploiting anxiety at the awesome technological power of the German politico-military machine, and at the informal alliance between the three Eastern autocracies. Europe now appeared torn between efficient Prussian militarism, the bloody 'socialism' of the Commune and a resilient papacy; unsurprisingly, therefore, optimism at home about the triumph of English constitutional and commercial principles in Europe waned dramatically, and there was a panic about the inadequacy of British defence in spring 1871. Though the panic died away, criticism of 'blinkered' commercialism did not. Gladstone's plans for further defence and tax cuts continued to be frustrated by opposition within the cabinet, and the consequence was that the government badly lost direction.

Similarly, the effect of the European tensions of 1870–1 on domestic politics was to bring out the ideological divisions within the Liberal

---

[82] *Collected works of Bagehot*, VIII, 65.

party that had been checked under Palmerston. The efficiency of Prussian centralism demonstrated the benefits and problems of state intervention; the excesses of the Commune added further to fears about the effects of 'democracy'; the quarrels between the papacy and the continental secular powers increased the difficulties of governing Ireland. I aim to argue elsewhere that these debates paralysed Gladstone's first government and made it impossible to devise an effective policy on which Liberals could fight the 1874 election.[83]

In these two ways, then, the European crisis of 1870-1 wrecked the Palmerstonian Liberal coalition and contributed to the Liberal defeat in 1874. But the Liberal party experienced a remarkable resurgence in the late 1870s; Victorian constitutional and moral Liberalism was to enjoy an Indian summer. The reason for this is quite simple. The Liberals desperately needed another Napoleon III. And they found one in Disraeli.

It is nearly forty years since the publication of the best discussion of the Liberal criticism of the 'imperialism' of Disraeli's government of 1874-80, a discussion that deserves more attention than it receives.[84] My aim here is to show that the criticism drew deeply on the traditions of mid-Victorian Liberalism that I have outlined, and for that reason became a cry of real substance for the party.

The Liberal criticism of the Disraeli government, and specifically its foreign policy, started from the basis that Disraeli, like Napoleon, was a 'conspirator', an unprincipled adventurer. That is to say, he was motivated by a desire for personal fame and self-advancement from a lowly position, rather than by a firm grasp of the constitutional and moral values that defined an English patriot – the values that an upper-middle class Englishman could have acquired from the public school and university education which Disraeli lacked. (In other words there was a substantial amount of class, racial and religious snobbery in these Liberal judgements.) Disraeli did not understand that an *English* attitude to her global responsibilities was the reverse of 'imperialist'. England's European interests lay with peace, 'necessary and inevitable progress' and other common objectives of the continent.[85] But in 1878 Disraeli and Salisbury instead concluded a secret agreement with despotic Turkey, alienating the other powers. This low manoeuvre gained Britain the worthless territory of Cyprus, by 'force and fraud', and involved a 'most hazardous' extension of British responsibility in Asiatic Turkey.[86]

[83] There is also some material relating to these two paragraphs in J. Parry, 'Gladstone, Liberalism and the Government of 1868-74', in *Gladstone Centenary Essays*, ed. D.W. Bebbington and R. Swift (Liverpool, 2000), 94-112.

[84] Koebner and Schmidt, *Imperialism*, ch. 6.

[85] M. E. Grant Duff, *Foreign Policy* (1880), 16.

[86] Lowe, 'Imperialism', 462-4.

Then at the Congress of Berlin Disraeli consistently supported 'the side of servitude, of reaction, and of barbarism'.[87] Between 1877 and 1879 he sought military glory for its own sake, roused the spectre of war with Russia, and then engaged in one with Afghanistan, talking of pursuing 'natural boundaries'. This policy, disguising the 'deficiencies of the Government' with a 'shabby ... war spirit' was in 'servile imitation of the Imperialism of the Second Empire', and similarly threatened eventual nemesis by over-extending national responsibilities.[88] The less scrupulous Liberals had no hesitation in arguing that the other driver of Disraeli's foreign policy was money – as befitted a Jew.[89] Disraelian imperialism could be compared to the decadence of the Roman and the Second Empires, in that great power was surrendered to financiers and their private interests. This conclusion was particularly apparent from the purchase of the Suez Canal shares in 1875, and the enormous commission given to the Rothschilds – old friends of Disraeli – who arranged it (over £150,000 in all for a loan of £4m for three months).[90] Liberals also argued that the government's drift towards interference in Egypt had been influenced by bondholders who sought the maintenance of their interest payments after the bankruptcy of 1875.[91] Vested interests distorted policy to selfish ends, while government recklessly frittered away the money given it in trust by taxpayers – in the teeth of a depression, thus prompting the warning that Rome's greatness had been crushed by excessive taxation.[92] Liberals, then, could raise the old cry of retrenchment and combine it with alarm about the growth of 'plutocracy' in English society.[93] The 1880 election was won on a tide of indignation at the way in which Conservatives had besmirched British political life.

Moreover, Liberals criticised Disraeli's tendency towards 'personal government' or 'personal rule' at home.[94] Disraeli was accused of neutering parliament, first because his Conservative majority was apathetic and acquiescent, secondly by regularly obstructing Liberal domestic reform proposals, and thirdly by his willingness to bypass it altogether – most famously when the government transferred Indian army troops to Malta at a time of great tension with Russia in spring 1878, claiming that

---

[87] W. E. Gladstone, 'England's Mission', *Nineteenth Century*, 4 (Sept. 1878), 561–2.

[88] Harcourt, *Hansard*, 243, 767–8, 13 Dec. 1878.

[89] A. S. Wohl, ' "*Dizzi-ben-Dizzi*": Disraeli as Alien', *Journal of British Studies*, 34 (1995), 375–411.

[90] N. Ferguson, *The World's Banker: The History of the House of Rothschild* (1998), 822–4.

[91] See e.g. the debate initiated by Goldsmid, 11 Aug. 1879, in *Hansard*, 249, 681 (one of several).

[92] Lowe, 'Imperialism'.

[93] For Gladstone and Lowe on plutocracy, see e.g. W.E. Gladstone, 'The County Franchise and Mr Lowe Thereon', *Nineteenth Century*, 2 (Nov. 1877), 554.

[94] E.g. Jacob Bright, 1878, in Williams, *Contentious Crown*, 132.

this did not require the authority of parliament. To deploy forces of the Crown in Europe without the consent of the Commons betrayed a fundamental Whig principle of 1688–9.[95] It also reminded Liberal critics not only of Napoleon's gesture politics but also of the subject races which provided Rome's military strength in her decadence.[96] Disraeli was accused of subverting other English constitutional traditions too – by his flattery of the court and apparent subservience to it. In particular the Royal Titles Act of 1876 – known to be the queen's personal wish – made her Empress of India, bestowing on her a foreign title which seemed to demonstrate the imperial claim to be above the law rather than the respect for free institutions which was expected of a modern constitutional monarch.[97] The queen's displays of partisanship, notoriously her visit to Hughenden in December 1877, added to Liberal complaints. Moreover, Disraeli's foreign policy seemed to pander to the acquisitive thirst of a jingo mob. The creator of household suffrage in 1867 made no attempt to teach the people he had enfranchised the 'lessons of self-denial and self-restraint' which had traditionally conserved England's global strength – let alone to found his policy on Christian conceptions of morality. The Conservatives were 'the materialists of politics'.[98] 'Imperialism' or 'sham-caesarism' seemed an apt description of a system in which influence was exercised by an alien conspirator, a class-bound Court, a selfish plutocracy and an unrepresentative, un-Christian, spendthrift mob rather than by rational public debate and a respect for freedom.[99] Disraeli's habitual 'depreciation of Parliamentary institutions' threatened to erode the basis of England's greatness, the 'habit of self-government', and to make a great empire 'little'.[100] As Gladstone said at Midlothian, 'what we are disputing about is a whole system of Government'.[101]

VI

Hugh Cunningham once suggested that from the late 1870s 'patriotism and Conservatism became firmly linked'.[102] I, however, wish to argue that the 1880 election saw a clash between two visions of patriotism,

---

[95] Hartington 20 May 1878, *Hansard*, 240, 264.

[96] See e.g. the remarks in *The Spectator*, cited in N. Vance, *The Victorians and Ancient Rome* (Oxford, 1997), 230; Harcourt, 20 May 1878, *Hansard*, 240, 335.

[97] J.W. Pease, 20 Mar. 1876, *ibid.*, 228, 313.

[98] Grant Duff, *Foreign Policy*, 50–3; Gladstone, 'England's Mission', 569–70.

[99] It was partly to make this political point that Liberal backbenchers led the protests against the idea of a memorial to the Prince Imperial in Westminster Abbey, 'the national Valhalla', and blocked it: 8 Aug. 1879 and 16 July 1880, *Hansard*, 249, 531 and 254, 698.

[100] F. Seebohm, 'Imperialism and Socialism', *Nineteenth Century*, 7 (Apr. 1880), 727; Gladstone, 'England's Mission', 584.

[101] W.E. Gladstone, *Midlothian Speeches 1879*, ed. M.R.D. Foot (Leicester, 1971 edn), 50.

[102] H. Cunningham, 'The Language of Patriotism', in *Patriotism*, ed. Samuel, 1, 75.

and that the crushing Liberal victory at that election demonstrated the continuing supremacy of the primarily constitutional conception of Englishness that I have stressed in this paper – a set of constitutional and moral values with which the Liberals had been associated for thirty years and that united a remarkable range of people in 1880, from Robert Lowe and the Whig peerage to radicals and Dissenters.[103] The Liberals stood for the revival of constitutional propriety, parliamentary government, financial accountability and a rational foreign policy. They stood for the extension of decentralised government by breaking the control of a narrow class over the counties, and for land and parliamentary reform in order to prevent the threat that a French-style deferential peasantry would return a powerful unthinking Conservative bloc. And they stood for the articulation of a moral conscience on a variety of issues ranging from temperance to prostitution. The year 1880 was not, as is sometimes said, a new departure for the Liberal party but the beginning of the end of a long and successful tradition.

The party fell apart in the 1880s, essentially because circumstances at home, in Ireland and abroad ensured that Liberals could no longer agree on how to apply these constitutional and moral assumptions to key questions of government in any of these areas. That decline of a common Liberal philosophy is closely related to a much bigger trend in the 1880s, the ebb of national self-confidence about the superiority of British constitutional arrangements relative to other European countries. It was no longer so easy to claim that Britain had found the secret of domestic political harmony when Irishmen were bombing in London and murdering British politicians in Dublin. It was no longer so easy to emphasise the sense of shared national citizenship when Britain now suddenly had one of the least democratic franchises in Europe. It was no longer so easy to claim that free trade and British commerce would achieve a peaceful conquest of Europe, when American imports were rising to flood-level proportions and the European powers were busily building up their tariff walls. It was no longer so easy to take pride in the lack of state intervention in education, housing and health when economic growth and political stability could not be taken for granted.

I would suggest that constitutional definitions of national identity were no longer so astonishingly effective after the 1880s – though it is important to recognise that they continued to resonate at many points in British politics, and arguably still do. It is a moot point whether the predominant way of defining national identity shifted, in the 1880s and

---

[103] Though the party could unite, it was, once again, for different reasons. While the majority probably saw the Conservatives as the target, some radicals followed Harrison in seeing the 'imperialist' enemy as the whole 'military and commercial aristocracy of England', who had been implementing a policy of conquest and force against native peoples for a generation: 'Empire and humanity', *Fortnightly Review*, 27 (Feb. 1880), 295.

1890s, from the constitution to the empire and indeed to what is often called 'imperialism'. That is arguable, but merits more careful investigation. My concern in this paper has been to stress that British national identity between 1850 and 1880 was not much celebrated by reference to the empire as such, and certainly not by reference to 'imperialism', but was conceived overwhelmingly in terms of the glory of the English constitution and its effects on national character. This can be fully seen only if British politics is presented in some sort of European context. That is not to say that it was necessary for Napoleon III to exist in order for Englishmen to celebrate their constitutional superiority. Many of the prejudices aired in the 1850s derived from political and economic comparisons between Britain and the continent that would have been made in any event. Nor was the constitutional definition of national identity a recent invention. Rather, it was embedded in collective experiences and myths reaching far into the past; that was why it was so widely held, and so effective as a political language. The significance of Napoleon III's presence on the international scene was that it provided a set of very potent images and stereotypes which allowed mid-Victorians to confirm the assumptions that they had a series of powerful reasons for holding anyway. In doing so it shaped the politics of a generation.

CHURCHILL IN THE TWENTY-FIRST CENTURY

A Conference held at the Institute of
Historical Research, University of
London, 11–13 January 2001

INTRODUCTION

By David Cannadine and Roland Quinault

THIS conference considered major aspects of Winston Churchill's career and re-assessed his contribution to modern history from the perspective of the twenty-first century. For this purpose a diverse group of historians was brought together who are all experts either on Churchill or on issues with which he was closely associated. Since few people are still alive who personally knew Churchill, the opportunity was also taken to ask Tony Benn MP, Lord Carrington, Lord Deedes and Lady Soames to give us their recollections of him. We are deeply grateful to them for sharing with us their vivid and insightful memories of Churchill. We also gratefully acknowledge the assistance the conference received from the Institute of Historical Research and the Royal Historical Society. Their support was appropriate because Churchill was made an Honorary Vice-President of the Royal Historical Society in 1936 (for his biography of his famous ancestor John Churchill, duke of Marlborough) and he passionately believed in the value of historical study of the kind promoted by the Institute of Historical Research.

The conference marked the centenary of Churchill's maiden speech in parliament on 18 February 1901. That was a bravura performance by a young man of twenty-six which inaugurated a parliamentary career remarkable for its length, range, controversy and distinction. Churchill was an MP for sixty-two years; he was a member of two Liberal, three coalition and four Conservative governments; he was prime minister for over eight years; he held most of the high offices of state other than the foreign office; he twice changed his party allegiance, yet he ended his career with approbation from across the political parties and the nation. He was also an international statesman of the first importance.

During his long career, Churchill spawned a vast mass of speeches, writings, correspondence and memoranda – a cornucopia of evidence which historians are still digesting. Characteristically, Churchill got in first by writing his own accounts of his early colonial adventures and of the two world wars. Uniquely among the great figures of the twentieth century, Churchill engaged with history both as a man of action and as a man of letters: he first made history as an actor, and then he wrote history as an author. In this sense, he lived his life both forwards and backwards, and it was this complex encounter, with the present and the past, with the present as the past and with the past as the present, which makes his career doubly fascinating both for historians and the wider public.

History mattered deeply to Churchill, partly because it provided him with his own identity and justification and partly because it gave him an invaluable perspective on the present. All his major historical works were concerned, not only with the past, but also with his own time and with himself. His life of Lord Randolph Churchill was both a display of filial piety and a justification of his own controverisal early career in politics. *The World Crisis* was not just a history of the First World War, but also a defence of his own conduct, especially over the Dardanelles. Churchill's biography of the first duke of Marlborough was another work of ancestral veneration, but it was also a comment on European politics in the 1930s. His six-volume history of the Second World War was not only a sweeping grand narrative, but also a very personal account which was coloured by events after, as well as before, the conflict. *A History of the English-Speaking Peoples* ranged back over two millennia, but it also reflected Churchill's contemporary hope that the Anglo-American alliance would save the world.

Since Churchill's death there have been innumerable studies of his life and policies ranging from scholarly to popular biographies. Most of them have drawn on the official biography and companion volumes begun by Winston's son, Randolph Churchill, and continued by Sir Martin Gilbert – a work of truly Churchillian proportions. All scholars of Churchill are much in their debt. The Churchill Archives Centre at Churchill College Cambridge has played an invaluable role in cataloguing his papers and making them available for scholars, while the International Churchill Society has promoted the study of Churchill around the world.

Nevertheless, as time passes, knowledge of Churchill is declining in the wider community. Despite, or perhaps because of the way Churchill was venerated by an earlier generation, there exists today a great deal of ignorance and prejudice about him which was symbolised by the daubing of his statue in a recent demonstration. Churchill, moreover, has been somewhat sidelined in school and university curricula – edged out, ironically, by the very dictators he successfully opposed. This is strange not least because Churchill had a more lasting influence than either Hitler or Stalin on the modern world order. Even in America, where admiration of Churchill has been more vocal and bi-partisan than in Britain, there has lately been some change of mind. For example, *Time* magazine, which voted Churchill the man of the half century in 1950, declined to name him the man of the century in 2000 because of his domestic and imperial record.[1]

[1] *Time*, 31 December 1999.

Churchill, of course, is not and should not be above criticism, but by now it should be possible to re-assess him in a balanced way which avoids hagiography on the one hand and caricature on the other. Churchill himself was well aware that his reputation – like those of other politicians – would be re-assessed after his death. In his biography of his father, Lord Randolph Churchill, published in 1906, he wrote:

> A politician's character and position are measured in his day by party standards. When he is dead, all that he achieved in the name of party, is at an end. The eulogies and censures of partisans are powerless to affect his ultimate reputation. The scales wherein he was weighed are broken. The years to come bring weights and measures of their own.[2]

Churchill returned to this theme of posthumous re-appraisal in his eulogy of Neville Chamberlain late in 1940:

> It is not given to human beings, happily for them, to foresee or to predict to any large extent the unfolding course of events. In one phase men seem to have been right; in another they seem to have been wrong. Then again, when the perspective of time has lengthened, all stands in a different setting. There is a new proportion, there is another scale of values. History with its flickering lamp stumbles along the trail of the past, trying to reconstruct its scenes, to revive its echoes, and kindle with pale gleams the passions of former days.[3]

As this passage implies, Churchill was quite prepared to be re-evaluated by historians with new perspectives and values providing they took into account the character and circumstances of his own life and times. The challenge now facing historians of Churchill is twofold. First, they have to re-assess Churchill according to 'the weights and measures' of our new century, in which he will be remembered, not primarily for personal reasons, but because of his lasting contribution to history. Secondly, they have to place Churchill firmly in the context of his own era, which witnessed tragedies and triumphs on a greater scale than our own.

---

[2] Winston S. Churchill, *Lord Randolph Churchill* (1907), 823.
[3] Winston S. Churchill, *The Unrelenting Struggle* (1942), 12 November 1940, 1–2.

THE THREE CAREERS OF WINSTON CHURCHILL
By Paul Addison

FOR twenty years after the Second World War Winston Churchill's status as 'the greatest living Englishman' was seldom questioned. Biographers celebrated his life, contemporaries paid tribute in their memoirs, and potters designed Churchill toby jugs adorned with quotations from his speeches. As a general rule, historians had little to say about him. They regarded events since 1914 as too recent for historical enquiry: hence the leading authority on Churchill's life and times was the great man himself. His six volume history *The Second World War*, was generally accepted as a definitive interpretation.

Since Churchill's death in 1965, custody of his memory has passed gradually out of the hands of contemporaries and into the hands of historians and historically minded biographers. For many years all other work was overshadowed by the publication in eight volumes (1966–88) of the official biography, a stupendous work begun by Randolph S. Churchill and triumphantly completed by Martin Gilbert. But Churchill was a subject of growing interest and controversy and by the 1990s books and articles were pouring from the press. In his recent bibliography Professor Eugene Rasor lists and annotates some 3,099 relevant items – though, admittedly, he has cast his net widely.[1]

This expanding literature was accompanied by a diversity of interpretations which sometimes produced explosions of controversy. The spectrum of opinion ran all the way from historians who still thought of Churchill as 'the saviour of his country' in 1940 to historians like John Charmley who maintained that his war leadership was responsible for the destruction of Britain as a great power.[2] The arguments between admirers of Churchill on the one hand, and critics on the other, were many-sided. At one level there were separate if overlapping controversies about major events in which Churchill had been involved. Professor Rasor lists fifteen major areas of controversy, including the Dardanelles, allied intervention in Russia, the General Strike and the Second Front, but others, such as Tonypandy, the strategic bombing offensive, or Churchill's role in Anglo-American relations, could easily be added. The many articles and monographs which dealt with such topics were

---

[1] Eugene L. Rasor, *Winston S. Churchill 1874–1965: A Comprehensive Historiography and Annotated Bibliography* (2000).

[2] John Charmley, *Churchill: The End of Glory* (1993).

also contributions to a larger controversy about Churchill's place in history and the role of myth and reality in the making of his reputation. Here again, a number of different but related questions were involved; biographical questions about the nature of the man himself, and historical questions about the consequences of his actions.

At the beginning of the twenty-first century Churchill's reputation is in the melting-pot. In place of the national icon of the mid-twentieth century we have a multiplicity of competing images and a confusingly disconnected debate. It seems unlikely that historians will ever agree on the subject, but they may perhaps succeed in clarifying the issues. The differing premises on which assessments of Churchill are based are scattered through the pages of biographies, or half buried in the dense undergrowth of learned articles. The rest of this article is an attempt to outline, in a more explicit and systematic fashion, the contours of one view of Churchill.[3]

Churchill's active political life spanned a period of more than half a century, beginning with his election to the House of Commons in 1900, and ending with his resignation from the premiership in 1955. It was a life twice transformed by world war: the two great turning-points were 1915 and 1940. In a career of many snakes and ladders 1915, the year of Gallipoli, was the longest of the snakes on which he landed. For a time his career and reputation lay in ruins and it was only through heroic feats that he managed partially to restore them. The year of Britain's 'finest hour', 1940, turned out to be the longest of the ladders. It took him to heights of fame and glory achieved by no other British politician of the twentieth century. But the two world wars were not only turning-points in Churchill's fortunes: they were turning-points in the roles he played. Between 1905 and 1915 Churchill was one of the most prominent figures in the Liberal governments of Campbell Bannerman and Asquith. But the First World War led to the disintegration of the Liberal party and after 1918 Churchill metamorphosed into one of the most bellicose Tory politicians of the interwar years. He was always to remain a Tory and indeed became leader of the party in 1940. But after 1940 he was reincarnated as a national hero and international statesman.

In a sense, therefore, Churchill's political life consisted of three careers within a career. Since he was twenty-five when he was first

---

[3] Any concise overview is bound to resemble a ten-minute production of *Hamlet*. Quite apart from the fact that so much has to be left out, many problematical issues have to be touched on lightly, and assertions made with only brief reference to the evidence on which they are based. Nor is there space fully to acknowledge my debt to the work of other historians and biographers. I am, however, very grateful to Roland Quinault for his comments on the lecture of which this article is a revised version.

elected to parliament in 1900, forty when he fell from office in 1915, and sixty-five when he became prime minister in 1940, the three careers also corresponded approximately with youth, middle age and old age. Like most attempts to divide the past neatly into the periods, this is no doubt a simplification, but it does highlight one of the main problems in any interpretation of Churchill's life: the paradoxes and contradictions. Here was a politician who travelled all the way from the left wing of the Liberal party to the right wing of the Conservatives, to become in the end a symbol and embodiment of national unity. Here too was a politician who was frequently written off up to 1939 as the most dangerous and irresponsible of decision-makers, hailed after 1940 as the greatest strategist and statesman of the age.

How are such apparent contradictions to be explained? The thesis adopted here is that that Churchill's character and opinions, his repertoire of political roles, and his view of the world, were largely settled by 1915. Of course he continued after 1915 to grasp new problems and frame new policies. But he was to remain, as he was later to write, 'a child of the Victorian age', and a statesman attached to the social and imperial order which existed before the First World War. Within himself, therefore, Churchill changed little after 1915. His second and third careers were to a great extent repetitions of the first, but in new historical contexts which transformed the significance of his actions.

A parallel line of reasoning applies to the history of Churchill's reputation. Churchill in 1940 was the very same man he always had been. But perceptions were changed by a new historical context in which aspects of 'Winston' which had previously been regarded as flaws were transformed into precious virtues and strengths. The consequence was that a politician whose career had frequently been written off during the 1930s as a failure was now hailed as the most triumphant and victorious of statesmen.

Compulsive ambition, colossal egotism, prodigious energy, a thirst for adventure – such were the characteristics blazingly apparent in the young Winston Churchill. Like other young men in a hurry, Churchill was hungry for office and aiming for the greatest prize of all, the premiership. Far from concealing the fact, he talked noisily of his ambition to get to the top and his calculations of how to get there. But Churchill's ambitions always extended beyond the possession of office and power. He believed that he was a man of destiny. He saw himself at some future date performing great deeds on the stage of history. To Churchill therefore, office was not an end in itself, but a means to an end: the winning of great political victories, the achievement of great reforms, the saving of the nation. At a house party in January 1915 Margot Asquith heard him exclaim: 'My God! This is living history.

Everything we are doing and saying is thrilling – it will be read by a thousand generations: think of that!'[4]

Churchill's drive for power was harnessed to the workings of a brilliant mind which, at this period, may well have been at the height of its powers. It was no accident that he was the most highly paid war correspondent of the day, or generally recognised as one of the most formidable of orators. The speed with which he mastered new subjects, and the fertility of his writing, put him in the same league as his friend H.G. Wells. By 1906 he was the author of six books of which two – *The River War* and *Lord Randolph Churchill* were major works ranking with those of professional historians. In politics he schooled himself, between 1900 and 1915, in the politics of free trade and protectionism, colonial affairs, social reform, the House of Lords, Ireland, grand strategy and foreign policy. His intelligence, however, operated through a rapid process of impressionism rather than slow and methodical analysis. According to Anthony Storr, Churchill's character matched Jung's description of a psychological type, the 'extraverted intuitive', who is 'never to be found among the generally recognized reality values, but is always present where possibilities exist'.[5] His cabinet colleagues, Grey and Birrell, feared that 'the tendency in him to see first the rhetorical potentialities of any policy was growing and becoming a real intellectual and moral danger'.[6]

Churchill's dynamism was one of the reasons why he was able to embark on a political career so early in life. The other, of course, was the fact that he was born into the governing class – the son of Lord Randolph Churchill, and grandson of a duke. But if he was an aristocrat he was also an adventurer who relished the company of other adventurers, most of whom were self-made men like F. E. Smith, Beaverbrook and Lloyd George. Through his mother, meanwhile, he was half-American and the grandson of a Wall Street financier. All in all, Churchill was closer in spirit to the City of London and the world of 'gentlemanly capitalism' than he was to the vanishing world of the landed estate. Beatrice Webb, meeting him for the first time in 1903, described him as 'more the American speculator than the English aristocrat ... He looks to high finance to keep the peace ... the cosmopolitan financier being the professional peacemaker of the modern world, and to his mind the acme of civilisation.'[7]

The young Winston Churchill was also a fervent believer in the

---

[4] Martin Gilbert, *Churchill: A Life* (1991), 294.

[5] Anthony Storr, 'The Man' in A.J.P. Taylor *et al.*, *Churchill: Four Faces and the Man* (Harmondsworth, 1973), 231.

[6] Lucy Masterman, *C.F.G. Masterman: A Biography* (1939), 128.

[7] Norman and Jeanne MacKenzie (eds.), *The Diary of Beatrice Webb*, II: *1892–1905* (1983), 287–8, entry for 8 July 1903.

British Empire. A more humane imperialist than many of his contemporaries, he was aware of. the arrogance and cruelty which sometimes disfigured British rule, and did his best to mitigate them.
Nevertheless he drank deeply of the heady imperialism of the 1890s.
His late Victorian vision of the hierarchy of races and the 'civilising
mission' of the British, was intensified by his experience of the 'barbarism' and 'fanaticism' of the Pathans on the north-west frontier of
India and the Dervishes of the Sudan. The war in South Africa, by
contrast, was for Churchill a 'White man's war' in which it would be
wrong to employ non-white troops against a European enemy.[8] As he
explained to the House of Commons in 1906, there were five black
inhabitants of South Africa for every one white. The 'black peril' was
'as grim a problem as any mind could be forced to face' and 'the one
bond of union' which might lead to a reconciliation between British
and Boer settlers.[9]

The fact that Churchill had been a soldier before entering politics
was ever present in the minds of his contemporaries. His experience of
the South African war had convinced him that civilians like himself
understood the principles of warfare as well or better than the generals.
It is not clear whether he believed in hereditary genius but the example
of his ancestor, the first duke of Marlborough, was always before him
and he felt that he possessed a special flair. As he wrote to his wife,
Clementine, after attending a military field day in May 1909: 'These
military men vy often fail altogether to see the simple truths underlying
the relationship of all armed forces ... Do you know I would greatly
like to have some practice in the handling of large forces. I have much
confidence in my judgment on things, when I see clearly, but on
nothing do I seem to *feel* the truth more than in tactical combinations.'[10]

In party politics young Winston was initially a Tory, but inwardly
unreliable. He thought of himself principally as the son and heir of
Lord Randolph Churchill: in his eyes a far-sighted Tory statesman with
strong radical and popular sympathies who had been ill-treated by the
leaders of the party. Never a wholehearted Tory, he wrote to his mother
from India in 1897: 'I am a Liberal in all but name. My views excite
the pious horror of the Mess. Were it not for Home Rule – to which I
will never consent – I would enter Parliament as a Liberal. As it is –
Tory Democracy will have to be the standard under which I shall
range myself.'[11] Churchill's ambivalence in party politics reflected a

[8] Randolph S. Churchill, *Winston S. Churchill: Companion*, 1, part 2 (Boston, 1967), 1216,
Churchill to Joseph Chamberlain, 16 November 1900.
[9] Randolph S. Churchill, *Winston S. Churchill: Young Statesman 1901–1914* (1967), 164.
[10] Mary Soames (ed.), *Speaking for Themselves: The Personal Letters of Winston and Clementine
Churchill* (1998), 23, Winston to Clementine, 30 May 1909.
[11] Randolph S. Churchill, *Winston S. Churchill*, 1 (1966), 318, Winston to Lady Randolph,
6 April 1897.

deeper truth. His creed was egotism – the right to express his own opinion on the merits of every issue. He was sceptical of party doctrine and resented the constraints they placed on the statesmanship of great men. As A.G. Gardiner wrote of him in 1914: 'More than any other man of his time, he approaches an issue without mental reserves or the restraints of party calculation or caution. To his imperious spirit a party is only an instrument. *Au fond* he would no more think of consulting party than the chauffeur would think of consulting the motor car.' Hence Churchill's partiality for coalitions of kindred spirits, free from the demands of the more partisan wings of the two main parties. His political ideal, he explained to Rosebery in 1902, was a 'Government of the Middle ... free at once from the sordid selfishness and callousness of Toryism one the one hand, and the blind appetites of the Radical masses on the other.'[13]

Churchill could rightly claim that in crossing the floor of the House to join the Liberals in 1904 he was acting in defence of a cause the Conservatives were abandoning – free trade. But his change of parties cost him dear. In the eyes of the Conservatives he was a shameless opportunist, a turncoat and a cad. The Liberals, though grateful for the loan of his talents, could never forget his Tory and military origins. Most implausible of all, so it seemed, was Churchill's role as radical and social reformer in alliance with David Lloyd George. The campaigns they waged in favour of welfare reforms, land taxes and the People's Budget seemed indistinguishable to the Tories from demagoguery and class warfare. But whereas Lloyd George had impeccable credentials as a radical, Churchill's attacks on his own class, and his professions of concern for 'the left-out millions', exposed him to charges of hypocrisy.

He was, in fact, more consistent in his political beliefs than was generally recognised. He had entered the House of Commons as an old-fashioned radical preaching Victorian political economy. As Churchill saw it, competitive capitalism was the mainspring of economic and social progress. His commitment to free trade and rejection of protectionism followed logically on from this and gave him a legitimate pretext for joining the Liberals, even if other motives were involved. His adoption after 1906 of the 'New Liberalism' marked his conversion to policies of welfare reform intended to provide a 'safety net' or 'minimum standard' below which the poor would not be allowed to fall. But as Churchill was careful to explain, his fundamental belief in the virtues of the market was undiminished. 'The existing organisation of society', he declared, 'is driven by one mainspring – competitive

[12] A.G. Gardiner, *Prophets Priests and Kings* (1914), 234.
[13] Paul Addison, *Churchill on the Home Front 1900–1955* (1992), 26.

selection. It may be a very imperfect organisation of society, but it is all we have got between us and barbarism ... I do not want to see impaired the vigour of competition, but we can do much to mitigate the consequences of failure.'[14] Welfare reforms were therefore the antithesis of socialism, which he condemned in no uncertain terms. Churchill, in other words, was preaching the virtues of a Darwinian society, but one in which the winners behaved mercifully towards the losers. Nor was this a temporary posture on Churchill's part. We have only to look at the reforms Churchill introduced at the Admiralty in the conditions of the lower deck, or at the way he behaved as an officer towards his men on the western front in 1915, to see at once that he was a genuine paternalist who wished to improve the lot of the underdog.

The radical agenda of Churchill and Lloyd George included attempts to cut the army and navy estimates, and something very close to an alternative foreign policy of friendship with Germany. This too might appear out of character, but only if we picture Churchill as a perpetual militarist prophesying conflict. For much of the Edwardian period he was confident that the long European peace would continue. It was nonsense, he declared in 1908, to talk of the inevitability of war between Britain and Germany.[15]

Churchill was to remain one of the leading members of a Liberal cabinet up to 1915. He continued therefore to champion Liberal policies such as Irish Home Rule, and to belabour the Tory opposition. But from 1910 onwards there were a number of signs that he was moving to the Right. Why was this? The most plausible explanation is that changing political circumstances brought out two hitherto latent aspects of Churchill's political identity: the conservative statesman, defending the social order; and the military leader, inspired by a sense of destiny.[16]

In the first of the two general elections of 1910 the Liberals lost their overall majority and became dependent on the votes of the Labour Party and the Irish Nationalists. Later in the year Liberal and Conservative leaders entered into secret but abortive negotiations for the establishment of a coalition. Although the negotiations fell through they marked a turning-point in Churchill's political attitudes. Whereas previously Churchill and Lloyd George had been leading the radical wing of the Liberals in alliance with Labour, Churchill now hoped for some kind of reconciliation or agreement with the Conservatives. He

[14] Michael Freeden, *The New Liberalism: An Ideology of Social Reform* (1978), 161.

[15] Robert Rhodes James (ed.), *Winston S. Churchill: His Complete Speeches, 1897–1963* (8 vols., New York, 1974), II, 1085, speech of 14 August 1908.

[16] Arguably the most accurate term for Churchill is 'Whig' and we should think of him as Whig with both radical and conservative aspects which alternated in response to events. But this seems to me too complex a formula for the purpose of this article.

continued to speculate hopefully on the prospects for a coalition, and made strenuous but fruitless efforts to repair his own relations with the Conservatives by defusing the Irish question – which eventually blew up in his face.

Two likely explanations for this rightward shift present themselves. The year 1910 marked the beginning of the 'great industrial unrest' which preceded the First World War. Churchill, who as home secretary was the minister responsible for the maintenance of law and order, drew a sharp distinction between purely industrial disputes, in which he claimed to be neutral, and syndicalist attempts to coerce the government through 'direct action' or a general strike, which he regarded as assaults on the constitution. Whether or not syndicalism posed a serious threat, Churchill certainly believed that it did. Thoroughly alarmed by the national rail strike of August 1911, he despatched troops on his own authority to key points of the railway network. Together with his conduct of the Tonypandy affair, his actions were strongly condemned in the House of Commons by Keir Hardie and Ramsay MacDonald. Churchill was becoming anti-Labour, and Labour anti-Churchill.

The other likely explanation of Churchill's retreat from radicalism after 1910 was a growing pessimism about Anglo-German relations. At the Home Office the information he received from the intelligence services convinced him that Britain was honeycombed with German spies, a real or imagined danger that inspired some of his more illiberal measures, such as the Official Secrets Act of 1911. He became fearful of German intentions, an anxiety redoubled by the Agadir crisis of 1911. In Churchill's view, the prospect of a major war strengthened the case for the creation, out of the Liberal and Conservative parties, of a 'national party' committed both to land reform and conscription.[17] It also awoke in him the soldier and strategist. Many years later Sir Ralph Hawtrey recalled an incident which occurred in 1910 or 1911, when he was motoring down to Brighton with Churchill and Lloyd George: 'Churchill began to talk about the next war. He described how, at the climax, he himself, in command of the army, would win the decisive victory in the Middle East, and would return to England in triumph. Lloyd George quietly interposed, 'And where do I come in?'[18]

The moment war broke out in August 1914 Churchill began to intervene in the conduct of naval operations. In October he went to see Asquith, begged to be relieved of the Admiralty and given a high military command. 'His mouth waters', Asquith wrote, 'at the sight and thought of Kitchener's new armies. Are these "glittering commands" to

[17] Addison, *Churchill on the Home Front*, 159.
[18] Martin Gilbert, *In Search of Churchill* (1994), 175.

be entrusted to "dug-out trash", bred on the obsolete tactics of 25 years ago ... he was quite three parts serious and declared that a political career was nothing to him in comparison with military glory.'[19] Asquith refused and Churchill sought instead for some means by which the Royal Navy could achieve a decisive breakthrough. The consequence, of course, was Gallipoli, the moment of truth at which Churchill's sense of destiny was thwarted by political reality.

Though Churchill was only partly to blame for Gallipoli he was made into the scapegoat while Asquith and Kitchener, who were equally if not more responsible, held on to their posts. To some extent, of course, Gallipoli was only a pretext for the removal of a politician whose bumptious and aggressive style had made numerous enemies and few friends. His maverick role in party politics had thoroughly alienated the Conservatives without winning the trust of the Liberals. The Conservatives therefore insisted on his removal from the Admiralty as a precondition of their entry into a coalition government, while the Liberals made little attempt to defend him in his hour of need.

Churchill's downfall was also the result of growing doubts about his judgement. How long such doubts had existed, and how far they were shaped by malice and distortion, is very difficult to say. But they were real enough and focused on the very field in which Churchill felt that his abilities were strongest: military operations and strategy. They seem to have been crystallised for the first time by Churchill's role in the defence of Antwerp in October 1914. 'Winston', Lloyd George declared, 'is becoming a great danger ... Winston is like a torpedo. The first you hear of his doings is when you hear the swish of the torpedo dashing through the water.'[20]

Few professional politicians doubted that Churchill possessed elements of genius. Even Bonar Law, who greatly disliked and distrusted him, acknowledged his outstanding abilities. But Gallipoli confirmed a consensus among the political elite that Churchill was a genius *manque*, and the qualification was lethal. The missing component in the otherwise wonderful mechanism of the Churchill brain was *judgement*: hence there was always a danger that he would plunge his companions into disaster. It was an assumption that might well permit Churchill to return to office in a subordinate post, but it ruled out a Churchill premiership as unthinkable.

By the time that peacetime politics returned in 1918 Churchill had

---

[19] Michael and Eleanor Brock (eds.), *H.H. Asquith: Letters to Venetia Stanley* (Oxford, 1982), 266, letter of 7 October 1914.
[20] John M. McEwen (ed.), *The Riddell Diaries 1908–1923* (1986), 91–2, entry for 10 October 1914.

recovered sufficiently to be included in the postwar coalition, but he was a wounded figure heavily dependent on the good will of Lloyd George. At the same time he found himself entering a new political world. At home the Liberal party was fatally divided and the Labour party emerging as the main alternative to the Conservatives. The electorate, which now included women over the age of thirty, had increased in size from seven million in 1910 to twenty-one million in 1918. There was a resurgence of industrial militancy and with it the renewed threat of a general strike. The British Empire was shaken by nationalist movements in India and Egypt, paralleled by the revolt of Sinn Fein in Ireland. The most fundamental challenge of all was the Bolshevik revolution of 1917, which threatened to spread from Russia into the heart of central Europe. From about 1921 onwards the worst of the immediate crisis was over and a period of relative stability followed, but it was also clear that the pre-1914 political order had vanished.

What was Churchill's role? There were flashes of the old radicalism especially during his period as Chancellor of the Exchequer. Although he eventually succumbed to the pressure to restore the Gold Standard at the pre-war rate of parity between the pound and the dollar, it was not without interrogating his advisers about the effects on industry and employment. He resumed with relish the role of champion of peace, retrenchment and reform. He cut naval expenditure, put the Ten-Year Rule on a revolving basis in 1928, and insisted that there was no danger whatever of a war with Japan. When the great slump occurred, he came up with the idea of an economic parliament. Churchill also developed new international themes. At the end of the First World War, and again during the world slump, he proclaimed the idea of the common heritage and destiny of Britain and the United States. In 1930 he put the case for a United States of Europe – one in which Britain would play little part.

In spite of such forward-looking moments the general character of Churchill's response to the postwar world was clear. 'Don't you make any mistake', he said to Lloyd George, 'you're not going to get your new world. The old world is a good enough place for me, & there's life in the old dog yet.'[21] Much of his political life between the wars consisted of a prolonged rearguard action, first as a coalition Liberal, and later as a Conservative, against the new political forces released by the First World War. The pattern was set at the very beginning of the period by his response to the Bolshevik revolution.

Anti-Bolshevism was the material from which Churchill fashioned a

[21] A.J.P. Taylor (ed.), *Lloyd George: A Diary by Frances Stevenson* (1971), 196–7, entry for 17 January 1920.

new political identity after 1919, and the foundation on which he built
a new career. No other cause for which he stood brought so many
aspects of his politics into a single, concentrated focus. In the first
instance it united Churchill the military leader, conducting the British
war of intervention in Russia, with Churchill the conservative statesman,
engaged in an ideological crusade against a creed which represented
the antithesis of everything he stood for. Since Churchill claimed that
the Kremlin was fomenting nationalist revolts against British rule in
Ireland, Egypt and India, it also involved the defence of the imperial
order. At home the intelligence services provided Churchill with evidence of Bolshevik interference in industrial disputes and the payment
of subsidies to the socialist *Daily Herald.* Churchill could therefore argue
that hard-line anti-socialism in domestic affairs was the necessary
counterpart of anti-Bolshevism abroad. Anti-Bolshevism therefore gave
Churchill a new and powerful rationale for his favourite project of a
Centre Party or permanent coalition of Liberals and Conservatives. It
also supplied him with a rich if dubious source of propaganda against
the Labour party. During the general election of October 1924 he
declared: 'Spellbound by the lure of Moscow, wire-pulled through
subterranean channels, Mr Ramsay MacDonald and his associates have
attempted to make the British nation accomplices in Bolshevik crimes.'[22]

Churchill's strident anti-Bolshevik, anti-socialist line was of crucial
importance in restoring him to favour with the Conservatives. He
continued to pursue a strong anti-Soviet line throughout his period as
Chancellor of the Exchequer in the Baldwin government, and into the
1930s. In Churchill's view fascism was the consequence of communism
and the necessary antidote to it. Hence his praise for the government
of Mussolini, whom he described in a speech to the Anti-Socialist
Union in 1933 as 'the greatest law-giver among living men'.[23] In the
opening stages of the Spanish Civil War he leaned strongly towards
Franco and the Nationalist side. With unconscious irony he also
declared in a debate in the House of Commons in 1937: 'I will not
pretend that if I had to choose between Communism and Nazi-ism, I
would choose Communism.'[24] In foreign affairs, this was exactly the
choice he would make and was, perhaps, making already.

Anti-Communism was not the only front on which Churchill fought
for the old world against the new. Throughout the 1920s he defended
the commanding heights of free trade against the protectionist wing of
the Conservative party. When the free trade cause was fatally under-

[22] Martin Gilbert, *Churchill: A Photographic Portrait* (1974), photos nos. 168–9.
[23] Martin Gilbert, *Winston S. Churchill*, v (1976), 457.
[24] David Carlton, *Churchill and the Soviet Union* (Manchester, 2000), 57. This very
stimulating and original book seems to me to overstate the consistency of Churchill's
hostility to the Soviet Union.

mined by the Slump, and he was compelled to abandon it, he put himself at the head of the India diehards in opposition to the policies of Baldwin, the leader of his own party.

For the first time in thirty years Churchill found himself acclaimed at gatherings of the constituency activists of the Tory party. But his relationship with the Conservatives between the wars was highly reminiscent of his relationship with the Liberals up to 1915. Churchill's views were often indistinguishable from those of the average Tory, but for all that he remained an independent grandee in a contractual relationship with the party, or whichever section of the party he was allied with at the time. There was, however, one important difference between the Liberal and the Tory phases of his career. During the Liberal phase there was always the possibility, if he could manage it, of rejoining the Conservatives. But once he had rejoined them in 1924 there was nowhere else for him to go. His fate, therefore, was entirely in the hands of the Conservative party. Over India and again over the question of rearmament Churchill demonstrated that he could attract the support of powerful bodies of Tory opinion. But as ever the support he obtained was strictly related to the issue in question. He never managed to convert it into a personal following based on trust in his judgement or faith in his political philosophy. When he came out in opposition to the Munich agreement in October 1938 his only supporters in the House of Commons were Brendan Bracken, Duncan Sandys and Robert Boothby. His isolation in the winter of 1938–9 was almost complete: this was the true period of exile in the wilderness. By January 1939, therefore, Churchill's career as a party politician was at an even lower ebb than it had been in the naval estimates crisis of January 1914, when he had almost been driven out of the Cabinet.

Churchill was still haunted by Gallipoli. Ever since 1915 he had struggled to set the record straight, defending his actions in evidence to the Dardanelles Commission and later at very great length in his book *The World Crisis*. To some extent he succeeded. Much, though not all of the blame, was lifted from his shoulders, and there was always a minority school of thought which praised Churchill as the author of a brilliant strategic conception that failed only through poor execution. No matter: 'Gallipoli' was shorthand for the charge which Baldwin Chamberlain and their allies continued to level against him in the 1930s: lack of judgement. Churchill, of course, denied this, but there was some truth in it. Impulsive, rhetorical and visionary, he tended to confuse the desirable with the attainable. Both his war of intervention in Russia and his India campaign were quixotic affairs in which his imagination parted company with reality.

As for the Opposition, the Labour Party was as hostile to Churchill between the wars as the Conservatives had been in the Edwardian age and ironically for the same reason: he was perceived as a dangerous enemy in the class war. In March 1933 the *Daily Herald* carried a cartoon of Churchill entitled 'Nazi movement: local version', depicting Churchill, dressed as a stormtrooper, giving the Nazi salute.[25] By the late 1930s Churchill was putting out olive branches to Labour but with little success. Three weeks after Munich Robert Fraser, a leader-writer for the *Herald*, wrote to Hugh Dalton: 'There is only one danger of Fascism ... and that will come if Chamberlain is overthrown by the Jingoes in his own party, led by Winston, who will then settle down, with his lousy and reactionary friends, to organise the nation on Fascist principles for a war to settle scores with Hitler.'[26]

Churchill's appointment as Prime Minister marked the beginning of a revolution in his reputation. In retrospect it is a revolution we tend to take very much for granted as the inevitable consequence of inspiring leadership in a time of national crisis. While that certainly is part of the explanation it is not the whole story. It scarcely diminishes Churchill to point out that in one sense he was supremely fortunate in 1940. Having been out of office for most of the 1930s he could not be held responsible for Britain's plight: this time the scapegoats were the 'men of Munich'. The circumstances of the time were such that what had previously been regarded as weaknesses or flaws in his make-up now became strengths. Few now complained that he was a warmonger or a would-be Napoleon: the zeal with which he waged war was now a precious asset. Nor was it any longer a black mark against him that he thought of himself as above party. What better recommendation could there be for the leader of a government of national unity? As for the allegation that he was an impossibilist, an impossibilist was exactly what was called for in 1940. Churchill's profound but irrational faith in victory was infectious and exhilarating and turned out to be right.

The year 1940 therefore transformed perceptions of Churchill, but this is not to say that sceptics and opponents disappeared. With the general public Churchill proved to be phenomenally, though not universally, popular. As for the political elite, most politicians and officials seem to have developed a great admiration for Churchill, but working as they did in close proximity with the great man they were always aware of his faults, and there were rows behind the scenes of which the general public knew nothing at the time. The effect of 1940, therefore, was to create something of a gulf between the war hero of the popular press, and the brilliant but fallible being who inhabited the corridors of power. Within the political elite, attitudes varied according

[25] Gilbert, *Churchill: A Photographic Portrait*, photo no. 200.
[26] Addison, *Churchill on the Home Front*, 324.

to the individual concerned and the state of the war at the time. As one defeat succeeded another during 1941, and the first half of 1942, there was much grumbling and plotting behind the scenes. In October 1941 Sir John Dill, the Chief of the Imperial General Staff, showed Sir John Reith an album of photographs of the Atlantic meeting between Churchill and Roosevelt. According to Reith's diary Dill said: ' "Our empire is worth saving. We must save it if we can from what others may do with it." "What do you mean?" I asked. There was a picture of Churchill on the page before us. He stabbed at it with his thumb. "That".' Dill was succeeded as Chief of Staff by Alan Brooke, whose love–hate relationship with Churchill was recorded in his diaries. 'God knows where we should be without him', Brooke wrote on 4 December 1941, 'but God knows where we shall go with him!'[28]

When they were eventually published, in two volumes edited by Arthur Bryant in 1957 and 1959, the diaries produced a sense of shock. They revealed for the first time the difference between the insider's view of Churchill and the wartime public image, and called into question the majestic self-portrait contained in his own *The Second World War*. The sensation would have been even greater but for the fact that some passages had been tactfully deleted. Thus in September 1944 Brooke wrote: 'He knows no details, has only got half the picture in his mind, talks absurdities, and makes my blood boil to listen to his nonsense. The wonderful thing is that three quarters of the population of the world imagine Churchill is one of the great strategists of history, a second Marlborough, and the other quarter have no conception of what a public menace he is.'[29]

The publication of the diaries marked the beginning of a more realistic assessment of Churchill's war leadership. The subsequent historiography is far too extensive to summarise here but the main tendency has been to demonstrate that after 1940, as before, Churchill's career was a very uneven mixture of success and failure. The war, however, raised Churchill's activities to a much higher plane, so it is more appropriate to employ the terms he himself used in the title of the last volume of his war history: 'Triumph and Tragedy'.

As a war leader Churchill can be assessed both as a military leader and as a statesman. On the military side his role has been analysed by historians such as Stephen Roskill, who is severely critical of his interference in naval operations, and John Keegan, who praises Churchill's overall grasp of grand strategy in Europe, while recognising that

[27] Charles Stuart (ed.), *The Reith Diaries* (1975), 281, entry for 2 October 1941.
[28] Arthur Bryant, *The Turn of the Tide 1939–1943* (1943), 299.
[29] *Daily Telegraph*, 24 January 2001.

he was badly mistaken about the Far East.[30] The sinking of the *Prince of Wales* and the *Repulse*, and the loss of Singapore, are not easily explained away. Churchill, it seems, was never quite the military genius he imagined himself to be. But the sources of triumph and tragedy have to be sought elsewhere.

Churchill's primary objective in World War Two was the defeat and destruction of the Third Reich. This was both a military and a political goal and it was Churchill's greatest strength as a war leader that he pursued it with single-minded tenacity. And whatever mistakes he made along the way, he achieved his aim. Between 1940 and 1943 it was Churchill who determined the main course of British and later Anglo-American strategy in Europe, and by May 1945 the Third Reich lay in ruins.

This was his triumph, but the price was much higher than he expected. The objective of defeating and destroying Nazi Germany led Churchill to abandon or undermine the conservative statesmanship for which he had stood between the wars. Since 1919 he had marked out clear-cut lines of resistance to the Labour party, the Soviet Union, and the enemies of imperial rule. During the Second World War he was no more in favour of socialism, communism, or the dissolution of the empire than he had been before. But he was compelled to wage war by coalition. This entailed first of all the establishment of a coalition government at home, with the Conservative party in alliance with Labour, the trade unions, and liberal reformers like Beveridge. On a global scale it involved the creation of a Grand Alliance in partnership with the United States and the Soviet Union. As a war leader, therefore, Churchill was compelled to compromise with forces whose ambitions were at odds with his own, and became the reluctant agent of policies of which he would have disapproved in peacetime. In 1942, for example, under pressure from Labour but also from Roosevelt, he was obliged to send Sir Stafford Cripps to India with an offer of self-government after the war. The Cripps mission failed, and repressive measures were adopted, but the pledge of self-government remained.

The Anglo-Soviet alliance, meanwhile, led to the virtual suppression of all public criticism of the Soviet regime. Churchill himself was silent about all those aspects of the communist system he had once denounced with such passion: nor could he admit in public to knowledge of Soviet atrocities like the massacre in the Katyn Woods. He was equally powerless to prevent the advance of the Red Army into eastern Europe, the annexation by Stalin of Polish territory, or the establishment of satellite regimes. On the home front, meanwhile, Labour and the Left

---

[30] Stephen Roskill, *Churchill and the Admirals* (1977); John Keegan, 'Churchill's Strategy' in Robert Blake and W.R. Louis (eds.), *Churchill* (Oxford, 1993), 327–52.

exercised much power and influence, more no doubt than Churchill realised until his defeat in the general election of 1945. The advance of socialism at home was, perhaps, the least of his problems, but in the end it reinforced all the others by depriving him of any direct role in the post-war settlement of the world.

Churchill had one great post-war aspiration of his own: the establishment of an Anglo-American world order on the basis of an ever closer union of the two great branches of the 'English-Speaking Peoples'. In 1943, when his hopes of Anglo-American harmony were at their zenith, he even proposed the establishment after the war of a common citizenship. The irony was, of course, that one of the war aims of the Roosevelt administration was the liquidation of the British Empire, and the expansion of American power and influence at the expense of Britain. By the end of 1943 it was clear to Churchill that he could no longer rely on American co-operation. As he explained to Violet Bonham Carter: 'When I was at Teheran I realized for the first time what a very *small* country this is. On the one hand the big Russian bear with its paws outstretched – on the other the great American Elephant – & between them the poor little British Donkey – who is the only one that knows the right way home.'[31]

As a war leader, therefore, Churchill tended to undermine and negate his *alter ego*, the conservative statesman. The self-cancelling process was exacerbated by his immersion in military affairs to the exclusion of almost everything else. For the most part he postponed the discussion of post-war questions, both domestic and international, until it was too late to do very much about them. The price Churchill paid for victory was partly due to the fact that for long periods the soldier in him displaced the statesman altogether.

After 1945 Churchill harboured doubts about the extent of his wartime achievement. 'Historians', he mused, 'are apt to judge war ministers less by the victories achieved under their direction than by the political results which flowed from them. Judged by that standard I am not sure that I shall be held to have done very well.'[32] This is only one of a number of melancholy post-war reflections such as his remark to Clark Clifford on the train to Fulton in 1946: 'America has now become the hope of the world. Britain has had its day ... if I were to be born again, I'd want to be born an American.'[33] As old age

---

[31] Mark Pottle (ed.), *Champion Redoubtable: The Diaries and Letters of Violet Bonham Carter 1914–1945* (1999), 313.

[32] Tuvia Ben-Moshe, *Churchill: Strategy and History* (1992), 329. Ben-Moshe's own fundamental criticism of Churchill is that he lacked long-term political aims and therefore failed to integrate strategic and political objectives.

[33] Paul Addison, 'Winston Churchill's Concept of the English-Speaking Peoples' in Attila Pok (ed.), *The Fabric of Modern Europe: Studies in Social and Diplomatic History* (Nottingham, 1999), 115.

advanced and the 'Black Dog' took possession of him, Churchill began to fear that his life's work had been in vain.

There is no need to endorse this verdict. For Churchill and indeed for Britain the price of victory was high but the price of defeat would have been very much higher: the permanent establishment of a Nazi-controlled Europe of which Britain itself might eventually have become a part. In the final analysis there are two reasons why Churchill deserves to be remembered as an exceptionally great man. First of all, he was right in all essentials about the rise of Nazi Germany, and without him all might have been lost in 1940. Secondly, whether he was right or wrong over one particular question or another, he was a great man in himself, in all three of his careers. When he died the Labour politician, Michael Foot, wrote an obituary that was sharply critical of many aspects of Churchill's record. But he also wrote:

> Seen from any angle the scale of the figure on the vast canvas is stupendous. Not merely does Churchill bestride the century; not merely has he been a foremost performer in British and world politics for a longer period than almost any rival in ancient or modern times. The same giant lineaments are revealed when his particular faculties are examined. His vitality, his brainpower, his endurance, his wit, his eloquence, his industry, his application, were superabundant, superhuman. The first and last impression left by the Colosseum concerns its size. So with Churchill: the man was huge.[34]

In the summer of 1939 Churchill was invited by Julian Huxley to see the giant panda at the London Zoo. Churchill gazed at the animal for a long time, then shook his head approvingly and said: 'It has exceeded all my expectations ... and they were very high.'[35] For historians, it seems to me, Churchill is just like the giant panda. He exceeds all our expectations.

[34] Michael Foot, *Loyalists and Loners* (1986), 168.
[35] Julian Huxley, *Memories* (Harmondsworth, 1972), 237.

CHURCHILL AND DEMOCRACY
By Roland Quinault

CHURCHILL'S views on democracy – both in theory and in practice – are of interest for many reasons. He played a leading role in the ideological battles between democracy and dictatorship in the first half of the twentieth century and he was one of the principal architects of the modern democratic world order. Yet Churchill was widely regarded, particularly in the middle phase of his career, as a reactionary and anti-democratic figure. This conundrum will be examined by considering Churchill's attitude to the concept of democracy and democratic reform – both at home and abroad – over his long career. Churchill was born in 1874 when the great majority of adults in Britain were still disenfranchised and he died in 1965 the year when the Voting Rights Act ended electoral racial discrimination in the United States. Thus his life roughly spanned the period during which universal suffrage democracy became the basis of political legitimacy in the western world.

Churchill's engagement with democracy began early in his life. In his famous address to the US Congress, in 1941, he declared:

> I was brought up in my father's house to believe in democracy. 'Trust the people' that was his message ... Therefore I have been in full harmony all my life with the tides which have flowed on both sides of the Atlantic against privilege and monopoly and I have steered confidently towards the Gettysburg ideal of 'government of the people by the people for the people'.[1]

When Winston was born, however, the political outlook of his father, Lord Randolph Churchill, was still strongly conservative. In 1878, for example, Lord Randolph complained that recent Tory legislation was based 'upon principles which were purely democratic'.[2] It was not until 1884, that Gladstone's introduction of a new Parliamentary Reform Bill prompted Randolph to embrace the principle of democracy, albeit it for conservative ends: 'Trust the people ... and they will trust you – and they will follow you and join you in the defence of the Constitution

[1] Winston S. Churchill, *The Unrelenting Struggle: War Speeches* (1942), 334: 29 December 1941.
[2] *Parliamentary Debates* (hereafter *Parl. Deb.*), 3rd series, 238, (1878), 907.

against every and any foe. I have no fear of democracy.'[3]

Thereafter Randolph was generally associated, in the public mind, with the concept of 'Tory democracy', which he defined, somewhat paradoxically, as both 'a democracy which supports the Tory party' and a government inspired 'by lofty and by liberal ideas'.[4] Randolph's concept of Tory democracy had a profound and lasting influence on Winston's political ideology. He considered that Tory democracy was his father's 'central idea', but conceded that it was 'necessarily a compromise ... between widely different forces and ideas'.[5]

In 1897 – two years after his father's death – Winston privately confessed that he was 'a Liberal in all but name' but went on to state that because he opposed Irish Home Rule, 'Tory Democracy will have to be the standard under which I shall range myself.' At the same time, he advocated manhood suffrage, universal education, payment of members and a progressive income tax.[6] In some contemporary notes, however, he expressed some pragmatic reservations about the extension of democracy:

> Ultimately 'one man, one vote' is logically and morally certain'. The question as to the rate at which we move to so desirable a goal is one which depends on local and temporary circumstances ... I would extend the franchise to the whole people not by giving votes to the ignorant and indigent, but by raising those classes to the standard when votes may be safely given. This will take time ... The principle is one of levelling up.[7]

Churchill also expressed opposition to female suffrage on the grounds that it would increase hysterical faddism and religious intolerance and make women the dominant power in the community.[8]

When Churchill began his parliamentary career as a candidate at Oldham, in 1899, he described himself a Tory democrat and declared that the Tory democracy was 'the backbone of the party'.[9] After his election for Oldham in 1900 he continued to regard himself as a

[3] Winston S. Churchill, *Lord Randolph Churchill* (1907) 239: speech at Birmingham, 16 April 1884.

[4] *Ibid.*, 240: speech at Birmingham, 9 April 1888. See also: Roland Quinault, 'Lord Randolph Churchill and Tory Democracy 1880–1885', *Historical Journal*, 22 (1979), 141–65.

[5] Churchill, *Randolph Churchill*, 237–8, 821.

[6] Randolph S. Churchill, *Winston S. Churchill* (hereafter Randolph Churchill, *Churchill*): *Companion*, I, part 2 (1967), 751: Winston Churchill to Lady Randolph Churchill, 6 April 1897.

[7] *Ibid.*, 767: notes on the Annual Register.

[8] *Ibid.*, 765.

[9] Robert Rhodes James (ed.), *Winston S. Churchill: His Complete Speeches, 1897–1963* (8 vols., New York, 1974) (hereafter Churchill, *Speeches*), I, 33–5: Oldham, 24, 26 June 1899.

democratic Tory, even when mixing with aristocratic friends and relatives.[10] His cousin's wife, the duchess of Marlborough – the American heiress, Consuelo Vanderbilt – thought that Churchill 'represented the democratic spirit so foreign to my environment, and which I deeply missed'.[11]

Churchill's conversion to Liberalism, in 1904, strengthened his faith in democracy. In 1905 he introduced a motion to reduce the duration of parliaments from seven to five years in order to strengthen the authority of the legislature against the increasing power of the executive.[12] He also favoured longer general election campaigns and a second ballot to 'secure a proper majority representation'.[13] Churchill believed that tariff reform could only be defeated by 'the sledge hammer of democracy' – a massive vote for free trade at the polls.[14] This was achieved by the 1906 'Liberal landslide' and thereafter Churchill used the term 'democracy' as a synonym for mass support for Liberalism.[15]

Churchill's conversion to Liberalism was followed by a change of heart on female suffrage. In 1904 he voted in favour of extending existing franchise rights to women on an equal basis.[16] However his support for some female suffrage was undermined by the actions of the suffragettes, who disrupted his election meetings in 1906, 1908 and 1910. He responded by denouncing their tactics as undemocratic.[17] Churchill observed that 'the frenzy of a few' was no substitute for the 'earnest convictions' of millions.[18] He described the 1910 Female Suffrage Bill as 'anti-democratic' because it proposed to enfranchise propertied women rather than wage earners. He preferred to enfranchise either a proportion of women from all classes or all adults over twenty-five.[19]

When Churchill became a Liberal, he also became an outspoken critic of the House of Lords. As a young Tory, he had shewn no partiality for peers as politicians, but he had regarded the House of Lords as a bulwark of the constitution.[20] In 1904, by contrast, he complained that the Lords had become 'the merest utensil of the Carlton Club'.[21] When the peers rejected the Liberal Education Bill,

[10] *Parl. Deb.* 4th series, 89 (1901), 409.

[11] Consuelo Balsan, *The Glitter and the Gold* (1953), 103.

[12] *Parl. Deb.*, 4th series, 150 (1905), 363–6.

[13] Churchill, *Speeches*, I, 538: Manchester, 8 Jan. 1906.

[14] Churchill, *Speeches*, I, 396: Newcastle, 5 Dec. 1904.

[15] Churchill, *Speeches*, II, 1158 : Nottingham 29 Jan. 1909.

[16] *Parl. Deb.*, 4th series, 131 (1904), 1366.

[17] Churchill, *Speeches*, I, 530: Cheetham, 5 January 1906.

[18] Churchill, *Speeches*, I, 1335: Dundee, 18 Oct. 1909.

[19] *Parl. Deb.*, 5th series, 19 (1910), 224.

[20] Randolph Churchill, *Churchill: Companion*, I, part 2, 698: Winston Churchill to Lady Randolph Churchill, 4 Nov. 1896; Churchill, *Speeches*, I, 44: Shaw, 28 June 1899.

[21] *The Times*, 22 Oct. 1904.

Churchill denounced the hereditary composition, landed character and partisan politics of the Lords. He counselled the Liberals to pass 'one or two good Radical Budgets', create new peers and 'educate the country on the constitutional issues involved' before they confronted the Lords.[22] The Lords' rejection of the 1909 Budget incensed Churchill who believed that 'the whole foundation of democratic life depended on the control of the finances being wielded by the House of Commons'.[23] He claimed that the past prominence of hereditary peers merely reflected the extent to which power had been engrossed by a 'small, limited and unrepresentative class'.[24] Churchill wrote to Asquith early in 1911:

> We ought to go straight ahead with the Parliament Bill & carry it to the Lords at the earliest date compatible with full discussion. We ought as early as possible to make it clear that we are not a bit afraid of creating 5000 peers – if necessary ... our representatives would be far more capable & determined politicians than the Tory nobles.[25]

When the Parliament Bill was introduced, Churchill declared that as the nation advanced, the influence and control of the peers should be reduced.[26]

The passage of the Parliament Bill precipitated a new crisis over Irish home rule. Churchill gradually abandoned his opposition to home rule after he became a Liberal and from 1908 he supported it on broadly democratic grounds. Speaking in 1912, on the Home Rule Bill, he stated that the great majority of the Irish people had a right to a parliament of their own. He acknowledged 'the perfectly genuine apprehensions of the majority of the people of north-east Ulster', but denied that they had the right 'to resist an Act of Parliament which they dislike'.[27] He regarded the Unionists' threats to prevent home rule as a challenge to democracy:

> This will be the issue – whether civil and Parliamentary government in these realms is to be beaten down by the menace of armed force ... It is the old battle-ground of English history ... From the language which is employed it would almost seem that we are face to face with a disposition on the part of some sections of the proprietary

[22] Churchill, *Speeches*, I, 717: Manchester, 4 Feb. 1907.
[23] Churchill, *Speeches*, II, 1393: Bolton, 7 Dec. 1909.
[24] *The Times*, 18 Dec. 1909.
[25] Randolph Churchill, *Churchill: Companion*, II, part 2 (1969), 1031: Winston Churchill to Asquith, 3 Jan. 1911.
[26] *Parl. Deb.*, 5th series, 21 (1911), 2029.
[27] *Parl. Deb.*, 5th series, 37 (1912), 1719.

classes to subvert Parliamentary government and to challenge all the civil and constitutional foundations of society.[28]

Churchill denounced the self-styled 'party of law and order' for acting above the law and setting a bad example to the British democracy 'millions of whom are ... repeatedly urged to be patient under their misfortune until Parliament has the time to deal with their problems'.[29] Churchill's condemnation of the Unionists for undermining parliamentary goverment paralleled his contemporary criticisms of the suffragettes, syndicalists and anarchists and was a precedent for his later stance towards other groups who believed in direct, as opposed to parliamentary action.

In 1912 Churchill was moved by reports of heroic self-sacrifice during the sinking of the Titanic:

> The whole episode fascinates me. It shows that in spite of all the inequalities and artificialities of our modern life, at the bottom – tested to its foundations, our civilisation is humane, Christian, & absolutely democratic.[30]

Churchill's faith in the democratic spirit of the age was reinforced by a much greater tragedy – the outbreak of the First World War:

> It is well that the democratic nations of the world – the nations ... where the peoples own the Government and not the Government the people – should realise what is at stake. The French, English and American systems of government by popular election and Parliamentary debate ... are brought into direct conflict with the highly efficient imperialist bureacracy and military organization of Prussia. That is the issue ... no sophistry can obscure it.[31]

Germany, however, was more democratic than Russia with whom Britain and France were allied during the war. Consequently Churchill welcomed the Russian revolution of February 1917 as a victory for democracy which strengthened the Allied cause:

> All the countries whose Governments owned the people, as if they were a kind of cattle, are on one side, and the countries where the people owned the Government, which are controlled by free citizens acting through Parliamentary institutions, and based on popular

---

[28] Churchill, *Speeches*, III, 2230: Bradford, 14 March 1914.

[29] *Parl. Deb.*, 5th series, 61 (1914), 1577.

[30] *Speaking for Themselves: The Personal Letters of Winston and Clementine Churchill*, ed. Mary Soames (1998), 65: Winston to Clementine, 20 April 1912.

[31] Churchill, *Speeches*, III, 2236: press release, 29 August 1914.

elections, are on the other ... Governments must never again own the people in any part of the world.[32]

In 1918 Churchill hailed the Armistice as an ideological, as well as a military, victory: 'We have beaten the Germans not only out of their trenches. We have beaten them out of their political system.'[33] Britain's own democratic credentials had been strengthened by the 1918 Reform Act which nearly tripled the electorate and enfranchised women over thirty. Churchill played no part in this reform and wrote before the 1918 general election:

The only uncertain element is the great one, this enormous electorate composed of so many of the poorest people in the country. I am pretty confident, however, that we shall secure very large majorities indeed.[34]

His confidence was justified and this bolstered his faith in democracy. In 1919 he boasted to MPs: 'We are elected on the widest franchise obtaining in any country in the world.'[35]

The interwar years provide the acid test of Churchill's commitment to democracy. His strong opposition to the Russian Bolsheviks, British Socialists and nationalists in the empire, together with his return to the Conservatives, led many Left-leaning contemporaries to question his commitment to democracy. For example, David Low, the political cartoonist, wrote of Churchill in the early 1920s: 'A democrat? An upholder of democracy? Um-ah-yes ... when he was leading it. Impatient with it when he was not.'[36] This view has been implicitly endorsed by many historians like Maurice Cowling, who argued that Churchill, after the First World War, abandoned 'the rhetoric of progress for the rhetoric of resistance'.[37] In fact, Churchill's political ideology remained essentially the same as it had been before the war – what changed was the political context, both at home and abroad, in which he operated.

Churchill's hostility to the Bolsheviks was prompted mainly by his distaste for their undemocratic and violent methods. He wrote to a Dundee constituent in December 1918:

With regard to Russia, you have only to seek the truth to be assured of the awful forms of anti-democratic tyranny which prevail there

[32] Churchill, *Speeches*, III, 2562: Dundee 21 July 1917.
[33] *Ibid.*, 2643: Dundee, 26 Nov. 1918.
[34] Martin Gilbert, *Winston S. Churchill* (hereafter Gilbert, *Churchill: Companion*), IV, part I (1977), 429: Winston Churchill to Clementine Churchill, 27 Nov. 1918.
[35] *Parl. Deb.*, 5th series, Commons, 114 (1919), c. 1254.
[36] David Low, *Low's Autobiography* (1956), 146.
[37] Maurice Cowling, *The Impact of Labour 1920–24* (1971), 166.

... The only sure foundation for a State is a Government freely
elected by millions of people, and as many millions as possible. It is
fatal to swerve from that conception.[38]

In 1920 Churchill denounced Lenin and Trotsky because they had
dissolved the Russian parliament and established an autocratic regime
which was not 'fit company for a democratic government like ours'.[39]
He declared that his hatred of the Bolsheviks was founded, not on their
'silly system of economics' or 'absurd doctrine of ... equality', but on
their 'bloody and devasting terrorism'.[40]

Churchill's critique of Bolshevism had more force than many of his
radical contemporaries were prepared to admit, but it led him to favour
one anti-Commmunist who was hardly a democrat. On a visit to Rome,
in 1927, Churchill praised Mussolini:

> Your movement has abroad rendered a service to the whole world.
> The greatest fear that ever tormented every Democratic or Socialist
> leader was that of being outbid or surpassed by some other leader
> more extreme than himself. It has been said that a continual
> movement to the Left, a kind of fatal landslide towards the abyss,
> has been the character of all revolutions. Italy ... provides the
> necessary antidote to the Russian virus.[41]

Churchill's comments were partly prompted by the need for good
Anglo-Italian relations, but he clearly preferred Italy to be Fascist,
rather than Communist.[42] His stance reflected the new ideological
polarity in Europe, but it also echoed a personal concern which he had
first voiced thirty years before. In his only novel, *Savrola*, written in
1896, Churchill traced, in his own words, 'the fortunes of a liberal
leader who overthrew an arbitrary Government only to be swallowed
up by a socialist revolution'.[43] His early fear that the principal threat
to democracy came from the Left, not the Right, was later reinforced
by the Bolshevik revolution. Nevertheless Churchill, in his Rome speech,
stressed that Britain had a very different way from Mussolini of dealing
with Bolshevism and when he returned home, he declared that *all*
forms of tyranny – aristocratic, theocratic, plutocratic, bureaucratic,
democratic – were equally odious.[44]

Churchill's postwar Irish policy was broadly consistent with his

---

[38] Winston S. Churchill, *The Aftermath* (1941), 48–9.
[39] Churchill, *Speeches*, III, 2937–8: Dundee, 14 Feb. 1920.
[40] *Parl. Deb.* 5th series, 131 (1920), 1728.
[41] Churchill, *Speeches*, IV, 4126: Rome, 20 January 1927.
[42] A point Churchill later acknowledged in 1944, see: *Parl. Deb.*, 5th series, 406 (1944),
938.
[43] Winston S. Churchill, *My Early Life* (1943), 169.
[44] Churchill, *Speeches*, IV, 4213: Albert Hall, 6 May 1927.

prewar democratic stance. He wrote to Lloyd George in 1918: 'I have always shared your view that home rule should be give to that part of Ireland which so earnestly desires it and cannot be forced upon that which at present distrusts it.'[45]

The IRA's subsequent campaign against the British authorities aroused Churchill's usual pugnacity and hostility to political violence. Nevertheless – as Paul Addison has pointed out – Churchill neither initiated, nor sought to prolong, British coercion in Ireland which he regarded as a prelude to a settlement, not an alternative to one.[46] He accepted the right of the Ulster Unionists to decide their own fate, but he continued to hope for the re-union of Ireland within the British Empire.[47]

In Britain, Churchill's postwar objective was to forge a progressive alliance between what he called 'the democratic forces in the Conservative party and the patriotic forces in the Liberal and Labour parties'.[48] He justified the continuance of Lloyd George's coalition government by referring to his father's call for a Tory democratic government animated by liberal ideas.[49] After the fall of the coalition, in 1923, he told Sir Robert Horne:

> I am what I have always been – a Tory Democrat. Force of circumstance has compelled me to serve with another party but my views have never changed and I should be glad to give effect to them by rejoining the Conservatives.[50]

In 1924 Churchill called for Conservative co-operation with 'a Liberal wing on the lines of 1886' which would 'afford the nation the guarantee it requires against retrogression'.[51] At the 1924 general election, Churchill stood as a 'Constitutionalist' candidate for Epping. In his election address he compared his position to that of the Liberal Unionists in 1886 and also observed:

> I am entirely opposed to minority rule ... the will of the majority ... is the only healthy foundation of the State ... 'Trust the people!' These words of Lord Randolph Churchill ... embody and express the fundamental principles of British national life and government.[52]

[45] Gilbert, *Churchill: Companion*, IV, part 1, 411: Churchill to Lloyd George, 9 Nov. 1918.
[46] Paul Addison, 'The Search for Peace in Ireland', in *Churchill as Peacemaker* ed. James W. Muller (Cambridge, 1997), 197–202.
[47] For a wider consideration of Churchill's Irish policy see Mary C. Bromage, *Churchill and Ireland* (Notre Dame, Indiana, 1964).
[48] Churchill, *Speeches*, III, 2816: London, 15 July 1919.
[49] *Ibid.*, 2816–7.
[50] Martin Gilbert, *Winston S. Churchill*, V (1976), 8: Riddell's diary, 30 May 1923.
[51] *The Times*, 8 March 1924.
[52] *The Times*, 13 Oct. 1924.

After the election, Churchill joined Baldwin's new Conservative government as Chancellor of the Exchequer. In 1925 he concluded a major speech to the Primrose League, by endorsing his father's belief in 'Government of the people, for the people, by the people'.[53]

The postwar rise of Labour did not undermine Churchill's faith in democracy, partly because he had prewar experience of confronting Labour. He had personally been opposed by Labour candidates at every election since 1908 and his opposition to socialism went back even further. In 1906 he had claimed that moderate Liberalism enlisted 'hundreds of thousands upon the side of progress and popular democratic reform whom militant socialism would drive into violent Tory reaction'.[54] In 1908 he had stressed the fundamental dichotomy between Liberal and socialist principles – a view which he re-stated in 1922: 'Socialism is the negation of every principle of British Liberalism'.[55] In the same speech he observed:

There never was a Government yet erected that would own the people as a Socialist government would. No Tsar, no Kaiser, no Oriental potentate has ever wielded powers like these. When the only employer in the country is the state, a strike becomes a rebellion. No strikes therefore can be tolerated.[56]

Nevertheless Churchill did not question the democratic right of the Labour party to seek a majority at the polls.[57] When Ramsay MacDonald formed the first Labour government in 1924, Churchill wrote to congratulate him and received an appreciative reply. Yet Churchill's antipathy to socialism remained as strong as ever and in 1926 he expressed the fear that a future Labour government would try to implement socialism and thus curtail 'our liberty'.[58]

Churchill regarded the General Strike in May 1926 as a threat to democracy because it attempted 'to compel Parliament to do something which it otherwise would not do'. He predicted that the conflict would end either 'in the overthrow of Parliamentary Government or its decisive victory'.[59] After the end of the strike, Churchill declared that 'government by talking ... is better than government by shouting and ... by shooting'. He denied that 'the age of democracy spells ruin to Parliamentary government' and claimed that parliament was 'the greatest instrument for associating an ever-widening class of citizens

[53] Churchill, *Speeches*, IV, 3592: the Albert Hall, 1 May 1925.
[54] Churchill, *Speeches*, I, 675: Glasgow, 11 Oct. 1906.
[55] *Churchill: Speeches*, I, 146–8: Dundee, 4 May 1908; IV, 3306: Dundee, 8 April 1922.
[56] Churchill, *Speeches*, IV, 3306: Dundee, 8 April 1922.
[57] Churchill, *Speeches*, III, 2943: Dundee, 14 Feb. 1920.
[58] Churchill, *Speeches*, IV, 3821: Bolton, 21 Jan. 1926.
[59] *Parl. Deb.*, 5th series, 195 (1926), 124.

with the actual life and policy of the State'.[60] Nevertheless Churchill was not keen on extending citizenship to young women. In 1927 he initially opposed the Equal Suffrage Bill because he feared it would harm the Conservative party at the polls, but he later decided to support it 'on the well known principle of making a virtue of necessity'.[61] He declared: 'we must not only trust the people ... but trust the whole people'.[62]

In his 1930 Romanes lecture, Churchill observed that parliamentary government 'seems to lose much of its authority when based upon universal suffrage' and that many European parliaments had been undermined:

> Democracy has shown itself careless about those very institutions by which its own political status has been achieved. It seems ready to yield up the tangible rights hard won in rugged centuries to party organizations, to leagues and societies, to military chiefs or to dictatorships in various forms.[63]

Churchill believed that the British parliament, by contrast, had retained both its power and prestige and provided 'the closest association yet achieved between the life of the people and the action of the State'. Nevertheless he doubted whether, even in Britain, the right economic decisions could be reached by 'institutions based on adult suffrage', since no single political party would adopt necessary, but unpopular, economic policies for fear of their electoral consequences. Consequently he recommended the creation of a subordinate 'Economic parliament' made up of businessmen and technocrats.[64]

The financial crisis of 1931 confirmed Churchill's fears about the limitations of modern democracies:

> Democracy as a guide or motive to progress has long been known to be incompetent. None of the legislative assemblies of the great modern states represent in universal suffrage even a fraction of the strength or wisdom of the community ... Democratic governments drift along the line of least resistance, taking short views, paying their way with sops and doles ... Never was there less continuity or design in their affairs, and yet towards them are coming swiftly changes which will revolutionize for good or ill not only the whole economic

[60] Churchill, *Speeches*, IV, 3968–9: Westminster, 26 May 1926.
[61] Gilbert, *Churchill: Companion*, V, part 1 (1979), 958–60: Churchill's Cabinet memorandum, 'The Question of extending Female Suffrage', 8 March 1927. *Speaking for Themselves*, 315: Winston to Clementine, 22 Oct. 1927.
[62] Churchill, *Speeches*, IV. 4333: Chingford, 24 Oct. 1927.
[63] Winston S. Churchill, 'Parliamentary Government and the Economic Problem', in *Thoughts and Adventures* (1942), 194.
[64] *Ibid.*, 196–203.

structure of the world but the social habits and moral outlook of every family.[65]

Churchill's comments reflected contemporary dissatisfaction – on the left, as well as on the right – with parliamentary party politics. This feeling encouraged Ramsay MacDonald to form, in August 1931, a coalition national government. Churchill, like his father before him, favoured the concept of a national government, but he was excluded from its ranks. Nevertheless he welcomed the national government's landslide victory at the polls, on the grounds that 'universal suffrage has sent the largest majority of Tory members to Parliament which has ever been dreamed of'.[66] By 1934, however, Churchill had concluded that the dominance of the House of Commons by one party was 'most unhealthy'. He advocated constitutional changes including a 'weighted' franchise with extra votes for heads of households and fathers of families and the creation of 'a strong and effective Second Chamber' able 'to keep the main structure of our national life beyond the danger of sudden and violent change'.[67]

Churchill's opposition, in the early 1930s, to the Government of India Bill reflected his belief that Asia was unsuited to democracy. As a young officer in India, he had observed: 'East of Suez democratic reins are impossible. India must be governed on old principles.'[68] But Churchill did not believe that India should be governed in an arbitrary or coercive way. In 1920 he endorsed the enforced retirement of General Dyer after the Amritsar Massacre and observed:

> Our reign in India or anywhere else has never stood on the basis of physical force alone and it would be fatal to the British Empire if we were to try to base ourselves only upon it.[69]

In 1931 Churchill opposed the Indian policy of MacDonald's government because it was proposed to transfer many British responsibilities to 'an electorate comparatively small and almost entirely illiterate'. He claimed that the Congress party represented the elite Brahmins who 'spout the principles of western Liberalism and democracy, but ... deny basic human rights to the 60 million untouchables'.[70] Churchill preferred the Indian government to be responsible to Westminster which he considered was 'the most democratic parliament in the world.'[71]

[65] Churchill, 'Fifty Years Hence', in *Thoughts*, 236.
[66] Churchill, *Speeches*, v, 5089: Chingford, 30 October 1931.
[67] *Ibid*, 5319–20: Broadcast, 16 Jan. 1934. *Parl. Deb.*, 5th series, 253 (1931), 102–6.
[68] Churchill, *Churchill: Companion*, I, part 2, 751: Churchill to Lady Randolph Churchill, 6 April 1897.
[69] *Parl. Deb.*, 5th series, 131 (1920), 1731.
[70] Churchill, *Speeches*, v, 5007: Albert Hall, 18 March 1931.
[71] Churchill, *Speeches*, v, 4986: Epping, 23 Feb 1931.

Churchill's doubts about democracy in India were increased by the failure of democracy in much of Europe. He claimed that the supporters of Congress had been influenced by 'all those books about democracy which Europe is now beginning increasingly to discard'.[72] In 1935 he described the proposals contained in the Government of India Bill as the 'faded flowers of Victorian Liberalism which, however admirable in themselves, have nothing to do with Asia and are being universally derided and discarded throughout the continent of Europe'.[73] Churchill's reservations were shared by some maharajahs and members of the orthodox Hindu society, Varnashrama Swarajya, who believed that western democracy was unsuited to Indian traditions.[74]

Churchill's reluctance to apply democratic principles to India contrasted with his readiness to deplore the lack of them in Nazi Germany. Soon after Hitler became chancellor, Churchill observed that German parliamentary democracy, which had been a security for Europe after the First World War, had been replaced by a dictatorship characterised by militarism and anti-semitism.[75] In 1934 he pointed out that the Nazi government was free from 'those very important restraints which a democratic Parliament and constitutional system impose upon any executive Government'.[76] He feared that the apparent success of the Nazi regime posed a threat to the continuance of democracy throughout western Europe:

> We have to consider ... whether the Parliamentary Governments of Western Europe ... are going to be able to afford to their subjects the same measure of physical security, to say nothing of national satisfaction, as is being afforded to the people of Germany by the dictatorship which has been established there.[77]

Nevertheless Churchill continued to regard the Communists, as well as the Nazis, as a threat to democracy. At Paris, in 1936, he welcomed the opposition of the French, British and American democracies to both the Nazis and Communists. His speech was applauded as a 'magnificent defence of democracy'.[78] Churchill feared that in Spain, where civil war had broken out, the Communists were waiting to seize

[72] *Ibid.*

[73] *Parl. Deb.*, 5th series, 302 (1935), 1921.

[74] Winston S. Churchill, Chartwell Papers, Churchill College, Cambridge (hereafter Churchill Papers), CHAR: 2/193/41–45: Stanley Bratle to Churchill, 15 April 1933; 2/123/163–7: Maharajah of Alwar to Churchill 19 July 1922; 2/189/123: cutting from *The Times*, 22 Nov. 1932.

[75] *Parl. Deb.*, 5th series, 276 (1933), 2790.

[76] *Parl. Deb.*, 5th series, 286 (1934), 2071–2.

[77] *Parl. Deb.*, 5th series, 302 (1935), 1496.

[78] Churchill, *Speeches*, VI. 5788: Paris, 24 September 1936; Churchill Papers, CHAR 2/258/79: Arthur Cummings to Churchill, 24 Sept. 1936.

ower as they had done in Russia in 1917. He did not, however, endorse 'ranco's revolt against the Republican government for he believed that whoever wins in Spain, freedom and free democracy must be the osers'.[79] By the end of 1938 Churchill was more favourable to the 'epublican cause because he thought that the influence of the Comnunists and anarchists had waned. He feared that if Franco won he vould practise 'the same kind of brutal suppressions as are practised n the Totalitarian States'.[80]

In the late 1930s it was President Roosevelt, rather than Churchill, vho led the rhetorical campaign in the English-speaking world against he European dictators.[81] The president's peace initiative in 1938 nspired Churchill to issue his own call to the transatlantic democracies:

Have we not an ideology – if we must use this ugly word – of our own in freedom, in a liberal constitution, in democratic and Parliamentary government ... Ought we not to produce in defence of Right, champions as bold, missionaries as eager, and if need be, swords as sharp as are at the disposal of the leaders of totalitarian states.[82]

After the Munich agreement, Churchill claimed that the ideological antagonism between Nazidom and democracy strengthened the free world.[83] In April 1939 Churchill again echoed Roosevelt's recent defence of democracy by citing the British legacy of Magna Carta, Habeas Corpus, the Petition of Right, trial by jury, the English Common Law and parliamentary democracy.[84]

Churchill opposed Chamberlain's appeasement policy partly because he feared that it would undermine democracy in Britain:

I foresee and foretell that the policy of submission will carry with it restrictions upon the freedom of speech and debate in Parliament, on public platforms, and discussions in the Press, for it will be said ... that we cannot allow the Nazi system of dictatorship to be criticsed by ordinary, common English politicians.[85]

This fear had some foundation for Churchill's attack on the Munich

[79] Winston S. Churchill, *Step By Step* (1939), 51–2: 'The Spanish Tragedy, August 10, 1936'.

[80] *Ibid.*, 313: 'The Spanish Ulcer, December 30, 1938'.

[81] For a comparison between Churchill and Roosevelt's comments on democracy see: Roland Quinault 'Anglo-American Attitudes to Democracy from Lincoln to Churchill' in *Anglo-American Attitudes: From Revolution to Partnership*, ed. Fred M. Leventhal and Roland Quinault (Aldershot, 2000), 132–6.

[82] Winston S. Churchill, *Into Battle: War Speeches* (1945), 17–18: Manchester, 9 May 1938.

[83] Churchill, *Battle*, 58: broadcast to the USA, 16 Oct. 1938.

[84] Churchill, *Battle*, 100: London, 20 April 1939.

[85] *Parl. Deb.*, 5th series, 339 (1938), 371.

agreement led to calls for him to be disowned by his constituency association. But Churchill warned that parliamentary democracy would not survive if the constituencies returned subservient MPs and tried to stamp out independent judgement.[86]

When Churchill entered the Cabinet, at the outbreak of war in 1939, he called for tough measures which would convince the world that the democracies were more than a match for the dicatorships.[87] Throughout the war he remained convinced that democracy was on trial as much as dictatorship. In 1942 he told Roosevelt: 'Democracy has to prove that it can provide a granite foundation for war against tyranny.'[88] Yet Churchill's famous speeches in the summer of 1940 employed the old language of freedom, rather than the new language of democracy. Thereafter Churchill's use of specifically democratic rhetoric was constrained by contradictory pressures from Britain's two major allies. In 1941 Hitler's invasion of the Soviet Union provided Churchill with a welcome ally but undermined the democratic credentials of the anti-Nazi front. Soon afterwards, Churchill and Roosevelt signed the Atlantic Charter which, although it asserted the right of people to choose their own form of government, made no reference to democracy. This prevented embarrassment not only for the Soviet Union, but also for imperial Britain. When the US entered the war, Roosevelt privately called on Churchill to give independence to India, but he refused to consider the matter until after the war was over.[89] In 1944 Churchill even told Roosevelt that British imperialism 'has spread and is spreading democracy more widely than any other system of government since the beginning of time'.[90]

Churchill's most important wartime statement on democracy was made in opposition, not to the Nazis, but to the Communists. In December 1944 he defended British intervention in Greece and other parts of liberated Europe as action designed to ensure the rule of democracy, which he defined as free and secret voting for the candidate of one's choice. He claimed that throughout his life he had 'broadly' stood 'upon the foundation of free elections based on universal suffrage'. He accused the Communists of creating 'a swindle democracy ... which calls itself democracy because it is Left Wing':

---

[86] Churchill, *Battle*, 78: Waltham Abbey, 14 March 1939.
[87] Churchill, *Battle*, 133–4: broadcast, 1 October 1939.
[88] CHAR 20/70/79–80: Churchill to Roosevelt, 20 Feb. 1942.
[89] Lord Moran, *Winston Churchill: The Struggle for Survival 1940–65* (1966), 30–1.
[90] Warren F. Kimball (ed.), *Churchill & Roosevelt: The Complete Correspondence III. Alliance Declining February 1944–April 1945* (Princeton, 1987), 140: Churchill to Roosevelt, 21 May 1944.

Democracy ... is not based on violence or terrorism, but on reason, on fair play, on freedom, on respecting the rights of other people. Democracy is no harlot to be picked up in the street by a man with a tommy gun. I trust the people, the mass of the people, in almost every country, but I like to make sure that it is the people and not a gang of bandits ... who think that by violence they can overturn constituted authority, in some cases ancient Parliaments, Governments and States.[91]

The end of the war in Europe led Churchill to fear a renewed threat to democracy at home. The break-up of the coalition government led to a return to party politics and a general election at which Churchill re-issued a warning he had made twenty years before. He denounced socialism as a threat to liberty in Britain – 'the cradle and citadel of free democracy throughout the world' – and he even suggested that a Labour government would have to rely on some sort of gestapo.[92] Nevertheless he accepted Labour's landslide victory at the polls:

I avow my faith in Democracy, whatever course or view it may take with individuals and parties. They may make their mistakes and they may profit from their mistakes. Democracy is now on trial as it never was before, and in these islands we must uphold it, as we upheld it in the dark days of 1940 and 1941 ... While the war was on and all the Allies were fighting for victory, the word 'Democracy', like many people, had to work overtime, but now that peace has come we must search for more precise definitions.[93]

In 1946, in his famous Fulton speech, Churchill laid down the general principle that 'the people of any country have the right and should have the power by constitutional action, by free unfettered elections, with secret ballot, to choose or change the character or form of government under which they dwell'. He was mainly concerned with the lack of democracy behind the 'Iron Curtain' in Eastern Europe, but his exhortation to the British and American peoples to 'practise what we preach' implied that they should also defend democracy at home.[94] Later that year, Churchill denounced Socialist state control in Britain by an 'aristocracy of privileged officials' and in its place advocated 'a property-owning democracy'.[95] In 1947 Churchill criticised

[91] *Parl. Deb.*, 5th series, 406 (1944), 927–8.
[92] Winston S. Churchill, *Victory: War Speeches* (1946), 188–9: election broadcast, 4 June 1945.
[93] *Parl. Deb.*, 5th series, 413 (1945), 86.
[94] Winston S. Churchill, *The Sinews of Peace: Post-War Speeches* (1948), 97: Westminster College, Fulton, Missouri, 5 March 1946.
[95] *Ibid.*, 214: Conservative Party Conference, 5 Oct. 1946.

the 'we are the masters now' mentality of the Labour government:

> Democracy is not a caucus, obtaining a fixed term of office by
> promises, and then doing what it likes with the people. We hold that
> there ought to be a constant relationship between the rulers and the
> people. Government of the people, by the people, for the people
> still remains the sovereign definition of democracy. There is no
> correspondence between this broad conception and the outlook of
> His Majesty's Government.[96]

Churchill thus linked Labour with an unfavourable image of American
democracy: government by caucus.

At the 1950 general election, Labour was returned to power with a
narrow parliamentary majority, although it received fewer votes than
the combined total for Conservatives and Liberals. This led Churchill
to favour proportional representation which he had first endorsed in
1931 – when Labour had also been in office.[97] In 1950 he drew the
attention of parliament to the 'constitutional injustice' whereby
2,600,000 Liberal voters had returned only nine MPs.[98] But his call for
a select committee on electoral reform attracted no support from Tory
backbenchers.[99] Churchill was also out of step with many Tories in his
attitude to reform of the House of Lords. During the debate on the
1947 Parliament Bill, he reminded the House that he had actively
supported the 1911 Parliament Act, but he attacked the new Bill because
it retained the hereditary peers instead of introducing fundamental
reform.[100] In 1952 Lord Salisbury noted that Churchill regarded the
Lords 'as a rather disreputable collection of old gentlemen'.[101] When
Churchill retired from the premiership, he refused a peerage and in
1961 he supported Anthony Wedgwood Benn's attempt to renounce his
peerage and retain his seat in the Commons, which led to the 1963
Peerage Act.[102]

Churchill disliked the hereditary character of the House of Lords
but he regarded the elected House of Commons as 'the enduring
guarantee of British liberties and democratic progress'. In 1953 he told
MPs: 'We are not only a democracy but a Parliamentary democracy
and both aspects of our political life must be borne in mind.' He ever

[96] *Parl. Deb.*, 5th series, 444 (1947), 203.
[97] *Parl. Deb.*, 5th series, 253 (1931), 102–6.
[98] *Parl. Deb.*, 5th series, 472 (1950), 143–4.
[99] Stuart Ball (ed.), *Parliament and Politics in the Age of Churchill and Attlee: The Headlam Diaries 1935–1951*, Camden Fifth Series, vol. 14 (Cambridge, 1999), 622–3: diary entries for 7 and 9 March 1950.
[100] *Parl. Deb.*, 5th series, 444 (1947), 202.
[101] Moran, *Struggle for Survival*, 376: diary entry for 22 Feb. 1952.
[102] Winston Churchill, *Letter to Anthony Wedgwood Benn* (Bristol, 1961). See also Tony Benn's comments in the 'Churchill Remembered' section.

claimed 'that elections exist for the sake of the House of Commons and not that the House of Commons exists for the sake of elections'.[103] He regarded himself as the servant of the House of Commons and he opposed the American system which separated the executive from the legislature.[104]

During his second premiership, Churchill was still reluctant to extend democracy to the non-white population of the British Empire, particularly in Africa. In 1954 he observed to Eisenhower:

I am a bit sceptical about universal suffrage for the Hottentots even if refined by proportional representation. The British and American Democracies were slowly and painfully forged and even they are not perfect yet.[105]

Churchill's reference to the Hottentots echoed an 1886 speech by Lord Salisbury, who had argued that majority government could not be safely conferred on Hottentots, Indians or other non-Teutonic peoples.[106] Churchill was sceptical, not without reason, whether democracy could operate effectively in countries where there were high levels of poverty and illiteracy and no tradition of mass participation in institutional politics. Nevertheless he did not rule out democratisation in the colonies if the conditions were right. Indeed in 1953 British Guiana was given a constitution based on universal suffrage, although it was soon suspended after disturbances broke out. In the same year the possibility of giving autonomy to the Gold Coast was also considered, although Jock Colville doubted if Churchill was interested 'in the inhabitants of those parts'.[107] Churchill's preference for gradual democratisation reflected his historical perspective. His remark to Eisenhower about the slow and imperfect emergence of democracy in Britain and America was fully justified. Britain had only recently adopted a one person one value franchise and still retained an hereditary monarchy and second chamber, whilst in the USA many non-whites were still disenfranchised.

In 1914 Churchill expressed the hope that he had 'a firm grip of democratic principles'.[108] How justified was this claim with respect to his career as a whole? Churchill's commitment, in principle, to democracy in Britain never wavered, even in the interwar years. He always

---

[103] *Parl. Deb.*, 5th series, 520 (1953), 21–2.
[104] Winston S. Churchill, *The Unrelenting Struggle: War Speeches* (1942), 334: 29 December 1941; Sir John Colville, *Parliamentary Democracy: History and Practice* (Toronto, 1986), 7–10.
[105] Anthony Montague Browne, *Long Sunset: Memoirs of Winston Churchill's Last Private Secretary* (1996), 164.
[106] *The Times*, 17 May 1886: Salisbury's speech at St James's Hall, 15 May.
[107] Moran Diaries, 434: 14 July 1953.
[108] *Churchill: Speeches*, III, 2232 : Bradford, 14 March 1914.

believed that the fundamental source of political authority was the wil
of the people expressed through the medium of free and secre
parliamentary elections. However Churchill's commitment, in practice
to democracy in Britain was less impressive than his rhetoric. Althoug
he supported the principle of manhood suffrage, he did little to advanc
its implementation. He quickly accepted the principle of women
suffrage, but he opposed female franchise bills both before and afte
the First World War. Moreover Churchill was not entirely committee
to an equal franchise. Montague Browne noted Churchill's interest, i
the 1950s, in schemes for cumulative votes for heads of families an
others with special responsibilites, but thought that he did not seriousl
wish to put them into practice.[109] However Churchill had also propose
such schemes in the 1930s, which suggests that he had a fairly seriou
interest in them.

Churchill often expressed reservations about democracy. He did s
not only in the early 1930s – when democracy was being undermine
by economic and political developments – but also after the Secon
World War when western democracy had triumphed. In 1947 he calle
democracy 'the worst form of Government except all those others tha
have been tried'.[110] He thought that democracy was riddled with fault
and dangers, and a perpetual popularity contest, though it was stil
better than alternative systems.[111]

It is tempting to ascribe Churchill's reservations about democracy t
his ancestral Conservatism. Sir John Colville noted that Churchill wa
a strange mixture of radical and traditionalist and in that respect, h
resembled his father, Lord Randolph, who had wished, in Winston'
words, to reconcile 'the old glories ... of King and country ... wit
modern democracy'.[112] Winston certainly saw no contradiction betwee
democracy and monarchy. In 1943 he approved the marriage of th
exiled King of Yugoslavia on the grounds that it would give him
chance of perpetuating his dynasty and then added, incongruously, 'ar
we not fighting this war for liberty and democracy?'[113] Yet Churchill'
belief that monarchy and democracy were compatible was based o
more than just Conservatism. His hope, at the end of the Spanish Civi
War, that the restoration of a constitutional monarchy would end ol
emnities was vindicated by events after Franco's death.[114]

Churchill's reservations about democracy stemmed not just from hi

[109] Browne, *Long Sunset*, 180.

[110] *Parl. Deb.*, 5th series, 444 (1947), 207.

[111] Browne, *Long Sunset*, 180.

[112] John Colville, *The Fringes of Power*, 128; Churchill, *Thoughts and Adventures*, 42.

[113] Winston S. Churchill, *The Second World War*, v: *Closing The Ring* (1952), 571–2: Churchi
to the Foreign Secretary, 11 July 1943.

[114] Churchill, *Step By Step*, 334: 'Hope in Spain, 23 February 1939'.

Conservatism, but also from his Liberalism. In 1906 he noted that the 1884 Reform Act had been followed by twenty years of Tory ascendancy:

> Who could possibly have foreseen that ... enfranchised multitudes would constitute themselves the buttresses of privilege and property; that a free press would by its freedom sap the influence of debate and through its prosperity become the implement of wealth; that members and constituencies would become less independent, not more independent; that Ministers would become more powerful, not less powerful; that the march would be ordered backward along the beaten track, not forward in some new direction..."[115]

Churchill was a Liberal when he wrote this comment, but he made similar remarks in the 1930s when he was a Conservative.

Churchill also feared that democracy could breed jingoism and war. In 1901 he observed: 'Democracy is more vindictive than Cabinets. The wars of peoples will be more terrible than those of kings.'[116] In 1947, in an imagined conversation with his father, he said: 'We have had nothing else but wars since democracy took charge.'[117] This was ironic because Churchill believed that peace was the only secure foundation for democracy. In 1906 he observed that 'the first indispensable condition of democratic progress must be the maintenance of European peace'.[118] This conviction underlay his support for European unity both before and after the Second World War. In 1947 he declared: 'The whole purpose of a united democratic Europe is to give decisive guarantees against aggression.'[119]

Churchill's anti-Socialism, which tarnished his reputation as a democrat in the eyes of the Left, reflected his Liberalism more than his Conservatism. His belief that socialism was an inherently illiberal political system may seem excessive in retrospect, but it was borne out, during his lifetime, in half of Europe and much of the rest of the world. Even in postwar Britain, the growth of the socialistic state alarmed not just the Right, but also moderate Labour politicians like Roy Jenkins. Today, by contrast, New Labour in Britain and the new socialists in Europe have rejected the full-blooded socialism which Churchill so strongly mistrusted.

Churchill's reputation as a democrat was also undermined by his reluctance to democratise Britian's non-white empire. But his stance

[115] Churchill, *Lord Randolph Churchill*, 219.
[116] *Parl. Deb.*, 4th series, 93 (1901), 1572.
[117] Winston Churchill, 'The Dream', in Martin Gilbert, *Winston S. Churchill*, VIII (1988), 369.
[118] Churchill, *Speeches*, I, 671: Glasgow, 11 Oct. 1906.
[119] Winston S. Churchill, *Europe Unite: Speeches 1947 and 1948* (1950), 83: Albert Hall, 14 May 1947.

on this issue was shared by most of his parliamentary contemporarie
including many Liberals and some socialists.[120] His attitude was base
mainly on pragmatic considerations of culture, wealth, class, educatio
and stability rather than on racial prejudice, for even in Britai
Churchill only favoured a gradual 'levelling up' to full democrac
Nevertheless Churchill's stalwart defence of democracy during th
Second World War strengthened the post-war demand for democrac
throughout the Empire.

Churchill's attitude to democracy was essentially late-Victorian i
character. He favoured a democracy which was evolutionary, n
revolutionary; parliamentary, not plebiscitary; monarchical, not repul
lican, liberal not socialist. His outlook was indelibly influenced by h
father's concept of Tory democracy which, in turn, drew on th
Victorian Liberal tradition of Gladstone and Mill. Like them, Church
trusted 'the people' but was not entirely committed to electoral equali
and believed that legislation and administration should be in the han
of those able to lead. Churchill had great confidence in his own abiliti
in this respect and one of his favourite definitions of democracy w:
'the association of us all through the leadership of the best'.[121] Howeve
Churchill never forgot that he was a representative of the people. C
his eightieth birthday – at the height of his fame – he modestly observe
that it was the British people who had the lion's heart during the wa
while he merely had 'the luck to be called upon to give the roar'.[122]

[120] See the comments by Tony Benn MP and Lord Carrington in the 'Churcl
Remembered' section.
[121] Winston S. Churchill, *Stemming The Tide: Speeches 1951 and 1952* (1953), 82–3: Glasgc
18 May 1951.
[122] Winston S. Churchill, *The Unwritten Alliance: Speeches 1953 to 1959* (1961), 203: spee
at Westminster Hall, 30 November 1954.

CHURCHILL'S WRITING OF HISTORY: APPEASEMENT, AUTOBIOGRAPHY AND *THE GATHERING STORM*

By David Reynolds

CHURCHILL'S life was politics. His career as an MP ran, virtually unbroken, from 1900 to 1964 – almost the first two-thirds of the twentieth century. But although Churchill lived for politics, he lived by writing. Much of his income was earned as a journalist and author. At one end of the spectrum were scores of newspaper columns assessing contemporary events and politicians, summarising the plots of great novels, or just musing for money – as in 'Have You a Hobby?' or 'Are There Men in the Moon?' At the other extreme are large books such as the biographies of his father (1906) and of his martial ancestor, the first duke of Marlborough (1933–8), and his *History of the English-Speaking Peoples* (1956–8). Somewhere in between are autobiographical vignettes such as *The Malakand Field Force* (1898) and *My Early Life* (1930). But it is for his two sets of war memoirs that Churchill the historian is most remembered – six separate volumes on World War I (1923–31) and its aftermath, six more on World War II and its origins (1948–54).

J.H. Plumb observed that Churchill's historical work could be divided into two categories: 'formal, professional' histories and those dealing with 'contemporary events in which he himself was involved.'[1] Yet there is a sense in which, for Churchill, all history was autobiography. In July 1934, in an obituary of his much-loved cousin, 'Sunny', 9th duke of Marlborough, he wrote of 'the three or four hundred families which had for three or four hundred years guided the fortunes of the nation'.[2] Prominent among them, of course, were the Churchills, from the first duke via Lord Randolph to Winston himself. In his view, British history was a narrative of the deeds of great men (definitely men), and most of those men were intertwined with the saga of his own family. This approach to history and politics naturally privileges the significance of the individual and the uniqueness of events. By contrast, the thrust of most modern historiography has been to subsume the individual into

---

[1] J.H. Plumb, 'The Historian', in A. J. P. Taylor, *et al.*, *Churchill: Four Faces and the Man* (1969), 130. See also Maurice Ashley, *Churchill as Historian* (1968).
[2] Martin Gilbert, *Winston S. Churchill: Companion* (hereafter Gilbert, *CV*), v, part 2 (1981), 820. Like all students of Churchill, I am indebted to Martin Gilbert's volumes of biography and documents.

larger patterns (Marxism, the Annales school, the linguistic turn) or to emphasise the role of individual at the lower levels of society rather than through politics at the top.

Today, therefore, Churchill's philosophy of history is bound to seem somewhat outmoded. Yet his historical writings have been immensely influential, none more so than *The Second World War*, which between 1948 and 1954 was serialised in eighty magazines and newspapers worldwide, and went on to appear in hardback in fifty countries and eighteen languages.[3] Although Churchill was at pains not to describe his account as history, 'for that belongs to another generation', he expressed confidence that it was 'a contribution to history which will be of service to the future.'[4] Privately he was less diffident. He liked to say, on matters of controversy, that he would leave it to history but would be one of the historians. In the case of *The Second World War*, as Plumb observed, subsequent historians have moved down 'the broad avenues which he drove through war's confusion and complexity', with the result that 'Churchill the historian lies at the very heart of all historiography of the Second World War.'[5] At the beginning of the twenty-first century, how should this work be evaluated?

In this short essay, I shall confine myself to some reflections on the opening volume, *The Gathering Storm*, and particularly the first of its two books, entitled 'From War to War', which covers the period from 1919 to 1939. For it is in this volume – published in the United States in June 1948 and in Britain in October – that Churchill made perhaps his most enduring 'contribution to history', through his critique of appeasement in the 1930s. His aim was 'to show how easily the tragedy of the Second World War could have been prevented; how the malice of the wicked was reinforced by the weakness of the virtuous'. What he called 'this sad tale of wrong judgments formed by well-meaning and capable people' was intended to prove that the conflict was indeed 'The Unnecessary War'. His purpose, in short, was 'to lay the lessons of the past before the future'.[6] The Cassandra of the 1930s became the Thucydides of the 1940s.[7]

Before World War Two, 'appeasement', true to its French root remained a neutral or even positive term, denoting the satisfaction of grievances by means of negotiation. Thereafter it became a term of

---

[3] John Ramsden, *'That Will Depend on Who Writes the History': Winston Churchill as His Own Historian*, Inaugural Lecture, Queen Mary and Westfield College, London, 22 October 1996, 12.

[4] Winston S. Churchill, *The Second World War* (hereafter *SWW*) (6 vols., 1948–54), I, vii.

[5] Plumb, 'The Historian', 149.

[6] *SWW*, I, vii–viii, 14, 270–1.

Cf. D. C. Watt, 'Appeasement: The Rise of a Revisionist School?', *Political Quarterly* 36 (1965), 198.

abuse, signifying peace at any price; likewise 'Munich' is now a synonym for betrayal. The supposed 'lessons' of appeasement have haunted postwar policymakers in America and Britain, be it Harry Truman over Korea in 1950, Anthony Eden during the Suez crisis of 1956, George Bush after Iraq invaded Kuwait in 1990, or the Blair government during the Kosovo war of 1999.[8] Of course, Churchill did not teach those lessons single-handed. Three Beaverbrook journalists, including Michael Foot, had already indicted Britain's leaders of the 1930s in the aftermath of Dunkirk – so successfully that their polemic against the *Guilty Men* sold 200,000 copies in its first six months.[9] Two other books also published in 1948 – *Munich, Prologue to Tragedy* by John Wheeler-Bennett and *Diplomatic Prelude* by Lewis Namier – took a similar line to *The Gathering Storm*. But Churchill's account of the interwar years was in a class of its own, selling *its* first 200,000 British copies in only two weeks.[10] Lengthy serialisation in *The New York Times*, *Life* magazine, and *The Daily Telegraph* (the latter running to forty-two extracts over two months) brought its principal themes to a huge audience. Nor was there anyone of comparable stature to defend appeasement. Britain's three premiers of the 1930s had all died discredited, without having written their memoirs – Ramsay MacDonald in 1937, Neville Chamberlain in 1940, and Stanley Baldwin in December 1947. Keith Feiling's official biography of Chamberlain, published in October 1946, did little to dispel the cloud of disapproval. What D. C. Watt has dubbed 'the Churchillian critique of appeasement' has held sway at a popular level for two generations.[11]

During that time, however, the historical documentation for the 1930s has changed dramatically. In the early 1970s, the official documents for the 1930s and World War Two became available at the Public Record Office under the new Thirty-Year Rule. Over the next decade a series of revisionist histories offered a more sympathetic account of the dilemmas faced by the appeasers. By the early 1980s, the interwar volume of Martin Gilbert's official biography, plus three massive companion volumes of documents, had provided much greater information about Churchill's views in the 1930s. And in the late 1990s, Churchill's original papers from the 1930s and 1940s were opened to

[8] Ernest R. May, *'Lessons' of the Past: The Use and Misuse of History in American Foreign Policy* (New York, 1973), 80–2; Anthony Eden, *Full Circle* (1960), 514–18 (where he uses the same image of a gathering storm); Alex Danchev, 'The Anschluss', *Review of International Studies*, 20 (1994), 97–101; David Reynolds, *Britannia Overruled: British Policy and World Power in the Twentieth Century* (second edn, 2000), 293.

[9] 'Cato', *Guilty Men* (reprint edn, 1998), xv.

[10] See Churchill College Archives Centre, Cambridge, Winston Churchill papers (hereafter CHUR), 4/24B, f. 334.

[11] Watt, 'Churchill and Appeasement', in Robert Blake and Wm Roger Louis, eds., *Churchill* (Oxford, 1993), esp. 199–201.

public inspection. Thus, from the vantage point of the early twenty-first century, historians can view appeasement, Churchill and *The Gathering Storm* from a new perspective. This essay, part of the larger project on the war memoirs, is a contribution to that reappraisal.

Given its historiographical impact, it is ironic that *The Gathering Storm* nearly did not appear. Churchill's basic contract was for four volumes, not six. Volume one was initially intended to run to the end of 1940 – a period eventually covered in two volumes. As late as January 1947, he envisaged only five chapters to take the reader from 1919 to the outbreak of war in September 1939. One chapter would survey the period 1919 to 1934, a second would deal with the rise of Hitler, 1931–8, and a third would examine British rearmament up to 1939. After a chapter devoted to Munich, one more, entitled 'The Interlude', would take the reader up to the outbreak of war.[12] It was not until Churchill began seriously to work on the interwar years during 1947 that the scope of this part of the book expanded dramatically, with outlines for eleven chapters, seventeen and even twenty-four chapters, before contracting down to the final twenty-one.

Self-evidently, five sketchy chapters about the appeasement era in a volume running to December 1940 would have had far less impact than the eventual first book of *The Gathering Storm*. Indeed the title itself, so evocative for Churchill's thesis, only emerged late in the day. Until October 1947, Churchill's working title was 'The Downward Path', for which he then substituted 'Toward Catastrophe'. Both of these seemed too negative to his publishers, particularly in the United States, given that the chapters were supposed to form the overture to his belated entry into Number Ten Downing Street. On 30 January 1948, just a few weeks before serialisation was to begin, Churchill was still canvassing suggestions for the title. It was his veteran literary agent, Emery Reves, who came up with the phrase 'The Gathering Storm'. This conveyed the sense of looming danger in a suitably 'crescendo' form.[13]

Why did the thrust of *The Gathering Storm* emerge relatively late in the day? There are, I think, three main reasons, each of them illustrative of Churchill the historian – the sources at his disposal, his method of writing and his sensitivity to the present.

As with most of his books since the biography of his father, Churchill employed a team of researchers. For *The Second World War*, this was an immensely distinguished team. Its anchor was William Deakin, a professional historian and Oxford don, who had particular responsibility

---

[12] See outlines in CHUR 4/74, f. 24 and CHUR 4/75, f. 1.
[13] CHUR 4/74, ff. 43, 61, and CHUR 4/24B, ff. 317–319; cf. Martin Gilbert, *Winston S. Churchill*, VIII (1988), 394–5.

for political and diplomatic matters. The naval side was handled by a retired officer, Commander Gordon Allen. For military affairs and high policymaking, Churchill used General Hastings Ismay, wartime military secretary to the cabinet, and General Sir Henry Pownall, who had been on the secretariat of the committee of imperial defence from 1933 to 1936 and was vice-chief of the imperial general staff in 1941. Ismay and Pownall were particularly well connected. The former was 'devilling' for Churchill even before he retired from the cabinet office in November 1946, while Pownall was a member of the advisory panel for the official military histories of the war, which gave him ready access to confidential material. Moreover, Churchill's prestige and connections also opened doors that would have been closed to ordinary historians.

In consequence, the source material for volume one is not simply Churchill's own documents from the period, as one might expect in the case of someone who was out of office. It also includes inside information of high quality on specific topics. For instance, on comparative air strengths in the 1930s, Pownall obtained statistical data from official contacts in France and the air ministry historical branch, while Churchill wrote direct to General Carl Spaatz, head of the Army Air Force in Washington, who had commanded the AAF in Britain in 1942. From half a dozen American agencies, Spaatz collated US data on German air strength.[14] To take another example, Churchill's account of Anthony Eden's resignation as foreign secretary in February 1938 drew on the diary of Oliver Harvey, Eden's private secretary, and on comments by several government ministers of the time. It was even checked by the cabinet secretary, Norman Brook, against the cabinet minutes. Consequently, Churchill was able to reveal for the first time that Eden's breach with Chamberlain occurred over policy towards the United States as well as Italy – ironically giving the world a far fuller account of this episode than Eden himself had done hitherto. In short, Churchill's indictment of appeasement was that of an outsider blessed with inside information. This was the case for the prosecution garnished with evidence from the defence.

The wealth of information that became available to Churchill is, I think, one reason why his account of the 1930s expanded so dramatically and why he found it difficult to control. A second reason is the way Churchill worked: he did not marshal that mass of information until late in the day. His preoccupation in 1946 and the first half of 1947

---

[14] See correspondence in CHUR 4/140A: the graph comparing French and German output of first-line aircraft, printed as appendix E of *The Gathering Storm*, was based on material provided via Pownall's friend, General Alphonse-Joseph Georges – *ibid.*, ff 23–32.

was the summer and autumn of 1940, when he was in power and Britain's fate lay in the balance. Meanwhile, his researchers were compiling essays on specific topics, using the official documents to which they had access as well as published sources such as the Nuremburg trials. At the same time, they were collating Churchill's own documents from the 1930s, particularly his speeches and correspondence with government ministers. These were printed as galleys at an early stage, allowing him to cut and paste lengthy quotation into his text. This was Churchill's standard method of writing his histories. After absorbing the material, he would start to cast it in his own mould, usually in lengthy late-night orations as he paced up and down his study at Chartwell – a pair of secretaries taking turns with the shorthand, research assistants in attendance to give factual advice. He wrote, as he liked to say, 'from mouth to hand'.[15]

But this was an incremental process. Not only the documents but also Churchill's own text were produced as galley proofs: he preferred to revise from the printed page, often doing minor corrections in bed first thing in the morning. These galleys went through three, four or even five versions, with titles such as 'Almost Final', 'Provisional Final' and 'Final' (to which the caveat was added, in large type: 'Subject to Full Freedom of Proof Correction'). Since no publisher would tolerate such a costly method of editing, Churchill did this at his own expense (out of the munificent advances), using the Chiswick Press, a branch of the publishers Eyre and Spottiswoode.[16] The eventual book was set up in new type from those galleys by his publishers, often very late in the day. This, incidentally, helps explain the numerous printing errors in the British edition of *The Gathering Storm*, which had to be rectified at the last minute by two pages of corrections and then a further errata slip. Some of these errors were deeply embarrassing. On page fifty-six of the first edition we are told that the French army was 'the poop of the life of France'. That is corrected on the errata slip: 'For "poop" read "prop".'

Gradually Churchill's dictated narrative put flesh on his documentary skeleton. But it was a common complaint – from his researchers, his publishers and not least his wife – that the bones still tended to show through. With so much of the material emanating from others, and with political duties as leader of the opposition taking up a good deal of time, Churchill found it hard to get his mind round the whole book. It usually required a special vacation, paid for by his publishers, at which Churchill, plus secretaries and members of his research team, engaged in what was known as 'bulldozing' the final text. This entailed

[15] Robert Rhodes James, *Churchill: A Study in Failure* (Harmondsworth, 1973), 31.
[16] By June 1947 he already owed them over £1,400 – CHUR 4/24A, f.145.

pruning the quotations, or relegating them to the ever-swelling appendices, and ensuring that Churchill's own voice came through clearly. For the first volume, the bulldozing was done in the warmth and opulence of the Mamounia Hotel in Marrakesh between 11 December 1947 and 18 January 1948 (his wife stayed behind to enjoy the austerity of an Attlee Christmas). From Marrakesh, corrected galleys were sent almost daily to the Chiswick Press, and new proofs received with equal frequency. It was only at this late stage that the book took coherent shape.

As Churchill bulldozed the 1930s, he brooded on the 1940s. In mid-November, he received a message from Henry Luce, the owner of *Life* magazine, who was still unhappy that the mass of documents marred the 'architectural sense' and impeded 'analytical insight'. Churchill replied defensively that he had so far been assembling the material in chronological order and had not yet had time 'to read Book I through at a run'. This he said he would do at Marrakesh. The analytical point he intended to bring out was that 'in those years there happened exactly what is happening today, namely no coherent or persistent policy, even in fundamental matters, among the good peoples, but deadly planning among the bad. The good peoples, as now, drifted hither and thither, to and fro, according to the changing winds of public opinion and the desire of public men of medium stature to gain majorities and office at party elections.'[17]

Churchill had used the phrase 'The Unnecessary War' at least as early as October 1940. He deployed it publicly in a major speech in Brussels in November 1945.[18] So the basic theme was not new. But his conviction that the conflict had resulted, in large measure, from a failure of political leadership sharpened in 1946–8 amid the deepening Cold War. For Hitler, read Stalin (each engaged in 'deadly planning'); for Baldwin, read Attlee (those 'public men of medium stature'). In his 'Iron Curtain' speech at Fulton in March 1946 he insisted that there 'never was a war in all history easier to prevent by timely action', adding 'I saw it all coming and cried aloud to my own fellow-countrymen and to the world, but no one paid any attention.' And so, said Churchill, 'one by one we were all sucked into the awful whirlpool. We surely must not let that happen again.' The analogies were reiterated in his political speeches during 1948, at the same time as his account of the 1930s unfolded in newspaper articles and then in volume form. The Berlin crisis, he told a mass rally of 100,000 Tories in June 1948,

[17] Luce to Churchill, 18 Nov. 1947, and Churchill to Luce, 22 Nov. 1947, quoted in Gilbert, *Churchill*, VIII, 357–8.
[18] John Colville, *The Fringes of Power: Downing Street Diaries, 1939–1955* (1985), 278; Robert Rhodes James (ed.), *Winston S. Churchill: His Complete Speeches, 1897–1963* (hereafter Churchill, *Complete Speeches*) (8 vols., New York, 1974), VII, 7251, 16 Nov. 1945.

'raises issues as grave as those which we now know were at stake at Munich ten years ago. It is our hearts' desire that peace may be preserved, but we should all have learned by now that there is no safety in yielding to dictators, whether Nazi or Communist.'[19]

It was this political moral, painfully apt for contemporaries, that gave the first book of Churchill's war memoirs its emotional power. Several readers went so far as to liken the story to a classical tragedy.[20] The gathering storm, clearly discerned on the horizon by men of vision, was ignored by politicians of lesser stature. How does Churchill's account stand up to scrutiny fifty years on? How far was he aware of its deficiencies at the time? In addressing these questions within a brief compass, I shall focus on four main issues: leadership, defence, foreign policy, and domestic politics.

Who were these mediocre leaders, blind to the gathering storm? Not surprisingly, Churchill is kind to the Conservative government of 1924–9, in which he was chancellor of the exchequer. This is a period of 'very considerable recovery' at home and genuine 'distinction' in foreign policy, particularly thanks to Treaty of Locarno. In 1929, 'the state of Europe was tranquil, as it had not been for twenty years, and was not to be for at least another twenty'. Thereafter the rot set in. The prime minister from 1929 to 1935 was Ramsay MacDonald, but Churchill has little to say about him. In the book, MacDonald is a shadowy figure, 'brooding supinely' and in a state of 'increasing decrepitude' over a predominantly Tory government after 1931.[21]

In *The Gathering Storm* the culpable figures are MacDonald's successors as premier, Stanley Baldwin and Neville Chamberlain. (They were also the two Tory leaders who kept Churchill out of office during the 1930s. The best Churchill can say for Baldwin is that he was 'the greatest Party manager the Conservatives ever had'; we are told that he 'took no active share in foreign policy' apart from his 'well-known desire for peace and a quiet life.'[22] Although Churchill did not write the famous index entry on Baldwin ('confesses putting party before country'), that summed up his sentiments. Whereas Baldwin was indicted for lethargy, political opportunism and indifference to foreign affairs; Chamberlain's crimes were hubris, illusions and mental rigidity. If Baldwin wanted to be left in peace, Chamberlain wanted to make peace. In dealing with Hitler, Churchill argues, this was folly of the highest order. He single

[19] Quotations from Churchill, *Speeches*, VII, 7292–3 (5 March 1946) and 7671 (26 June 1948).
[20] For instance, Alfred Duff Cooper to WSC, 5 August 1948, CHUR 4/19; Sir Harold Butler, 'Mr Churchill and the Unnecessary War', *The Fortnightly*, 163, Oct. 1948, 227.
[21] *SWW*, I, 30, 52.
[22] *SWW*, I, 26, 187.

out Chamberlain's 'long series of miscalculations, and misjudgments of men and facts', though acknowledging that his 'motives have never been impugned'.[23] In Churchill's account, each man, for different reasons, wreaks appalling damage – from indolence or arrogance, they facilitated Hitler's resistible rise and thus an unnecessary war.

There is, however, a tension in Churchill's account. Baldwin was premier from 1935 to 1937, Chamberlain from 1937 to 1940. On Churchill's own admission, it was during the period 1931–5 that 'the entire situation on the Continent was reversed'. He says that 'once Hitler's Germany had been allowed to rearm without active interference by the Allies and former associated Powers, a second World War was almost certain'. (An earlier draft even used the word 'inevitable'.)[24] The years 1931–5 was the MacDonald era – hence Churchill's concern to represent Baldwin as 'the virtual Prime Minister' during that period.[25] But the main way in which he resolves the tension is to highlight a series of missed opportunities *after* 1935. In today's jargon, book one of *The Gathering Storm* is at times almost an exercise in counterfactual history.[26]

At the beginning of chapter eleven, for instance, he depicts 'a new atmosphere in England' in early 1936. The obvious breakdown of collective security and a general backlash against the Hoare–Laval pact dividing up Abysssinia had, he argued, created a cross-party consensus that was 'now prepared to contemplate war against Fascist or Nazi tyranny'. Yet the government stuck to its 'policy of moderation, half-measures and keeping things quiet'.[27] Critically, there was no reaction to Hitler's re-occupation of the Rhineland in March. In an early draft of the end of chapter thirteen, Churchill had written: 'Nothing could have stopped Hitler after the seizure of the Rhineland except a very serious war.' In the published text, however, this categorical judgement is heavily qualified: 'Many say that nothing except war could have stopped Hitler after we had submitted to the seizure of the Rhineland. This may indeed be the verdict of future generations. Much, however, could have been done to make us better prepared and thus lessen our hazards. And who shall say what could not have happened?'[28]

A second putative 'turning point' occurs at the end of 1936, where Churchill juxtaposes Baldwin's now notorious speech of 'appalling

---

[23] *SWW,* I, 173–4, 255.
[24] *SWW,* I, 52 and 148; cf. CHUR 4/85, f.4.
[25] *SWW,* I, 94.
[26] It is worth noting that in 1931 Churchill contributed a long essay under the title 'If Lee Had Not Won the Battle of Gettysburg' to a collection entitled *If It Had Happened Otherwise.*
[27] *SWW,* I, 147–8.
[28] CHUR 4/87, f. 65; cf. *SWW,* I, 186.

frankness' to the Commons on 12 November and the crisis over Edward VIII's abdication the following month. Through the 'Provisional Semi-Final' version Baldwin's speech was placed as the climax of an earlier chapter on the loss of air parity from 1933 to 1936. This documented Baldwin's February 1934 pledge that Britain would keep abreast of Germany, his denials of Churchill's warnings that parity had been lost, his May 1936 'confession' that it had and, finally, his 12 November admission that, had he gone to the country on a rearmament platform, the outcome would have been certain defeat. In this form, the chapter had enormous power as a cumulative indictment of Baldwin. But at the 'Provisional Final' stage, Churchill sacrificed that in order to play up another turning point. He moved the November material into a later chapter on 1936–7, 'The Loaded Pause', and there followed it with a two-page account of the Abdication (previously a single sentence at the end of the draft on 'Air Parity'). In this treatment, Baldwin's 'appalling frankness' in admitting 'that he had not done his duty with regard to national safety because he was afraid of losing the election' is described as 'an incident without parallel in our Parliamentary history'. The impression produced on the House was 'so painful that it might well have been fatal' to Baldwin but for his adroit handling of the king's affair. Just at this moment, asserts Churchill, the cross-party forces for 'Arms and the Covenant' that he had been marshalling were on the verge of a breakthrough. But the contrast between Baldwin's shrewd judgement of public opinion and Churchill's pleas that the king be given time (to get over his infatuation) turned the tables for the two of them. Churchill wrote that the forces he had gathered on defence were 'estranged or dissolved' and that 'I was so smitten in public opinion that it was the almost universal view that my political life was ended.'[29]

Undoubtedly Baldwin did retrieve himself over the Abdication, but historian Paul Addison is surely right that Churchill greatly exaggerated the effect of the crisis on the 'Arms and the Covenant' movement. 'The reason why his campaign faltered after December 1936 was that 1937 saw a relaxation of Anglo-German tensions' that lasted until the Austrian Anschluss in March 1938.[30] Nevertheless, Churchill's interpretation has become widely accepted. Even more so has his version of what Baldwin told the Commons on 12 November. In *The Gathering Storm* Churchill's extracts from Baldwin's speech and his own commentary imply that Baldwin was referring to the 1935 election. In fact, as Baldwin's full text makes clear, he was referring to 1933–4, in the wake of the notorious 'pacificist' victory at the East Fulham by-

[29] *SWW* I, 169–71; cf. CHUR 4/81.
[30] Paul Addison, *Churchill on the Home Front, 1900–1955* (1992), 323.

election and was contrasting that with his success in gaining a mandate in 1935 on a clear, if cautious, platform for rearmament. All this was said by Baldwin in justification of his aphorism that 'a democracy is always two years behind the dictator'. Reginald Bassett suggested, just after *The Gathering Storm* appeared that Churchill was following a long line of writers who had quoted selectively and misleadingly from Baldwin's speech.[31] In fact, it is possible that Churchill was in their vanguard. As drafts make clear, the highly expurgated version of Baldwin's speech used in *The Gathering Storm* was taken verbatim from Churchill's June 1938 collection of speeches entitled *Arms and the Covenant*. There the editor, his son Randolph, had appended some of Baldwin's words on 12 November 1936 to Churchill's own 'locust years' speech the same day.[32] Ellipsis points in this text indicate two explicit omissions from Baldwin's words, but there are, in fact, three other unacknowledged gaps. Although proof copies of *Arms and the Covenant* do not survive in Churchill's papers, Winston made it clear to Randolph that 'I must have the final word in a matter which so closely concerns myself, upon what goes in or out.'[33] Whoever was responsible, this was an early and accessible version of the 'appalling frankness' speech, on which others may well have relied. In 1948 *The Gathering Storm* was following the pack hunting Baldwin, but *Arms and the Covenant* may have started them running a decade before.

Underpinning Churchill's account of the years 1936–8 is his hopeful estimate of potential German resistance to Hitler. Repeatedly he asserts or implies that a firmer stand by Britain and France would have destroyed Hitler's credibility and triggered a military putsch. This is evident in his treatment of the Rhineland crisis of 1936 and can be seen particularly in the key chapter about Munich. Churchill was confident that, if Britain and France had taken a tough line over Czechoslovakia, the German generals would have mounted a *coup* against Hitler. He took seriously their assertions to this effect at the Nuremburg trials and also under private interrogation, as relayed by Ismay from British military sources in Germany, particularly those of General Franz Halder, then army chief of staff. But readers of Churchill's draft questioned his interpretation. Sir Orme Sargent, the deputy under-secretary at the foreign office and critic of Munich in 1938, warned against 'overrating the possibility of an army revolt in September 1938 ... the generals were repeatedly planning revolts; but at the last

---

[31] R. Bassett, 'Telling the Truth to the People: The Myth of the Baldwin "Confession"', *The Cambridge Journal*, II, I (Oct. 1948), 84–95, especially 95, note 1. See also Keith Middlemas and John Barnes, *Baldwin: A Biography* (1969), 969–73.

[32] *SWW*, I, 169; cf. CHUR 4/81, f.175, and *Arms and the Covenant*, 385–6.

[33] WSC to Randolph, 3 April 1938, Chartwell Trust papers, CHAR 8/598, ff. 1–2 (Churchill College, Cambridge).

moment they drew back, either because the situation was too favourable for Germany, or because it was so unfavourable that they could not as patriots play into the hands of the enemy'.[34] From inside Churchill's research team, Deakin also advised him not to 'put too much store on Halder's account', while Pownall said he had found no corroborative evidence in the foreign or cabinet office records and warned that 'Halder, as you know, is apt to "shoot a line"'.[35] In response, Churchill softened his tone. The phrase 'We now know for certain what was happening on the other side' became 'We may now look behind the brazen front which Hitler presented to the British and French governments.' Echoing Sargent, he added the qualification that 'the generals were repeatedly planning revolts, and as often drew back at the last moment for one reason or another'. He also acknowledged: 'It was to the interest of the parties concerned after they were prisoners of the Allies to dwell on their efforts for peace.' But he retained a lengthy version of the generals' story and noted that it 'has been accepted as genuine by various authorities who have examined it. If it should eventually be accepted as historical truth, it will be another example of the very small accidents upon which the fortunes of mankind turn.' He summed up 'The Tragedy of Munich' as follows: 'Hitler's judgment had been once more decisively vindicated. The German General Staff was utterly abashed ... Thus did Hitler become the undisputed master of Germany, and the path was clear for the great design.'[36]

Here is an excellent example of Churchill's principles of interpretation: contingency not determinism, an emphasis on individuals rather than broad forces, and the ostensible deference paid to 'history' while seducing future historians. Of course, Churchill's counterfactuals remain imponderable, but it is a tribute both to his vision and his craftsmanship that many of his turning points are the ones that scholars still ponder.[37] Although *The Gathering Storm* had not ended historical debate – far from it – Churchill was eminently successful in shaping the agenda.

[34] Sargent to WSC, 15 Dec. 1947, CHUR 4/141A. f. 126. Sargent was also drawing on the comments of his colleague Ivone Kirkpatrick, who had served in the Berlin Embassy in 1933–8.

[35] Memos by Pownall [20 Sept. 1947], and Deakin, undated [early 1948], in CHUR 4/91, ff. 98, 120–1.

[36] *SWW*, I, 243–6, 250; cf. CHUR 4/91, f. 113.

[37] For instance, Hitler's most recent biographer highlights the importance of the Rhineland occupation in 1936 for the Führer's domestic position and, while admitting it is 'an open question' whether the 'ill-coordinated' plotting in 1938 'would have come to anything', argues that the 'legacy of Munich was fatally to weaken those who might even now have constrained Hitler', Ian Kershaw, *Hitler* (2 vols., 1998, 2000), I: 589–91, II: 123–5.

In shaping it, but not setting it in stone. If we look at Churchill's treatment of appeasement, we can see how *The Gathering Storm* is at odds with the revisionism of historians writing after the archives became open in the early 1970s.

On fundamental issues of defence and diplomacy, Churchill was, of course, essentially right. In the early 1930s he repeatedly urged that it was folly for the victors either to disarm or to allow Germany to rearm while German grievances had not been resolved. His whistle-blowing about the pace of German air rearmament after 1933 helped galvanise the government into belated action over air defence and his lurid warnings about Hitler's intentions were amply vindicated by the unfolding of events. The first book of *The Gathering Storm* documents Churchill's public statements about Hitler and his secret intelligence about German rearmament, often leaked by anxious officials, validating both against evidence from postwar sources. The official biography develops these themes with rich detail. But there is more to say on these matters. Air rearmament was not the totality of defence issues, nor the Nazi threat the sum of 1930s diplomacy.

It is now clear that Churchill was not so much a lone voice calling for rearmament in the 1930s but one of a number of actors – in office, officialdom, the military and parliament – engaged in a complex bureaucratic battle to shift the government from its early ignorance and complacency about the growth of the Nazi airforce. The leaks to Churchill were only a facet of this struggle, in which, for instance, Chamberlain shared Churchill's priorities more than Baldwin's. Yet even today, and certainly in the 1930s, reliable evidence is lacking for the growth of Hitler's Luftwaffe during its early years. Even numbers of aircraft, where the data exists, are an insufficient guide. What matters are serviceable front-line planes, in other words combat aircraft for which the Luftwaffe had fuel, spare parts and trained pilots to keep in the air in time of war. On these criteria, Richard Overy, a historian of the German war economy, has argued that Churchill exaggerated German potential, for instance predicting in September 1935 a total of 2,000 first-line aircraft by October 1936 and possibly 3,000 a year after that. In fact, says Overy, the figure was less than 3,000 even in September 1939. In any case, the statistics were not used at the time as precision weapons but rather as bludgeons to create alarm and thus provoke action. Churchill admitted as much in *The Gathering Storm*. 'I strove my utmost to galvanise the Government into vehemence and extraordinary preparation, even at the cost of world alarm. In these endeavours no doubt I painted the picture even darker than it was.'[38]

[38] R. J. Overy, 'German Air Strength 1933 to 1939: A Note', *Historical Journal*, 27 (1984), 465–71, esp. note 5; *SWW*, I, 180.

234   TRANSACTIONS OF THE ROYAL HISTORICAL SOCIETY

Churchill and others were partly victims of German disinformation, spread assiduously by General Erhard Milch and staff in the air ministry. But their exaggerations about the potential of the Luftwaffe were reinforced by exaggerated fears about bombing itself. During the course of the Second World War, 147,000 people were killed or maimed in the whole of the United Kingdom as a result of aerial bombardment.[39] But when Churchill addressed the Commons in November 1934 he predicted that, in seven to ten days of intensive bombing, at least 30,000 to 40,000 Londoners would be killed or maimed and that, 'under the pressure of continuous air attack', at least three or four million people would flee the metropolis for the surrounding countryside. In July 1936, he was even more alarmist. As part of delegation of senior MPs to see Baldwin, his estimates for bomb tonnage and casualty rates implied figures of 5,000 dead and 150,000 wounded from a single all-out raid on London.[40] Churchill was not alone in such fears. What Uri Bialer has called 'the shadow of the bomber' hung over British life throughout the 1930s. Writing in 1966, Harold Macmillan recalled that 'we thought of air warfare in 1938 rather as people think of nuclear warfare today'. That was not mere popular paranoia, stirred up by H. G. Wells, Bertrand Russell, and the like. In October 1936 the Joint Planning Sub-Committee of the Chiefs of Staff estimated that 20,000 casualties might be expected in London in the first twenty-four hours of an air attack, rising within a week to around 150,000.[41]

As Wesley Wark has shown, the exaggerations of German air strength and of the potency of bombing, to which Churchill contributed, had a counter-productive effect on the government. Having underestimated the German air threat in 1933–6, Whitehall swung to the opposite extreme in 1936–8. The fear of German airpower was much in the minds of both the chiefs of staff and Chamberlain himself as they debated whether to take a stand over Czechoslovakia. In reality the German air staff had concluded that they could not deliver a knock-out blow against Britain. But, as Chamberlain told his cabinet after his second visit to Hitler in September 1938 (and only his second round-trip in a plane), as he flew back up the Thames toward London 'he had imagined a German bomber flying the same course, he had asked himself what degree of protection they could afford to the thousands of homes which he had seen stretched out below him, and he had felt that we were in no position to justify waging a war today in order to prevent a war hereafter'.[42]

[39] Basil Collier, *The Defence of the United Kingdom* (1957), 528.
[40] Winston S. Churchill, *Arms and the Covenant* (1938), 172–3; Gilbert, *CV*, v, part 3, 273–4.
[41] Harold Macmillan, *Winds of Change, 1914–1939* (1966), 575; Uri Bialer, *The Shadow of the Bomber* (1980), 130.

The frenzied mid-1930s debate about the 'air menace' therefore helped galvanise RAF modernisation, but it also induced diplomatic paralysis. Moreover, it diverted attention from the other two services, particularly the army – a consequence deplored at the time by none other than Henry Pownall, then an army bureaucrat![43] A British Expeditionary Force for France and Belgium was low on Churchill's list of priorities. When he spoke of his 'Grand Alliance' with France, he meant 'the Union of the British Fleet and the French Army, together with their combined Air Forces'. Or, as he put it in the early 1930s, 'Thank God for the French Army.'[44] It is also worth noting that, in contrast with his passion for air rearmament, Churchill was slow to support peacetime conscription. Although this issue was popular with many local Conservative associations during 1938 and was pushed strongly by dissident MPs such as Leopold Amery, Churchill did not speak out on the matter and only signed two of the five Commons motions about national service introduced between July 1938 and April 1939. At late as 18 April 1939, after Hitler had devoured Czechoslovakia and Britain had guaranteed Poland, Churchill was not among sixty-five MPs (many of them Tories, including his son-in-law Duncan Sandys) who demanded 'immediate acceptance of the principle of the compulsory mobilisation of the man, munition, and money power of the nation'. Compulsory national service had socialistic undertones and ran against national custom, but Churchill's reticence also reflected his preoccupation with the air and sea, not the land. He wrote in a newspaper article in May 1938, 'if our Fleet and our Air Force are adequate, there is no need for conscription in time of peace. No one has ever been able to give a satisfactory answer to the question: "What do you want conscription for?"'[45]

As Donald Cameron Watt has observed, Churchill's rearmament campaign 'never focused on the issues that might have made an impact on German military opinion – military arms production, conscription, a Continental commitment'.[46] Air rearmament had a bias towards isolationism – the defence of the United Kingdom. Greater resources

[42] Wesley K. Wark, *The Ultimate Enemy: British Intelligence and Nazi Germany, 1933–1939* (Oxford, 1986), ch. 3; Cab 42 (38), 24 Sept. 1938, CAB 23/95 (Public Record Office, Kew).

[43] Pownall blamed 'Air Panic', whipped up by Churchill and others, for the July 1934 cutback in funds for the army expansion programme. See Martin Gilbert, *Winston S. Churchill*, v (1976), 553 note.

[44] Both of these remarks are quoted in *SWW* I, respectively 179 and 59.

[45] N.J. Crowson, *Facing Fascism: The Conservative Party and the European Dictators, 1935–1940* (1995), 158–63; cf. 'Future Safeguards of National Defence', *News of the World*, 1 May 1938, in Michael Wolff, ed., *The Collected Essays of Sir Winston Churchill* (4 vols., Bristol, 1976), I, 402.

[46] Watt, 'Churchill and Appeasement', 204.

for the army would have implied a continental strategy, projecting British power across the Channel. In all this, of course, Churchill was broadly at one with Chamberlain, most politicians and public opinion. That is why in May 1940 there were only 10 British divisions alongside 104 French, 22 Belgian and 8 Dutch on the Western Front. Such were the ghosts of the Somme and Passchendaele that in 1934 MacDonald had decreed that the words 'Expeditionary Force' not be used in public statements or even official documents. As the military critic Basil Liddell Hart wrote of the Western Front of 1914–18, 'It was heroic, but was it necessary? It was magnificent, but was it war?'[47] Churchill agreed that, even if Britain had to fight, a repeat of Flanders Fields would indeed be an unnecessary war. What he does *not* say about rearmament in *The Gathering Storm*, therefore points us on to his equivocations about mass invasion of the continent in later volumes of memoirs. And his refrain, 'Thank God for the French Army' – which only voiced the unspoken assumptions of most policymakers – reminds us that he, like they, never imagined the collapse of the Western Front in 1940. In short, one might argue that Churchill's warnings against appeasement in the 1930s played a part in helping win the Battle of Britain, but they did nothing to avert the prior disaster of the Battle of France.

On foreign policy, as on defence, Churchill's retrospective concentration on Germany (informed by the events of 1940) distorts the diplomacy of the 1930s and, at times, his own part in it.

Since the revisionism of the 1970s, it is a commonplace of historical scholarship that British policymakers discerned a potential three-front threat in the 1930s. The menace of German airpower at home was reinforced by Japan's challenge to Britain's substantial interests in China and Southeast Asia and by Italy's threat to the Eastern Mediterranean and the Suez lifeline to India. Japan was, in fact, the main concern in the early 1930s, after its invasion of Manchuria, and this prompted the beginnings of British rearmament. Although the revival of German power, especially in the air, took precedence after Hitler gained power in 1933, in 1936–7 it was the combination of Mussolini's empire-building in Ethiopia and the outbreak of the Spanish Civil War that preoccupied ministers and focused their attention on the Mediterranean. Not until 1938, with first the Austrian Anschluss and then the Czech crisis, did Germany in Europe return to centre-stage. But policymakers could not ignore the fact that, from July 1937, Japanese and Chinese forces were locked in a major war across eastern China.

In *The Gathering Storm*, however, Churchill's eyes are fixed on Berlin. After a couple of pages on the Manchurian crisis in chapter five, there is virtually nothing about events in Asia. Only from a minute by

[47] Brian Bond, *Liddell Hart: A Study of His Military Thought* (1976), 68 and 85.

Churchill when first lord of the admiralty in February 1940, printed in an appendix, does one learn that Japan had 'for two and a half years been engaged in a most ruinous war in China'. The almost total omission of the Far East from the volume was noted by Denis Kelly, one of Churchill's junior research assistants, very late in the day, on 8 January 1948. At his suggestion a brief reference to Japan's signature in 1936 of the Anti-Comintern Pact was inserted in chapter twelve. Asked for his advice, Deakin suggested on 31 January that the Japanese story should be dealt with as 'an introduction to their entry into war' in 1941. 'All right', Churchill agreed, and the matter was relegated to volume three.[48]

Although there is more reference to Mediterranean affairs in *The Gathering Storm*, they do not bulk large. To a considerable extent, as Robert Rhodes James observed thirty years ago, this mirrors Churchill's perspective in the 1930s. Warning the Commons about the real priorities as the Abyssinian crisis deepened in October 1935, Churchill pointed to German rearmament: '*There* is the dominant factor; *there* is the factor which dwarfs all others.'[49] Contrary to many League enthusiasts, notably Eden, Churchill was not keen to make Italian aggression a major moral and political issue. In Europe, Mussolini (about whom Churchill continued to make complimentary references in public) was a potential bulwark against German expansion. Churchill endorsed the Stresa agreement of April 1935, which committed Britain, France and Italy to maintaining the independence of Austria. On the other hand, Churchill could see the dangers to the League's credibility if its council in Geneva decided on half-hearted sanctions against Mussolini, which then failed. That could irreparably damage the League's role in containing Germany. At the height of the furore over the Hoare–Laval Pact, Churchill was vacationing in Spain and North Africa. 'Looking back', he wrote in *The Gathering Storm*, 'I think I ought to have come home', speculating that he might have been able to marshal the anti-government forces and bring down 'the Baldwin régime'. More likely, as historian Graham Stewart has observed, his speeches and correspondence at the time suggest that he (and many in the government) was genuinely undecided as to whether 'Geneva or Stresa represented the best hope of containing Germany.' Keeping away from Westminster allowed him to stay on the fence.[50]

The Spanish Civil War merits only a brief discussion in chapter twelve of *The Gathering Storm*. There Churchill presents the two sides as

[48] *SWW*, 1, 67–9, 168, 598; cf. CHUR 4/141B, ff. 311–13.

[49] Rhodes James, *Churchill*, 328–9.

[50] *SWW*. 1, 144; cf. Graham Stewart, *Burying Caesar: Churchill, Chamberlain and the Battle for the Tory Party* (1999), 243.

equally barbarous and states: 'In this quarrel I was neutral.' His main point is to endorse the official policy of non-intervention, on the grounds that, 'with all the rest they had on their hands the British Government were right to keep out of Spain.'[51] In the early months of the Civil War, however, Churchill definitely leaned towards Franco and 'the Anti-Red' forces, as he often called them. 'I am thankful the Spanish Nationalists are making progress', he told his wife in September 1936, adding that it would be 'better for the safety of all if the Communists are crushed'. The following April he admitted to the Commons that, despite his attempts to remain neutral, 'I will not pretend that, if I had to choose between Communism and Nazi-ism, I would choose Communism.'[52] Churchill, it should be remembered, remained a visceral anti-Bolshevik. Although he did not agree with many of the Tory right that Nazi Germany might be used to contain Bolshevism, it is possible that in 1936–7, with Hitler less menacing after the Rhineland crisis, Churchill's sense of priorities may temporarily have wavered. In February and April 1936, Popular Front governments came to power with Communist support in Spain and then France. In Spain, the election began the descent to civil war; in France, the ensuing rift between left and right seemed, at times, to presage something similar. Reiterating the need for Britain and France to keep out, he hinted in an article in August 1936, of deeper fears. A 'revivified Fascist Spain in close sympathy with France and Germany is one kind of disaster. A Communist Spain spreading its snaky tentacles through Portugal and France is another, and many may think the worse.'[53] It has often been observed that Churchill's lack of ideological zeal about Italy and Spain distanced him from many of his potential allies on the centre and left who supported the League. It is also possible that at times in 1936–7, he was uncertain about the greatest international dangers. Not until 1938–9, with Hitler on the march again and Franco in the ascendant, did he state clearly that a Fascist victory in Spain would be more dangerous to the British Empire.

On the other side of the diplomatic fence, Churchill tended to exaggerate the potential for a 'Grand Alliance' against Germany. This is a familiar point and can be discussed more briefly. With regard to France, it remains a matter of debate how far British appeasement was the reason or the pretext for French inertia in the 1930s. Churchill, as usual, includes qualifying passages that carefully straddle this divide. 'More than once in these fluid years French Ministers in their ever-

[51] SWW, I, 167.
[52] Gilbert, Churchill, v, 785; Churchill, Speeches, vi, 5850.
[53] See Rhodes James, Churchill, 406–9, quotation from 407; cf. David Carlton, Churchill and the Soviet Union (Manchester, 2000), 50–61.

changing Governments were content to find in British pacifism an
excuse for their own. Be that as it may', he adds, 'they did not meet
with any encouragement to resist German aggression from the British.'
And in characteristically counter-factual mode, he leaves the reader
with the impression that, over the Rhineland and on other occasions,
British resolve could have tipped the balance. Yet most historians of
the period tend to locate relations with Britain in a complex of factors –
political, economic and military – that shaped French policy.[54]

On the Soviet Union, Churchill plays up signs of Soviet readiness to
intervene in the Czech crisis of 1938. Again this issue remains a matter
of controversy, but such evidence as has been gleaned from the Soviet
archives strongly suggests that Stalin did not intend to take independent
action to save Czechoslovakia and that he had not decided what to do
if the French honoured their treaty obligations, thereby bringing his
own into play. Churchill again registers the necessary qualifications,
notably on Soviet good faith, but the weight of his account in chapters
sixteen and seventeen is on the 'astonishing' degree of 'indifference –
not to say disdain' displayed by British and French leaders towards the
Soviet Union. For this, he adds in an allusion to the Nazi-Soviet Pact,
'we afterwards paid dearly'.[55] In support of his theme, he highlights a
public declaration by Maxim Litvinov, the Soviet foreign minister, at
the League of Nations and also private assurances made to him by
Ivan Maisky, Stalin's ambassador in London, which Churchill passed
on to the Foreign Office. (At an earlier stage, Churchill had a whole
draft chapter entitled 'The Maisky Incident'.) Churchill also wrote of
the 'intimate and solid friendship' between the Soviet Union and the
Czech state, arguing that Stalin felt 'a very strong desire to help' the
Czechs. This, he suggested, stemmed largely from 'a personal debt' felt
to President Eduard Benes because the latter had forwarded intelligence
of German contacts with the Soviet military, which triggered Stalin's
purges in 1937. In the original draft Churchill accepted unequivocally
that there was a genuine plot: 'This was in fact the great military and
Old-Guard-Communist conspiracy to overthrow Stalin, and introduce
a regime based on a pro-German policy.' Deakin persuaded Churchill
to replace 'in fact' with 'a part of' and 'great' with 'so-called'. Deakin
also proposed a qualification that the information supplied by Benes was
probably planted by Soviet intelligence, in the hope that transmission by
the Czechs would make it more credible to the paranoid Stalin, but

[54] SWW, I, 151; cf. Anthony Adamthwaite, Grandeur and Misery: France's Bid for Power in
Europe, 1914–1940 (1995), 22–31.
[55] SWW, I, 239–40; cf. Igor Lukes, Czechoslovakia between Stalin and Hitler: The Diplomacy
of Edvard Beneš (Oxford, 1996), chs. 4 and 7; Zara Steiner, 'The Soviet Commissariat of
Foreign Affairs and the Czechoslovakian Crisis in 1938: New Material from the Soviet
Archives', Historical Journal, 42 (1999), 751–79.

Churchill relegated the qualification to a footnote and added that it was 'irrelevant'. Even after Deakin's editing, this anecdote (which Benes had told Churchill in 1944) added immensely to what Churchill called 'the salient fact for the purposes of this account', namely 'the close association of Russia and Czechoslovakia, and of Stalin and Benes'.[56]

In contrast with later volumes of the memoirs, the United States does not bulk large in *The Gathering Storm*. It is, however, striking that one of Churchill's most trenchant criticisms of Chamberlain occurs over his handling of President Roosevelt's offer in January 1938 to convene an international conference to explore the basis of a general peace settlement. This cut across Chamberlain's plans for bilateral negotiations with Hitler and Mussolini, so the prime minister asked Roosevelt to delay his initiative. A few days later, pressed by Eden, he invited the president to go ahead. It is unlikely that Roosevelt had anything substantial in mind when he made his offer. But Churchill asserted: 'We must regard its rejection – for such it was – as the last frail chance to save the world from tyranny otherwise than by war.' That Chamberlain, he went on, in mounting incredulity, 'should have possessed the self-sufficiency to wave away the proffered hand stretched out across that Atlantic leaves one, even at this date, breathless with amazement'. Here, transparently, the Cold War context of *The Gathering Storm* shows through. After the intimate wartime alliance, after lend-lease and the Marshall Plan, it was indeed hard to recall the depths of suspicion entertained in 1930s Britain about American isolationism. Chamberlain's 1937 aphorism, that it was 'always best and safest to count on nothing from the Americans except words', was then an axiom in most of Whitehall and Westminster. In a way Churchill did not intend, he was right to say about British handling of the Roosevelt initiative: 'One cannot to-day even reconstruct the state of mind which would render such gestures possible.'[57]

Together with his counterfactuals, Churchill's tendency to simplify the international scene in the 1930s – reducing several storm clouds into one – is a central weapon in his attack on British appeasement. But the clarity of Churchill's indictment derives not just from his simplification of events abroad. One of the most notable features of book one of *The Gathering Storm* is what he *doesn't* say about politics at home.

The 1930s are now conventionally dubbed Churchill's 'wilderness years'. He used that phrase on the last page of *The Gathering Storm*,

[56] *SWW*, I, 224–6; cf. Deakin and WSC notes on CHUR 4/90, f. 45.
[57] *SWW*, I, 196–9; cf. David Reynolds, *The Creation of the Anglo-American Alliance, 1937–1941: A Study in Competitive Co-operation* (1981), 16–23, 31–2, 297.

where he referred to 'eleven years in the political wilderness', but it was popularised by Martin Gilbert's book *Winston Churchill: The Wilderness Years* and the related eight-part TV series shown on both sides of the Atlantic in 1981–2.[58] Historian Alastair Parker has, however, questioned the appropriateness of this term, arguing that in the 1930s Churchill tempered his criticism of the Government's foreign policy because of his persistent hopes of returning to office.[59] As recent historians of the Tory party have shown, the politics of the 1930s were more fluid than our impression of 'the era of Baldwin and Chamberlain' now suggests. However it may look in retrospect, therefore, Churchill did not expect to stay on the backbenches for more than a decade. Little of this emerges in *The Gathering Storm*.

Churchill's campaign against the government's India policy in the early 1930s seems, in retrospect, to be a quixotic flourish by an incorrigible diehard. But it is now clear that much of the Tory party was unhappy about the proposed devolution and that in early 1931 and again in mid-1934 the Government was in serious danger over its India Bill. Had Samuel Hoare, then spoken of as a future premier, not successfully covered up his manipulation of evidence to the Select Committee on India in 1934, Churchill might well have succeeded in his hope of evicting Baldwin and joining a reconstituted national government led by Austen Chamberlain. Yet, although the India Bill dominated British politics in 1933–5, filling 4,000 pages of Hansard with over fifteen million words, it is hardly mentioned in *The Gathering Storm*. To do so would have detracted from Churchill's focus on Germany. It would also have signalled Churchill's political motives, encapsulated in the celebrated Commons exchange when Leo Amery characterised Churchill's India policy with the Latin tag, 'Fiat iustitia ruat caelum.' Translate, demanded Churchill, whereupon Amery responded, to gales of laughter: 'If I can trip up Sam, the Government is bust.'[60]

A new chapter opened in the summer of 1935, with the India Bill passed and Baldwin now prime minister. Churchill eagerly anticipated that the autumn election would produce a smaller majority for the national government, more attention by Baldwin to the Tory right and,

---

[58] Gilbert also used *The Wilderness Years* as the title for the 1981 volume of documents on 1929–35 that accompanied his official biography. In 1994, however, Sir Martin observed that the phrase now seemed to him 'less apposite' because, as the 1930s wore on, Churchill 'became a kind of one-man unofficial opposition', backed by a 'Cabinet' of former colleagues and civil servants, many of whom fed him information about Britain's defence weakness. Thanks to them, 'his wilderness years had been fully inhabited', Martin Gilbert, *In Search of Churchill* (1994), 109, 135.

[59] R.A.C. Parker, *Churchill and Appeasement* (2000), xi, 65, 261–2.

[60] See Stuart Ball, *Baldwin and the Conservative Party: The Crisis of 1929–1931* (1988); Stewart, *Burying Caesar*, esp. chs. 4–6, Amery quotation from 179.

in consequence, a cabinet post for himself, ideally the admiralty. He alludes to these hopes in *The Gathering Storm*, but represents his exclusion from office after the election as providential. '[N]ow one can see how lucky I was. Over me beat the invisible wings.' He takes the same line when relating how Baldwin passed over him for the new post of minister for the co-ordination of defence in March 1936. Although again admitting disappointment, Churchill wrote: 'This was not the first time – or indeed the last – that I have received a blessing in what was at the time a very effective disguise.'[61]

At the time, however, Churchill's passion for office was intense. On 8 March, the day after Hitler occupied the Rhineland, he called on Neville Chamberlain, then chancellor of the exchequer. According to Chamberlain's diary Churchill said 'he was in a very difficult position' because Stanley Baldwin did not propose to announce the name of the new minister until after the Commons debate on the Rhineland. Churchill said he 'wanted to make a "telling" (I understood in the form of a fierce attack on S.B.) speech if he were ruled out from the post, but not if there were any chance of its being offered him'. Chamberlain, who privately regarded this inquiry as 'an audacious piece of impertinence', declined to give any sign. On 10 March Churchill pulled his punches in the Commons, making little reference to the Rhineland while offering a broad and, in Chamberlain's words, 'constructive' survey of the defence scene. His reward, however, was the appointment of Sir Thomas Inskip on 14 March.[62]

For the remainder of Baldwin's premiership Churchill acknowledged, albeit bitterly, that he had no chance of office. But when Neville Chamberlain succeeded Baldwin in May 1937, Churchill's hopes revived and this again affected his handling of foreign policy. Rearmament was now gaining momentum, Hitler was relatively quiet, and Churchill persuaded himself that the government was moving towards his policy of arms and the covenant. Then came Eden's resignation as foreign secretary in February 1938, mainly over conversations with Italy but also over Chamberlain's handling of Roosevelt's recent initiative. In *The Gathering Storm* Churchill devotes a whole chapter to Eden's departure as a major turning point. This begins with a stark statement of policy differences between Chamberlain and Eden. It ends with one of the most vivid purple passages in *The Gathering Storm*, when Churchill recalls

[61] *SWW*, I, 141, 157.

[62] Parker, *Churchill and Appeasement*, 82–5. Interestingly, Baldwin had used a similar tactic during the crisis over the Hoare-Laval pact the previous December, pre-empting a possible assault from Austen Chamberlain, the Tory elder statesmen and backbench critic, by hinting that Austen might succeed Samuel Hoare at the Foreign Office. Once the parliamentary crisis had passed, the post was then offered to Eden. See Crowson, *Facing Fascism*, 58–65.

receiving the news of Eden's resignation while at Chartwell on the evening of 20 February. Throughout the war, he tells his readers, he never had any trouble sleeping, even in the darkest days of 1940. But that night 'sleep deserted me. From midnight till dawn I lay in my bed consumed with emotions of sorrow and fear', thinking of this 'one strong, young figure standing up against long, dismal drawling tides of drift and surrender'. But now, said Churchill, 'he was gone. I watched the daylight slowly creep in through the windows, and saw before me in mental gaze the vision of Death.'[63]

Early drafts of this chapter, however, lacked the stark introduction and conclusion. One version opened with a passage of somewhat faint praise of Eden, later moved to page 190, and ended with Churchill's speech to Commons after Eden's resignation. In the book, this appears in the next chapter. Churchill's reworkings made the episode more dramatic. One of Churchill's readers, Lord Vansittart, who had been Eden's permanent under-secretary until December 1937, questioned Churchill's polarity between Eden and Chamberlain. Vansittart argued that the former was more concerned about Italy than Germany ('the *real* issue') and that, in consequence, the resignation was mistimed: Eden 'played his one big card at the wrong moment'.[64] Privately Churchill may have shared some of these reservations. The story of the sleepless night is not unique to *The Gathering Storm*: Churchill told it at least twice in private in 1945–6. But when he did so at Yalta the reason he gave for his sleeplessness was subtly different. 'I was too excited', he told Eden. 'It was a grand thing to do, but I never felt it was done in the right way. More could have been made of it.'[65] In fact, Churchill was often scathing about Eden in private during the 1930s. 'I think you will see what a lightweight Eden is', he told his wife in January 1936, after Eden was appointed foreign secretary. And in February 1940 Churchill went so far as to say 'he would rather have Chamberlain than Eden as Prime Minister by eight to one'.[66]

In the light of recent research, the whole Churchill–Eden–Chamberlain triangle in 1938 looks very different from Churchill's account, written, it should be remembered, after Eden had served for most of the 1940s as Churchill's wartime foreign secretary and then as his

[63] *SWW*, I, 201; drafts of chapter fourteen in CHUR 4/88.

[64] Vansittart to WSC, 10 Nov. 1947, CHUR 4/141A, f. 102.

[65] Lord Moran, *Winston Churchill: The Struggle for Survival, 1940–1965* (1968), 261; cf. Halifax, diary, 7 Mar. 1946, Hickleton papers, A 7.8.18 (Borthwick Institute, York). Back in 1943, Halifax recorded, Churchill also 'waxed eloquent over Anthony's resignation in 1938; said that he had staged it badly and hadn't made any effort to work with all the powerful factors (such as Winston!) who would have co-operated' (Diary, 23 May 1943, A 7.8.12.)

[66] WSC to Clementine, 11 Jan. 1936, Gilbert, *CV*, V, part 3, 11; Cecil H. King, *With Malice toward None: A War Diary*, ed. William Armstrong (1970), 22.

deputy leader in the postwar opposition. In 1938 Churchill viewed Eden's resignation from the foreign office as a shock, but not a mortal blow to his hopes of working with Chamberlain. Although abstaining in the opposition's vote of censure, Churchill was also the fourth Tory MP to sign a round-robin expressing continued support for Chamberlain and his policy.[67] In the summer of 1938 he still believed that a satisfactory agreement could be reached over the Sudetenland. As for his relations with Eden, the two men kept their distance from each other. The former Foreign Secretary, over twenty years Churchill's junior and icon of the Tory left not the right, was reluctant to associate himself with Churchill, now widely seen as one of yesterday's men. Eden was also trying to avoid political isolation and muted his criticisms to make himself credible for renewed office when Chamberlain was forced to broaden his government.

It was not until after Munich that Churchill's opposition to Chamberlain became unqualified. Again he abstained in the Commons, but this time only after being dissuaded from actually voting against his own leader. By contrast, both Eden and Leo Amery, the other leading critic of Chamberlain, were almost persuaded by the premier's final speech in the Munich debate to vote with the government rather than abstain, and they made conciliatory noises in private to Number Ten. Churchill did nothing of the sort this time, unlike February. In fact, he dramatised his opposition by sitting ostentatiously in the Commons chamber while the votes were counted. His ringing denunciation of Munich as 'a total and unmitigated defeat' contrasted with Eden's more tempered criticisms.[68] While Eden continued to pull his punches during 1938–9, Churchill eclipsed him as the most trenchant critic of appeasement. The government U-turn in March 1939 and the guarantees to Eastern Europe were seen as vindication of Churchill not Eden. In September 1939 a top job for Churchill was essential if the government were to seem serious about the war. He was given the admiralty and a seat in the new war cabinet. Eden, by contrast, although a former foreign secretary, could be fobbed off with a non-cabinet portfolio at the dominions office.

In retrospect, it was the end of his 'wilderness' decade. But throughout the 1930s, Churchill had agitated for office, both from frustrated ambition and from frustrated conviction, amply justified after 1939, that he could make a difference. His problem was tactical: was criticism or cooperation the best route back? Under both Baldwin and

[67] N.J. Crowson, 'Conservative Parliamentary Dissent over Foreign Policy during the Premiership of Neville Chamberlain: Myth or Reality?', *Parliamentary History*, 14 (1995), 322–3.
[68] Crowson, 'Conservative Parliamentary Dissent', 326–7. More generally see Parker, *Churchill and Appeasement*, chs. 8–10, and Stewart, *Burying Caesar*, chs. 11–13.

Chamberlain, the prophetic voice was often muted. At times, book one of *The Gathering Storm* is almost history with the politics left out.

Churchill's self-image of apolitical rightness in *The Gathering Storm* grated on some contemporaries. Lord Halifax, successor to Eden as foreign secretary, remarked to Chamberlain's aggrieved widow: 'I fancy the main purpose of the book is not only to write history, but, also, to "make a record" for W.S.C.' In a particularly nasty review, entitled 'Churchill's "Mein Kampf"', Michael Foot, the Beaverbrook journalist and co-author of *Guilty Men*, wrote of Churchill clothing his 'personal vindication in the garb of history ... In 500 pages Churchill hardly allows himself one admission of weakness or false judgment on his own part.' Foot added: 'The whole book, of course, is vastly more enjoyable and instructive than Hitler's *Mein Kampf*. But in personal conceit and arrogance there is some likeness between the two.'[69]

As I have indicated in this essay, Churchill had indeed written a political memoir. His propensity for counterfactuals, his isolation of the German air threat from the mass of international problems facing British governments in the 1930s, and his simplification of the politics of that decade were all exercises in self-vindication. I have also tried to show how, despite his disingenuous disclaimer, this war memoir represented 'history'. The documents at his disposal, the stature he had attained as war leader and the lessons he drew from the past for the future all helped give his words an extra authority.

There was another reason for that authority – one worth dwelling on in conclusion since the thrust of this essay may seem to have belittled Churchill's achievement in *The Gathering Storm*. The most significant counterfactual in book one is Churchill's claim that Britain would have been wiser to fight Hitler in September 1938 over Czechoslovakia rather than a year later over Poland. At the end of the chapter entitled 'Munich Winter', he devoted three pages to this question.[70] Churchill had to acknowledge the core of the retrospective case for appeasement, namely that the extra year allowed Britain to modernise the RAF with Hurricanes and Spitfires and deploy the essential Chain Home Radar system. During the drafting he prepared an essay on how the Battle of Britain would have gone if fought a year earlier, in which he was forced to conclude: 'As the Battle of Britain was won on a very narrow margin in 1940 it may be argued that it might have been lost if fought in 1939.'[71] In consequence, perhaps, he dropped this little setpiece from

[69] Halifax to Anne Chamberlain, 13 April 1948, Hickleton papers, A 4.410.18.4; Michael Foot, 'Churchill's "Mein Kampf"', *Tribune*, 8 Oct. 1948, 7.

[70] *SWW*, I, 218, 263–5.

[71] CHUR 4/92, f. 119.

the book and recast the air material. In the book he emphasised that, despite the danger of air raids on London, there was 'no possibility of a decisive Air Battle of Britain' until Hitler had occupied France and the Low Countries and thereby obtained bases in striking distance of southeast England. Churchill also insisted that the German army was not capable of defeating the French in 1938 or 1939. 'The vast tank production with which they broke the French Front did not come into existence till 1940.' His conclusion, therefore, was that 'the year's breathing-space said to be "gained" by Munich left Britain and France in a much worse position compared to Hitler's Germany than they had been at the Munich crisis.' This was the greatest 'what if' in *The Gathering Storm*. Although its force was diminished by Churchill's cascade of counterfactuals and by his exaggeration elsewhere of the potency of airpower and of the Luftwaffe, most military historians would now agree with his verdict: 1938 was the time for confrontation, not negotiation.[72] On the big issue, Churchill was, quite simply, right.

We should remember, however, that Churchill was not against appeasement *per se*. Occasionally in *The Gathering Storm* he does use the word in a pejorative sense: ' "Appeasement" in all its forms only encouraged their aggression and gave the Dictators more power with their own peoples.' But this is one of only a handful of explicitly negative references.[73] Moreover, when setting out some 'principles of morals and action which may be a guide in the future', he argues that those seeking 'peaceful compromise' are 'not always wrong. On the contrary, in the majority of instances they may be right, not only morally but from a practical standpoint.' The follies Churchill describes in *The Gathering Storm* are essentially those of men not methods. As his conduct of wartime relations with Stalin shows, he was not averse to negotiating with dictators. He returned from Yalta in February 1945 momentarily hopeful that the agreements would stick. 'Poor Nevil[l]e Chamberlain believed he could trust Hitler', he told his ministers. 'He was wrong. But I don't think I'm wrong about Stalin.'[74] Even when these agreements broke down, his line was not war but negotiation from strength. His address at Fulton in March 1946, now indelibly known as the Iron Curtain speech, was actually entitled 'The Sinews of Peace'. And when in December 1950, at the critical moment of the Korean war, Prime Minister Clement Attlee promised that there would be no appeasement, Churchill set out his own position to the Commons: 'Appeasement in itself may be good or bad according to the cir-

[72] *SWW*, I, 265; cf. Williamson Murray, *The Change in the European Balance of Power, 1938–1939: The Path to Ruin* (Princeton, 1984), ch. 7.
[73] *SWW*, I, 194; cf. pp. 261, 271, 372, 381.
[74] Hugh Dalton diary, 32: 28 (23 Feb. 1945) (British Library of Political and Economic Science, London).

cumstances. Appeasement from weakness and fear is alike futile and fatal. Appeasement from strength is magnanimous and noble and might be the surest and perhaps the only path to world peace.' His efforts as prime minister in 1951–5 for a new 'summit' to achieve détente, analysed by John Young, were a continuation of this philosophy, for which he now used the term 'easement'.[75]

By then, however, the forces arrayed against him were too strong. These included the foreign office, the Eisenhower administration and the Kremlin, not to mention his own stroke in June 1953. But there was yet another reason for his failure. As I noted at the start of this essay, Churchill lived a double life as politician and writer. In *The Gathering Storm* he transformed the fluid politics of the 1930s into enduring history. But during his second premiership Churchill again strove to make history as actor not author. By then, however, the 'lessons' of appeasement had become too strong. The images of Baldwin and Chamberlain, of the Rhineland and Munich, had become part of Western culture. And for that *The Gathering Storm* was, in large part, responsible. In the 1950s, one might say, Churchill was a prisoner of history – his own history of the 1930s. It proved easier to make history than to unmake it.

[75] Gilbert, *Churchill*, VIII, 574; John Young, *Winston Churchill s Last Campaign: Britain and the Cold War, 1951–1955* (Oxford, 1996), esp. 8–10, 323–4.

CHURCHILL AND THE BRITISH MONARCHY[1]

By David Cannadine

In early April 1955, on the eve of his retirement as prime minister, Sir Winston Churchill gave a farewell dinner at 10 Downing Street, at which the principal guests were Queen Elizabeth II and the duke of Edinburgh. At the end of the evening, as he escorted his sovereign to her car, the cameras caught the leave-taking scene: Churchill, full of years and honour, wearing the Order of the Garter which she had given him, and the Order of Merit which her father had bestowed, bowing to the queen, whom he had earlier saluted as 'the young, gleaming champion' of the nation's 'wise and kindly way of life'.[2] This sunset tableau, combining regal youth and statesmanly age, was reminiscent of Winterhalter's picture, painted one hundred years before, which had depicted the venerable duke of Wellington doing homage to the young Victoria, to Prince Albert, and to their son, Prince Arthur of Connaught, on the first of May 1851.[3] For Churchill, like the Iron Duke before him, was not only her majesty's greatest subject: he was also an ardent admirer of the institution of monarchy, and of the person and the character of the last British sovereign he himself would live to serve. Indeed, according to his wife, Clementine, he was 'Monarchical No 1'.[4]

This was scarcely surprising. For Churchill was born and grew up in what he later recalled as 'the days of Queen Victoria and a settled world order', when politics, society and government were still largely dominated by the monarchy, aristocracy and gentry, and by the pageantry and spectacle that were associated with them. This was Churchill's world where, as C.F.G. Masterman noted, 'a benign upper class dispensed benefits to an industrious, bien pensant and grateful

---

[1] This is, despite the overwhelming mass of pertinent material, a strangely neglected subject, with the honourable exception of P. Ziegler, 'Churchill and Monarchy', in R. Blake and W.R. Louis (eds.), *Churchill* (Oxford, 1994), 187–98, to whose pioneeringly perceptive essay this account is much indebted.

[2] Robert Rhodes James (ed.), *Winston S. Churchill: His Complete Speeches, 1897–1963* (8 vols., 1974) (hereafter *Speeches*, I–VIII), VIII, 8645–6.

[3] N. Frankland, *Witness of a Century: The Life and Times of Prince Arthur, Duke of Connaught, 1850–1942* (1993), 1–2.

[4] Randolph S. Churchill and Martin Gilbert, *Winston S. Churchill* (8 vols., 1966–82) (hereafter *Churchill*, I–VIII), VIII, 570; J.R. Colville, *The Fringes of Power: Downing Street Diaries, 1939–1955* (1985), 128.

working class'.[5] Thus understood, Britain was a 'complex society', which 'descended through every class of citizen' from the monarchy at its apex to the workers, in their 'cottage homes', at the bottom, and it was because he saw it in this way that Churchill 'accepted class distinction without thought'.[6] Yet for all his deeply rooted belief in 'a natural social, almost a metaphysical order, a sacred hierarchy which it was neither possible nor desirable to upset', Churchill's relations with the British royal family were more complex and controversial than that serene sunset encounter with his sovereign suggests.[7] The too-ings and fro-ings of his party-political allegiancies, combined with his decade of unrelieved opposition during the 1930s, meant there were times when he and the British crown were placed on contrary sides on the great issues of the day. And despite his devotion to the institution of monarchy Churchill sometimes found individual sovereigns difficult to deal with and expressed disparaging opinions which they, reciprocally, were also inclined to entertain of him.

As a politician and statesman, Churchill's relations with British sovereigns were also much influenced by his historical sense of how the monarchy had evolved, and by his constitutional sense of what the monarchy ought to be and ought to do. During the first phase of his political career, until his fall in the aftermath of the Dardanelles disaster he tended to see Edward VII and George V as obstructing his Liberal reforming zeal. In the interwar years, the collapse of the great continental ruling houses, combined with his own growing conservatism meant Churchill became more appreciative of the stabilising virtues of the British crown, and it was this very appreciation which clouded his judgement at the time of the abdication. But this divisive episode meant that in 1940, there were many fences to mend between the unexpected monarch and the unexpected prime minister, and it was only when this had been accomplished during the Second World War that the final and mutually admiring phase of crown–Churchill relations was established. 'King and country, in that order', noted Lord Moran, 'that's about all the religion Winston has.'[8] But it was not always in that order; and Churchill's opinions sometimes seemed more heretical than orthodox.

[5] Churchill, VIII, 371; D. Cannadine, Aspects of Aristocracy: Grandeur and Decline in Modern Britain (1994), 156.

[6] V. Bonham Carter, Winston Churchill as I Knew Him (1965), 161; Lord Butler, The Art of the Possible (1971), 156; P. Addison, Churchill on the Home Front, 1900–1955 (1992), 47, 52–3 211, 311–15, 439; W.S. Churchill, Marlborough: His Life and Times (2 vol. edn, 1947) (hereafter Marlborough, I–II), I, 915–16.

[7] I. Berlin, Mr Churchill in 1940 (nd), 12, 17, 36–7. The origins of the kingly and hierarchical social order were sketched out in W.S. Churchill, A History of the English Speaking Peoples (4 vols., 1956–8) (hereafter ESP), I–IV, I, 53, 122, 136–38.

[8] Lord Moran, Winston Churchill: The Struggle for Survival 1940–1965 (1966), 192.

I

Churchill's view of the British monarchy was grounded in the classic
Victorian histories by Macaulay, Froude, Gardiner and Carlyle that he
had initially encountered as a Harrow schoolboy and later read as a
self-educating subaltern in Bangalore; and they were set out, virtually
unchanged, in his *History of the English-Speaking Peoples*, which was largely
written during the late 1930s, although it was not published until he
was in retirement.[9] Notwithstanding the title, which implied that
attention would be given to ordinary men and women, it was essentially
a brightly lit cavalcade of the great public figures who had made up
the nation's story, and it was headed and dominated by kings and
queens. They formed a varied and diverse collection, and Churchill
judged them confidently, crisply and critically. There were outstanding
leaders in war and forceful adminstrators in peace, such as Alfred the
Great, William the Conqueror, Henry II, Richard I, Edward I, Henry
V, Henry VII, Elizabeth and William III.[10] But many monarchs were
personally inept and politically disastrous, among them Stephen, John,
Richard II, Richard III, Mary Tudor, James II, George III and George
IV. As Robert Rhodes James rightly notes, 'Churchill's histories are
populated with the Good and the Bad' – and of none was this more
true than his history of the English-speaking monarchy.[11]

Yet amidst this constantly shifting kaleidescope of royal dynasties,
national alliances and sovereign individuals, two general themes did
stand out. One was that, despite the delinquencies of many individual
monarchs, the English crown was a sacred, mystical, almost metaphysical institution, which connected the past, the present and the
future, and which proclaimed the unity and identity of the nation. As
Lord Moran recalled, 'the history of England, its romance and changing
fortunes, is for Winston embodied in the royal house'.[12] A second was
that, while European nations preferred (or suffered) kings and queens
who were generally despotic and absolute, the English evolved a more
admirable form of 'constitutional and limited monarchy'. Thanks to
parliament, which represented the nation as a whole, and the later
advent of the two party system, the sovereign's power was progressively
eroded in a succession of episodes which were milestones in the
advancing story of English liberties, extending from Magna Carta to

[9] J.H. Plumb, 'Churchill: The Historian', in *idem, The Collected Essays of J.H. Plumb*, I,
The Making of an Historian (1988), 240–3.
[10] *ESP*, I, XIII–XIV, 92–6, 131–40, 157–69, 178–89, 224–43, 315–24; II, 13–21, 82–95, 106–
115; III, 3–22.
[11] *ESP* I, 152–3, 190–202, 289–307, 378–95; II, 76–81, 304–13; III, 131–2, 135–43, 193; IV,
12–15, 32–3; Robert Rhodes James, *Churchill: A Study in Failure, 1900–1939* (1970), 312.
[12] Moran, *Struggle for Survival*, 399.

the Glorious Revolution of 1688 and beyond. The result was a happy
compromise, a 'permanent parliament and a docile monarchy', whereby
the sovereign reigned above the battle of party, while the Lords and
Commons legislated and the politicians governed.[13]

   This, then, was the British crown, as it had evolved and developed
by the end of Victoria's reign, when young Winston was first learning
about it. He had no doubt that she had been a great queen, who 'in
spite of her occasional leanings', was 'a constitutional sovereign', who
'represented staunchness and continuity in British traditions', and who
'set a new standard for the conduct of monarchy which has ever since
been honourably observed'.[14] In institutional (and Tory) terms, the
crown embodied the nation's history, continuity and identity in its
symbolic functions and ceremonial activities; and in practical (and
Whig) terms, it was a convenient constitutional device, which left the
people free to elect their representatives through whom they governed
themselves. But during her reign, the monarchy also acquired two
important new functions. Thanks to the happy home life of Victoria
and Albert, it provided a moral example to the nation, of decent and
dutiful domesticity, in a way that had not been true for much of the
Stuart and Hanoverian dynasties. And Victoria was not only the head
of the British nation but also became the 'great presiding personage'
of the British Empire. Largely on account of Disraeli's initiative and
imagination, hers had become an imperial monarchy, the focus and
cynosure of a diverse and far-flung British community, extended across
the seas and around the world, which was united in fealty to the queen
empress.[15]

   This monarchy – by turns Tory and Whig, mystical and functional,
symbolic and constitutional, individual and familial, national and imperial – was in the full flower of its late-Victorian confidence and ostentation
as Churchill was growing up. It seemed an apt expression of the
British genius for organic constitutional evolution and working political
compromise, it was widely envied around the globe, and in this
particular settlement and configuration, it lasted the whole of his long
life.[16] For Churchill, and notwithstanding the occasional difficulties of
incompetent individuals or malevolent monarchs, it was beyond doubt
the best of all possible worlds. 'Our ancient monarchy', he observed
on the birth of Prince Charles in 1948, 'renders inestimable services to

[13] Plumb, 'Churchill', 227–9; *ESP*, II, 166, 178, 190, 219, 261–3, 271, 293–303, 314–2; *ESP*, III, VIII.
[14] *ESP*, IV, 45, 225.
[15] *ESP*, VI, 43–5, 224–5, 230–1, 298–9.
[16] D. Cannadine, 'The Context, Preformance and Meaning of Ritual: The British Monarchy and the "Invention of Tradition", c. 1820–1977', in E.J. Hobsbawm and T.O. Ranger (eds.), *The Invention of Tradition* (Cambridge, 1983), 120–60.

our country and to all the British Empire and Commonwealth of Nations.' And it did so because it was 'above the ebb and flow of party strife, the rise and fall of ministries and individuals, the changes of public opinion and fortune'. Domestically, it presided, 'ancient, calm and supreme within its functions, over all the treasures that have been saved from the past, and all the glories we write in the annals of our country'. And internationally, it provided 'the mysterious ... the magic link which unites our loosely bound but strongly interwoven Commonwealth of nations, states and races'.[17]

But Churchill never forgot that while the mystical, unifying, moral and imperial functions of the monarch were important, the whole thrust of English history had been to bring about a state of affairs where the king's government was carried on by minsters, who were primarily answerable to parliament, rather than to the crown. 'The royal prerogative', he insisted to his wife in 1909, 'is always exercised on the advice of ministers, and ministers and not the crown are responsible, and criticism of all debateable acts of policy should be directed to ministers, not to the crown.' He made the same point about parliament's pre-eminence thirty years later, when he bluntly informed the exiled duke of Windsor that 'when our kings are in conflict with our constitution, we change our kings', as had happened in 1688 – and as had happened again in 1936.[18] And in 1947, in *The Dream*, his imaginary conversation with his father, Churchill explained that the monarchy had survived because 'they took the advice of ministers who had majorities in the House of Commons'. This was the British monarchy as limited, constitutional, parliamentary monarchy. It put the crown in its place, and in political (though not social) terms, that was a subordinate place. Honouring the sovereign was right and good; but being governed by the sovereign had long since been given up.[19]

II

Such were Churchill's history and theory of the British monarchy: how, then, did his relations with successive British monarchs work out in practice? During his early years, young Winston enjoyed the sort of friendship which in those days was commonplace between the scion of a great ducal house and the royal family, characterised by a paradoxical combination of closeness and distance, approval and disapproval – and with eyes firmly to the main chance. His parents pulled strings with the duke of Cambridge, the queen's cousin and commander in chief of

[17] *Speeches*, VII, 7743; VIII, 8337.
[18] *Churchill*, II, 327; V, 1037.
[19] *Churchill*, VIII, 366; *ESP*, II, 267.

the British army, to get their son his commission, initially intended to
be in the infantry, but subsequently in the cavalry. Such shameless
lobbying was customary in high social circles at that time; but these
were also the years of Victoria's imperial apotheosis, by which the
young Churchill was deeply and lastingly affected. In Diamond Jubilee
year, he was serving in India, and as he read accounts of how the
queen had been made an empress, his romantic ardour was roused: 'I
must', he told his mother, 'array myself with those who "love high
sounding titles", since no title that is not high-sounding is worth
having.'[20]

But as someone with a career to establish and a reputation to make
young Winston generally saw British royalty in terms of professional
contacts and social connection. In 1898, he sent the prince of Wales a
copy of his first book, *The Story of the Malakand Field Force*, and he
professed himself 'Tory enough' to be delighted at the recipient's
favourable response. Soon after, the prince wrote again, advising him
(rather shrewdly, as things turned out) that the 'parliamentary and
literary life' would suit him better than 'the monotony of military life'
and they continued to correspond while Churchill was in South Africa
during the Boer War.[21] When he took up his 'parliamentary and literary
life' in earnest, by becoming an MP for Oldham, he was soon invited
to Balmoral. 'I have been very kindly treated here by the king', he
reported to his mother, 'who has gone out of his way to be nice to
me.' As Churchill began to make a reputation as colonial under-
secretary, Edward expressed delight that he was becoming 'a *reliable*
minister and above all serious politician, *which can only be obtained by
putting country before party*'. And when he became engaged, the king sent
him a congratulatory telegram, and gave him a gold headed malacca
cane as a wedding present.[22]

But Churchill's drive, brashness, ambition, opportunism, self-absorp-
tion and egotism soon grated on his sovereign, and as he moved from
being a junior Conservative backbencher to a junior Liberal minister
Edward reluctantly concluded that he was 'almost more of a cad in
office than he was in opposition'.[23] In 1909, when president of the
board of trade, Churchill made common cause with the chancellor of
the exchequer, Lloyd George, to reduce the amount spent on the army

[20] *Churchill*, I, 75, 147–50, 205, 227, 242–3, 336.
[21] *Speeches*, VI, 6552; *Churchill*, IRI, 381–2, 420–1; Randolph S. Churchill and Martin
Gilbert, *Winston S. Churchill: Companion Volumes* (5 vols., 1966–82) (hereafter *CV*, I–V), *CV*
I, part 2, 763, 1231–2; P. Magnus, *King Edward the Seventh* (Harmondsworth, 1967), 330–1.
[22] *Churchill*, II, 52, 158–9, 160–1, 211, 271, 274; Magnus, *Edward the Seventh*, 432.
[23] J. Vincent (ed.), *The Crawford Papers: The Journals of David Lindsay, Twenty-Seventh Earl
of Crawford and Tenth Earl of Balcarres, 1871–1940, During the Years 1892 to 1940* (Manchester
1984), 83; K. Rose, *King George V* (1983), 112; Magnus, *Edward the Seventh*, 432.

in favour of old age pensions. The king responded by suggesting to the prince of Wales that Churchill's initials, WC, 'are well named'. When he made a speech in September 1909, attacking dukes as 'unfortunate individuals' and 'ornamental creatures' who were part of a 'miserable minority of titled persons who represent nobody', the king's private secretary, Lord Knollys, took the extraordinary step of writing to *The Times* to protest. Churchill was unrepentant. 'He and the king must really have gone mad', he retorted. 'This looks to me like a rather remarkable royal intervention, and shows the bitterness which is felt in those circles. I shall take no notice of it.' But Knollys was no less unforgiving. 'The very idea', he wrote, of Churchill's acting 'from conviction or principle ... is enough to make anyone laugh.'[24]

The same contrasts in attitude and behaviour were apparent during the early years of the reign of George V. As home secretary, Churchill successfully oversaw the trial for criminal libel of Edward Mylius, who claimed that George V had secretly married in Malta in 1890; and the king found his nightly reports of Commons proceedings 'always instructive and interesting'.[25] But while George V recognised Churchill's zeal and energy, he shared his father's view that he was 'irresponsible and unreliable'. In 1908, he had told Churchill that he did not consider Asquith to be a gentleman. As he later admitted to Lord Esher, he should never have said such a thing, 'but Winston repeated it to Asquith, which was a monstrous thing to do, and made great mischief'.[26] There were also difficulties arising from the reports of the Commons proceedings, as when Churchill observed that 'there are idlers and wastrels at both ends of the social scale'. George V opined that such views were 'very socialistic'; but Churchill stood by the offending phrase and objected to receiving 'a formal notification of the king's displeasure'. Peace was eventually restored; but the sovereign's private secretary saw this as further evidence that Churchill was 'a bull in china shop', while *he* continued to think the royal reproof unjust and a sign that the king lacked political impartiality.[27]

When Churchill moved to the admiralty, matters did not improve. The new first lord was a party politician and a zealous reformer; the king was a former naval person, head of the armed services, and a staunch believer in tradition and precedent. Churchill wanted to name a ship 'HMS Oliver Cromwell': not surprisingly, George V took violent exception to thus commemorating the regicide. Churchill then proposed 'HMS Pitt': but the king wouldn't have that, either. In both cases,

---

[24] Magnus, *Edward the Seventh*, 473, 506; *Churchill*, II, 326–7, 338–9.

[25] H. Nicolson, *King George V: His Life and Reign* (1967), 71; Rose, *George V*, 83–4; *Churchill*, II, 373–5, 382–3, 418–23, 426, 436.

[26] *Churchill*, II, 670–1; *Churchill*, III, 87; Nicolson, *George V*, 138; Rose, *George V*, 71.

[27] *Churchill*, II, 433–9; Rose, *George V*, 76, 111–12.

Churchill grudgingly gave way. 'I have always endeavoured to profit from any guidance His Majesty has been gracious and pleased to give me', he wrote rather stiffly and unconvincingly after this second royal rebuff.[28] Thereafter, their relations remained tense, as Churchill made no secret of his view that George V was a dim reactionary, and the king made it plain that Churchill was rude and inconsiderate. When he objected to the first lord's proposal to withdraw battleships from the Mediterranean to safeguard British waters, in May 1912, Churchill exploded to his wife: 'The king talked more stupidly about the navy than I have ever heard him before. Really it is disheartening to hear this cheap and silly drivel with which he lets himself be filled up.'[29]

These two monarchs disliked Churchill because they thought he was insufficiently respectful of their person and their prerogative, while Churchill objected to inappropriate royal interference in matters which were wholly within the realm of parliament and government. As a result, the crown and court were firmly against him by the time war broke out in 1914, and thereafter, relations deterioriated still further. When Churchill rashly assumed command at Antwerp, Lord Stamfordham opined that he must be 'quite off his head!' And when he urged the reappointment of Lord Fisher as first sea lord, George V objected on the (not unreasonable) grounds that he was seventy-three and lacked the confidence of the navy; but Churchill insisted and the king had to give way.[30] All of which meant that his downfall over the Dardanelles disaster in 1915 was greeted at Buckingham Palace with scarcely concealed relief. 'It is', Queen Alexandra informed her son, 'all that stupid, young foolhardly Winston C's fault.' And the king agreed. Churchill had become 'impossible', a 'real danger', and he was 'delighted' and 'relieved' that he had gone. So was his son, the prince of Wales and future Edward VIII: 'It is a great relief to know Winston is leaving the admiralty', he wrote to his father.[31] Thus ended the first phase of Churchill's involvement with the British crown, which scarcely presaged the mutual admiration that would characterise their relations by the last two decades of his life.

III

It was during the 1920s and 1930s that Churchill's attitudes towards the British monarchy became generally more appreciative and admiring. Like many pre-1914 Liberals, the First World War left him saddened

[28] Churchill, II, 646–54; CV, II, part 3, 1764; Rose, George V, 160–1.

[29] Churchill, III, 87–8; Rose, George V, 160.

[30] Churchill, III, 86–7, 120, 150–1, 383–4.

[31] Churchill, III, 454, 473; CV, III, part 2, 939; Rose, George V, 189; P. Ziegler, King Edward VIII: The Official Biography (1990), 78.

and uncertain, and looking out on a social, political and international landscape so brutally transformed that it bore little resemblance to the Edwardian *belle époque*, with its settled values, historic institutions, venerable titles and great estates. 'Injuries', he later wrote, 'were wrought to the structure of human society which a century will not efface, and which may conceivably prove fatal to the present civilisation.'[32] The ruling houses of Germany, Russia and Austria-Hungary had been fixed points around which much of Europe's history had revolved. Now they were gone, and the Spanish monarchy followed in 1931. Deprived of these symbols of order, tradition and continuity, 'woven over centuries of renown into the texture of Europe', the continent lapsed into anarchy, civil war, revolution and dictatorship (whether fascist or communist). Even Britain was not entirely free of this contagion: great aristocratic families were no longer as secure or prominent as they had been before 1914, and universal democracy threatened to get out of hand.[33]

These changes, in continental circumstances and in Churchillian perceptions, help explain the substantial transformation in his relations with King George V. For he no longer regarded the British sovereign as the ignorant, blimpish reactionary of his Liberal days, but as the embodiment of decency, duty and tradition, in a world of strife, anarchy and revolution; and for his part, the king now warmed to Churchill both as an old friend and fellow Conservative. The solution of the Irish problem seems to have had a great deal to do with this. Churchill greatly admired the 'unswerving sense of devotion' the king displayed in visiting Belfast in June 1921 when he urged Irishmen to 'forgive and forget', and the king applauded Churchill's 'skill, patience and tact' in seeing the Irish Treaty through in the following year. Thereafter, while Churchill was chancellor of the exchequer, their relations remained friendly, and when he visited Balmoral in 1927, Churchill 'enjoyed myself very much' and had 'a very good talk about all sorts of things'. And when holidaying at Deauville, he observed the Shah of Persia at the gaming tables, dissolutely 'parting with his subjects' cash'. 'Really', he observed to Clementine, 'we are well out of it with our own gracious monarch!'[34]

Churchill developed these views more fully in an obituary notice of

[32] Cannadine, *Aspects of Aristocracy*, 156–7; M. Cowling, *Religion and Public Doctrine in Modern England* (Cambridge, 1980), 320–8; *Churchill*, IV, 914–15; W.S. Churchill, *The World Crisis: 1915*, (1923), 17; idem, *The World Crisis: The Eastern Front* (1931), 82; *Speeches*, V, 5291.
[33] W.S. Churchill, *The World Crisis: The Aftermath* (1929), 18, 31; idem, *The Eastern Front*, 17.
[34] Rose, *George V*, 337; Rhodes James, *Study in Failure*, 120; *Churchill*, IV, 790–1; *Churchill*, V, 244, 303, 700–1.

George V, which he reprinted in *Great Contemporaries*.[35] In the course of the reign, great changes had destabilised the world: empires and monarchies had fallen; dictatorship and anarchy had flourished; democracy had become incontinent and unfettered. Yet, 'at the heart of the British Empire', there was 'one institution, among the most ancient and venerable, which, so far from falling into disuetude or decay, has breasted the torrent of events, and even derived new vigour from the stresses'. 'Unshaken by the earthquakes, unweakened by the dissolvent tides, though all be drifting', the 'royal and imperial monarchy stands firm.' This was 'an achievement so remarkable, a fact so ... contrary to the whole tendency of the age', that it could not be 'separated from the personality of the good, wise and truly noble king whose work is ended'. He was 'uplifted above class-strife and party-faction'; he never feared British democracy; he reconciled labour and socialism to the constitution and the crown; he 'revivified the national spirit, popularized hereditary kingship'; and in so doing won the affection of his subjects and the admiration of mankind. 'In a world of ruin and chaos', Churchill concluded, 'King George V brought about the resplendent rebirth of the great office which fell to his lot.'[36]

But then the crown passed to King Edward VIII, whom Churchill had known (and admired) for a long time. As home secretary, he had participated at the 'beautiful and moving ceremony' at Carnarvon Castle in 1911 when Edward was invested as prince of Wales, and he had met him soon after at Balmoral. Edward's delight and relief at Churchill's fall in 1915 was soon abandond, and he reverted to his earlier belief that Churchill was 'a wonderful man with great powers of work'.[37] During the 1920s, Churchill helped the prince with speech writing and speech making, he sent him copies of *The World Crisis* as the volumes appeared, they corresponded about public affairs and played polo together, and in 1932, the prince contributed to the cost of the Daimler that Churchill was bought by his friends on his return from America. Four years later, Edward was king, and Churchill wrote him a gracious and grandiloquent letter, offering 'my faithful service and my heartfelt wishes that a reign which has been so nobly begun may be blessed with peace and true glory' and that 'in the long swing of events, Your Majesty's name will shine in history as the bravest and best beloved of the sovereigns who have worn the island crown'.[38]

[35] W.S. Churchill, *Great Contemporaries*, (1942 edn), 245–56.
[36] This was not the first time Churchill had written appreciatively about the king, having earlier produced a film script for Alexander Korda to commemorate George V Silver Jubilee: *CV*, v, part 2, 962–4, 989–1031.
[37] *CV*, ii, part 2, 1099; part 3, 1781; Ziegler, *Edward VIII*, 46.
[38] *Churchill*, iv, 525, 682–3; *Churchill*, v, 7, 809; *CV*, v, part. 1, 42–3, 1065–6; *CV*, v, part 3, 34–5; *Speeches*, v, 5291.

These hopes were sincere and heartfelt, and rested on an exaggerated sense of the king's virtues, with a blind eye turned to his faults (especially his support of appeasement); but they were nullified by the abdication. In taking the king's side against the government, and allaying himself with the legendarily mischievous Lord Beaverbrook, Churchill may have been seeking to embarrass Baldwin and the national government. This was certainly the view of his critics, but his motives were more deeply grounded and disinterested than that.[39] He was a loyal friend, especially when the going got rough, and he sympathised with the king's wish for a happy home life to accompany the glitter and pomp of his lonely public position. Moreover, England had been through its constitutional revolution in 1688, and in the uncertain 1930s, neither the country nor the monarchy needed any repetition of that disruption and disturbance. And he was sure that, given time, the king would repent of his passion for Mrs Simpson, and thus retain (and adorn) his throne. On the basis of this analysis, Churchill's course was clear. With Baldwin's knowledge and consent, he rallied to the king, seeking to boost his morale, and urging him to be discreet in his relationship with Mrs Simpson. And he tried to play for time, out of fear that undue pressure or excessive haste might lead the king to make the wrong decision (abdication and marriage), and in the hope that given time and chance, he might do the right thing, and renounce her.[40]

In championing the king, Churchill did his own reputation untold harm, with the public, the politicians, and the court. In a period of mounting tension and anxiety, his plea for extra time was patently unrealistic; he failed to appreciate that Edward had already decided to give up the throne; and he seriously misjudged the character of the sovereign and the mood of the country, which was turning decisively against the king. On 7 November 1936, he rose in the Commons to plead that 'no irrevocable step be taken'. The House turned angrily on him; the speaker ruled him out of order; he shouted at Baldwin that 'you won't be satisfied until you've broken him'; and he stormed out of the chamber. Within three days, the king had abdicated, but Churchill, though shocked and disappointed, stood by him. Following Baldwin's announcement in the Commons, he praised Edward's 'qualities of courage, of simplicity, of sympathy and, above all, of sincerity rare and precious' which, he felt sure, 'might have made his reign glorious in the annals of this ancient monarchy'.[41] He helped to compose the ex-king's abdication broadcast, he was convinced his policy had

[39] *Churchill*, v, 809–31; Rhodes James, *Study in Failure*, 269–77; Vincent, *Crawford Papers*, 573–7, 580.
[40] *Churchill*, v, 810–11; *CV*, v, part 3, 450–4; Vincent, *Crawford Papers*, 577; Colville, *Fringes of Power*, 716; Ziegler, *Edward VIII*, 302–27.
[41] Colville, *Fringes of Power*, 196; *Speeches*, vi, 5820–2.

been the right one, and he remained deeply unhappy at what had occured. 'I believe', he wrote to Lloyd George at Christmas, when it was all over, 'the Abdication to have been altogether premature and probably quite unnecessary. However, the vast majority is on the other side.'[42]

But while Churchill remained personally loyal to the duke of Windsor (as Edward VIII became), he recognised that the monarchy had to be carried on, and the throne had to be supported. In the aftermath of the abdication, he served on the Commons select committee charged with arranging the civil list for King George VI and Queen Elizabeth. The government expected him to cause further trouble over making financial provisions for the duke; but on learning of his substantial private fortune, Churchill agreed that the matter should be dealt with privately, so as to avoid the public embarrassment of parliamentary discussion. When the Committee's proposals were presented to the Commons, in March 1937, Churchill made a stirring speech in support of 'the honour and dignity of the crown'.[43] He believed the crown should be well provided for because 'the glitter and splendour of ceremonial pageant' was popular and exciting, and helped associate the mass of the people with the state. But he also insisted that 'the ancient constitutional monarchy of this country' was 'the most effective barrier against one man power or dictatorship, arising whether from the right or from the left'. Embodying tradition and custom, and sustained by parliament, it brought decency and security to national life, and provided 'that element of unity, of the present with the past', which was 'the greatest hope of our freedom in the future'.[44]

IV

By the end of 1936, Churchill respected and revered the British throne as a powerful institution providing a beneficient antidote to contemporary chaos: and after seeing King George VI and Queen Elizabeth crowned at Westminster Abbey, he admitted to Clementine, 'You were right. I see now the "other one" wouldn't have done.' He published an effusive article on the new monarch in the *Strand Magazine* in May 1937, and in a speech in the following year opined that 'the king and his family play a part in our modern life more helpful and more fortifying to the state than in any former age'.[45] But this realistic recognition of royal realities did not mean he abandoned the duke.

[42] *Churchill*, v, 828, 831; *CV*, v, part 3, 489, 493–4.

[43] R. Rhodes James (ed.), *'Chips': The Diaries of Sir Henry Channon* (1967), 128.

[44] *Speeches*, vi, 5847–9.

[45] Ziegler, 'Churchill and the Monarchy', 194; *CV*, v, part 3, 519, 651–3, 1530; *Speeches*, vi, 6017.

Indeed, Henry Channon believed that Churchill was 'pro-Windsor to the end'. They exchanged letters regularly in the months after the abdication; Randolph Churchill was one of the few English friends who attended the wedding of the duke and duchess; and early in 1939, Churchill himself visited the Windsors in the south of France. When war broke out, and Churchill was recalled to the government as first lord of the admiralty, the duke wrote to him, 'not as a minister of the crown, but more as a father'. And on one occasion, they met in the basement secret room of the admiralty, where the disposition of the British navy was recorded. Lord Crawford – the embodiment of responsible respectability – was not at all amused.[46]

So, in the aftermath of the abdication, Churchill was scarcely *persona grata* with the new king, the new queen, or the new court. George VI and Elizabeth had heartily loathed Wallis, and regarded any supporters of hers as enemies of theirs; and so, with equal vehemence, did Queen Mary. Indeed, they viewed the social circle centring around Emerald Cunard, Henry Channon and Winston Churchill as embodying all that was worst of the vulgar, morally suspect, American forces that seemed to be corrupting British society.[47] And these pro-Edward-and-Wallis delinquencies were further compounded by the fact that Churchill was implaccably anti-Chamberlain and anti-appeasement. The new king and queen, by contrast, were devoted supporters of the prime minister. They shared his strong sense of decent moral values, and he appeared with them on the balcony of Buckingham Palace after he returned bearing 'peace with honour' from Munich. When Chamberlain resigned on 10 May 1940, George VI told him he had been 'grossly unfairly treated' and 'greatly regretted' his going, while Queen Elizabeth wrote saying 'how deeply I regretted your ceasing to be prime minister. I can never tell you in words how much we owe you'.[48]

Chamberlain's departure was bad enough for the king and queen: the prospect that he might be followed by Churchill seemed even worse. His devotion to the institution of monarchy was not in question; but although he signed himself, as first lord of the admiralty, 'Your Majesty's faithful and devoted servant and subject', it was precisely that faith and that devotion to George VI which seemed so conspicuously lacking. Along with most of the British establishment, the king preferred

[46] *Churchill*, v, 853, 855–6, 1035, 1037; *CV*, v, part 3, 634–5; *Churchill*, vi, 12–13, 154; M. Gilbert, *The Churchill War Papers* (2 vols., 1993–4) (hereafter *WP*, i–ii), i, 369–70, 376–7, 776, 1070; Vincent, *Crawford Papers*, 604; Rhodes James, *'Chips'*, 122.

[47] *CV*, v, part 3, 673–4; W.S. Churchill, *The Second World War* (6 vols., 1948–54) (hereafter *SWW*, i–vi), i, 172; Rhodes James, *'Chips'*, 60–1, 80–3, 90–1.

[48] *Churchill*, vi, 313; J.W. Wheeler-Bennett, *King George VI: His Life and Reign* (1965), 443–4; S. Bradford, *The Reluctant King: The Life & Reign of George VI, 1895–1962* (New York, 1989), 274–9; A. Roberts, *Eminent Churchillians* (1994), 10–40.

Halifax as Chamberlain's successor. He was decent, religious, landed, a fox hunter and a family friend. Churchill, by contrast, was widely regarded as 'a cad', 'a 'half breed', a 'dictator', a 'rogue elephant', 'the greatest adventurer in modern political history'.[49] Jock Colville, the scion of a courtly family, and private secretary to Neville Chamberlain, was singularly unimpressed by Churchill's 'record of untrustworthiness and instability'. And his mother, Lady Cynthia Colville, who was a lady-in-waiting, received a letter from Queen Mary saying she hoped her son would remain with Chamberlain and not go to the new prime minister. Had these people known that the duke of Windsor had sent Churchill a letter of congratulation, thanking him for his 'great measure of practical and sympathetic support in the past', and clearly expecting more of the same in the future, they would have been even more alarmed.[50]

Such was the extent of courtly opposition when Churchill took office in May 1940, an appointment to which George VI was himself initially 'bitterly opposed'. The fact that Churchill immediately insisted – despite firmly expressed royal misgivings – in making the dreaded Lord Beaverbrook minister of aircraft production, and the no-less unrespectable Brendan Bracken a privy councillor, only seemed to confirm the establishment's worst fears, namely that the 'gangsters' and the 'crooks' were now in charge.[51] The new prime minister was not always scrupulous in keeping the king informed, and he was often infuriatingly unpunctual for royal audiences or luncheons. 'He says he will come at six, puts it off until 6.30 by telephone, then comes at seven', noted Colville. Chamberlain had been considerate and deferential, and the king and queen felt 'a little ruffled by the offhand way' in which Churchill treated them.[52] Moreover, he soon established himself as the personification of Britain's unity and resolve, and as the nation's supreme warlord and grand strategist, which meant he inevitably upstaged the king. For he was eloquent, charismatic and heroic, which George VI was not. 'The King and Queen feel Winston puts them in the shade', recorded Mrs Ronald Greville. 'He is always sending messages for the Nation which the King ought to send.'[53]

Nevertheless, their relations gradually improved. 'As the war pro-

[49] Cannadine, *Aspects of Aristocracy*, 161, and references cited there.
[50] Colville, *Fringes of Power*, 29, 121–3, 130.
[51] Roberts, *Eminent Churchillians*, 14–15, 38–41; Colville, *Fringes of Power*, 145; Ziegler 'Churchill and the Monarchy', 194; R. Blake, 'How Churchill Became Prime Minister', in Blake and Louis (eds.), *Churchill*, 273; *Churchill*, VI, 316, 453–4; Bradford, *Reluctant King* 312–14.
[52] Ziegler, 'Churchill and the Monarchy', 195; Colville, *Fringes of Power*, 160, 211 *Churchill*, VI, 560, 716; *Churchill*, VII, 655.
[53] Rhodes James, *'Chips'*, 272; Colville, *Fringes of Power*, 211, 467; Bradford, *Reluctant King* 340.

ceeded', Jock Colville recalled, 'the King and Queen became as devoted to Winston as he consistently was to them.' George VI soon came to recognise the vigour and brilliance and sheer indispensability of his wartime leadership: 'I must confess', he wrote when giving permission in July 1941 for Churchill to leave the country to meet Roosevelt off Newfoundland, 'that I shall breathe a great sigh of relief when you are safely back home- again.' And, although titanically busy, Churchill regularly lunched with the king at Buckingham Palace, and sent the royal family presents on their birthdays and at Christmas.[54] In 1941, the king publicly expressed his confidence in his prime minister by making him lord warden of the Cinque Ports, and Churchill was 'much attracted by the historic splendour of the appointment', which had been held by the younger Pitt, Wellington and Palmerston. So close did their friendship become that when Churchill wrote his wartime memoirs, he noted with pride that was as much familial as personal, that 'as a convinced upholder of constitutional monarchy I valued as a signal honour the gracious intimacy with which I, as first minister, was treated, for which I suppose there has been no precedent since the days of Queen Anne and Marlborough during his years of power'.[55]

One indication of this is that throughout the war, his letters to his sovereign displayed what Ben Pimlott has rightly described as 'extravagant courtesy', and 'exaggerated shows of deference'.[56] Here is one example. Early in 1941, George VI sent his best wishes for the new year, adding that he had 'so much admired all you have done during the last seven months as my prime minister'. Churchill replied that the sovereign's support had been 'a constant source of strength and encouragement'; that he had served the king's father and grandfather as a minister; that his own father and grandfather had served Queen Victoria; but that the king's 'treatment of me has been intimate and generous to a degree that I had never deemed possible'. The war, he concluded, putting things in a broader and more optimistic perspective, had 'drawn the throne and the people more closely together than was ever before recorded', and George VI and Queen Elizabeth were 'more beloved by all classes and conditions than any of the princes of the past'.[57] Such letters, almost Disraelian in their flattering eloquence, were warmly received at Buckingham Palace; and George VI did his best to reciprocate the same elevated sentiments, even though he could not match the same high style.

[54] Colville, *Fringes of Power*, 211, 323; *Churchill*, VI, 961, 1148; Wheeler-Bennett, *George VI*, 446–7 525–6.

[55] *SWW*, II, 335; Colville, *Fringes of Power*, 439–40.

[56] B. Pimlott, *The Queen: A Biography of Queen Elizabeth II* (1996), 81, 173.

[57] *SWW*, II, 554–5; Wheeler-Bennett, *George VI*, 467. For another, similar letter from Churchill to the king in 1943, see Wheeler-Bennett, *George VI*, 564–5.

But while Churchill's faith and devotion were as sincerely felt as they were eloquently expressed, he had not obtained supreme power with any intention of sharing it with his sovereign. He kept the king fully supplied with the appropriate papers, and was impressed by his thorough mastery of them; but they were for information only.[58] From the outset, Churchill paid great attention to parliamentary opinion, he regularly (if reluctantly) deferred to his chiefs of staff, and in the later stages of the war, he found it increasingly difficult to get his way with Roosevelt and Stalin. But as his intransigence about Beaverbrook and Bracken had signalled early on, he never seems to have changed his mind on a major matter of wartime policy or personnel at the behest of his sovereign. Only in smaller matters did the king occasionally insist, and the prime minister reluctantly give way. This was memorably demonstrated at the time of the D-Day landings, which Churchill was determined to watch at first hand from a nearby cruiser squadron. The king thought this was too great a risk, and in the end he prevailed. But even then, Churchill insisted that this in no sense overturned the general principle that as prime minister he alone could decide which theatres of war he should visit.[59]

Two other members of the British royal family took up Churchill's time during the war years, one of whom was the duke of Windsor, who was hoping for better times now he had a friend at 10 Downing Street.[60] But while Churchill remained personally sympathetic, this was another of those rare instances where he also had to take note, in what was a difficult and delicate family matter, and at a time when he himself was barely established in power, of the wishes of the king and queen. In July 1940, the duke and duchess were in Lisbon, having fled from France before the advancing German army. It was rumoured they were the object of Nazi plots and schemes, which made it imperative to get them out of the country. The duke wanted to return home, and to an important job. But the king, Queen Elizabeth and Queen Mary, were determined 'to keep him at all costs out of England'. Caught in the middle of this royal row, Churchill offered the duke the Governorship of the Bahamas, and urged him to go there directly. It was a deft solution to a difficult problem. 'He'll find it a great relief', observed Lord Beaverbrook of the duke. 'Not half as much as his brother will', replied Churchill. 'I have done my best', the prime minister told the duke, who recognised that he had. But in keeping him out of the country, Churchill also mended his own damaged fences with the king and queen.[61]

[58] Bradford, *Reluctant King*, 305.
[59] *SWW*, v, 546–51; Wheeler-Bennett, *George VI*, 600–6.
[60] P. Dixon, *Double Diploma* (1968), 115.
[61] Colville, *Fringes of Power*, 183–4, 211; Bradford, *Reluctant King*, 434–9.

The very different challenges presented by the career considerations of the king's cousin, Lord Louis Mountbatten, were a great deal easier for Churchill to deal with. For here his task was not reluctantly to relegate a tainted royal to the margins of events, but enthusiastically to propel a glittering royal towards the centre of affairs. As well as being the great-grandson of Queen Victoria, Mountbatten was young, brave, gallant, confident and dashing – an ambitious, well-connected officer after Churchill's own heart. Moreover, he was the son of Prince Louis of Battenberg, who had been obliged to resign as first sea lord in October 1914 when Churchill had been first lord of the admiralty on the wholly groundless accusations that because of his German 'birth and parentage', he was unpatriotic in his sympathies.[62] So Churchill had many reasons for wishing Lord Louis well, and he did just that, making him successively chief of combined operations in 1941, and supreme allied commander in South East Asia two years later, positions of exceptional seniority to be given to an impetuous (and foolhardy?) sailor who was only in his early forties. And with the end of the war in the Far East approaching, Churchill clearly anticipated giving Mountbatten further preferment and promotion. 'We will talk about your future', he told him, 'as I have great plans in store.'[63]

It was a sign of Churchill's transformed relations with the British monarchy, no less than of his triumphs as war leader, that on 8 May 1945, he appeared on the balcony of Buckingham Palace with King George VI and Queen Elizabeth. 'We have', he observed, in moving a loyal address to the king in the Commons, 'the oldest, the most famous, the most honoured, the most secure and the most servicable monarchy in the world.' It was, he insisted, 'an ancient and glorious institution', and 'the symbol which gathers together and expresses those deep emotions and stirrings of the human heart which make men travel far to fight and die together.'[64] But then Churchill was turned out at the general election, and the king was as dismayed to lose his prime minister as he had been reluctant to appoint him five years before. 'I was shocked at the result, and I thought it most ungrateful to you personally after all your hard work for the people', he wrote, with a fine indifference to the conventions of constitutional impartiality. 'I shall miss your counsel to me more than I can say.' He duly offered Churchill the Order of the Garter (which he refused) and later the Order of Merit (which he accepted).[65]

[62] *Churchill*, II, 551–2, 631–2; *Churchill*, III, 147–53; Nicolson, *George V*, 333.

[63] P. Ziegler, *Mountbatten: The Official Biography* (1985), 49, 132–3, 165–57, 168–9, 176–8, 216–24, 299; Colville, *Fringes of Power*, 127; *Churchill*, VIII, 100.

[64] *Churchill*, VIII, 174; *Speeches*, VII, 7164–5.

[65] *Churchill*, VIII, 109, 114–15, 177–8; Wheeler-Bennett, *George VI*, 635–7, 645, 650; Bradford, *Reluctant King*, 377–8.

V

Unlike the great duke of Marlborough, Churchill had been dismissed by the electorate rather than by his sovereign, and thereafter he remained a firm favourite with the British royal family, by many of whom he was now regarded more 'as a friend' than as an ex prime minister. The king continued to consult him about speeches and letters, Churchill sent copies of his history of the Second World War as successive volumes appeared, and he spoke effusively in parliament on the occasion of their majesties' silver wedding.[66] He was delighted when Princess Elizabeth became engaged to Lieutenant Philip Mountbatten; in seconding the Commons address of congratulation, he noted that the monarchy and the royal family, 'play a vital part in the tradition, dignity and romance of our island life'; and when he arrived (late) for their wedding in Westminster Abbey, 'everyone stood up, all the kings and queens'.[67] Churchill also remained a foul-weather friend to the duke of Windsor: he unavailingly supported his search for an honorary post at the British Embassy in Washington; and Winston and Clementine celebrated their fortieth wedding anniversary with the duke and the duchess in the south of France in 1948.[68]

On Churchill's return to power in October 1951, the king was as pleased to see him back as he had been dismayed in 1940. 'In Winston's approach to the throne', Lord Moran reported, 'his sense of history invested the monarch with a certain mystique, so that he always spoke of the royal house with touching reverence.'[69] The death of George VI in January 1952 moved him deeply, and his broadcast and parliamentary eulogies were vibrant with emotion: 'during these last months, the king walked with death, as if death were a companion, an acquaintance, whom he recognized and did not fear'. And he saluted him for being 'so faithful in his study and discharge of state affairs, so strong in his devotion to the enduring honour of our country, so self-restrained in his judgement of men and affairs, so uplifted above the clash of party politics'. In short, his conduct on the throne was 'a model and a guide to constitutional sovereigns throughout the world today, and also in future generations'. But what Churchill meant by that was revealing: George VI 'mastered the immense daily flow of state papers', and this made 'a deep mark' on the prime minister's mind; but he never suggested the king made any serious impact on government policy.[70]

[66] Marlborough, II, 912–13; Moran, Struggle for Survival, 312; Churchill, VIII, 390–1, 446–7, 491, 760–1; Speeches, VII, 7632–3.

[67] Speeches, VI, 7541; Churchill, VIII, 340–41; Rhodes James, 'Chips', 418.

[68] Ziegler, Edward VIII, 505; Churchill, VIII, 174, 207, 232–5, 267–8, 409–10, 431, 450; Marlborough, I, 906–11.

[69] Pimlott, The Queen, 173; Moran, Struggle for Survival, 414, 421.

[70] Moran, Struggle for Survival, 341, 372–4; Colville, Fringes of Power, 640; Churchill, VIII, 696–701; Speeches, VIII 8336–7.

The prime minister's feelings towards the king were genuinely warm; and with his successor, all was even more sweetness and light. Churchill had first met Princess Elizabeth at Balmoral in 1928, when she was two. She was, he told Clementine, 'a character', with 'an air of authority and reflectiveness astonishing in an infant'. Now she was queen, and the ageing prime minister saw himself playing Melbourne to her Victoria. He was the experienced world statesman, with an authority matchless and unrivalled; she, by contrast, was the young sovereign, new to her great responsibilities. The prime minister wore a frock coat and top hat for their (increasingly lengthy) weekly audiences, they talked about polo, horses, and his early life as a subaltern in India, and he returned 'overflowing with her praises'.[71] The queen, for her part, was 'very fond' of her first prime minister; she enjoyed his company at the races and at Balmoral; she gave him the Order of the Garter, which he had previously declined from her father; and she commissioned a portrait bust by Oscar Nemon to be placed in Windsor Castle. Mutual admiration could scarcely go further, and was one of the reasons why Churchill determined to stay on to be the high priest of the secular-cum-sacred splendours of her coronation.[72]

Among the greatest pleasures of Churchill's second premiership were the opportunities to give public expression to his romantic feelings for the institution of monarchy, and for the person of the new monarch. When saluting Elizabeth's accession, he hoped her reign would witness 'a golden age of art and letters', and a 'brightening salvation of the human scene'. On the evening of her coronation, he described the queen as 'a lady whom we respect because she is our queen, and whom we love because she is herself'. And when she returned from her six-month Commonwealth tour in May 1954, Churchill was even more expansive. The 'gleaming episode' of this 'royal pilgrimage' had, he averred, cast a 'clear, calm, gay and benignant' light 'upon the whole human scene', and he assigned 'no limits to the reinforcement which this royal journey may have brought to the health, the wisdom, the sanity and hopefulness of mankind'.[73] Small wonder that on Churchill's eightieth birthday, the whole royal family bought him a present of four silver wine coasters. 'You have been, and are, such an inspiration to our people', the queen mother wrote in congratulation, 'and we are all *very* proud of you' – a complete and conspicuous *bouleversement* from the

---

[71] *Churchill*, v, 303; *CV*, v, part 1, 1349; Rhodes James, *'Chips'*, 474; Moran, *Struggle for Survival*, 403, 484, 607; Pimlott, *The Queen*, 193–4; S. Bradford, *Elizabeth: A Biography of Her Majesty the Queen* (1996), 220–2, 226–7.

[72] Moran, *Struggle for Survival*, 404, 414, 450–1, 472, 547; *Churchill*, v, 763–5, 770–1, 822–4, 852, 874, 884, 886–7, 914, 942, 993.

[73] *Speeches*, VIII, 8487, 8567.

damning opinions she had entertained of him fifteen years before.[74]

But there was also serious and sensitive royal business with which Churchill as prime minister had to deal. Much of this concerned two familiar figures: the duke of Windsor, who remained a problem, and Lord Mountbatten, who had recently become one. The duke still wanted an official job; but there was nothing Churchill could do, try as he might (and he clearly did). He also wanted to attend Queen Elizabeth's coronation, but Churchill strongly and successfully advised against.[75] As for Lord Mountbatten: he was convinced that the marriage of his nephew to Princess Elizabeth meant the Mountbattens had become Britain's ruling house when the princess became the queen. But Churchill (strongly urged on by Queen Mary and Alan Lascelles) took the greatest exception to this idea, and the name of Windsor remained. The prime minister probably needed no encouragement, having taken against Mountbatten since 1945, partly because of his treatment of the princes in India, and partly because of his oft-repeated Labour sympathies. As a result, Churchill was less sympathetic to Mountbatten's determined wish to be first sea lord than he might once have been, and it was only towards the very end of his premiership that Churchill appointed him to the office from which his father had resigned forty years before.[76]

At the same time, a new royal reign, and a new royal generation brought with them new problems for Churchill. There was the question of televising the coronation, to which the cabinet and the queen were initially opposed, and which the prime minister thought would be too great a strain for the young monarch. Eventually, they were all forced to change their minds in response to public opinion. There was the problem of Princess Margaret, who wished to marry the divorced Peter Townsend: Churchill was initially favourable, believing 'the course of true love must always be allowed to run smooth'; but he was persuaded by his wife that this would be an error of judgement comparable to that of the abdication, and he threw his weight (and the cabinet's) against the scheme.[77] There was also the future of the queen mother: on the death of her husband, she inclined to retire into private life, but Churchill persuaded her otherwise, and even held out the prospect that she might become governor general of Australia. And there was the need to assuage the duke of Edinburgh, who had felt slighted when told that his wife had not taken his surname. At the very end of his

[74] *Churchill*, VIII, 1072–6.

[75] *Churchill*, VIII, 979; Ziegler, *Edward VIII*, 539–40, 549, 551; Bradford, *Elizabeth*, 184, 310–11, 343–4; Colville, *Fringes of Power*, 670, 675.

[76] *Churchill*, VIII, 672–3; Ziegler, *Mountbatten*, 502–3, 512, 523–4, 681–2; Pimlott, *The Queen*, 183–6; Bradford, *Elizabeth*, 176–8; Colville, *Fringes of Power*, 637, 641–2, 760.

[77] Pimlott, *The Queen*, 205–7, 218–20; Bradford, *Elizabeth*, 182–3, 204–5.

prime ministership, in March 1955, Churchill suggested to the cabinet that Philip might be created a prince of the United Kingdom, a proposal eventually carried through by Harold Macmillan two years later.[78]

By then, Churchill was well into his retirement, which had begun in April 1955. He had declined the dukedom which his sovereign offered him in his final audience, and he conspicuously refused to give 'advice', believing that the choice of his successor was a matter for the monarch alone. (In fact, of course, it was no such thing: Eden had for years been Churchill's acknowledged heir-apparent, and Churchill had advised George VI of that in June 1942.) And the queen not only attended his farewell dinner: she wrote to him in her own hand, thanking him 'with deep gratitude' for all his services as her first (and favourite) prime minister, a position in her affections that he has retained to this day. 'I had a lovely letter from her', Churchill told Lord Moran, 'eight pages in her own writing. It took me a whole morning to reply.'[79] Thereafter, sovereign and subject continued to correspond, he sent her copies of the *History of the English Speaking Peoples*, he dined occasionally at Buckingham Palace, and the queen consulted him about the succession to Eden in 1957, when he recommended Harold Macmillan in preference to R.A. Butler on the grounds that he was the more decisive.[80]

The queen's affection for her first and favourite prime minister were fully displayed on his death in January 1965, when she behaved impeccably, and with great generosity and imagination. For it was at her instruction, and with parliament's acquiesence, that Churchill was given a state funeral – arrangements which represented a conspicuous reversal of the previous occasion, when parliament had had to petition the (extremely reluctant) Queen Victoria to accord a similar honour to Gladstone.[81] Setting aside all precedent and precedence, Elizabeth II attended in person (something even Victoria had not done for Wellington, and would never have dreamed of doing for the Grand Old Man) to mourn the passing of her greatest subject, as did almost the entire royal family – with the exception of the still-unforgiven duke and duchess of Windsor.[82] Appropriately enough, one of the most memorable images from that day was of the British monarch and her family

[78] *Churchill*, VIII, 722; Colville, *Fringes of Power*, 646; Bradford, *Elizabeth*, 275.

[79] *Churchill*, VII, 125; *Churchill*, VIII, 1123–8; Colville, *Fringes of Power*, 709; Bradford, *Elizabeth*, 228; Moran, *Struggle for Survival*, 653.

[80] Moran, *Struggle for Survival*, 710; Pimlott, *The Queen*, 258; Bradford, *Elizabeth*, 236; *Churchill*, VIII, 1177–8 1193–4, 1223, 1227, 1313, 1330–1, 1333.

[81] H.C.G. Matthew, 'Gladstone's Death and Funeral', *The Historian*, 57 (Spring 1998), 20–4; *Hansard*, fourth series, vol. LVIII, cols. 69, 80, 123–6, 265, 415; *Hansard*, fifth series, vol. 705, cols. 667, 679.

[82] *The Sunday Telegraph*, 31 January 1965.

gathered together in a royal tableau on the steps of St Paul's, saluting Churchill's coffin as it was carried away.

VI

As with many aspects of Churchill's public life and political career, his relations with British monarchs constitutes a rich and varied story, which unfolded at several different levels. There was a high rhetorical plane of history, drama, romance and sentiment, only equalled among British prime ministers by Disraeli. From this grandiloquent perspective, Churchill regarded successive sovereigns as national symbols and imperial icons, whose affairs he was proud to conduct, and whose encouragement, recognition and admiration he deeply cherished. At another level, and this was especially demonstrated in his instinctive feelings towards the duke of Windsor, the widowed Queen Elizabeth, the humiliated Prince Philip and the matrimonially troubled Princess Margaret, Churchill had a genuine sense of the loneliness, sadness and tragedy which was never far from the public pomp and glitter of the throne. And at yet a third level, of workaday politics and practical affairs, he often saw individual monarchs as flawed personalities, political opponents and tiresome nuisances, with inflexible attitudes, reactionary opinions and obscurantist instincts.

In practice, this meant that virtually everything was negotiable – and re-negotiable. For, as Churchill had earlier put it in his life of Marlborough, 'when kings forswear their oaths of duty and conspire against their peoples, when rival kings or their heirs crowd the scene, statesmen have to pick and choose between sovereigns of fluctuating values, as kings are wont to pick and choose between politicians according to their temporary servicableness'.[83] As the record shows, 'picking and choosing between sovereigns' was how Churchill spent much of his political life. Among British monarchs, his opinions of Edward VII, George V, Edward VIII and George VI all underwent serious and significant modification. Only Queen Victoria and Queen Elizabeth II seem to have been the beneficiaries of his unstinted admiration. And, of course, what was negotiable from Churchill's side was also negotiable from the monarchy's side: Edward VII and George V certainly changed their minds about Churchill, and so, even more significantly, did George VI and Queen Elizabeth, as initial alarm was replaced by 'temporary serviceableness' and eventually by lifelong admiration. For just as he came to modify his opinion of them in the light of events, so they in turn came to alter their opinion of him.

[83] *Marlborough*, 1, 298.

Constitutional monarchy, like political activity, was very much the art of the possible.

But not everything was negotiable. Above all, the principle and practice of 'constitutional monarchy' was, for Churchill, inviolate. The crown was to be revered and respected as an institution, and individual sovereigns might be courted and flattered with Disraelian artifice, but 'the supremacy of parliament over the crown' was, for Churchill, the cardinal axiom of British political life, and of his political practice. As he put it in his *History of the English Speaking Peoples*, the monarch was 'the instrument of parliament', the king was 'the servant of his people', and the Commons was 'the dominant institution of the realm'.[84] Accordingly, it was 'the duty of the sovereign to act in accordance with the advice of his ministers', and Churchill never wavered in this belief. To be sure, he was prepared to give way, throughout his career, on minor matters: the naming of ships in the royal navy, the employment of the duke of Windsor, his own attendance at the D-Day landings. But in all great matters – the personnel of politics, domestic statecraft, the grand strategies of war and peace – he was determined to prevail, and, as Philip Ziegler notes, 'it is hard to think of a single instance in which Churchill changed his views or his course of action on any important question in accordance with his perception of the wishes of the monarch of the time.'[85]

From one perspective, there was an extraordinary symmetry and completeness to Churchill's relations with the British monarchy. He began his public life at the end of the reign of one great queen, and he ended his public life at the beginning of what he felt sure would be the reign of another. 'I', he observed on her accession, 'whose youth was passed in the august, unchallenged and tranquil glories of the Victorian era, may well feel a thrill in invoking, once more, the prayer and the anthem, "God save the queen".'[86] So, indeed, it had been; and so, indeed, he did. But from another perspective, the serenity of these final years was late happening and hard won. Of course, and as befitted the grandson of a duke, he had never been a social revolutionary: even before 1914, one perceptive contemporary had opined that the 'whole tenor of his mind' was 'anti-radical'.[87] But in his early liberal, crusading years, he seemed on the side of radical reform to an extent which made successive sovereigns uneasy, and he also carried with him an accumulation of personal shortcomings which meant monarchs were disinclined to trust him – a hostile view which his misguided loyalty to

[84] *Speeches*, VI, 5821; *ESP*, II, 262.
[85] *Speeches*, VI, 5821; Ziegler, 'Churchill and the Monarchy', 198.
[86] *Speeches*, VIII, 8338.
[87] Vincent, *Crawford Papers*, 319.

Edward VIII seemed amply to vindicate. Only as he got closer to the British throne in the reigns of King George VI and Queen Elizabeth II, did he come to see virtues in them and, reciprocally, they in him.

But there were also deeper trends and feelings at work. For as the first half of the 'terrible twentieth century' followed what he regarded as its uniquely dreadful course of 'woe and ruin', Churchill did become more socially and politically conservative, which meant he increasingly regarded the institution of monarchy as the best available antidote to the excesses of democracy, revolution, dictatorship, fascism and communism, by which the world seemed blighted. That the British crown remained, despite all this, stable and secure became, by contrast, a source of singular pride and gratification to him. It defied the course of history, and in his years of power and triumph, Churchill took great delight in helping and encourging it to become even 'stronger than in the days of Queen Victoria'. 'No institution', he told Lord Moran on the accession of Elizabeth, 'pays such dividends as the monarchy.' Small wonder that at his funeral, the queen's wreath bore the appreciative inscription 'In grateful remembrance: Elizabeth R.' For she, like her parents, had much to thank him for.[88]

[88] *Churchill*, VIII, 366, 1364; Moran, *Struggle for Survival*, 372.

CHURCHILL AND THE TRADE UNIONS

By Chris Wrigley

WINSTON CHURCHILL combined a rhetoric of Tory democracy with a shrewd political realism in his approach to the trade unions. When class conflict was strong and law and order under threat, as in 1911–26, the rhetoric evaporated and Churchill became the champion of the anxious propertied classes. So much so that his persistent Dundee opponent, Edwin Scrymgeour, observed during the 1922 general election campaign, shortly after Mussolini took power in Italy, that it would not surprise him in the event of civil war in Britain 'if Mr Churchill were at the head of the Fascisti party'.[1] While this view ignored Churchill's deep commitment to democracy and the British constitution, it did reflect concerns about his apparent revelry in the role of Defender of Order. Yet both before and after 1911–26 his approach to the trade unions was emollient.

Trade unions were an important pressure group which could affect his political prospects in Oldham, where he first sought and secured a parliamentary seat. In going for Oldham he was attempting to put into practice, and to benefit from, Tory democracy. His father, Lord Randolph Churchill, had been personally encouraged by Disraeli and had taken up his mantle when proclaiming Tory democracy. As Lord Randolph put it in 1885, the Tory Party's 'great strength can be found, and must be developed, in our large towns as well as in our country districts'.[2] Winston Churchill advanced on Oldham believing he was carrying on where his father had left off.[3] 'I am a Tory Democrat', he stated early on in the 1899 by-election campaign. 'I regard the improvement of the condition of the British people as the main aim of modern government.' To this ringing declaration he added qualifications sufficiently ample to have equalled Disraeli in such matters: 'I shall therefore promote to the best of my ability all legislation which, without throwing the country into confusion and disturbing the present concord, and without impairing that tremendous energy of production on which the wealth of the nation and the good of the people depend, may yet

[1] Martin Gilbert, *Winston S. Churchill*, IV (1975) 879.
[2] At Cambridge University Carlton, 6 June 1885; Winston S. Churchill, *Lord Randolph Churchill*, I (1906), 295.
[3] See *inter alia*, Robert Rhodes James, *Churchill: A Study in Failure 1900–1939*, (Harmondsworth, 1973), 19–23, and Roy Foster, *Lord Randolph Churchill* (Oxford, 1981), 390–6.

273

raise the standard of happiness and comfort in English homes.'[4]

Winston Churchill stood in a double by-election for the two-member Oldham constituency with James Mawdsley. He was one of the first, quite possibly the first, trade unionists with whom Churchill had substantial contact. The young aristocrat running in harness with the trade unionist was very Young England. Initially, Churchill was going to run with Robert Ascroft, who was well known to Oldham's textile workers as solicitor to the Amalgamated Association of Card Blowing and Ring Room Operatives and for his part in negotiating wage agreements in 1889 and 1890 and helping to resolve the major 1892-3 cotton lock-out. With Ascroft's sudden death, the Conservatives triggered a double by-election with Mawdsley as the candidate whom it was hoped would pull the textile workers' votes to the Conservatives. Churchill believed he was part of a winning combination, writing to his mother on 25 June 1899, 'Owing to the appearance of a Tory Labour candidate it is quite possible we shall win.'[5]

The candidature of Mawdsley with Churchill is a very interesting episode illustrating Churchill's attitudes towards trade unionists and trade unionism. On the one hand, Churchill and Mawdsley shared many views. On the other, one can wonder if the young Churchill grasped – or was even interested in – Mawdsley's political views. In *My Early Life* he wrote of Mawdsley as 'a Socialist' and of a partnership between 'a "scion" of the ancient British aristocracy' and a socialist, a view echoed by Randolph Churchill in the official life and by Robert Rhodes James in the *Complete Speeches*. Peter Clarke in *Lancashire and the New Liberalism* rightly noted that Mawdsley's social reform programme amounted mostly to municipal control of utilities, as he put it, his 'claims were utilitarian and they were pitched low'.[6] By 1930, when he wrote *My Early Life*, Churchill was clear enough about what then constituted socialism. Thirty years earlier, Mawdsley was only a socialist in the dubious sense of favouring state intervention and regulation of industry, of a measure of collectivism.

Mawdsley was a bigger trade union figure and more of a Conservative than most writers about Churchill have realised. He was a member of the TUC's executive body, its parliamentary committee, 1882-3, 1884-90 and 1891-7, and was the TUC's chairman in 1886. He also served on the Royal Commission on Labour, 1891-4. He was a notable anti-

[4] At Oldham, 26 June 1899; Robert Rhodes James (ed.), *Winston S. Churchill: His Complete Speeches, 1897-1963* (8 vols., New York, 1974) (hereafter *Complete Speeches*), I, 35. Paul Addison, *Churchill on the Home Front* (1992).

[5] Randolph S. Churchill, *Winston S. Churchill: Companion*, I (1967), 1009, 1022, 1024-5 and 1028-30.

[6] Winston S. Churchill, *My Early Life*, (1930), chapter 17. Randolph S. Churchill, *Winston S. Churchill*, I, (1966), 444-5.

socialist, resigning from the parliamentary committee in 1890 in protest at the growing influence of New Union socialists in the TUC. Then he deemed socialist ideas fit only for the 'scum of London'. In 1895 he was instrumental in forging a cotton and coal alliance which changed the TUC rules so as to undercut many of the socialists.[7] In the general election of that year he was the conduit for 'Tory gold' to reach an Independent Labour party candidate, providing the money on a no questions asked basis.[8] Churchill would have found Tom Mann or Bob Smillie very different kinds of 'socialist' from Mawdsley. Nevertheless, Mawdsley was an effective trade union leader and was one who believed he could secure more labour regulation in parliament by working through the existing parties.

The young Churchill's approach to trade unionism combined a Tory democrat desire to do something for working people, provided it did not affect the competitiveness of industry, with a concern to maintain social stability. As early as 1897 he had held forth on industrial relations at the time of the great engineering lock-out. Appropriately, his audience was a Primrose League gathering at Bath. Then he had talked vaguely of some form of profit sharing, but one which would make the workers willing to suffer income losses in bad economic times.[9] In the 1899 by-election he was explicit that Tory democracy benefited the existing social order. 'For many years the Conservative Party has guarded the interests of labour', he told an Oldham audience, 'Their efforts have not been without reward, for Tory democracy has now become the stoutest bulwark of the constitution.'[10]

Churchill's attitude towards labour all his life had this element of *noblesse oblige*, but such benevolence was tempered by an expectation of good behaviour in return. The aristocratic expectations of playing a leading role in events and for others to minister to his needs was strong in him. Charles Masterman commented of him, 'He desired in England a state of things where a benign upper class dispensed benefits to an industrious, *bien pensant*, and grateful working class.'[11] Although mostly a kind man, Churchill had been brought up to expect employees to provide service, and quickly. Even his warmest admirers on occasion shuddered at his sometimes insensitive treatment of waiters, valets,

[7] A. Bullen, 'The Making of Brooklands' in Alan Fowler and Terry Wyke (eds.), *The Barefoot Aristocrats* (Littleborough, 1987), 99. Alan Fowler, 'Lancashire to Westminster: A Study of Cotton Trade Union Officials and British Labour, 1910–39', *Labour History Review*, 64, 1 (1999), 1–22. H.A. Clegg, A. Fox and A.F. Thompson, *A History of British Trade Unions Since 1889*, I, (Oxford, 1964), 115, 256 and 259.

[8] Sir James Sexton, *Sir James Sexton: Agitator* (1936), 146.

[9] On 26 July, 1897 at Claverton Down, Bath; *Complete Speeches*, I, 27.

[10] On 26 June 1899; *Complete Speeches*, I, 36.

[11] Quoted in Rhodes James, *Churchill*, 45.

chauffeurs and others.[12] One recalled with dismay his ringing for service, observing that when you want a drink you should ring, and keep ringing until it appears. Such an outlook was not in harmony with trade union notions of the dignity of labour. He also had a patrician, indeed Whig, attitude towards history. His historical writings do not deal much with the common man or woman. 'War, politics, violence, these are the stuff of Churchill's history: but glorious not nasty' was one way J.H. Plumb put it. On another occasion, more in caricature, he wrote of Churchill's history as 'a saga world of killer patricians, entangled by tradition and events in a few human decencies'.[13]

As well as this aristocratic outlook and his notions of Tory democracy, a further major aspect of Churchill's attitude to the trade unions was a deep-rooted belief in market forces and individualism. Churchill spoke of the economic struggles between nations when commenting on the 1897 engineering lock-out.

> Whoever is right, masters or men – both are wrong, whoever might win, both must lose. In the great economic struggle of nations no quarter is ever shown to the vanquished. Every individual has, no doubt the right to buy the best goods in the cheapest market, and if British manufacturing cannot produce goods for export at the lowest price in the market our trade ... would simply go to the German emperor...[14]

He long remained an articulate expounder of the merits of free market forces. In October 1906, in one of his celebrated social reform speeches, he commented:

> The existing organisation of society is driven by one mainspring – competitive selection. It may be a very imperfect organisation of society, but it is all we have got between us and barbarism ... and great and numerous as are the evils of the existing condition of society in this country, the advantages and achievements of the social system are greater still. Moreover that social system is one which offers an almost indefinite capacity for improvement ... I do not want to see impaired the vigour of competition, but we can do much to mitigate the consequences of failure. We want to draw a line below which we will not allow people to live and labour, yet above which they may compete with all the strengths of their manhood.[15]

[12] Maurice Ashley, *Churchill As Historian*, (1968), 9.
[13] In a book review in *The Spectator*, 1964, partly reprinted in J.H. Plumb, *The Making of an Historian: The Collected Essays of J.H. Plumb* (Brighton, 1988), 226.
[14] At Claverton Down, Bath, 26 July 1897; *Complete Speeches*, I, 27.
[15] At Glasgow, 11 October 1906; Winston S. Churchill, *Liberalism and the Social Problem* (1909), 82.

He echoed these words in a speech to the 1947 Conservative party conference.

Like Lloyd George, Churchill was more concerned to help the underdogs of society, not labour which was organised. With the Trade Boards Act, 1909, he made what he emphasised was an exceptional modification to laws of supply and demand to ensure 'adequate minimum standards' in sweated trades, 'where ... you have no organisation, no parity of bargaining, the good employer is undercut by the bad and the bad employer is undercut by the worst; [and where] the worker, whose livelihood depends upon the industry, is undersold by the worker who only takes up the trade as a second string'. This Act initially covered 200,000 workers, of whom 140,000 were women and girls, in tailoring, box-making, lace making and chain making.[16]

But what of trade unions? He himself was a great individualist. In a speech to a well-to-do audience in November 1901, he lamented, 'In trade vast and formidable combinations of labour stand against even vaster and more formidable combinations of capital, and, whether they war with each other or co-operate, the individual in the end is always crushed under.' He declared, 'I believe in personality.'[17] Yet as a Conservative MP he favoured the reversal of the Taff Vale Judgement, 1901, being one of seventeen Conservative MPs to vote for a TUC backed bill in 1903.[18] When the Bill was moved again in 1904, he supported it observing that although 'it was difficult to find a logical reason for relieving trade unions of their responsibilities and leaving them their power', there was the practical reason that the pre-Taff Vale legal position had enabled the trade unions to function well, being 'less violent and unjust' than before, and had not damaged the economy. He commented of the 1875 legislation that it 'was the work of a Tory government; it was introduced by so good a Tory as Lord Cross, had the *impimatur* of Disraeli; and was one of the great agencies by which ... the Tory democracy had been built up in this country'.[19]

While such comments might be construed as examples of his ability to manufacture plausible arguments to meet his current political needs, more probably they reflect his views. For he was to make very similar points after the Second World War. Moreover, in the period before

[16] House of Commons Debates, fifth series, vol. 4, col. 388, 28 April. (The passage is rephrased in *Liberalism and the Social Problem*, 240.) Addison, *Churchill on the Home Front*, 78–9.
[17] At the Philomathic Society dinner, Liverpool, 21 November 1901; *Complete Speeches*, I, 109.
[18] F. Bealey and H. Pelling, *Labour and Politics 1900–1906* (1958), 204. Addison, *Churchill on the Home Front*, 42.
[19] In the House of Commons; *House of Commons Debates*, fourth series, vol. 133, col. 999, April 1904.

1911 it is sometimes overlooked that his contact was with the more moderate trade unionists in industries marked on the whole by less tumultuous industrial relations: the textile workers of Oldham, Manchester and Dundee. Later, in 1911–26, he was to be alarmed by militant miners, railwaymen, dockers and engineers.

In the Edwardian period he readily praised the level-headedness of trade unionists. Thus, in October 1906, he said that if any group could claim to speak for the working classes,

> it is the trade unions that more than any other organisation must be considered the responsible and deputed representatives of Labour. They are the most highly organised part of labour; they are the most responsible part; they are from day to day in contact with reality...
>
> The fortunes of the trade unions are interwoven with the industries they serve. The more highly organised trade unions are, the more clearly they recognise their responsibilities; the larger the membership, the greater their knowledge, the wider their outlook.[20]

Two years later, when he elaborated on these comments, he went so far as to reconcile the trade unions to his belief in individualism. At Dundee, when proclaiming them as 'the bulwarks of a highly competitive industrial system', he commented,

> Trade unions are not socialistic. They are the antithesis of socialism. They are undoubtedly individualistic organisations, more in the character of the old Guilds, and much more in the culture of the individual, than they are in that of the smooth and bloodless uniformity of the masses.[21]

Yet in these years Churchill, as after 1945, was explicit as to the importance of the right to strike. Thus, for instance, he observed in November 1904,

> It is most important for the British working classes that they should be able if necessary to strike – although nobody likes strikes – in order to put pressure upon the employers for a greater share of the wealth of the world or for the removal of hard and onerous conditions, but in the socialist state no strike would be tolerated.[22]

On several occasions in the period before 1911, Churchill spoke on what David Metcalf has dubbed the trade unions 'sword of justice'

---

[20] At Glasgow, 11 October 1906; *Liberalism and the Social Problem*, 72–3. For similar sentiments specifically linked to the cotton trade unions, see his speech at Oldham, 21 October 1903; *Complete Speeches*, 1, 219.

[21] At Dundee, 4 May 1908; *Complete Speeches*, 1, 1030.

[22] In a speech to working men in the Liberal Club, Coatbridge; *Complete Speeches*, 1, 384.

role. In January 1908, when speaking of the Liberal government's social reforms, Churchill observed, 'While I believe in the advantages of a competitive system under which man is pitted against man, I do not believe in allowing men to be pitted against each other ruthlessly until the last drop of energy is extracted, and there the trade unions come in as safeguards and checks.'[23] Earlier, when opposing tariff reform, he had argued that tariffs would give big profits to employers and destabilise industrial relations. He explained, 'We are told that wages were to be raised. If they are, it can only be through the pressure of the trades unions.'[24]

In his early career Churchill was willing to listen to local trade union leaders and to come to his own judgement on issues. When he was seeking election in Oldham in 1899, J.R. Clynes, then secretary of Oldham Trades Council, led a trades council delegation to press on him various labour issues. Clynes later recalled,

I found him a man of extraordinarily independent mind, and great courage. He absolutely refused to yield to our persuasions, and said bluntly that he would rather lose votes than abandon his convictions.[25]

Yet later, in 1903, Churchill was convinced of the justice of reversing the Taff Vale Judgement after a correspondence with Clynes.

In looking at Churchill's attitudes to trade unionism it is especially important not to read back the later importance of the Labour party or TUC to the pre-1911 period. Both Churchill and Mawdsley were able to contemplate British politics with a trade union movement attaching itself to the existing parties, as in the USA. For Mawdsley, it was possible to pursue labour concerns in parliament through any party, but his preference was for the Conservative party. For Churchill in 1899, it was easy to herald Mawdsley's emergence as a parliamentary candidate as marking 'the birth of a new party which has for a very long time been in the minds of a great section of our fellow-countrymen – a Conservative Labour Party'.[26]

While favourable to trade unionism in these years, Churchill was very hostile to socialism. He proclaimed the necessity of private property and decried state employment as a recipe for low output. He frequently created caricatures of socialism to jeer at in his speeches. Of the fiery socialist Victor Grayson, he observed, 'The socialism of the Christian era was based on the idea that "all mine is yours", but the socialism of

[23] At Manchester, 22 January 1908; *Complete Speeches*, I, 873.

[24] At Oldham, 21 October 1903; *Complete Speeches*, I, 219.

[25] J.R. Clynes, *Memoirs 1869–1924* (1937), 97. Others later commented on this characteristic; for example, W.H. Thompson, *I Was Churchill's Shadow*, (1951), 169.

[26] At the Co-operative Hall, Greenacres, Oldham on 29 June 1899; *Complete Speeches*, I, 45.

Mr Grayson is based on the idea that "all yours is mine".[27] When Charles Masterman suggested that Keir Hardie would go to heaven quickly, Churchill replied, 'If heaven is going to be full of people like Hardie...well, the Almighty can have them to himself.'[28]

Like Lloyd George, Churchill was well aware of the growth of the SPD in Germany. In a speech to a working-class audience in the Liberal club at Coatsbridge in November 1904 he contrasted, in a traditional Liberal manner, the quality of the British constitutional system with that of Germany. In Britain he said they 'should try to improve the lot of the masses of the people through the existing structure of society rather than by the immediate demolition of that structure and the building up of an entirely new system'. In contrast, he asserted, 'If I were in Germany I would be a socialist myself. I would be against militarism, conscription, the high protective tariff, and the despotic form of government ...'[29] In this Churchill was in tune with prevailing working-class sensitivities. In the more democratic states, working-class politics was predominantly moderate (as in Britain, France and the USA), whereas under the more repressive regimes it was more revolutionary (as in Russia and Germany).

Churchill was very aware of the power of the propertied classes in Britain, France and the USA. He might have added Germany to his list. In such countries he felt the stability of the state rested on the 'vast numbers of persons who are holders of interest-bearing, profit-bearing, rent-earning property, and the whole tendency of civilisation and of free institutions is to an ever-increasing volume of production and an increasingly wide diffusion of profit'. He predicted that in such societies revolution would provoke counter-revolution. He argued that Liberalism offered the alternative to class war, as through gentle reforms it would enable British society 'to slide forward, almost painlessly ... on to a more even and more equal foundation'. He elaborated the historic function of the Liberal party: 'By gradual steps, by steady effort from day to day, from year to year, Liberalism enlists hundreds of thousands upon the side of progress and popular democratic reform whom militant socialism would drive into violent reaction.'[30] In this Churchill unknowingly was predicting his own political trajectory in the face of militant trade unionism at home and Bolshevism abroad.

Winston Churchill became much involved in industrial relations while president of the board of trade (April 1908–February 1910) and

[27] At Cheetham, 22 January 1908; *Complete Speeches*, 1, 874.
[28] Lucy Masterman, *C.F.G. Masterman: A Biography* (1939), 164 (in late September or early October 1910).
[29] At Coatsbridge, 11 November 1904; *Complete Speeches*, 1, 384.
[30] At Glasgow, 11 October 1906; *Liberalism and the Social Problem*, 77–8.

then home secretary (February 1910–October 1911). At the board of trade Churchill utilised the knowledge of several trade union leaders when he was preparing industrial reforms. In the case of safety in the mines, Churchill responded to both the recommendations of the Royal Commission on Accidents in Mines and representations from the TUC and mining trade unions.[31]

He was also, like Lloyd George before him, very willing to adopt a high profile in trying to resolve industrial disputes. Soon after taking office he set out to strengthen the board of trade's powers of intervention beyond the powers in the 1896 Conciliation Act. One proposal considered was the introduction of a version of the Canadian Lemieux Act, so that the board of trade could appoint a court of inquiry and introduce a cooling-off period while a settlement was sought.[32] While this failed to gain support from either side of industry, Churchill pressed on with the formation of a standing court of arbitration, which he saw as 'consolidating, expanding and popularising the working of the Conciliation Act'.[33] Churchill tried hard, but unsuccessfully, to achieve agreement to a new sliding scale in the cotton industry, in order to provide 'a more scientific process' for resolving differences than the persistent strikes and lock-outs.[34]

Churchill continued to express sympathy and support for trade unionism after he went to the home office. This was most notably the case with the Trade Union Bill, 1911 (which was passed in 1913 and substantially undid the Osborne Judgement, 1909, which had undercut trade union political funds). Then, in May 1911, Churchill declared,

I consider that every workman is well advised to join a trade union. I cannot conceive how any man standing undefended against the powers that be in this world could be so foolish, if he can spare the money from the maintenance of his family, not to associate himself with an organisation to protect the rights and interests of labour, and I think there could be no greater injury to trade unionism than that the unions should either be stripped of a great many strong and independent spirits ... or that they should split into rival bodies and that attempts should be made to make party trade unions – Liberal

[31] See, for instance, his speech to a deputation from the Parliamentary Committee of the TUC and some mining unions at the Home Office, 21 April 1910; *Complete Speeches*, II, 1556–7.
[32] Chris Wrigley, 'The Government and Industrial Relations' in Chris Wrigley (ed.), *A History of British Industrial Relations 1875–1914* (Hassocks, 1982), 145–6. E. Wigham, *Strikes and the Government 1893–1974* (1976), 22.
[33] Memorandum, 1 September 1908; Randolph S. Churchill, *Winston S. Churchill: Companion*, II, part 2 (1969), 836–8.
[34] Report of a conference at the Board of Trade, 4 March 1909; *Complete Speeches*, II, 1181–3.

and Socialist party trade unions – and so break the homogeneity and solidarity of the great trade union movement.[35]

However, by this time Churchill's sympathy with labour was beginning to diminish, and in cabinet he had opposed reversing the Osborne Judgement.

At the home office Churchill was responsible for law and order, causes dear to his heart, and as violence associated with industrial disputes escalated, so Churchill's emphasis on order put him in conflict with many trade union activists. Yet, in the earlier big disputes, Churchill still went out of his way to praise the solid trade union majority. After the riots in Tonypandy Churchill stated in the Commons that he believed that they were the work of 'rowdy youth and roughs from outside' not 'the well-educated, peaceable, intelligent and law-abiding class of men', the miners of South Wales.[36] Later in 1911 he spoke of most railwaymen being part of 'a self-respecting and respectable class' who 'have been all for peace and order throughout'.[37] In these remarks he was not only respecting the Lib-Lab voters but stating his own view.

The controversy over Churchill's role or non-role in the deaths of trade unionists in South Wales, at Llanelli not Tonypandy, has distracted attention from the part he delighted in playing in these industrial conflicts. As home secretary, as he was not slow to assert, his role was not to judge who was right or wrong but to maintain the peace. Though having made statements to that effect, he frequently promptly indicated his view. Thus, in the case of the Newport docks strike of May–June 1910 he made it clear he felt the employer was being unreasonable, whereas in the case of the 1910 South Wales coal strike he observed, 'both seemed to have behaved very unreasonably. Both sides seem to be intent on quarrelling without the slightest regard to the common interest and without paying any attention to the public welfare which is gravely compromised by their action.'[38] In practice he often annoyed both sides of industry, for his heart was with those enforcing law and order, the police and the soldiers.

J.R. Clynes, who was often a shrewd judge of people, wrote in the 1930s of Churchill, 'Churchill was, and has always remained, a soldier in mufti. He possesses inborn militaristic qualities, and is intensely proud of his descent from Marlborough.'[39] Churchill was more interested in efficient operations of the police and the soldiers, and asserting order,

[35] House of Commons Debates, fifth series, vol. 26, cols. 1017–8, 30 May 1911. Addison, Churchill on the Home Front, 145–7.

[36] House of Commons Debates, fifth series, vol. 21, col. 239, 7 February 1911.

[37] House of Commons Debates, fifth series, vol. 29, col. 2247, 18 August 1911.

[38] House of Commons Debates, fifth series, vol. 18, col. 73–80, 22 June 1910, and vol. 20, col. 416, 24 November 1910.

[39] Clynes, Memoirs, 1, p. 97.

than helping businessmen *per se*. In 1911 he appears to have found the notion that the police may have used excessive force, including on women and children, hard to believe.[40] He was also a warm champion of the conduct of the soldiers. Of the troops in South Wales, he commented that soon 'they did not look upon the whole body of strikers as if they were wild beasts, as they were described in so many of the London newspapers ... In a week they were playing football matches with them...'[41]

However, if this was shades of the general strike, so was Churchill's concern to maintain transport and food supplies. At the end of unrest in London in mid 1911, Churchill informed the Commons, 'If the strike continued a regular system of convoys would have had to be organised.' He also stated that it would be 'the duty of the government in the event of the paralysis of the great railway lines upon which the life and food of the people depend, to secure to the persons engaged in working them full legal protection ...'[42] With industrial unrest spreading, accompanied by more violence, Churchill became increasingly alarmist about transport strikes leading to a serious social breakdown in Britain. Four days after the national rail strike of 18–19 August 1911, in which Churchill had deployed large numbers of soldiers in London and thirty-two cities and towns, he made a notably alarmist speech in the Commons. In it he graphically recounted the disastrous effects in the Euphrates in the fifteenth century when the Nimrod Dam broke, after which thousands of people 'were wiped from the book of human life'. He then commented, 'These are the considerations which it is no exaggeration to say have to be borne in mind at the present juncture.' He referred to the recent dock and rail disputes observing of the industrial north and midlands,

it is practically certain that a continuance of the railway strike would have produced a swift and certain degeneration of all the means, of all the structure, social and economic, on which the life of the people depends. If it had not been interrupted it would have hurled the whole of that great community into an abyss of horror which no man dare to contemplate ... I am sure the House will see that no blockade by a foreign enemy could have been anything like so effective in producing terrible pressures on these vast populations as the effective closing of those great ports coupled with the paralysis of the railway service.[43]

[40] For instance, in response to George Lansbury's questions, 10 August 1911; *House of Commons Debates*, fifth series, vol. 29, cols. 1360–1.

[41] *House of Commons Debates*, fifth series, vol. 21, col. 236, 7 Feb 1911.

[42] *House of Commons Debates*, fifth series, vol. 29, cols. 1987 and 1991, 16 August 1911.

[43] *House of Commons Debates*, fifth series, vol. 29, cols. 2323–34, 22 August 1911.

Churchill was very taken aback by the pre-First World War strikes in key sectors of the economy. At the board of trade in 1909 he had been disconcerted at the response to a threat to pass emergency legislation to refer a mining dispute to compulsory arbitration. Sir George Askwith, the board of trade's conciliator, recalled, 'As he was leaving the room, Mabon, the famous Welsh leader, turned on him with the remark, in a strong Welsh accent, "Mr Churchill, you cannot put 600,000 men into prison." '[44] At the time of the 1911 national rail strike, he was dejected when the men rejected Lloyd George's proposed settlement, commenting, 'The men have beaten us ... We cannot keep the trains running. There is nothing we can do. We are done!' But when Lloyd George secured a settlement Churchill telephoned him regretting it, commenting, 'I'm very sorry to hear it. It would have been better to have gone on and given these men a good thrashing.'[45]

By July 1911 Churchill was anxious about industrial relations generally. According to Asquith's cabinet report to the king on 21 July he raised the issue with his colleagues, referring to 'the almost daily outbreak of strikes, direct and sympathetic, accompanied by a growing readiness to resort to violence, and imposing heavy labour responsibilities both on the police and military'. He called for a public inquiry perhaps chaired by the prime minister, 'into the causes and remedies for these menacing developments'.[46] His colleagues agreed with his concern, but did not set up a public inquiry.

Churchill's concern was to do with more than a wave of strikes. He was alarmed by rioting crowds, in South Wales, London and Liverpool in particular. In the case of Liverpool he was not alone among ministers, Herbert Samuel writing to his wife in August 1911, commented 'Liverpool is verging on a state of revolution.'[47] The king took the same view. Churchill noted that in Liverpool and elsewhere poor people often joined in the unrest. In the House of Commons he read out the chief constable's report which stated that in Liverpool, the riot began with a fringe of the crowd at the great demonstration of the National Transport Workers' Federation, 'the fringe at this corner consisted no doubt of the roughs from the adjoining Irish district, always ready for an opportunity to attack the police'.[48] Churchill, like his former leader Lord Salisbury, had forebodings about social disintegration. He often had an aristocratic concern about Robespierre and the French Revo-

[44] Lord Askwith, *Industrial Problems and Disputes* (1920), 131.
[45] Masterman, *Masterman*, 207–8.
[46] Asquith's report to the King, 21 July 1911; Asquith Papers, 6, f. 58. The king shared Churchill's anxieties as revealed in Asquith's Cabinet Paper on Industrial Unrest, 8 September 1911; PRO, CAB 37/107/107.
[47] Samuel to his wife, 17 August 1911; Samuel Papers, A157, f. 615.
[48] *House of Commons Debates*, fifth series, vol. 29, col. 1989, 16 August 1911.

lution, if not about Napoleon whom he greatly admired. He was easily teased by Lloyd George and Masterman. At the time of the 1909 People's Budget, Lucy Masterman recorded,

... they began talking wildly, absolutely in fun, of the revolutionary measures they were proposing next: the guillotine in Trafalgar Square; and nominating for the first tumbril. Winston, whose sense of humour is not very quick, became more and more indignant and alarmed...[49]

As Paul Addison has commented, Churchill in the summer of 1911 'fatally compromised' his standing as a radical reformer as he adopted 'a belligerent posture' and a determination that 'the spirit of insubordination must be broken'.[50] Churchill remained on the side of those wanting a tough stance, not a settlement through legislation, during the big 1912 coal dispute.[51] However, by this time he was at the admiralty and so in charge of one of the armed forces.

Churchill dealt again with labour as minister of munitions during the First World War. As in the Second World War, he was readily willing to make concessions to the trade unions if these would secure greater effort for the needs of the war. In August 1917 he responded to pressure from the skilled engineering unions to drop proposals to extend dilution of labour to private work. Instead he pushed quickly through parliament an emollient Munitions of War Amendment Bill, which included the abolition of the much-hated leaving certificate (needed from employers before workers could leave for other employment) and gave the minister of munitions powers to increase skilled workers' hourly rates of pay in order to remove financial inducements for skilled men to transfer to more highly paid less skilled work (mostly on piece rates).[52]

Churchill made use of these powers again in the autumn of 1917 to try to remedy the widespread and ominously growing grievances over pay. In so doing he displayed a lack of awareness of the sensitivity of altering some groups of workers' pay. He unleashed a series of strikes as workers not included in the initial 12.5 per cent pay rises strove to restore their differentials (their relative position with regard to pay). In November the matter was deemed so urgent by Lord Milner, Churchill

---

[49] Masterman, *Masterman*, 139.

[50] Addison, *Churchill on the Home Front*, 150.

[51] Asquith's Cabinet report to the king, 16 March 1911; Asquith Papers, 6, f. 119.

[52] Chris Wrigley, *David Lloyd George and the Labour Movement* (Hassocks, 1976), 203. Chris Wrigley, 'The Ministry of Munitions: An Innovatory Department' in Kathleen Burk (ed.), *War and the State* (1982), 32–56.

and others that the war cabinet was summoned half an hour earlier to deal with it.[53]

In the succeeding months the government was forced to concede further pay rises to other groups, with Churchill and the civil servants trying to protect the public purse. On one occasion a Belfast engineer spoke of Dr Macnamara and Churchill at the admiralty with regard to dockyard labour, 'whenever he [or Macnamara] went as Secretary for a shilling for the "bottom dog" he was always received in the finest manner; Mr Churchill was always in favour of giving a shilling to the "bottom dog" '. To this, the civil servant Sir Thomas Munro responded, 'Mr Churchill's generous instincts have to be a little curbed by those of us here.'[54] Churchill, having unleashed the initial pay awards, himself pressed on iron and steel trade union officials that in wartime, with employers able to pass costs on, the old check on pay rises had gone and the state had to be firm. When he learned in January 1918 that a general extension of 7.5 per cent in pay was about to be authorised, he wrote to Lloyd George stating this was 'too foolish' and that such a concession should not be given 'on the eve of a tussle with labour which may lead to strikes instead of keeping it as a counter for bargaining a peace with'.[55] However, in such moves Churchill was trying to bolt the stable door after the horse had galloped out and run away. The 12.5 per cent pay rise episode did nothing to enhance Churchill's reputation for dealing with labour.

Churchill's time at the ministry of munitions was also marked by him being impressed by the effectiveness of the Ministry's interventionist role in industry. At a dinner to mark his departure from the Ministry, Churchill commented,

> I have not been quite convinced by my experience of the Ministry of Munitions that socialism is possible, but I have been very nearly convinced. I am like one of those people who are trembling on the border-line between individual enterprise proceeding in fierce competition in all industries, and a vast organised machinery of production supported and equipped by all that is best in the nation and proceeding on calculation and design to multiply enormously the prosperity of the whole people. I am bound to say, I consider, on the whole, the achievements of the Ministry of Munitions con-

[53] Maurice Hankey to Lloyd George, 17 November 1917; Lloyd George Papers F/23/1/28. Wrigley, *David Lloyd George*, 219–22.

[54] Conference with the Belfast engineers, 22 November 1917; PRO MUNS-82–342/23. Munro had been one of the three commissioners who enforced dilution on the Clyde in 1916.

[55] Conference with the iron, steel and bricklayers unions, 3 January 1918, PRO MITNS79–341/12. Churchill to Lloyd George, 21 January 1918; Lloyd George Papers, F/8/2/4.

stitute the greatest argument for state socialism that has ever been produced. Nothing like it has ever been attempted in any part of the world.[56]

This was a long way from his pre-war anti-state stereotyping, as expressed in November 1904 when he stated, 'Whenever we have men working on assured and fixed salaries drawn from the state we can be quite certain that while they do their duty they will not over-exert themselves.'[57]

After the end of the First World War Churchill took similar political postures towards industrial unrest to those he had adopted during the serious industrial unrest of 1911. While again he showed some caution in deploying troops in industrial disputes, he was emphatic that where strikes threatened food supplies or utilities he was willing to take strong measures. In February 1920 when the cabinet was in alarmist mood about major strikes leading to serious unrest, Churchill was a vigorous supporter of the emergency transport system, observing 'It is not strike-breaking, it is feeding the people.' He also stated that while the Territorial Army could not be used in a strike or local riot 'but if there was a grave national emergency then there could be a Royal Proclamation and the Territorial Force would be embodied and available'.[58]

Nevertheless, he continued to see trade unionism as a bulwark against revolution. When supporting recognition of the Railway Clerks Association in February 1919, he commented,

> the trade union organisation was very imperfect, and the more moderate its officials were the less representative it was, but it was the only organisation with which the government could deal. The curse of trade unionism was that there was not enough of it, and it was not highly enough developed to make its branch secretaries fall into line with head office. With a powerful union either peace or war could be made.

However, at that time of acute industrial unrest even Bonar Law, the Conservative leader, observed that 'the trade union organisation was the only thing between us and anarchy, and if the trade union organisation was against us the position would be hopeless'.[59]

---

[56] At a dinner given by the higher staff of the Ministry of Munitions, 22 January 1919; PRO MUNS-12–200/53.

[57] At Coatsbridge, 11 November 1904; *Complete Speeches*, II, 383. Even allowing for the different audiences, this displays a notably different view.

[58] Notes of a cabinet meeting, 2 February 1920; K. Middlemas (ed.), *Thomas Jones: Whitehall Diary*, II (Oxford, 1969), 99–103. See also P. Dennis, 'The Territorial Army in Aid of the Civil Power in Britain', *Journal of Contemporary History*, 16 (1981), 705–24.

[59] Chris Wrigley, *Lloyd George and the Challenge of Labour* (Brighton, 1990), 117.

Churchill's deeper fears of mob rule and revolution were accentuated by developments in Russia from October 1917 and in Central Europe in 1918–19. Such fears seem to have prompted alarmist talk and action on his part, all the more worrying to those who did not share his concerns as he held the office of secretary of state for war. As Paul Addison has aptly put it, 'Churchill's Marlborough complex was coupled with a primal hatred of the Bolshevik revolution.'[60]

While Churchill was very much a *bona fide* anti-Bolshevik and anti-socialist, like Lloyd George he was very willing to play up anti-Labour fears to encourage middle-class voters to continue to feel a need for the coalition government. At Loughborough on 4 March 1922, he warned, 'A socialist will coax and wheedle you and argue you into ruin, and the Communist will ram ruin down your throat with a bayonet on the Russian plan.'[61] Also, given the massive swings to Labour in London county council and then borough elections in 1919 and 1920, Churchill had additional political reasons for promoting Conservative–Liberal coalition politics at the local level as well as 'fusion' nationally. Moreover, there was a consistency in both his tough line in favour of 'order' and his continuing support for social reform, including housing and unemployment measures as well as supporting special taxes on war wealth.

This pattern was repeated in his period as chancellor of the exchequer in Baldwin's 1924–9 government. He remained vehemently anti-Communist, be it the Third International or the Communist party of Great Britain, and anti-socialist. Hence, in January 1927, his praise for Mussolini's 'triumphant struggle against the bestial appetites and passions of Leninism'.[62] He continued to pretend publicly that Ramsay MacDonald and the other Labour party leaders were wolves in sheep's clothing, whereas most were sheep in sheep's clothing, with the odd sheep in wolf's clothing. He also hoped to push forward with some social reforms, notably in the areas of housing and pensions, such as he had pressed for in the past as part of his Tory democracy or pre-war Radicalism.[63] By 1924 he had written off the trade unions as Labour supporters, and consistent with his view in cabinet on the Osborne Judgement in 1911, he favoured making trade unionists contract-in to the unions' political levy. Yet he maintained his view (to use Gladstone's phrase) that working people should be 'within the pale of the constitution' and that state funding would enable them to exercise 'to the full their constitutional rights and to being continuously assimilated into the British parliamentary system'.[64]

[60] Addison, *Churchill on the Home Front*, 211.
[61] Martin Gilbert, *Winston S. Churchill*, IV, 772.
[62] Addison, *Churchill on the Home Front*, 274.
[63] Diary entry, 28 November 1924; Jones, *Whitehall Diary*, I, 307.

With the general strike Churchill identified the mass action as a constitutional outrage while he deemed the coal strike a legitimate industrial action. As in 1911 he revelled in the law and order operational side of the dispute, again urging heavy troop presence, even with tanks and machine-guns, where there was anticipated to be serious unrest. Four years later, in *My Early Life*, he claimed his behaviour was consistent with earlier crises. He wrote,

> I have always urged fighting wars and other contentions with might and main till overwhelming victory, and then offering the hand of friendship to the vanquished. Thus, I have always been against the pacifists during the quarrel and against the Jingoes at the close ... I thought we ought to have conquered the Irish and then given them Home Rule; that we ought to have starved the Germans and revictualled their country; and that after smashing the General Strike, we should have met the grievances of the miners.[65]

Certainly, after the general strike Churchill tried to find compromises acceptable to both sides of the coal industry. However, as Paul Addison has emphasised, having failed he proposed forcing a settlement on the miners, with 'all relief to their families to cease within one week' for men who refused to return to work.[66]

Churchill's tough line with strikers in disputes which he deemed to threaten the social fabric of society made many leaders of the British Labour movement deeply suspicious of him. This was not assuaged for many by his anti-Nazi and anti-appeasement policies before the Second World War. Churchill, however, built on his First World War experiences at the ministry of munitions when he sought extra labour for admiralty war work. In January 1940, after referring to his experience in the First World War, he said, 'Millions of new workers will be needed, and more than a million women must come boldly forward into our war industry' and emphasised, 'Here we must specially count for aid and guidance upon our Labour colleagues and trade union leaders.'[67] As prime minister when speaking of the trade unions' co-operation in suspending restrictive practices 'which have taken generations to win', he specifically referred back to his own blunders of 1917, saying that he 'survived many of its political vicissitudes,

[64] Addison, *Churchill on the Home Front*, 269.
[65] Churchill, *My Early Life*, quoted in Robert Rhodes James, 'Introduction', *Complete Speeches*, I, 18–19.
[66] Addison, *Churchill on the Home Front*, 268.
[67] Speech at Free Trade Hall, Manchester, 27 January 1940; Martin Gilbert, *The Churchill War Papers*, I (1993), 695. On bringing trade union and employer representation to the Admiralty to help ensure large numbers of extra merchant ships, see *House of Commons Debates*, fifth series, vol. 369, cols. 1923–36; 27 February 1940.

including the $12\frac{1}{2}$ per cent, which, at any rate, you will admit was we
meant'.[68]

Churchill, like Lloyd George in December 1916, needed Labour
support to fight the war. George Isaacs, a trade unionist and Labou
MP who was to be Attlee's minister of labour, 1945–51, later commente
of Churchill accession to the premiership in 1940,

> It must be stressed that the readiness of the trade unions to suppo
> the government and to set aside their old quarrels with Churchi
> was due in large measure to the fact that in Bevin they had
> personality who could meet the Prime Minister on level term
> Bevin, as Minister of Labour, was a necessary condition for th
> partnership...[69]

For Churchill, Bevin soon became a rock he could rely on. As Ala
Bullock has observed, 'Bevin was a new discovery in whom he rec
ognised at once a toughness of mind, a self-confidence and strength c
will which matched his own.'[70] Within five months of Bevin enterin
the government Churchill raised him to the war cabinet and kept hir
there, very much as a man who could take on much power in a crisi
While Churchill was not uncritical, he admired Bevin and his abilit
to ensure increased industrial output. Churchill observed frankly in Ju
1941, that 'he is producing ... though perhaps on rather expensiv
terms, a vast and steady volume of faithful effort, the like of which ha
not been seen before'.[71] Churchill certainly warmed to the trade unio
support for the war, paying warm tribute to their role in 1940 an
afterwards.[72] He was especially pleased to note the far fewer strike
than in the First World War. After one of his speeches before leadin
trade unionists, his principal private secretary observed that he though
Churchill got on better with them than with the Tories. According t
Eric Seal, Churchill replied, 'yes, they have a certain native virility
although he found himself in sympathy with the Tories on theoretic
matters like free enterprise and the rights of property'. When Sea
commented that the trade unionists 'were essentially conservative an
not much of the pale intellectual about them', Churchill agreed.

[68] Speech to employers and members of the TUC gathered in honour of US ambassado
Gilbert Winant; 27 March 1941; Martin Gilbert, *The Churchill War Papers*, III (2000), 40g
10.

[69] George Isaacs, 'Churchill and the Trade Unions' in Charles Eade (ed.), *Churchill*
his Contemporaries (1953), 383.

[70] Alan Bullock, *The Life and Times of Ernest Bevin*, II (1967), 4.

[71] *House of Commons Debates*, fifth series, vol. 373, cols. 1278–9, 29 July 1941. Bulloc
Bevin, II, 67.

[72] Churchill to Luke Fawcett, 4 September 1941; Gilbert, *The Churchill War Papers*, II
1158.

[73] Martin Gilbert, *Winston S. Churchill*, VI, 1044.

CHURCHILL AND THE TRADE UNIONS 291

Churchill generally disliked socialists, especially middle-class ones, but admired pragmatic trade union leaders.

After the victorious end of the war but the Conservative defeat in the general election, Churchill continued to take a positive view of the trade unions. To the respect for their role in the war was added Churchill's need to woo working-class voters if a Conservative return to office was to be achieved. In the post-war years Churchill reverted to his old language of Tory democracy. Thus at the 1947 Conservative party conference, after referring to Disraeli and his legislation, Churchill declared,

> The trade unions are a long-established and essential part of our national life ... we take our stand by these pillars of our British Society as it has gradually developed and evolved itself, of the right of individual labouring men to adjust their wages and conditions by collective bargaining, including the right to strike ...

At the 1950 Conservative party conference he returned to this theme.

> The salient feature of this conference has been the growing association of Tory democracy with the trade unions. After all it was Lord Beaconsfield and the Tory Party who gave British trade unionism its charter, and collective bargaining coupled with the right to strike. I have urged that every Tory craftsman or wage-earner should of his own free-will be a trade unionist, but I also think he should attend the meetings of his trade union and stand up for his ideas instead of letting only socialists and communists get control of what is after all an essentially British institution.[74]

He also defined Conservative economic and social policy in phraseology very similar to that he used in the Edwardian period.

With his return to office in 1951, with fewer votes than the Labour party but a majority of seats, Churchill did not want to resurrect his own or the Conservative party's anti-trade union image. Nor did he wish for strikes which could disrupt the recovery of the British economy. He took up the suggestion from a Conservative party central office official that Sir Walter Monckton would be an ideal, emollient minister of labour.[75] Churchill briefed Monckton not to bring about confrontations with public-sector trade unionists, least of all the miners. Churchill himself pressed Monckton to avoid railway strikes on two

[74] Printed in Chris Wrigley, *British Trade Unions 1945–1995* (Manchester, 1997), 44.
[75] According to his private secretary, when Tom O'Brien, a trade union Labour MP, congratulated Churchill on Monckton's appointment, 'That was a suggestion straight from the Holy Ghost, Prime Minister', Churchill grinned and replied, 'From an even higher source than that'. It turned out the initial suggestion came from George Christ of Central office. Anthony Montague Browne, *Long Sunset* (1995), 131.

occasions, the latter in December 1954 being an occasion when Monckton otherwise intended not to give way.[76] Churchill also personally
cultivated senior trade union figures, including Vincent Tewson, the
general secretary of the TUC; this included invitations to social events
at Downing Street. His government also outdid Attlee's in the number
of trade unionists appointed to various consultative committees.[77] This
policy secured industrial peace, even if commentators at the time and
several historians subsequently have questioned its wisdom given the
rising inflation and declining relative competitiveness of British industry
in these years.

Perhaps the most notable feature of Churchill's attitude to the trade
unions was the sheer longevity of many of his attitudes. 'Tory democracy' or 'One nation' views were recurring themes, though if – as
was notably the case at times in 1911–26 -he felt industrial unrest was
threatening the social fabric of society, he was very willing to smash
'the enemy within'. George Isaacs in 1953 rightly observed, 'Sir Winston
is an individualist in an aristocratic tradition' but 'he cannot be regarded
as a "typical" capitalist or even a "typical" aristocrat.'[78] Churchill's
background, including the martial tradition of his illustrious ancestor,
the first duke of Marlborough, is very important. As well as his father,
another figure whom he much admired at the turn of the century and
who influenced his outlook was Lord Rosebery; a Whig peer who was
an Imperialist abroad, a social reformer at home and who, incidentally,
successfully offered conciliation and succeeded in settling the massive
1893 coal lock-out.

Churchill's ideas about trade unions and a free market economy
were not novel. Notions of resolving industrial clashes through joint
consultation were widespread in his period, and were shared by many
trade unionists such as Arthur Henderson, Ben Turner, J.R. Clynes,
David Shackleton and Ernest Bevin. He was notable for being a
president of the board of trade who was pro-active, who stretched the
voluntaryist provisions of the 1896 Conciliation Act as far as they would
go and made some attempts to extend such powers by additional
legislation. In this he was presenting himself centre stage much as his
successful predecessor, David Lloyd George, had done. Churchill, faced
with what he deemed serious unrest, was more belligerent than Lloyd
George. With the national rail and coal disputes of 1912 Churchill
busied himself with securing law and order while Lloyd George was
skilful in negotiating deals which unlocked the disputes. Churchill was

[76] Addison, *Churchill on the Home Front*, 427–9.
[77] Anthony Seldon, *Churchill's Indian Summer* (1981), 29, 199 and 568–9. V.L. Allen, *Trade Unions and Government* (1960), 34 and 304.
[78] Isaacs, 'Churchill and the Trade Unions', 389.

less well tuned-in to the delicacies of industrial relations than Lloyd George, as was dramatically illustrated with the way he blundered in out of his depth over the 12.5 per cent pay increases in 1917. Yet, when he felt industrial disputes were not menacing the fabric of society and he was not full of anti-red sentiments, Churchill worked towards Tory democrat aspirations of industrial peace and harmony.[79]

[79] I am grateful to Stefan Berger, Chris Williams, Neil Wynne and their colleagues for their comments on an early version of this essay, given at the Department of History, University of Glamorgan, Research Seminar, 13 December 2000.

CHURCHILL AND THE PREMIERSHIP
By Peter Hennessy

A POLITICAL and literary life of such extraordinary longevity, variety and richness of vocabulary leaves anyone seeking a consistent theme among any of Winston Churchill's verbal puddings with a bowlful of paradox. The conduct of the premiership and the management of cabinet government are no exceptions. Among the papers his no. 10 private office produced for Harold Macmillan in the summer of 1960 when his appointment of a peer (Alec Home) to the foreign secretaryship led to accusations of excessive prime ministerialism,[1] is a Hansard extract for 1938 in which Churchill defends the appointment by Chamberlain of Lord Halifax to the same post on the grounds that the prime minister sat in the House of Commons. 'What is the point of crying out for the moon', Churchill inquired of the Lower House, 'when you have the sun and you have that bright orb of day from whose effulgent beams the lesser luminaries drive their radiance?'[2] And his most famous characterisation of the premiership seems to treat it as a post of licensed overmightiness. 'The loyalties', he declared in his war memoirs, 'which centre upon number one are enormous. If he trips he must be sustained. If he makes mistakes they must be covered. If he sleeps he must not be wantonly disturbed. If he is no good he must be pole-axed'[3] – a case, to adopt a phrase of John Ramsden's, of 'autocracy tempered by assassination'.[4]

Yet Churchill was a considerable romantic about the linked notions of collective discussion and cabinet government. During his last, early 1950s premiership, he told his doctor, Lord Moran, that: 'I am a great believer in bringing things before the Cabinet. If a minister has got anything on his mind and has the sense to get it argued by Cabinet he will have the machine behind him.'[5] As we shall see, he was attempting

---

[1] Among Macmillan's critics, interestingly enough, was the man who had cuckholded him and served as Churchill's Parliamentary Private Secretary in the 1920s, Robert Boothby. Lord Boothby, 'Parliamentary Decline: Way to Bring Back Members' Power,' *Daily Telegraph*, 4 August 1960.
[2] Public Record Office, PREM 5/233, Bligh to Macmillan, 22 July 1960. Churchill had developed his sun-and-stars metaphor during a Commons debate on Halifax's appointment on 28 February 1938.
[3] Winston S. Churchill, *The Second World War, Vol. 2, Their Finest Hour*, (1949), 15.
[4] Conversation with Professor John Ramsden, 2 January 2001.
[5] Lord Moran, *Winston Churchill: The Struggle for Survival 1940/1965*, (1968), diary entry for 28 April 1953.

in his peacetime premiership at least, to bring even the most sensitive issues such as nuclear weapons policy, to the full cabinet for proper discussion before decision in a manner unmatched by most other prime ministers since Britain became (or aspired to become) an atomic power.

But, as with most premiers, one must not lose sight of the irritation that easily arises when the prime ministerial will is not allowed to triumph. As he wrote in another passage of his war memoirs: 'All I wanted was compliance with my wishes after reasonable discussion.'[6] And of that same war cabinet of whom he declared tearfully on its dissolution in May 1945 that 'The light of history will shine on every helmet',[7] he had earlier opined to one of his military aides (on his way back from the Casablanca Conference early in 1942) that: 'It [the war] was now so straightforward that even the Cabinet could handle it.'[8]

Churchill's conduct of his wartime premiership has been hugely researched, exhaustively written-up and widely read about and absorbed. His peacetime premiership rather less so, for understandable reasons, and it is upon the 1951 to 1955 occupancy of no. 10 Downing Street that I wish to concentrate in this paper though much of it will be couched in a running comparison with his style and approach to the job during the Second World War (not least because he was very prone to this himself during his 'recidivist' premiership, to borrow Roy Jenkin's phrase[9]).

It is too simple, however, to juxtapose the 1940–5 and 1951–5 Churchill premierships in terms of a straight contrast between war and peace. However absorbed he was by the task of licking Hitler and Hirohito, Churchill had to devote at least some of his time and nervous energy to thinking about domestic reconstruction as well as a new postwar global geopolitics, increasingly so from the spring of 1943 when the Beveridge debate began to make the political weather at home. Equally, the nature of the east–west conflict (and the exchange of shot and shell in Korea until the armistice of July 1953) meant that his 'Indian Summer'[10] premiership was conducted against the backdrop of a Cold War which might tip catastrophically not just back into the kind of total war with which Churchill was only too familiar but into what Arthur Koestler called 'total war's successor Absolute War'.[11]

[6] Winston S. Churchill, *The Second World War*, IV (1951).

[7] Ben Pimlott (ed.), *The Second World War Diary of Hugh Dalton, 1940–1945* (1986), p. 865, diary entry for 28 May 1945.

[8] Sir Ian Jacob quoted in the *Calgary Herald*, 20 May 1971. I am grateful to Professor John Ramsden for this gem.

[9] Roy Jenkins, 'Churchill: The Government of 1951–1955', in Robert Blake and Wm Roger Louis (eds.), *Churchill: A Major New Assessment of his Life in Peace and War* (Oxford, 1993), p. 491.

[10] Anthony Seldon, *Churchill's Indian Summer: The Conservative Government, 1951–55* (1981).

[11] Arthur Koestler, *The Yogi and the Commissar and Other Essays* (1945), 256.

For Churchill lived his life after July 1945 in the shadow of a mushroom cloud in a sense that was true of no other of the king's (and from February 1952) the queen's subjects. He remains the only British prime minister to have authorised the use of a nuclear weapon against a human target. For under the terms of the 1943 Quebec Agreement, the concurrence of the British prime minister was required before atomic bombs could be dropped on Japan. By the time they exploded above Hiroshima and Nagasaki in August 1945, Mr Attlee was in Downing Street, but it was Churchill who initialled the minute on 1 July 1945, without consulting the cabinet or ministers collectively, which gave British approval for the weapon to be used if the Alamagordo test proved successful.[12] As is well known, the best of his failing energies were devoted in his last premiership to an attempt to ease the Cold War before the atomic weapon's immensely more destructive successor – the hydrogen bomb – brought what Churchill called an 'equality of ruin'[13] to both east and west.

This uneasy limboland between war and peace crops up often in his no. 10 files. Sometimes it appears among his machinery of government papers. For example, when finally accepting the force of argument deployed against the idea of peacetime 'overlord' ministers by both his cabinet secretary, Sir Norman Brook,[14] and the leader of the opposition, Clement Attlee,[15] Churchill told the House of Commons in the autumn of 1953 that he 'had no experience of being Prime Minister in time of peace and I attached more importance to the grouping of Departments so that the responsible head of the Government [i.e. himself as PM] would be able to deal with a comparatively smaller number of heads than actually exists in peacetime.'[16] Yet in a letter to Lord Woolton, one of the 'supervising' ministers whose 'overlordship' (of food and agriculture) he terminated in September 1953, Churchill said: 'I am myself convinced that the system which the Opposition describes as "the rule of the Overlords" is not necessary now that the *war emergency* [my italics] has receded and the [Korean War-related] Armament programme is spread.'[17]

Churchill's last term can best be seen, I think, as a premiership conducted in the shade of four overlapping shadows: he lived it and

[12] PRO, PREM 11/565, 'Record of Events Leading to Dropping Bombs on Hiroshima and Nagasaki', Cherwell to Churchill, 29 January 1953.
[13] PRO, PREM 11/669, draft Cabinet paper on 'Two-Power meeting with the Soviet Government.'
[14] PRO, CAB 21/2804, 'Supervising Ministers,' Brook to Churchill.
[15] House of Commons, *Official Report*, 3 November 1953, col. 15.
[16] *Ibid.*, col. 20.
[17] PRO, PREM 5/225, 'Ministerial Appointments. Ministry of Sir Winston Churchill (Conservative)', Part 3, Churchill to Woolton, 2 September 1953.

operated it in the long shadow cast by his Second World War experience (the 'overlords' were but one manifestation of this); the lengthening and deepening effect of Britain's waning relative power, of which he was acutely conscious, was the second ('You cannot ignore the facts for they glare upon you', he told Anthony Montague Browne, one of his private secretaries[18]); the potentially devastating shadow of the hydrogen bomb, the third; and, finally, his own growing physical infirmity marred many a working day and night especially after his stroke in July 1953.

Prime ministerial recidivism must be the sweetest of sensations, not least because of its rarity (a catharsis shared in the postwar period only be Churchill and Harold Wilson). And part of the joy of Churchill's restoration in October 1951 was the pleasure he took in reconstructing as far as he could both the honorary extended family notion of no. 10 (having those officials around him bonded by shared and past experience) and his peculiar working methods of both the twilight kind (failing to distinguish between night and day) and direction by the vividly worded philippic of a prime minister's minute (though he did not resume the use of those famous red 'Action This Day labels which the no. 10 messengers had lovingly exhumed for him[19]). As Jock Colville, the only one of the wartime private secretaries who did return to no. 10 (as joint principal private secretary with the incumbent, David Pitblado), put it, ' "Auld Lang Syne" was ringing out along the Whitehall corridors.'[20]

In addition to Colville, Churchill was consoled by another familiar face of wartime officialdom in the autumn of 1951 in the person of Norman Brook, the cabinet secretary. It was Brook who had to bear the brunt of a good deal of nonsense from his prime ministerially born-again chief who had taken it into his head that both the machinery of government and its minders had been progressively blighted by some kind of Attleean virus in the years and months since his eviction from no. 10 on 26 July 1945.

As Colville expressed it many years later:

When Churchill returned as Prime Minister in 1951, he had long since reached the age [he was a month short of his 77th birthday] at which new faces are palatable. He inherited Mr Attlee's Private Secretaries. Arriving at 10 Downing Street with Sir Norman Brook he flung open the door connecting the Cabinet Room to the Private Secretaries' Offices ... He gazed at them, closed the door without

---

[18] Peter Hennessy, *Muddling Through: Power, Politics and the Quality of Government since 1945* (1996), 202.

[19] John Colville, *The Fringes of Power: Downing Street Diaries 1939–1955* (1985), 634.

[20] *Ibid.*, 633.

saying a word, shook his head and proclaimed to Norman Brook: 'Drenched in socialism'.[21]

It did not stop there. He badgered Brook for weeks to shrink what he seemed to regard as the Whitehall equivalent of feather-bedded nationalised industries – a bloated cabinet committee system.[22] There was some justification for this, but Brook had to make the case *for* cabinet committees as the best way of co-ordinating government business in peacetime – a development of Second World War practice for postwar purposes as described and advocated in the Anderson Report produced by a coalition cabinet committee and presented to Churchill himself in May 1945.[23]

Brook's attempts to sell the virtues of the Andersonian system were complicated by Churchill's determination to revive the wartime practice of 'overlords' as a way of both co-ordinating swathes of government activity and reducing the burden on himself as head of government with the added bonus of allowing a smaller cabinet to be constructed. This 'overlord' question continues to resonate half-a-century later. As I write in the run-up to the general election of 2001, thought is being given in no. 10 and the cabinet office to the *break-up* of John Prescott's 'overlordship' of environment, transport and the regions and to the possible *creation* of overlordships on 'social exclusion' and other areas. Brook's successor-but-five as cabinet secretary, Sir Richard Wilson, is known to have found the paper Sir Norman had waiting for Churchill on the subject in October 1951 of particular interest.[24]

Brook's objections to the idea of peacetime 'supervising ministers', as they were termed at the time, was very similar to those expressed by John Anderson in the last days of the wartime coalition government. The idea, Brook told Churchill in late of October 1951, was 'fraught with serious difficulties both constitutional and practical' because it was difficult to reconcile with individual ministerial responsibility, it was inconsistent with the principle that policy should be formulated by those with the responsibility for carrying it out. Furthermore, the 'supervising minister' concept rested on the assumption that policy could be divorced from administration and it was contrary to the traditions of cabinet government that one cabinet minister should be subordinate to another.[25]

There was a Whitehall complication, too. 'Supervising ministers'

---

[21] John Colville, *The Churchillians* (1981), 64.
[22] The toing and froing between Churchill and Brook is vividly preserved in PRO, PREM 11/174, 'Request by Prime Minister for List of all Committees in Whitehall...'
[23] PRO, PREM 4/6/9, 'Cabinet Organization. Report of the Machinery of Government Committee', May 1945.
[24] Private information.
[25] PRO, CAB 21/2804, Brook to Churchill.

would be served by officials whose knowledge of the subject matter was less than that possessed by civil servants working to subordinate ministers. Outside bodies, too, would be influenced by the new dispensation seeking to sway the overlords rather than the overlorded. It would be better, Brook advised his new boss, to seek co-ordination through standing cabinet committees of a kind Churchill himself had developed during the war and Mr Attlee had continued in the years since 1945.[26]

Unusually for Brook, his machinery-of-government advice was disregarded. But for the opposition of Anderson himself (offered what Anderson – by this time, Lord Waverley – thought a nonsensical overlordship of the treasury, the board of trade and the ministry of supply[27]), Rab Butler as chancellor would have been reduced to what Robert Hall of the cabinet office's economic section called the status of 'a tax collector'.[28]

Churchill's tenure at the exchequer in the 1920s had left remarkably little trace on him and not just in his failure to appreciate the impossibility of reviving in peacetime the economic and industrial overlordship Anderson himself had operated as Wartime lord president of the council – when a kind of prime minister-for-the-Home front (the 'automatic pilot,' Churchill had called him[29]) – through the lord president's committee, a powerful instrument with a vast reach over virtually all aspects of a siege economy Britain within which the Treasury found itself in unaccustomed eclipse.[30]

During his twilight premiership, Churchill almost matched his opposite number, Attlee, in being 'tone deaf'[31] to the resonances of modern economic policy and its making. Appointing John Boyd-Carpenter financial secretary to the treasury in October 1951, he confessed: 'I was Chancellor of the Exchequer ... for five years and ... I never understood it.'[32] He was quite incapable, for example, of judging on its merits the huge row over 'Operation Robot' during the run-up to the 1952 budget, the eventually abandoned scheme for a 'dirty float' of the pound as a way of easing the chronic pressure on the balance of payments. And how he must have hated being asked to distinguish between production

[26] *Ibid.*
[27] John. W. Wheeler-Bennett, *John Anderson, Viscount Waverley* (1962), 352.
[28] Alec Cairncross (ed.), *The Robert Hall Diaries, 1947–1953* (1989), 176, diary entry for 29 October 1951.
[29] C.R. Attlee, *As It Happened* (1954), 14.
[30] Lord Robbins, *Autobiography of an Economist* (1971), 172; D.N. Chester, 'The Central Machinery for Economic Policy' in D.N. Chester (ed.), *Lessons of the British War Economy (1951)*, 23.
[31] This was the description of Attlee used by his President of the Board of Trade, Harold Wilson. Harold Wilson, *A Prime Minister on Prime Ministers* (1977), 297.
[32] Hennessy, *Muddling Through*, 188.

and productivity at an election meeting in North-East London by a local grammar schoolboy, the future Labour MP, John Garrett.[33]

But what of the 'overlordships' which *were* created? It is possible to discern no fewer than five if one includes Field Marshal Lord Alexander brought back from the governor-generalship of Canada to preside over the service ministries as minister of defence, Lord Swinton as minister of materials and Lord Cherwell as overseer of atomic energy, both civil and military. Only two, however, feature in both the declassified files and the parliamentary debates as carriers of the label – Lord Woolton, the Lord President, and Lord Leathers who carried the grand title of secretary of state for the co-ordination of transport, fuel and power. Both were businessmen and both had been engaged in wartime overlording, Leathers as minister of war transport and Woolton, with considerable success, as minister of food.

Neither relished the non-jobs their 1951–3 incarnations turned out to be[34] and it is plain that Churchill never understood either what they were up to (or were supposed to be up to). In one of the most engagingly frank pieces of archive in his No. 10 files for 1951–5, Churchill, as late as August 1953 in a 'SECRET AND PERSONAL (Not to be shown to anyone else)' minute for Brook and the head of the civil service, Sir Edward Bridges made two requests:

1. Please find out the exact relation of the functions of the Secretary of State for the Co-ordination of Transport, Fuel and Power with the work of the respective Ministers concerned. Let me have if possible a diagram.

2. Let me have a short report, one page, on how in practice these are working and what would be the consequences of abolishing, as is my intention, the new office we created when the Government was formed. What arrangements for the co-ordination of business of these Departments are needed as part of the ordinary mechanism of the Cabinet and its Committees.

The minute is capped by a wonderfully wittly ironic extra plea to the two grand technicians-of-state: 'A statement should also be prepared showing how wise and necessary this was and how what has been achieved justifies me (a) in having created, and (b) in now abolishing the post in question. This might extend to 500 words.'[35]

---

[33] For details of 'Robot' see Alec Cairncross, *Years of Recovery: British Economic Policy 1945–51* (1985), 234–71. For Garrett and his question at the meeting in Woodford, I am grateful to Mr Garrett for sending me his unpublished article, 'My Life with Labour', in December 2000.

[34] Peter Hennessy, *The Prime Minister: the Office and its Holders since 1945* (Harmondsworth, 2000), 194.

[35] PRO, PREM 5/225. Churchill to Bridges and Brook, 9 August 1953.

Why did Churchill, as it were, persist with his 'overlord' experiment over the first two years of the 1951–5 premiership despite Brook's counsel? A sense of failing powers, as Paul Addison has suggested,[36] and a lack of personal touch on home front problems which presented him from doing overmuch co-ordinating himself plus, maybe, a mistaken belief that Leathers' patch could somehow make sense of the nationalisations of the 1945–8 period. The unhappy outcome has, in general terms, deposited 'overlords' alongside 'inner cabinets' in the 'failed attempts' file of those who have sought to streamline cabinet government in more recent times – perhaps wrongly.

The failing personal powers were painfully and frequently apparent to those on the inner circle even before the stroke of the summer of 1953. Though there is an ever-present danger of portraying Churchill in his premiership-of-shadows incarnation in parody terms as a kind of walking (or tottering) off-licence-cum-pharmacy, it was quite inevitable that a great trencherman and bottleman in his late seventies would find a 1950s workload pretty unsustainable. As he admitted to Harold Macmillan, 'at every cabinet today there are discussed at least two or three problems which would have filled a whole session before the first war'.[37] And as Colville confided to Lord Salisbury a few months before Churchill's stroke: 'I hate to be disloyal, but the PM is not doing his work. A document of five sheets has to be submitted to him as one paragraph, so that many points of the argument are lost.'[38]

For all the scattergun nature of the memos he fired off to ministers, often over-reacting madly to what he read in the newspapers,[39] Churchill was surely right, having decided it was his 'duty' to resume the premiership despite living 'most of the day in bed',[40] to focus his remaining energies on the Cold War and Britain's role, ever harder to sustain, as both an easer of east-west tensions (especially after the death of Stalin in March 1953 when he felt powerfully aware of his being the sole survivor of the wartime 'Big Three' of Yalta[41]) and as a potential restrainer of the United States (particularly with John Foster Dulles at the state department from January 1953[42]).

The Cold War was the most powerful single shaper of the style of his final premiership in a number of interrelated ways. Firstly, and this is often overlooked, he had to direct one last British contribution to a

[36] Hennessy, *Muddling Through*, 189.

[37] Macmillan Diary, Western Manuscripts Department, Bodleian Library, University of Oxford. D.25. entry for 22 February 1953.

[38] Moran, *Struggle for Survival*, 401, diary entry for 22 February 1953.

[39] Hennessy, *The Prime Minister*, 183.

[40] Moran, *Struggle for Survival*, 366, diary entry for 20 September 1951.

[41] Hennessy, *The Prime Minister*, 203.

[42] PRO, PREM 11/669.

substantial war — Korea. Here he operated a mixture of personal diplomacy, individual direction and attention to detail which caught his eye that was very much a micro version of the great days of 1940 to 1945.[43] For example, he was deeply ill at ease with the use of napalm in Korea informing Alexander in August 1952 that: 'We should make a great mistake to commit ourselves to approval of a very cruel form of warfare affecting the civilian population.'[44]

A similar, and striking, outburst of fastidiousness affected him when he was reminded that the old wartime deception organisation, the London controlling section, under its new covername of the directorate of forward plans, had engaged in a dash of disinformation ahead of the first British atomic test off the Australian coast in the autumn of 1952 using *The Sunday Express* as its willing (and knowing) instrument. He threw a fit of constitutionalism about it (as he had when he discovered Attlee had managed to conceal £100m of expenditure on developing the bomb from parliament[45]). He recoiled from the deception as:

> The idea of stimulating, through an inspired article, information both true and false, so mixed up as to be deceptive, to any particular newspaper, [as it] is not one hitherto entertained in time of peace. Certainly no departure from the principle that tells the truth or nothing should be made except upon direct ministerial responsibility as an exception in the public interest.[46]

Churchill became the first British prime minister to have a nuclear weapon at his sole disposal when a 'Blue Danube' atomic bomb was delivered to RAF Wittering in November 1953.[47] But it was the over one thousand times more powerful hydrogen bomb (America's Russia's and, when ready, Britain's) that truly preoccupied him during his last years in no. 10. He fully appreciated the degree to which the nuclear question was a prime ministerial one.

[43] On this theme, I am indebted to my former student, Tom Dibble. Tom Dibble, 'The Importance of Being Winston: A Study of the Churchill Government and the Korean War October 1951–July 1953,' unpublished undergraduate thesis, Department of History, QMW, 1996.

[44] PRO, PREM 11/115, Churchill to Alexander, Prime Minister's Personal Minute, M 444/52, 8 December 1952.

[45] PRO, CAB 21/2281B, Churchill to Bridges, Prime Minister's Personal Minute M140c/51, 8 December 1951.

[46] PRO, PREM 11/257, 'Request by Prime Minister for Report from Minister of Defence on Organisation which is Maintained for Misleading Enemy about Our Future Plans and Intentions' Prime Minister's Personal Minure, M 439/52, Churchill to Brook, 16 August 1952. The article appeared as John L. Garbutt, 'Tactical atom bomb exercise planned', *Sunday Express*, 17 August 1952.

[47] Brian Cathcart, *Test of Greatness: Britain's Struggle for the Atomic Bomb* (1994), 273.

Yet, he subjected the making of a British H bomb decision to full cabinet discussion no less than three times in the summer of 1954,[48] and kept the queen fully informed of developments.[49] The horrifying potential of the nuclear age was made plain in a pair of cabinet papers which went to all cabinet ministers. The first of these reached them in the weeks spanning the decision to manufacture a British H Bomb and took the form of a paper from the chiefs of staff pulling together the implications for future defence policy of recent changes in both international politics and military technology on each side of the Iron Curtain.[50] The second was a bone-chilling report on the consequences for both the survivability of government and the UK's civilian population after a thermonuclear war which Churchill and his defence minister, Macmillan, commissioned in December 1954 from a highly secret Whitehall group chaired by William Strath of the cabinet office.[51] Its findings were circulated 'for their personal information' to cabinet ministers during Churchill's very last days in Downing Street.[52]

Churchill, building on the chiefs of staff argument that 'Our scientific skill and technological capacity to produce the hydrogen weapon puts within our grasp the ability to be on terms with the United States and Russia',[53] sold the indispensability of a *British* H Bomb to the cabinet with the argument 'that we could not expect to maintain our influence as a World Power unless we possessed the most up-to-date nuclear weapons'.[54] The minutes suggest that it was restraining an over-adventurous United States in the Far East (these were the years of the stand-off over Formosa, Quemoy and Matsu) as much as deterring the Soviet Union[55] that drove Churchill to insist on this means of ensuring Britain paid the price of sitting at what he called 'the top table'.[56]

Clearly here the 'glaring facts' of Britain's decline from super-powerdom could be – and were – ignored by Churchill as, in his mind, the H Bomb, at one bound, gave Britain the capacity to narrow the gap between London and both Washington and Moscow thereby

---

[48] PRO, CAB 128/27, CC (54) 47th Conclusions, 7 July 1954; CC (54) 48th Conclusions, 8 July 1954; CC (54) 53rd Conclusions, 26 July 1954.

[49] PRO, PREM 11/747, 'Churchill to HM Queen', 16 July 1954.

[50] This paper was retained by the Cabinet Office until 1999. PRO, CAB 129/69, C (54) 249, 'United Kingdom Defence Policy', 22 July 1954.

[51] PRO, DEFE 13/45, 'The Defence Implications of Fall-Out from a Hydrogen Bomb, Macmillan to Churchill, 13 December 1954.

[52] *Ibid.*, Lloyd to Eden, 21 April 1955.

[53] PRO, CAB 129/69, C (54) 249.

[54] PRO, CAB 128/27, CC (54) 47th conclusions.

[55] *Ibid.*, CC (54) 48th conclusions.

[56] He used these words to Sir Edwin Plowden on being told by Plowden that the UK had the capacity to make the thermonuclear weapon. Hennessy, *Muddling Through*, 105–6.

creating the continuing possibility of the UK being the skilful resolver of the great confrontation between the USA and the USSR. This latter element of the gilt-edged possibility the cabinet failed to buy. For in that same nuclear-tinged summer of 1954, Churchill received probably his roughest ever treatment at the hands of his full cabinet over his attempts at personal diplomacy with both Eisenhower and the post-Stalin leadership while out of the cabinet's restraining reach on the *Cunarder* returning home with his doubting foreign secretary, Anthony Eden, from his Washington discussions.[57]

In the end it was the Russians who snatched the summit prize from Churchill.[58] But, until the very last hours of his premiership, he behaved as if it still might be there for the grasping. For what was there left by way of honours for Churchill to crave? The Nobel Peace Prize. The Nobel Prize for Literature (which he *did* receive for the war memoirs) was no compensation.[59]

It is almost inconceivable now that a man or woman in their late seventies could fill the British prime ministership, however titanic their prior achievements. Nor could the country be run from a bed. For me the element of the Churchill style of premiership which will linger in my own mind when senescence comes to call will be the bedroom scenes of 1951–5 which, between them, throw into relief all four of the shadows in which, by this time, the grand old man lived and toiled. For there in no. 10 he would work, unless the chairmanship of cabinet or a committee intruded, until shortly before lunch, an unlit Havana in his mouth, the bed covered in papers with a secretary from the 'garden room' beside it to take dictation. Also in attendance would be a member of the private office, Rufus, the halitosis-afflicted poodle at the PM's feet and his beloved budgerigar, Toby, performing aerobatics above.[60]

Toby, like his master, was plainly agitated at the prospect of getting his mind round the frailties of the British economy and would become noticeably more excited when the chancellor, Rab Butler, came to brief the recumbent Churchill. He would zoom round the room while opening his bowels in mid-flight in such a fashion that he could lay a deposit on Rab's bald head. On one occasion, the private secretary, Anthony Montague Browne, saw the chancellor out as he mopped his head with a silk handkerchief emitting an accompanying sigh of, 'The things I do for England...'[61]

[57] Martin Gilbert, *Never Despair: Winston S. Churchill, 1945–1965* (1988), 1018–36.
[58] *Ibid.*, 1036.
[59] Hennessy, *Muddling Through*, 194.
[60] *Ibid.*, 1036.
[61] Anthony Montague Brown, *Long Sunset: Memoirs of Churchill's Last Private Secretary* (1995), 14.

In the last months of the premiership, Harold Macmillan was summoned to the bedroom to discuss the horrors of thermonuclear war. That night in his diary he recorded an extraordinary scene in which Toby managed to upstage even the H Bomb. The bird began the meeting sitting on top of Churchill's head. Occasionally he would drop down to take sips from the whisky and soda beside the PM's bed. 'Really', wrote Macmillan,

> he is a unique dear man with all his qualities and faults ... The bird flew about the room; perched on my shoulder and pecked (or kissed my neck) ... while all the sonorous 'Gibbonesque' sentences were rolling out of the maestro's mouth on the most destructive and terrible engine of mass warfare yet known to mankind. The bird says a few words in a husky voice like an American actress...[62]

Never again will no. 10 be enlivened by such grand and glorious eccentricity or by such appealing furred and feathered friends.

[62] Macmillan diary. D. 19, diary entry for 26 January 1955.

CHURCHILL AND THE CONSERVATIVE PARTY
By Stuart Ball

THE words 'Churchill' and 'party' lie in uneasy company. Winston Churchill is regarded as the least orthodox and party-minded of all those who stood in the front rank of British politics during the twentieth century, always navigating by his own compass. This view is shaped by Churchill's remarkable egotism and the well-known incidents of his career: the two changes of party allegiance, the coalitionism of 1917–22, the rebellious 'wilderness' years of the 1930s, and the premiership almost above party in 1940–5. It has been reinforced by the preponderance of biography in the writing about Churchill, and especially by those which regard him as a 'great man'. Churchill tends to be removed from his political context and separated from his peers, and there is a reluctance to see him in any conventional light. As a result, by far the most neglected aspect of Churchill's life has been his party political role, and in particular his relationship with the Conservative party.[1]

There are several reasons for this. It is the antithesis of those aspects which most attract admirers and authors – this is the Churchill of the 'Gestapo' speech, not of 'blood, toil, tears and sweat'.[2] Seeing him as a party politician is in conflict with the picture of the lone hero, the

[1] The only discussions are Lord Blake, 'Churchill and the Conservative Party', in Crosby Kemper (ed.), *Winston Churchill: Resolution, Defiance, Magnanimity* (Columbia, Mo., 1995), 141–56, a brief narrative treatment which does not go beyond 1940, and the more specific study by John Ramsden, 'Winston Churchill and the Leadership of the Conservative Party 1940–51', *Contemporary Record*, 9, no. 1 (1995), 99–119; the latter's volume in the Longman History of the Conservative Party series, *The Age of Churchill and Eden 1940–57* (1995), provides further analysis and is the most valuable exploration of this theme after 1940. Paul Addison, *Churchill on the Home Front 1900–55* (1992), is unusual in concentrating on domestic politics and makes many important points, but still leaves Churchill's relationship with the party in the background; it excludes discussion of the India revolt and thus has a comparatively short examination of 1929–39, and like most works gives less weight to the 1945–55 period. A recent substantial study by Graham Stewart, *Burying Caesar: Churchill, Chamberlain and the Battle for the Tory Party* (1999), focuses on Churchill's career during the 1930s.
[2] None of the twenty-nine essays in the last major collection, Robert Blake and W.R. Louis (eds.), *Churchill* (Oxford, 1993), discussed Churchill's relations with the Conservative party. There is a similar pattern in the various biographies, whether it is the orthodox narrative of the massive volumes of the official life, summarised by Martin Gilbert in *Churchill: A Life* (1991), or the revisionism of John Charmley, *Churchill: The End of Glory* (1993). The most recent brief synthesis, Ian Wood, *Churchill* (Basingstoke, 2000), does not even have an entry for Conservative party in the index.

unique and iconoclastic. At the same time, Churchill does not stand for any particular brand of Conservatism, and his name does not figure within the party in the same way as Disraeli, Baldwin, Macmillan, Thatcher and even (in more intellectual circles) Salisbury. Since 1945 Conservatives have certainly been glad to hail him as their own, but they raid his past for little other than the summer of 1940. Churchill is seen as a great man *of* the party, rather than a great figure *in* it, and his legacy is unclear. It is easy to say that Churchill was not an 'orthodox' Conservative, as if Conservatism was reducible to some formulaic recipe. In fact, there were three strands in Churchill's outlook which he shared with most Conservatives of his era. First was the Empire and Britain's world role; for this Churchill had an instinctively positive outlook and a sense of mission. Second was the independent spirit of the British people; the 'Tory democracy' of Disraeli and Lord Randolph, resting upon practical measures but never to be stifled or circumscribed. The third theme was a guarantor of this: a balance between the classes, without the dominance of one over the others – as needful in the taming of the unchecked House of Lords as it was in the danger of socialism.

The aim of this paper is to examine the most important themes and issues in Churchill's relationship with the Conservative party, concentrating on the period between his return to the fold in 1924 and the second premiership of 1951–5. It seeks to ask questions which are rarely raised, and to offer some different perspectives.[3] His position cannot be assessed if it is treated too much in isolation – for example, was Churchill any more 'in the wilderness' in the 1930s than Amery or the fourth marquess of Salisbury, or was he less constructive as opposition leader in 1945–51 than Balfour had been after the previous landslide defeat in 1906–11? Churchill was far from flawless as a party politician, but his abilities have been undervalued. A successful political career needs not just oratorical and executive talent, but also an awareness of relationships and the ability to work with others. Churchill is not known for the latter, but the problem is that because in his case

[3] The monographs on party and political history are more helpful than any biographies. In addition to Ramsden, *Age of Churchill and Eden*, and Stewart, *Burying Caesar*, see Stuart Ball, *Baldwin and the Conservative Party: The Crisis of 1929–31* (London and New Haven, 1988); Gillian Peele, 'Revolt over India', in *The Politics of Reappraisal 1918–39*, eds. G. Peele and C. Cook (1975), 114–45; Carl Bridge, *Holding India to the Empire: The British Conservative Party and the 1935 Constitution* (New Delhi, 1986); Maurice Cowling, *The Impact of Hitler: British Politics and British Policy 1933–40* (Cambridge, 1975); Neville Thompson, *The Anti-Appeasers: Conservative Opposition to Appeasement in the 1930s* (Oxford, 1971); N.J. Crowson, *Facing Fascism: The Conservative Party and the European Dictators 1935–40* (1998); Paul Addison, *The Road to 1945: British Politics and the Second World War* (1975); Kevin Jefferys, *The Churchill Coalition and Wartime Politics 1940–45* (Manchester, 1991); and Anthony Seldon, *Churchill's Indian Summer: The Conservative Government 1951–55* (1981).

the ability and egotism were more strikingly evident, he is treated as if he was of an entirely different breed.

An assumption which colours many views of Churchill is that he did not appreciate party political realities. This is untenable: Churchill was a constituency MP for several decades, and showed that he was well aware of the limits of party tolerance in the 1930s. He sat through many local functions, delivered speeches around the country, attended as many conferences as most ministers in this era, and was present at party meetings. He was aware of how the parliamentary Conservative party worked, and of the backbench groups and committees. Churchill had a better understanding of the role of party than was displayed by Lloyd George, Austen Chamberlain, Mosley, Beaverbrook and Stafford Cripps between 1918 and 1939, and his awareness of its importance was shown by his desire to underpin the Lloyd George coalition by the fusion of its followers into a single party. He also had a better feel for what the Conservative party and the public would accept than was demonstrated by Austen Chamberlain in 1922, Hoare in 1935, and Balfour and F.E. Smith more generally; the latter burned his boats more irretrievably than Churchill without leaving the party. However, in the interwar period Churchill tended to underestimate the resilience and adaptability of parties. He thought that a major crisis was likely to lead to the parties breaking up and realigning; in other words, that party in general was a constant part of the landscape, but the particular parties in their present forms were not. Up to 1939 he seemed often to be looking for a repeat of the upheaval of the 1880s which had been so crucial in his father's career. In December 1929 he thought 'that all three parties would go into the melting pot within the next two years and come out in an entirely different grouping', but when this happened in August 1931 he was not in a position to take advantage of it.[4]

There is some basis for the traditional view, especially during the Second World War. There is no doubt that Churchill wanted most of all to succeed as a war leader, and that all else was secondary. This was partly due to his patriotism and the peril which the nation faced; with invasion a real danger, party matters naturally had little call on his time. Anything which disrupted national unity or took attention away from the war effort was disliked – particularly party frictions, and later plans for postwar reconstruction. It is also true that Churchill was comfortable with coalition, and not only in wartime. He always wished to broaden the base of the government and form a ministry of all the talents. However, his desire to continue the coalition into peacetime was based upon the assumption that Labour would still be the junior

[4]Jones to Bickersteth, 23 Dec. 1929, *Thomas Jones: Whitehall Diary, Vol. 2: 1926–30*, ed. K. Middlemas (Oxford, 1969), 229.

partner, whilst the end of the war would allow more Conservative involvement on the home front. This expectation was not unreasonable in 1944–5, given Lloyd George's victory in 1918 and Labour's limited advance in the 1930s. Churchill did not spurn party as the working means of British political life, or the nature of the Conservative party as such – but he sought to broaden it, to hold the centre and contain Labour. He favoured a coalition arrangement when the elements were more equally balanced, as in 1918–22, and fusion and absorption when not, as in the Woolton-Teviot agreement with the Liberal Nationals and the offer of a cabinet post to Clement Davies, the Liberal leader, in 1951. In seeking to widen the Conservative base, and to appeal to former Liberals on the basis of moderate reformism, Churchill was following the same course as Baldwin had before him.

Churchill's tactics were often more cautious than his oratorical style might suggest. Its memorable vigour obscures the fact that his moves were generally as carefully rehearsed as his major speeches – where hours of work lay behind any apparent spontaneity. However, whilst there is no doubt that Churchill had a gift for words and an original turn of phrase, no one has ever suggested that he was a skilled tactician. If anything, the view is quite the opposite – that his decisions were poor and his judgement flawed, and that this was his area of greatest weakness. This derives mainly from three events – the failure of the Gallipoli campaign in 1915, the rejection of his charges against Hoare and Derby by the committee of privileges in 1934, and the shouting down of his speech in the abdication crisis in 1936. Yet, in the first two of these at least, it could be said that his case was sound enough and need not have led to such a setback. The abdication speech was a failure to understand the mood of the hour, but even so too much should not be construed from one blunder. In any long parliamentary career there are speeches which fall flat or have unintended results, and Churchill had no more stumbles than most. Baldwin is often considered to have been a master of the moods of the House and the currents of public opinion, but in reality his touch was as erratic as Churchill's. Churchill's approach was based upon an almost mid-Victorian concept of the importance of opinion in the House of Commons and the degree of independence of the backbench MP. Before he became leader himself, he hoped for a definition of party loyalty which was based broadly upon principles and sentiments rather than narrowly upon the present leaders. Although he was generally disappointed, throughout the century similar expectations have been held by figures from different generations, backgrounds and parties, including Mosley, Bevan, Powell, Jenkins and Heseltine.

Churchill's main forum was parliament, and only secondarily did he go beyond that to address a wider party audience. Given that in the

Conservative party policies were made by the leaders and that the strongest influence upon them was exerted by or through the parliamentary party, this was a sensible strategy. However, few excluded figures have had more than a handful of regular followers, even if they have been able to muster greater support during a crisis. Rebellions tend to occur on issues rather than in support of a personality, however respected or popular; the rebel vote of 1922 was not *for* Bonar Law any more than that of 1975 was *for* Thatcher or that of 1990 *for* Heseltine – although in each case a credible alternative leader was needed, as Meyer's failure in 1989 demonstrates. So it is not surprising that the India rebels or the anti-appeasers did not wish to be thought of as Churchill followers even when they applauded his speeches. The point of note about Churchill's two campaigns in the 1930s is not that they did not involve more Conservative MPs, but rather that they gathered so many. This was particularly the case with India, perhaps the largest sustained internal rebellion the Conservative party has ever seen – but it is also true of the smaller and less consistent band of anti-appeasers, for they were still larger than the Suez group of the 1950s, the Profumo rebels or Powellites of the 1960s, the resisters of the poll tax in the 1980s, or the Maastricht rebels in the early 1990s.

The most significant period of Churchill's relationship with the Conservative party begins with his return to the fold in 1924. Churchill's predominant theme since 1918 had been anti-Socialism, and the changes in the political landscape left him with no other natural home. His return was encouraged by the new party leader, Stanley Baldwin, and in the 1924 general election he was returned as Conservative MP for Epping, a safe seat near London.[5] Conservative doubts about Churchill in the 1920s were not due to his prewar years as a Liberal or his crossing of the floor in 1904. Much of prewar politics seemed remote by 1924, and the only leading figure of that era who was still active, Balfour, was one of the strongest proponents of Churchill's return. Indeed, it is this connection which links to the real concern about Churchill in the 1920s – his leading role in the Lloyd George coalition, and the suspicion that he would intrigue for its revival. The fear of a returned coalition was a constant theme in Conservative politics from 1922 to 1935, with plots and conspiracies being frequently suspected – and not just by such paranoid minds as J.C.C. Davidson.[6]

Any reservations were certainly not because Churchill was not

---

[5] Churchill contested the election as a 'Constutionalist', but he was the offically sanctioned candidate of the Epping Conservative Association and was regarded as such by Central Office (which had helped him secure the candidacy).

[6] *Memoirs of a Conservative: J.C.C. Davidson's Memoirs and Papers 1910–37*, ed. R.R. James (1969), 213, 215, 309–10; *Parliament and Politics in the Age of Baldwin and MacDonald: the Headlam Diaries 1923–35*, ed. Stuart Ball (1992), 68, 140, 150–1, 189.

Conservative enough in his views.[7] As the hammer of the Reds at home
and abroad since 1918, he was if anything too much to the right. Given
the tone which Baldwin wished to set in 1924, putting Churchill in any
cabinet post was an ambivalent step. The danger that Churchill might
give the government too belligerent a face may also help to explain
Baldwin's decision to offer him the exchequer. Although prominent, it
was less politically sensitive than other departments, as it was less in
direct contact with Labour and the trades unions and had no immediate
role in executing foreign or imperial policy. The treasury was less of a
danger than a return to the home office would have been (if Joynson-
Hicks caused problems with the ARCOS raid, consider the fireworks
that Churchill might have set off), or ministries such as labour, health
or even education; the board of trade was critical on tariff and
safeguarding issues, whilst giving Churchill a military department would
have been more unacceptable to party opinion and given him not
enough to do – considerations which also applied to the imperial and
non-departmental posts respectively.

The strategy worked well: the treasury kept Churchill occupied and
returned his attention to his best regarded field of domestic reform,
where he worked as effectively with Neville Chamberlain as any two
such powerful colleagues and partial rivals have in any other ministry.
The appointment as chancellor did not go to Churchill's head; he had
plenty of ideas, but put the greatest emphasis upon loyalty to Baldwin
and being a reliable member of the cabinet team. He delivered good
but not too showy or individualistic, debating performances.[8] He
cultivated Conservative MPs, and was aided in this by the large influx
of new members in 1924. In 1925 the clash with Bridgeman over the
naval budget aroused a few fears of coalitionist plots, but the admiralty's
case was not conclusive whilst the need for economy was strong. The
Economy Bill which Churchill delivered in March 1926 was a response
to backbench and constituency pressure, although the savings identified
fell well short of the sweeping reductions for which – however unreal-
istically – the party clamoured.

Churchill was happy with the course of the 1924–9 government on
social reform and conciliation.[9] His stance on the general strike was
the same as Baldwin's: that this was a challenge to the constitution and
must be defeated. If there was a difference, it was only in the vigour

[7] For example, his anti-Socialist views were set out in a long letter to *The Times*, 18
Jan. 1924, at the formation of the first Labour government.
[8] See Neville Chamberlain's rather patronising assessment at the end of the first session,
Chamberlain to Baldwin, 30 Aug. 1925, Martin Gilbert, *Winston S. Churchill: Companion*
(hereafter Gilbert, *Churchill: Companion*), v, part 1 (1979), 533–4.
[9] See his response to Baldwin's speech on the trade union levy bill, Churchill to
Clementine Churchill, 8 Mar. 1925, *Companion Documents, Volume V (Part 1)*, 424.

of the tactics and language used, and throughout the strike Churchill accepted and discharged the tasks which he was given. Although he supported Baldwin's decision not to legislate in 1925, Churchill was more in tune than his leader with Conservative opinion on the trade union levy, another key theme of the mid 1920s. He was in favour of the change to 'contracting in' even before the general strike, and had no disagreement with the terms of the 1927 Trade Disputes Act. Another matter on which the rank and file felt strongly was strengthening the House of Lords as a bulwark against an overriding Socialist majority, and here again Churchill was of the same mind as the centre and right of the party. The de-rating scheme which he developed with Neville Chamberlain in 1927–8 was the centrepiece of the government's unemployment strategy. Although the reform failed to generate public enthusiasm, it had something to offer both urban and rural Conservatives and was well attuned to mainstream party opinion.[10] By the election of May 1929, Churchill had established a fairly secure position in both the party and the cabinet; if the Conservatives had won, he would have been seen as a positive member of the team which had secured victory. Whilst Baldwin was considering a reshuffle which would have moved him from the Treasury, there was no intention or pressure to leave him out of the next cabinet.[11] A change of post was not a snub or unwelcome; there were more creative opportunities elsewhere, and now that Churchill had worked his passage the party would be willing to give him greater latitude.

The Conservative defeat in 1929 left the Liberals holding the parliamentary balance, and Churchill was willing to seek an arrangement with them to block Labour or remove them from office after a few months. He was not the only Conservative to consider this, but few others were willing to deal directly with Lloyd George, or thought that Lloyd George would set a feasible price. Nevertheless, the revival of coalitionism, or even the rumour of it, damaged Churchill's position. Although Churchill was fairly effective in replying to Snowden in set-piece debates such as the 1930 budget, in general he did not shine on the opposition front bench; Baldwin was not alone in thinking that he had 'made one blunder after another'.[12] However, he was not the only former minister who found adapting to opposition difficult, and Austen Chamberlain and Baldwin were even more indifferent performers. The

[10] Amery diary, 24 Apr. 1928, *The Leo Amery Diaries, Volume 1: 1899–1929*, eds. J. Barnes & D. Nicholson (1980), 547.

[11] Neville Chamberlain diary, 11 Mar. 1929, Neville Chamberlain MSS, Birmigham University Library; Churchill's own recollections, Amery to Baldwin, 11 Mar. 1929, Gilbert, *Churchill: Companion*, v, part 1, 1431, 1444–45.

[12] Amery diary, 26 May 1930, *The Empire at Bay – The Leo Amery Diaries, Volume 2: 1929–45*, eds. J. Barnes and D. Nicholson (1988), 72.

revival of protectionist feeling in the Conservative party in 1929–30 was not as difficult for Churchill as might have been expected. Now back in the party mainstream, he was ready to take a more flexible view. The problems of the slump undermined the certainties of many defenders of free trade, and whilst he was still reluctant to put duties on food imports, he was not prepared to quit the front bench over this.[13] He was sensitive to the move of party opinion towards tariffs and imperial preference in the winter of 1929–30 and developed his own position alongside it, closing rather than widening the gap.[14] It is significant that when Beaverbrook was identifying the barriers to be overcome in the spring and summer of 1930, Churchill had faded into the background; Salisbury and even Percy offered more resistance, until the attack moved on to Davidson and ultimately Baldwin.

Churchill's eclipse in 1929–31 was not mainly due to the renewal of the tariff issue, or even his opposition to Baldwin's line on India. There was a third factor which affected a considerable number of the 1924–9 cabinet: the feeling against the 'old gang', and the desire to refresh the Conservative front-bench. Fanned by Beaverbrook as part of his efforts to remove obstacles to his protectionist Empire Crusade, this became a forceful pressure during 1930.[15] Inclusion in the 'old gang' was not so much a matter of age alone, but rather of style, outlook, and length of career. It affected most those who seemed to have late Victorian roots or mentalities, and so included Austen Chamberlain, Joynson-Hicks, Churchill, Salisbury and Percy, but not Neville Chamberlain, Hoare and Cunliffe-Lister. Churchill was thus only one amongst several who were washed into a backwater by this tide of party feeling. As this pressure mounted at the end of 1930, his attention turned to the India question. It was not a deliberate search for a weapon to use, but rather that the dwindling chances of his inclusion in the next cabinet removed the counterbalance to his strong convictions on this issue. In November 1929 Churchill had been deeply unhappy when Baldwin supported the Irwin Declaration of eventual dominion status, but he remained a loyal member of the front-bench team until his resignation in January 1931.[16] His departure was not a leadership bid; like Eden in 1938, Thorneycroft in 1958 and Heseltine in 1986, it was the only reaction left when an

[13] Addison, *Churchill on the Home Front*, 294, 296–9; Churchill to Baldwin, 14 [not sent] & 16 Oct. 1930, Gilbert, *Churchill: Companion*, v, part 2 (1981), 191–4.

[14] Nicolson diary, 23 Jan. 1930, *Harold Nicolson: Diaries and Letters 1930–64*, ed. Stanley Olson (1980), 14–15. He was happy to accept the referendum policy announced by Baldwin on 4 Mar. 1930 and the advance to the 'free hand' in September and October 1930, and in the budget debates of April 1931 gave public support to introducing tariff for revenue and negotiating purposes.

[15] Ball, *Baldwin and the Conservative Party*, 115, 116, 159–61.

[16] *Ibid.*, 114–117; Hoare to Irwin, 13 Nov. 1929, Gilbert, *Churchill: Companion*, v, part 2, 111.

existing tension was stretched to breaking point. He remained loyal on other issues in 1931, and sought to help in the party's attacks on Labour.[17]

At the height of the tariff crisis in September 1930, Churchill had warned Baldwin that he cared about India 'more than anything else in public life'.[18] He was unwilling to go beyond the Simon Commission's proposals for limited regional devolution, and was appalled when the first Round Table conference ended in January 1931 with a commitment to a federal constitution including areas of native control of the central government. A few days later, on 26 January, Baldwin gave firm support to this in an ill-judged speech which dismayed Conservative MPs. He had barely consulted his front-bench colleagues, and several were angry and upset. Churchill resigned the next day, and during the following weeks sought to draw back the party's position.[19] This had some effect: despite scoring some debating points at Churchill's expense, Baldwin sounded a more careful note in his next speeches in March 1931. Between 1931 and 1935 Churchill was not using India to overthrow Baldwin and seize the leadership – not because he did not want it, but because he knew that it was not likely to be obtained in that way. Although there were a few moments when the tide of party feeling swung towards Churchill's views on India, he would not have been Baldwin's replacement. Any successor would need the support of most of the front bench and have to be able to command wider and deeper confidence amongst MPs and the constituencies than Churchill did. As the crisis of March 1931 showed, the most likely new leader would have been Neville Chamberlain.[20]

Churchill had been aware since 1929 that Chamberlain might be Baldwin's eventual successor, blocking his own chances and providing a less congenial style of leadership.[21] He had considered retirement and concentrating on making his family's financial situation more secure, even before the depression hit his investments in late 1929. In fact, he largely followed through with this, adopting a kind of semi-retirement. During the 1930s Churchill followed his own course first and foremost, and took remarkably little account of the views of others. This could be ascribed to egotism and lack of judgement, but makes more sense

[17] Churchill to Boothby, 21 Feb. 1931, *Companion Documents, Volume V (Part 2)*, 275. He delivered a powerful attack on MacDonald in the debate on the Trades Disputes Bill just after his resignation, although this could also be seen as a bid to win over Conservative MPs.

[18] Churchill to Baldwin, 24 Sep. 1930, Gilbert, *Churchill: Companion*, v, part 2, 186.

[19] Ball, *Baldwin and the Conservative Party*, 121–2, 134; Churchill had a favourable reception at the N[ational] U[nion] Central Council, 24 Feb. 1931.

[20] Ball, *Baldwin and the Conservative Party*, 135–6 201.

[21] Churchill to Clementine Churchill, 27 Aug. 1929, Gilbert, *Churchill: Companion*, v, part 2, 61–62.

as the conduct of someone who feels above the fray of the day-to-day struggle. Churchill's course was closest to that of the 'elder statesman', combining experience which should be deferred to with some detachment from the government, though not hostility.[22] This gave him the licence to concentrate on issues of particular interest, and explains the nature of his interventions. His attendance at the House was intermittent, and the habit of delivering a prepared speech and then departing was not calculated to draw in the many new members who hardly knew him. He expected to offer advice and be heard at the highest level, and to be given privileged access to information in certain areas; he played a part behind the scenes, and over air defence was certainly not 'in the wilderness'. At the same time, Churchill was giving much more of his time and energy to activities outside politics. Some of these were to make money, but others were leisure; the involvement in Chartwell, and the painting – which unlike his writing was never intended to produce income. His absence from the fray at the crucial party conference of 1934, cruising in the Mediterranean and painting was not a tactical move but a reflection of other priorities.

It is wrong to regard Churchill as being isolated or excluded after 1931, although this is the romantic myth of the 'wilderness years'. This implies that his omission from the national government in 1931 was a consideration in its making, rather than the natural consequence of his resignation from the front bench and the limited number of ministerial places available for Conservatives in a coalition. This false perspective results from viewing events as if the political world revolved around Churchill, and assuming that such a giant could only have been marginalised by the deliberate efforts of the 'pygmies' who ruled the national government. The truth is more ordinary; he was one of a number of Conservative ex-ministers whose position and influence had declined, and who were peripheral to the events of August to November 1931. Several who were still members of the business committee found no place, such as Steel-Maitland, Peel and Amery, whilst Austen Chamberlain and Hailsham were marginalised. Nor was Churchill unusually detached from his party, being no further removed than Heseltine in 1986–90 and less so than Bevan in the early 1950s, Cripps in 1939, Austen Chamberlain in 1922–3, or Powell after 1968. Another perspective on Churchill's position in the 1930s is offered by a comparison with the two most recent Conservative chancellors of the exchequer. He was more in touch with the party mainstream on India

---

[22] He was described in these terms by Harold Nicolson as early as January 1930 Nicolson diary, 23 Jan. 1930. This does not mean that 'elder statesmen' do not harbour hopes of a recall to the cabinet; Austen Chamberlain's position – which was more similar to Churchill's in 1929–35 than is ususually recognised – is an example of this.

than Kenneth Clarke has been on Europe since 1997, and more respected and listened to than Norman Lamont after 1993, despite the latter's Euroscepticism. The closest parallels to Churchill's position were Balfour after 1911 and Gladstone after 1874 – for certainly he did not rule out the chance of a recall to high office, although he expected not the leadership but a cabinet post related to defence.

Churchill's conduct during the 1930s makes little sense if he really was aiming to seize the party leadership or bring down the national government. In 1931 Amery noted: 'I imagine that his game is to be a lonely and formidable figure available as a possible Prime Minister in a confused situation later on.'[23] This would have been a remote and wildly speculative strategy, but Churchill's independent course was open to misinterpretation, and the suspicion that he was seeking to overthrow the leadership was a handy weapon to use against him. However, if this was his purpose, then his judgement was deeply flawed and his tactics foolish beyond belief. His campaign over India was conducted separately from the other heavyweight former ministers who might have been allies, such as Austen Chamberlain and Salisbury. Churchill's onslaught drove them towards an ineffective middle ground, and consolidated party moderates behind Baldwin and Hoare. Mainstream opinion regarded Churchill's intemperate language and forecasts of doom as exaggerated, and their excess made the official policy more credible. Up to 1933 Churchill made little effort to appeal directly to the Conservative grass roots, and by then the firmer regime of Willingdon as viceroy provided a less worrying state of affairs in India than had been the case in 1929–31. Nor was there any real attempt to canvass Conservative MPs in general, and the rebels acted according to their own personal agendas. As the 'diehards' did not view Churchill as their leader and were often ineffective in debate, they were hardly a suitable basis for a leadership bid.

Churchill was far from being opposed to the national government in principle, for it was precisely the sort of cross-party anti-Socialist pact that he had been looking for in the 1920s. His opposition to the India policy and urging of rearmament can obscure the fact that he was in agreement on the broad range of domestic policy.[24] India would not, in any case, have been the issue on which to divide the national government. Agreement since the Irwin Declaration in 1929 had enabled Baldwin and MacDonald to feel that they could work together

[23] Amery diary, 30 Jan. 1931, *Empire at Bay*, 146.
[24] For example, his support and praise for Chamberlain's budget in 1936: Addison, *Churchill on the Home Front*, 320. This contrasted with the manifesto of the five Conservative MPs who resigned the whip over India in 1935: Atholl, Todd, Astbury, Nall and Thorp to Baldwin, 1 and 21 May 1935, Baldwin MSS 107/82–7 and 91–4, Cambridge University Library.

in August 1931, and India was one of the main factors in the latter's
decision to remain in office. The round table policy was subscribed to
by Labour and Liberal figures in the government, and was further
reinforced when Irwin joined the cabinet in June 1932. There was no
significant cave amongst the Conservative ministers on India, or fault
line between them and the other parties; if this was an attempt to
weaken the national government, then it was misguided in attacking
one of its most cohesive fronts. Although Conservative activists in the
constituencies were disturbed, especially where they had economic or
personal links with India, public opinion generally was little moved.
Nor was this an issue upon which to make alliance with Lloyd George
or appeal to the middle ground, and some combination of mavericks
from all sides was never likely.

Churchill's campaign over India was focused almost obsessively upon
that single issue, and he was determined to fight to the bitter end.[25]
Although he was defeated, his strategy was not unsound. At the outset
he made such effective use of the Conservative party's official backbench
India Committee in March 1931 that Baldwin was nearly toppled from
the leadership.[26] After the national government's landslide majority in
1931, it became clear that success was not likely to be achieved through
parliamentary dissent alone. From the summer of 1932 the focus was
widened to the constituencies; rejection of the policy by the National
Union would not bind the leadership, but it would be a difficult
barrier to surmount.[27] Churchill's link with Rothermere was not foolish:
contrary to myth, the party crisis of 1929–31 had showed how much
impact a campaign conducted by the likes of the *Daily Mail* could have
on the Conservative grass roots, especially in the safer seats of middle-
class south and middle England. The official line was opposed by large
minorities at the central council and annual conference meetings in
1933 and 1934, and seventy-nine Conservative MPs voted against the
second reading of the India Bill in February 1935, even though on all
these occasions the issue was made one of confidence in the leadership.
In April 1934 Hoare admitted that 'not thirty' Conservative MPs were
strong supporters of the Bill, whilst 'the great mass is very lukewarm'.[28]

Churchill's decision in 1933 to refuse a place on the joint select
committee considering the white paper was not a mistake, as it would
have muzzled him during the key months of the struggle, but there
were other tactical errors.[29] In March 1933 his speech in the debate on

[25] Churchill to Croft, and to Carson, 31 Mar. 1933, Gilbert, *Churchill: Companion*, v, part
2, 558–9; Cazalet diary, 19 Apr. 1933, in Robert Rhodes James, *Victor Cazalet* (1976), 154.
[26] Ball, *Baldwin and the Conservative Party*, 144–5.
[27] Stewart, *Burying Ceasar*, 153.
[28] Hoare to Willingdon, 20 Apr. 1934, Gilbert, *Churchill: Companion*, v, part 2, 769–770.
[29] On the Select Committee, see the discussion in Stewart, *Burying Ceasar*, 157.

the white paper was wrecked by an unproven allegation that the government was manipulating and coercing the Indian civil service. More serious damage resulted from his accusation in April 1934 that Derby and Hoare had interfered with evidence submitted to the select committee. This was not a mistake in itself and could easily have led to Hoare's downfall; only packing the investigating committee and other dubious tactics saved him and possibly the government.[30] However, the rejection of Churchill's case when the committee of privileges reported in June reinforced views of his unfitness for office and made him almost a pariah. On this and other occasions, he was vulnerable to claims that he was seeking the destruction of the national government.[31] Nevertheless, Churchill was not alone in making mistakes. It was Page Croft – who had been campaigning within the Conservative party since Edwardian days, and should have known better – who breached unwritten conventions in sending propaganda directly to constituency delegates before the 1933 conference.[32] Although he was dammed by the involvement of his son, Randolph, Churchill was very doubtful about using the by-election tactic which backfired at Wavertree and Norwood by letting Labour in.

The proper test is not whether a revolt reverses a policy or brings down a government, for it is exceptionally rare for resistances in the Conservative party to have such results. The fall of the coalition in 1922 was the product of an unusual combination of issues and groups on a wide front. More limited effects are the norm, and it is these with which the India campaign should be compared. Churchill's campaign affected government policy in several ways – in its timing, in its presentation, and to some extent in its content. It certainly put down a marker beyond which concessions could not be made, placing the emphasis upon safeguards, limited powers and the counterbalancing role of the princely states. The India campaign achieved more than the protectionist pressure to apply tariffs to iron and steel in the late 1920s, or the Suez group in the 1950s, or the opponents of the common market in 1970–1, or the critics of the poll tax in the late 1980s. The closest parallel is with the opponents of the Maastricht treaty in the Major period, and if the 'Eurosceptics' achieved more this was mainly due to Major's vulnerable majority after the 1992 election. The India campaign was fought under the largest-ever government majority; whilst this might give some MPs more latitude to express dissent, it ensured that there were many more who could be counted on for loyal

[30] C. Bridge, 'Churchill, Hoare, Derby, and the Committee of Priveleges: April to June 1934', *Historical Journal*, 22 (1979), 215–27.

[31] Hoare to Willingdon, 17 & 31 Mar. 1933, Gilbert, *Churchill: Companion*, v, part 2, 549–50, 557–8.

[32] Lord Croft, *My Life of Strife* (1949), 232–4.

support. Even so, the leadership had to take care, and there were several alarming moments between February 1931 and March 1935.

Churchill's developing concern about air defence in 1934–36 was shared by many within the Conservative party who feared that disarmament had gone too far. He was not the only senior figure inside or outside the government to urge swifter rearmament, although he was the most persistent and public in expressing his views. Once again there were doubts about his intentions and judgement, but the charge of scaremongering was largely deflated by German statements about the size of their air force. Churchill had seemed wild and emotional about India, but more sober and informed over rearmament and later appeasement. His tactics were less confrontational and he was building support in 1935–6, especially on the need for a ministry of supply to manage the rearmament effort. He dearly hoped to get this post, and from October 1935 to March 1936 moderated his public statements to facilitate this. However, Baldwin was concerned that he would be unwilling to accept the necessary compromises and become a disruptive force in the government. Churchill's public criticisms of the Nazis meant that his return would send a signal which conflicted with the government's efforts to negotiate peaceful resolutions of disputes. For these reasons, Baldwin and later Chamberlain decided against bringing Churchill back into the cabinet in peacetime. However, many of those who did not consider Churchill to be the best man for the job still agreed with him over the need for greater vigour in defence preparations.

The abdication crisis at the end of 1936 was a setback for Churchill, reviving the criticisms of his lack of judgement and the suspicions that he was intriguing to bring down Baldwin and the National Government. Churchill was dismayed to be shouted down in the Commons on 7 December 1936, but the storm was as brief as it was intense. Some fences were mended with more judicious words on 10 December, and two days later Churchill delivered one of his most effective speeches on defence.[33] The impact of the crisis should not be exaggerated, for his diminished impact and support in 1937 owed more to the better international atmosphere.[34] Even so, the choice of Churchill to second Neville Chamberlain's formal election as party leader in May 1937 was not just a symbol of unity, but also a sign that Churchill counted for something in Conservative politics. Chamberlain's accession to the premiership was welcomed as a positive step, and most Conservatives were persuaded that his purposeful drive for appeasement offered the

[33] Winterton diary, 12 Dec. 1936, in Earl Winterton, *Orders of the Day* (1953), 223; Amery diary, 10 Dec. 1936, *Empire at Bay*, 433.

[34] Addison, *Churchill on the Home Front*, 323.

best prospect of avoiding war. Rearmament still mattered, but visible progress was being made and the government was more readily accorded the benefit of the doubt. The eclipse of Churchill by the end of 1937 was a product of Chamberlain's success, for they could not both be right in their prescriptions. Churchill's message had now become predictable and its negativity was unwelcome. Conservative opinion in parliament and the constituencies rejected the anti-appeasement case because it seemed likely to lead to war rather than prevent it. Churchill's real period of isolation was the eighteen months from the autumn of 1937 to March 1939. He was discounted by the majority of Conservative opinion, and kept at a distance by the mainly younger and left-wing group of anti-appeasers who looked to Eden. Churchill was reduced to a small group of supporters who were little liked or respected: principally Bracken, Sandys and Boothby, with Spears and Macmillan in the outer circle. It is this which gives rise to descriptions of Churchill as a 'lonely figure', although dissident former ministers rarely have more than a couple of brave souls closely linked to them in parliament.[35]

Even so, during this period he was still listened to, and it was only in the months between the Munich settlement and the occupation of Prague in March 1939 that the atmosphere became bitter. An open breach and resignation of the whip seemed possible after his speech in the Munich debate and his vote with Labour on the ministry of supply issue on 17 November 1938. It was also in this period that he encountered serious opposition within his constituency association, threatening his position as a Conservative candidate. Whether or not central office had a finger in the pie, the local unrest was genuine.[36] Dissent was strongest in some of the branches, but Churchill retained the crucial support of his chairman and the central executive. He followed a prudent strategy, and was not in as much danger as other less prominent anti-appeasers such as Vyvyan Adams, Paul Emrys-Evans and the duchess of Atholl. Doubts about the Munich settlement and especially the wisdom of further appeasement were more widespread than appeared on the surface; although only Duff Cooper resigned from the cabinet, several others wavered. There were threats of resignation from junior ministers such as Crookshank, and a feeling that this had been far from 'peace with honour'.[37] After the occupation of Prague in March 1939, German conduct provided the vindication of experience and the anti-appeasers became the realists. In the summer months of 1939 the Conservative

---

[35] Blake, 'Churchill and the Conservative Party', 153.
[36] Colin Thornton-Kemsley, *Through Winds and Tides* (Montrose, 1974), 93–7; David Thomas, *Churchill: The Member for Woodford* (Ilford, 1995), 91–111.
[37] Crookshank diary, 30 Sep.–6 Oct. 1938, Crookshank MSS, Bodleian Library.

newspapers pressing for Churchill's return to the cabinet were led by the Baldwinite loyalist Lord Camrose's *Daily Telegraph*.

His conduct at the admiralty after the outbreak of war damped fears about his motives and judgement, and he was careful to give unmistakable public loyalty to Chamberlain. This was carried through to Churchill's speech in the Norway debate itself, and was an essential foundation for his acceptance by the party as prime minister in May 1940. Kingsley Wood's support of Churchill may show that ambition resides in every breast, but it also demonstrated his acceptability to party centrists of a different background and outlook. There was still much fear and bile from those most closely linked to Chamberlain, as shown by Butler's comments to Colville on 10 May.[38] However, Churchill's purge of the old guard and elevation of the excluded was far from sweeping, and driven more by the need for efficiency and the pressure of the moment. The dropped or sidelined were mainly those who had not shone in wartime posts or become a liability, such as Hoare, Simon, Stanley and Elliot, and a few younger figures who had not made a strong mark one way or another, such as Wallace. There was no exclusion which seemed unjust or aroused resentment, and most of the inclusions were not provocative.

The events of May to October 1940 focused attention upon Churchill at his best, and when Neville Chamberlain's health unexpectedly collapsed in the early autumn, no other successor as party leader would have been credible. The myths of the prewar decade had already begun to be woven around Churchill: when he became leader in October 1940, *The Times* pointed to the improbability of this outcome because his 'unorthodoxy has so often brought him into conflict with his party'.[39] But how true was this view, influenced as it was by the immediate past? Churchill's conflict as a young backbencher had been through holding to an old orthodoxy in the face of a new, of being a recusant Tory. As a Coalitionist after 1917 he had worked in harmony with the orthodox strain of Conservatism which was dominant up to 1922. In the 1920s he was soundly in the Conservative mainstream; along with the majority of the cabinet and most MPs he resisted the pressure of the minority to extend safeguarding to iron and steel before 1929, and then was careful to move with the protectionist tide in 1930–1. His India campaign was solidly Tory – indeed for many too hidebound in outlook – and his doubts were privately shared by many who voted for the official line. The pressure for swifter rearmament did not conflict with Conservative feeling generally in 1934–8; this was why it embarrassed the leadership,

[38] Colville diary, 10 May 1940, *The Fringes of Power: Downing Street Diaries 1939–55*, ed. J. Colville (1985), 122.

[39] *The Times*, 10 Oct. 1940; Ramsden, 'Churchill and the Leadership', 99.

who felt constrained by the broader public mood of disarmament. On appeasement Churchill was in conflict with the party leader, Chamberlain, and the major figures around him, and in unfriendly tension with central office. Over the abdication crisis and during the Munich settlement he was for a few days or weeks seriously out of step with a powerful mood in Conservative parliamentary and constituency opinion. However, as with India, the case which he put forward was closer to Conservative instincts and self-image than Chamberlain's pursuit of Gladstonian arbitration in search of an elusive concert of Europe. Many Conservatives were uneasy about appeasement, and felt that Britain was being disregarded and humiliated – a mood which spread as the sheer relief at avoiding war over Czechoslovakia wore off. As leader after 1940, Churchill was orthodoxly Conservative – the usual line of criticism is that he was not forward-looking enough.

There were two areas of tension between Churchill and the parliamentary party between 1940 and 1945. Significantly, the first and most important was a national rather than a party concern: the strategic direction of the war. Doubts emerged as military setbacks and problems in war production continued during 1941, and this became more acute during the most difficult period from late 1941 to the end of 1942. Conservative MPs were unhappy about the influence of Churchill's personal circle, in particular Beaverbrook and Bracken, and the lack of orthodox Conservatives in the cabinet.[40] The 1922 Committee provided a forum for concern, but would not support any direct attack on Churchill. This was demonstrated at the lowest point after the fall of Tobruk in June 1942, when the lack of Conservative support for the vote of censure in the Commons led its proposer, Wardlaw-Milne, to offer to withdraw it before the debate.[41] Conservative MPs did not want a different leader, but a more responsive and effective government. The feeling that Churchill paid too little attention to Conservative opinion was also balanced by consensus about the priority of the war. Thus an audience of 150 Conservative MPs at a lunch for Churchill organised by the 1922 Committee in 1941 cheered his declaration that no party would sacrifice more in the interests of victory. The turn of the tide in the war at the end of 1942 removed the pressure on Churchill, and his continuance in office was never again in doubt. That the concern had been for nation and not faction was shown by the fact

[40] 1922 Cttee., 23 July 1941. See also the comments of Hacking and Dugdale, the retiring and incoming Party Chairmen, in March 1942, Collin Brooks diary, 12 Mar. 1942, Addison, *Churchill on the Home Front*, 361; Butler's comments to Chuter Ede, Ede diary 25 Feb. 1942, *Labour and the Wartime Coalition: From the Diary of James Chuter Ede 1941–45*, ed. K. Jefferys (1987), 57; Amery diary, 27 Feb. 1944, *Empire at Bay*, 969.

[41] Headlam diary, 30 June 1942, *Parliament and Politics in the Age of Churchill and Attlee: the Headlam Diaries 1935–51*, ed. Stuart Ball (Camden Sth series, 14, 1999), 322.

that the critics of the previous months were the most pleased and reassured by the news of victory.[42]

The second area of tension concerned domestic policy; this became more important from 1942 onwards, but never threatened Churchill's position. In 1942 and 1943 Conservatives were restive over some extensions of state direction on the home front, especially when promoted by Labour ministers; there was particular hostility to the coal rationing scheme and a revolt against Bevin's Catering Wages Bill led by the former party chairman, Douglas Hacking. After the Beveridge Report, and especially in the later stages of the war, it was measures of postwar reconstruction which were most controversial. Finally, there was the concern about the lack of any distinctive Conservative policies, especially as the prospect of an election drew nearer. Churchill was not unsympathetic to Conservative resistance to creeping Socialism, and party pressure led to some compromises.[43] However, his reaction to Conservative dissent on agreed matters or awkward aspects of the war, such as the equal pay vote in March 1944 or the problems of Poland and Greece in the winter and spring of 1944–5, was much more impatient. His continued priority was to avoid any controversies which distracted from the war effort or threatened wartime unity. Thus he was hostile to R.A. Butler's efforts to reform education as well as unhappy over the need to set out postwar plans. Part of the problem was certainly Churchill's understandable wish to retain his unique stature as a prime minister almost above party. He felt ambivalent about his role as party leader, and attracted to continuing the wartime coalition. Uncertainty over this continued up to May 1945; as long as the possibility remained open, Churchill was opposed to anything which tended to emphasise separateness – such as distinctively party statements or a more forceful approach to by-elections after Conservative losses in 1944.[44] Together with his exhaustion in 1944–5, this inaction left the Conservatives committed to the coalition's reconstruction proposals without gaining any credit for them. Although a party conference was held in March 1945, it had little impact. When the election eventually was held on party lines, the manifesto had to be improvised hastily and was presented without the word 'Conservative' appearing: it was 'Mr Churchill's declaration of policy', and electors were asked to 'Vote National'. Lacking other ammunition, Churchill turned to the par-

[42] Report of Churchill's Parliamentary Private Secretary, Harvie-Watt, 13 Nov. 1942, Ramsden, *Age of Churchill and Eden*, 32.

[43] Churchill minuted 'good' on his PPS's report of Conservative opposition to the coal scheme: Ramsden, *Age of Churchill and Eden*, 33. He also shared Conservative dislike of left-wing broadcasts on the BBC, and of current affairs discussion in the army: Addison, *Churchill on the Home Front*, 346.

[44] 'Party Truce', Whips' files, in Ramsden, 'Churchill and the Leadership', 102.

tisanship of the misjudged 'Gestapo' broadcast and the Laski affair –
more red herring than red peril. However, although the vocal young
radicals of the Tory reform committee had been swept by enthusiasm
for planning, Churchill was in tune with most Conservative candidates
on economic and social policy.

The most common charge against Churchill is that he neglected his
responsibilities as party leader in wartime, but both Asquith and Lloyd
George had had little time to spare for Liberal organisation during the
First World War. There were clear limits to the advisability of party
activities in wartime, and it was Chamberlain and Hacking who
mothballed central office and set the tone for the interpretation of
the party truce in 1939–40, despite being apparently more partisan
Conservatives. A recurring theme from Churchill's address to the party's
central council in March 1941 to the annual conference four years later
was the need to sacrifice party interests in wartime.[45] In any case, there
was little Churchill could have done to prevent the tide of feeling
against the 'guilty men' of Munich which swept the country in 1940–2,
and the election verdict was even more a punishment of Baldwin and
Chamberlain than a rejection of Churchill. There is no suggestion that
Churchill was the primary cause of defeat even if some of his actions
or inactions, such as the 'Gestapo' speech or being unwilling to hold
party conferences, may have contributed to its extent. More could have
been done by way of propaganda and election preparations, including
a swifter return for local party agents from war service and a less
cautious and sober manifesto. However, it strains credulity to argue
that the defeat would have been avoided if Churchill had apportioned
his attention differently between 1940 and 1945.

Churchill's standing as the wartime saviour protected him from
criticism within the Conservative party after the election defeat. The
rank and file did not wish to lose his leadership, whilst MPs and the
shadow cabinet recognised that he could not be forced out. It was
thought that he might decide to fold his tent after the defeat, and that
age and health meant that he might not be able to stay for long. In
fact, ambition to reverse the defeat soon restored Churchill's vigour,
whilst his constitution held up until the major stroke of 1953. He
remained leader until 1955 – a longer tenure than Baldwin, and only
just surpassed by Thatcher. Yet he is never thought of as a 'party'
leader in the same sense, even though the years from 1940 to 1955 were
the most productive phase of his career. The period as leader of the
opposition has been especially neglected; this is partly due to the general
theory that it is governments which fail rather than oppositions succeed,

[45] Speeches at NU Central Council, 27 Mar. 1941; NU annual conference, 15 Mar.
1945.

but still more to the belief that Churchill had little to do with the recovery – indeed, that it was achieved almost despite him.[46] The picture which emerges from the memoirs of the shadow cabinet is that he was absentee, reactionary in outlook, difficult to deal with, and imprudent in his parliamentary onslaughts. The image of Churchill in 1945–51 is that of the self-indulgent rambles at the fortnightly shadow cabinet lunches at the Savoy: a poor manager of meetings and men, out of touch with modern realities, lacking a coherent strategy and disliking detail. Yet Churchill was actually a vital part of the equation in 1945–51 – not least because his role and contributions did not duplicate the style and activities of his colleagues. His known reluctance to move too far to the left was reassurance to the party mainstream, which was always dubious about the novel panaceas offered by bright young men. At the same time Churchill wanted to win, and was willing to make the compromises necessary to do so.

Churchill made an effective start in the new House on 16 August 1945 and at his meeting with Conservative MPs on 21 August, but his strategy was little more than criticising the government and waiting for them to make mistakes. His absences in the winter of 1945–6 and the confusion of command which followed produced a critical reaction in the 1922 Committee, but matters improved in 1946 with Eden discharging the role of deputy leader. From the spring of 1946 Churchill began to attack the government over shortages, ration cuts and mismanagement, linking these hardships with Socialist nationalisation, but he left it to Eden and others to present the party line in debates on social and welfare measures in 1945–7. However, it is likely that it was criticism of austerity rather than reassurance on welfare which brought voters – and especially women – back to the Conservatives in 1950, and so Churchill's priorities were not misguided. In 1946 he gave way to rank-and-file pressure for a fresh and authoritative definition of policy, which led to the *Industrial Charter* of 1947. Churchill wanted to avoid giving hostages to fortune in specific pledges, but the content was principles rather than promises; whilst he remained doubtful and out of sympathy with it, he did nothing to block it. The November 1947 local elections showed large Conservative gains, and they held a consistent lead in the opinion polls through 1948. When Labour appeared to be recovering ground in early 1949, and especially after the failure to win the Hammersmith South by-election in March, party anxieties recurred and but were swiftly steadied. Churchill listened to the criticisms of the 1922 Committee once again, and the shadow cabinet agreed on 1 April to draw up a full policy statement. This time, with the election on the horizon, Churchill took a close interest in the

---

[46] This is the concluding analysis of Ramsden, 'Churchill and the Leadership', 117.

drafting, though the substance was a reworking of the various charters. Not long after, further gains in the May 1949 local elections and the economic difficulties which led to devaluation in September restored Conservative morale. His leadership during the election campaigns of 1950 and 1951, and of the opposition during the eighteen months between, has not attracted criticism. When the Conservatives returned to office in 1951 with the cautionary but workable majority of seventeen, it was Churchill's victory as much as anyone's. The policy pamphlets and committee minutes which lie in the archives are easily overvalued, whilst growing membership and larger staffs are the result of improving party fortunes rather than the cause. It may be that opposition is as much about waiting carefully for the government to run into difficulty, and that Churchill's wish to keep his powder dry was not unwise. Certainly, when the party was next in opposition in 1964–70 an extensive policy review did not result in confidence during the 1970 election campaign or a successful government afterwards.

In Paul Addison's view, between 1949 and 1953 Churchill 'led the Conservative Party with great vigour and flair towards the middle ground of politics'.[47] He was more successful at navigating the way back from defeat in 1945 than Balfour was after 1906, and hit fewer shoals than Hague has done since 1997, although admittedly the economic fortunes of the Attlee and Blair governments are poles apart. In comparison to the equivalent defeats of 1906 and 1997, after 1945 there was greater cohesion and sense of purpose. It is too easy to account for this by saying that the tariff issue for Balfour or Europe for Hague were more divisive and difficult to deal with – this may be so, but they were also not handled as well. There were tensions too after 1945, not least between the rump of Chamberlainite backbenchers who felt slighted after 1940 and the anti-appeasers who had risen above them, and between the young upstarts of the Tory reform committee and the staid provincial businessmen. Whilst mistakes and troubles are easy to detect and apportion the blame for, their absence is close to invisible, and the credit likely to be taken by whoever is the busiest bee around – in this case Butler and Woolton, and perhaps Macmillan as well. Churchill's strategy was to give the lead on the major occasions, such as votes of censure, the party conference and mass rallies like that at Blenhiem in August 1947, and to delegate the detail. However, his intermittent attendance at the House remained an issue: in March 1949 a senior backbencher considered that Churchill 'is not really a party man – all he wants is to get back to power – people are beginning to realize this'.[48]

[47] Addison, *Churchill on the Home Front*, 387.
[48] Headlam diary, 7 Mar. 1949.

Whilst his interest in policy and his parliamentary performances can be criticised, Churchill was more successful in the appointments which he made as party leader. Taken as a whole, his record in this area is at least as good as other leaders, and perhaps better than any except Bonar Law. Even if he sometimes favoured candidates from his own circle, it is significant that he could be persuaded to choose someone from the mainstream who would enjoy wider confidence.[49] The role of R.A. Butler in the wartime policy exercise and in being given charge of the Conservative research department after 1945, is only the most visible example of this. For the party chairmanship, Churchill first appointed Dugdale, a former Baldwin protégé who was widely liked, and then when he fell ill chose Assheton; both were at least equal in capacity to the other Chairmen appointed since the post was created in 1911.[50] Woolton may not have been Churchill's first thought to succeed Assheton after the 1945 defeat, but still he appointed and supported him. If his appointment had been a flop Churchill would surely have been criticised, and so on the same principle he deserves his share of credit for Woolton's successes. Churchill's choices of chief whips combined orthodoxy with effectiveness: Stuart managed the delicate task of the wartime coalition period well, whilst the out-numbered opposition performed reasonably well from 1945 to 1950. In 1950–1 Labour's narrow majority was worn down, whilst in 1951–5 a fairly small Conservative majority was never seriously troubled. This cannot be put down entirely to Labour's Bevanite problems, and perhaps Buchan-Hepburn is the unsung success of Tory chief whips. Whilst failure in 1945 has obscured the fact that Churchill made sound party appointments, so in a different way did recovery in 1950 and 1951. The problem here is not criticism of his team, but the fact that they take all the credit – especially Butler and perhaps Macmillan on policy, and Woolton and perhaps Maxwell-Fyfe on organisation.

Churchill was also a good constructor of cabinets, given that all prime ministers have limited material to work with. The 1940 ministry had to be a compromise between the old guard and fresh faces, with room made for Labour. It worked competently enough through 1940, and was progressively adjusted thereafter. The 'caretaker' government of 1945 is sometimes unfairly dismissed, but it was a sound and capable team. Most of all, the quality of the 1951 cabinet – most purely Churchill's own – was unusually high, and stands well in comparison with the Conservative teams which returned to office in 1915 or 1979.

[49] Ramsden, 'Churchill and the Leadership', 111.

[50] With the exception of the special and temporary status of Neville Chamberlain as Chairman in 1930–31; see Stuart Ball, 'The National and Regional Party Structure', in A. Seldon and Stuart Ball (eds.), *Conservative Century: the Conservative Party since 1900* (Oxford, 1994), 174–5.

As well as a few prestigious outside figures such as Earl Alexander of Tunis, there was a mixture of old and new talent. The great offices were in strong hands: for Butler at the treasury and Eden at the foreign office, 1951–5 was to be the high point of their careers, and Maxwell-Fyfe at the home office was suitable and effective. As the government continued a new generation of ministers gained their spurs, including Thorneycroft, Macleod, Lennox-Boyd, Heathcoat Amory, Eccles, and Peake.

Two principal themes run through this paper. The first is that Churchill was much closer to mainstream Conservative opinion than is generally recognised. This is particularly the case for 1923–9, but it is also largely true for 1930–9 when he was in line with the national government on many areas of domestic policy. On the particular issues where he differed, his instincts and reservations were shared by many, even if they did not trust him personally or express open dissent. Hardly any Conservatives were keen on the India policy; where Churchill failed it was through the lack of a convincing alternative, which left the majority of the party uneasily trusting the 'men on the spot' in Westminster and India. Most Conservatives wanted faster rearmament as the foundation for a firmer stance which would end the humiliations swallowed from Abyssinnia and the Rhineland to the Tientsin crisis of June 1939. By 1939 Churchill was seen to stand for this, and reservations about him lessened considerably between March 1939 and May 1940. During the war Churchill provided the kind of patriotic and unifying leadership which the Conservative party admires, and his relegation of partisanship was fully in tune with party sentiment. Conservatives did not feel that they should be operating during the party truce in the way in which Labour was, but that Labour should be acting as they did. Between 1945 and 1955 Churchill led the Conservatives from the mainstream. He did not lean too far in the direction of planning and interventionism, or sound reactionary notes which would deter middle opinion. This pragmatic approach was continued after 1951, and there is little doubt that the uncontroversial course which the Churchill government followed was satisfactory and reassuring to the party as a whole.

The second theme is that Churchill was a more capable party politician and effective Conservative leader than has previously been acknowledged. This should not be regarded as tarnishing his reputation or diminishing his stature, even if it means that he is set less apart from others. Churchill should be seen as a man who spent a lifetime in politics in an age when they were dominated and defined by parties. His wartime approach to the party leadership was not necessarily unsound, and the party appointments made then and later were above the average in capacity and effectiveness. The criticism of his opposition leadership has some parallels with Neville Chamberlain's impatience with Baldwin, for it is the same difference of outlook between the grasp of detail and the appreciation of atmosphere and timing. If the leader bears the ultimate responsibility for the party's fortunes, then Churchill is due the credit for his part in the postwar recovery. Alone amongst Conservative leaders – except perhaps Bonar Law in 1922 – Churchill tends not to be given much credit for the election victory gained under his command. Yet the margin in 1950 was close and the victory in 1951 a narrow one, and it may well be that another leader – which would almost certainly have been Eden – might not have kept his nerve or had the stature to succeed. His contribution to his peacetime ministry of 1951–5 also tends to be overshadowed, partly due to the stroke which affected its second half. Churchill's course between 1946 and 1955 was consistent and coherent, revolving around the defence of freedom against an enchroaching state. This was the common link between his strong line on the Cold War and warnings of the danger of Communism abroad, and his support for the liberty of the individual and free markets at home against Socialist planning and bureaucracy. He was able to maintain a clear and distinctive Conservative identity, without either echoing the discredited past of the 1930s or losing touch with moderate opinion. It was under Churchill that the identification of the Conservatives with normality, stability, prosperity and opportunity was strongly established in the postwar era. This was the foundation not just for three consecutive terms in government from 1951 to 1964, but for the predominant role of the Conservative party in British politics in the decades to follow.

CHURCHILL AND THE TWO 'EVIL EMPIRES'

By David Carlton

Introduction

When, on 22 June 1941, Nazi Germany invaded the Soviet Union, Winston Churchill's public response was immediate and unambiguous: in a broadcast to the nation he proclaimed that 'any man or state who fights on against Nazism will have our aid ... It follows, therefore, that we shall give whatever help we can to Russia and the Russian people.' He also referred to his own past as an opponent of Communism: 'I will unsay no word that I have spoken about it, but all this fades away before the spectacle which is now unfolding.'[1] This seminal broadcast has cast a long shadow both backward and forward from 1941 in its effect on how most historians and biographers have seen Churchill's attitude to the two principal dictatorships of the twentieth century.

Looking backward, the following assumptions have tended to be made:

- that Churchill's celebrated hostility to the early Bolshevik state was largely shaped, as in 1941, by strategic calculations centring on British national interest – with the Soviet leaders condemned above all for withdrawing Russia from the common war against Wilhelmine Germany.
- that Churchill was clear once Adolf Hitler had come to power in Germany that the Soviet Union must be courted as a potential ally and that he never wavered from this conviction until, after many vicissitudes, the Soviet Union finally acquired this status as a result of Nazi Germany's attack upon it in June 1941.
- that Churchill's obsessional hostility to Nazi Germany meant that after becoming prime minister in May 1940 he never contemplated a compromise peace with the state that for him represented the sole embodiment of the threat to create a 'new dark age'.

Looking forward from 1941, the following assumptions about Churchill have also tended to command broad support:

[1] *The Times*, 23 June 1941.

- that Churchill had confidence in the Soviets' ability to stand up to the German invasion; attempted sincerely to work in a co-operative spirit with Josef Stalin during the remainder of the war; and, despite some inevitable differences, looked forward to a postwar world built on the Anglo-Soviet 'Percentages Agreement', on the Yalta Declaration and on other agreements reached among the big three.
- that Churchill's criticisms of the Soviet Union and of Communism made at Fulton, Missouri, in March 1946 were offered more in sorrow than in anger and were aimed at creating an Anglo-American framework for 'containment' of any further Communist expansionist designs rather than at a confrontation with Moscow over East European developments that had already taken place beyond the 'Iron Curtain'.
- that Churchill's last premiership (1951–55) was marked by a sincere bid to achieve a lasting *détente* with the Soviets – especially after Stalin's death in March 1953; and that his desire for summitry, unimaginatively blocked by President Dwight Eisenhower and by some members of the British cabinet, farsightedly pointed the way to the eventual ending of the Cold War a quarter of a century later.

Here a challenge will be offered to these various assumptions in the expectation that historians in the twenty-first century will prove increasingly ready to look at a Churchill largely shorn of mythology. And the thesis will be advanced that Churchill, despite tactical trimming, was an adamantine enemy of the Soviet Union from its birth until his retirement in 1955; and that his desire to confront Nazi Germany, though genuine enough, amounted for him to no more than a second-order crusade.

Intervention

Churchill, in common with other British ministers in David Lloyd George's coalition government, reacted to the Bolshevik Revolution of 1917 by supporting collective Allied intervention in order to try to force Russia back into war against Germany. This in practice meant backing the white forces led by A. V. Kolchak, Anton Denikin, and others. But once the struggle with Germany had ended in November 1918 the main reason for British intervention appeared to Lloyd George and most of his colleagues to have ended, although there was uncertainty about how precipitately to withdraw from Russia. At this point Churchill's role became crucial. According to one traditionalist historian, Roland Quinault:

The British troops in Russia became Churchill's direct responsibility when he was appointed Secretary of State for War [and Air] in January 1919. He immediately decided to withdraw the British troops stationed at Murmansk and insisted that all British troops in Russia should abstain from active operations against the Bolsheviks. By the end of 1919 Churchill had reduced the number of British troops in Russia from 40,000 to 2,000. However, he wanted to 'protect as far as possible those who had compromised themselves in the common cause of the Allies and of Russia herself', and he authorised the despatch of surplus stocks of munitions to the anti-Bolshevik forces.

Churchill's hostility to the Bolsheviks stemmed first and foremost from their desertion of the Allies. There is little evidence to support Lloyd George's allegation that Churchill's 'ducal blood revolted against the wholesale elimination of Grand Dukes in Russia'.[2]

This treatment is, however, open to challenge. For it glosses over the fact that Churchill was thought by Lloyd George and other leading colleagues, including Chancellor of the Exchequer Austen Chamberlain, to have been an extremist on the subject of Russia. Churchill was in their eyes during 1919 and 1920 frequently guilty of pursuing his own agenda, namely that of seeking to expand rather than to contract the British presence in Russia and of wanting to eliminate the Bolshevik experiment for ideological reasons. As he put it in a public speech on 11 April 1919: 'Of all the tyrannies in history, the Bolshevist tyranny is the worst, the most destructive, and the most degrading. It is sheer humbug to pretend that it is not far worse than German militarism.'[3] Churchill's colleagues seem not to have endorsed this line and certainly they were not minded to prolong British intervention on ideological grounds alone. On 29 July 1919, for example, Lloyd George called in the war cabinet for early withdrawal from Archangel and Murmansk but Churchill said that 'he was very sorry to be associated with such an operation'. Lloyd George responded that 'it was a mistake to treat the present operations as though they were a campaign against Bolshevism' and claimed that the war cabinet had accepted the view that 'it was not our business to interfere in the internal affairs of Russia'. And he even singled out Churchill for criticism in front of his colleagues, saying:

If the Allies had decided to defeat Bolshevism, great armies would have been required. The small British force in Russia had not been sent there for this purpose. It was true that one member of the

[2] Roland Quinault, 'Churchill and Russia', *War and Society*, 9 (1991), 103.
[3] *The Times*, 12 Apr. 1919.

Cabinet had always urged this policy, but he himself [Lloyd George] had always protested against it.[4]

The war cabinet backed the prime minister and hence troops were withdrawn from Archangel and Murmansk against Churchill's wishes. The latter continued, however, to plead for support for Denikin in the South. Again Lloyd George moved against him – sending this harsh letter of reprimand on 22 September 1919:

> I wonder whether it is any use my making one last effort to induce you to throw off this obsession, which if you will forgive me for saying so, is upsetting your balance ... The reconquest of Russia would cost hundreds of millions. It would cost hundreds of millions more to maintain the new Government until it had established itself. You are prepared to spend all that money, and I know perfectly well that is what you really desire. But as you know that you won't find another responsible person in the whole land who will take your view, why waste your energy and your usefulness on this vain fretting which completely paralyses you for other work?[5]

Even after this Churchill continued to rail, often in public, against the line of his own colleagues well into 1920. But Lloyd George, sorely tried, chose not to dismiss him. Rather he and his entourage began privately to deride him. On 16 January 1920, for example, the prime minister told Sir Henry Wilson, the chief of the general staff, that 'Winston has gone mad.'[6] And on the following day Frances Stevenson, the prime minister's secretary and mistress, recorded in her diary: 'He [Churchill] has arrived [in Paris] simply *raving* because of the decision of the Peace Conference with regard to trading with Russia, which absolutely and finally ruins his hopes of a possible war in the East. At times he became almost like a madman.'[7]

The extent to which Churchill 'lost his balance' on the subject of the early Soviet Union is, then, too little recognised. But one historian who stands out as an exception is Clive Ponting. He has collected some of Churchill's wilder utterances in this early phase:

> He told the House of Commons ... 'Bolshevism is not a policy; it is a disease. It is not a creed; it is a pestilence.' This image of Bolshevism as a disease was one of Churchill's favourites. In the *Evening News* in

[4] War cabinet minutes, 29 July 1919, CAB 23/11, Public Record Office [hereafter PRO].

[5] Lloyd George to Churchill, 22 Sept. 1919, Churchill Papers, in Martin Gilbert, *Winston S. Churchill: Companion*, IV (1977) 869.

[6] Diary of Henry Wilson, 16 Jan. 1920, in *ibid.*, 1004.

[7] *Lloyd George: A Diary by Frances Stevenson*, ed. A.J.P. Taylor (1971), 197.

July 1920 he wrote of 'a poisoned Russia, an infected Russia, a plague bearing Russia'...

The Bolsheviks were also a 'league of failures, the criminals, the morbid, the deranged and the distraught'. In a speech in the Connaught Rooms in April 1919 they were a 'foul combination of criminality and animalism'. Animals were another favourite source of imagery. In a speech in Dundee in November 1918 Bolshevism was described as 'an animal form of Barbarism' and its adherents were 'troops of ferocious baboons amid the ruins of cities and the corpses of their victims' although the 'bloody and wholesale butcheries and murders [were] carried out to a large extend by Chinese executioners and armoured cars'. Again in a speech at the Mansion House in February 1919 he spoke of the 'foul baboonery' of Bolshevism ... although a month later the Bolsheviks were portrayed as vampires.[8]

The singularity of this language, at least in a British context, is surely what is so striking. It suggests that Churchill's approach to the Soviet Union was fundamentally different from that of other leading figures, however conservative, in the British political elite. The question at issue, therefore, is whether he ever really changed.

Churchill in the wilderness: responding to Nazi Germany

One viewpoint – broadly shared also by Martin Gilbert, William Manchester and many other historians – has been succinctly presented by Quinault:

Churchill's attitude to Communist Russia changed after Hitler's accession to power in Germany. This development convinced Churchill that Britain and France should seek a rapprochement with Soviet Russia. In July 1934, after warning about German rearmament, Churchill welcomed the pacific tone recently adopted by [Maxim] Litvinoff, the Soviet Commissar for Foreign Affairs. After Hitler's re-militarisation of the Rhineland in 1936, [Maurice] Hankey [the cabinet secretary] noted that, 'In view of the danger from Germany' Churchill had 'buried his violent anti-Russian complex of former days'. Churchill told Ivan Maisky, the Soviet envoy in London, that Hitler was the greatest threat to the British Empire and that he wanted therefore to rebuild the entente of the First World War between Britain, France and Russia. Churchill interpreted Stalin's purges as a 'lurch to the right' by a regime which had reason to fear

[8] Clive Ponting, *Churchill* (1994), 229–30.

German aggression. Consequently, he had no wish for Britain and France to support a Nazi crusade against Soviet Communism.

Events in 1938 increased Churchill's desire for cooperation with the Soviet Union. After the Anschluss with Austria, Churchill declared that although he detested Russia's form of government, it should not be shunned by Britain ... But Chamberlain responded to the new crisis over Czechoslovakia by seeking an understanding with Hitler, rather than with Stalin. After Chamberlain's visit to Hitler in September 1938, Churchill observed that the premier's fundamental mistake had been his refusal to take Russia into his confidence.[9]

All this is, however, a great oversimplification. First, Churchill's initial response to the appointment of Hitler as German chancellor was to favour a British retreat into isolation. On 14 March 1933, for example, he stated in the House of Commons; 'I hope and trust that the French will look after their own safety, and that we shall be permitted to live our life in our island ... without again being drawn into the perils of the Continent of Europe. But if we wish to detach ourselves, if we wish to lead a life of independence from European entanglements, we have to be strong enough to defend our neutrality.'[10] If he did not favour at this stage any alliance with France, we may be sure that the thought of alliance with the Soviet Union would have been wholly repugnant to him. For as recently as 17 February 1933 he had addressed the Anti-Socialist and Anti-Communist Union in these terms:

I hope we shall try in England to understand a little the position of Japan, an ancient state with the highest state sense of national honour and patriotism and with a teeming population and a remarkable energy. On the one side they see the dark menace of Soviet Russia. On the other the chaos of China, four or five provinces of which are actually now being tortured, under Communist rule.[11]

Secondly, Churchill did not use language about Hitler and the Nazis in their first years in power that was in any way comparable to that with which he had assailed the Bolsheviks in their early years. For example, he wrote of the Führer as late as 1935: 'We cannot tell whether Hitler will be the man who will once again let loose upon the world another war in which civilization will irretrievably succumb, or whether he will go down to history as the man who restored honour and peace of mind to the great Germanic nation and brought it back serene,

---

[9] Quinault, 'Churchill and Russia', 107. See also, for example, Martin Gilbert, *Prophet of Truth: Winston S. Churchill, 1922–1939* (1976) *passim*; and William Manchester, *The Caged Lion: Winston Spencer Churchill, 1932–1940* (1988), *passim*.

[10] *Hansard*, 14 Mar. 1933, CCLXXV, col. 1820.

[11] *The Times*, 18 Feb. 1933.

helpful and strong, to the forefront of the European family circle.'[12]

Finally, we need to recognise that any moves Churchill did make towards a rapprochement with the Soviets were cautious in character and subject to reversal. It is true that between 1934 and mid-1936 he did speak in public along lines that suggested possible Soviet involvement in collective security arrangements designed to check Germany and he even had some private meetings with Soviet Ambassador Maisky. But he was careful not to propose an Anglo-Soviet alliance and he did not endorse France's alliance with Moscow.

In the summer of 1936, however, he seems to have had second thoughts about the desirability of even limited British association with the Soviets. For he became greatly agitated by the outbreak of the Spanish Civil War and hoped fervently that General Francisco Franco would defeat the 'Red'-leaning government. Moreover, he came to believe that the Soviets had a considerable measure of responsibility for creating the polarised situation in Spain. On 5 November 1936, for example, he vigorously condemned Soviet 'intrigues' there as 'insensate folly'. He elaborated:

> so far as I have been able to ascertain, there is practically no doubt that an enormous influence in creating revolutionary conditions in Spain was the most imprudent and improvident action of Soviet Russia. I say that it would be quite impossible for the free nations of the western world to interest themselves in the fate of Russia, let alone make incursions on her behalf, if she continues to present herself in this guise. It would be a crime to call upon French or British soldiers, or upon the good peoples of these two countries, to go to the aid of such a Russia.[13]

And Churchill was not even apparently unwilling to rule out that Nazi Germany might have to be utilised as a counter against 'such a Russia'. For on 4 August 1936 he was sent a private letter by an intimate friend, General Sir Hugh Tudor, who argued as follows:

> The situation in Europe certainly seems to be getting worse. Spain is a new complication. If the rebels win the Fascist group will be strengthened in Europe, and Spain may line up with Italy and Germany.
>
> If the red Government wins Bolshevism will come very near us. With Spain Bolshie, France half Bolshie, and Russia subsidising our communists are we going to line up with them and Russia?
>
> I know how important even vital our friendship with France is, but I feel many in England would rather make a strong western pact

[12] Winston S. Churchill, *Great Contemporaries* (1937), 203.
[13] *Hansard*, 5 Nov. 1936, cccxvii, col. 318.

with Germany and France and let Germany settle Russia and Bolshevism in her own way. No doubt Germany would *eventually* be stronger after defeating Russia but in the meantime we and France would have time to get our defences right; and it would take years before Germany would be in a position to make war again, nor do I suppose she would want to having got a satisfactory expansion. Even Germany cannot like war.

Russia deserves what is coming to her, as she will never stop undermining capitalistic governments in every way she can. If she is left alone, in 10 years or so she will be the strongest power on earth and *she* may want to take in India and may be a more dangerous enemy than Germany.[14]

Churchill's remarkable reply read:

I have, as you divine, been much perturbed in my thoughts by the Spanish explosion. I feel acutely the weight of what you say ... I am sure it represents the strong and growing section of Conservative opinion, and events seem to be driving us in that direction.[15]

This surely is proof that the traditional view of Churchill's attitude to the 'two evil empires' in the 1930s is oversimplified. And more evidence is to be found in 1937, when Churchill told the House of Commons that 'I will not pretend that, if I had to choose between Communism and Nazi-ism, I would choose Communism.'[16]

By 1938–39, it is true, Churchill had returned to the line that the Soviets should be courted with a view to using them to contain Germany. In the meantime, however, Franco had won the Civil War in Spain and Neville Chamberlain had taken over as prime minister without offering Churchill a cabinet post. Had these matters gone otherwise maybe Churchill would have found himself in the camp of the 'appeasers' of Germany rather than working with the British Left for an arrangement with Moscow.

The 'Finest Hour'

'Churchill [on becoming prime minister on 10 May 1940] at once defined British war aims, or rather he laid down a single aim: the total defeat of Hitler and the undoing of all Germany's conquests.'[17] This,

---

[14] Tudor to Churchill, 4 Aug. 1936, Churchill Papers, in Martin Gilbert, *Winston S. Churchill: Companion*, v (1982) 306–7.

[15] Churchill to Tudor, 16 Aug. 1936, *ibid.*, 313.

[16] *Hansard*, 14 Apr. 1937, cccxxii, col. 1063.

[17] A.J.P. Taylor *et al.*, *Churchill: Four Faces and the Man* (1969), 36.

according to A.J.P. Taylor in 1969, was Churchill's unwavering approach to the Second World War. And this version of history still commands widespread acceptance. But the war cabinet minutes and Neville Chamberlain's diary point to a more complicated reality.

What is now known is that at the time of Dunkirk, Churchill seemingly agreed with his colleagues Chamberlain (the lord president of the council) and Lord Halifax (the foreign secretary) that a settlement with Germany was desirable in principle, provided that satisfactory terms could be obtained. The essential point was, in Halifax's words, that 'matters vital to the independence of this country were unaffected'. There was certainly no insistence, as Taylor supposed, on 'the total defeat of Hitler and the undoing of all Germany's conquests'. On the contrary, Churchill himself stated that he would not object in principle to negotiations 'if Herr Hitler was prepared to make peace on the terms of the restoration of German colonies and the overlordship of Central Europe'. And at one point he went even further. For, according to the war cabinet minutes, he said on 26 May 1940 'that he would be thankful to get out of our present difficulties, provided we retained the essentials of our vital strength, even at the cost of some cession of territory'.[18] That he had in mind cession of British territory is made clear in Chamberlain's diary entry for 27 May, in which he recorded that the prime minister had told his colleagues that 'if we could get out of this jam by giving up Malta and Gibraltar and some African colonies he would jump at it'.[19]

This does not mean, however, that Churchill and Halifax were in complete agreement. But what actually divided them was apparently a rather narrow point: whether and when acceptable peace terms might be on offer. Halifax conceded that the matter was 'probably academic' but he nevertheless favoured accepting a French proposal jointly to invite neutral Italy to try to discover how severe Hitler's terms might be. For the foreign secretary was conscious that if the war continued, 'the future of the country turned on whether the enemy's bombs happened to hit our aircraft factories'. According to the war cabinet minutes, 'he was prepared to take the risk if our independence was at stake, but if it was not at stake he would think it right to accept an offer which would save the country from avoidable disaster'. Churchill, on the other hand, thought that Germany, with France on the point of collapse, would not at this juncture be willing to make such an offer; and he was concerned that it would have a deplorable effect on national morale if it became known that a fruitless bid for such an offer had

<hr />

[18] War cabinet minutes, 26, 27, and 28 May 1940, CAB 65/13, PRO.
[19] Neville Chamberlain Diary, 26 May 1940, in Clive Ponting, *1940: Myth and Reality* (1990), 107.

been made. Chamberlain then found a formula acceptable to both Halifax and Churchill. According to the war cabinet minutes, he said: 'While he thought that an approach to Italy was useless at the present time, it might be that we should take a different view in a short time, possibly even a week hence.' He then proposed framing a reply to the French, 'which, while not rejecting their idea altogether, would persuade them that now was the wrong time to make it'.[20]

The French disregarded this advice from London and appealed to Benito Mussolini to act as mediator on their behalf. But he refused. It must therefore remain a matter for speculation whether, if Mussolini had acted otherwise, Hitler, given that his primary interest had always lain in the East, would have offered the kind of terms that Churchill's war cabinet could have accepted. As it was, the Battle of Britain went ahead. And when its outcome proved sufficiently favourable to the British to allay their worst fears the war cabinet had no difficulty in uniting on the policy of continued unambiguous prosecution of the war.

An admirable 'revisionist' verdict on all this has been offered by historian David Reynolds:

> there can be little doubt that, contrary to the mythology he himself sedulously cultivated, Churchill succumbed at times to the doubts that plagued British leaders in the summer of 1940 ... The Churchill of myth (and of the war memoirs) is not always the Churchill of history. Scholars working on the 1930s and World War II have long been aware of this discrepancy, but it deserves to be underlined in view of the dogged rearguard action fought by popular biographers and television producers. Contrary to national folklore, Churchill did not stand in complete and heroic antithesis to his pusillanimous, small-minded political colleagues. British leaders in the 1930s and World War II all faced the same basic problem of how to protect their country's extended global interests with insufficient means at their disposal. The various policies they advanced are not to be divided into separate camps – appeasers and the rest – but rather on different points of a single spectrum, with no one as near either extreme as is often believed. This is true of the Chamberlain era; it is also true ... in 1940. In private Churchill often acknowledged that the chances of survival, let alone victory, were slim. He also expressed acceptance, in principle, of the idea of an eventual negotiated settlement, on terms guaranteeing the independence of the British Isles, even if that meant sacrificing parts of the empire and leaving Germany in command of Central Europe ...

[20] War cabinet minutes, 28 May 1940, CAB 65/13, PRO.

This is not in any sense to belittle Churchill's greatness. On the contrary. My contention is that the popular stereotype of almost blind, apolitical pugnacity ignores the complexity of this remarkable man and sets him on an unreal pedestal.[21]

What we may, therefore, conclude for our purposes is that Churchill was not so very inflexible concerning Nazi Germany in 1940 any more than he had been in 1936–37. This needs to be borne in mind as we return to a study of his attitude towards the Soviet Union in the aftermath of Barbarossa.

From Barbarossa to Potsdam

Churchill's famous broadcast of 22 June 1941 gave the impression, which has largely endured, that he welcomed the Soviet Union as an ally and was willing to disregard past differences. In private, however, Churchill spoke at times in terms that would have shocked most of those who listened to his broadcast. On the previous evening, for example, he had told his private secretary, John Colville, that 'Russia will assuredly be defeated'. So his offer of aid may have amounted to little more than posturing. Or, as he put it to Colville, 'if Hitler invaded Hell he would at least make a favourable reference to the Devil!' Then on the next day he privately 'trailed his coat for [Stafford] Cripps [the British ambassador in Moscow], castigating Communism and saying that the Russians were barbarians'. He added, according to Colville, that 'not even the slenderest thread connected Communists to the very basest type of humanity'.[22]

All of this suggests that in June 1941 Churchill had by no means

[21] David Reynolds, 'Churchill and the British "Decision" to Fight On in 1940', in *Diplomacy and Intelligence during the Second World War*, ed. Richard Langhorne (Cambridge, 1985), 165–6. See also David Carlton, 'Churchill in 1940: Myth and Reality', *World Affairs*, 161 (1993–4), 97–103.

[22] John Colville, *The Fringes of Power: Downing Street Diaries, 1939–1955* (1985), 404–5. A decade later Colville recalled that Churchill had declared in the presence of various guests at Chequers, including Cripps, Lord Salisbury, Anthony Eden, Sir John Dill (the chief of the imperial general staff) and Gilbert Winant (the American ambassador): 'I will bet anybody here a Monkey [£500] to a Mousetrap [a sovereign] that the Russians are still fighting and fighting victoriously, two years from now' Martin Gilbert, *'Never Despair': Winston S. Churchill, 1945–1965* (1988), 550. But there appears to be no contemporary documentation supporting this claim; and Colville's published diary does not refer to it. Apart, however, from the chance that Colville's memory may have played him false, there is also the possibility that in the presence of so many witnesses Churchill did not feel able to say that the Soviets would 'assuredly be defeated' lest his 'defeatism' become widely known. Thus his wholly private words to his Private Secretary, as recorded in the latter's contemporary diary, surely give us a much better guide to his real expectations.

changed his mind about the evil that the Soviet Union represented and
that he did not expect or perhaps even desire to see the Soviets among
the victors at the end of the Second World War. What he actually
anticipated was that the Americans would soon join the war and that
the Soviets would soon leave it. Then the Anglo-American combination
would proceed to defeat Germany and be able to reconstruct the
entire European continent on liberal-capitalist lines. His optimism was
naturally reinforced in December 1941 when Hitler capriciously declared
war on the United States. But it was to be cruelly dispelled during 1942
and 1943 as a result of the Soviets' great military victories on the
Eastern Front.

Churchill probably never fully recovered from the blow that came
with the realisation that the Soviets would be a principal victor in the
'good' European war he had backed so volubly in 1939. His son
Randolph recalled a conversation with Harold Macmillan:

> He [Macmillan] described how in Cairo in 1943 Churchill suddenly
> said to him late one night: 'Cromwell was a great man, wasn't he?'
> 'Yes, sir, a very great man.' 'Ah,' he said, 'but he made one terrible
> mistake. Obsessed in his youth by fear of the power of Spain, he
> failed to observe the rise of France. Will that be said of me?' He was
> of course thinking of Germany and Russia.[23]

Churchill was, however, clear by 1943 that, with the Soviets and the
Americans now being Britain's allies, the war against Germany would
be fought to a finish. But for him this crusade was by no means enough
to give him a sense of true fulfilment. Hence he was soon seen by
many of his intimates to be devoting at least as much of his attention
to frustrating Soviet designs, real or imaginary, as to defeating Germany.
One of his obsessions concerned the fate of Greece: in order to save
her from Communism he entered into a bilateral negotiation with
Stalin during 1944 involving the ruthless abandonment of Romanians,
Bulgarians and anti-Communist Russian prisoners-of-war. But none of
this was based on a genuine desire to co-operate with the Soviets but
was driven by hatred and fear on Churchill's part. In this he undoubtedly
differed from most members of the British elite.[24]

Another episode that indicated how eager Churchill was, well before
Nazi Germany's final collapse, to frustrate Soviet designs, as he saw
them, concerns Spain. This little-known drama surprisingly does not
feature in either Churchill's own war memoirs or in Gilbert's authorised
biography. It began on 16 October 1944, when Britain's retiring

[23] Randolph S. Churchill, *Winston S. Churchill*, II (1967), 283.
[24] On the attitude of the British elite in this period see Martin H. Folly, *Churchill, Whitehall and the Soviet Union, 1940-1945* (Basingstoke, 2000).

ambassador in Madrid, Lord Templewood (formerly Sir Samuel Hoare), with all the authority of an ex-foreign secretary, urged in a memorandum sent to the foreign office that the British, American and Soviet governments send a warning to Franco that Spain must reform its internal regime or face economic sanctions.[25] Foreign Secretary Anthony Eden found this idea attractive and, to Churchill's fury, asked that the matter be raised in the war cabinet. By 4 November Clement Attlee, Labour's leader, was taking the same line. He feared, he stated in a memorandum, that Britain was in danger of being regarded as the Franco regime's sole external supporter among the victors and he accordingly urged a change of direction: 'We should use whatever methods are available to assist in bringing about its downfall. We should, especially in the economic field, work with the United States and France to deny facilities to the present regime.'[26] That both Washington and Paris, given the left-wing mood then prevailing in both capitals, would have been willing to co-operate was of course not in doubt.

Churchill's first response was to confront Eden privately. The prime minister had, above all, been dismayed by a foreign office draft intended for despatch to the US government which had argued that 'if the present unsatisfactory position is allowed to crystallise we may therefore eventually be faced with a new Spanish civil war as the only means of getting rid of the present regime'.[27] This seemed to him to amount to the promotion of Communism. He accordingly drafted a candid minute for his foreign secretary, dated 10 November, which tells us something of his contempt for the foreign office and much about his fear of Europe-wide Communism at a time when most observers would have assumed that he would be concentrating on the defeat of Germany and Japan. First, he stated: 'I am no more in agreement with the internal government of Russia than I am with that of Spain, but I certainly would rather live in Spain than Russia.' He then argued that economic sanctions would not lead to a benign transition to a more liberal order in Spain. He added: 'What you are proposing to do is little less than stirring up a revolution in Spain.' He then set the matter in the wider European context:

Should the Communists become masters of Spain we must expect the infection to spread very fast through Italy and France ... I was certainly not aware that the Foreign Office nursed such sentiments...

I can well believe that such a policy as you outline would be hailed with delight by our Left Wing forces, who would be very glad

[25] Llewellyn Woodward, *British Foreign Policy in the Second World War* (5 vols., 1970–76), IV, 30.

[26] Attlee memorandum, 4 Nov. 1944, WP(44)622, CAB 66/57, PRO.

[27] Draft telegram, 9 Nov. 1944, FO 371/39671/C15949, PRO.

to see Great Britain in the Left Wing of a doctrinal war. I doubt very much, however, whether the Conservative Party would agree once the case was put before them, and personally I should not be able to seek a fleeting popularity by such paths. I should of course be very glad to see a Monarchical and Democratic restoration, but once we have identified ourselves with the Communist side in Spain which, whatever you say, would be the effect of your policy, all our influence would be gone for a middle course.[28]

This minute also deserves to be considered in the context of the British domestic scene. For maybe the prime minister intended it to be understood by Eden as a preliminary to a possible resignation threat. Certainly it should not be forgotten that the House of Commons in 1944 still had a clear majority of Conservative MPs who had been elected in 1935 and who had shown little sympathy for the Left in the Spanish Civil War.

Eden, however, was defiant and made clear his resentment at Churchill's charging the foreign office with having Communist sympathies. In an unusually pompous minute dated 17 November the foreign secretary replied:

It was certainly not my desire to provoke or to precipitate a revolution in Spain ... You also raised in your minute the general question of opposition to Communism. I hope I have satisfied you that it is far from Foreign Office intention to foster Communism in Spain. I think I ought to add that Foreign Office policy has never tended towards fostering Communism anywhere else...[29]

Matters came to a head at a meeting of the war cabinet on 27 November. Decisive to the outcome was Attlee, who was now evidently reluctant to confront Churchill. Perhaps tabling a memorandum had been sufficient for his purposes, which may have been to appear to be broadly in step with Labour party thinking. At all events, the cabinet minutes recorded him as having 'expressed his entire agreement with the action proposed by the Prime Minister'.[30] This amounted to no more than the despatch to Franco of a hostile message which indicated that Spain would not be allowed to participate in the peace negotiations nor to join the future United Nations. Thus Churchill had frustrated those who favoured economic sanctions and who wanted, in his words, to 'make suggestions to the [US] State Department to beat up the Spaniards'.[31]

[28] Churchill minute no. M1101/4 to Eden, 10 Nov. 1944, FO 371/39671/C16068, PRO.
[29] Eden to Churchill, 17 Nov. 1944, FO 371/39671/C16068, PRO.
[30] War cabinet minutes, 27 Nov. 1944, CAB 65/48, PRO.
[31] Churchill minute no. M1254/4 to Eden, 31 Dec. 1944, PREM 8/106, PRO.

There were limits, however, to what Churchill could achieve in Europe as a whole. For it had become obvious to him by 1943 at the latest that any all-out anti-Soviet crusading on his part would henceforth have to be in a joint partnership with the president of the United States. But during the closing stages of the war he was compelled to see that neither Franklin Roosevelt nor Harry Truman was minded to confront the Soviets. On this matter Averell Harriman was eventually to reflect perceptively:

> It is important to remember that we still had a war to win in the Pacific; our military plans called for a massive redeployment of American troops from Europe to the Far East. I am not persuaded that by refusing to withdraw from the Elbe we could in fact have forced the Russians to allow free elections, and the establishment of freely elected governments, in Eastern Europe...
>
> There was no way we could have prevented these events in Eastern Europe without going to war against the Russians ... But I cannot believe that the American people would have stood for it, even if the President had been willing, which he was not.[32]

Churchill's sense of frustration was further compounded in July 1945 when during the Potsdam Conference he had to hand over the premiership to Attlee following Labour's landslide election victory.

Advocating a US nuclear ultimatum to Moscow

In opposition Churchill seemed to have expected that as an *eminence grise* he would gradually be able to steer both Attlee and Truman on matters relating to the Soviet Union. Immensely encouraged by the emerging East–West tension and by signs of increasing American robustness, he accordingly risked his reputation in March 1946 at Fulton with his dramatic warning about Communism. He also called for a special relationship between the United States and the British Empire, which would enable the two countries 'to walk forward in sedate strength'.[33] This sounds like an endorsement of the containment policy which, at George Kennan's suggestion, the Truman administration was about to adopt towards the Soviet bloc. But Churchill had a hidden agenda during the early Cold War years: he actually favoured not containment but a confrontation with Moscow before the Americans lost their A-bomb monopoly.

As early as the Potsdam conference in July 1945 Sir Alan Brooke,

---

[32] W. Averill Harriman and Elie Abel, *Special Envoy to Churchill and Stalin, 1941–1946* (New York, 1975), 479.

[33] *The Times*, 6 Mar. 1946.

the chief of the imperial general staff, had noted the delight with which Churchill had received the news that the Americans had successfully tested an atomic bomb: 'He had at once painted a wonderful picture of himself as the sole possessor of these bombs and capable of dumping them where he wished, thus all-powerful and capable of dictating to Stalin.'[34] Of course he had to know that only the Americans were actually going to possess these weapons in the immediate postwar years but this was a mere detail: for he seems to have assumed that, whether as prime minister or as leader of the opposition, he would be able to persuade the Americans to do his bidding.

By 8 August 1946 he was confiding to his doctor, Lord Moran, what he envisaged:

> We ought not to wait until Russia is ready. I believe it will be eight years before she has these bombs. America knows that fifty-two per cent of Russia's motor industry is in Moscow and could be wiped out by a single bomb. It might mean wiping out three million people, but they [the Soviets] would think nothing of that.[35]

And gradually he made his views known to an ever larger circle.

Among those he approached were Conservative politicians Macmillan, Eden and Robert Boothby. To Eden, for example, he wrote in September 1948:

> I have felt misgivings and bewilderment ... about the policy of delaying a real showdown with the Kremlin till we are quite sure they have got the atomic bomb. Once that happens nothing can stop the greatest of all world catastrophes.[36]

And overseas leaders canvassed included J.C. Smuts of South Africa and Mackenzie King of Canada. According to King's diary entry for 25 November 1947, Churchill 'thought America would, as indeed she should, tell the Russians just what the United States and the United Kingdom were prepared to do in meeting them in the matter of boundaries, seaports etc., but let them understand that if they were not prepared to accept this, their cities would be bombed within a certain number of days'.[37]

The Americans were also of course aware of what Churchill proposed. He wrote, for example, to General Dwight Eisenhower on 27 July 1948 urging that the West should use its possession of overwhelming force

---

[34] Arthur Bryant, *Triumph in the West* (1959), 373–4.
[35] Lord Moran, *Winston Churchill: The Struggle for Survival, 1940–1965* (1966) 315.
[36] Churchill to Eden, 12 Sept. 1948, Churchill Papers, in Gilbert, '*Never Despair*', 422.
[37] *The Mackenzie King Record*, IV: *1947–1948*, eds. J.W. Pickersgill and D.F. Forster (Toronto, 1970), 236–7.

to compel them not merely to quit Berlin and all Germany but to retire entirely to within their own borders: failure to do this would make a third world war inevitable.[38] And US ambassador in London Lewis Douglas reported in the same sense to his government:

> You probably know his [Churchill's] view, that when the Soviets develop the atomic bomb, war will become a certainty ... He believes that now is the time, promptly, to tell the Soviet that if they do not retire from Berlin and abandon East Germany, withdrawing to the Polish frontier, we will raze their cities. It is further his view that we cannot appease, conciliate, or provoke the Soviets; that the only vocabulary they understand is the vocabulary of force; and that if, therefore, we took this position they would yield.[39]

Only once, however, did Churchill risk advancing his views in public. This was at the Conservative party conference held in Llandudno in October 1948. He declared that 'the Western nations would be far more likely to reach a lasting settlement, without bloodshed, if they formulated their just demands while they had the atomic power and before the Russians had it too'. 'We ought', he proclaimed, 'to bring matters to a head and make a final settlement.' He added: 'We ought not to go jogging along improvident, incompetent, waiting for something to turn up, by which I mean waiting for something bad for us to turn up.'[40] Much of the British public and media may not have grasped that this amounted to a call for a threatened immediate military 'showdown'. But *The Times* at least saw the point and did not minimise the risks involved. Its editorial contained this passage:

> it is extremely unlikely that just the threat of the bomb would make Russia consent to a settlement on western terms. No great and proud nation will negotiate under duress: Britain and the United States have rightly refused to do so in the case of Berlin. It is unreasonable to suppose that Russia will willingly negotiate on the division of the world under threat of nuclear bombardment.[41]

After this Churchill showed considerable restraint in public. And even in private Churchill's approach was soon to change with the successful testing of a Soviet atomic bomb in 1949. For his own country, unlike as yet the United States, was now vulnerable to atomic retaliation.

[38] Churchill to Eisenhower, 27 July 1948, Churchill Papers, in Gilbert, '*Never Despair*', 422.

[39] *Papers Relating to the Foreign Relations of the United States, 1948*, III: *Western Europe*, United States Department of State (Washington, DC, 1974), 90–1.

[40] The full text of Churchill's speech at Llandudno is in *Winston S. Churchill: His Complete Speeches, 1897–1963*, ed. Robert Rhodes James (8 vols., New York, 1974), VII, 7707–17.

[41] *The Times*, 11 Oct. 1948.

All the same, he never entirely abandoned his belief in the case for precipitating a 'showdown'. As late as 4 May 1954 Moran reported him as having said:

> The danger is that the Americans may become impatient. I know their people – they may get in a rage and say: ... Why should we not go it alone? Why wait until Russia overtakes us? They could go to the Kremlin and say: 'These are our demands. Our fellows have been alerted. You must agree or we shall attack you.' I think if I were an American I'd do this. Six years ago in my Llandudno speech I advocated a show-down. They had no bombs then.[42]

All of this surely calls into question Sir Michael Howard's verdict on Churchill at the time of Fulton:

> Churchill was no cold warrior. Wary as he had been of Soviet ambitions and objectives, he had gone to extreme lengths – in the eyes of some, too extreme – to conciliate his wartime ally. He had established – so he believed – a warm relationship with Marshal Stalin. He was sensitive to the security needs of the Soviet state. Most of all, he had a deep respect and affection for the Russian people and a grateful recognition for all they had suffered in the common cause.[43]

As for Churchill's view during the immediate postwar years as to the relative demerits of the two 'evil empires', we find him saying in a public meeting in New York on 25 March 1949:

> We are now confronted with something which is quite as wicked but much more formidable than Hitler, because Hitler had only the Herrenvolk stuff and anti-Semitism. Well, somebody said about that – a good starter, but a bad stayer. That's all he had. He had no theme. But these fourteen men in the Kremlin have their hierarchy and a church of Communist adepts whose mercenaries are in every country as a fifth column.[44]

Advocating summitry

By the time Churchill returned to the premiership in October 1951 the Soviets had successfully tested an atomic bomb of their own and this inevitably meant that even he, as leader of a country now vulnerable

[42] Moran, *Winston Churchill*, 545.
[43] Michael Howard, 'Churchill: Prophet of Détente', in *Winston Churchill: Resolution, Defiance, Magnanimity, Good Will*, ed. R. Crosby Kemper III (Columbia, Missouri, 1996) 177–88.
[44] *Complete Speeches*, VII, 7800.

to nuclear bombardment, could no longer plausibly call for decisive 'showdown' with the ultimate enemies of civilisation in Moscow; and in any case Truman would on past form have been unimpressed. The rest of Churchill's time in politics was thus, on this reading, to be a sad anticlimax.

Many historians, however, do not favour this interpretation. For they believe that Churchill in the 1950s became something of an optimist about the Soviets – particularly in the aftermath of Stalin's death. Hence, he called for an early summit in order to explore with the 'new look' leaders in Moscow the prospects for *détente* – an approach frustrated mainly by Cold War Americans. Gilbert, for example, has written:

> On 6 April [1955] Churchill resigned. A decade [*sic*] of seeking amelioration with the Soviet Union, and a summit to set in train a wider negotiated détente, was over. It had been his last, his most sustained, and least successful foray into international affairs.[45]

In urging summitry, however, Churchill was probably motivated primarily either by a desire to hang on to office or to leave office in a spectacular fashion rather than by a genuine belief in any change in Moscow. Historian John Young was at one time tempted to offer an explanation along these lines (though at a later date he seems to have become more inclined to take Churchill's protestations of sincerity at face value):

> The Prime Minister may not have sought détente purely in order to make a reputation as a great peace-maker, but there was a degree of vanity behind his interest in easing tensions with Russia and this blinded him to some of the problems with his policy – particularly the reaction his ideas would have on [Konrad] Adenauer's policy in Germany and on the French government's efforts to secure EDC [the European Defence Community] ... After mid-1953 he claimed that it was the hope of reaching a *modus vivendi* with Moscow that kept him in office, but it is difficult to know whether this was a reason or a rationalization for remaining as premier.[46]

Even less complimentary to Churchill was the contemporary verdict of Sir Evelyn Shuckburgh of the foreign office. He wrote in his diary on 24 July 1953:

---

[45] Martin Gilbert, 'From Yalta to Bermuda and Beyond', in *Churchill as a Peacemaker*, ed. James W. Muller (Cambridge, 1997), 332.

[46] John W. Young, 'Cold War and Détente with Moscow', in *The Foreign Policy of Churchill's Peacetime Administration, 1951–1955*, ed. John W. Young (Leicester, 1988), 75. The note of scepticism is missing in John W. Young, *Winston Churchill's Last Campaign: Britain and the Cold War, 1951–55* (Oxford, 1986).

The more I think of it, the more I disapprove of W.S.C. fostering this sentimental illusion that peace can be obtained if only the 'top men' can get together. It seems an example of the hubris which afflicts old men who have power, as it did Chamberlain when he visited Hitler. Even if you do believe in the theory, surely you should keep this trump card in your hand for emergency and not play it out at a time when there is no burning need, no particularly dangerous tension (rather the reverse) and your opponents are plunged in internal struggles and dissensions. It is hard to avoid the conclusion that W.S.C. is longing for a top-level meeting before he dies – not because it is wise or necessary but because it would complete the pattern of his ambition and make him the father of Peace as well as of Victory. But it would do no such thing unless he were to make concessions to the Russians which there is no need to make, in return for a momentary and probably illusory 'reduction of tension'. After that splendid achievement he would die in triumph and we should all be left behind in a weaker position than before.[47]

Moreover, a minute sent by Churchill to Eden in December 1953 has come to light which Gilbert did not use in his authorised biography and which surely serves to show what an unreconstructed anti-Soviet Churchill privately remained even in his final years in office. He feared that the French would refuse to ratify the EDC project (intended to permit West German rearmament) and that as a consequence the vexed Americans might redeploy their forces in Europe to peripheral areas. He accordingly wrote:

We are all agreed to press EDC through. President Eisenhower rejects the idea that if it continues to be indefinitely delayed an arrangement can be made to include a German army in NATO. It must be EDC or some solution of a 'peripheral' character. This would mean that the United States would withdraw from France and occupy the crescent of bases from Iceland, via East Anglia, Spain, North Africa, and Turkey, operating with atomic power therefrom in case of war. The consequence would be a Russian occupation of the whole of defenceless Germany and probably an arrangement between Communist-soaked France and Soviet Russia. Benelux and Scandinavia would go down the drain. The Americans would probably declare atomic war on the Soviets if they made a forcible military advance westward. It is not foreseeable how they would deal with a gradual, though rapid and certain Sovietisation of western Europe à la Czechoslovakia. It is probable that the process would be gradual so that Sovietisation would be substantially effective

[47] Evelyn Shuckburgh, *Descent to Suez, 1951–56* (1986), 91–2.

and then war came. Thus we should certainly have the worst of both alternatives.

If the United States withdraws her troops from Europe, the British will certainly go at the same time. The approach of the Russian air bases and the facilities soon available to them west of the Rhine would expose us, apart from bombing, rockets, guided missiles etc, to very heavy paratroop descents. We must have all our available forces to garrison the Island and at least go down fighting.

The French should realise that failure to carry out EDC (unless they can persuade the United States to try the NATO alternative) would leave them without any American or any British troops in Europe, and that a third World War would become inevitable. It would be conducted from American peripheral bases, and as the Russian armies would be in occupation of Western Europe all these unhappy countries would be liable to be American strategic bombing points. Whatever happens Great Britain will continue to resist until destroyed. In three or four months or even less after the beginning of atomic war the United States unless out matched in Air Power will be all-powerful and largely uninjured with the wreck of Europe and Asia on its hands...[48]

These are not the words of a serious pioneer of *détente*. For with great certitude they depict the Soviets as unreformable creatures of tireless aggression. In fact they represent the convictions of the visceral anti-Soviet that Churchill had never ceased to be since the first days of the Bolshevik Revolution. In short, his anti-Nazi phase, for which ironically he will always be principally remembered, was for him something of a digression, however necessary, in his extraordinarily long career. Thus, once the Battle of Britain had been won and the Americans had entered the war, the struggle to defeat Germany became for him no more than a second-order crusade. For in his own eyes at least the contest with Soviet Bolshevism was what gave his political life the greatest continuity and meaning.[49]

[48] Churchill to Eden, 6 Dec. 1953, PREM 11/618, PRO.
[49] This paper is based on a much longer study, namely David Carlton, *Churchill and the Soviet Union* (Manchester, 2000). I am grateful to its publisher, Manchester University Press, for permission here to draw on material and arguments which first appeared there.

CHURCHILL AND THE AMERICAN ALLIANCE
By John Charmley

THE influence of Churchill's account of the appeasement years on the public mind has long been recognised and has been rehearsed here by David Reynolds. Equally influential in moulding the present view of the past has been the account of the Anglo-American alliance given by Churchill in *The Second World War*. One healthy change that the twenty-first century might bring is a less romanticised and more realistic account of the so-called special relationship. Like all good revisionism, this essay will attempt to clear away some of the rich Churchillian detritus, before trying to trace some of the outline of a different version of events. Such, however, is the artistry of the Churchillian version, and so strong the need of the British to believe it, that only the boldest of seers would wager on the chances of it being dislodged in the near future.

Churchill was, of course, himself half-American, one of a number of products of what one historian has termed the 'gilded prostitution' of the 1870s when American heiresses fulfilled the dynastic ambitions of their parents by marrying into the British aristocracy. In his early manhood there was a vogue for what was called 'Anglo-Saxonism', stimulated by America's aggression against the Spanish Empire.[1] In 'The White Man's Burden', Kipling welcomed his fellow Anglo-Saxons to the responsibilities of imperialism. The British colonial secretary, Joseph Chamberlain, himself married (at the third time) to an American, looked forward to a partnership of the Anglo-Saxon races. But this fashion proved transient. The experience of working with the Americans at the end of the First World War, and more especially of the moralising of Woodrow Wilson and the return of America into isolation, ensured that for most of the interwar period, a quite different attitude obtained. This is captured nicely in a protest made by the cabinet secretary, Sir Maurice Hankey, to Balfour in 1927: 'Time and time again we have been told that, if we made this concession or that concession, we should secure goodwill in America. We have given up the Anglo-Japanese Alliance. We agreed to pay our debts and we have again and again made concessions on this ground. I have never seen any permanent results follow from a policy of concession. I believe we are less popular and more abused in America than ever before, because they think us

---

[1] John Charmley, *Churchill's Grand Alliance* (1995), 3 and references given there.

weak.'[2] So, when Neville Chamberlain wrote that 'It is always best and safest to count on nothing from the Americans except words',[3] he was reflecting a common assumption of his generation of politicians, and one that was not always unspoken.

How different has been the rhetoric of British leaders since 1945. To a very large extent this change was wrought by Churchill. We can discern the early signs of this in *The Gathering Storm* when in the best Whig fashion he used hindsight to distort the reality of events in early 1938 by making Roosevelt's fatuous offer of an international conference into a great lost opportunity. Viewed through the lenses of the Second World War, the idea that an American alliance in 1938 might have helped to prevent the war did not look as ridiculous as it appeared in 1938 when Chamberlain rightly commented that there was everything to be said for Churchill's idea of the grand alliance – until you examined it.[4] Churchill, having thus early established the centrality of the American alliance to any sensible British policy, goes on to delineate the steps by which, once prime minister himself, he was able to woo America bring her into the war, and forge therein an alliance of the most intimate nature. From this far from bald but convincing narrative it would be impossible to guess that what had happened was that the appeasement of Germany had been followed by the appeasement of the United States.

It is a mark of the success of the Churchillian version of events that even the application of the loaded word appeasement to Anglo-American relations should cause hackles to rise. The Churchillian grand narrative disguised the reality of British decline by portraying it as a passing of the torch to another branch of the English-speaking peoples. Any twenty-first century revisionism will have to deal not only with the literary power of Churchill's Anglo-American alliance, but also the psychological need that it filled. After all, why question an account of a relationship that most British prime ministers have described as 'special'; surely they cannot all be wrong? To this there are two answers. Firstly, those prime ministers who have subscribed to the idea of the special relationship have, by so doing, underwritten their own importance and that of the United Kingdom, which is the main reason why it has had such resonance in post-war British politics. Secondly, not all prime ministers have, in fact, gone along with the Churchillian version Eden, who of course suffered from the reality of Britain's declining power in 1956, and Edward Heath who saw another path for Britain

[2] British Library, Balfour Papers, Add. MS. 49704, Hankey to Balfour, 29 June 1927.
[3] Birmingham Universrty Library, Neville Chamberlain Papers, NC 18/1/1032, Neville to Hilda Chamberlain, 19 December 1937.
[4] John Charmley, *Churchill: the end of glory* (1993), 330–3 and references there.

to follow, declined to join in the Americanophilia, as did the laconic Clement Attlee. An additional problem in revising the Churchillian narrative lies in the feelings of Americanophilia naturally generated in generations of British historians who have reason to be grateful to American archives and American funding. This has not led to an uncritical approach to the Anglo-American relationship, but it has, perhaps, generated a tendency to see it as essentially benign for Britain. This all serves to disguise what might be clearer to the future revisionist, which is that A.J.P. Taylor may well have been right when he called the 1939–45 conflict 'the war of the British Succession'.

It would take an effort of revisionism beyond imagination to argue that the Anglo-American alliance was unnecessary. Churchill's own line of defence against accusations of appeasement tended along this line, with the addition that he seldom sacrificed anything of importance and obtained, in return concessions of great value.[5] This is certainly the impression left on any reader of *The Second World War*. Difficult though it has proved to break away from the Churchillian version of the war, a less sanitised version of the Anglo-American alliance suggests what the outlines of such an attempt might be in this area. In the confines of a short essay it is possible to do only two things: the first is to subject some of the key elements in the Churchillian canon to critical scrutiny; and the second is to examine more sceptically the implication that no very heavy price was paid by the British for American co-operation.

Churchill liked to imply that America's eventual entry into the war was the product of his prolonged and ardent wooing; cause and effect are not, however, as clear as this. When Churchill rallied his colleagues behind the policy of staying in the war despite the collapse of France, the argument that America's entry into the conflict was imminent was crucial. Indeed, David Reynolds cites it as one of the 'wrong reasons' for Churchill adopting the 'right policy'.[6] Wrong though he was, Churchill undoubtedly believed what he told the cabinet; the problem is that he continued to hold this belief for the next eighteen months, during which America repeatedly declined to enter the war. This certainly presented Churchill the historian with a problem, not least since during that period Britain made a number of concessions to the United States; but he was equal to the challenge and created one of his most effective myths. In *The Second World War*, the period between the fall of France and Pearl Harbor is portrayed as one in which America edged closer and closer to entering the war. Any concessions

[5] Charmley, *Churchill's Grand Alliance*, chapter 8, for examples.
[6] D. Reynolds, 'Churchill and the British "Decision" to fight on in 1940: Right Policy, Wrong Reasons', in *Diplomacy and Intelligence During the Second World War*, ed. R. Langhorne (1985), 147–67.

made by Britain were nothing more than what was demanded if that process was to gather momentum, and they were more than justified by that 'most unsordid act', lend-lease. This is an interesting version of events, but hardly definitive.

The historian who claims to divine truly Roosevelt's intentions between May 1940 and December 1941 is brave to the point of self-delusion. Roosevelt made and unmade sense from day to day; he was a politician who erected ambiguity and ellipsis into an art form. These were qualities Churchill scarcely discerned, and ones his literary style was unable, in any event, to portray. Churchill's bold, swift narrative was filled with Macaulayesque characters, and in it, FDR became the soldier of freedom. Roosevelt's admirers were naturally delighted with this portrait and saw no reason to question it. His Republican opponents had their own reasons for finding it acceptable, because it confirmed the views of those who had always suspected that Roosevelt had dragged America into the war on Britain's coat-tails. In the absence of any demand for a more nuanced version of Roosevelt, it took a good deal of time for one to emerge.[7] Alongside the firm lines of the older portraits, the lineaments of another Roosevelt have emerged clearly enough to hazard a few generalisations. This Roosevelt is also an opportunist, but about means rather than ends. His objectives remain fluid enough to irritate historians who wish to pin him down, but they are discernible in the sort of broad outlines Roosevelt himself indulged in. His ultimate commitment was to the creation of a world safe for America and Roosevelt saw no reason why the application of liberal and democratic principles on a global scale should not achieve that objective. This Roosevelt shared Churchill's commitment to the defeat of the evils of fascism, but he was flexible about how that would be achieved. For a long time he hoped that Britain would be able, in Churchill's plangent phrase, to 'finish the job' if America provided the 'tools'; American entry into the war might be necessary, or it might not be, either way, Roosevelt kept his options open and Churchill's hopes as high as he dared. He was not, however, committed to many of the things for which Churchill and the British were fighting. Roosevelt had no time for the British Empire or for imperialism on the British model; he was equally opposed to the sort of autarchic trading system the British had created for their Empire since 1932. These things were obstacles to the sort of world Roosevelt wanted, and between 1940 and 1945 he did his best to use Britain's dependence upon America to remove them. Churchill's Roosevelt is a paladin of freedom whose eventual failure at Yalta could be partially forgiven as it was redeemed by his earlier actions. He was a fit partner for Churchill and the inheritor of the white man's burden. Concessions made to such a figure in the name of hastening America's entry into the war were not only forgivable, they were laudable.

Churchill himself was prepared to make a virtue out of necessity. As he told General de Gaulle in early 1944: 'Look here! I am the leader of a strong, unbeaten nation. Yet every morning when I wake my first thought is how I can please President Roosevelt, and my second is how I can conciliate Marshall Stalin.' Why, he asked, did de Gaulle's first thought appear to be how he could snap his fingers at the British and the Americans.[8] De Gaulle had already given the definitive reply to Churchill's question back in November 1942, namely that it was his task to look after French interests, not those of other Powers. As Eden later sadly commented, if de Gaulle had seemed 'contumacious, especially to our American allies, perhaps we should have learnt from it. Some of the faults of later years might have been avoided if we had shown more of the same spirit.'[9] The historian of the twenty-first century might find this comment more resonant than his predecessors have done. Were Anglo-American war aims as identical as Churchill thought? Was America's participation in the war so conditional that it depended upon a drip-feed of concessions from the British? Was Britain's role in the war after 1941 as glorious as the Churchillian legend would have it, or was she, in effect, squeezed by her allies for their own ends?

The Churchillian grand narrative avoids the need for such questions by implying a connection between British concessions and America's involvement in the war. It is difficult to establish such a direct connection. It is clearly not impossible to argue that the bases for destroyers deal, lend-lease and the Atlantic Charter were all milestones on the road to war, since that was exactly what Churchill did, but other interpretations are possible and may more plausibly be linked with the more nuanced picture of Roosevelt with which the twenty-first century will replace the heroic simplicities of Churchill's portrait. In essence the president was establishing American hemispheric hegemony and securing for his country what Lord Curzon would have called a *glacis*, that is a buffer zone of security. Perhaps, as some have argued, Roosevelt's decision to allow American destroyers to convoy British ships was a provocative move to create an 'incident' that would precipitate America's entry into the war. However, since this had not

[8] Martin Gilbert, *Winston S. Churchill*, VII (1986), 646.
[9] Lord Avon, *The Eden Memoirs, volume II. The Reckoning* (1965), 250.

happened by December 1941, such a hypothesis neither confirms nor denies Churchill's narrative thrust. What is undeniable is that it was Hitler's actions rather than those of Churchill that actually brought America into the war. Still, for a mythologist of Churchill's capacity and skill, *post hoc* and *propter hoc* were easily elided, especially since it could be asked whether Britain had actually conceded anything of importance in return for such an excellent result.

The triumph of the Rooseveltian world order has made the formulation of such a question as problematic as answering it. Its values have become hegemonic in western societies, and most of us take its precepts for granted: free trade, anti-imperialism, the transcendence of the values of democracy and of toleration, these truths we hold as self-evident. That the war helped their progress, and that Britain helped win the war that achieved this result, we take as a legitimate source of pride. This is, perhaps, Whig history with a vengeance. The British were fighting not to create the commonwealth of the reign of Elizabeth II, and a modern, progressive, multi-cultural society, but to preserve the empire of Victoria and the values which it represented and held dear. We may now hold such things cheap and abhor imperialism. We may feel that empire was a doomed cause and rightly so, and feel little grief at its passing; nor do we pronounce elegies for the end of imperial preference. We do not regret the decline and fall of the old social order with its inequalities and its indefensible hierarchies, its prejudices and its conservatism. None of this should blind us to the fact that for those who were fighting the war to defend the world they knew and loved, there was indeed a price exacted for the American alliance. Men such as the secretary of state for India, Leo Amery, and the colonial secretary, Lord Lloyd, saw America as a rival as well as an ally. For them, as for many of their ilk, the concessions demanded by Washington were not easily distinguished from extortion. Will the historian of the twenty-first century allow more space for their version of the Anglo-American relationship before Pearl Harbor?

When Churchill renewed his plea to Roosevelt for more destroyers at the end of July 1940, the president's agreement was conditional on long leases on the British bases in the Caribbean. Eden described it as a 'grievous blow at our authority and ultimately ... at our sovereignty'.[10] That stout imperialist and ally of Churchill's, Lord Lloyd, accused the Americans of resorting to gangster tactics.[11] The professional diplomats had, however, already come up with the excuse that would underpin every other concession that Britain would make: 'the future of our

[10] Public Record Offce, London, Prime Minister's Papers, PREM. 3/476/10, Eden minute, 29 December 1940.
[11] Charmley, *Churchill's Grand Alliance*, 430.

widely scattered Empire is likely to depend upon the evolution of an effective and enduring collaboration between ourselves and the United States.'[12] This platitude was not accompanied by any query about whether the United States wanted to underwrite the British Empire. In fact, in return for bases described by Roosevelt as 'of the utmost importance to our national defence',[13] the British received out of date destroyers, and far from the fifty promised, by the end of January 1941, only two of them had turned up. To argue that the concession on the British side was only symbolic is both to underrate the importance of symbol and to attribute a late twentieth-century consciousness to men born in the reign of Queen Victoria.

The second item in the Churchillian catalogue, lend-lease, seems less in need of the aid of the word symbolic; without it Britain could not have stayed in the war. The 'most unsordid act' actually had a good deal of shoddiness about it. Writing a year before Pearl Harbor, Churchill revealed his own unspoken assumptions when he told Roosevelt that he believed 'you will agree that it would be wrong in principle and mutually disadvantageous in effect if, at the height of this struggle, Great Britain were to be divested of all saleable assets so that after victory was won with our blood ... we should stand stripped to the bone'.[14] Roosevelt did not agree in the slightest. His secretary of state, Cordell Hull, had spoken about using 'American aid as a knife to open up that oyster shell, the empire';[15] and that was precisely what the Roosevelt administration attempted to do. Even Churchill bridled at Roosevelt's proposal to send a destroyer to Simonstown to pick up the last of Britain's gold reserves,[16] and although he finally decided not to protest formally, he did not dissent from Beaverbrook's view that the Americans had taken advantage of Britain's situation to 'exact payment to the uttermost for all they have done for us.'[17] It was entirely legitimate for the Americans to promote their national interests in this way, as it was for them to force the British to sell off their overseas assets at bargain-basement prices to obtain lend-lease; whether it is accurate to portray the process as one of 'mixing together' might well be questioned more by the twenty-first century than it has been thus far.

The notion of Roosevelt pursuing a policy of his own devising that was compatible with British interests only up to a point is strengthened

[12] PRO, War Cabinet Memoranda, Cab. 66/10, WP(40)276, 18 July 1940.
[13] E. Roosevelt (ed.), *The Roosevelt Letters*. III (1953), Roosevelt to David Walsh, 22 August 1940, 329–30.
[14] W. Kimball (ed.), *Churchill and Roosevelt: the Complete Correspondence* (hereafter: *Churchill–Roosevelt Correspondence*) (Princeton, 1984) I, Churchill to Roosevelt, 7 December 1940, 108.
[15] Kimball, *The Juggler*, 49.
[16] PRO, PREM. 4/17/1, Churchill minute, fos. 93–4.
[17] PREM. 4/17/1, Beaverbrook memorandum, fos. 104–6.

by the Atlantic Charter. Such has been the success of the new order of which the Charter was the harbinger in the postwar era that it is difficult to recapture just how radical it was. One of the anxieties of the Roosevelt administration in the summer of 1941 was that with the entry into the war of the Soviet Union, the British would enter into commitments that would prejudice the creation of the sort of world order America wanted.[18] The Atlantic Charter, so lauded in the official Churchillian version of the Anglo-American relationship, came as a bolt out of the blue at the time. British historians, struck either by its now platitudinous nature, or by Churchill's version of it, have shown a lack of curiosity about its origins. These lie in Roosevelt's determination to avoid the fate of Woodrow Wilson. He was well aware of the allegations of his opponents that American aid was simply subserving British imperial interests; the Charter was the answer to them. Article 3, which provided for 'the right of all peoples to choose the form of government under which they live', struck at the very heart of imperialism. Churchill's declaration that it did not apply to the British Empire was unilateral in nature, and there is no sign that the Americans agreed with him, even if it was hardly politic to say so. Article 4, providing for all nations to have 'access of equal terms to the trade and to the raw materials of the world', was the pure doctrine of Hull's free trade beliefs and ran directly counter to the economic beliefs of the party upon whose support Churchill's premiership rested.

Churchill's justification for signing up to the Charter followed the usual lines. After explaining away the exemptions he claimed for the Empire, Churchill argued that nothing much had been conceded; in return, the president had promised to become 'more provocative' towards Germany, which surely heralded a swift American entry into the war.[19] By the end of August Churchill was telling Roosevelt of the 'wave of depression' created in Britain by his own repeated statements to the American press that the Atlantic meeting was not the prelude to America's entry into the war. It may be that Roosevelt's comments were made for domestic purposes and that the impression he had left on Churchill at the conference was the correct one, but to assume this to be the case because of the assumption that Roosevelt was moving America towards war, is to go down a perilous road. That, of course, does not mean that Roosevelt's remarks to Churchill might not have reflected his own views, but it suggests caution about assuming that it was so because Churchill's portrait of Roosevelt demands that it should have been so. Roosevelt was well aware of the part Churchill's leadership

---

[18] Charmley, *Churchill's Grand Alliance*, 32–3, 36–7.
[19] Franklin D. Roosevelt Library, Private Secretary's File, Safe File, Atlantic Charter (1), Box 1, Churchill to Harry L. Hopkins, 29 August 1941.

played in keeping Britain in the war and he wanted to do nothing to jeopardise it. Roosevelt's actions in late 1941 certainly lend themselves to the Churchillian version of events, namely that he was becoming more and more provocative with a view to creating an incident with Germany that would bring America into the war; but they might also be read as efforts to bolster Churchill and to keep the British in the war.

If the historian of the twenty-first century might approach Churchill's narrative of the prelude to America's entry into the war with a more sceptical eye, asking questions about the compatibility of Anglo-American objectives, and taking more account of those who thought a real price was being paid to Washington for aid that could have been had more cheaply, then he will have to admit, nonetheless, that Churchill's claims for influence over the direction of allied grand strategy in 1942 stand up to scrutiny. The Mediterranean strategy was undoubtedly his brain-child, which no doubt accounts for the controversy it has generated over the years. But those who would use it as yet another stick with which to beat Churchill will have to take into account the fact that it succeeded for reasons that were also unconnected with him. Churchill's own explanation, couched in terms of the role his relationship with Roosevelt allowed him to play, is only part of the story. Had there been no more to it then, after General Marshall's visit to London in March 1942, the western allies would have found themselves preparing for an invasion of France. But Churchill's agreement to Marshall's plans had come only because of a conviction that they were impossible to implement – as proved to be the case. The Alliance, and the Americans, needed an operation in 1942, and since most of the available troops were British and in North Africa, that effectively dictated the main theatre of operations. The Anglo-American failure to clear to the Germans out of Tunisia before May precluded a cross-Channel invasion in 1943, which then gave Churchill's preferred strategy a prolonged lease of life. However, for all Churchill's claims for the influence that he gained through his relationship with Roosevelt, he was unable to persuade the Americans of the merits of continuing with a campaign in the Adriatic for 1944.

Was it, however, true that even in return for America's agreement to the Mediterranean Strategy in 1942 and 1943, Churchill surrendered nothing of great value? An answer to this requires us to go beyond the tramlines laid down in *The Second World War*. One of the great differences between Churchill's account of the war and that given in the other great personal account of it, de Gaulle's *Mémoires de Guerre*, is that where the latter is largely an account of the political struggle to determine the future of France, Churchill's concentrates upon the war itself. When Eden attempted to engage Churchill in serious debate in late 1942 about the future of British foreign policy, he received the discouraging response that he hoped that such 'speculative studies will be entrusted to those on whose hands time hangs heavy', commending to him the recipe of Mrs Glass for jugged hare – 'First catch your hare'.[20] It could be argued that too much should not be built upon such a remark, except for the fact that throughout the war the foreign secretary, Anthony Eden, found it impossible to get Churchill to engage in serious planning for the postwar era. To set against that a few musings by Churchill to his private secretary in 1940, and his appointment of his son-in-law, Duncan Sandys, to a postwar planning committee, smacks of special pleading. One could simply dismiss Eden's complaints had they been made once or twice, but they are a constant refrain throughout the war.

Eden told his colleagues in 1942 that the absence of any 'guiding principle' for British foreign policy was a 'grave weakness'. Both of Britain's main allies treated the vagueness of British policy with suspicion; America and Russia naturally suspected imperialist ambitions were being hidden from them, whilst the European governments in exile were 'puzzled by an apparent inability on our part to give them the kind of lead, to provide for them the kind of focus, which they have come to realise they must have if they are to survive'.[21] The argument that Britain had no alternative to following what America and the Soviet Union wanted is more convincing applied to 1945 than it is in 1942. Indeed it was this consciousness of a limited window of opportunity that prompted Eden to try to persuade Churchill to map out a vision for British foreign policy; it might have to be deviated from, but without such a vision the danger of drifting into the American slipstream was only too apparent.

Churchill's refusal to enage in such a debate does not mean that he had no thoughts. As he told Eden in response to his 'Four power plan', his thoughts rested 'primarily in Europe – the revival of the glory of Europe, the parent continent of the modern nations and of civilisation'; unfortunately 'the war has prior claims on your attention and mine.'[22] Moreover, when it came to the 'greatest' problems, intimate cooperate with America would be necessary, and it was upon that that his heart was set.[23] Nor were his hopes here modest ones. If one characteristic of Whig history is the tracing of clearer lines between the past and present than actually existed, another is the airbrushing out of inconvenient facts. The speech that Churchill gave on the hills of old

[20] PREM. 4/100/7, M.461/42, Churchill to Eden, 18 October 1942.
[21] PREM. 4/100I7, WP(42)516, 'The Four Power Plan', Eden memorandum, 8 November 1942.
[22] PREM. 4/100/7, M.461/42, Churchill to Eden, 18 October 1942.
[23] PREM. 4/100/7, M.474/2, Churchill to Eden, 21 October 1942.

Missouri on 5 March 1946 is usually known by the title of its striking metaphor, 'the Iron Curtain' speech, but it is in fact entitled the 'Sinews of Peace'. Although posterity has focused upon its message about the Iron Curtain, the main theme of the speech was the renewal of a plea for Anglo-American unity. That plea had been made in a major speech Churchill had given at Harvard in September 1943, but which fails to get any mention in the war memoirs. There Churchill made it plain that when he talked about 'unity' he meant 'union'. Churchill advocated the healing of the breach made in the reign of George III and looked forward to an Anglo-American union with a common legal system and a common currency.[24] That this did not happen should not disguise from us Churchill's hope that it would, or the price it exacted in terms of having an independent British foreign policy. No where was this price heavier than in it was in Anglo-French relations.

Churchill shared Eden's view that British interests demanded the restoration of French power, not least as a counterweight to possible Soviet 'preponderance';[25] indeed, it was partly to that he had built up General de Gaulle. However, Churchill's pursuit of the American special relationship served to wreck Britain's relations with de Gaulle, and with it short circuited any attempt to evolve a constructive policy towards the future organisation of Europe. There was little point Churchill having inchoate ideas about a 'Council of Europe' if the effect of his American policy was to prevent their execution. Indeed, following my leader where Washington was concerned landed the British in a good deal of hot water, before pouring the cold remnants over plans for European unity. De Gaulle's policy of asserting France's interests regardless of Anglo-American feeling had brought American enmity from the moment he irritated Cordell Hull by occupying the islands of St Pierre and Miquelon in 1941. Those anti-Vichy French exiles who had fallen out with de Gaulle (or never been in with him) tended to wash up on the shores of the New World where they provided the state department with a colourful collection of anti-Gaullist rumours. The state department was never sure whether de Gaulle was a crypto-fascist (he was a general after all) or a Communist pawn, but they were clear, as was Roosevelt, that the Allies should have as little truck with him as possible.[26] This meant, in practice, not just keeping him out of Operation TORCH, but co-operating with the Vichy collaborationist, Admiral Darlan.

The crisis caused by the Darlan affair is absent from Churchill's

---

[24] *The Times*, 7 September 1943.

[25] M. Kitchen, *British Policy towards the Soviet Union during the Second World War* (1986), 151, quoting Churchill to Sir Alexander Cadogan, 2 April 1943.

[26] On all of this see, J. Charmley; 'British Policy towards General de Gaulle, 1942–1944' (Oxford D. Phil, thesis, 1982).

account of the war, but at the time it raised a storm of protest. Progressive opinion in Britain and America reacted very badly to it, with Attlee warning about the reaction of the Labour movement, and Eden of its effect on Anglo-Soviet relations.[27] Churchill, however, preferred to go along with Roosevelt, who opined that the French were a 'very silly people' and that de Gaulle 'really did not know what the opinion of France is or who represents France'.[28] The result was that the Western allies ended up setting up Darlan as the *chef d'état* of a French North Africa that owed allegiance to Marshal Petain, whilst Churchill, in a secret session of the House of Commons, excoriated de Gaulle as 'one of those Frenchmen who have a traditional antagonism against the English'.[29] Whatever the truth of that observation, Churchill and Roosevelt's treatment of de Gaulle ensured that he would indeed have such an antagonism. The assassination of Darlan on Christmas Eve 1942 provided a way out of a situation that was damaging relations between Britain and Russia as well as with de Gaulle, but again, Churchill chose to follow Roosevelt's policy of promoting General Giraud as Darlan's replacement, rather than breaking with the Vichy regime in North Africa; indeed, much to the fury of the Gaullists, the Americans even brought in fresh Vichy collaborationists such as Marcel Peyrouton to help run what was, in effect, an American puppet government in North Africa. In May 1943, Churchill even agreed, at Roosevelt's behest, that the time had come to break with de Gaulle, although the announcement of a union between the Gaullists and the forces of the American-backed General Giraud prevented this.

Roosevelt seemed to class France along with 'Spain and Italy as a Latin power with no great future in Europe', but in Eden's eyes Britain should have no truck with such a view. If Britain was to contain Germany after the war then a strong and friendly France was 'indispensable for our security whether or not the United States collaborates in the maintenance of peace on this side of the Atlantic'. This meant doing 'everything to raise French morale and promote French self-confidence'. There were, he told Churchill in July 1943, points beyond which 'we ought not to allow our policy' to be governed by the Americans: 'Europe expects us to have a European policy of our own, and to state it.'[30] Churchill had already made it clear that he did not propose to 'allow our relations with the United States to be spoiled through our proposed patronage of this man ... whose accession to

[27] PRO, Foreign Office General Correspondence, Series 371/32144/Z9714 for sheafs of protests. See also Cab. 66/32, WP(42)576, Eden memorandum, 11 December 1942.
[28] PRO. Avon Papers, FO 954/29 part II, Oliver Lyttelton's record of a meeting with Roosevelt, November 1942.
[29] Gilbert, *Churchill VII*, 277–78.
[30] PRO. FO 371/36301/Z8225, draft memorandum, 12 July 1943 by Eden.

power in France would be a British disaster of the first magnitude.'[31] Eden thought that the deliberate snubbing of de Gaulle by the Americans and by Churchill 'would make him a national hero' inside France, as well as fatally damaging Anglo-French relations.[32] Churchill would have none of this. He was not, he told Eden, willing to 'mar those personal relations of partnership and friendship ... between me and President Roosevelt ... by which... the course of our affairs has been most notably assisted' for a 'budding Fuhrer' like de Gaulle.[33] Although Eden was able to prevent this hostility from actually leading to a breakdown in Anglo-French relations, he could not prevent the damage caused by de Gaulle's conviction that as long as Churchill had anything to do with it, Britain would put the American alliance before her commitments to Europe.

The danger in this line was pointed out to Churchill by his old friend, Duff Cooper, who was appointed as ambassador to the French Committee of National Liberation in late 1943, when he asked him on the eve of D day whether he could be sure that 'having sacrificed ... [French] friendship and the hegemony of Europe out of friendship to the United States', the latter would not retreat into isolationism.[34] The answer, of course, was that he could not, but that did not prevent him from continuing to alienate de Gaulle at every opportunity. At a famous meeting with the general on 4 June 1944, Churchill made unambiguously plain his preference for America and Roosevelt over Europe and de Gaulle. Despite assurances to the general from both Eden and Bevin that Churchill's views were purely personal, the Frenchman had already drawn his own conclusion that Britain preferred being an American client state to trying to lead Europe.[35] Duff Cooper argued passionately that Britain would 'emerge from this war with greater honour than any other country' and that the 'leadership of Europe' awaited her if she would only take it.[36] In May, and again in December 1944, he advocated Britain taking the lead to organise a Western European Union, only to be frustrated because Eden thought it might displease the Soviets whilst Churchill thought that the Americans would not like it.[37]

Churchill's record of deferring to the American dislike of de Gaulle continued right down to his refusal to recognise any French Provisional

[31] FO 371/36047/Z6026, Churchill to Eden, 23 May 1943.
[32] *The Reckoning*, diary entry, 8 July 1943, 397.
[33] PREM. 3/181/8, Churchill draft paper, 13 July 1943.
[34] FO 37/42134/Z3307, Cooper to Churchill, 25 April 1944.
[35] Charmley, *Churchill's Grand Alliance*, 569–70 for the various sources for this conversation.
[36] John Charmley, *Duff Cooper* (1986), 186–187.
[37] Charmley, *Churchill's Grand Alliance*, 539–540 for the references.

government until Roosevelt himself suddenly, and without consulting Britain, decided to do so in October 1944. It damaged British interests in both a short and a long-term way. In the first instance it helped prevent Churchill from actually doing anything effective about his ideas about a 'Council of Europe'. In the second place it encouraged a belief that there was a dichotomy between constructive engagement with Europe and the special relationship. Constructive engagement with Europe was not possible because it would mean transgressing American policy towards de Gaulle, and it was also unnecessary because Britain's continuance as a Great Power depended upon America not upon her relationship with Europe. Churchill may have indulged in 'Morning thoughts' and after-dinner conversations about Europe, he certainly wished to see it as one of 'regional councils' of the United Nations, but Roosevelt wanted no 'regional councils', so naturally he got his way on that, as he did on policy towards France.

One of the other areas where Churchillian deference to Roosevelt exacted its price was in British policy towards the USSR, a topic on which the views of the twenty-first century might well differ from those prevailing hitherto. Any attempt to argue, as Eden did, for a constructive engagement with Soviet Russia is likely to founder on the reality of the Cold War. In its hindsight both Eden's eagerness to offer Stalin his 1941 frontiers, and Churchill's belief that Stalin was a man of his word, can be made to look very like appeasement.[38] It may well be that there never was any chance of Anglo-Soviet relations avoiding the freezer, but Eden's attempt to win Stalin's goodwill by granting his demand for a recognition of the frontiers of June 1941 was not without its merits. In the first place, as Eden himself pointed out, if the war was to be won it was highly likely that it would because Soviet troops were already in possession of the territory lost in 1941, and since the Western Allies would be unable to take it from the Soviets, they might at least have whatever benefits might accrue from such a recognition before it became inevitable.[39] There was naturally a good deal of suspicion of British intentions on the Soviet side, and these were hardly likely to be dispelled by a British refusal to recognise the 1941 frontiers, especially if that were to be followed by no 'Second Front' in Europe until 1944. However, unfortunately for Eden, Churchill was in America when his proposals came through. Roosevelt's confidant, Sumner Welles later called Eden's proposed treaty a 'Baltic Munich', and stigmatised Russian demands as 'indefensible from every moral standpoint and equally indefensible from the standpoint of the future

[38] Most recently here see D. Carlton, *Churchill and the Soviet Union* (2000).
[39] *The Reckoning*, 295–297.

peace and stability of Europe'.[40] This exaggeratedly moral outburst avoided addressing Eden's assertion that if German military power was destroyed 'Russia's position on the Continent will be unassailable'. As Rab Butler put it: 'our refusal to concede their claim to certain territories in Central Europe – the future of which without them we are unable to influence – will tend to maintain that atmosphere of suspicion which has for so many decades affected Anglo-Soviet relations';[41] and so it proved.

For all Churchill's interest in forging a special relationship with Roosevelt and the Americans, the evidence suggests that Roosevelt's interest lay in trying to create one with Stalin. Roosevelt's own belief was that the Soviet system was evolving in a manner favourable to his own plans. It was, he thought, 'increasingly true that the Communism of twenty years ago has practically ceased to exist' and that the 'current system is more like a form of the older socialism'.[42] He told Churchill in March 1942 that 'I think I can personally handle Stalin better than either your Foreign Office or my State Department. Stalin hates the guts of all your top people. I think he likes me better, and I hope he will continue to do so.'[43] Roosevelt's concept of the United Nations had no place in it for Churchillian regional councils, it depended rather upon Stalin co-operating in a single global organisation with the 'Four Policemen' controlling its activities. Churchill's acceptance of that model in August 1943 at Quebec marked, in the words of William H. McNeill, the surrender 'of whatever hopes he once had of pursuing an independent postwar policy. Instead of 'relying on Britain's own strength and the support of a friendly and consolidated Europe, Churchill decided to pin his hopes upon America'.[44] That Roosevelt's hopes were pinned on Stalin emerges from any study of the last two years of the war that can steer between the Scylla of the Churchillian version and the Charybdis of Cold War hindsight.

By mid-1943, Roosevelt had decided that he needed a bilateral meeting with Stalin, something that shocked Churchill who tried to persuade him against the idea.[45] Roosevelt had been advised by ambassador Joseph Davies that Stalin distrusted Churchill as an old-fashioned imperialist, and Roosevelt, with his invincible belief in himself, thought that he might, face to face, be able to persuade the Soviet leader to try to achieve his territorial objectives without, in the process,

[40] FDR Library, A.A. Berle Papers, diary, Welles to Berle, 4 April 1942.
[41] PRO. FO 945/25, SU/42/26, Butler to Eden, 13 March 1942.
[42] Charmley, *Churchill's Grand Alliance*, 33.
[43] *Churchill–Roosevelt Correspondence*, I, Roosevelt to Churchill, 18 March 1942, 421.
[44] William H. McNeill, *America, Britain and Russia 1941–1946* (1953), 323.
[45] *Churchill–Roosevelt Correspondence*, II, Churchill to Roosevelt, 28 June 1943, 283–284.

offending 'democratic public opinion.'[46] At Tehran, Roosevelt exerted himself to reassure Stalin that America was not going to gang up with the British, telling him that America would not fight him over the future of Poland, and assuring him that whatever Churchill thought, there would be an invasion of France in 1944. In language calculated to appeal to Stalin's realism, Roosevelt told him that the essential thing over Poland was to make Soviet claims in a way which did not upset western opinion, especially his own Polish-American voters. In return, Stalin responded warmly to Roosevelt's ideas for a global United Nations, with both of them rejecting Churchill's view that such a body should be organised on a regional basis. They also agreed on the insignificance of France in a future Europe and on the possible disposal of the French and Italian colonial Empires.[47] The two men even joined in having a little fun at Churchill's expense, teasing him about the future of Germany and suggesting that its entire general staff should be taken out and shot. It was little wonder that Churchill should later have said that it was at Tehran that he had realised for the first time 'what a small nation we are. There I sat with the great Russian bear on one side of me with paws outstretched, and on the other side the great American buffalo, and between the two the poor little English donkey who was the only one ... who knew the right way home.'[48] That last comment did him far more honour than he deserved. In fact, far from Churchill's wooing of Roosevelt paying off in terms of increased influence on American policy, the last eighteen months of the war witnessed both a diminution in British influence and growing signs of stress.

Here the twenty-first century historian may have to part company with the rhythms of the Churchillian grand narrative. An investigation of the internal politics of the Roosevelt administration after the election victory in November 1944, and a study of Anglo-American divergences over Greece and Italy, might reveal a story different in tone and content from the one with which we are familiar. Harry Hopkins had warned Lord Halifax before Roosevelt's re-election in November that the British might well be better off with a Republican victory. The Republicans would 'give you a free hand in India, in Europe and in the Middle East. You will have no embarrassing insistence on this or that in Saudi Arabia and all the other places where you have been accustomed to having your own way. It won't be like that with Roosevelt after the elections.'[49] Nor was it. As Halifax noted in December, there was a

[46] Elizabeth Kimball Maclean, 'Joseph P. Davies' (Ph.D. thesis, University of Michigan, 1986, p. 340, citing Davies' diary, 13 May 1945).
[47] See Charmley, *Grand Alliance*, 78–80 for detailed argument on this theme.
[48] John W. Wheeler-Bennett, *Action This Day* (1967), 96.
[49] FO 371/38550/AN4451, Michael Wright letter, 14 November 1944.

real 'desire for a brand new 100% American foreign policy'.[50] This manifested itself in protests against the reactionary nature of British policy in Greece and Italy, It was all very well for Churchill to protest (in the case of Greece) 'we have a right to the President's support',[51] but that did not make it forthcoming. As Harry Hopkins warned, whilst the administration wanted a 'strong Britain', they 'had ideas of their own on many question which might differ from ours and were not going to be an amenable junior partner. At best, Britain could hope to be 'America's outpost on the European frontier, the sentinel for the New World.'[52] This is not to imply that Anglo-American relations were heading for a breakdown, but it is to question the assumption that Britain gained great influence in Washington as a result of Churchill's deference to the president.

Instead of the real picture, an increasingly assertive America whose policy was unamenable to British guidance, Churchill provides us with an artistically more satisfying conclusion to his story of the Anglo-American alliance. The tragedy in the title of volume six of the war memoirs is, of course, Roosevelt's refusal to heed Churchill's advice after Yalta and to take a firm stand against Soviet designs in Eastern Europe. Argument will always rage over Roosevelt's actions at Yalta, but there seems no reason to disagree with the interpretation that it was essentially an attempt to fudge a settlement in a climate where too much clarity would only expose divisions within the Grand Alliance. As for Churchill's self-proclaimed prescience, there was not much sight of it either before or immediately after the conference. For all his wooing of Roosevelt, the president refused to have a pre-Yalta bilateral meeting with Churchill and preferred to set himself up as the mediator between the British imperialists and the Soviet Communists. His own summary of his policy towards Stalin can hardly be bettered: I think if I give him everything I possibly can and ask for nothing from him in return, noblesse oblige, he won't try to annex anything and will work with me for a world of democracy and peace.'[53] This may, as the president's enemies allege, be a sign of his naïveté, but equally it reflected his belief that he, and he alone, could find a way to give Stalin what he wanted without breaking the Grand Alliance. Moreover, if Roosevelt was naïve, Churchill was no better, returning from Yalta declaring that Stalin was a man who could be trusted.[54] As the signs multiplied, at least in British eyes, that things might not be so optimistic,

---

[50] FO 371/38551/AN4618, Halifax to Foreign Office, 10 December 1944.

[51] *Churchill–Roosevelt Correspondence*, III, Churchill to Hopkins, 10 December 1944, 451.

[52] FO 371/38550/AN4451, Michael Wright letter, 14 November 1944; Charmley, *Grand Alliance*, pp. 117–118.

[53] F. Harbutt, *The Iron Curtain* (1986) p. 42.

[54] *Churchill–Roosevelt Correspondence*, III, Churchill to Roosevelt, 5 April 1945, p. 613.

Eden concluded that British policy was a 'sad wreck'.[55] Although gloomy, that was not a bad summary. Because of the onset of the Cold War and its effect on the historiography of the period from 1945 to 1947, it is easy to anticipate events and forget that for much of that period the British were anxious about America's refusal to help them against the Soviet, as well as indignant at America's refusal to bail them out financially except at a price. In short, the dividends from Churchill's policy were minimal. The argument that American participation in NATO contradicts such a conclusion is only tenable on the assumption that the British influenced American policy in that direction. For that, as for so many of the assumptions behind the myth of the Special Relationship, evidence is wanting. America came into the Cold War for her own reasons, not because the British persuaded her to do so.

Such, in brief, are the outlines of an alternative version of the Anglo-American alliance. The chances of it winning acceptance should not be rated highly. The Churchill myth was benign in a way that the British needed, and that need shows no sign of ending. It provided them with a gentle and even generous way of stepping down from power and accepting American leadership. When the Cold War came it was easy, as Churchill's memoirs showed, to ignore the 'sad wreck' of the hopes of 1945 and to construct a straight line between 1941 and the Truman doctrine. Churchill himself contributed another step on the road with his Iron Curtain speech, which everyone could conveniently forget had met with a largely hostile reception when it had been given. Parts of the Churchill myth even became true over time. With the decline of empire and the creation of the welfare state the British polity did become more liberal and democratic in tone, and the influence of American popular culture added a new dimension to the Anglo-American relationship. Of course, as Churchill belonged to the class, which saw most to deplore in these developments, it was not surprising that some of its members viewed his achievement with ambiguous feelings.

Churchill resembles Disraeli in many respects, not least in leaving behind a protean legacy that allowed his successors to link an unimagined future with his imagined past. The American illusion allowed the British ruling elite to pretend, to themselves and to their electorate, that Britain was a great power. The costs and consequences of that we live with today; some will welcome it, others not, but we cannot pretend to a neutrality on that part of the Churchillian legacy. More than that, by encouraging the belief that the road to power lay through Washington, Churchill's myth encouraged British statesmen, including himself during his peacetime premiership, to neglect Europe

[55] *The Reckoning*, p. 525.

in favour of the special relationship. This ignored the lessons to be drawn from the fact that twice in one generation Britain had found Europe so important that she had had to stake her imperial might on its freedom. Those voices raised in the first half of the 1940s to argue that Britain should take advantage of the unique position she had won in Europe to lead its unification were ignored in favour of Churchill's grander narrative. A more measured appreciation of the successes and failures of the American alliance might have encouraged a more realistic politics about Europe. Still, we should not complain too loudly. Churchill may have written history the way it ought to have been, but at least he paid it some regard and great respect – which is more than some of our modern politicians do.

CHURCHILL AND EAST–WEST DETENTE

By John W. Young

AS with many aspects of his career, Churchill's attitude towards the Soviet Union and Communism has generated considerable debate.[1] The same statesman who urged war on the Bolshevik regime in 1919 – likening it to 'troops of ferocious baboons' or 'a culture of typhoid'[2] – also urged co-operation with Stalin in the 1930s; he spent his last years in office calling for a summit meeting to reduce Cold War tensions, having himself stirred up those tensions with the 1946 Fulton Speech, where he coined the term 'Iron Curtain'. Where one historian has concluded that 'ideologically-based anti-Sovietism and anti-Communism were Churchill's most abiding obsession for some forty years', placing emphasis on the rhetoric of the intervention period[3]; another historian recognises that Churchill's language never reached such intensity again, that he sought to work with Stalin despite the latter's purges and that even the Fulton Speech praised the Soviet war effort, welcoming 'Russia to her rightful place among the leading nations of the world'.[4]

Few will doubt that Churchill genuinely detested Communism. By aiming at the destruction of monarchy, aristocracy, parliamentary democracy and private property, as well as the British Empire, its ideology was directed against all that he cherished. But there is a debate about whether ideological differences made Churchill 'obsessive' in his anti-Communism or whether he was capable of a more subtle approach to the subject. This essay concentrates on his pursuit of a summit in the 1950s and argues that, in fact, his desire for détente was quite consistent with his anti-Communism. However, once the USSR had the atomic bomb, he realised that Communism was most safely undermined, not by war but by diplomacy, trade and security agree-

[1] I am grateful to the British Academy for providing financial support for the research that led to this article.

[2] Martin Gilbert, *Winston S. Churchill*, IV (1975), 227 and 257.

[3] David Carlton, *Churchill and the Soviet Union* (Manchester, 2000), 200 and see 201–2 for the emphasis on 1919–20.

[4] Ian S. Wood, *Churchill* (2000), chapter 4; and, for the Fulton Speech, Randolph S. Churchill, *The Sinews of Peace* (1948), 93–105.

ments that would 'infiltrate' the Soviet bloc and eventually dissolve totalitarianism from within.[5]

Churchill and the USSR before 1950

As his political life developed, and particularly after 1929, Churchill increasingly focused on foreign, imperial and defence issues. He had a view of international affairs that best fits within the 'realist' school of analysis: countries are involved in a struggle for power in an anarchic environment; under the logic of the 'balance of power', the weak must band together if the strong are to be resisted; and alliances and armed forces are a better guarantee of survival than international law or organisations. His complaint against the appeasers in the 1930s was not that they negotiated with Hitler but that they did so from a position of weakness, that they 'neither prevented Germany from rearming, nor did they rearm themselves in time ... and they neglected to make alliances'.[6] Yet Churchill also believed that certain groups of countries could share a common outlook, hence his interest in co-operation with the 'English-speaking' Dominions, in European unity and in a 'special relationship' with America. He believed in promoting trade links as a way to ensure peace, he favoured active diplomacy and, partly because he believed in the balance of power, he was ready to respect the sphere of influence of rival states – so long as they did not impinge on Britain's. In December 1950 he even declared that, while 'Appeasement from weakness and fear is ... fatal. Appeasement from strength is magnanimous ... and might be the surest way to peace.'[7] This may seem to be at odds with his dislike of totalitarianism, but in fact it was not in contradiction to it, because, alongside his *realpolitik*, Churchill also had a faith in humanity that told him that repressive regimes could not last forever.

Where the USSR was concerned Churchill's realism led him to accept, by the 1930s, that it would exist for some time and was an essential component in any anti-German balance of power. Roland Quinault has argued that this was consistent with Churchill's view of

[5] I first made the case that Churchill accepted 'the division of Europe in the short-term whilst hoping eventually to see a withering away of Soviet Communism' in *Winston Churchill's Last Campaign* (Oxford, 1996), quote from vi–vii; but I was deeply indebted to two earlier works: Kenneth Thompson, *Winston Churchill's World View* (Baton Rouge, 1983); and S. J. Lambakis, 'The Soviet Union and Churchillian Diplomacy' (Ph.D. thesis, Catholic University of America, 1990).

[6] Martin Gilbert, *Winston S. Churchill*, v (1976), 999.

[7] Robert Rhodes James (ed.), *Winston S. Churchill: His Complete Speeches, 1897–1963* (8 vols., New York, 1974), 8143.

Russia since before the 1917 revolution; that he had a 'persistent belief that Russia was a major and essential element in the international community ...' and 'always regarded Russia as a natural ally of Britain and other powers who wished to check German ascendancy in Europe'.[8] His dealings with the USSR during the Second World War are still the focus of much debate. In his memoirs, written as the Cold War began, he naturally portrayed himself as a tough opponent of Stalin, an approach some historians have followed.[9] But others argue that Churchill's military strategy for most of the war was not well geared to limiting Soviet influence at the end of it.[10] Two of the most detailed studies of wartime policy towards the USSR see him as uncertain in his overall approach: for Martin Kitchen, the prime minister genuinely sought a good working relationship with Stalin, underestimated the revolutionary content of Soviet policy and, even in 1945, wavered over taking a firmer stand; while for Martin Folly, Churchill was quite prepared in the last months of the war to talk sharply to the Soviets' when he felt agreements were being broken, but at the Potsdam summit in July he was 'hardly ... uncompromising'. In particular the prime minister looked positively on Stalin's desire for a warm-water port, giving the Soviets access to the world's oceans.[11]

The most controversial of Churchill's wartime dealings with Stalin was the so-called 'percentage deal' of October 1944, the essence of which was that Britain preserved Greek independence of Moscow while the Soviets gained predominance in Romania and Bulgaria. As John Charmley has argued, the 'percentage deal' was no aberration but an attempt to secure a deal on spheres of influence in Europe that would restrain Stalin's ambitions and provide the basis for Britain and the USSR to work together after the war.[12] Faced by a deteriorating position in the Balkans, and with the US unwilling to engage in such divisions of territory, the prime minister put his faith in secret diplomacy, a head-to-head meting and a spheres of influence arrangement that fitted his *realpolitik*. Such an approach was to be revived by him when he returned to the premiership in 1951. Indeed, in 1953 Churchill was even to recall the October 1944 visit to Moscow as 'the highest level

[8] Roland Quinault, 'Churchill and Russia', *War and Society*, 9 (1991), 99.

[9] For example, Richard G. Kaufman, 'Winston Churchill and the art of statecraft', *Diplomacy and Statecraft*, 3 (1992), 175.

[10] The thesis is best argued in T. Ben-Moshe, *Churchill: Strategy and History* (1992) or in John Charmley, *Churchill's Grand Alliance* (1995), chapters 3–14.

[11] Martin Kitchen, *British Policy towards the Soviet Union in the Second World War* (1986); Martin Folly, *Churchill, Whitehall and the Soviet Union* (2000), quote from 164.

[12] Charmley, *Grand Alliance*, 102–3. For other discussions of this episode see P.G.H. Holdich, 'A Policy of Percentages?' *International History Review*, 9 (1987), 28–47; and John Kent, *British Imperial Strategy and the Cold War* (Leicester, 1993), 23–33.

we ever reached' in Anglo–Soviet relations.[13] In the meantime, however, after losing office in the very midst of the Potsdam conference, Churchill was to become known, not for his desire to co-operate with the Soviets, but for urging resistance to them.

In the aftermath of the war Anglo-Soviet relations quickly became strained, not least over spheres of influence in the Near East. By November 1945 Churchill was advocating an alliance with America because the 'fact that ... the English-speaking world is bound together, will enable us to be better friends with Soviet Russia ... that realistic state.'[14] Four months later Churchill made his Fulton Speech, with its condemnation of the 'Iron Curtain' and its call for a 'special relationship between the British Commonwealth ... and the United States'. Although the image of the Iron Curtain became part of Cold War rhetoric, the logic of the speech was typical of Churchill's established outlook on the world: the Soviets were a threat, but 'there is nothing they admire as much as strength' and an Anglo-American alliance was necessary to deter them. But at the same time he spoke of his 'strong admiration ... for the valiant Russian people', advocated 'frequent and growing contact with them' and hoped that Western strength would pave the way for an East–West 'settlement'.[15] Over the following few years Churchill supported the unity of the West under American leadership, particularly with the Marshall plan and Atlantic alliance, while also referring to hopes of an East–West settlement. But he had radically different views, even in his own mind, about how to bring such a settlement about.

With the diplomatic breakdown between the USSR and the Western allies in late 1947, and especially during the dangerous months of the Berlin blockade, Churchill privately pressed an idea that had been forming in his mind for some time. Concerned that America's atomic monopoly would not last and fearful that the Cold War must at some point become hot, he wanted to force Stalin to accept a 'reasonable' settlement by threatening the USSR that – if they did not accept such a settlement – they would be subjected to nuclear attack. This was a dangerous twist to the logic of 'negotiation from strength' but Churchill avoided stating it baldly in public and he was far from being alone in such ideas. Various Americans advocated a pre-emptive strike against the USSR, if only to avoid a worse conflict later, and one air force general was sacked in 1950 for publicly urging this. Fortunately President Truman never accepted such logic. In London the idea of a showdown

[13] Lord Moran, *Winston Churchill: The Struggle for Survival* (1966), diary entry of 24 February 1953.
[14] Martin Gilbert, *Winston S. Churchill*, VIII (1988), 166–7.
[15] Churchill, *Sinews of Peace*, 93–105.

was contemplated by, among others, the chiefs of staff, Harold Macmillan and even the philosopher – and later anti-nuclear campaigner –
Bertrand Russell.[16] 'Either we must have a war against Russia before
she has the atom bomb', Russell once told an audience of schoolboys,
'or we will have to lie down and let them govern us.'[17]

Return to power, 1950–2

Even as he was privately contemplating a 'showdown' Churchill's
speeches were developing in parallel an alternative, long-term strategy
for securing victory in the Cold War. At the Party conference in
October 1948, a few months into the Berlin blockade he spoke against
'false hopes of a speedy ... settlement with Soviet Russia' and came
the closest he ever did in public to urging a 'showdown'; but he also
hoped that, if the USSR could be opened to 'the ordinary travel and
traffic of mankind', then it could lead 'the spell of ... Communist
doctrines to be broken.'[18] And in 1949, in New York, he said that the
Kremlin 'feared the friendship of the West' because 'free and friendly
intercourse' with the outside world would destroy Communism.[19] 'Contacts and trade', Martin Gilbert has written, 'these were the twin tracks
of Churchill's search for a way to ease the East–West divide.'[20] With
the end of the US atomic monopoly later that year, and the growing
danger thereafter of a Soviet nuclear strike on Britain, the desirability
of a 'showdown' became less attractive and it was the alternative ideas,
of opening contacts with the Soviets as the way to break down the Iron
Curtain, which came to the fore in Churchill's thinking. This was most
noticeable in his February 1950 election address in Edinburgh, where
he called for a 'parley at the Summit', which would be 'a supreme
effort to bridge the gulf between the two worlds, so that each can live
their life ... without the hatreds of the Cold War'. It was the first time
the word 'summit' had been used to describe an East–West leaders'
meeting and (like 'Iron Curtain') it soon became part of popular
vocabulary. But it would be wrong to contrast the messages of Edinburgh
and Fulton: just as the earlier speech had praise for Stalin and hoped
for a settlement of differences, so the later one condemned Soviet
expansionism and emphasised the importance of the US nuclear arsenal

[16] Young, *Last Campaign*, 23–28.
[17] Caroline Moorehead, *Bertrand Russell* (1992), 469.
[18] Randolph S. Churchill, *Europe Unite* (1950), 409–24.
[19] Randolph S. Churchill, *In the Balance* (1951), 32–9.
[20] Martin Gilbert, 'From Yalta to Bermuda and Beyond: In Search of Peace with the
Soviet Union', in James W. Muller (ed.), *Churchill as Peacemaker* (Cambridge, 1997), 322.

for Western defence.[21] It should also be noted that, as Churchill made clear in another speech some months later, one purpose of a summit would be 'to bring home to the ... Soviet government the gravity of the facts which confront us all'.[22] Thus, even if a nuclear attack were not actually to be threatened by the West, the danger of nuclear war was still seen as the way to induce Stalin to settle his differences with his former allies.

Once again the key to understanding Churchill's thinking was the concept of negotiation from strength. Both elements were generally present in his speeches but the precise balance between them, and the specific proposals that fleshed them out, varied according to the international situation and political needs at home. Despite helping to proclaim the Cold War, Churchill had 'a world view which was quite different to the one the Americans had adopted'; he condemned Communist tyranny and would resist it, but he was also imbued with the British diplomatic tradition that you might have to coexist with those you despised.[23] On returning to Downing Street in 1951 Churchill continued to believe that Communism must be resisted, that the West must be strongly armed – not least with a formidable nuclear arsenal – and that Britain must work closely with America. But he had no desire for a relentless anti-Communist crusade, he wanted to avoid a Soviet nuclear strike on Britain and he hoped to develop diplomatic, personal and trade links as ways of breaching the Iron Curtain.

Despite the Edinburgh speech, and similar calls from Churchill for a summit during the October 1951 election, he returned to power in the wake of taunts from the Labour party that he was a warmonger. These may have reinforced his determination to make his name as a great peacemaker, his reputation as a war leader being secure. His age (he was seventy-six) and his ill health (he had suffered a stroke in 1949) suggested he might not be in power long, but the very arteriosclerosis from which he suffered also made him more set in his ways. Had he been, at heart, an obsessive anti-Communist then it would have been abundantly obvious at this point, given his condition; but in fact he was to focus much of his energy before retirement on a relaxation of tension with the Soviets, undermining their rule through a policy of moderation rather than threat.[24] In early November he sent a message of 'Greetings' to Stalin[25] and told the Commons that there should be

[21] James, *Churchill Speeches*, 7285–93.
[22] *Ibid.*, 8048–50.
[23] Charmley, *Churchill's Grand Alliance*, 265.
[24] On the effect of Churchill's ill health see J. M. Post and R. S. Robins, *When Illness Strikes the Leader* (New Haven, 1993), 18–20, 43–5 and 67–8.
[25] Public Record Office [hereafter PRO], FO 371/94841/134, Churchill to Stalin, 4 Nov. 1951.

'an abatement of the Cold War by negotiation at the highest level.'[26] He was not alone in hoping for such a relaxation. Anthony Eden, also believed in active diplomacy to break down barriers, was prepared to make spheres of influence arrangements with the Soviets and, having returned to the foreign office, devoted his first major international speech, at the UN on 12 November 1951, to a plea for 'a truce to name-calling' in the Cold War.[27] The foreign office drew up a paper late in the year, on fighting the Cold War in the long-term, which seemed to echo Churchill's approach in some ways: the West must first seek an 'equilibrium between the two blocs'; it should then be ready for a 'period of coexistence' in which limited agreements could be possible; and eventually, if there were a 'change in the nature of the ... Soviet regime', there could be a 'genuine settlement.'[28] It soon became clear, however, that even if they shared Churchill's long-term hopes, Eden and the foreign office disliked the idea of an early summit, on a loose agenda, that put the ageing, ailing prime minister in the spotlight. Instead, the professional diplomats preferred talks at foreign ministers' level, on fixed topics, with careful preparation.

His own poor health and the scepticism of the foreign office were not the only problems to face the prime minister. Far more difficult to overcome was the negative attitude of the Truman administration. For Churchill the American alliance was essential to negotiation from strength, and he wanted an early visit to Washington in to establish a close working relationship with the White House. But Cold War fears were at their height in America, where McCarthyism was gathering pace. US planners saw little chance of fruitful talks with the USSR at present and they ruled out a summit meeting, at least until a settlement was achieved to the Korean War, which had been raging for over a year. They were also concerned that any relaxation of tension would undermine efforts to rearm the West, and especially the process of rearming West Germany. The US had proposed West German rearmament in late 1950 and had thereby stirred up a major controversy in the Atlantic alliance. France and other European countries eventually agreed to proceed only on the condition that German troops were securely lodged in a supranational European Army. Negotiations for a 'European Defence Community' (EDC) got underway in 1951 but any sign that the Cold War was ending could lead the French, in particular, to argue that the whole effort should be abandoned.[29]

Given the American position, it is unsurprising that Churchill's visit

[26] James, *Churchill Speeches*, 8296–7.
[27] Young, *Last Campaign*, 44–6 and 49–52.
[28] FO 371/125002/4, PUSC(51)16 (17 Jan. 1952).
[29] Based on Young, *Last Campaign*, 53–62 and 67–72.

to Washington in January 1952 saw no progress towards talks with
Stalin. When Churchill suggested that a tough Western policy towards
the USSR merely helped to solidify the Stalinist system, the US
secretary of state, Dean Acheson, dismissed the argument.[30] The Soviet
issue, originally placed first on the agenda, was not actually discussed
until the end of the visit, when Truman was quick to set out his doubts
about an early summit. He did reassure Churchill that America was
not planning a 'showdown' with Moscow, however, and in return the
prime minister said that, with regard to a Summit 'he would not do
anything ... to make things more difficult for the President'. This
meeting was noteworthy for making clear, once more, that Churchill's
desire for a summit was part of a broader campaign to undermine
Soviet power: the British record shows that time was devoted to the
issue of a 'psychological warfare' campaign to provoke division inside
the Eastern bloc.[31] After his North American visit, Churchill was well
aware that, with the start of the US election campaign, little progress
was possible on a summit. In March 1952 therefore he barely expressed
interest in the 'Stalin note', a Soviet proposal to sign a German peace
treaty on condition that a reunited Germany was neutralised between
East and West. In any case, the Stalin note seemed no more than a
last-ditch attempt to prevent the EDC Treaty being signed (an event
that occurred in May).[32] His enthusiasm for a summit revived over
summer, however, when it became obvious that the next American
president might be his old wartime colleague, Dwight Eisenhower. In
August, Churchill contemplated a summit with Eisenhower and Stalin,
where the Potsdam conference – still unfinished business for the prime
minister – 'would be reopened'.[33] But the signs from the American
election did not necessarily favour détente. The campaign was overshadowed by the bloody deadlock in Korea, McCarthyism was at its
most intense and John Foster Dulles (Eisenhower's chief spokesman on
foreign policy) emphasised the need to 'liberate' those living under
Soviet rule.[34]

[30] *Foreign Relations of the United States* [hereafter *FRUS*], *1952–4*, vol. *VI* (Washington,
1986), 530–42; Dean Acheson, *Present at the Creation* (1970), 597–9.
[31] PRO, CAB 134/3058, minutes of fifth plenary meeting (18 Jan. 1952); *FRUS, 1952–
4, VI*, 846–9.
[32] See Rolf Steininger, *The German Question: the Stalin Note of 1952 and the problem of
reunification* (New York, 1990).
[33] J. Colville (edited by J. Charmley), *The Fringes of Power: 10 Downing Street diaries* (1985),
650 and see 654.
[34] But Eisenhower did moderate his own line as the election approached: see Robert
A. Divine, *Foreign Policy and US Presidential Elections, 1952–60* (New York, 1974), 50–56.

Stalin's death and the call for a summit, 1953

In January 1953 Churchill arrived in New York to see Eisenhower, now president-elect. As in the meetings with Truman, the prime minister's purpose was both to establish a close working relationship and explore US views on détente. But again he left disappointed: for, while Eisenhower had expressed a readiness to hold a summit, he also suggested it need not involve the British![35] In late February the president spoke in public of a possible meeting with Stalin, without mentioning Britain: this led Churchill to tell the Commons, on 3 March, 'I should be quite ready at any time to meet President Eisenhower and Marshal Stalin . . .'[36] Ironically, however, it was the death of Stalin, only three days later, which really opened the way for Churchill's campaign for a summit. The new 'collective leadership' in Moscow was keen to install itself in power without any external complications and, within a week, made several statements that it wanted to settle international problems peacefully.[37] Churchill wasted little time in suggesting to Eisenhower that a summit should now be proposed but was rebuffed, the president arguing that the 'collective leadership' would merely use such an occasion for propaganda purposes.[38] In Washington, Dulles, now secretary of state, championed the view that now was the time to put pressure on the Soviets, not relax it; and this view tended to win out over the president's more positive approach. It took six weeks before Eisenhower made a public statement – the 'Chance for Peace' speech – welcoming the Kremlin's desire for peace but demanding hard evidence of its good intentions. Specifically, the US wanted to see an end to the Korean War, peace in Vietnam (where France was engaged in a colonial war with Communist-led nationalists) and the signature of an Austrian peace treaty.[39]

In London the foreign office, too, was sceptical about any real change in Soviet policy.[40] But Churchill continued to hope for détente, writing to Eisenhower on 11 April that 'there is a change of heart in Russia'

---

[35] PREM 11/422, record of meeting (8 January 1953); *FRUS, 1952–4, Secretary of State's Memoranda of Conversations* (microfilm, Washington, 1952); and see Colville, *Fringes*, 662–3.

[36] *Public Papers of the Presidents of the United States: Dwight D. Eisenhower, 1952* (Washington, 1960), 69–70; Hansard, *House of Commons Debates, Volume 512*, cols. 17–19.

[37] Denise Folliot (ed.), *Documents on International Affairs, 1953* (1956), 1–2, 8–9 and 11–13.

[38] Peter Boyle, *The Churchill–Eisenhower Correspondence, 1953–5* (Chapel Hill, NC, 1990), 31–2.

[39] Folliot (ed.), *Documents*, 45–51; and on the debates that preceded the speech see especially Walter W. Rostow, *Europe after Stalin* (Austin, Texas, 1982).

[40] But Eden did consider the possibility of meeting the Soviets at foreign minister's level. See Young, *Last Campaign*, 135–6 and 142–9.

and objecting to parts of the 'Chance for Peace' speech.[41] Only a few days later the prime minister's ability to shape British policy was strengthened when Eden was forced into hospital for a gallstones operation that went terribly wrong, forcing him into temporary retirement for several months. Churchill then took control of the foreign office himself and used a speech in Scotland on 17 April to speak of a 'new breeze blowing on the tormented world'.[42] He sent a number of messages to Eisenhower over the following weeks, suggesting either a summit or 'a personal contact' with Moscow. But the president was opposed to both these ideas.[43] So, on 11 May an exasperated Churchill used a speech on foreign affairs in the Commons to call for 'a conference on the highest level ... between the leading powers without long delay'. The details of what the summit would discuss were left deliberately vague, Churchill preferring to work to an open agenda. Junior ministers from the foreign office were only shown the speech a few hours before it was delivered. Eisenhower was not consulted at all.[44]

It has been claimed that Churchill 'did *not* have in view' any 'concrete agreements' between East and West in the 1950s; and that he did not 'advocate that the West should make any concessions ... on any of the great issues of the day ...'[45] This is simply mistaken. In fact, Churchill did seek concrete advances, not least a relaxation of East–West trade limits (discussed below). He was also ready to concede the creation of a Communist regime in North Vietnam in 1954, telling a US official that it made no sense to clash with the Soviets on 'the fringes' of the world.[46] But, most controversially of all, in the 11 May speech he advocated a 'new Locarno' pact for Europe, which would relax tensions in Central Europe and give the USSR a sense of security, not least by removing the danger of German irredentism. 'Russia has a right to feel assured that ... the ... Hitler invasion will never be repeated ...' This was not a one-sided concession, for his hope was that, under the new system, 'Poland will remain a friendly power ... though not a puppet state' of the Soviet Union. But the idea caused a furore in West Germany, where the Adenauer administration was within six months of an election. The problem for Adenauer was that the 'new Locarno' proposal, however it was pursued, spelt political danger. If it were to involve mutual recognition of Germany's existing borders, that would also mean acknowledging East Germany's existence and put off German

[41] Boyle, *Correspondence*, 41–2.
[42] James, *Churchill Speeches*, 8465–70.
[43] Boyle, *Correspondence*, 46–55.
[44] *House of Commons Debates, Volume 515*, cols. 883–98; Anthony Nutting, *Europe Will Not Wait*, 50.
[45] Carlton, *Soviet Union*, 203.
[46] PREM 11/645, record of conversation with Radford, 26 April 1954.

reunification for the foreseeable future: steps which Bonn – and Washington – were unwilling to take and which would alienate German voters. But if Germany had to be reunified before the 'new Locarno', then that threw open the whole issue of a German peace treaty.[47] For at least one German historian, the proposal suggested that Churchill was ready to sacrifice West Germany's alliance with the West in order to achieve stability in Europe.[48] After discussions with Adenauer later in May, Churchill avoided further public debate over the 'new Locarno' idea but continued to urge it in private meetings.[49]

Adenauer was not the only Western leader to be dismayed by the 11 May speech and it was soon clear that Churchill could not 'bounce' his allies into a summit. In Paris there was grave concern, not only that talk of a relaxation of Cold War tensions would undermine the government's attempts to ratify the EDC treaty, but also that Churchill intended to exclude France from a summit. As a result the French asked Eisenhower to arrange a three-power Western summit to try to control the British leader's ambitions. The president, equally concerned at the situation, agreed to do so. He won Churchill over to the idea partly by agreeing to hold the 'Western summit' on the British territory of Bermuda. Arranging this conference then proved difficult because the French government almost immediately fell from office, plunging France into weeks of political crisis.[50] The conference had still not met when, on 23 June, Churchill suffered an even more grievous blow, a crippling stroke, which forced him to avoid public appearances. Yet even without these problems, the idea of a summit might have come to nothing. Evidence from the Soviet archives suggests that, while ready to improve bilateral relations with Britain, the 'collective leadership' was cautious in its dealings with Churchill. The 11 May speech made little impact in Moscow, mainly because it was felt he would be unable to force a change of policy on Washington.[51]

Soviet policy was itself thrown into confusion in mid-June by the so-called 'Berlin rising'. It is now clear that this event, which in fact affected much of East Germany, was partly triggered by hopes of some Soviet leaders for a radical change of policy. In particular, Lavrenti

[47] Konrad Adenauer, *Errinerungen, 1953–5* (Stuttgart, 1966), 204–9.
[48] Klaus Larres, *Politik der Illusionen: Churchill, Eisenhower und die deutsche Frage* (Gottingen, 1995), 127–33; also Klaus Larres, 'Integrating Europe or ending the Cold War? Churchill's Post-War Foreign Policy', *Journal of European Integration History*, 2 (1996), 34–9. Other discussions of the 'New Locarno' proposal include Anthony Glees, 'Churchill's Last Gambit', *Encounter*, 64 (April 1985), 27–35; and Jurgen Foschepoth, 'Churchill, Adenauer und die Neutralisierung Deutschlands', *Deutschland Archiv*, 12 (1984), 1286–1301.
[49] Young, *Last Campaign*, 164–6 and 193.
[50] Based on Young, *Last Campaign*, 166–76.
[51] Uri Bar-Noi, 'The Soviet Union and Churchill's Appeals for High-Level Talks, 1953–4,' *Diplomacy and Statecraft*, 9 (1998), 112–18.

Beria, chief of the secret police, was ready to contemplate the reunification and neutralisation of Germany.[52] Churchill's reaction to the
rising – which occurred just before his stroke – was astonishing, but
very revealing of the extent to which he wanted to pursue détente: he
complained when allied representatives in Berlin condemned the Red
Army's crushing of the rising; he even told one British general that the
Soviets had the right to enforce martial law 'in order to prevent anarchy
...'[53] As it was the rising proved a further blow to any hopes of a 'thaw'
in the Cold War. Following Churchill's stroke, the Bermuda conference
had to be postponed. Instead, Lord Salisbury became acting foreign
secretary and went to Washington to discuss the international situation
with Dulles and the French foreign minister, Georges Bidault. With the
last two opposed to a summit with the Soviets, it was agreed instead
to seek an East–West foreign ministers' meeting on a precise agenda,
including the German problem. But, in the wake of the Berlin rising
the Soviets were keen to stabilise their position in East Germany before
opening the German question for debate with the West. As a result,
they stalled on the idea of a foreign ministers' meeting for several
months.[54]

The renewed campaign and a Cabinet crisis, 1953–4

As Churchill recovered from his stroke, the drive to obtain what he
now called 'easement', linked to the idea of a summit, became one of
the very few issues that interested him. To the despair of his fellow
ministers, the hope of achieving an improved international atmosphere
became the prime motive for the leader's refusal, despite his deteriorating health, to hand over to Eden – who had himself recovered
from illness by October 1953. Some might argue that détente became
a mere rationalisation of Churchill's desire to cling to office; and in
such a character the mix of selfish and idealistic motives was doubtless
complex. But his commitment to détente, and particularly his wish for
a summit, was already obvious *before* his stroke and the tenacity with
which he pursued his aim, especially in mid-1954, shows that it
motivated him strongly. As he explained to Eisenhower (who remained
unmoved by the argument), there was no question 'of being fooled by
the Russians'; Churchill was all too aware of the military threat they
posed to Western Europe; but he believed that the Western alliance
was solid enough to negotiate from a position of strength now, and

[52] See Amy Knight, *Beria* (Princeton, 1994), 191–4.
[53] PRO, FO 800/822, Churchill to Coleman, 22 June.
[54] Based on Young, *Last Campaign*, 184–202.

that time would lead to 'the ebb of Communist philosophy ...'[55] Some hope of progress was given by the end of the Korean War in July and Churchill told the party conference on 10 October – the occasion that marked his return to active political life – that he was staying in office 'not because of love of power' but because of his hopes of 'sure and lasting peace'.[56] Soon after that he succeeded in reviving the proposal for a 'Western summit' and a date of early December was set for the Bermuda conference.

Any hope that Churchill had of persuading the US and French governments to accept the specific idea of a summit with the Russians was undermined in late November when Moscow finally accepted the proposal for a four-power foreign ministers' meeting. This was arranged for Berlin in late January. The claim, that Churchill 'spent a large portion' of the Bermuda meeting, arguing for a summit.[57] With any diplomatic talks now destined to occur between foreign ministers, what Churchill did focus on was general arguments for a détente policy: the fact that the West was strong enough to pursue this; the desirability of testing whether there was a real change of policy in the Kremlin; the wisdom of providing Moscow with security guarantees in Europe; and his belief that trade and personal contacts could be used to 'infiltrate' the Iron Curtain and undermine Communism from within. But Eisenhower stated that the Kremlin was a 'whore' who had done no more than change her appearance in recent months and the French made it quite clear that signs of a 'thaw' were weakening the Western alliance, by undermining support in the French parliament for the EDC.[58] Churchill, though never enthusiastic about the EDC, reluctantly recognised that it must be passed if Western unity were to be preserved and 'peace through strength' pursued. If it were not passed, then the US could fall back on a 'peripheral' defence strategy, leaving continental Europe open to Communist advances.[59] This would undermine the very Western position of strength that he saw as essential to successful dealings with Moscow.

Churchill complained that the Bermuda communiqué showed not 'the slightest desire for the success of the (Berlin) conference ...'[60] Sure enough the foreign ministers' gathering quickly became deadlocked on the future of Germany. But Churchill urged Eden to avoid a complete

---

[55] Boyle, *Correspondence*, 82–6.

[56] James, *Churchill Speeches*, 8494–7.

[57] M. Steven Fish, 'After Stalin's Death: the Anglo-American Debate over a New Cold War', *Diplomatic History*, 10 (1986), 352.

[58] Based on Young, *Last Campaign*, 222–9.

[59] PREM 11/618, Churchill to Eden, 6 Dec.

[60] PREM 11/418, Churchill to Eden, 7 Dec.

breakdown and bid the Soviets 'au revoir and not goodbye'.[61] He got his wish. Before Berlin closed on 18 February, it was agreed that there should be another foreign ministers' conference a few months later in Geneva, to discuss Far Eastern problems. Before this conference met, Churchill's hopes of moving the negotiations to leaders' level received encouragement from an unexpected source: the Kremlin. There were now signs that elements in Moscow realised Churchill might genuinely be aiming at a relaxation of tension the prime minister, Georgi Malenkov, wanted to exploit and, in March, a member of the Soviet embassy approached Churchill's son-in-law, Christopher Soames, saying a meeting between the two premiers was possible.[62] This was welcome to Churchill, but he felt he should visit Eisenhower first, in order to win him over.[63] Before looking at how the proposal developed, however, it is important to note that Churchill's efforts to improve East–West relations in another area, that of trade, also reached their height at this time.

Apart from advocating a summit meeting and a 'new Locarno', Churchill's campaign for détente included one other main proposal: a reduction of East–West trade limits. In 1950, Western countries had created the Co-ordinating Committee (COCOM), which agreed on lists of goods that would be banned or subjected to quantitative limits in trade with the Communist bloc. The issue had become a source of US-European disagreement, with the Americans pressing for tougher limits than European governments felt necessary.[64] Eisenhower's election seemed to promise a fresh approach and there has been considerable debate about how successful the President was in pushing a new policy. Eisenhower, like Churchill, saw détente in the trade field as a way to create 'centrifugal' forces in the Soviet bloc: freer trade would create ties between Eastern European counties and the West. But he met strong opposition in Washington and, in October 1953, merely proposed to cut 'peripheral' items from COCOM lists.[65] For Churchill this was

[61] PREM 11/664, Churchill to Eden, 15 Feb.

[62] Bar-Noi, 'Soviet Union', 122–4.

[63] See especially Moran, *Struggle for Survival*, diary entry of 8 April 1954.

[64] On the background to this issue see especially: A. Dobson, *The Politics of the Anglo-American Economic Special Relationship* (Brighton, 1988), 125–34; V. Sorenson, 'Economic Recovery Versus Containment: the Anglo-American Controversy over East–West trade, 1947–51', *Co-operation and Conflict*, 24 (1989), 69–97; and F. M. Cain, 'Exporting the Cold War: British Responses to the USA's Establishment of COCOM, 1947–51', *Journal of Contemporary History*, 29 (1994), 501–22.

[65] For praise of Eisenhower on trade see: P. Funigiello, *American-Soviet Trade in the Cold War* (Chapel Hill, NC, 1988), 77; and R. M. Spaulding, 'A Gradual and Moderate Relaxation of Tension: Eisenhower and the Revision of American Export Control Policy', *Diplomatic History*, 17 (1993), 224. But for a critical view: T. E. Forland, ' "Selling Firearms to the Indians": Eisenhower's Export Control Policy', *Diplomatic History*, 15 (1991), 226–33.

not enough. In January he told the Cabinet that 'increased trade with the Soviet bloc would mean, not only assistance to our exports, but greater possibilities for infiltration behind the iron curtain'.[66] Then, on 25 February (despite pressure from Dulles to avoid such a step[67]) he pressed for a reduction of COCOM lists in a speech to the Commons. The speech is widely accepted as a turning point in the story of East–West trade.[68] It allowed Eisenhower to push his own administration towards compromise and by August COCOM lists had been almost halved. 'The main impetus behind the revisions, though, came not from Eisenhower, but from Winston Churchill.'[69] Once again he had proved ready to speak out publicly on East–West contacts, risking an argument with the US; and trade relaxations were to prove the only concrete success of his pressures for détente.

Churchill's hopes of a two-power summit with Malenkov came to nothing in mid-1954, largely because of the same problems he had faced before: opposition from within his own government and from the US, and suspicion from the Soviets. But in the process he demonstrated the extraordinary lengths to which he was prepared to go in order to achieve his last political dream. He faced an initial delay because of the difficulty in timetabling his visit to Eisenhower. This did not take place until late June, largely because it needed to be dovetailed with a recess in the Geneva conference, so that Eden and Dulles could also be in Washington. Once he saw Eisenhower, Churchill won a remarkable *coup*. The American leader agreed there could be a bilateral meeting.[70] The exact reason for this fateful concession is unclear; but of course Eisenhower had earlier reserved his own right to meet the Soviets on a bilateral basis. On the sea-voyage home Churchill, armed with Eisenhower's approval, drafted a message to Moscow, enquiring whether they would welcome a visit from him. Despite some doubts from Eden, the message was sent off immediately, without the cabinet or foreign office being consulted. But such devious methods only ensured that, when Churchill arrived home in July, there was a cabinet crisis. Some ministers, already exasperated with their chief's declining mental state, his inefficient leadership of government and personal

[66] CAB 128/27, CC(54)3rd (18 Jan.).
[67] FO371/111207/29, Berlin to FO, reporting Dulles-Eden conversation, 18 February.
[68] James, *Churchill Speeches*, 8535–6; G. Adler-Karlsson, *Western Economic Warfare* (Stockholm, 1968), 91; Forland, 'Selling Firearms', 223; Spaulding, 'Moderate Relaxation', 241–2.
[69] Ian Jackson, 'The Eisenhower Administration, East–West Trade and the Cold War', *Diplomacy and Statecraft*, 11 (2000), 135; and see 129–35 on the 1954 talks. In general see also John W. Young, 'Winston Churchill's Peacetime Administration and the Relaxation of East-West Trade Controls', *Diplomacy and Statecraft*, 7 (1996), 125–40.
[70] FO371/125143/59, record of meeting, 25 June; *FRUS, 1952–4, VI*, 1079–80.

obsessions were determined to resist his latest attempt to circumvent cabinet government.

The opposition was led by Salisbury, who threatened to resign, but Eisenhower also helped the prime minister's critics by expressing surprise at the speed of his approach to Moscow. After some bitter clashes the cabinet agreed, on 9 July, to await the outcome of the Geneva conference before deciding how to proceed. But this simply put off the hour of decision: Geneva, though it resulted in a settlement of the Indo-China war, did nothing to shift Churchill and Salisbury from their positions vis-à-vis a summit. A cabinet meeting on 23 July was as acrimonious as any earlier in the month and it still seemed as though the government could fall apart. Churchill's behaviour at this time, his determination to seek a bilateral meeting and his willingness to offend so many key ministers, argues against those who question the sincerity of his interest in détente.[71] What eventually saved cabinet unity, and ended Churchill's hopes of a Moscow visit, was the behaviour of the Kremlin. The Soviet foreign minister, Vyacheslav Molotov was especially sceptical about a bilateral meeting, partly because the Soviets still harboured doubts about Churchill's intentions, but also, it seems, because any summit would strengthen the hand of Malenkov within the collective leadership. By 24 July Molotov had persuaded his fellow ministers to sidestep the issue and call instead for four-power talks on a European-wide security system.[72] It was this initiative that allowed the embattled Churchill to back away from a bilateral summit and end the mounting criticism within his own ranks. He now wrote to Molotov arguing that the Soviet proposals were at odds with a bilateral meeting and withdrew the suggestion of one.[73]

End of office

Despite his defeat Churchill, was unapologetic about his search for détente. On 3 August he circulated a cabinet paper, arguing that two decades of peace would bring profound changes within the Communist bloc On 18 August came another, suggesting he might initiate a bilateral meeting again, once EDC was approved.[74] But it was at this point that the Achilles heal of the Atlantic alliance was fully exposed. On 31 August the French assembly refused to ratify the EDC treaty and threw the Western alliance into confusion. Hopes of a negotiation with Moscow from a position of strength were lost and Churchill's remaining

---

[71] Based on Young, *Last Campaign*, 270–84.
[72] Bar-Noi, 'Soviet Union', 124–7.
[73] PREM 11/670, Churchill to Molotov, 26 July.
[74] CAB 129/70, C(54)263 (3 Aug.) and 271 (18 Aug.).

months as premier were dominated by the results of the action. Only in late December did the national assembly approve a plan for German entry into NATO, but the French senate did not follow suit until March. By then Churchill's summit hopes had suffered another blow, with the fall from power of Malenkov. In the wake of this, and with a general election looming, the British premier, too, agreed to set a date for his departure. In mid-March he did think again about a summit, but this time Eden showed forceful opposition, and Churchill finally retired on 7 April.[75] His most famous public statement about East—West relations during these months was his erroneous claim, in a short speech at Woodford in November, that he ordered the stockpiling of weapons in Germany in 1945 for use against the Soviets. The theme of Woodford was actually negotiation from strength, the basis on which he always planned his march to the summit. But his plea for 'closer contact with Russia' was drowned out in the ensuing press furore over the German weapons.[76]

Ironically, Churchill resigned only months before the first East—West summit since Potsdam, ten years before. The solution of the problem of German rearmament put the West in the position of strength for negotiations that he had sought. At the same time the Kremlin saw advantages in a meeting: the new predominant figure, Nikita Khruschev, believed this would solidify his hold on power; and, by signing a treaty in May that neutralised Austria, the Soviets hoped to demonstrate that a similar solution was possible for Germany. In concluding the Austrian State Treaty, Moscow fulfilled the last of the conditions that Eisenhower set for a summit in the 'Chance for Peace' speech. But the US was not keen on a conference and it was Eden who pressed most for one. Facing a general election, the new premier saw this as one way of ensuring a Conservative victory. 'How much more attractive a top-level meeting seems when one has reached the top', remarked Churchill.[77] The summit, held in Geneva in mid-July, seemed to improve the international atmosphere – there was much talk of 'the spirit of Geneva' – but produced no concrete breakthrough.[78] The problems of German reunification, European security, disarmament and East—West contacts were only discussed there in outline. Detailed talks were held at a separate foreign ministers' conference three months later and, as Churchill had always predicted, such a conference produced only

[75] Based on Young, *Last Campaign*, chapter 12.
[76] James, *Churchill Speeches*, 8598, and see 8609–22 for a subsequent exchange with Labour critics in the Commons.
[77] Harold Macmillan, *Tides of Fortune* (1969), 587.
[78] See Gunter Bischof and Saki Dockrill (eds.), *Cold War Respite: the Geneva Summit of 1955* (Baton Rouge, 2000).

390 TRANSACTIONS OF THE ROYAL HISTORICAL SOCIETY

deadlock.[79] Undismayed, Churchill continued to urge détente for a time, notably in a 1956 speech in Aachen, where he wanted to break down 'bloc politics' and work for a new 'Unity of Europe', in which the Eastern countries would regain their independence.[80]

Conclusion

Michael Howard has described Churchill as a 'prophet of détente', someone who 'looked beyond the hostile ideology of the Soviet state to the evolution of the Russian people themselves' and who recognised 'their growing restiveness at the deprivation enforced by the regime, a restiveness only likely to increase as their contacts with the West multiplied ...'[81] Howard's short essay does not look in detail at Churchill's ideas beyond his calls for a summit and it would be unhistorical to draw too close a parallel between the Cold War in the 1950s and the situation two decades later, when East–West relations were dominated by the effects of mutually assured destruction and the Vietnam War. But it is certainly possible to see Churchill as an early representative of those, more numerous in later decades, who argued that the safest way to fight Soviet Communism was to engage in contact with it and try to break down the hold it had on the peoples of the Eastern bloc. The specific subjects that Churchill emphasised in his campaign for détente – the need to avoid nuclear war, the desirability of a recognised dividing line in Europe (the 'new Locarno') and an expansion of trade between the two blocs – were paralleled in the 1970s by the SALT negotiations, the talks on security and co-operation in Europe and the relaxation of trade limits. Henry Kissinger, a prime architect of 1970s détente took some interest in the British statesman's ideas, seeing them as far-sighted, if somewhat incoherent.[82] Yet Churchill also seems to have had the main attributes of a particularly *European* approach to détente, later identified with Charles de Gaulle or Willy Brandt: a desire to restrain the US from extreme action, to avoid a crusading form of anti-Communism and to mediate between Washington and Moscow; a readiness to engage in trade and talks with the Eastern bloc, to respect the other side's sphere of influence and to develop an ordered relationship with them; and an acceptance of the

[79] John W. Young, 'The Geneva Conference of Foreign Ministers, October–November 1955: Acid Test of Détente', in Bischof and Dockrill (eds.) *Cold War Respite*, 271–91.
[80] James, *Churchill Speeches*, 8674–6.
[81] Michael Howard, 'Churchill: Prophet of Détente', in R. Crosby Kemper III (ed.), *Winston Churchill* (Columbia, 1996), 177–88, quote from 188.
[82] Henry Kissinger, *Diplomacy* (1994), 506–14.

reality of European division in the short term whilst hoping for the breakdown of Communism in the long term.[83]

It is easy to list the main reasons why, notwithstanding his formidable international reputation, Churchill's attempts to initiate détente resulted only in a relaxation of certain trade controls. His own ill health was one factor, particularly his stroke in 1953. Increasingly, his worsening health, his lack of energy and tendency to become obsessed with one issue, made cabinet ministers anxious both to end his hopes of a summit and to be rid of him. In any case, the foreign office never liked the idea of an East—West summit with an open agenda and neither did the Americans. Churchill vastly overestimated his own influence, and the power of his country, when he felt he could act as the Cold War's mediator. US opposition was highly significant, because Churchill wanted to negotiate with the Soviets from a position of strength and that demanded a united Western alliance. But France (because of its desire to secure a European Army) and West Germany (because of Adenauer's opposition to reunification on the basis of neutralisation) were also fearful of Churchill's aims. Even the USSR showed little interest in his schemes. Indeed, Uri Bar-Noi's work in the Soviet archives provides 'proof that Churchill's attempts to bring about a relaxation of the Cold War were greeted with distrust and scepticism' in Moscow. Malenkov did consider meeting the British premier, but Molotov and others were 'neither interested in a three-power summit, nor ... inclined to hold ... Anglo-Soviet talks ... They were mistrustful of Churchill's intentions and had doubts as to whether he had the ability to persuade his American allies to modify their Cold War diplomacy'.[84]

In a sense, Molotov's position was quite justified. Churchill's anti-Communism cannot be doubted, nor can his deep commitment to the American alliance. However, he was a highly complex character whose personal ambition, approach to international relations and understanding of British national interests led him to dedicate the last few years of his active political career to reducing Cold War tensions. There was an *apparent* paradox here but not an actual one. For it was only his belief in the strength of the Anglo-American position, including the position of a superior nuclear capability that allowed him to contemplate negotiations with Moscow: these had to be pursued from a position of strength. And his hope was that détente, through allowing peaceful penetration of the Soviet bloc, would eventually contribute to its withering away. Thus, while he might want to lower the dangers of an East—West conflict in which Britain would be a prime nuclear target,

---

[83] See the definition in Kenneth Dyson (ed.), *European Détente* (1986), 2–5.
[84] Bar-Noi, 'Soviet Union', 111–12.

he was actually still *fighting* Soviet totalitarianism, a point that some historians of the subject even now fail to grasp.[85] Trade, personal contacts and security arrangements like a 'new Locarno', might mean the survival of Communism in the short-term; but in the long-term Churchill believed that it was a doctrine that could not survive. In December 1952 he even told his private secretary, John Colville, that the latter, if he lived his normal span, would see the collapse of Communism in Eastern Europe.[86] It was not a bad estimate: Colville died in 1987.

[85] For example, Carlton, *Soviet Union*, 162–96 and 202–4.
[86] Colville, *Fringes of Power*, 657–8.

CHURCHILL REMEMBERED

Recollections by Tony Benn MP, Lord Carrington, Lord Deedes and Mary Soames

[The following is a transcription of a panel discussion chaired by Professor David Cannadine in the Chancellor's Hall, Senate House, University of London, on Thursday 11 January 2001].

TONY BENN: Time does funny things to your memory. For the whole of my childhood Winston Churchill was a political giant, but my grandfathers always referred to him as 'young Winston', because one of them was born in 1850 (I never knew him) and the other in 1863, eleven years before Winston was born. All three of them, both my grandfathers and my father, sat with Winston when he was a Liberal before the First World War, and although it may sound impertinent, in our family we always referred to him as Winston, never Churchill, it was just Winston: 'What did Winston say', 'Young Winston' and so on. I had the honour of sitting with him for fourteen years in the House of Commons and have recollections of that time.

Churchill's early politics, the politics of before the First World War, were of course quite radical Liberal politics. The historians will correct me if I am wrong, but I think he set up the labour exchanges, and therefore had an idea that labour had rights. Was he involved in the troops going to the Rhondda? In Wales there is still a recollection of that. But I quoted him regularly in the House of Commons, because in 1914, as first lord of the admiralty, at the time the navy was shifting from having coal-fired ships to oil-fired, he nationalised British Petroleum, and when I did the same with the British National Oil Corporation I used to entertain the House of Commons with the exact words that Winston used in 1914. He bought the Anglo-Iranian Oil Company for £2 million (BP) and he used the most powerful language about how multi-national trusts were squeezing the government of the day and so on. He was well to the left of New Labour, but that covers a very wide range of opinion!

My mother in 1914, it must have been just after the outbreak of the First World War (her father was a member of course at the time) was in the gallery of the House of Commons when Churchill, as first lord of the admiralty, made a statement about some naval engagement. I have never checked it in Hansard and many stories are not true, but I think this one must be. She used to repeat as best she could the phrase he used. He said, 'And I hope the whole Housh will be glad to hear that the German shubmarine wash purshued and shunk' – and that was her recollection of young Winston.

Of course in the 1920s Churchill, as chancellor of the exchequer, followed a policy now being followed by the present chancellor: then it was called the gold standard, now it is called prudence. But he followed a policy which undoubtedly did him an enormous amount of damage among his contemporaries, because it was thought that that absolute purity of economic policy contributed to the difficulties that came in 1929, and I have often thought that if Winston had died in 1931 the recollection of him would have been probably as a failure, even though it would have been quite untrue, whereas of course he lived to achieve far greater things.

Winston was of course a Liberal Imperialist. My father, who was secretary for India 1929–31, had a number of clashes with Winston in the House of Commons. I was introduced to Mr Gandhi in 1931, when I was six years old, I was taken by my father to see him – I have no recollection of what he said or anything I said, which would not have mattered – but I was much impressed by the way in which he took an interest in children. I think I am right that Churchill described him as 'the naked fakir loping up the steps of the viceregal lodge to parley on equal terms with the representative of the King-Emperor'. And I have a video of Winston from the 1930s, in which he talks about 600 million poor benighted Indians, who depended on the empire to preserve their society. That was his position and although it is easy now to dismiss imperialism, it was part of the whole philosophy that illuminated the thinking not just of Conservatives but of many Liberals as well.

The first time I ever heard him speak was in 1937, when my father, who had been defeated in 1931, was re-elected and he took me to the House of Commons as a twelve-year-old boy, introduced me to Lloyd George, and I sat in the gallery and I heard Winston warn about the Nazis. In our household the hostility to Neville Chamberlain and appeasement was enormous and the admiration for Winston was very, very great. When he went back to the admiralty in 1939, before he became prime minister, a message was sent out 'Winston is back', so the navy knew he was there, and then, of course, when he took over after the famous Norway debate, he provided absolute inspiration to everybody. I lived in London during the blitz and I remember it very well indeed. The speeches that he made really did inspire us. On his eightieth birthday when he made a speech, which I attended, at Westminster Hall, you were probably there Mary Soames (was that when the picture was given to him which subsequently came to an unfortunate end?), he dismissed his role. He said: 'People say I was the lion. The British people were the lion and I was privileged to give the roar.' I remember that very modest account of his interpretation of his role as a political leader.

There is a family story here you will allow me perhaps to tell. In the summer of 1940, when the war was really going very, very badly, there was a big discussion in the press as to whether children should be sent to America. My brother David, who was then twelve, wrote a letter to my mother saying 'I would rather be bombed to fragments than leave this country'. My mother wrote to *The Times* about it. Brendan Bracken drew this to Winston's attention and in the middle of this period of war Winston, in his own hand, wrote a letter to my mother about it. My brother has this letter, the copy is in the Churchill Library in Churchill College, Cambridge, and he sent my brother a copy of *My Early Life*. Now you think of a prime minister having time to write a manuscript letter at that period in history! It is just an indication of the extraordinary qualities of the man.

About a year later, when Winston and Clem [Attlee] were in coalition, Winston said to Clem 'We need a few more Labour peers' and so Clem said to my dad 'Would you like a peerage?' My dad was then sixty-four or something, he had rejoined the air force because he felt during the war you had to fight and not be a parliamentarian – he ended up as an air gunner before they caught up with him, because he had been a pilot in the First World War. He took the peerage, he didn't consult me, which made me very angry, but he asked my elder brother, because of course in those days there were no life peerages, and my elder brother didn't care one way or the other. Then my brother was killed in 1944, so by the time I got into Parliament in 1950 as a member of the House of Commons my father was already seventy-three, but the local Labour constituency association very sweetly never raised the matter of the peerage at the selection conference, though I did tell them.

Dingle Foot once told me a marvellous story about the difference between a cabinet that Winston presided over and a cabinet presided over by Clem. Dingle was parliamentary secretary at the ministry of economic warfare, a very junior job, and he was occasionally brought into the cabinet with some issue that had to be clarified. He said when Winston was in the chair, which was most of the time, he had the opportunity of hearing the most brilliant historical summary of the whole history of the human race, culminating in the period they had reached, and he said 'I left the Cabinet without knowing what I had to do.' When Clem was in the chair he would say 'Right minister, what is it', 'Right, agreed, right', and he said 'I left the Cabinet about two minutes later, knowing exactly what I had to do.' Churchill's quality of historical analysis is difficult if you want a quick decision, but it is the only thing which makes politics tolerable.

The other thing I remember about the war was Winston's attitude to the alliance with the Soviet Union, because he had been a bitter critic of the Russian Revolution. But as soon as Hitler attacked Stalin in 1941 Winston came out one hundred per cent for the Anglo-Soviet alliance. I have copies of the magazine *British Ally*, which was published in English here and in Russian in the Soviet Union, and his support for the Soviet Union when they were bearing the brunt of the war was one of the factors that interested me.

Now we come to the end of the war. I was on a troopship coming back in 1945 and I heard his broadcast saying 'If Labour was elected a Gestapo would be introduced.' Clem, whatever his weaknesses, wouldn't harm a fly, but it was an indication that Winston in campaigning mode was capable of using fairly strong language. Actually he and Clem got on very well together. I think they had the same nanny at one time or another.

When I was elected an MP Clem was prime minister, but a year later Winston became prime minister again. In those days you could actually ask the prime minister a question and get an answer, a thing that is inconceivable nowadays, and I remember asking him a question about atomic weapons and I got a perfectly straightforward answer about the nature of our relationship with the United States. Clem Attlee came up to me afterwards and said 'You had *no* right to ask that question without consulting me. I am the only one who knows what the arrangements were', which was probably true. I think almost a couple of days after I was elected was the famous occasion when Winston pursued Clem over the question of an American admiral. Under the arrangements, before NATO I suppose, an American admiral was put in charge of the Atlantic fleet and Winston absolutely tore Clem into shreds at prime minister's question time. That was the day Mrs Attlee had asked the new MPs to tea, so I went to Number 10, very excited as a new MP, and Vi Attlee turned on Clem with absolute brutality and said 'You made a fool of yourself, why didn't you know the answer to the question that Winston was putting', and Clem scuttled out like a mouse, because he was so frightened of Vi!

In 1951, when Winston got back into power, he appointed Walter Monckton as Minister of Labour. Now Walter was a member of parliament for Bristol and I travelled down on the train with him at one stage and he gave a marvellous account of the occasion when Winston appointed him. 'All he said to me was "Walter, I want you to look after the home front" ', and that phrase, to deal with the whole of labour in terms of 'the home front' during a war, seemed to me very characteristic. Lady Violet [Bonham Carter], who I knew of course, adored Winston. I think he went to speak for her in the 1951 election and she said at the meeting 'A cat may look at a king.' She was a Liberal and he was a Conservative, but those were the early days of 'the third way'.

When it was clear I was going to be thrown out of the Commons when my dad died, I wrote to Winston: 'Dear Prime Minister, you refused a peerage, can you help me with my problem' and so on. And he wrote me a lovely letter back, saying 'I think yours is a very hard case, I think people *should* be able to give up their peerages.' He did add 'and resume them later', because coming from aristocratic stock the idea of giving them up forever would be a bit much! So I wrote to him and thanked him and said 'Can I publish your letter' and he said 'I can't, because it has to be confidential because I am Prime Minister.' But the day he resigned I wrote to him again and I said, 'Dear Sir Winston, now you are not in office, could I publish your letter' and do you know, within twenty-four hours of retiring, when he must have had ten million letters, he arranged to send me the same letter for publication. And when I was thrown out of the Commons and I fought a by-election, I must have been the only Labour candidate, I circulated 25,000 copies of a photocopy of Winston's letter, which played some part in getting me re-elected – and then of course thrown out again. The only time I ever spoke to him personally, I went up to thank him at the end of a vote at 10 o'clock and he said to me 'You must carry on' and I owe a lot of the victory that ultimately came to that.

I am very proud that my sons Stephen and Hilary, who is now a member of parliament, saw him from the gallery in the House of Commons. And of course I remember the 1945 election, which I forgot to mention, when we canvassed Number 10, before the Thatcher gates were up, and Jeremy Hutchinson, the Labour candidate, with me driving the loudspeaker van (which is much harder than flying a plane) went to Number 10, to the front door. Jeremy Hutchinson said 'I am the Labour candidate and I have got the electoral register here and there is a Mr Churchill I want to canvass', and the whole domestic staff were brought out, it was like *Upstairs, Downstairs*. The butler in the front said 'We are all Conservative in this house' and a maid at the back with a little bonnet, I give her full marks, said 'And we would lose our jobs if we weren't!'

I am very, very proud to have been a contemporary of Winston and to have known him. His memory will remain as an example of someone who believed what he said, said what he believed, did what he said he would do if he got there, even if you didn't agree with any of it.

LORD CARRINGTON: I think it was a very great pity that Tony Benn was encouraged by Winston Churchill to leave the House of Lords: we could have done with him, after that splendid speech he had made. I think that Bill Deedes and I are the only surviving members of the last Churchill administration. I must tell you that I was there in a very humble capacity, as parliamentary secretary to the Ministry of Agriculture and Fisheries and I can't say that I spent much time at that time in the cabinet room seeing the prime minister. In fact I think I only went into the cabinet room twice during that particular time and so you must forgive the inadequacy of what I have to say.

I would just like to say one or two things about what Winston Churchill meant to my generation, those of us who were growing up in the 1930s. Of course he was a very controversial figure. He was a hero in my home, partly because of his policy against appeasement, partly because my family were also Liberal Imperialists and they agreed with him about India. But of course in a way what he was saying at that time was against the mainstream feeling in the Conservative Party and in the Labour party, generally speaking, and I think that there were great doubts amongst ordinary people about his judgement, which I suppose in a way was reinforced when he supported the duke of Windsor at the time of the abdication crisis. He was I think to some extent mistrusted in the country, and even when he became prime minister, though most of us were rather pleased that a real leader was going to be prime minister rather than Neville Chamberlain.

My first cousin, Jock Colville, who was private secretary to Neville Chamberlain and so to speak inherited Winston Churchill at Number 10, in his diaries (which he should never have written) really made it quite clear what trepidation those at Number 10 felt when Winston Churchill arrived as prime minister. The diaries are very frank and I know they are true, because he used to talk to me about it. It didn't take him very long to realise what a mistake he had made.

For me and my generation, my fellow officers, it was a very great relief that we felt that we then had (I was in the army at the time) a man who was a leader, a fighter, with a soldier's reputation and with the power to inspire our partners. Those of us who were alive at that particular time will never forget the debt that we owe him. I mean, his voice on the radio, his unmistakable figure, that wonderful billycock hat that he wore, the boiler suit, the formidable face, the personification of resistance − it was impossible to believe in defeat when he was there.

At the time, in 1940, I was commanding a very great military outfit, the demonstration platoon at the Small Arms School in Hythe, and when we were not doing demonstrations and teaching people how to fire weapons we spent every night on the beaches at Hythe, which was a place where the Germans might have landed. In my platoon I had forty-eight men, three bren guns, forty-five rifles and my pistol, and we had three-and-a-half miles of beach. You won't believe this, but it simply never occurred to me that we were going to be defeated. I was really in a way rather sorry for the Germans if they arrived on my beach! I am quite sure that that spirit was very largely due to Winston Churchill: the feeling that we had a leader who inspired us and was determined that we weren't going to be beaten. Of course we didn't understand the problem, but it seemed to me then and it seems to me now that we were in good hands and that those now who are very critical about what happened simply weren't alive at the time and don't know what we who were there felt about him.

After the war I took my seat in the House of Lords, rather against my wishes, but I didn't have the guts of Tony Benn. I remember that when I first took my seat I decided to go and look down at the House of Commons from the peers' gallery at all these extraordinary figures whom one had known about during the war, who seemed larger than life, because there they had been headlines in the paper. I was quite convinced that they were going to look quite different from ordinary human beings, that they had bigger heads and haloes and were grander in every respect than ordinary people. I was deeply disappointed when I looked down from the Peers' Gallery to find that they were very ordinary people – with two exceptions. One (sitting on the opposition benches) was Winston Churchill, who looked quite different from everybody else in his bow tie and his black short coat and the pinstripe trousers and that extraordinary head and the sort of bulldog expression. He looked quite different from anybody else on the Conservative benches. And on the Labour government benches, there was Ernest Bevin, who also looked quite different from anybody else. He looked like some gigantic benign frog, but he looked a big man. Those were the two who, in my judgement, stood out.

Looking back on that, what a very difficult time that must have been for Winston Churchill. He must have felt how ungrateful the British public were to him when, after five or six years of war, he was defeated at the [1945] election. Whatever the reasons were, he behaved with remarkable generosity at that time.

About a year later, I became a whip in the House of Lords and there was a custom that the leader of the Conservative party came and had lunch once a year with the chief whip and the whips. Winston Churchill came along and we sat in the dining room of the House of Lords, and of course we looked at him with great awe because of his reputation. He was obviously either bored or in a very bad temper, or both, and for the first course and the meat course he never really spoke at all, he just sat there looking thoroughly bored and disagreeable. We were getting more and more uncomfortable and shifting about in our seats, when in through the door of the House of Lords dining room came Bessie Braddock, who, as some of you may remember, was rather large and had a considerable reputation. Winston Churchill looked at her as she went by and then she disappeared. He said 'Ah, there goes that constipated Britannia', and he was so pleased with this comment that he then became absolutely a different person and we saw something of the magic and the fascination of his personality.

Then when he became prime minister again in 1951, I must say it never occurred to me that anybody was going to offer me a job. So on the day after the election I was not waiting at the end of a telephone for Randolph Churchill to pretend that he was the prime minister and offer me a job. But I was, if one can be so politically incorrect, out shooting partridges at home. About 3 o'clock in the afternoon somebody came running up from the house and said to me 'Number 10 wants you on the telephone.' I was a bit surprised, so I hurried back and rang up Number 10 and I was put through and waited, and there was the prime minister on the end of the telephone. He said 'I hear you have been shooting partridges' and I said 'Yes, prime minister'. He said 'Would you like to join my shoot?' And there I was, appointed as parliamentary secretary to the ministry of agriculture and food. Now can you imagine the prime minister today ringing up the most humble parliamentary secretary to ask him if he would take a job in his government? I thought it was the most extraordinary thing to do, and something which I shall never forget.

About a couple of years later, there was a terrible scene, a terrible crisis, in Critchell Down. This was a situation in which the lines of the graph had crossed between the rights of the private owners of property and the need to produce maximum production of food. The ministry of agriculture, and I indeed, had taken the view that maximum production of food, because we still had rationing, was more important than the rights of the owners. But now the rights of the owners became more important than the production of food. There was a terrible scandal and everybody was blamed and Tom Dugdale, my boss, resigned. I thought since I had been wrong too I had better resign as well, so I put in my resignation. I was sent for by the prime minister to the cabinet room and he said to me 'You put in your resignation.' I said 'Yes prime minister'. 'Do you want to resign from my government?', he said. I said 'Well no, of course I don't.' He said 'Well, then you'd better not.' So that was that! And when he said that to you you certainly didn't contradict him.

Parliamentary secretaries didn't very often go to the cabinet, but when Tommy Dugdale or someone was away, I remember going to a cabinet meeting in which there was a discussion about whether or not we were going to take rationing off sweets or off meat, I can't remember which it was. Gwyl Lloyd George, who was the minister of food, said that he felt that it was not possible to remove rationing, because we didn't have enough supplies and it was impossible to do it. But I remember the prime minister saying 'We said we were going to do it and we *will* do it, so that's that.' Of course it was done and it was perfectly alright, but it was an example of the conviction and the courage that he had. He was determined to get rid of the bureaucracy and constraints and regulations and all those things that were inevitable in a time of war and which hung on after the war.

I suppose you could say that he stayed on too long as prime minister, but then, who doesn't? I mean, they all do. I suppose the only one who didn't really was Harold Wilson, I think probably he was the only one. I don't know whether he regretted it, but certainly in my Australian days, when I was in Australia, Bob Menzies resigned and he regretted it forever afterwards, because he disliked all his successors so much. I think there is a compulsion on people in high places not to like their possible successors and to stay as long as they can. So I think that that was probably true, and anyway, my party has a great history of disloyalty to its leaders. Everyone, from Winston Churchill downward, has been stuck in the back by a knife. Eden, Alec Home, Ted Heath, Margaret Thatcher, John Major, they have all been, so I suppose to some extent the prime minister of the day has to ignore that.

Just one final thought. There is a fashion now to judge people of a different generation by the standards and customs and thoughts of the present generation. Now I think that is a very difficult and wrong thing to do. How can you really judge what people felt like when they were born 130 or 140 years ago and were brought up in totally different circumstances and totally different customs than those which you find today. I think those critics of Winston Churchill sometimes seem to ignore that. That is certainly so about his feelings about Liberal imperialism and all the rest of it, people now don't understand. One example of this relates to Churchill's views on Europe. When I was at NATO I had to go to Zürich and make a speech and I thought it would be quite a good idea to read that famous speech Churchill made in Zürich, in which most people now think that he was advocating British membership of the European Union. If you read the speech, of course, he wasn't doing anything of the kind. What he was saying was that people should be magnanimous in Europe, Europe must get together and forget what happened. But Britain was quite removed from that: we were not part of Europe, we were part of an alliance which had won the war with the Americans, the Europeans had not really been enormously successful in the war, we defeated the Germans, the French had been defeated, the Italians had been rather ambivalent one way or the other, and there wasn't a particular reason why he felt that we should join Europe. We had an empire; Churchill was brought up in the days when a quarter of the land surface of the world was coloured red and was British. That is the sort of thing that people nowadays seem to me not to understand about people of his generation.

What an extraordinary man Churchill must have been. of all the people that I have ever met in my life I think that I admire him most of all, and I think he did more than anybody I know to enable all of us to live the sort of lives that we live now. For me it was a privilege to have known him as distantly as I did and I am very happy I did.

LORD DEEDES: I did have a certain amount to do with Winston in the 1930s, mainly over India, because *The Morning Post*, the newspaper I was on, worked together with Winston against self-government for India. But I don't want to dwell on that so much, what I want go dwell on is a quality in Winston, one single quality which I have come greatly to admire and which I think is very much underrated. It came into my mind very forcibly the other day when I was looking through a volume which has just appeared, Martin Gilbert's volume *1941, The Churchill Papers*. It is an enormously thick book and it carries all the papers connected with Winston in 1941. It put in my mind, reading through these papers in 1941, something that Field Marshal Wavell once said. Wavell said he thought that the prime requirement for any general was mental robustness. Now in my view that was a quality which Winston had abundantly and in my belief that mental robustness was an enormous factor in his getting through the war and getting us through as well. I want to dwell on this, because I think it is a much rarer quality in politics now than most people believe.

I want to dwell on the year 1941, not at all a cheerful year. In fact if you think about it, between Winston taking over in 1940 and the Battle of Alamein in October 1942, which is roughly twenty-eight months, there weren't really many happy days in the course of those two-and-a-half years. And throughout that period, Winston had to run the war and govern the country, with a stream of bad news, much of which we knew nothing about. I can remember (I was a soldier at the time like Peter Carrington) getting pretty depressed at various times during that period. But for Churchill, who was privy to countless setbacks, difficulties, disasters of which the rest of the world knew nothing, it must have been a supreme test of mental robustness.

Let's just go through some of the factors that weighed on his mind. First of all, I think hardest to bear of all, was the bombing that began almost as soon as he took office, the lives lost and the destruction it created. There is a passage in the 1941 papers of a visit by Winston to Plymouth after it had been bombed four nights out of five. Winston was appalled by what he saw and at the same time got a warning from various people that the country would not be able to put up with much more of it. Imagine that weight of thought on the mind. When he left Plymouth he kept saying to Jock Colville and others with him 'I never saw the like', he really was profoundly upset.

After the bombing, factor two, the sinking at sea by U-boats, with which Churchill was amply familiar because he knew all about it from the First World War. He knew quite well that the U-boat campaign against the ships bringing supplies to this country could ditch us. There was the position in France, this is the third factor. How to deal with Vichy; what to do about the French navy; what, above all, to do with General De Gaulle who, for all his great patriotism, was extremely tiresome through a great part of the war to Winston. Then there loomed, this is the fourth factor, over much of this period the threat of invasion, which was acute in 1940, slightly relieved in 1941 and when Russia was attacked by Germany probably faded into the background. But that was a factor constantly to be borne in mind. There was the need to rebuild our army after the defeat at Dunkirk, not simply for war in the desert, which was to take place, but ultimately for a return to Europe. Then after Russia was attacked by Germany in 1942, constant pressure from Stalin for more support and eventually a call for a second front long before we were ready for it. Churchill was under constant pressure from Stalin to open up the second front.

There was also a critical House of Common, with many of the loyalists, remember, in those days absent in uniform. Those loyal to Churchill, many of them were away from the House, they were in uniform and they were involved in the war. There is this passage, I think in June 1941, from Chips Channon's diary: 'On all sides one hears increasing criticism of Churchill, he is undergoing a noticeable slump in popularity and many of his enemies, long silenced by his personal popularity, are once more vocal.' Crete had been a great blow there. That is another factor to weigh on the mind and keep somebody from sleep. There was the ever urgent problem of keeping American on our side, until Pearl Harbor, and giving us as much neutral aid, pseudo-neutral aid, as they could be persuaded to do.

Now my list is not complete, but there are nine constant anxieties, any one of which really would be enough to absorb the human mind, constantly nagging, constantly nagging at Churchill's mind. And from this flood of anxiety, if you think about it, really no relief at all. I can't think of any time in our history when a prime minister was subjected to such an unrelieved burden. In the First World War, you may remember, the duty in a sense was shared – Asquith in a sense did the first half of the war, Lloyd George did the latter part. In the Second World War Winston bore responsibility from 1940 until the finish. Although he had the wit to devise recreation of his own sort, it wasn't much to live on. What he really enjoyed at Chequers was a good film and probably his favourite film was a film about Nelson and Lady Hamilton made by Alexander Korda, whom he knighted in 1942. Churchill really enjoyed a thoroughly sentimental film, but that was about the only recreation he got. He enjoyed his meals, he enjoyed good company, his sleeping hours were eccentric but then they were what he needed.

George VI found the burden of the war very heavy indeed and got very depressed. Churchill and the king used to have lunch once a week at Buckingham Palace – rather a frugal lunch I may say. But anyway, that weekly talk, in the presence of Queen Elizabeth the Queen Mother, was mutually supporting.

Winston's life before 1940 was very much a preparation for what really amounted to a tremendous threat to his sanity. He began his career as a subaltern, he fought in a number of wars, he was at Omdurman (I have been there at that battlefield, I know exactly how he was involved in the Lancers charge), he had big setbacks at the Dardanelles when he was first lord of the admiralty, he left the government to go into the front line. There is a very good story about why Winston went into the front line. He was with the Grenadier Guards, who were dry at battalion headquarters. They very much liked tea and condensed milk, which had no great appeal to Winston, but alcohol was permitted in the front line, in the trenches. So he suggested to the colonel that he really ought to see more of the war and get into the front line. This was highly commended by the colonel, who thought it was a very good thing to do.

Churchill's mental robustness was also much tested during what is called his wilderness years: he was out of office 1929 to 1939, quite a long time for a man with his abilities. There was the battle over India, which I was faintly involved in, and the battle over rearmament just before the war. Now some will argue that when I talk about mental robustness I am talking about courage, which of course is not in question. But not quite, because few men, no matter how courageous, could have sustained the constant adversity of the first twenty-eight months of that war and emerge from it as triumphantly as he did. There were men in history who showed the same quality, but most of them were altogether more roughly hewn than Winston. There were plenty of men who were less sensitive, they didn't have a cat sleeping on their bed, they didn't keep a pet canary like Winston. There was a very gentle side to Winston, which is rarely matched with people of such resolution. And the men who were in a sense as mentally robust as Winston, they weren't given as readily to tears as Winston, who cried very easily, showing a side of his nature which many people didn't suspect was there. That seems to me the amazing feature of this mental robustness: the fact that it was a nature which had an altogether softer side, an altogether kindlier, more thoughtful side than anyone might suppose. It was not a ruthless temperament, it was not a brutal temperament, it was a sensitive temperament mixed with mental robustness. And in my judgement, no one has ever really assessed sufficiently what that mental robustment meant for this country at the most critical time in its life. That fact alone has led me, the more I think about it, very close to believing in destiny.

LADY SOAMES: I have to say it has been a great thrill for me and very moving to sit here with former colleagues and friends of my father and to hear their different approaches to him. Given the distinguished audience we have got here I feel rather nervous, but I would like just to pick out two aspects of my father's life – one about his character and the other which is a slight sort of fancy on my part about him.

I want to talk about my father's quality of naturalness, which as a matter of fact has been brought out very much, both by Tony Benn and by Peter Carrington. This quality was apparent principally of course to his family, colleagues and friends. He was extremely natural and almost, I would say, entirely lacking in hypocrisy. I can truthfully say that he was the least pompous person I have ever met in my life. Even as his standing and fame grew, his public and private persona remained very much the same and many of those who knew him, both in private and public, have testified to what I can only call the sort of oneness of his character. His engaging, almost uninhibited frankness of expression and candour often I think quite surprised people, who were accustomed to more guarded and more circumspect public figures.

I remember an occasion when this was strongly demonstrated. I was accompanying my father after the war, during his second prime ministership. He was going somewhere tremendously important to be received, I am not sure it wasn't to have a freedom or perhaps a degree or something. I think my mother must have been away and I was in charge, and I was appalled to realise that we were going to be extremely late, so I was much embarrassed, and my father even seemed a little bit fussed, the way he kept looking at the turnip (which he called his watch) – 'we are going to be very late'. So when we got there I thought 'oh dear, glum faces'. Not at all. Charming people on the doorstep, mayors in robes and gold chains, and everybody saying 'Oh prime minister of course we quite understand'. My father got out and said 'I am so sorry I am late', 'Oh no prime minister, we quite understand, we quite understand last minute matters of state held you.' So I thought how wonderful, how divine they are, they have held him out this excuse without him having to say anything, feeling much relieved. To my horror I saw papa going rather pink, which was always a sort of sign that he was going to say something very truthful. He went very pink and he said 'Well, that is most kind of you, but I have to say I started late.' It was so unnecessary, I was quite cross with him!

But it was this very characteristic of an often unguarded spontaneity which he was aware of himself, and I think in his later life, when, particularly at mealtimes, he liked to feel that he could talk in an unguarded way, it caused him very much to prefer small groups of what came to be known as the golden circle, which was the group of his family and closest colleagues and friends. He was always wary, until he got to know them, of strangers. He preferred a small company, which did not include strangers with ears avidly pricked up for quotes, watchful eyes and wagging tongues.

He was blessed in that for him the boundary line between work and recreation was smudged. His life's main work was a natural expression of his gifts for heroic action, oratory and writing. And his naturalness and zest for life were among his most attractive characteristics, of which those of us who were fortunate enough to be close to him were the lucky beneficiaries. As a child at Chartwell I was one of these, although of course for a long time I took my luck for granted. But he was such fun to be with and Chartwell was his playground: landscaping, creating waterfalls and lakes, bricklaying, though I have to say that the charms of being a bricklayer's mate palled fairly soon for me, because moments of boredom caused inattention, which caused dropping of heavy bricks on small toes. So I used to retreat howling to the house quite often.

My father's love and concern for animals, whether farm, wild or domestic, was particularly appealing to a child. My vivid and happy memories are of a man whose zest for life made quite ordinary things exciting, and who despite all other preoccupations and heavy burdens never quite gave up his toys. Among my fondest adult memories of my father in extreme old age is of him on high summer days at Chartwell, sitting for long periods in front of the buddleia bushes, which he had caused to be planted for their delectation, watching the butterflies quivering and hovering, and keeping delighted tally of the red admirals, the tortoiseshells and the painted ladies, which he recognised and knew quite clearly.

The other thing I want to talk about is of how most of us probably envisage my father. For none of us here, or indeed anywhere, can recall Winston Churchill other than as a middle-aged or very old man. Our instant image of him is of a formidable and now legendary war leader, a venerable statesman crowned with honours, the hero of our finest hour. But I like sometimes to try to imagine my father as he must have been as a young man and to try to recapture the sheer dash and dare and determination of the young Winston. Although at Harrow he had not distinguished himself at games, or indeed at anything else very much, he won the public schools' fencing competition – no mean feat. And he must have been superbly fit after his training at Sandhurst as a cavalry officer. He was a brilliant polo player; long days in the saddle on the North-West Frontier; several brushes with death, and in the Sudan the cavalry charge at Omdurman. Then in South Africa the Boer War, the armoured train, his imprisonment and escape, which rang throughout the world, putting him on the front pages where he would remain for the rest of his life. All these adventures were also grist to his emerging skill as writer: pen and sword. Of course to a number of people, particularly senior officers in the field, young Churchill was insufferably bumptious, a medal hunter with an overplus of vitamin I.

But I want to end my contribution by just reminding myself and, if I may, you, of the effect the younger Winston Churchill could have on people. His army days over, the emerging politician soon to be controversial, jumping ship from Tory to Liberal, but already the star quality shone in him obviously, and was recognised by for instance at least one sophisticated observer: Lady Violet Asquith, who met him for the first time at a party in 1906. She was 19, a young woman quite accustomed to the company of brilliant people. He was 32, in his first ministerial office in her father's government. She would write: 'Until the end of dinner I listened to him spellbound. I can remember thinking this is what people mean when they talk about seeing stars. I was transfixed, transported, into a new element. I knew only that I had seen a great light. I recognised it as the light of genius.'

At the time of Winston and Clementine's engagement, his prospective mother-in-law, Lady Blanche Hozier, wrote to an old friend, the poet Wilfred Scawen Blunt: 'He is so like Lord Randolph, he has some of his faults and all of his qualities. He is gentle and tender and affectionate to those he loves, much hated by those who have not come under his personal charm.' And Sir Edward Grey took a charitable view of Winston after colleagues in 1908 had complained that he talked too loudly and too much at cabinets. Similar complaints, I may say, would emerge and are recorded on other occasions down the years. But Sir Edward took the long view and amicably ironic wrote: 'Winston very soon will become incapable from sheer activity of mind of being anything in a Cabinet but Prime Minister.' He also thought young Churchill was a genius, and forecast that his faults and mistakes would be forgotten in his achievements. I think that that long-ago prophecy has largely come true.

CHAIRMAN (DAVID CANNADINE) I thank all our speakers for such a marvellously varied and yet consistent set of memoirs of Churchill.

Question: I was very interested by Lord Carrington's remarks about the disloyalty of Conservatives to their leaders. I don't know whether the story is true, of Churchill sitting on the government benches after the war when a young Conservative MP came up and sat next to him and said 'Mr Churchill, isn't it wonderful to be here amongst all our friends, and across the floor are the enemy', and Churchill growled back 'No my boy, across the floor are the opposition, the enemy is all around you.' My question is to Tony Benn: would that apply today to Tony Blair?

TONY BENN: I think the difference between the Labour and Conservative parties is that the Labour party elects a leader, argues with them from the day they are elected and keeps them until they want to go. The Tory party worship their leader and put a knife between their shoulderblades just as soon as they fail. Now that is the difference. Tony Blair could go on until he is 95, we have never got rid of a leader, but we make life very difficult for them while they are there. But the Conservative party's loyalty, I mean six minutes' standing ovations for Mrs Thatcher, and then we knew that Michael Heseltine was sharpening his penknife. We have never got rid of a leader to the best of my knowledge. Ramsay went, thank God, but that was a different consideration. I met him in 1930 at Number 10 and he offered me a chocolate biscuit, and since then I have looked at Labour leaders with chocolate biscuits very suspiciously and I am getting a lot of them at the moment!

Question: Can I tempt Bill Deedes into saying something about Churchill, *The Morning Post* and India in the mid-1930s?

LORD DEEDES: What happened was, the government determined upon self-government for India quite early on and this came to fruition in the early 1930s. Winston was convinced that it was a false step, not only provincial autonomy would go wrong, but the centre would go wrong, and with I suppose about twenty-five Conservative members on his side and the backing of *The Morning Post* and occasionally *The Daily Mail*, we had this campaign that ran for a couple of years whether or not India should be granted self-government. In fact the Government of India Bill, 356 clauses, was seen through by Sam Hoare and Rab Butler as his number two while all this was going on. In defiance of Winston's wishes, self-government for India was postponed because of the war but was in a sense statutorily arranged before the war broke out.

I of course had sympathy with Winston. I was at the Wavertree by-election where Randolph fought and worked with the Churchill family up there, and I had developed sympathy with the whole thing. But I have since come to see that it was probably a mistake to think that India should not have self-government. It was a misjudgement, you can't alter that fact. Baldwin in a sense was right about it. I think it came out of Winston's great affection for India, his early days on the North-West Frontier, it was from the best motives. But I have to say in all honesty, although I supported the campaign – I was India correspondent for *The Morning Post* for a while – I do think it was a misjudgement.

LORD CARRINGTON: This has got not much to do with Churchill, but I think it is quite interesting about India. In 1947, when the India Independence Bill was going through parliament, it arrived in the House of Lords. The House of Lords was then opposed to independence for India, very largely I think because so many of them had been influenced by Winston Churchill, and this rather derided character Halifax got up to speak and it is almost the only occasion in all the time that I have been sitting in the House of Lords when one speech turned the whole debate. Because of that speech the House of Lords passed the second reading of the India Bill, and it was really rather a notable occasion. He did make the most magnificent speech.

TONY BENN: Halifax, as Lord Irwin, was viceroy of India from 1929–31 when my father was secretary of state. I got from the India Office library the full correspondence between Halifax, this very High-Church Conservative, and my dad, who was a radical man, and the account of India at the time is absolutely fascinating. Irwin was respected in India, because when he arrived it was Good Friday and he wouldn't meet anybody for religious reasons, and the Indians said 'here must be an Englishman who believes in his religion', which surprised them very much indeed. Irwin arranged for Gandhi to come to London for the round-table conference, which is when I met him. I was in the House of Lord when the royal assent was given to the India Independence Act, at the moment when the title emperor of India jumped into the dustbin of history, because after that of course no king of England was emperor of India. As for what Peter Carrington says about Halifax, I must go and read it because sometimes one speech *does* make a difference and if he says that influenced such a reactionary body as the House of Lords it must have been quite a speech.

Question: Mr Benn, you were in the House when the Conservatives came back in 1951. One of the first acts of Churchill was to get rid of everything that was on the Festival of Britain site. Can you comment on what you felt about that at the time?

TONY BENN: I remember the Festival of Britain very well. It was an attempt of course to boost our morale after the war. I think the first exhibition we had was 1946, called Britain Can Make It, and then there was the Festival of Britain, which was as controversial as the Dome. It was actually very successful. I went to the opening and I enjoyed it very much – the skylon, the dome and so on. But Churchill had it cleared. I daresay he wanted the South Bank free of memories. What he would have done with the wheel (the London Eye) now I do not know. But can I just add one thing that came out of Mary Soames's account: what a tremendous sense of fun he had. At Chequers, when I stayed there, a Dutch painting was pointed out to me, in the corner of which Winston had painted a mouse. Another occasion I remember was when he got up at a very critical moment of a debate, it must have been as leader of the opposition, and Attlee was very worried that Winston rose. And Winston said 'If the Right Honourable gentleman wonders about me, I am looking for my zuzubes', he had lost them, and he took one and dragged it down towards him. An enormous sense of fun he had. On one occasion a Labour member had one of these enormously elaborate question – 'Does the Right Honourable gentleman, recognising and remembering and take into account' and so on and so on – it went on about two minutes, and Winston said 'Yes sir' and sat down and he completely deflated the questioner. I think his sense of fun was something that did make him enormously attractive and free of pomposity, and these are the things you remember about people after you have forgotten the political arguments.

Question: One of the greatest blows that Churchill suffered from was of course the defeat in the 1945 election. Lord Deedes, Lord Carrington and Mr Benn had served in the forces during the war, and Churchill believed that the forces voted largely against him. Do you believe that was so, and if so, why was it so?

LORD DEEDES: I would very much like to answer that question. In my view in 1945 Winston was a victim of the between-the-wars government, the National Government that came into office in 1931 on the resignation of a Labour government, a government in which he had no part at all. What the country remembered in 1945 was the best part of three million unemployed during the 1930s – I am not blaming the government, but it happened – that was a major, major factor; laxity over rearmament; Munich, all of which Winston opposed. And I have always believed that the verdict in 1945 had more to do with the record of the government in the 1930s of which Winston was not part, than any kind of comment upon Winston himself.

TONY BENN: Can I confirm that. I was coming back in a troopship in

the summer of 1945 and we had a political debate on board the
troopship and I was the Labour candidate. There is no doubt whatever
that all the troops on board that ship, including people who had served
with General Slim in Burma and so on, were undoubtedly in favour
of a change. But they weren't anti-Winston, and I think what Bill
Deedes says is absolutely right: people said 'never again, we are never
going back to the means test, we are never going back to unemployment,
we are never going back to fascism, we are never going back to that,
we want a new Britain'. And remember this, war does funny things. I
think somebody said it is 99 per cent boredom and 1 per cent moments
of real danger, so you had masses of time to talk. I learned much more
as an aircraftsman second class in Rhodesia and in Egypt than ever I
learned at university, because you met people, you talked and talked,
and a lot of the discussion during the war was political – what is the
war about, what are we going to do afterwards, what is the postwar
world going to be like.

I remember on the troopship going out, this was earlier, going to
the officer commanding troops and I said 'We want to have a discussion
on War Aims.' The colonel said to me, I was the most junior, an
aircraftman second class was probably known as a private, 'Well Benn,
if you have a discussion on War Aims, I hope there will be no politics'.
I said 'Oh no sir, certainly not!'

I have a funny feeling, and this is the difference between the left and
the right. I think the right in Britain was fighting the Germans and the
left was fighting fascism. That is quite an important difference. We
were fighting to see that the ideas of fascism never came, whereas for
some people this was teaching the Hun another lesson because they
wouldn't learn from the defeat of 1918. I don't know that others will
agree, but that was certainly the way that I saw it and my family saw
it, and I would be interested to know whether Bill Deedes would go
along with that second part.

LORD DEEDES: Good point.

LORD CARRINGTON: If I may just say, in my squadron in France in 1945
there was not one single man who would vote for the Conservative
party, not one. This was partly due, as Bill Deedes and Tony Benn
have said, to the fact that quite a large number of them were
unemployed before the war and had had a pretty awful time, and they
remembered it. It was also a fact, which perhaps is not particularly
creditable, that quite a number of them thought that if they voted
Labour they would still get Winston Churchill as the prime minister.
Thirdly, there was an appalling publication called *ABCA*, which was
edited by Dick Crossman and which was pure Labour party propa-

ganda, and which we had to go and tell our squadron was the be-all and end-all and the absolute truth in the future. It was the most wonderful Labour party propaganda there has ever been.

LORD DEEDES: As we are reminiscing, they offered me the editorship of *ABCA*, but I turned it down.

TONY BENN: Mind you, we never thought we'd win the election. During the whole campaign in 1945, when I was driving a loudspeaker van in Westminster when I got back from Egypt, not one of us thought we'd win. There were no opinion polls to mislead us, there were no spin doctors to confuse us, and we all thought we had lost. I was at Transport House when the results came out, it was two weeks if you remember after polling day, and I was sitting there in the dark watching the results on an epidiascope, and we couldn't believe it. And out of the bright light into the room came Clem, who had flown back from the meeting at Potsdam, and I saw his face when he heard he was prime minister. The BBC man came up to me and said 'Will you say "three cheers to the prime minister"', for which I was too shy, but Clem was astonished that he had won. So in a sense that confirmed that it wasn't an anti-Winston vote in any way at all.

Question: I want to put a trivial question and a very serious one. I was inspired by Mary Soames' account of the young Winston to ask a question about the very young Winston. Perhaps you can only answer by checking backwards from what you know. If I recall rightly one of the great stories of his early life is that when he was a very young officer the London County Council had put up screens in the music hall to try to cut down the competition and make them somewhat more respectable places, and as a very young officer Churchill was said to have led a gang of young officers and men to knock down these screens. I wonder if this was just a sign of pluck and dash, that he'd like to be at the head of an exciting escapade, or whether there was a more or less conscious and principled gesture against sexual puritanism going on.

LADY SOAMES: No, I am sure you are reading too much into it. I think it was just unseemly larkiness on the part of a lot of perhaps young officers out for an evening. I really refuse to have political correctness cast on my father as long ago as that! I can't throw any light on it, it was before even my time.

D.C. WATT: Coming back to the 1945 general election, if there hadn't been a party truce during the war the results of the 1945 election would be much clearer. The whole country's revulsion was not against Winston Churchill at all, but against the Tory party, the Tory party organisation and the kind of candidates they preferred in the 1930s and during the war.

Question: Churchill believed in a Liberal and Conservative axis, now we have a Labour and Liberal axis. Do you think the Conservative party should try and get back to the Churchillian position and ally more with the Liberals?

LORD DEEDES: This relates to something that Lord Carrington said. One cannot compare the mood, the attitude, the thinking of the Liberal party of Winston's day with the party of today, it is simply not comparing like with like. The Liberal party of Winston's time and the Liberal party of today are two totally different handkerchiefs. People stick to their names and change their views. That is why Winston Churchill changed his own view and joined the Conservative party. The past is no guide whatsoever as to what might happen now, that is the point I want to make.

LORD CARRINGTON: Without being party political, if I were a member of the Liberal party I would be very anxious about what their leadership is doing, because it seems to me that they lay themselves open really to 'what is the point of voting Liberal, you might as well vote Labour'.

TONY BENN: Well, that raises a very big question. If I were a Conservative I would say that, of course, I fully understand that. But I think of Churchill and Macmillan, and to some extent Ted Heath, as One Nation Tories, who would have a lot in common with the Liberal party. Even Clem Attlee, it used to be said he was a typical major from the First World War: it was the horses first, the men second and the officers last. That was the way he saw it, a very responsible view. Macmillan's view was much influenced by the fact that he fought in the First World War and then saw the people with whom he had fought being thrown into unemployment in the interwar years. Harold Macmillan's book *The Middle Way* would lead to expulsion from the Labour party of today, because he said we have to plan our economy. So the politics are very complicated. Of course there always were Simonite Liberals. You know what they said about John Simon – he sat on the fence so long, the iron had entered into his soul. But he was a man who was really a natural Conservative, and ended up of course as Conservative lord chancellor, but he had been a Liberal in the old days and then the Simonites moved over with MacDonald in 1931. It is very complex. Normally, the more progressive of the two parties is destroyed by any coalition, which is why Lloyd George destroyed the Liberal party by going into coalition after the First World War and why my dad would never touch a coalition with a bargepole. He didn't believe in that type of politics, designed to get power and not to do anything.

LORD CARRINGTON: You are coming round to my point of view!

TONY BENN: We might agree about the rapid reaction force as a force undermining NATO, but I won't go into that either.

CHAIRMAN: I think there is a danger that agreement is going to break out and we should probably stop at that point. But before we do so, let me ask each member of our panel if they have a final brief thought.

TONY BENN: The wonderful use of language. It came home to me very much, because of the famous speech he made about the RAF – 'Never in the field of human conflict has so much been owed by so many to so few.' Shortly after that, the BBC had the week's good cause and a Labour MP called Geoff Muff, who later became Lord Calverly, gave the broadcast, and I have never forgotten the words with which he finished. He said 'I cannot put our debt to the Royal Air Force better than the words used by our own Prime Minister. Never since wars began have such a relatively large number of people been indebted to such a relatively small number!'

LORD DEEDES: I will end up by offering you a bit of advice that Winston once gave a very timid Conservative candidate. I was not at the lunch, but the candidate took a sip of Winston's claret and said 'A very nice wine, sir'. And Winston turned to him and said 'Sip burgundy, swill claret.' Keep it in mind!

CHAIRMAN: It has been a great pleasure for me to find myself, wholly by association, sitting in such an illustrious and anecdotally memorable company this evening. We have all been informed, moved, amused and entertained in spectacular style. I ask you to join with me in thanking Tony Benn, Lord Carrington, Lord Deedes and Mary Soames for their marvellous memories of Winston Churchill.

ROYAL HISTORICAL SOCIETY:
REPORT OF COUNCIL
Session 2000–2001

Officers and Council

- At the Anniversary Meeting on 24 November 2000, Professor J.L. Nelson succeeded Professor P.J. Marshall as President after the Meeting.

Professor Nelson wrote in the Spring 2001 "Newsletter" 'If Peter Marshall thought it an impossible act to follow as incoming President after Rees Davies, the successor's successor is doubly daunted! In key aspects, Peter has continued and extended Rees's initiatives: the Society's publishing activities have thriven mightily in the past four years with the new *Studies in History* series, the splendid new edition of the *Handbook of British Dates*, and *Camdens* and *Transactions* that go from strength to strength; and the presidential voice, clear yet never strident, and firm even when accompanied by a chuckle, has been heard on an ever-growing range of public issues where History has a stake.'

'Yet a good President will always lever an individual stamp on the Society's collective life. The Fellowship has grown, and not by chance. Peter has done more than urge us all at every possible opportunity to make it our business to recruit suitably qualified applicants – he has set a shining example by himself sponsoring no fewer than 58 new Fellows in the past four years. Nor is it a coincidence that many of these have been from beyond Europe or have interest in extra-European history. Just before and just after the beginning of his presidency, two of the Society's conferences signalled interests close to Peter's heart: the history of women and gender and the history of empires and of the formation of identities by non-Europeans under colonial rule. Attenders at either or both those conferences will recall the difference made by Peter's enthusiastic engagement.   Now and in the future, the impetus he has given to a significantly widened inclusion of exponents of public history must enrich the Society further still.'

'In the Council Room, the portraits of the presidential ancestors, en masse, can seem intimidating. The adjective is not one that comes to mind in Peter's case (and I suspect it won't be the word for his portrait) – though when needed, there is steel beneath the unfailing courtesy and unassuming cheeriness. His qualities in office have proved awe-inspiring, to be sure, and for his successor, plain inspiring too, but Peter as president has been above all an enabler and a welcomer aboard. His has been exactly the right kind of leadership to set the Society's course as, hopes aloft but with charts in constant need of updating (part of our trade, after all), we move out into a new millennium.'

- Professor A.G. Jones succeeded Professor D.S. Eastwood at Literary Director; the remaining Officers of the Society were re-elected.
- The Vice-Presidents retiring under By-law XVII were Professor M.J. Daunton and Professor P.J. Hennessy. Professor C.D.H. Jones and Professor R.D. McKitterick were elected to replace them.
- The Members of Council retiring under By-law XX were Professor J.M. Black, Dr. C.R.J. Currie and Dr. J.P. Martindale; Professor A.E. Goodman resigned mid-term. In accordance with By-law XXI, amended, Professor J.A. Green, Professor H.E. Meller and Professor R.J.A.R. Rathbone were elected in their place.
- Professor D.S. Eastwood succeeded Professor M.J. Daunton as Convenor of the *Studies in History* Editorial Board.
- The Election of Officers Subcommittee convened during the year proposed that Professor Julian Hoppit succeed Professor Kathleen Burk as Honorary Treasurer. Professor Hoppit consented to Council's request that his name be put forward to the Society's Anniversary Meeting on 23 November 2001 with effect from that date.
- The Society's staffing arrangements have changed within the year. The Executive Secretary is now ably assisted by the Administrative Secretary, Mrs. Helen Combes.
- MacIntyre and Company were appointed auditors for the year 2000-2001 under By-law XXXIX.
- Cripps Harries Hall continue to manage the Society's investment funds.

Activities of the Society during the Year.

- At the end of 2000, an excellent piece of news for the Society was the success of its British History Bibliographies Project, with the Institute of Historical Research as co-applicant, in gaining a further three years' AHRB funding for online development. The Project's General Editor, Ian Archer, was congratulated on this success. The award of £246,596 from the AHRB's Resource Enhancement Scheme will allow the Society to mount an on-line version of the Bibliography to be hosted by the Institute of Historical Research. Not only does this mean that the project's funding is secure until the end of 2003, but it will make the database of approximately

300,000 works on the history of Britain and Ireland and the British overseas published up to 2000 available to scholars, teachers, students, independent researchers, all over the world free of charge. The site will go live in May 2002, and free access should mean that the Bibliography will become a staple item on scholars' desktops, vastly increasing the reach of the resource. The data will thereafter be up-dated at regular intervals. On-line publication of the bibliography will also enable the project to develop cross-searching facilities with other databases; it is hoped that we can play a key role in developing convergence between on-line resources of interest to historians. In the longer term, searches on individuals, for example, will generate not only bibliographic data but also take the user to a New DNB entry and details of the archival holdings relating to the individual.

The Project's first AHRB grant came to an end in December 2000, and for the current year the project is supported by funds in hand. The task of re-editing the 19000 titles in the 1993-6 Annuals to provide the complete searching facilities (e.g. inclusion of time fields) has been completed. The refinement of the thesaurus is an ongoing operation, and considerable progress has been made with the geographical indexing scheme. The use of the new 'journals-awareness' service, BL-INSIDE, has enhanced our journal searching facilities, although we continue to depend on the good offices of the Library staff at the Institute of Historical Research for a large number of journals and physical checking of items for relevance.

- The Society's website - www.rhs.ac.uk, set up with the kind co-operation of the Institute of Historical Research. It is now fully operational. Details of the Society's latest activities including its prizes, publications, meetings, grants including its research support schemes (including application forms) can be found there, as well as application forms for both the Fellowship and Membership and the current List of Fellows, Corresponding Fellows, Associates and Members with their research interests.
- The Society has continued to be closely involved with archival issues of importance to historians. The Society's Archives Group, under the supervision of the Honorary Secretary, continued to provide a regular forum for the Society's archival interests. The group has been of great assistance to Council.
- Responses have been made to:

  o an invitation from Resource to comment on a consultation paper with the UK Archives Community; the need to move towards positive action on archives was emphasised.
  o an invitation from the National Heritage Memorial Fund to

comment on its quinquennial performance review consultation
paper.

- ○ an invitation from the Public Record Office to comment on
  the Government Policy of Archives Draft Action Plan
- ○ an invitation from the Department for Culture, Media and
  Sports to respond to the Quinquennial Review of the Historical
  Manuscripts Commission: Stage One; the Society's response
  stressed the need to keep the HMC in its present form as an
  independent public body.
- ○ a request for support from Manchester Central Library, regarding the fate of archives in public libraries.

● The Society instigated a series of meetings with a small committee
  of representatives from the Society and British Library personnel,
  initially to discuss the dispotal of newspapers and the BL's foreign-
  language acquisitions' policy. This has proved extremely valuable,
  and further meetings are planned on a widening range of issues.
● The Society has continued to be concerned this year with:

- ○ the nomination of board members and panel convenors to the
  Arts and Humanities Research Board Funding Group and
  panellists to the Board
- ○ relations with the Quality Assurance Agency/History Bench-
  marking Group
- ○ the Arts and Humanities Research Board's review of its
  postgraduate awards, especially the problems of attracting
  students to postgraduate study, especially where the acquisition
  of languages and other technical skills requires extended preparation, the gap between the Ph.D. and the first academic job
  and the increasing significance of mature students.
- ○ Advisory Council on the Reviewing Committee on the Export
  of Works of Art Review of Graduate Studies
- ○ representation at the Historical Association Schools Conference
  A-level Forum
- ○ National History Week 2002, proposed by the Historical Association.

● The Society has forged improved links with the History at the
  Universities Defence Group, particularly regarding redundancy and
  closures in University History Departments
● The Society continued its close involvement with the British
  National Committee of the International Committee of Historical
  Sciences. The Committee having provided financial support for 33
  scholars from Britain, attendance of British historians at the 19th

Quinquennial Congress at Oslo, on 6th - 13th August 2000 was good and the Congress was a great success.

- The 20th Quinquennial Congress will be held in Sydney in 2005, and the President welcomes suggestions for themes and sub-themes. It was also hoped that grants could be available for British historians to attend.

Meetings of the Society.

- Five papers were given in London this year and two papers were read at locations outside London. Welcome invitations were extended to the Society to visit the history departments at the Universities of Exeter and Stirling. What has become an established pattern was followed on these visits; Members of Council meet with the departments to discuss issues of interest to historians before the paper is delivered. The Society always receives a warm welcome and generous hospitality from the universities that it visits and is very grateful to them for their kindness.

- The Colin Matthew Memorial Lecture for the Public Understanding of History - previously known as the Gresham Lecture - was given to a very large and appreciative audience by Professor Roy Porter at St. Anthony's Church, Holborn on 'The British Enlightenment: Then and Now'. These lectures are given in memory of the late Professor Colin Matthew, a former Literary Director and Vice-President of the Society.

- The President [Professor P.J. Marshall] and Executive Secretary had attended a reception at the Ards Arts Centre/Town Hall, Newtownards, to mark the publication of *Transactions*, Sixth Series, Volume 10, containing the papers read at the joint conference in Belfast with the history department of the Queen's University and the Public Record Office of Northern Ireland from 9th – 11th September 1999. The Society was pleased to present a copy of the publication to Mr. Michael McGimpsey, Minister for Culture, Arts and Leisure.

- A conference on 'Churchill in the twenty-first century' was held at the Institute of Historical Research, London, on 11th – 13th January 2001. Over 80 delegates attended, and a selection of the papers read at the conference will be published in *Transactions*, Sixth Series, Volume 11, to be published in November 2001.

- From 19th – 20th April 2001 the Society joined with the Department of History of the University of York, at The King's Manor, York, to host a conference on 'Historians and their Publics'; the latest in a series of colloquia on professional issues and held regularly each spring. The next, 'Conflicting Loyalties: The Responsibilities of the

Historian' is planned for Saturday 16thFebruary 2002 at the School
of Oriental and African Studies, University of London, Thornhaugh
Street, Russell Square Street, London.

- A conference, 'English Politeness: Conduct, Social Rank and Moral
Virtue, c.1400-c.1900',, is planned to be held at The Huntington
Library, San Marino, California, U.S.A., on 14th – 15th September
2001.

- A conference, 'Architecture and History', to be held jointly with
the Society and the Society of Architectural Historians of Great
Britain will be held at the University of Sheffield on 5th – 7th April
2002.

Prizes

The Society's annual prizes were awarded as follows:

- The Alexander Prize was not awarded in 2001.
- The David Berry Prize for 2000, for an essay on an approved topic
of Scottish history, attracted three entries. The Prize was awarded
to Fraser Macdonald for his essay 'St. Kilda and the Sublime'. The
judge's citation read:

A compelling and absorbing essay that explores the tensions between the St.
Kilda that was seen and described by Victorian travellers, and the St. Kilda
that was lived and worked on by the islanders themselves. Rather than being
perched 'on the edge of the world', the island society, and its religious and
social organisation, was 'an emblem of Presbyterian polity' at a time when
a modern sense of Scottish nationality was being forged. Drawing on a
number if disciplines, including historical geography, the essay is nonetheless
accessible and richly illustrated.'

- The Whitfield Prize for a first book on British history attracted 20
entries. The generally high quality of the entries was again commended by the assessors.

The Prize for 2000 was awarded to Adam Fox for his book <u>Oral
and Literate Culture in England, 1500-1700</u> [OUP].

Proxime accessit was Bruce Campbell for his book <u>English Seignorial
Agriculture, 1260-1450</u> [CUP].

The judges wrote:

'The Whitfield Prize for a first book on British history attracted 20 entries.
Over half were of a high or very high quality.

The judges had a difficult task to reduce a short list of seven down to a
winner. After much consideration they awarded the prize to a well-researched,

lively and innovative study of oral and written culture. This is a very wide-ranging book, going from popular speech and proverbial wisdom to ballads and rumours. It combines scholarship with 'readability'. It is an outstanding first book.'

• Thanks to a continuing generous donation from The Gladstone Memorial Trust, the third Gladstone History Book Prize for a first book on a subject outside British history was awarded. The number of entries increased this year to 19.

   The prize for 2000 was awarded to Matthew Innes for his book State and Society in the Middle Ages: The Middle Rhine Valley, 400 - 1000 [CUP].

   Proxime accessit was Rebecca Spang for her book The Invention of the Restaurant [Harvard University Press].

   The judges wrote:

   'Innes' study works outwards from a dense body of material associated with the monastery of Lorsch in the eighth and ninth centuries towards a radical reformulation of conventional views of the relationship between central' and 'local' power in the Carolingian era. Innes shows how the dichotomy public-private leads to anachronistic assumptions of an implicit teleology in the actions of early medieval rulers, who were not in fact either engaged in state creation or in delegating supposedly public power down to aristocratic officials in the localities -- the power exercised and competed for by local aristocrats had its own dynamic. In a strong field, Innes' work stood out for its intellectual vigour, informed by wide reading in political theory and comparative history as well as in the immediate subject matter, and for the elegantly controlled manner in which detailed source-specific argument was related to the overall thesis of the book and vice versa.'

• In order to recognise the high quality of work now being produced at undergraduate level in the form of third-year dissertations, the Society has instituted, in association with History Today magazine, an annual prize for the best undergraduate dissertation. Depart-ments are asked to nominate annually their best dissertation and a joint committee of the Society and History Today select in the autumn the national prizewinner from among these nominations. The prize also recognizes the Society's close relations with History Today and the important role the magazine has played in dis-seminating scholarly research to a wider audience.

   First prize was awarded to Lucy Marten-Holden from the University of East Anglia for her essay: 'A study into the siting and landscape context of early Norman castles in Suffolk';

Second prize was awarded to Alison Rosenblitt, from Wadham College, Oxford for her essay: 'Symmetry and asymmetry in Anglo-Saxon Art'

Third prize was awarded to Jennifer Brook from the University of Newcastle for her essay 'I forgive you in advance": Pasternak and the publication of Dr. Zhivago'

At the kind invitation of the Keeper, all entrants and their institutional contacts were invited to a celebratory lunch and a behind the scenes visit to the Public Record Office in January 2001. Approximately twenty candidates and tutors attended.

An article by the first prize-winner presenting her research appeared in *History Today* in the fiftieth anniversary edition in April 2001.

● Frampton and Beazley Prizes for A-level performances were awarded following nominations from the examining bodies:

Frampton Prizes
  ○ The Associated Examining Board: awarded jointly to:
    Daniel Donaghy, Ridge Danyers College, Cheadle Hulme and Arlene Garvin, Clarendon House Grammar School, Ramsgate, Kent
  ○ Edexcel Foundation incorporating the London Examination Board:
    Catherine L. Long, Simon Langton Girls' School, Canterbury
  ○ Northern Examinations and Assessment Board:
    Andrew Counter, Stockport Grammar School
  ○ Oxford and Cambridge School Examinations Board:
    no candidate was nominated this year
  ○ University of Cambridge Local Examinations Syndicate:
    no candidate was nominated this year
  ○ University of Oxford Delegacy of Local Examinations:
    no candidate was nominated this year
  ○ Welsh Joint Education Committee:
    Iwan Williams, Ysgol Gyfun Ddwyieithog Dyffryn Teifi, Llandysul, Ceredigion.

Beazley Prizes
  ○ Northern Ireland Council for the Curriculum Examinations and Assessment: Fiona M. Von Orsen, Rathmore Grammar School
  ○ Scottish Examination Board:
    Robin Vandome, Boroughmuir High School, Edinburgh.

Publications

- *Transactions*, Sixth Series, Volume 19 was published during the session, and *Transactions*, Sixth Series, Volume 11 went to press, to be published in November 2001.

- In the Camden, Fifth Series, *Parliament and Politics in the Age of Churchill and Attlee: The Headlam Diaries, 1935-1951*, ed. Stuart Ball (No. 14). *British Envoys to Germany, 1816-1866. Volume 1: 1816-1829*, ed. Sabine Freitag and Peter Wende (No. 15) and *An Appeasement Diary: A.L. Kennedy and The Times*, ed. Gordon Martel (No. 16) were published during the year. *Parliaments, Politics and Elections, 1604-1648*, ed. C.R. Kyle and *Remembrances of Elizabeth Freke*, ed. R.A. Anselment went to press for publication in 2001-2002.

- The Society's *Annual Bibliography of British and Irish History, Publications of 1999*, was published by Oxford University Press during the session, and the *Annual Bibliography of British and Irish History, Publications of 2000* went to press, to be published in 2001.

- The *Studies in History* second series continued to produce exciting volumes. As scheduled, the following volumes were published during the session,

  - *Massacre at the Champ de Mars: Popular Dissent and Political Culture in the French Revolution* by David Andress,
  - *Cheshire and the Tudor State, 1480-1560* by Tim Thornton;
  - *French Exile Journalism and European Politics, 1792-1814* by Simon Burrows;
  - *The Practice of Penance, 900-1050* by Sarah Hamilton.

  - *The Drawing Down of the Blinds: The Commemoration of the Great War in the City and East London, 1916-1919* by Mark Connelly;
  - *The Moravian Church and the Missionary Awakening in Eighteenth-Century England* by John Cecil Strickland Mason;
  - *Liberalism and the Land Issue, c.1885-1931*, by Ian Packer;
  - *Electoral Reform at Work: Local Politics and National Parties, 1832-1841*, by Philip J. Salmon;
  - *Peasant and Soldier in French Popular Culture, 1700-1870*, by David Hopkin;
  - *Power and Border Lordship in Medieval France: the county of Perche in the eleventh and twelfth centuries*, by Kathleen Thompson; and
  - *Henry VIII, the League of Schmalkalden and the English Reformation* by Rory McEntergart

  are all due to be published in the next session.

- These latter volumes will all feature in a launch to be held after the Anniversary Meeting and Presidential Address on 23rd November 2001. As in previous years, the membership of the Society will be invited to attend.

- From 1ˢᵗ July 2000, volumes in *Studies in History* series were offered to the membership at a favourable discounted price. 216 accepted the offer for volumes published during the year, and approximately a further 200 copies of the volumes to be published in the year 2001-2002 were ordered. We look forward to an increase in the number of volumes sold to the membership as the scheme becomes more established.

Papers Read

- At the ordinary meetings of the Society the following papers were read:

  o 'Yeats at War: poetic strategies and political reconstruction from the Easter Rising to the Free State'
    Professor Roy Foster (5ᵗʰ July 2000: Prothero Lecture)
  o 'The impact of Napoleon III on British politics, 1851-1880'
    Dr. J.P. Parry (20ᵗʰ October 2000 at the University of Exeter)
  o 'Some Pardoners' Tales: The Earliest English Indulgences'
    Professor Nicholas Vincent (26ᵗʰ January 2001)
  o 'Orientalism and the Ottoman City: Salonica and the Western Traveller in the Nineteenth Century'
    Professor Mark Mazower (2ⁿᵈ March 2001 at the University of Stirling)
  o 'Individualizing the trans-Atlantic slave trade: the biography of Mahommah Gardo Baquaqua of Djougou [1854]'
    Professor Robin Law (30ᵗʰ March 2001)
  o 'The myths of the South Sea Bubble'
    Dr. Julian Hoppit (18ᵗʰ May 2001)

- At the Anniversary meeting on 24ᵗʰ November 2000, the President, Professor P.J. Marshall, delivered an address on 'Britain and the World in the Eighteenth Century: IV. The turning-outwards of Britain".
- At the Conference entitled 'Churchill in the Twenty-First Century' held jointly with the Institute of Historical Research, London, at the IHR, on 11th – 13ᵗʰ January 2001:

  o Introduction David Cannadine and Roland Quinault
  o The Three Careers of Winston Churchill Paul Addison
  o Churchill and Democracy Roland Quinault
  o Churchill's Writing of History: Appeasement, Autobiography and 'The Gathering Storm' David Reynolds
  o Churchill and the British Monarchy David Cannadine
  o Churchill and the Trade Unions Chris Wrigley

- ○ Churchill and the Premiership Peter Hennessy
- ○ Churchill and the Conservative Party Stuart Ball
- ○ Churchill and the two 'Evil Empires' David Carlton
- ○ Churchill and the American Alliance John Charmley
- ○ Churchill and the East-West Detente John W. Young
- ○ Churchill Remembered Tony Benn MP, Lord Carrington, Lord Deedes and Mary Soames

Finance

The Society continues to enjoy a healthy financial state overall, in spite of a decrease in the endowment from £2,693,805 in June 2000 to £2,336,292 in June 2001, a decrease of £357,513. Our net investment income has decreased from £90,389 to £85,411 in the same period, primarily as a result of the following factors: first of all, the substantial decline in the telecoms sector and its related effects; and secondly, the continuing and growing decline in global economic growth. Council continues to support a rigorous control of expenditure across the Society's activities. The Society this year had an operating deficit of £32,545, compared with an operating deficit for last year of £24,637, an increase of £7,908.

Council records with gratitude the benefactions made to the Society by:

- ○ Mr. L.C. Alexander
- ○ The Reverend David Berry
- ○ Professor Andrew Browning
- ○ Professor C.D. Chandaman
- ○ Professor G. Donaldson
- ○ Professor Sir Geoffrey Elton
- ○ Mr. E.J. Erith
- ○ Mrs. W.M. Frampton
- ○ Mr. A.E.J. Hollaender
- ○ Professor P.J. Marshall
- ○ Mr. E.L.C. Mullins
- ○ Sir George Prothero
- ○ Professor T.F. Reddaway
- ○ Miss E.M. Robinson
- ○ Professor A.S. Whitfield

Membership

- • Council was delighted to acknowledge the awards in the Honours' Lists during the year, to Fellows, Professor Norman Davies [CMG],

Professor M.R.D. Foot [CBE], Professor E. Ives [CBE] and Professor Paul Kennedy [CBE].
- The wording for the criteria for the Fellowship and the Membership
  was revised during the year in order to extend eligibility to a wider
  range of persons contributing to historical scholarship. A new
  criterion for the Fellowship was added, reading: 'those who have
  made a major contribution to historical scholarship in a form other
  than publication; for instance, the organisation of exhibitions,
  collections, or conferences, or by the editing of local history serials'
  and to the Membership was redefined as 'those engaged in advanced
  historical scholarship and research, or teaching history in higher or
  further education, or who have rendered many years of service to
  history at national or local level'.
- Council was advised and recorded with regret the deaths of 4
  Honorary Vice-Presidents, 5 Fellows, 1 Life Fellows, 8 Retired
  Fellows, 1 Corresponding Fellow and 2 Associates. These included

  > Dr. G.E. Aylmer – Honorary Vice-President and former Presi-
  > dent
  > Professor H.R. Loyn – former Vice-President and Member of
  > Council
  > Miss K. Major – Honorary Vice-President
  > Dr. E. Miller – Fellow
  > Sir Steven Runciman – Honorary Vice-President
  > Sir Richard Southern – Honorary Vice-President and former
  > President.

- 118 Fellows and 13 Members were elected. The membership of the
  Society on 30 June 2001 numbered 2547, comprising 1748 Fellows,
  480 Retired Fellows, 22 Life Fellows, 8 Honorary Vice-Presidents,
  91 Corresponding Fellows, 102 Associates and 102 Members.
- The Society exchanged publications with 15 Societies, British and
  Foreign.

Representatives of the Society

- Professor M.R.D. Foot who represents the Society on the Committee to advise the publishers of *The Annual Register* expressed
  concern during the year regarding its future, but after further
  discussion these concerns were allayed at rest for the present.
- Professor R.D. McKitterick agreed to represent the Society on
  behalf of the HE sector at the termly meetings of the Qualifications
  and Curriculum Council, in response to an invitation from the
  Qualifications and Curriculum Authority
- Dr. W. Childs agreed to represent the Society on the history steering

group for a new Qualifications and Curriculum Authority project to look at issues in the 4–19 geography and history curricula.
- Professor L. Jordanova replaced Dr. A.M.S. Prochaska on the Advisory Council of the reviewing committee on the Export of Works of Art;
- Professor K. Brown was asked to replace Professor A.L. Brown on the University of Stirling Conference.
- The representation of the Society upon various bodies was as follows:

  ○ Mr. M. Roper, Professor P.H. Sawyer and Mr. C.P. Wormald on the Joint Committee of the Society and the British Academy established to prepare an edition of Anglo-Saxon charters;
  ○ Professor N.P. Brooks on a committee to promote the publication of photographic records of the more significant collections of British Coins;
  ○ Professor G.H. Martin on the Council of the British Records Association;
  ○ Dr. G.W. Bernard on the History at the Universities Defence Group;
  ○ Professor C.J. Holdsworth on the Court of the University of Exeter;
  ○ Professor D. d'Avray on the Anthony Panizzi Foundation;
  ○ Professor M.C. Cross on the Council of the British Association for Local History; and on the British Sub-Commission of the Commission International d'Histoire Ecclesiastique Comparée;
  ○ Miss V. Cromwell on the Advisory Board of the Computers in Teaching Initiative Centre for History; and on the Advisory Committee of the TLTP History Courseware Consortium;
  ○ Dr. A.M.S. . Prochaska on the National Council on Archives;
  ○ Professor R.A. Griffiths on the Court of Governors of the University of Wales, Swansea;
  ○ Professor W. Davies on the Court of the University of Birmingham;
  ○ Professor R.D. McKitterick on a committee to regulate British co-operation in the preparation of a new repertory of medieval sources to replace Potthast's *Bibliotheca Historica Medii Aevi*;
  ○ Professor J. Breuilly on the steering committee of the proposed British Centre for Historical Research in Germany.

- Council received reports from its representatives.

Grants

- Council was pleased to be able to contribute grants of £500 each to the

- The Maitland Memorial at Poets' Corner, Westminster Abbey; the President attended the installation of the memorial on 4th January 2001, and Council was proud of the Society's participation in such a worthy venture.

- The Henry Loyn Endowment Fund for a lecture in his honour to be held at the Centre for the Study of Medieval Society and Culture, Cardiff University periodically.

- The Royal Historical Society Centenary Fellowship for the academic year 2000-2001 was awarded equally to Laura Napran registered for a PhD at Pembroke College, Cambridge and is working on a thesis entitled 'Marriage Contracts in the North of France and the South Low Countries in the Twelfth Century', and Catherine Kropp, registered at Cambridge University, working on a thesis entitled 'The Refugee and Immigration Issue in Austria-Hungary and Great Britain in the 1880s: Russian Jews in Foreign and Domestic Policy'. The Research Support Committee agreed that Miss Kropp should also receive the award of £1,000 donated last year by The Mercers' Company, to assist her research.

- The Society was delighted to accept with deep gratitude from Professor Peter Marshall the most generous donation of a sum sufficient to cover the stipend for a one-year Research Fellowship at the Institute of Historical Research, similar to the existing Royal Historical Society Centenary Fellowship, in the financial year 2001-2002. Professor Marshall hoped to be able to donate future sums to fund a similar fellowship every other year in future. Whilst placing no restrictions on the place of origin of the Fellow, Professor Marshall hoped that it might be possible to award the fellowship to a student from a Commonwealth country. Council agreed that the award would be known as the Peter Marshall Fellowship.

- The Society's Research Support Committee continued to provide grants to postgraduate students for attendance at short-term training courses or conferences, funding towards research within and outside the United Kingdom and to assist the financing of small specialized historical conferences, especially where there is substantial involvement of junior researchers. Grants during the year were made to the following:

Training Bursaries:

○ Marie-Clare BALAAM, University of Wolverhampton
25th Anniversary Conference of the Social Science History Association, Pittsburgh, Pennsylvania, 26th-29th October 2000.

○ Mathew CLEAR, University of Sussex
International Medieval History Conference held at Kalamazoo, USA on 3rd – 6th May 2001.

○ Anastasia FILIPPOUPOLITI, University of Leicester
20th International Scientific Instrument Symposium to be held at the Royal Academy of Sciences, Stockholm, Sweden 15th – 19th October 2001.

○ Jorge Luis GIOVANNETTI-TORRES, University of North London
"Intra-Caribbean Migration: the Cuban Connection (1899 to the present) held at the University of the West Indies, Mona Campus, Jamaica.

○ Fiona Janet Louise HANDLEY, University College, London
World Archaeological Congress held at Kura Hulanda, Curacao, Dutch Antilles on 23rd – 29th April 2001.

○ Carolyn Ruth HARLAND, University of Aberdeen
"Locating the Victorians" Conference held at Imperial College, London on 12-15th July 2001.

○ Barbara HATELY-BROAD, University of Sheffield
Annual conference of the Society for Military History held in Calgary, Canada on 24th –27th May 2001.

○ Rebekah Francis HIGGITT, Imperial College, London
"Locating the Victorians" Conference held at Imperial College, London on 12-15th July 2001.

○ Alexandra JACKSON, King's College, London
27th AAH Annual Conference held at Oxford Brookes University on 29th March – 1st April 2001.

○ Rebecca JENNINGS, University of Manchester
Pacific Coast Conference on British Studies held to the University of California on 6th – 8th April 2001.

○ Andrew Christopher KING, University of Durham
International Medieval Conference to be held at the University of Leeds, 9th – 12th July 2001.

○ Markos KOUMADITIS, King's College, London
31st International Symposium of the Modern Greek Studies Association held at Georgetown University, Washington DC, U.S.A., 25th – 28th October 2001.

○ Christopher James OTTER, University of Manchester

"Locating the Victorians" Conference held at Imperial College, London on 12-15th July 2001.

○ Caterina PIZZIGONI, King's College, London
XXIII International Conference of Latin Americanists held at Peruga, Italy on 4th – 6th May 2001.

○ Shira Danielle SCHNITZER, Balliol College, Oxford
Varieties of Political Belief in Britain, 1832 – 1914" conference held at the University of Sunderland 28th – 30th June 2001.

○ Paula Regina STILES, University of St Andrews
International Medieval History Conference held at Kalamazoo, USA on 3rd – 6th May 2001.

○ Guy Alexander THOMAS , SOAS, University of London
Multidisciplinary Conference on Cameroon at Rice University, Houston, Texas, U.S.A. on 6th – 8th April 2001.

○ Rodanthi TZANELLI, University of Lancaster
"Tourisms, Identities, Conflicts and Histories" Conference held at the University of Central Lancashire 21st – 23rd June 2001.

○ Emma Louise WINTER, St Catherine's College,Cambridge
"Romantic Nationalists 1750 – 1850" conference held at the University of Surrey, Roehampton 28th June – 1st July 2001.

Research Fund: Research within the United Kingdom

○ Laurence LUX-STERRIT, University of Lancaster
Visit to archives in York and London.

○ David Andrew James MACPHERSON, Birkbeck College, London
Visit to archives in Ireland.

○ Ian James Forrester MORTIMER, University of Exeter
Visits to various archives in England.

○ Vivian Betty NEWMAN, University of Essex
Visits to various archives in England.

○ Susan Kathryn PARKINSON, University of Lancaster
Visit to various archives in England.

○ Marie PASCHALIDI, University College, London
Visit to PRO, Kew.

○ Kimberley A PERKINS, University of Aberdeen
Visits to various archives in Scotland.

○ Peter John PRANGLEY, University of Northumbria
Visit to archives in London.

○ Simone SELVA, University of Sussex
Visit to archives in London.

○ Yang Chien TSAI, University of Leicester
Visit to archives in London.

○ Diana Margaret TWINNING, London School of Economics
Visits to archives in England, Wales and Scotland.
○ Robert Murray Yeaman WATSON, University of Dundee
Visit to various archives in Scotland.

Research Fund: Research outside the United Kingdom

○ Stephanie Lyn BATESON, University of Sheffield
Visit to archives in the USA.
○ Craig Michael BEESTON, University College, Oxford
Visit to archives in USA.
○ John BULAITIS, Queen Mary Westfield, London
Visit to archives in France.
○ Wai Keung CHAN, SOAS, London
Visit to archives in London.
○ Criseyda Elizabeth COX, Balliol College, Oxford
Visit to archives in France and Italy.
○ Christopher DAVIDSON, University of St Andrews
Visit to archives in the Arab Emirates.
○ Ulrike EHRET, Kings College, London
Visit to archives in Germany.
○ Lars FISCHER, University College, London
Visit to archives in the Netherlands.
○ Keimelo GIMA, Royal Holloway, London
Visit to archives in Australia and Papua, New Guinea.
○ Zoe Ann GREER, University of Newcastle Upon Tyne
Visits to archives in USA.
○ Alexandra JACKSON, University of Aberdeen
Visit to archives in France.
○ Andrew Edward JOHNSTONE, University of Birmingham
Visit to archives in USA.
○ Nikolas KOZLOFF, St Anthony's College, Oxford
Visit to archives in Venezuela.
○ Paul Myer LEVANTHAL, University of St Andrews
Visit to archives in Israel.
○ Stefania LONGO, University College, London
Visit to archive in Italy.
○ Sloane MAHONE, Lady Margaret Hall, Oxford
Visit to archives in Africa.
○ Simon MARTIN, University College, London
Visit to archives in Italy.
○ Martin McELROY, Queen's University, Belfast
Visit to archives in Republic of Ireland.
○ Sueng-Keun OH, University College, London
Visit to archives in Italy.

o Nicola PIZZOLATO, University College, London
   Visit to various archives in USA.
o Noelle PLACK, University of Birmingham
   Visit to archives in France.
o Matteo RIZZO, SOAS, University of London
   Visit to archives in Africa.
o Camilla RUSSELL, Royal Holloway, London
   Visit to Vatican archives, Italy.
o Shira Danielle SCHNITZER, Balliol College, Oxford
   Visit to archives in Israel.
o Paula STILES, University of St Andrews
   Visit to archives in the Arab Emirates.
o Karine Nathalie VARLEY, Royal Holloway, London
   Visit to archives in France.
o Emma Louise WINTER, St Catherine's College, Cambridge
   Visit to archives in the Republic of Ireland.

Workshop Fund:

o 'Cultural Encounters and Resistance: the United States and
   Latin America, c1890-1950' held at University College, London
   29th – 30th June 2001 (Christopher ABEL).
o 'Cathedrals in the Middle Ages' conference held at University
   of Nottingham 28th April 2001 (Julia BARROW).
o 'Retailing and Distribution History: New Studies' workshop
   held at the University of Wolverhampton 16th May 2001 (John
   BENSON).
o 'Gender and Conflict in the Middle Ages c400- 1550) held at
   the York University, 5th- 7th January 2001 (Cordelia BEATTIE
   and Isabel DAVIES).
o 'Rethinking Women and Politics in Early Modern England'
   conference held at the University of Reading, 16th –17th July
   2001 (James DAYBELL).
o 'Disordered Families: Britain and Europe, 1600 – 1800', conference held at Warwick University 13th May 2000 (Martin
   FRANCIS).
o 'Metamorphosis: Gender, History and the Body' conference
   held at the University of Essex, 16th June 2001 (Wendy
   GAGEN).
o 'John Stow, Author, Editor and Reader' conference held at
   Corpus Christi College, Oxford, 30th March – 1st April 2001
   (Alexandra GILLESPIE).
o 'Desire in History' conference held at the IHR, University of
   London, 12th July 2001 (Hannah GREIG).

o 'Emigrant Homecomings: the Return Movement of British and Irish Emigrants, c1700-c2000 held at the University of Aberdeen, 12th – 14th July 2001. (Marjory HARPER).

o 'National Identities and Parliaments, 1660- 1860' Neale Lecture and Colloqium held at University College, London, 9th-10th March 2001 (Julian HOPPIT).

o 'Political Identities in Britain and Western Europe 1200 – 1500' conference held at University of Durham, 28th – 30th August 2001 (C.N.JONES).

o 'The Permissive Society and its Enemies' conference held at the School of Advanced Studies, University of London, 9th-11th July 2001 (Harriet JONES).

o 'Nationalism and Identity in the Third Republic in France' conference held at Keele University 6th – 8th July 2001 (Barbara KELLY).

o 'The Conception and Representation of Space in the Early Middle Ages' conference held at Newnham College, Cambridge, 25th November 2000 (Rosamund McKITTERICK).

o 'Seeing Gender: Perspectives on Medieval Gender and Sexuality' to be held at King's College, London 4th- 6th January 2002 (Robert MILLS).

o Reformation Studies Colloquium to be held at the University of Exeter 8th – 10th April 2002 (Andrew SPICER).

o 'The History of Consumption: Interdisciplinary Perspectives' conference held at the University of Sussex, 25th – 28th March 2001 (P.M.THANE).

ORS awards

o Merav MACK, Lucy Cavendish College, Cambridge
o Izabella ORLOWSKA, SOAS, London.

28 September, 2001

THE ROYAL HISTORICAL SOCIETY
FINANCIAL ACCOUNTS
FOR THE YEAR ENDED 30 JUNE 2001

haysmacintyre
Chartered Accountants
Registered Auditors
London

THE ROYAL HISTORICAL SOCIETY
REPORT OF THE COUNCIL OF TRUSTEES
FOR THE YEAR ENDED 30 JUNE 2001

The members of Council present their report and audited accounts for the year ended 30 June 2001.

PRINCIPAL ACTIVITIES AND REVIEW OF THE YEAR

The Society exists for the promotion and support of historical scholarship and its dissemination to historians and a wider public. This year, as in previous years, it has pursued this objective by an ambitious programme of publications – a volume of Transactions, two volumes of edited texts in the Camden Series and a volume in the Guides and Handbooks series, a new edition of a Handbook of Dates, have all appeared, by the holding of meetings in London and at universities outside London at which papers are delivered, by the sponsoring of the joint lecture for a wider public with Gresham College, by distributing over £20,000 in research support grants to 97 individuals, and by frequent representations to various official bodies where the interests of historical scholarship are involved. It is Council's intention that these activities should be sustained to the fullest extent in the future.

RESULTS

The Society experienced a difficult year with total funds decreasing from £2,693,805 in June 2000 to £2,336,292 in June 2001, a decrease of £357,513. This was largely due to a down turn in the stockmarket.

FIXED ASSETS

Information relating to changes in fixed assets is given in notes 2 and 3 to the accounts.

INVESTMENTS

The Society has adopted a "total return" approach to its investment policy. This means that the funds are invested solely on the basis of seeking to secure the best total level of economic return compatible with the duty to make safe investments, but regardless of the form the return takes.

The Society has adopted this approach to ensure even-handedness between current and future beneficiaries, as the focus of many investments moves away from producing income to maximising capital values. In the current investments climate, to maintain the level of income needed to fund the charity, would require an investment portfolio which would not achieve the optimal overall return, so effectively penalising future beneficiaries.

The total return strategy does not make distinctions between income and capital returns. It lumps together all forms of return on investment – dividends, interest, and capital gains etc, to produce a "total return". Some of the total return is then used to meet the needs of present beneficiaries, while the remainder is added to the existing capital to help meet the needs of future beneficiaries.

RESERVES POLICY

The Council have reviewed the Society's need for reserves in line with the guidance issued by the Charity Commission. They believe that the Society requires approximately the current level of unrestricted general funds to generate sufficient total return, both income and capital, to cover the Society's expenditure in excess of the members' subscription income on an annual basis. A substantial level of unrestricted reserves of £2,141,200 is therefore necessary to ensure that the Society can run efficiently and meet the needs of current and future beneficiaries.

The Society restricted funds consist of a number of different funds were the donor has imposed restrictions on the use of the funds which are legally binding. The purposes of these funds are set out in note 1.

STATEMENT OF TRUSTEES' RESPONSIBILITIES

The Charities Act of 1993 requires the Council to prepare accounts for each financial year which give a true and fair view of the state of affairs of the Society and of its financial activities for that year. In preparing these accounts, the Trustees are required to:

- select suitable accounting policies and apply them consistently;
- make judgements and estimates that are reasonable and prudent;
- state whether applicable accounting standards have been followed, subject to any material departures disclosed and explained in the accounts;
- prepare the accounts on the going concern basis unless it is inappropriate to presume that the Fund will continue in business.

The Council is responsible for ensuring proper accounting records are kept which disclose, with reasonable accuracy at any time, the financial position of the Society and enable them to ensure that the financial statements comply with the By-laws of the Society and the disclosure regulations. They are also responsible for safeguarding the assets of the Society and hence for taking reasonable steps for the prevention and detection of error, fraud and other irregularities.

MEMBERS OF THE COUNCIL

Professor J L Nelson, PhD, FBA	– President
Professor P Mandler, MA PhD	– Honorary Secretary
Professor A D M Pettegree, MA, DPhil, FSA	– Literary Director
Professor A G Jones, MA, PhD	– Literary Director
Professor K Burk, MA, DPhil	– Honorary Treasurer
D A L Morgan, MA FSA	– Honorary Librarian
Professor A J Fletcher, MA	– Vice-President
Professor C J Wrigley, PhD, LittD	– Vice-President
Professor D Cannadine, MA DPhil, FBA	– Vice-President
Professor P A Stafford, DPhil	– Vice-President
Professor J A Tosh, MA, PhD	– Vice-President
Mrs S J Tyacke, CB FSA, Hon PhD	– Vice-President
Professor C D H Jones, DPhil	– Vice-President
Professor R D McKitterick, MA, PhD, LittD	– Vice-President
I W Archer, MA DPhil	– Member of Council
G W Bernard, MA, DPhil	– Member of Council
Professor J C G Binfield, OBE, MA, PhD, FSA	– Member of Council
Professor R H Trainor, MA, DPhil	– Member of Council
W R Childs, MA, PhD	– Member of Council
Professor M L Dockrill, MA, BSc (Econ), PhD	– Member of Council
Professor V I J Flint, MA DPhil	– Member of Council
Professor J L Miller, MA, PhD	– Member of Council
Professor C M Andrew, MA, PhD	– Member of Council
J E Burton, DPhil	– Member of Council
Professor T A Reuter, MA, DPhil	– Member of Council
Professor J A Green, DPhil	– Member of Council
Professor H E Meller, PhD	– Member of Council
Professor R J A R Rathbone, PhD	– Member of Council

MEMBERS OF COUNCIL

At the Anniversary Meeting on 24 November 2000, Professor J L Nelson was elected President in accordance with By-law XVI, replacing Professor P J Marshall; Professor A G Jones was elected Literary Director in accordance with By-law XVIII, replacing Professor D S Eastwood; the remaining Officers of the Society were re-elected.

The Vice-Presidents retiring under By-law XVII were Professor M J Daunton and Professor P J Hennessy. Professor C D H Jones and Professor R D McKitterick were elected to replace them.

The Members of Council retiring under By-law XX were Professor J M Black, Dr C R J Currie and Dr J P Martindale, Professor A E Goodman having resigned mid-term. Following a ballot of Fellows, Professor J A Green, Professor H E Meller and Professor R J A R Rathbone were elected in their place.

STANDING COMMITTEES 2001

The society was operated through the following Committees during 2001—

Finance Committee	Professor C M Andrew	
	Mr P J C Firth	– non Council Member
	Professor P Mathias	– non Council Member
	Professor R J McKetterick	
	Professor R H Trainor	
	The six Officers	
Membership Committee	Professor J C G Binfield	
	Professor H Meller	
	Professor J Miller	
	*Professor P Stafford	
	The six Officers	
Publications Committee	Professor J A Green	
	Professor C D H Jones	
	Professor T A Reuter	

REPORT OF THE AUDITORS
TO THE MEMBERS OF THE ROYAL HISTORICAL SOCIETY

We have audited the accounts on pages 441 to 447 which have been prepared under the historical cost convention, as modified by the revaluation of fixed asset investments, and the accounting policies set out on page 443.

RESPECTIVE RESPONSIBILITIES OF THE COUNCIL OF TRUSTEES
As described on page 2 the Trustees are responsible for the preparation of accounts. It is our responsibility to form an independent opinion, based on our audit, on those accounts and to report our opinion to you.

BASIS OF OPINION
We conducted our audit in accordance with Auditing Standards issued by the Auditing Practices Board. An audit includes examination, on a test basis, of evidence relevant to the amounts and disclosures in the accounts. It also includes an assessment of the significant estimates and judgements made by the Board of Trustees in the preparation of the accounts, and of whether the accounting policies are appropriate to the Society's circumstances, consistently applied and adequately disclosed.

We planned and performed our audit so as to obtain all the information and explanations which we considered necessary in order to provide us with sufficient evidence to give reasonable assurance that the accounts are free from material misstatement, whether caused by fraud or other irregularity or error. In forming our opinion we also evaluated the overall adequacy of the presentation of information in the accounts.

OPINION
In our opinion the accounts give a true and fair view of the state of the Society's affairs as at 30 June 2001 and of its incoming resources and application of resources for the year then ended, and have been properly prepared in accordance with the Charities Act 1993.

haysmacintyre
Chartered Accountants
Registered Auditors

Southampton House
317 High Holborn
London
WC1V 7NL

28 September 2001

THE ROYAL HISTORICAL SOCIETY

BALANCE SHEET AS AT 30TH JUNE 2001

	Notes	2001 £	2001 £	2000 £	2000 £
FIXED ASSETS					
Tangible assets	2		1,600		2,810
Investments	3		2,250,106		2,619,660
			2,251,706		2,622,470
CURRENT ASSETS					
Stocks	1(c)	42,136		29,340	
Debtors	4	13,212		42,115	
Cash at bank and in hand	5	75,018		70,120	
		130,366		141,575	
LESS: CREDITORS					
Amount due within one year	6	(45,780)		(70,240)	
NET CURRENT ASSETS			84,586		71,335
NET ASSETS			2,336,292		2,693,805
REPRESENTED BY:	20				
Unrestricted – General Fund			2,141,200		2,467,587
Restricted – E.M. Robinson Bequest			114,330		116,678
Restricted – A.S. Whitfield Prize Fund			44,895		49,758
Restricted – BHB 2 Andrew Mellon Fund			35,867		59,782
			2,336,292		2,693,805

Approved by the Council on 28 September 2001

President:

Honorary Treasurer:

The attached notes form an integral part of these financial statements.

THE ROYAL HISTORICAL SOCIETY

CONSOLIDATED STATEMENT OF FINANCIAL ACTIVITIES FOR THE YEAR ENDED 30 JUNE 2001

	Notes	Unrestricted Funds General Fund £	Restricted Funds E M Robinson Bequest £	Restricted Funds A S Whitfield Prize Fund £	BHB/ Andrew Mellon Fund £	2001 Total £	2000 Total £
INCOMING RESOURCES							
Members' subscriptions							
—net		53,543	—	—	—	53,543	63,165
—tax recovered on Deeds of Covenant and Gift Aid		1,163	—	—	—	1,163	3,191
		54,706	—	—	—	54,706	66,356
Donations and legacies	7	13,813	—	—	—	13,813	11,461
Total Voluntary Income		68,519	—	—	—	68,519	77,817
Royalties and reproduction fees		61,568	—	—	—	61,568	48,197
Total Income before investment income		130,087	—	—	—	130,087	126,014
Investment income		96,909	3,650	1,314	—	101,873	106,971
Gross Incoming Resources in the Year		£226,996	£3,650	£1,314	—	£231,960	£232,985
RESOURCES USED							
Grants and prizes payable	8	(32,205)	—	(1,000)	—	(33,205)	(35,175)
Direct charitable expenditure	9	(156,614)	—	—	(23,915)	(180,529)	(172,351)
Administration expenses	10	(50,771)	—	—	—	(50,771)	(50,096)
Total Resources used		(239,590)	—	(1,000)	(23,915)	(264,505)	(257,622)
Net Incoming/Outgoing Resources (Operating surplus)		(12,594)	3,650	314	(23,915)	(32,545)	(24,637)
Net Gains and Losses on Investment Assets		(313,793)	(5,998)	(5,117)	—	(324,968)	101,626
Net Movement in Resources in Year		(326,387)	(2,348)	(4,863)	(23,915)	(357,513)	76,989
Balance Brought Forward at 30 June 2000		2,467,587	116,678	49,758	59,782	2,693,805	2,616,816
Balance Carried Forward at 30 June 2001		£2,141,200	£114,330	£44,895	£35,867	£2,336,292	£2,693,805
Unrealised Surpluses included in above balances		£177,667	£43,018	£19,645	£—	£240,330	£616,372

THE ROYAL HISTORICAL SOCIETY

Notes to the Accounts for the Year Ended 30 June 2001

ACCOUNTING POLICIES

(a) *Basis of accounting*

The financial statements have been prepared in accordance with the Charities (Accounts and Reports) Regulations October 1995, the Statements of Recommended Practice 'Accounting by Charities' and applicable accounting standards issued by UK accountancy bodies. The particular accounting policies adopted are described below. The financial statements are prepared under the historical cost convention, as modified to include fixed asset investments at market value.

(b) *Depreciation*

Depreciation is calculated by reference to the cost of fixed assets using a straight line basis at rates considered appropriate having regard to the expected lives of the fixed assets. The annual rates of depreciation in use are:

| Furniture and equipment | 10% |
| Computer equipment | 25% |

(c) *Stock*

Stock is valued at the lower of cost and net realisable value.

(d) *Library and archives*

The cost of additions to the library and archives is written off in the year of purchase.

(e) *Subscription Income*

Subscription Income is recognised in the year it became receivable with a provision against any subscription not received.

(f) *Investments*

Investments are stated at market value. Any surplus/deficit arising on revaluation is charged to the income and expenditure account. Dividend income is accounted for on a received basis.

(g) *Publication costs*

Publication costs are transferred in stock and released to the income and expenditure account as stocks are depleted.

(h) *E.M. Robinson bequest*

Income from the E.M. Robinson bequest is used to provide grants to the Dulwich Picture Gallery.

(i) *A.S. Whitfield Prize Fund*

The A.S. Whitfield Prize Fund is used to provide an annual prize for the best first monograph for British history published in the calendar year.

(j) *Donations and other voluntary income*

Donations are recognised on a received basis.

(k) *Grants payable*

Grants payable are recognised in the year in which they are paid.

(l) *Allocation of administration costs*

Administration costs are allocated between direct charitable expenditure and administration costs on the basis of the work done by the Executive Secretary.

TANGIBLE FIXED ASSETS

	Computer Equipment	Furniture and Equipment	Total
	£	£	£
Cost			
At 1st July 2000 .	29,742	1,173	30,915
Additions	—	—	—
At 30th June 2001	29,742	1,173	30,915
Depreciation			
At 1st July 2000 .	26,932	1,173	28,105
Charge for the year .	1,210	—	1,210
At 30th June 2001	28,142	1,173	29,315
Net book value			
At 30th June 2001	£1,600	£—	£1,600
At 30th June 2000	£2,810	£—	£2,810

All tangible fixed assets are used in the furtherance of the Society's objectives.

3. INVESTMENTS

	General Fund £	Robinson Bequest £	Whitfield Prize Fund £	Total £
Market value at 1st July 2000	2,345,286	108,351	42,393	2,496,0:
Additions	310,510	—	—	310,5:
Disposals	(441,181)	—	—	(441,1:
Unrealised (loss)/gain on investments	(309,668)	(5,998)	(5,177)	(320,8:
	1,904,947	102,353	37,216	2,044,5:
Cash awaiting investment	171,122	22,093	12,375	205,5:
Market value at 30th June 2001	2,076,069	124,446	49,591	2,250,1:
Cost at 30th June 2001	£1,898,402	£81,428	£29,946	£2,009,7:

4. DEBTORS

	2001 £	2000 £
Trade debtors	—	29,3:
Other debtors	7,079	6,9:
Prepayments	6,133	5,8:
	£13,212	£42,1:

5. CASH AT BANK AND IN HAND

	2001 £	2000 £
Deposit accounts	75,188	76,2:
Current accounts	(170)	(6,1:
	£75,018	£70,1:

6. CREDITORS: Amounts due within one year

	2001 £	2000 £
Trade creditors	3,164	48,7:
Sundry creditors	20,087	5,8:
Subscriptions received in advance	16,301	10,8:
Accruals and deferred income	4,823	5,4:
	£45,780	£70,2:

7. DONATIONS AND LEGACIES

	2001 £	2000 £
A. Browning Royalties	81	1:
G.R. Elton Bequest	3,243	6,6:
Donations and sundry income	6,182	2,2:
Conference fees and funding	4,307	2,3:
	£13,813	£11,4:

GRANT AND PRIZES PAYABLE	Unrestricted Funds £	Restricted Funds £	Total 2001 £	Total 2000 £
Alexander Prize	—	—	—	1,583
Grants	2,300	—	2,300	100
Research support grants (note 14)	20,830	—	20,830	21,178
Young Historian Scheme HA A-Level	—	—	—	4,039
Centenary fellowship	7,975	—	7,975	6,275
A-Level prizes	700	—	700	600
A.S. Whitfield Prize	—	1,000	1,000	1,000
E.M. Robinson Bequest				
— Grant to Dulwich Picture Library	—	—	—	—
Gladstone prize	400	—	400	400
	£32,205	£1,000	£33,205	£35,175

DIRECT CHARITABLE EXPENDITURE	Unrestricted Funds £	Restricted Funds £	Total 2001 £	Total 2000 £
Publishing costs (Note 15)	73,821	—	73,821	93,234
Purchase of books and publications	2,720	—	2,720	2,609
Binding	5,356	—	5,356	4,352
Prothero lecture	467	—	467	403
Studies in History				
— Executive editor's honorarium	4,667	—	4,667	4,875
— Executive editor's expenses	1,462	—	1,462	960
— Sundry expenses	1,948	—	1,948	1,628
Other publications (Note 16)	11,051	—	11,051	11,041
British Bibliographies	—	6,481	6,481	4,186
Salaries, pensions and social security	31,360	17,434	48,794	27,006
Computer consumables, printing and stationery	7,688	—	7,688	7,152
Meetings and travel	10,423	—	10,423	10,511
Conference costs	5,651	—	5,651	4,394
	£156,614	£23,915	£180,529	£172,351

ADMINISTRATION EXPENSES	Unrestricted Funds £	Restricted Funds £	Total 2001 £	Total 2000 £
Salaries, pensions and social security	13,440	—	13,440	10,504
Postage and telephone	1,923	—	1,923	2,147
Bank charges	1,514	—	1,514	1,542
Audit	9,526	—	9,526	6,265
Investment Broker	16,462	—	16,462	16,582
Insurance	978	—	978	999
Depreciation	1,210	—	1,210	2,601
Circulation costs	5,718	—	5,718	9,456
	£50,771	£—	£50,771	£50,096

The average number of staff employed during the year was 2 (2000: 1)

INSURANCE POLICIES	2001 £	2000 £
The Society was charged with the following amounts relating to committee and employees' liability:		
Employees liability	78	78
Public liability	78	78
	156	£156

COUNCILLORS' EXPENSES
During the year travel expenses were reimbursed to 30 Councillors attending Council meetings at a cost of £6,270 (2000: £6,207).

13. AUDITOR'S REMUNERATION

	2001 £	200 £
Audit fee	4,400	4,
Other services	1,828	1,

14. GRANTS PAID

During the year the Society awarded grants to a value of £20,830 (2000: £21,178) to 84 (2000: 92) individ (Note 8).

15. PUBLICATIONS

	Transactions Sixth Series £	Camden Fifth Series £	Guides and Handbooks Costs £	Camden Classic Reprints £	Tot £
Cambridge University Press					
Opening stock	2,199	7,688	2,574	16,879	29,3
Printing	14,594	27,872	1,168	—	43,6
Off prints	2,408	—	—	—	2,4
Carriage	518	1,159	—	—	1,6
Closing stock	(3,994)	(17,234)	(4,047)	(16,861)	(42,1
	15,725	19,485	(305)	18	34,9
Society's costs	—	—	7,423	—	7,4
Paper					11,4
Sales commission					19,9
					£73,8

16. PUBLICATIONS

	2001 £	200 £
Other publications cost		
Annual Bibliography	14,809	15,
Less: royalties received	(3,758)	(4,
	£11,051	£11,

17. LEASE COMMITMENTS

The Society has the following annual commitments under non-cancellable operating leases which expire:

	2001 £	200 £
Within 1–2 years		
Within 2–5 years	2,326	1,
	£2,326	£1,

18. LIFE MEMBERS

The Society has ongoing commitments to provide membership services to 22 Life Members at a cos approximately £42 each per year.

UNCAPITALISED ASSETS

The Society owns a library the cost of which is written off to the Statement of Financial Activities at the time of purchase.

This library is insured for £150,000 and is used for reference purposes by the membership of the Society.

ANALYSIS OF NET ASSETS BETWEEN FUNDS

	B.H.B. General Fund £	E.M. Robinson Bequest Fund £	A.S. Whitfield Prize Fund £	Andrew Mellon Fund £	Total £
Fixed Assets	—	—	—	1,600	1,600
Investments	2,076,070	124,446	49,590	—	2,250,106
	2,076,070	124,446	49,590	1,600	2,251,706
Current Assets					
Stocks	42,136	—	—	—	42,3136
Debtors	9,225	—	—	3,987	13,212
Cash at bank and in hand	27,304	—	—	47,714	75,018
	78,665	—	—	51,701	130,366
Less: Creditors	(13,535)	(10,116)	(4,695)	(17,434)	(45,780)
Net Current Assets	65,130	(10,116)	(4,695)	34,267	84,586
Net Assets	£2,141,200	£114,330	£44,895	£35,867	£2,336,292

THE ROYAL HISTORICAL SOCIETY
THE DAVID BERRY ESSAY TRUST

BALANCE SHEET AS AT 30TH JUNE 2001

	2001 £	2001 £	2000 £	2000 £
FIXED ASSETS				
1,117.63 units in the Charities Official Investment Fund				
(Market Value £12,752: 2000 £11,444)		1,530		
CURRENT ASSETS				
Bank Deposit Account	10,155		9,557	
CREDITORS:				
Amounts falling due within one year	(1,405)		(1,079)	
NET CURRENT ASSETS		8,750		8
NET ASSETS		10,280		10
REPRESENTED BY:				
Capital fund		1,000		1
Income and expenditure reserve		9,280		9
		£10,280		£10

INCOME AND EXPENDITURE ACCOUNT

	2001 £	2001 £	2000 £	2000 £
INCOME				
Dividends		391		
Bank Interest Receivable		207		
		598		
EXPENDITURE				
Prize awarded		(250)		
Travel expenses		(76)		
Excess of income over expenditure for the year . .		272		
Balance brought forward		9,008		9
Balance carried forward		9,280		9

The fund has no recognised gains or losses apart from the results for the above financial periods.

Approval on behalf of the Royal Historical Society on the 28 September 2001.

1. ACCOUNTING POLICIES
   Basis of accounting.
   The accounts have been prepared under the historical cost convention. The late David Berry, by his dated 23rd April 1926, left £1,000 to provide in every three years a gold medal and prize money for the essay on the Earl of Bothwell or, at the discretion of the Trustees, on Scottish History of the James Stua to VI, in memory of his father the late Rev. David Berry.
   The Trust is regulated by a scheme sanctioned by the Chancery Division of the High Court of Justice c 23rd January 1930, and made in action 1927 A 1233 David Anderson Berry deceased, Hunter and Anoth Robertson and Another and since modified by an order of the Charity Commissioners made on 11 Jan 1978 removing the necessity to provide a medal.
   The Royal Historical Society is now the Trustee. The investment consists of 1117.63 Charities O Investment Fund Income with units. The Trustee will advertise inviting essays every year of the three period.)
   A resolution was approved by the Charity Commission on the 16 August 1999 changing the purpose o Charity to provide an annual prize of £250 for the best essay on a subject, to be selected by the candi dealing with Scottish History, provided such subject has been previously submitted to and approved by Council of The Royal Historical Society.

REPORT OF THE AUDITORS TO THE TRUSTEES OF THE DAVID BERRY ESSAY TRUST

We have audited the accounts on page 448 which have been prepared under the historical cost convention and accounting policies set out on page 448.

pective responsibilities of the Council and Auditors
The Trustees are required to prepare accounts for each financial year which give a true and fair view of the e of affairs of the Trust and of the surplus or deficit for that period.
n preparing the accounts, the Trustees are required to:
elect suitable accounting policies and then apply them consistently;
nake judgements and estimates that are reasonable and prudent;
repare the accounts on the going concern basis unless it is inappropriate to presume that the Trust will continue in business.
The Trustees are responsible for keeping proper accounting records which disclose with reasonable accuracy at time the financial position of the Trust. They are also responsible for safeguarding the assets of the Trust and ace for taking reasonable steps for the prevention and detection of fraud and other irregularities.
As described above the Trustees are responsible for the preparation of accounts. It is our responsibility to form independent opinion, based on our audit, on those accounts and to report our opinion to you.

is of opinion
We conducted our audit in accordance with Auditing Standards issued by the Auditing Practices Board. An lit includes examination, on a test basis, of evidence relevant to the amounts and disclosures in the accounts. lso includes an assessment of the significant estimates and judgements made by the Trustees in the preparation the accounts, and of whether the accounting policies are appropriate to the Trust's circumstances, consistently lied and adequately disclosed.
We planned and performed our audit so as to obtain all the information and explanations which we considered essary in order to provide us with sufficient evidence to give reasonable assurance that the accounts are free m material misstatement, whether caused by fraud or other irregularity or error. In forming our opinion we evaluated the overall adequacy of the presentation of information in the accounts.

nion
n our opinion the accounts give a true and fair view of the state of the Trust's affairs as at 30th June 2001 and ts surplus for the year then ended.

HAYSMACINTYRE
Chartered Accountants
Registered Auditors
London

September 2001